THE LOCRIAN MAIDENS

THE LOCRIAN MAIDENS

LOVE AND DEATH IN GREEK ITALY

James M. Redfield

PRINCETON UNIVERSITY PRESS   PRINCETON AND OXFORD

Library of Congress Cataloging-in-Publication Data

Redfield, James M., 1935–
     The Locrian maidens : love and death in Greek Italy / James
M. Redfield.
        p.   cm.
     Includes bibliographical references and index.
     ISBN 0-691-11605-9 (alk. paper)
        1. Marriage—Italy—Locri Epizephyrii (Extinct city)
     2. Women—Italy—Locri Epizephyrii (Extinct city)   3. Locri
     Epizephyrii (Extinct city)—Social conditions.   4. Locri
     Epizephyrii (Extinct city)—Social life and customs.   I. Title.
     HQ630.15.L63R43 2003
     306.81′0937—dc21   2002044720

British Library Cataloging-in-Publication Data is available

This book has been composed in Baskerville

Printed on acid-free paper. ∞

www.pupress.princeton.edu

Printed in the United States of America

10   9   8   7   6   5   4   3   2   1

For KPA _____

"PAST ALL ACCIDENT"

Contents

Preface

Origins

Epizephyrian Locri is a place and a topic I almost literally stumbled upon. In 1975 I was traveling with my friend Salvatore Maddi down the east coast of the Italian toe; we were doing a systematic survey of Greek colonial sites from Taras to Rhegion. In due order we came to Locri, and I was astonished—by the scale of the place, first of all, and then by the material in the Antiquarium. The following day I encountered Locrian art on the first floor of the Reggio Museum, where most of the surviving objects are kept: sculpture and little bronzes and terracottas. These are not great objects (the greatest surviving work of Locrian art, the Ludovisi Throne, is in Rome), but they collectively convey an idiosyncratic artistic personality, a sensibility that sets them apart. If I had to characterize this personality in a phrase I would call it a disciplined sensuality. I was also struck by the prominence in this art of women's things and of representations of women. It seemed immediately clear to me that the Locrians were different, and that this difference had something to do with their women. Shortly thereafter I came across Gunther Zuntz's *Persephone*, which introduced me to the Locrian *pinakes* and the Orphic gold tablets and Empedocles, and told me that there was indeed something different about west-Greek religion and that it had to do with a goddess. I had found the topic that would dominate my work for the next twenty-some years.

I was touring Greek colonial sites in the first place because I was interested in Greek culture and in its varieties. The textbook accounts of Greece are dominated by Athens, partly because from Athens we have the best material—although it is worth saying that our best material is from Athens partly because Athens has dominated the textbook accounts since ancient times. Furthermore it is worth remembering that for many Greeks of the classical period Athens was a kind of monstrosity, even a threat to civilization: too big, too rich, too powerful, too permissive in its social and political life. Athens was not (for the Greeks) a model Greek city, but a creative, possibly pernicious, departure from the model.

I was looking for that model, and I was looking in Italy because I thought that in their colonies the Greeks would best reveal their collective understanding of what a society should be: Faced with the task of creating cities in unfamiliar territory and against hostile indigenes, the founders had to be explicit in their choices. No wonder that the west-

ern Greek frontier introduced the geometric street plan, the rationaliz-
ation of territory through the cadastral survey, and the coherent law
code. More than one scholar has concluded the city-state was actually
invented in the West, and introduced from there into the mainland
home of the Greeks.

As I learned more about the Greek West, however, I learned something about the varieties of the colonial enterprise: The rationalism of
the planned communities was quite consistent with a certain wild creativity. On the Greek frontier—in the West, and to a lesser extent on
the Black Sea—originated Greek charismatic religion and philosophy,
cultural movements which in their origin were linked to radical political movements, although as they were transplanted to the Greek mainland they sank to the status of countercultural tendencies. All this was
more possible to the Greeks than it might have been to some other
peoples in that their self-conception had always been somewhat plu-
ralistic: Each city was expected to have its own *nomoi*, its own cultural
norms. The frontier, I came to see, was the laboratory where the limits
of this pluralism were tested.

The peculiarity of Epizephyrian Locri, its cultural particularity, I
therefore saw as proper to the frontier and as possibly intelligible in
terms of a general Greek repertoire of recurrent problems with alternative solutions. In this relation between generic challenge and specific
response I found my strategy for the book. This is a book about the
Greek city-state, focused on a particular atypical instance. At the same
time it is a book about Epizephyrian Locri, a place I hope almost literally to put on the map.

The Term Locrian

The term *Locrian* is ambiguous. The ambiguity is already in my title,
which refers both to the maidens sent from old-world Locris to Troy
(part 2) and to the Italian Locrian maiden celebrated by Pindar (part
3). This ambiguity will be extensively explored in the pages that follow.

Old-world Locris was an area—actually two discontinuous areas—
adjoining Boeotia and Phocis: Opuntian Locris faced Euboea and Ozolian Locris faced the Corinthian gulf. Italian Locris was an area just
north of the territory of Rhegion; it included the great city we call
Epizephyrian Locri, and also Medma, Hipponion, and at some periods
Temesa; these latter were normally politically independent but part of
the Locrian culture area. Recent evidence suggests that the Alcantara
valley to the north of Mt. Etna in Sicily was also included in the Locrian
cultural sphere.

Structure

It is not possible to approach Locri with a set of questions and then find out the answers to them. I have adopted a different strategy, beginning each section with a particular problem or text or even a particular object, something that can be defined or described with a degree of firm objectivity. I have then proceeded to talk about what is known about it and what can be reasonably deduced from this; I then go on to talk about the unanswered questions, what some plausible solutions might be, and how they might fit into a more general context. Often I conclude with some suggestions that are frankly imaginative. The next section starts over with something else that can be seen or otherwise securely established and with what is known about it, and once again works its way toward the hypothetical. My hope is that all these hypotheses, as they interlock, will to some degree support one another and that the whole will be more persuasive than its parts. I have come through the years to see Locri as a closed, even secretive, community where the kind of religion we call Orphic had become (uniquely for the Greeks) the established religion of the city, where marriage-exchange was the most important source of social coherence, and where marriage itself was understood in Orphic terms as the heroization of the bride. This core hypothesis was already laid out in a 1976 paper given to the Women's Caucus of the American Philological Association; it has taken a quarter of a century to refine and contextualize it.

For the past twenty-some years, each time I was invited to take part in a seminar or a conference, I have asked myself: "What has this topic to do with Epizephyrian Locri?" This volume is the result of that strategy; it contains pretty much everything (except for a few literary essays) I have written during that time, and substantial chunks have already been published. I have gone over each text revising it where I thought I could thereby avoid confusing or boring the reader, but I have not tried to turn it from a series of essays into a continuously unfolding argument. It is a series of "raids on the inarticulate," to borrow a phrase from T. S. Eliot.

The essays are divided into four parts, with introduction, excursus, and epilogue. The first part makes no explicit reference to the Locrians; it seeks to establish a cultural context by laying out the problem of women in the city-state. The second part is on the peculiar ritual of the old-world Locrians, and establishes some Locrian themes. In "On Development," the excursus at the center of the book, the context is socioeconomic. The third part is on Epizephyrian Locri, and the fourth develops the third in four iconographic essays. The epilogue concludes with some reflections on the relations of the Locrians to philosophy.

What I have to say about Locri is often hypothetical; given the evidence, it could hardly be otherwise. Most scholars who have worked with this material have sooner or later abandoned it; there are too many gaps. Locri requires a high tolerance for ambiguity. My hope is that these speculations will be plausible enough to be of some use, not only because plausible hypotheses usually stimulate thought, but also because the question of their plausibility may lead the reader to think more deeply about the general tendencies and limits of the Greek sociopolitical enterprise—particularly in relation to that sociopolitical question which was for them, as it is for us, fundamental: the status and roles proper to free women.

Unquestionably the Locrians were not like the others. If I have not found the difference that made the difference, then it is still to seek. I conclude with a formulation improvised in a university meeting by the late Paul Wheatley, a formulation that might well serve as the motto of the Committee on Social Thought: "A theory is not to be rejected on the basis of lack of evidence. A theory is not even to be rejected on the basis of adverse evidence. A theory is only to be rejected in favor of a better theory."

Acknowledgments ─────────────────────────────

WHEN A PROJECT has taken twenty years it is impossible to remember all the people who have helped. Among those who have provided, sometimes in contention, useful comments on some substantial part of this manuscript are Kathleen Atlass, Wayne Booth, Philippe Borgeaud, Claude Calame, David Cohen, Marcel Detienne, Christopher Faraone, James Fernandez, Elizabeth Gebhard, Emily Grosholz, Jonathan Hall, Pamela Haskin, Michael Jameson, Marylin Arthur Katz, Katie Kretler, Leslie Kurke, Bruce Lincoln, Paul Ludwig, Sabine MacCormack, James McGlew, Gregory Nagy, Wendy Olmsted, Gloria Ferrari, Richard Posner, Marshall Sahlins, Richard Seaford, Kendall Sharp, Laura Slatkin, Christiane Sourvinou-Inwood, David Tandy, Angela Taraskiewicz, Maggie Tuteur, J.-P. Vernant, Peter White, and Froma Zeitlin. I began the manuscript in 1986 during six months as a Fellow of the Stanford Humanities Center, and finished the rough draft during nine months as a associate of the same institution, in 1997–1998. In the interim I received two grants in aid of research from the College of the University of Chicago, and another from the Social Sciences Division, and also a travel-to-collections grant from the National Endowment for the Humanities. I am one of so many who have benefitted from steady and resourceful support of the humanities by Rich and Barbara Franke. Critical material support in the closing stages was provided by Patricia and Gary Fieger. My thanks to them all.

I owe a special debt to Arnaldo Momigliano, who encouraged this work in its earliest stages and whose memory I now evoke; I am only sorry I cannot show him the finished product.

Abbreviations

ABV	J. D. Beazley, *Attic Black-Figure Vase-Painters.* Oxford: Clarendon, 1956.
ARV	J. D. Beazley, *Attic Red-Figure Vase-Painters*, 2d ed. Oxford: Clarendon, 1963.
Baumeister, *Denkmäler*	A. Baumeister, ed., *Denkmäler des klassischen Altertums zur erläuterung des Lebens der Griechen und Römer in Religion, kunst und sitte.* Münich and Leipzig: R. Oldenbourg, 1885–1888.
BTCGI	G. Nenci and G. Vallet, eds., *Bibliografia topografica della colonizzazione greca in Italia e nelle isole tirreniche.* Pisa: Scuola normale superiore; Rome: École française de Rome, 1977–.
Buck, *Dialects*	C. D. Buck, *The Greek Dialects: Grammar, Inscriptions, Glossary.* Chicago: University of Chicago, 1955.
Daremberg-Saglio	C. Daremberg and E. Saglio, *Dictionnaire des antiquités grecques et romaines d'après les textes et les monuments.* Paris: Hachette, 1873–1919.
DK	H. Diels, and W. Kranz, eds., *Die Fragmente der Vorsokratiker*, 6th ed. Berlin: Weidmann, 1951–1952.
EAA	*Enciclopedia dell'arte antica, classica e orientale.* Rome: Instituto della Enciclopedia Italiana, 1958–1966.
FGH	F. Jacoby, ed., *Fragmente der griechischen Historiker.* Berlin: Weidmann, 1923–. (Vols. after 1940 published by E. J. Brill, Leiden.)
FPG	F.W.A. Mullach, *Fragmenta philosophorum graecorum.* Paris: Didot, 1881–1883.
IG	*Inscriptiones graecae.* Berlin: de Gruyter, 1873–.
Kern	Otto Kern, ed., *Orphicorum fragmenta.* Berlin: Weidmann, 1922.
LIMC	*Lexicon iconographicum mythologiae classicae.* Zurich: Artemis Verlag, 1981–1999.
LSJ	H. G. Liddell, R. Scott, and H. Stuart Jones, eds., *Greek-English Lexicon*, 9th ed. Oxford: Clarendon, 1940.

Meiggs and Lewis   R. Meiggs and D. Lewis, ed., *A Selection of Greek Historical Inscriptions to the End of the Fifth Century B.C.* Oxford: Clarendon, 1969.

Preller-Robert   L. Preller, *Griechische Mythologie*, 4th ed., rev. C. Robert. Berlin: Weidmann, 1894–1926.

RE   A. Pauly, G. Wissowa, and W. Kroll, *Real-Encyclopädie der classischen Altertumswissenschaft.* Various places: various publishers, 1893–.

Roscher   W. H. Roscher, *Ausführliches Lexikon der griechischen und römischen Mythologie.* Leipzig: Teubner, 1884–1937.

SEG   *Supplementum epigraphicum graecum.* 1923–.

Schmitt,   H. H. Schmitt, ed., *Die Staatsverträge des
Staatsverträge   Altertums 3: Die Verträge der griechisch-römischen Welt von 338 bis 200 v. Chr.* Munich: C. H. Beck, 1969.

SIG³   W. Dittenberger, *Sylloge Inscriptionum Graecarum*, 3d ed. Leipzig: S. Hirzelium, 1915–1924.

TLG   *Thesaurus Linguae Graecae.*

Tod   M. N. Tod, *A Selection of Greek Historical Inscriptions*, 2d ed. Oxford: Clarendon, 1946–1950.

Winter, *Terrakotten* F. Winter, ed., *Die Typen der figürlichen Terrakotten.* Vol. 3 of *Die antiken Terracotten, im Auftrag des Archäologischen Instituts des Deutschen Reichs*, ed. A. Kekulé. Berlin-Stuttgart: W. Spemann, 1880–1903.

THE LOCRIAN MAIDENS

Introduction ————————————————————————————

On Introduction

Every work of history appears to require an introduction. The oldest known to me is that of Hecataeus:

> Hecataeus of Miletus has the following story to tell. I have written this as I believe it to be true. But the stories of the Greeks are numerous and (to me at least) obviously ridiculous. (1 *FGH* 1)

The stories Hecataeus is about to tell are of the type we call mythical; nevertheless he appears here as the grandfather of history, not so much in his promise to tell a true story (a promise that is also made by myth) but in his passion to replace all other stories. It seems that a narrative becomes historical in its effort to correct the errors of previous narratives. No history is ever the first. The present work also is revisionist in that it aims to recover lost aspects of our classical past, with the hope that this recovery may expand our understanding of ourselves. As such a work is adversarial to whatever fixed opinions have up to now limited our understanding, I come before my audience with some apprehension. Let me explain.

We call fifth- and fourth-century Greece "classical" because we believe, with some reason, that we all come from there, that these people originated the civilization we call "Western." We also believe that the West invented modernism, now becoming the world civilization. Therefore we also believe that the classical West experienced a kind of "first modernism," which in some respects set the pattern for the post-Enlightenment modernism still in process. Of course all these beliefs also deserve effective revisionist criticism. Here, however, I intend something different; I accept (at least for the sake of argument) this notion of the classical, I take it as somewhat true that the Greek city-state was the social system within which the West originated, and I seek to extend our notion of the human possibilities of that system. We tend to talk of these possibilities in terms of Athens, or of Athens in contrast to Sparta; I here propose Epizephyrian Locri as a third type, a different way of being Greek. What gives this inquiry a justification beyond the antiquarianism of local history is the possibility that the Locrians may show us something about the Greeks that we had missed, and therefore something that we lost as we became Western.

The difference that made the Locrians different was (as we shall see) more than anything else something about their women. This has therefore become a book about women in the Greek city-state and thus begins my apprehension. After slavery, the Greek repression and political disenfranchisement of women have become in our time the most disreputable thing about the Greeks. Here I intend, however, neither to defend nor to denounce this fact, but to differentiate its meaning. I shall be describing a society, that of the *polis*, which everywhere foregrounded sex differences and turned them to social uses. Also (in the ethnographic tradition) I believe that it is not possible to describe a society accurately without a certain sympathy with its values, even when they conflict with other values that I hold. The ancients, so far as we can tell, rejoiced in sex differences, whereas we tend to see them as an unfortunate fact, something as far as possible to be overcome by technology and social practice. Our time has discovered that sex differences appear in culture only as they are socially constructed into those collective representations we call "gender"; for some reason it tends in our time also to be assumed that anything socially constructed is somehow illegitimate and oppressive.

Difference, the manner in which persons and groups define themselves in contrast to some defining "other," has become in our time a leading historical topic, and gender has become the leading instance of difference. By historicizing these differences we can then distance ourselves from tradition: No longer do we have to take it for granted that men and women must have radically different life chances, since we now know that those differences are not dictated by nature but are culturally and historically conditioned. From this point of view our classic tradition is one source of what is wrong with us, worth study only in order to disenthrall ourselves from it. But it seems to me that we need also to remember that a fact can be evaluated only in terms of values (including ours) that are themselves culturally and historically conditioned, that we, like the ancients, are the creators of our cultural world, and that we, like the ancients, created culture not to oppress us but to sustain us (even if it contains much oppression). The uneasiness produced by certain facts about this classic past we have otherwise been taught to admire may usefully lead us to reevaluate the past, but also to reevaluate our own values. In the interest of that project I proceed to a rather lengthy unhistorical introduction. I am going to say something about our own society and its values, and then I am going to imagine an alternative society that those values might invent.

Human Nature

The Enlightenment discovered human nature—not for the first time, certainly, but perhaps for the first time as an alternative to history. The revolutionary project of the Enlightenment was our liberation from history in the name of nature: As privileges and prejudices were swept away, the Rights of Englishmen—or even Saxon Liberties—would be replaced by those Natural Rights supposed to be self-evident; reason would sweep away monopolies, preferential arrangements, the whole historic amalgam in order to give play to individual choice in the service of natural desire—thus naturally producing the adjustment of the economy to human nature. Society would not be imposed on persons but would arise from their natural tendency to sociability. Such a society would for the first time be founded not on traditional relations but on individual needs, conceived as the ultimate human reality.

This Enlightenment project required a reevaluation of difference, a reevaluation that can be conveniently discussed in terms of the old sociological contrast between ascribed status and achieved status. Persons have ascribed status according to the categories into which they are born; nobility is ascribed status, as is caste, as is race. Achieved status, by contrast, comes to people in terms of what they do. Inherited wealth confers ascribed status; one achieves status by making money. To be sent to the right sort of school confers ascribed status; one achieves status by doing well enough there to get into the right sort of college. The ideology of ascribed status claims that persons are born with readily distinguishable natures; the ideology of achieved status asserts that the true nature of persons, their talents or absence thereof, are revealed only as they diversely come to success or failure.

The project of the Enlightenment was that careers be open to the talents; the result was to be what Jefferson called a natural aristocracy. Those who achieved status were then to be really superior. Our term for this "real" superiority is *merit*. The problems proposed by this term are not my topic here; suffice it to observe, first, that we are not at all clear what we mean by merit, so we tend to ascribe it to those who do in fact come out on top (a circularity that puts the system beyond criticism); second, that equal opportunity, even when it exists, does not produce equality but rather generates inequality according to a specific set of rules (a natural aristocracy is a type of aristocracy); and, finally, that, however meritocratic the society, merit is continually being redefined by those who have already succeeded in such a way that most of the time their own children will be judged meritorious. These therefore succeed partly owing to a favorable inheritance (they belong to the families that control the resources and make the rules); their achieved status is thus a mystification of ascribed status. Furthermore, a society in which this was not true would be a repellent and dysfunctional society in which people did not care about their children. Thus a natural (or at least very general) human tendency produces the mystification of historically contingent advantages in order to disguise them as natural superiority.

All this is only to suggest that the founding fathers did not after all find the way to a society freed from historically contingent inequities, and that our society, like all societies, falls short of its own expectations of itself. It is this fact about ourselves that suggests that we still have something to learn from the others, including our own past.

In pursuit of this project I here draw attention to an ambiguity in the term *human nature* that our post-Enlightenment ideology brings to the surface. Human nature seems to mean two different things. In the first place our nature is to be cultural; we are the creatures with reason or with the power of speech, or capable of symbolic predication (the terms differ, but the difference indicated is the same), and we recognize this quality in one another, thus finding a basis for communication, exchange, and compassion. I call this our philosophical nature. In terms of this distinctive quality of ours we can claim inalienable and self-evident rights: Nature, surely, makes nothing without a purpose, and since we have capacities we are entitled to explore them to fulfillment. Since we have the ability to deliberate we are entitled to define our own interest and pursue it. Since we can form a society we are entitled freely to participate in shaping the society we inhabit. Furthermore merit is to be defined in terms of these natural capacities; the reasonable, the sensible, the wise, the sympathetic are the really superior. A level playing field is one that we permit no other factors to influence.

Our biological nature, by contrast, is my name for those features of humanity that are characteristic of us as a type of animal, that are both culture-universal and specific (not necessarily unique) to us. It includes things such as upright posture and the opposable thumb, infantile dependency and the general shape of the life-cycle, the five senses, the necessity of dreams, the capacity for shame, and also those underlying structures that, according to neo-Cartesian linguistics, are common to all languages. These things are "of the body" but they are also of the mind; they are "hardwired" and, as they everywhere underlie the varieties of culture, they are normally taken for granted. But we could certainly in principle encounter rational beings with none of these things. Probably only at that moment would we begin to discover just how many of them there are. I remember reading somewhere that the mocking noise, "nyah nya-nyah nya-*nyah* nyah" is found everywhere irrespective of diffusion, and is therefore hardwired in the brain. Also those things that while far from universal, are independently invented in different places—things such as the wheel, the value of gold, the divine right of kings—are aspects of our biological nature; they are things that come naturally to our species and that another rational species might find impossible or incomprehensible.

Our philosophical nature is a philosophical idea and can historically be traced back to the origins of philosophy in the Pythagorean schools, which divided body from soul so completely that it was thought a human soul could inhabit a body of a different species. Our biological nature is more characteristic of the poets (and Aristotle among the philosophers); it sees our higher faculties—reason, sentiment, and the like—as functions of the body, and therefore sees the body as implicated in our intellectual and emotional life. A tall person sees the world differently from a short one (not that all tall persons are the same, but height is a factor); a man thinks differently from a woman.

Of all the aspects of our biological nature, the most significant is the division of the species into two sexes. By this I mean both that the overwhelming majority of human beings are obviously either male or female, and also that sexual difference, which in combination with infantile dependency gives each of us an "original" relation to a mother and/or mother-substitute, is the primary building block of social structure. The first difference we experience as we become socialized is the difference between mother and everyone else, and all societies find that mothers are normally female. This being the case, it is also true that the first gendered classification presented to most children is sameness with and difference from the mother.

All of this is "natural," which does not mean that it has to be immutable. From the point of view of technology, nature, including human nature, consists of those things that we do not yet know how to alter. And in fact we already have or are on the verge of having a technology that could change all this: Cloning techniques are about to make it possible to fertilize one woman from the cells of another. All the offspring of such unions would be female, and we could imagine a world in which this was the only form of conception, and the Y chromosome, considered a genetic defect, had been eliminated. Paradoxically enough, this would be the Final Solution of the Woman Question.

This fantasy is rich in science-fictional possibilities; careless pregnancy, for instance, would disappear; each conception would be the result of a planned technical and fairly expensive procedure, and childbirth would be definitively uncoupled from sexual enjoyment (which latter in any case might lose much of its importance). Let us assume that the incest taboo would be extended to cover self-fertilization, true cloning; this would secure each child two parents, only one of whom would be the birth mother. The resulting kinship system would be interesting, possibly generating sentences such as: "I have no cross-siblings, since my father couldn't carry a child." More generally, all social positions would be occupied, and since they would all be occupied by women, sex would have no social relevance. On the other hand motherhood would not disappear, and we could imagine important differences between those who chose to bear children and those who did not, and reasonably expect social expectations about the social correlatives of this choice: sex would disappear, but gender might not. Perhaps it is true, as David Gutmann has suggested, that children are protected by a transfer of the mother's aggression to the father, a transfer that helps her not to abuse her children, mother and child then being sheltered by male aggression turned outward in the service of the family. Such a differentiation might still be needed, and "mothers" and "fathers" would then be thought of as different kinds of people with different life-chances and appropriately different standing. It is only that "motherhood" would become a career open to the talents.

There is more to gender than this, and quite possibly less; the elimination of sex difference would surely bring into play the law of unintended (which is to say unpredicted) consequences. Here I am making only the point that it would be a further step in the great adventure of modernism, which involves among other things the substitution of achieved status for ascribed status, the shift, in the language of Sir Henry Maine, from status to contract. Most of us now feel that to ascribe a status to a human being in virtue of his or her sex is an injustice. This attitude of ours was completely unknown less than two hundred years ago. Would we now be ready (assuming that the costs could be met) to eliminate the possibility of such injustice by forever eliminating males? And if not, why not? Would such a society be a human society? It would unquestionably be composed of human beings.

"The principle of community," said Aristotle, "is difference." Society functions because it has a structure, and it is structured by an internal differentiation of functions. The question is: Should this differentiation be prior to social action, or its consequence? Achieved-status societies, which take the second choice, are experienced as dynamic, characterized by mobility and innovation; changes in status are possible and those who are disadvantaged are constantly seeking to join the advantaged. Such societies are suffused with hope and disappointment. Ascribed status, asserting that the social order is "natural," assures that certain social functions will be served by assigning them to some and at the same time denying them to others. The most perfected version of this solution is the Hindu caste system. Since (and this is the tragic reality of social structure) social difference always involves inequality, such prior assignment advantages one category to the disadvantage of others. At the same time, ascribed status shelters certain differentiations from competition and thus can promote continuity and peace. Max Weber remarked that the point of hereditary monarchy is to assure that the highest position in the state is already filled and is therefore out of reach. Ascribed-status societies, which put most positions out of the reach of most people, are relatively inert, characterized by custom and a sense of resignation. Since competition is minimized there are few losers. A society that ascribes gender (labeled as sex) at birth asks us to resign ourselves to our gender.

Sex and Gender

Gender, the social construction of sex, is the way we use sex-difference to ascribe status—mostly indirectly, by ascribing qualities. Men are (we are told) combative, women peaceable; men are rational, women emotional; men are progressive, women conservative; men are disciplined and demanding, women are nurturant and flexible; women stay inside and make a home while men go out and make history. Not that this particular set of oppositions is culturally universal—probably Hopi men are as peaceable as their women, and Japanese women no more conservative than their men—but every culture has made some important distinctions in their expectations of men and women. Women (unquestionably) make babies whereas men (we are generally told) make the rules. Many cultures associate fertility and the land with the female, while the juridical authority of males (except in our own post-Enlightenment society) is as near a culture-universal as makes no difference. In all these ways gender, as the accepted order of things, provides an a priori description of the person, leaving the developing individual with further choices of conformity (the manly boy and the womanly girl), deviance (the sissy and the tomboy), or transgression (cross-dressing and homosexuality). Sex is a bundle of facts; gender is a system of values. The social construction of sex into gender turns fact into value by giving anatomical information normative force.

In the single-sex society I have imagined, sex would disappear; everyone would be simply human. Gender would continue to be possible, however, and it might well be found necessary to invent it—just as single sex-societies, for example prisons or boarding schools, tend to create "female" and "male" categories within their membership. Ancient pederasty did something similar within the all-male political society in its contrast between the male lover and the womanlike beloved. In other words, we already know about gender in the absence of sex.

In fact the categorization might well be more rigid, just as we can expect a higher standard of discipline from a volunteer army than from an army of conscripts, and greater patriotism from the naturalized citizen than from the native. Similarly we might imagine that the "mothers" in a society of women would be held to a higher standard of nurturance than in ours; they would have chosen their role in full knowledge of the consequences. Perhaps a few maternally gifted women would be selected to have very large families, releasing the others to other life tasks; those selected would become a kind of elite corps of the nurturant—perhaps also scorned as "breeders."

This imaginary society, however, would have lost part of our genetic inheritance; whatever traits are carried on the Y chromosome would have become extinct. From the point of view of social allocation, such an extinction represents the loss of a talent pool. If males are on average better at anything, there will be fewer persons available to play the roles where this gift is useful. Quite possibly, however, this would be no loss, or perhaps the loss would be a price worth paying for the elimination of a difference that has been throughout history the source of so much tension.

More socially significant than the loss of male qualities, however, would be the loss of the difference itself. All the binary sorting that occurs at birth would cease; as this source of tension disappeared, others would arise. The struggle for personal identity, which now takes place in compliance with or resistance to a socially dictated sexual identity, would become yet more open-ended. And since, as we have observed, all social positions would still be occupied, the differences that generate social distance between positions would still have to be arrived at somehow. Since sex did not exist, it would be necessary, in a way, to invent it. All this suggests that so far from it being (natural) sex that makes (cultural) gender necessary, it is rather gender that makes sex culturally useful. Society siezes upon sex difference in the interest of structure.

Society, which is a structure, is hungry for difference, and therefore amplifies and distorts natural differences in the process of making them structurally significant. Of all natural differences, sex is culturally the most important. Our imaginary monosex society, however, has reminded us that from the point of view of nature males are the nearly unnecessary sex. Their role in the formation of the next generation is fleeting and could well be unacknowledged—except that their relation with children is acculturated (as it always is) through social institutions of tribe and family. Marriage, indeed, has been seen as an institution that enables women to secure the help of men in raising their young, although it might as well be seen as an institution that enables males to claim title to children and thereby have descendants. In any case it is clear that the cultural order seeks to overcome the uncertain relation of one generation of males to the next.

Males, in fact, are defined by their natural incapacity: Not all women, it is true, have babies, but no men do. Quite possibly it is to compensate for this inadequacy that males everywhere assert that what men do is important, what women do relatively unimportant. In any case the males have time on their hands and the energies thus spared are released to other purposes. Being largely useless in nature, males become the cultural sex par excellence. Thus originates the familiar analogy ("Ortner's Rule") that will resonate through these pages: male:female::culture:nature (Ortner 1974). Quite possibly the most important cultural use of sex is to code the culture/nature difference.

In a monosex society the most significant absence might be the absence of the difference itself. "The principle of community is difference" not only because a distribution of functions encourages exchange but also because differing stocks of information encourage communication. When the men build themselves a world of artificial ideals, then it is the job of the women to bring them down to earth; when the women are fierce in defense of their own brood, it is the job of the men to take the long view and interpret family interest in terms of universally defensible rules. Each of us in dealing with the opposite sex is required to deal with the world as mirrored to us by an opposition. Differences mediated are more powerful than either pole simply; this is the social application of the principle that what does not kill you makes you stronger. Perhaps this is the deepest motivation for the development of sex into gender: By an amplification of difference the society sets itself the strenuous challenge of mediation. Sex difference stretches and educates us; we find that society asks us both to assert the values of our own sex and to appreciate those of the other. The tension of opposites, the Heracleitan bow, may be a universal cosmic principle, and here it comes home to us. Since a fertile couple consists of both sexes and in most societies a couple is a basic social unit, this mediation is part of our most intimate experience. Perhaps the best reason for the elaboration of sex into gender is that by increasing the distance between the sexes it also strengthens the bond between those persons who successfully mediate this difference.

Furthermore, it is the elaboration of sex into gender that makes possible the mediation. Sex is a fact, whereas gender is a concept; facts do not go away unless altered by the application of technology, but concepts are freely manipulable. The woman who sets out to be one of the boys, the man in touch with his feminine side, these people are making effective use of generic concepts. Furthermore, categorical contrasts can be elaborated both metaphorically and analogically. In Greek the sun is male, the moon female, a point not unconnected with the fact that the sun is all-seeing, whereas the moon is associated with witchcraft and arcane influences. Rivers are male, they make the land fertile; springs are female and nymph-haunted. These elaborations can also be manipulated; they are liable to dialectical inversion. Female Greek earth gives rise to the mythical first kings, snake-tailed and bearded; from the sky falls the fertilizing dew, which is also a triad of maidens. The master analogy, male:female::culture:nature, is equally apt to dialectic. Culture is natural to us; nature as we understand it is a cultural product. As women are on the side of nature they are associated with process, whereas men are associated with structure; women thereby become agents of culturally transformative processes, they are mistresses of life and death, of weddings and funerals, and as such the more cultural sex. Males, by contrast, may be seen as more animalistic, less costumed and nuanced, and thereby closer to nature. The juridical authority of which they are so proud may come to be seen even by themselves as rigid and ill-adapted to reality, needing to be mercifully tempered by the woman's touch. Cultural categories, in fact, need not constrain us since they can always be used against themselves to open new possibilities. And it is by transforming existing categorizations that we work our way into the unfamiliar. In fact I have expanded on these generic categories at possibly quite unnecessary length—there is certainly little here that is original—because throughout the inquiry that follows they will be reformed, transformed and inverted, and continually recur.

Citizens and Women

Politically significant differences are those used to legitimate authority. In the first urbanization of the Bronze Age, in the Near Eastern and Chinese cities of palace and temple, these differences were largely ascribed and inherited; the resulting society was a relatively stable hierarchy. There was some mobility in the system as elite cadres recruited talented (male) members from below—a process eventually rationalized in ancient China through the examination system. This mobility, however, left the fundamental hierarchy in place; ministers served the king, and kings were gods or at the least had the mandate of heaven.

In that second urbanization which began around the Mediterranean in the Iron Age, in the urbanization of the Phoenicians, the Greeks, and the Etruscans, the hierarchical model began to be replaced by a second model, founded on the idea of citizenship, which is the idea that the highest place in the community is occupied by a group of peers. These persons then allocated authority among themselves primarily by organizing competition for office and other kinds of status—competition motivated by what the Greeks call *philotimia*. In this way achieved status became the leading principle of political structure. Authority was no longer seen as inherent in the person, but rather as belonging to the office; offices could be won and lost. To the victor—in political conflict, but also in athletics and in the arts—belonged the spoils of power and influence. Authority was thereby demystified; it was not a given within a cosmic order but rather the result of a transparently secular process. This was the well-known "contest system" of the Greeks. Certain forms of ascribed status endured: Ritual privileges could be inherited, and heroic ancestry counted for something. Ideally, however, all citizens began equal and became unequal through competition. Obviously some were richer than others, but wealth was not seen as conferring status directly; rather, like talent and luck, it was an advantage in the competition for status.

The political revolutions of the post-Enlightenment nation-states claimed a kinship on this point with the ancient cities; this is one of the things we mean when we call the second urbanism a "first modernism." The Enlightenment found in the Roman republic, and to a lesser degree in Greek city-states, an exemplum of demystified authority. Authority had been legitimated in those cities, as in the then-emerging modern world, by victories in free competition between citizens formally equal before the law. Thus the classical past was used as a model for our achieved-status society.

Citizenship itself, however, was in the classical city an ascribed status, acquired (except in newly organized cities) almost exclusively by inheritance; furthermore it was almost everywhere heritable exclusively by and through the father. No doubt this was merely the persistence of that dominance of males which had been equally characteristic of the first urbanization. (The oldest cities sometimes had female monarchs, but ministers of state were exclusively male.) Gender remained a political principle.

In our post-Enlightenment polity citizenship is seen as a condition proper to all, even though it can be enjoyed only by those with the luck to belong to a free community; it is the exercise of the inalienable rights implied by our philosophical nature. Nevertheless until very recent times, in conformity with the classical model, those rights could be exercised only by males. This anomaly gave rise to the Woman Question. It should not have been the same for the Greeks, since for them citizenship in its essence was proper only to certain sorts of people: freeborn Greek males. They therefore should have had no ideological problem about the exclusion of slaves and women.

Nevertheless the establishment of cities of free men seems very early to have given rise to the idea of the city of free women—most obviously in the ritual level, in the widespread ritual of the Thesmophoria, when the wives of the citizens withdrew for some days to form their own temporary polity, with women holding fictive offices named from those of the real city. This ritual representation is echoed in the literary imaginings of both Aristophanes and Plato. It seems that the Woman Question was already adumbrated in this first modernism. Of course Greeks, like all their predecessors, oppressed their women; their historic contribution to the oppression of women, however, seems to have been their bad conscience about it. Probably this happened because one aspect or precondition of an achieved-status society was a relatively low level of personal authority, and this cultural feature appeared in the household as well as the state. The Greek father was assuredly in principle the absolute ruler of his little domain, but in practice most seem to have held the kind of authority we see in the Homeric Zeus: continually contested and uncertainly effective. Sex difference, in fact, appears among the Greeks as an example of what we shall be call "normal danger," a difference that continually asserts itself in conflict and stands to be again mediated.

Why, then, did Greek men persist in maintaining sex difference as a social and political principle? Why did they not admit women to the polity as their equals? Perhaps because for them our biological nature had something normative about it. Surely our philosophical nature, which is more an aspiration than an actuality (we are not really all that rational, compassionate, etc.), is normative: Our special capacities confer upon our species certain species-universal rights and obligations. Our biological nature, however, is in its turn more than a set of limitations, of unsolved technical problems; it is also the kind of creature that we are, and there is indeed some health in an aspiration to fulfill one's creatureliness. A society in which everyone was the same sex would, from this point of view, not be a human society; it would lack an organizing principle that (unlike such parvenus as race and class) is far older than society itself, a principle that we share with most of the animals and even some of the plants. From this point of view, a society that has not coped in some way with the division of the species into two sexes has not coped with the problem of being human. The Greeks coped, somewhat shamefacedly, by relegating women to private life and saving the public sphere for males.

From the time of Hesiod onward women appear in Greek literature as a Problem—a problem that was partially solved in various ways by various constitutional and social arrangements. At Athens women were nearly annihilated in terms of public life—at least in theory; in practice they took a measure of revenge. At Sparta they were both liberated and excluded and, I shall argue, became vehicles for the repressed elements of that repressive regime. Their position at Locri is the central puzzle of this book; to anticipate a very long argument, I conclude that as vehicles for the transmission of status they were in that polity awarded a unique degree of respect (which need not imply liberty or even real appreciation), and that the exchange of women through marriage both maintained the social order and prefigured to the Locrians the joys of the world to come. The mediation of the difference between male and female therefore became a model for the mediation of the difference between life and death. It will be many chapters yet, however, before we are in a position to examine the arguments tending toward this conclusion.

This is a book that attempts its work on at least three different levels. In the first place, it attempts to identify a Locrian strand in the Greeks— and therefore in us. Second, it is a prolonged reflection on the social uses of sex and gender. Lastly, it attempts a mode of thought about society, founded on the proposition that the cultural life of society consists of the establishment and mediation of difference, and that mediation is dialectical.

Of all socially significant differences, sex is most deeply inscribed in the cosmic order. "Male and female created He them"; he did not create us rich and poor, slave and free, or even clever and slow. Male and female we are (nearly all the time) born; the question is what we are to make of this. The Greeks took it for granted that sex difference is essential in us and needs to be respected in the social order. Perhaps we in all our enlightenment still have something to learn from them in this, more particularly from the Locrian solution to the tensions and dilemmas thus created. Difference always carries with it inequality of power; that, perhaps, is the sociological version of original sin. But difference also makes possible complementarity and cooperation—providing that the parties are able to overcome their competitive will to power. When this happens, the difference of the parts becomes, in principle, the basis for the happiness of the whole. Perhaps we should think on this. After all, sex differences do still exist, and we still have to find some way to live with them. Possibly putting them to use is not the worst of all solutions, particularly if the uses are dialectical, which is to say, resourcefully ambivalent.

Part One

SEXUAL COMPLEMENTARITY

One

The Sexes in Cosmos and History

In the beginning, Hesiod tells us,[1] *there was only Space and Love and Earth and Hell. Space of herself bore male and female darkness, and these bore male and female light. Female darkness (Night) then of herself bore many children, a brood of dark and dangerous creatures; the youngest of her daughters, Strife, in her turn and of herself produced another such brood. Meanwhile Earth of herself bore Sky, Ocean, and the Mountains. Sky and Earth together then generated the Titans. Because Sky never ceased to press upon Earth these were unable to emerge. Therefore Earth gave Cronos, the bravest of these offspring, a sickle with which he castrated his father Sky. From the blood where it fell upon Earth grew another dark brood; the actual genitals fell into Ocean where they generated Aphrodite.*

Cronos's sister Rhea was subdued (dmētheisa) *by him and they bore six Olympian gods: Hestia, Demeter, Hera, Poseidon, Hades, and Zeus. As soon as each was born, however, Cronos swallowed the child. Finally Rhea substituted a stone for Zeus, the last-born. Therefore Zeus could grow up to overcome his father Cronos, and cast him into Hell. Zeus took charge of the universe and distributed* timai, *titles, honors, and functions, to the other gods. He also began to marry* (alochon theto), *beginning with a Titan named Craft* (Mētis), *marrying also the second-generation Titan Leto, mother of Apollo and Artemis, also his sister Demeter, mother of Persephone, several other Titans, and finally, as his only legitimate wife, his sister Hera, mother with him of Ares, Hebe, and Eileithuia. The Olympians, under the leadership of Zeus, then fought and won a war against the Titans and the universe became finally and definitively stable.*

Earth, however, had given Zeus a prophecy that his son by Craft was destined to be greater than himself. Therefore while Craft was still pregnant—with a daughter—he swallowed her. Thus the daughter, Athena, was born from the head of Zeus and the prophesied son never conceived. In revenge Hera bore of herself Hephaistus. Stability was tested when Hell produced his only child, coupling with Earth to produce the monster Typhon, whom Zeus defeated as the last threat to his sovereignty.

This is the story of the establishment of cosmic patriarchy: Zeus, "father of gods and men," takes control. In order to do so he had to

---

[1] This account is paraphrased from the *Theogony*, with very much detail omitted. For a more detailed account of the same material see Redfield (1993). The last section of this chapter, "Nature and Culture," is reprinted verbatim from that piece.

overcome his father, who before him had overcome his own father. Cronos, in fact, is the first "Oedipal" father in Greek myth: His son threatens to replace him and he tries to annihilate the child. So this is a story about the paradox of patriarchy: In order to be a patriarch one must be a father, that is to say, one must engender a next generation, which is a threat to the very authority it makes possible.

However the story is not only about fathers and sons; it is at least as much about the mothers, and their babies, and love. Love is one of the first beings, but love has no progeny; he is present throughout as the principle of cosmic progress. The universe has an erotic history, and evolves through parturition and coupling, that is to say, through kinship. First the mothers produce children without fathers, parthenogenetically. As the universe develops, however, this ceases to be possible: children require two parents. The children of Strife are the last fatherless children (except for Hephaistus).

This succession myth reaches its conclusion when Zeus avoids siring the son who would replace him by swallowing the mother; thereby Athena (who does have two parents) is born from the father. This anomaly produces a brief regression to birth from the mother alone when Hera in an attempt to claim equality with her husband produces Hephaistus. That child is however imperfect: crippled, childless, in various stories rejected by his mother and cuckolded by his wife. He is a token of his mother's subjection to Zeus.

Athena is the living token of the triumph of the father. She is, further, a virgin, a *parthenos*; she, Artemis, and Hestia alone among the goddesses are immune to the power of Aphrodite (*Homeric Hymn to Aphrodite* 7–33). Hestia, although both Apollo and Poseidon court her, refuses marriage and keeps to the house of Zeus; she (although she is his sister) plays the part of Zeus's prenubile daughter who tends the hearth and embodies the purity of the house. Artemis is the wild daughter, a huntress who strays about the mountains; she is highly sexual although unavailable, and surrounded by available nymphs. Artemis, that is, embodies the nubile daughter; she is eternally just this side of sexuality. Thus both Hestia and Artemis embody recognizable female roles.

Athena, by contrast, while certainly female, is not so in any recognizable way. Her resistance to sexuality, the *Hymn to Aphrodite* tells us, is part of her choice of war, the typically male activity. She also is patron of male crafts, of carpenters and of smiths who make armaments. At the same time, she is patron of weaving and women's crafts. She goes between the sexes. It is symptomatic that in epic the gods appear in mortal disguise appear as persons of their own sex—except for Athena; she can disguise herself as either male or female.

In terms of gender roles Athena is a monstrosity; the production of this monster is the necessary step toward closing down the process of generation and stabilizing the universe. The crippled Hephaistus is another cost of this closing down, as is the loveless, relatively infertile marriage of Zeus and Hera. Hera is the legitimate wife—indeed in Greek thinking she is the embodiment of legitimacy and sovereignty—and she alone cohabits with Zeus, but the others are the mothers of his more significant children.[2] Her relation with Zeus consists mostly of jealous wrangling.

The closing of cosmic development involves a transition from force to craft; Cronos is "crookedly crafty" and overcomes his father by a crafty ambush (arranged by Mother Earth). Zeus survives because of Rhea's crafty use of the stone, and is himself even craftier than his father; at last he incorporates Craft.

There is also a transition from rape to marriage: Sky's attentions to Earth are continual and uncontrollable; Cronos "subdues" Rhea; Zeus for the first time has wives; the gods are becoming a family. Furthermore Zeus distributes *timai*, functions and privileges, and bargains with them to secure his allies. Kinship is supplemented by negotiated relations. All in all the universe is becoming more civilized. Hesiod makes cosmic a fable that turns up in various forms all over the world: that order was achieved only when the men got control and displaced the women. As elsewhere, this involves a shift toward civil institutions. In Hesiod, as elsewhere, male is to female as culture is to nature.

On the other hand, in Hesiod the women do not go away; Marylin Arthur (Katz) points out that while the male authorities in Hesiod succeed each other, the women accumulate.[3] Earth, the first mother, is still with us and still fertile; indeed her coupling with Tartarus, a kind of negative Sky (as far below Earth as Sky is above her), produces the last challenge to Zeus's rule in the form of the monster Typhon. Aphrodite is the only deity from an earlier generation to achieve a place on Olympus; she is attended by Love (*Theogony* 201), one of the four primordial powers. A number of other females from the old order—most notably, Hecate—find a place with Zeus when he installs the new one.

The story, then, is not of the replacement of nature by culture, or the further forming of nature by its incorporation in culture; it is a story of the only partially successful repression of nature by culture. Zeus rules a natural order that he has not entirely mastered; the paternal power of Zeus rests on a perversion and inhibition of paternity: a

---

[2] Ares is (in Homer) "hated of gods and men"; Hebe is a servant, Eileithuia is an aspect of Hera in her role as patroness of childbirth.

[3] Arthur (Katz) (1982).

daughter born from the head and a son who is never conceived. On the other hand (as we shall see) his paternity is not over.

Pandora

Nature, expelled by the Olympian pitchfork, reasserts herself in the next phase of the story, when we turn to the relations of gods with mortals.

Once, Hesiod tells us,[4] *when gods and mortals still feasted together, there was a feast at Mecone at which Prometheus, a Titan, offered gods and men an ox. He craftily divided the beast into two portions, a small portion consisting of the meat, and a large portion consisting of the bones and fat. He then offered Zeus his choice of portions. Zeus knew he was being cheated; nevertheless he fell in with Prometheus's scheme and took the larger, less valuable portion. That is why beasts are divided at sacrifice: The bones and fat are burnt for the gods, while mortals get to eat the meat.*

Zeus then took his revenge on Prometheus by taking fire from us. Prometheus stole it back. Zeus then took further revenge for the theft of fire: He had formed from clay a beautiful maiden. Every god gave her a gift—of beauty, skill, speech—and therefore she is called "Allgifts," Pandora.

Prometheus had warned his brother Epimetheus not to accept any gifts Zeus might send, but when Pandora arrived Epimetheus was so swept away by her charms that he took her—and with her all the ills that flesh is heir to: labor, sickness, and scarcity. She was the first woman, and since her time, men are born of women and to toil.

Nor did Prometheus escape punishment; Zeus bound him.

There is no account in Hesiod of the origin of mankind, nor is there any account of how we were born before there were women; presumably we were born of the earth, or were immortal, or both. The feast at Mecone does seem, however, to be an account of the origin of sacrifice (although Hesiod does not say so). For the Greeks, burnt sacrifice was a way of making meat edible; domesticated animals were sacrificed, the meat of these animals was then eaten, and meat could not be eaten unless the animal had been sacrificed first.[5] Therefore the story is also about the origin of meat-eating, which is in the story evidently a novelty or Prometheus would not even think to succeed in his deception.

The story tells us that woman came to us "in exchange for [the theft of] fire"—in other words, because men have fire they have to have woman as well. The fire in question is evidently the sacrificial fire,

---

[4] This paraphrase conflates the versions of the Pandora story told in the *Theogony* 535–616, and *Works and Days* 42–105.

[5] There were certain exceptions to all these rules, but they remain the rules.

which is to say, the cooking fire.[6] So there seems to be some connection between birth through woman and the eating of meat.

Meat-eating is a source of anxiety because we are all made of meat; when eating animals we are eating others like ourselves in a modified form of cannibalism. The avoidance of cannibalism, says Hesiod (*Works and Days* 276–280) distinguishes humans from other species. This is not a natural rule (human flesh seems to be a healthy and, one hears, palatable food) but a cultural one. Cannibalism marks a frontier where our philosophical nature and our biological nature collide; it is the definitive conversion of the person into an animal. People rarely engage in it, and even when they do, it is never casual. It is everywhere troubling that people are both good to eat and good to think with, good to talk to and good to feed on.

On the other hand, people do generally eat meat. The opposite pole from cannibalism, vegetarianism, is certainly adopted by some but in no society is required of all. Anxiety about meat-eating, however, comes out in special rules. Generally it is expected that meat will be cooked; therefore the cooking fire becomes a key symbol of culture and all that distinguishes us from the other animals. The Greeks made the further requirement that the animal be sacrificed, and in this way shared with the gods and sanctified. On the other hand, sacrifice involved a division between the men's part and the gods' part, and the Prometheus story tells us that this commemorates the initial division between gods and men.[7] At sacrifice the Greeks wore crowns that marked them as sacrosanct and at the same time (according to Aeschylus) commemorated the bonds of Prometheus.[8]

Our flesh is our mortality. That which sustains our flesh is the food of our mortality—and this should especially be true of flesh made food. In any case the gods of the Greeks cannot eat and drink our food and drink; they consume the food and drink of immortality—ambrosia and nectar—which, indeed, would make us immortal too if we could get hold of them.

Because the gods cannot eat meat they can enjoy the sacrifice only in the form of the *knisē*, the savory smell that rises from burning the fat. Probably this is why Zeus allowed Prometheus to cheat him; he knew that Prometheus's arrangements were correct. Nevertheless Zeus is angry—probably at the fact that Prometheus brought in meat and mortality in the first place. In any case, Zeus, by taking away fire, tries to

---

[6] In contrast to the craft fire, which seems to be in the foreground in the *Prometheus Bound*.

[7] Cf. Vernant (1979).

[8] Brelich (1970).

make it impossible to eat meat in a cultural manner. Prometheus steals fire back, thus restoring us to both culture and mortality. Zeus then completes our mortal condition by sending us woman.

As flesh is the food of mortality, so to be born of flesh is the mortal mode of generation. Like roast meat, woman is (to Epimetheus) irresistibly delicious. Thus we bring our condition on ourselves, although in another sense it is brought upon us by the struggle between god and Titan that is going on over our heads. And our condition is characterized not only by mortality, but also by disease, toil, scarcity, and conflict. We live in the Age of Iron.[9]

The Pandora story reverses the trend of the succession myth; for the gods, the triumph of paternity is the achievement of structure; for us, paternity arrives as a punishment and opens before us the process of the generations. The gods repress nature and achieve a cultural order; we fall out of a purely cultural condition—all males, and immortal—into nature, characterized by mortality and women. Prometheus, who claims to be our friend, in fact inflicted this condition on us. Perhaps that is why Zeus is hostile to him from the beginning: Zeus can see that the real titanic project is to introduce mortality into the world, which is to say, to destabilize the cosmos.[10] In any case we fall from culture into nature as we come to be born of woman and must labor to induce the earth to yield us our livelihood.

Woman, of course, is (in the Greek view, where agriculture is man's work) like the earth; both become fertile when sown by the male. As we fall into nature we get close to the earth; therefore Pandora should be of the earth, earthy. In fact we have representations of Pandora rising from the earth, and once she is called "Anesidora," giver of gifts (also an epiklesis of Demeter and another name for the earth).[11] Therefore it has been suggested Pandora was originally an earth goddess, remodeled by Hesiod.[12] Our evidence for the earthy Pandora is, however, considerably later than Hesiod; I prefer to think that the tradition lapsed into this "error" because, for all Hesiod's protests to the contrary, Pandora's connection with the natural order was patent. She is an ambiguous figure, and we should expect ambiguity in representations of her.

Hesiod explains her name: "because all the gods gave her gifts." This is contrary to Greek onomastic tendencies, which would rather lead us

[9] In the *Works and Days* 174–178.

[10] In some other versions of the story Prometheus is the creator of humankind, sometimes in opposition to Zeus.

[11] Cf. Casanova (1979), pp. 66–67.

[12] Robert (1914).

to interpret her name as "giver of all gifts"—like *dotēr heaōn*, "giver of good things," a title of Demeter. Probably Hesiod is explicit in his idiosyncratic interpretation of the name because he wishes to insist on Pandora's artificiality. In Hesiod, as Pietro Pucci points out, Pandora is an artifact.[13] This reversal is critical for Hesiod's well-known misogyny. For him women are on the side of culture, in fact of luxury, which is an excess of culture; they are deceitful, greedy, expensive; they distract men from their work, which is their struggle with the earth, and consume the resources of that work, thereby making it harder.

Women nevertheless are necessary if a man is to have an son; otherwise "the residual heirs will disperse his resources" (*Theogony* 607–608). Note that Hesiod is talking not of natural land, freely available, but of property, cultural land. Nor is the point of the woman merely a child; Hesiod wants an heir. Therefore a woman is not enough; he must have a legitimate wife. But marriage is a cultural relation, and between persons. A married woman can demand her rightful share; unlike the land she has a mind of her own. It is this that Hesiod resents. The fertility of the woman links her to nature, but marriage-exchange situates her in culture, where she is a "speaking sign," in the phrase of Lévi-Strauss.

Therefore the rule male:female::culture:nature is, like all such structural analogies, dialectical: the opposite is also true—not as true, but also true.

Pandora's Children

Epimetheus married Pandora; their child was Pyrrha.[14] Prometheus also had a child: Deucalion. The identity of Prometheus's wife is variously given, but we are told by at least one source that she was Pandora.[15] Since Pandora was the first mortal woman, she seems the only creature available to be the mother of mortals. So it is plausible that she married both brothers, as she was surely sent to them both.[16]

Deucalion and Pyrrha were the sole survivors of the great flood that

[13] Pucci (1977).

[14] For sources see West (1985), p. 50n.35.

[15] The scholiast on Apollonios Rhodios 3. 1086 = Hesiod frag. 2 West.

[16] The scholiast on Homer *Od.* 10.2 (= Hesiod frag. 4 West) says that most people called Deucalion's mother Klymene (and this therefore was Prometheus's wife). In the *Theogony* (508) Klymene is Prometheus's mother. This scholiast also says that Hesiod gave the name of Prometheus's wife as Pryneie—a name that otherwise means nothing to us; could it be a mistake for Pronoia, a name of kindred meaning with Prometheus (Casanova 1979, 145)? Deucalion's mother in any case was clearly a problem—perhaps because the ancients, like a number of modern scholars, thought implausible a tradition that Prometheus married his nemesis.

Zeus sent to destroy us. They reinstituted sacrifice.[17] They repopulated the earth by throwing stones over their shoulders; the people sprung from these stones were the Leleges, an aboriginal people of Greece. They also had children of their own: Pyrrha bore Hellen "in name to Deucalion, but in fact to Zeus";[18] he was the ancestor of the Hellenes. Deucalion had a daughter Pandora; she bore to Zeus Graikos (Hesiod fr. 5 M&W), ancestor of the Epirote Greeks (after whom the Romans called the whole people Graeci). Another of Deucalion's daughters, Thuia, bore to Zeus Magnes, father of the Thessalians, and Makedon, father of the Macedonians. Zeus, in other words, coupled with the daughter and grandaughters of Pandora and produced various "first men," and thereby the peoples of Greece.

Through these unions—and the many more that follow—the high god reenters history. Several times Zeus has tried to destroy us; all the same, he cannot keep his hands off our women. Aphrodite works her will on him (*Hymn to Aphrodite* 39–40) and he breeds heroes who go on to make history. (Zeus provides an abbreviated catalogue in *Iliad* 14.313–328). Perhaps he does not do this any more, but every city in Greece included noble families who traced their lineage back to these families—the kings of Sparta to the most notable of all the heroic sons of Zeus: Heracles, who may even in the end have become a god. Heracles, Hesiod tells us (*Theogony* 526–530), finally rescued Prometheus from his punishment—not that Zeus was any less angry, but that his anger was outweighed by his desire that his own son achieve some truly significant act. In other words, Zeus's interest in his mortal offspring finally outweighs even his anger. If Zeus's anger was originally at Prometheus for introducing mortality into the world, then the outcome is that Zeus values particular mortals more than he hates mortality. In his masculine nobility Heracles is godlike—on his way to divinity—and in his way becomes on earth the male heir that Zeus could not have in heaven.

Thus it turns out that the structure achieved by Zeus gives way to process, that cosmos opens out into history, under the sign of Aphrodite—who already herself has all the feminine traits then passed on to Pandora: elaborate ornaments, wheedling words, deceptive wiles. These qualities are dangerous, but they enable women to charm men into sexuality, which makes babies. Therefore a man can have an heir and the farm can go on—or the great family, the family with heroic ancestors, can do more great deeds and make history. The nobility of males is their manliness, which is their difference from women, but in reach-

---

[17] Rudhardt (1970).
[18] West (1985), p. 53n.44.

ing across this difference women create couples, which are more powerful than men singly. Males make order, females reopen order to possibility.

Nature and Culture

Scholastic philosophy made a distinction between two kinds of nature: *natura naturata* and *natura naturans.* The first is the inner order of nature: From the music of the spheres down the great chain of being to the symmetrical opposition of the elements, nature coheres as a functioning system. The second is the inner tendency of nature to achieve that system. Whereas the first is displayed, for example, in the unity of an organism, the second shows itself in the tendency and capacity of the organism to grow, repair itself, and reproduce. The first is order, being; the second process, becoming. Both are primary realities, and both therefore are (for the Greeks) divine; Greek stories often tell in one way or another of the dialectic between these principles. In theogonic narrative they are in the contrast between paternity and maternity. On Olympus they are perhaps best represented by Zeus and Aphrodite; Zeus is god of order, communicated through meaningful signs (even the thunderbolt is usually interpretable), whereas Aphrodite's power is felt as an inner yielding, an inchoate experience. Yet Zeus also is subject to the power of Aphrodite, while Aphrodite is herself an Olympian and in the end subject to the rules.

In the logic of myth the assertion of a difference leads, as likely as not, to the discovery of each aspect under the sign of the other. We earlier identified order with culture, process with nature. Now we speak of them both as aspects of nature. Both also are aspects of culture. Culture surely establishes differences, asserts a stable structure of roles and obligations, but to shift roles and revise obligations is also cultural, and is the work of institutionalized processual structures, especially rituals. We can see that Lévi-Strauss's rule, "nature is continuous, culture discontinuous," holds only in this dialectical sense. Nature consists of form *and* matter, flux *and* information; as a system of forms, a cosmos, nature in fact presents a model for the cultural order. We might think of this as the cultural aspect of nature. Conversely culture provides modulations from stage to stage, "chromatic" passages, whereby the categories are subject to transformation. We might think of this as the naturalization of culture; these mediations allow us to live as cultural creatures in the real world.

On Greek Olympus, Zeus is male, Aphrodite female; this is as it should be. Women, who have the strange chromatic capacity to make one person into two, are everywhere the patrons of transformation. Greek women, in particular, took charge of the wedding and the funeral—which, along with childbirth, were the great rites of passage. Women similarly have a typical role as mediators; men make the rules and women figure out how to make them livable. Yet women also assert and enforce the rules; Dike and Eunomia are maidens. Hera, not Zeus, is the personification of sovereignty. Conversely rivers, fertile bull-headed deities, are male, and Zeus has no sooner abandoned us to nature by sending us Pandora than he recovers contact with us by seducing Pandora's daughters. From the point of view of sexuality, it is the males who are uncontrollable, the women who (in the best case) can set an example of order and restraint. Even Aphrodite could be, at Corinth, *poliouchos*, keeper of the city; women may be in some respects a problem to civil society, but from another point of view they will turn out to be critical to the maintenance of a civil order.

Two

Women in Civil Society

The Subjection of Women

That Greek males believed in the subjection of women is unquestionable; indeed we have just seen that their mythology tells us that the conquest by males of female powers is the foundation of civilization and quite possibly of the cosmic order itself. This theme is recapitulated in their folk histories: The *Oresteia*, for instance, tells how the disastrous situation produced in the king's house when the queen takes command is finally redressed when Athena, who "stands only for the male," succeeds in persuading the female Furies to serve the juridical authority of Athenian males. From antiquity to the present many have taken these stories to represent some kind of historical reality and have thought that some kind of early matriarchy was in fact replaced by patriarchy; there is actually no good evidence for this. It seems better to take these stories as social structure displayed in the form of narrative: They do not tell us that women were once in charge, but rather insist that, if they ever were, it would be a situation absolutely to be changed. The Greeks were nothing if not patriarchal, and if some of the women thought otherwise, we hear very little about it.

A number of recent studies have suggested that Greek patriarchy was in practice less than absolute: indeed ideology, so far from telling us what happened, is often evidence for its opposite. The insistence that women should be silent tells us that they were heard from; the insistence that they should stay indoors tells us that they wandered;[1] the insistence that they should obey without question tells us they were often resistant to male authority. Women at Athens could not, it seems, own or dispose of property, but Virginia Hunter has collected plenty of evidence that they sometimes did, in defiance of the rules.[2] Ideological insistence is often one pole of an ambiguous actuality.

---

[1] Cohen (1990). "Women of the privileged classes . . . are seen attending funerals, both private (Lys. 1.8) and public (Thu. 2.45), going to festivals (Lys. 1.20), gathering in the streets (Ar. *Ec.* 1–310, *Lys.* 1–253, *Th.* 792), visiting male relatives in prison (Lys. 13.39–41, And. 1.48), attending women's parties (Ar. *Ec.* 348–350, *Lys.* 700–702, *Th.* 795), visiting neighbors (Men. *Sam.* 35–38, Herod. *Mim.* 6, Theoc. 15), and, of course, going to the well (*h.Cer.* 105–107)." Pratt (2000), p. 51.

[2] Hunter (1994), pp. 21–29.

The ambiguous status of Greek women, however, relates not only to the gap between ideology and practice; it is also internal to the ideology itself. We have just seen this on the theogonic level: having suppressed the female element by swallowing one wife and antagonizing another, Zeus proceeds to reconnect mankind to nature by sending them the race of women, and he himself, with other gods, becomes subject to Aphrodite, last child of grandfather Uranus, and so reenters history. These women are—to the gods as to mortals—so attractive; both as problems and as motives they are powerful. They embody all the ambiguities of society's relation to that natural order to which we do and do not belong.

An isomorphic ambiguity can be observed on the political level: Women—certain women, that is—do and do not belong to the political community. The question can be put thus: Given that citizens are superior to other men, and men superior to women, what made women of citizen families superior to other women? Aristotle, after all, says that "women are one half of the free population (*eleutheroi*)" (*Politics* 1260b), and for Aristotle throughout the *Politics*, freedom, *eleutheria*, is one of the proper grounds for a claim to full citizenship, yet Aristotle never suggests that women should participate in political life. These women, it seems, both were and were not citizens.

The Freedom of Men

The Greeks tell us that whereas barbarian society is hierarchical a Greek polity is an association of equals. Barbarians are all slaves, since each is subject to another and all are subject to the king; Greek citizens are free, *eleutheroi*. This is a status founded on equality and similarity: *ep' isēi kai homoiai*; the sovereign (unless sovereignty has been usurped by a tyrant) belongs to some plurality of masterless men, no one of whom recognizes any juridical superior. Legitimate political authority belongs to the office, not the officeholder, and offices are taken in turns, which means that citizens alternate in superiority and inferiority. At Sparta, which was in many respects the prototypical city-state, we are told that the art most studied was *archein kai archesthai*, that of ruling and being ruled.[3] The Spartan knew how to give orders and how to take them.

Freedom, *eleutheria*, is for the Greeks not only distinct from but opposite to license; freedom is in fact rather associated with discipline.

---

[3] Plutarch *Moralia* 212c–d and Babbit in his Loeb edition of Plutarch ad loc.; see also Xenophon *Agesilaus* 2.16; in the philosophical tradition *archein kai archesthai* was the "lesson" (*epistēmē*) that the orderly citizen learned—see Xenophon *Cyropaedeia* 1.6.20, Plato *Laws* 643e; in the *Republic* (444d) it is equated with health.

The *locus classicus* on this point (the context is again Spartan) is Demaratus's response to Xerxes, who asked how it was that the Greeks would fight: His own subjects fought under the lash, but these strange free creatures seemed to have nothing to compel them. The Spartans, answers Demaratus,

> although they are free are not entirely free. They have a master, their law, and they fear it far more than your subjects fear you. And so they do whatever it commands. And it gives always the same command; it does not allow them to flee from any mass of people in battle; they must stay in the ranks and conquer or perish. (Herodotus 7.104.4–5)

Citizenship, that is, is an honorable condition, tested and proven by the risks of war. Military training is therefore the initiation proper to free manhood. The citizens in the fullness of manhood then demonstrate their equality and similarity in the hoplite phalanx, which is only as strong as its weakest link. All must stand together *en taxei*, in their assigned places. Those who fail the test receive harsh local names: "shield-thrower" at Athens, "trembler" at Sparta. The penalty is *atimia*, loss of political rights. Courage in combat is thus the minimal precondition of citizenship.

The warrior of the city-state, however (in contrast to the heroic warrior), while he sealed on the battlefield his membership in the group, did not there achieve exceptional status within it. The Greeks did award medals in recognition of exceptional battlefield achievements—*t'aristeia*—but in classical times war was seldom an arena in which men rose to notability. In fact, those who during the long Peloponnesian War proved themselves gifted commanders, such as Demosthenes and Brasidas, usually remained politically insignificant. In battle the ideological focus was on participation, not preeminence. Command in battle even in the fifth century continued to be given to those who had proved themselves elsewhere, by political success. Victory in debate, not combat, was the way to public recognition: Free (Greek) men (it was thought) assert themselves in speech. The citizen therefore is characterized by *parrhēsia*, which is not so much "freedom of speech" as "absence of deference." "*Parrhēsia* is proper to *eleutheria*," says Democritus (B 226 DK), "although the right moment for it is risky." The opposite of *parrhēsia* is *kolakeia*, flattery, which (like throwing away your shield) is symptomatic of fear. "Terror produces flattery" says Democritus (B 268 DK) "without goodwill." *Kolakeia* and *aneleutheria*, unfreedom, are more or less synonymous (Plato *Republic* 590b); the free man displays his free spirit in fearless speech.

Here again the Greeks defined themselves in contrast to the barbarous cities of the Near East. The Persian king was for them a tyrant, and like all tyrants expected to be flattered. Although his powers were absolute—it was the law of the Persians that the king could do whatever he liked (Herodotus 3.31)—he was, precisely because of his arbitrary power and associated deference, not truly free, which is to say, not capable of true political action. In a true political community a free man persuades others like himself as to the merits of his case; he thus exercises rational power (in contrast to the impulsive authority of the oriental monarchs). Issues are brought *es to koinon* or *es meson*, into a public meeting where they are debated; the free citizen has *isēgoria*, access to the floor, and *isonomia*, the equal protection of the laws. This juridical equality implies social similarity—that is to say, an egalitarian society marked by lack of deference. Therefore exceptional success of any kind is socially dangerous. Social discipline is enforced by envy, as political discipline is enforced by the fear of the law.

All this, of course, is an idealization and even so applies only to the narrow circle of the citizens. In no Greek city can these have been one quarter of the inhabitants, and in a wealthy commercial city like Athens they were probably less than 10 percent. The underage, in the first place, were excluded; under ancient demographic conditions these must have been close to half the population. Most citizens probably owned a slave or two, and some owned many; these were of course excluded. Also excluded were those between slave and citizen—aliens, who might be citizens somewhere else but not here, and freedmen, who ceased to be slaves without acquiring citizenship. Also excluded were women. It is on this exclusion that I focus here.

The Exclusion of Women

War and (political) speech define the specific manliness that is citizenship, and neither is proper for a woman. "War is for men to take care of—*polemos andressi melēsei*," in the Homeric phrase, which is or became a proverb.[4] When Hector uses this phrase to Andromache (*Il.* 6.492), he is not just telling her that she does not belong in combat: He is telling her that since she is not a warrior she is not entitled to opinions about the war. Similarly Telemachus excludes his mother (*Od.* 1.358): *muthos andressi melēsei*, "speech is for men to take care of." (He is about to summon a political assembly.) Later he adapts Hector's whole sentence (*Od.* 21.350–353)—as Alcinoos adapts it in order to recover the political initiative from his wife Arete (*Od.* 11.352). Similarly the phrase comes pat to Lysistrata's husband:

---

[4] See its awkward use in *Il.* 20.137, where men are in contrast to gods.

We stood it all as long as we could;
We kept on our good behavior, whatever you men did.
You never let us grumble. But we didn't like it!
After all we could see what was happening, and oftentimes here at home
We heard about the dumb decisions you made—on the biggest issues.
Although we were crying on the inside we'd ask with a laugh
"What was decided about the ratification of the treaty
In your meeting today?" "What's that to you?" my man'd say,
"Keep quiet." And I kept quiet. . . .
                          I did keep quiet.
Then we found out about some even worse decision
And we'd ask: "Honey, how'd you do something so stupid?"
And he'd give me a straight look, and say if I didn't stick to my spinning
I'd soon have a faceful of tears, "'war is for men.'"

                              Aristophanes *Lysistrata* 507–520[5]

"Silence is a woman's adornment (*kosmos*)" says Sophocles' Ajax to his wife when he wants her to stay out of his affairs (S.*Aj.* 293); this also is more or less a proverb.[6] The theme recurs in Andromache's description of herself as a good wife:

All ways we women have found out to be good,
These were my constant care under Hector's roof.
First—and whatever blame they do or don't
Bring against us women, this in itself provokes
Reproaches, when she doesn't stay indoors—
I gave up any such wish and stayed at home.
There in the house I never gave entertainment
To sophisticated female talk; wisdom was the teacher
Who tutored me well in private; that sufficed.
With silent tongue and peaceful eye I met
My husband; I knew where I should prevail
And when to leave the victory to him.

                              Euripides *Troades* 645–656

All this is of course another idealization; Andromache here is not so much good as goody-goody. In fact when she goes on to say how cheerfully she nursed the bastards produced by her husband's adultery, more than one Greek male, I suspect, would have thought her extravagant. In any case these formulations state not so much the rules to which women were actually held but rather what it meant not to be a

---

[5] Compare: ἱστοὶ γυναίκων ἔργα κοὐκ ἐκκλησίαι—Menander Sententiai 363 Jaekel.
[6] Aristotle *Politics* 1260a30; cf. S. Fr.. 61 Nauck, Heracleidæ 476f., Æschylus *Septem* 232 Democritus 274 Diels.

man. The manly world of the free citizens was secured by the suppression of women:

> When the woman's ways rule in the house
> The man is a slave, he is free no longer.
>
> Euripides Fr. 502 Nauck 4–5

A woman does have a sphere of her own—even Andromache knew there were places where she should prevail—but it is firmly delimited; a woman's place is in the home: invisible, inaudible, and under a man's control.

We remember the prayer of thanksgiving attributed to Socrates among others (Diogenes *Laertius* 1.33): first that he was born human and not a brute beast, then that he was a man and not a woman, third that he was Greek and not barbarian. All these "others" are excluded from the city[7]—or rather they are excluded from political life, from public speech, while remaining included in society at work. Barbarians are included in the role of slaves, and animals are included by being domesticated. (Aristotle *Politics* 1252b says that the ox is the slave of the poor.) Women, similarly, are included by being subordinated. Thus the socialization of women is often treated in metaphors of domestication, of horsebreaking or the subjection of the ox to the yoke.[8]

Although certain animals are naturally suited to domestication, these actually become domesticated only when included in society. Their "otherness" then becomes a specific social status. Similarly (for those Greeks who subscribed to the doctrine of natural slavery) barbarians are naturally suited to slavery, but they only become slaves when brought to Greece for that purpose. In their own place they are not free, since they are not citizens; they are either wild savages (neither ruling nor ruled) or in servitude to Oriental despots. However this servitude is not in the strict sense slavery, since the despots, not being citizens, are not free themselves. The true slave is the slave of the free man; that is why at Sparta, where the free man was most free (because most disciplined), the slave was most a slave (Critias fr. B37 DK). Similarly, for the Greeks, only Greek women are free women. The women of other nations are not, although in wild places they are wild and in the Orient show great independence and even rule their men. Barbarians after all are in a way all women; they lack the manly capacity for military discipline and free debate, and therefore are incapable of forming that specific relation with their wives that defines the free

---

[7] DuBois (1982b).
[8] Gould (1980), p. 53.

woman.[9] To be a free woman is to have a specific relation to a free society.

Domesticated animals and slaves are property; the free woman is not. She is, however, under supervision. She has a *kurios*, a guardian—her father, originally, then her husband (although the father retained certain rights[10]), and finally in widowhood her son or some collateral relative. *Kurios* is also the term for the guardian of an orphan, who exercises the rights and responsibilities of a parent. As one who must always have a *kurios* the woman is a kind of perpetual child.

At Athens women could not own property;[11] elsewhere they could, but even so transactions usually involved the consent of the *kurios*.[12] Similarly, the *kurios* represented the woman in the court. The scholiast to Aristophanes (ad *Knights* 965) tells us: "this is the usual way they summon a case to the law court, 'Ms. so-and-so and *kurios*'—which is to say, her husband." A woman was juridically hardly a person in her own right. Her respect for the male world, further, was expected to lead her to control herself. The kind of self-restraint we see in Andromache's description of herself is precisely characteristic of the *gunē eleuthera* (the phrase has many of the connotations of our "respectable woman"); "the outer house-door is the proper limit for a free woman" (Menander Fr. 546 11.3–4). If this restraint is lacking, women begin to stray; the Greek word for this is *anesis*. The *anesis* of women is always a negative fact, whereas "free woman" is an honorable title.[13] It seems that Greek women became free by being under restraint. But since they could take no part in war or politics where male freedom is earned and displayed, in what did their freedom consist?

---

[9] "Among barbarians the female and the slave have the same position. The reason is that they have not the natural capacity to command, so that their partnership is between male slave and female slave." Aristotle *Politics* 1252b.27. Just (1985), p. 188, commenting on this passage, remarks: "for Aristotle, among the undifferentiated mass of the barbarians not only was there no distinction between the characteristics of free men and slaves, but also none between those of men and women"—which is not quite what Aristotle says, but may well be what he meant.

[10] Hunter (1994), p. 15.

[11] Women at Athens could certainly inherit property; perhaps it is more accurate to say that they could own it but not dispose of it. Cf. de Ste. Croix (1970); Foxhall (1989).

[12] Schaps (1979).

[13] *Anesis* is the term used by both Plato (*Laws* 637c) and Aristotle (*Politics* 1270a1) for the (from the philosophic point of view, highly undesirable) license allowed women at Sparta. Cf., for the cognate verb, Plato *Comicus* Fr. 98:

> A woman, if you keep her
> Under constant discipline, is the best thing you can acquire;
> Let her loose and she becomes a thing of outrageous intemperance.

Sexual Discipline

The answer has something to do with the restriction of sexuality. Whereas the Greeks recurrently picture barbarism as a society where women are freely available, in a free Greek society free women are sexually unavailable except by marriage. The law, says Pausanias in Plato's *Symposium* (181e), forbids the love of free women. By implication, it permits the love of unfree women: slaves, certainly, but also those women who are "liberated" in the sense that they are not slaves, but not respectable because not in the care of their male kin. All women not so guarded are potentially available as prostitutes or otherwise; the statuses of *pallakē* (concubine), *hetaira* (courtesan), and *pornē* (whore) fade into each other, and it is in one or another of these, almost without exception, that we meet such unsupervised women in Greek literature. A generation ago we called these "loose women," which implied that they ranged freely; for the Greeks also they have (precisely in their lack of freedom) a freedom of action denied to the free woman:

> It is hard, Pamphile,
> For a free woman to battle with a whore.
> She can do more damage, she knows more, she is ashamed
> Of nothing, and she's better at flattering.

Menander Fr. 566

It was of course also possible (although discreditable) for a free woman to sell herself. It was even possible for her lawful husband to serve as her pimp. The law recognized this possibility by exempting the customer in such a case from the penalties against adultery ([Demosthenes] 59.67). Such a woman had forfeited the protections of a free woman. So also a man who sold himself lost the rights of a citizen: He could not hold office or speak in public (Aeschines 1.29). The penalty is the same as that for throwing away his shield in battle. The coward proves himself no free man; the male prostitute becomes androgynous (idem 110–111) and accepts the status of an unfree woman. The woman taken in adultery loses the right to take part in public rituals; she is "excluded from that sphere of public life which is the equivalent of politics for men."[14] In all three cases—coward, catamite, whore—the abandonment of a sociosexual role, the failure to remain *en taxei*, brings with it loss of citizenship.

The chastity of the free woman thus corresponds to the manly courage of the citizen. The freedom of women, like the freedom of men, is political: It is proper to the woman who holds her place in the social

---

[14] Cohen (1991), p. 225.

order and thereby performs a political role. We are told (Plutarch *Solon* 23) that a law of Solon permitted a father to sell his unchaste daughter as a slave. Once again, freedom turns on self-discipline. The man offers his life for the city, the woman saves her sexuality for legitimate marriage and then risks her life in the production of legitimate heirs. "I would rather stand three times beside my shield," says Medea, "than bear one child" (Euripides *Medea* 250–251). Statistics on mortality in childbirth and battle—at least before the Peloponnesian War—would almost certainly have supported her estimate of the relative risks. In this way we can interpret Vernant's rule that "marriage is to the young woman what war is to the young man."[15] Legitimate sexuality is the woman's honor.

It is "vile (*phaulon*) to lead a free girl (*parthenos eleuthera*) into error" (Menander *Dyskolus* 289–291). A man caught in the act with a free girl could theoretically be murdered with impunity by any of her close male relatives.[16] Sex with such a woman could be safely enjoyed only by those ready to accept the responsibilities of marriage.

On these matters, Sostratus,
Here's how I stand. Say one of my friends falls for
A courtesan. . . . I run right in and grab her.
I'm drunk, I start fires, there's not a word to be said.
Before even asking who she is, we've got to have her.
Delay's the thing that makes the passion grow
While a quick start comes to a quick conclusion.
Say that he talks of marriage, though, and of a free girl
Then I'm quite different. I inquire into her family,
Her life, her character. This time it's for keeps;
My friend will permanently remember how I handled the matter.

Menander *Dyskolus* 57–68

Prostitution is sex without consequences; marriage is sex with in-laws. The difference is the difference between market-exchange and gift-exchange: The first is a transitory relation entered into for the sake of the commodity, while in the second the commodity is exchanged in the service of—and as a symbol of—a continuing bond between the parties. The parties, further, are conceived not as persons but as lineages. Concubinage (as we shall see) could extend the sexual relation into a

[15] Vernant (1968).

[16] Cole (1984a). Cantarella (1991) and Foxhall (1991) have argued that *moicheia*, which we translate "adultery," was a term applied to the seduction of any free woman, and that it was primarily a crime against the authority of the *kurios*. It might be added that this conception has an epic prototype in Odysseus's reaction to the seduction of his serving-maids: He certainly feels it as a disgrace to himself and a pollution of his house.

lifelong commitment. Nevertheless, such a relation, for the Greeks, remained ephemeral precisely because it was a relation between persons. Marriage, by contrast, could give a man something no concubine could give him: legitimate children, that is to say, sons with two grandfathers. This meant, however, that his children were not entirely his own; his children were connected to their mother's family. His wife's brothers may take an interest in her sons and thus undermine the authority of their father (cf. Aristophanes *Clouds* 124). It is perhaps not consistent with Greek legal thinking to say that a married woman has rights, but she has legitimate claims and some ability to enforce them. This affects her relation with her husband.

> A courtesan is much warmerhearted than
> The woman you marry—what would you expect?
> Your wife sits tight with the legal right to despise you;
> The other knows she has to pay her way
> By being nice, or find some other fellow.

Amphis Fr. 1 Kock

The woman's freedom is not her liberty but her dignity, which entitles her to a mind of her own.

Women in Charge of Themselves

The contrast between wife and prostitute, however, like so many other contrasts in Greek society, is only ideally a polar opposition. In practice it turns out to be an overlapping spectrum of conditions.[17] At one extreme there are the slave women of the *ergasterion*, the "factory," available by the hour to any casual purchaser. At the other extreme of the unfree range were women who became the lifelong companions of their purchaser and who bore children recognized by the father. We even hear of "free courtesans," *hetairai eleutherai*, which would seem to contradict the rule that free women were available only by marriage. The explanation seems to be that these women were resident aliens. The speaker of the *Against Alcibiades* ([Andocides] 4.14) says that Alcibiades brought into the house "concubines both slave and free." When Plutarch uses this sentence in his *Alcibiades* (8.3) he interprets the phrase as "foreign and local."

Evidently the woman with the greatest independence was the one who was a free citizen of some other city. She had no master since she was not a slave; on the other hand her *kurios*, although he probably

---

[17] The best review of this spectrum is in Davidson (1998), especially chapters 3 and 4.

existed in law, was too far away to take an interest in her. Chrysis in Menander's *Samia*, who is just such a woman, is called an *eleuthera gunē*; the implication is that an Athenian who assaults her is likely to be in trouble with the law. In this intermediate situation between slave and citizen we can imagine that in a city like Athens a good number of women made independent lives—like the Woman of Andros in Terence's comedy (11. 69ff) who lived quietly by craft work until she drifted into prostitution. Such a woman was *eleuthera* but not a *politis*, a citizeness.[18]

Pericles' citizenship law of 451–450[19] would in principle have made an important difference to these women: Before that date they were available to Athenians as wives for the production of legitimate children, afterward not. However, such a woman could be properly married only if her suitor could locate her *kurios* and contract with him the *enguē*, the agreement between males which made the marriage legitimate. In practice, in the case of women who had drifted out into the world (as opposed to respectable foreign women encountered at Athens or elsewhere), this was likely to be difficult.

A case in point is that of Glykera in Menander's *Perikeiromene.* She and her twin brother Moschus had been exposed at birth because their mother died bearing them and their father did not think he could raise them. They were picked up by an old woman who raised Glykera herself and handed Moschus over to another woman in whose house he was raised. When Glykera reached womanhood, she was courted by a certain Polemon and lived with him as his wife. One day, while he was away at the wars, she was seen kissing in fond farewell a young man on her doorstep. When Polemon came home he heard of this. He did not know that this young man was actually her twin brother; he therefore became enraged, hacked off her hair, and went away. Glykera then left the house and moved in with her brother. Polemon, still convinced the young man is a seducer, then wants to steal her back, and receives some advice from an older friend:

—If this thing happened, Polemon, the way you people
Say it happened, and she'd been married to you. . . .

[18] On this term see Patterson (1986), p. 55.

[19] The bibliography on this law is enormous; so far no consensus has emerged. I tend to agree with Cynthia Patterson (1981) that this was unlikely to have been a law aiming to regulate marriage, but was rather part of an emerging emphasis on citizenship (rather than family) as the most significant status. The marriages that it would have discouraged, however, would mainly be those marriages with important foreign women—daughters of kings and tyrants, for instance—which in the sixth century had significantly enriched some leading Athenian families. See Humphreys (1974), pp. 93–94.

—What are you talking about, Pataikos?

—It does make a difference.

—I certainly thought we were married!

—Don't cry.

Who gave her to you?

—Gave her to me? She did.

—There you are.

She liked you at the time, perhaps, and now she doesn't.
She's gone away because of the improper way you treated
Her.

—What do you mean "improper"? That's
The hurtfulest thing you've said so far.

—You love her.
That I can plainly see. But it follows that what you're doing now
Is crazy. How are you going to steal her? Who are you trying
To abduct? She's in charge of her own affairs.
The only alternative for someone with your disadvantages,
Someone in love, is persuasion.

—And the guy who seduced her
While I was away, isn't he guilty?

—You can make a complaint
That he's done you wrong, if you can get him to respond.
If you use force, you're liable. This is not a case
For criminal sanctions but for appeal to arbitration.

Menander *Perikeiromene* 486–503

Because Glykera is an orphan of unknown parentage, because she has
been raised by a woman whose own status (at least in the play as we
have it) is unclear, because she lacks, so far as Polemon knows, the
kind of male relative who can execute an *enguē*, she belongs to no
one. If she goes off with another man that is not adultery. She is "in
charge of her own affairs," *hēautēs esti ekeinē kuria*. This is a paradox;
because she is her own *kuria*, she has none. Therefore Polemon cannot properly marry her; there is no one from whom he can acquire
title to her.

Thrasonides in the *Misoumenos* (37–40) seems to be in the same difficulty with respect to Krateia.[20] He says that he had "set her up as a free
woman" (*peritheis eleutherian*) and further specifies what this meant: He
"made her mistress of the house, gave her servants, jewelry, clothes."
These are the externalities—*himatia kai chrusia*—that represent the

---

[20] Turner (1977), l. A 45.

freedom of a woman; they lend respectability to an informal relationship.[21] Nevertheless he could not marry her, because she had no *kurios*; she was herself *kuria*. Just like Polemon, he says in frustration: "I thought she was my wife" (*gunaika nomisas*).[22]

Furthermore he is not altogether wrong about that. *Wife*, like *whore*, turns out to be for the Greeks a term that applies to several conditions. Fundamentally there is a contrast between two types of marriage: a marriage in which the woman is transferred from her father to her husband, and a marriage contracted between husband and wife. In the first type, a woman passes from one *kurios* to another, and in the case of divorce must return from the second to the first, bringing her dowry back with her. Her husband could send her away, or she could leave of her own accord (which was less discreditable to her). In practice the latter step was "virtually impossible without male support."[23] (We may well believe that in communities where women could own property and were therefore less dependent on the *kurios* they could more easily divorce their husbands on their own initiative.[24]) Glykera also needs male support and is fortunate enough to have a twin brother in a position to help her. She is not, however, under his tutelage, and her departure from the house is conceived as her independent act. Her marriage with Polemon is of the other type, which we may call "companionate."

Companionate marriage was recognized at Athens as early as the seventh century, since it appears in Draco's law of justifiable homicide, which allows one to kill without penalty a man caught in the sexual act with a "concubine (*pallakē*) kept for the sake of free children" (Demosthenes 23.53). Such a relationship could even be founded on an explicit contract.[25] The mythical prototype is the marriage of Jason and Medea; hence her insistence in Euripides' play on oaths sworn and service rendered—all of which, however, is of no use to her in the absence of nearby kindred of her own to defend her interests.[26]

If Glykera and Polemon had been Athenians and their marriage had continued in this form, their children would have been free Athenians,

---

[21] Cf. [Demosthenes] 59.35. A husband was expected to provide at least one servant: Theophrastus *Characters* 22.10, 28.4.

[22] For extensive comment on the legal implications of Thrasonides' protest, see Turner (1979).

[23] Rosivach (1984).

[24] Willetts (1969), p. 144 (Crete), and cf. Diodorus 12.18 for a law of Thurii attributed to Charondas.

[25] Harrison (1968), p. 46n.3, Wolff (1944), pp. 70–75, cf. Isaeus 3.39.

[26] Williamson (1990).

but illegitimate and under certain disabilities.[27] The daughters could be given in marriage to Athenians—so that their children would be legitimate.[28] The law explicitly barred illegitimate sons from being legitimated by adoption, however.[29] Therefore such sons could not be members of a phratry, and would not be able to enroll their own sons in a phratry in order to make them legitimate Athenians. Polemon, in other words, could not under this arrangement have legitimate children by Glykera. He could have legitimate grandchildren, but could not continue his own patriline. Legitimate children must be born of a legitimate wife (*damar*).[30] One could have only one legitimate wife at a time, but it was evidently possible to have both *damar* and *pallakē*, and for children of both families to be free—providing that the two families lived in separate households.[31]

The Freedom of Women

A legitimate wife was one married by *enguē* or *enguēsis*[32] (the two terms appear to be synonymous). This was a contract between father-in-law (or other qualified male—[Demosthenes] 46.18) and son-in-law whereby the bride was legally conveyed. The actual wedding was the execution of this contract by the physical conveyance of the bride to her husband's house (the *ekdosis*) and the consummation of the marriage (the *gamos*—this last word usually means "wedding" but can be more generally a name for the sexual act itself). The conveyance and consummation might be the occasion of an elaborate celebration, also called

[27] The play is apparently set in Corinth. However "it is the project of Athenian new Comedy, even when a play is set in a state other than Athens . . . only to permit marriages that conform to . . . Athenian marriage law. The Athenian audience must be presented with a play that celebrates and reinforces its double civic ascendance pieties. Love, which is initially made to appear to be a force that threatens the integrity of the descent group, is finally revealed to confirm it and act only in its support." Ogden (1996), p. 179.

[28] Vatin (1970), pp. 118–120.

[29] Wolff (1944), pp. 79–80.

[30] This archaic, poetic word occurred in Draco's code; since the Athenians never developed any other word for a legitimate (as opposed to companionate) wife it continued in use in the law and even in colloquial speech: see, e.g., Eupolis Fr. 158 (Nauck).

[31] There is evidence that Socrates had a *damar* named Myrto, and that Xanthippe was his *pallakē*: Fitton (1970).

[32] Or by *epidikasia* in the case of an heiress given in marriage by the court—see Isaeus 6.14.

gamos, but that celebration had no legal force; the *engue* and the consummation made the marriage.[33]

The bride was now a member of her husband's house and her children were members of his kindred. They belonged to the *anchisteia hierōn kai hosiōn*, those "closely related in matters sacred and profane." The *anchisteia* joined those linked by descent and by legitimate marriage, out to the degree of children of first cousins. It defined those who could inherit and as such included females, since it was possible for a male to inherit through his mother. The *anchisteia* also defined the group obligated to avenge a homicide and bury the kindred dead.[34] Perhaps they shared other ritual rights and obligations, although we know nothing of these.

The contrast between *gnēsios*, legitimate son, and *nothos*, bastard, was not in their relations to their fathers—indeed a *nothos* was his father's acknowledged son[35]—but in their different relation with their father's kindred, a difference created by the low status of the mother. That relation was monitored not by the *anchisteia*—a notional body that never met as such—but by the patrilinear descent group, the phratry.[36] These related males owned sacred property together and met on certain ritual occasions, particularly at the *apatouria*, (the name is obscure, but probably means "related to fatherhood"), the family festival par excellence. The phratry may have had a variety of ritual functions but (whatever its origins) it functioned in classical times primarily to keep track of the legitimacy of males. A man might give a feast, the *gamēlia*, to his phratry on the occasion of his marriage, and he was expected to seek from it the recognition of his legitimate sons.[37] This recognition was secured by membership in the phratry, which was open only to children of parents married by *engue*. Thus the son secured rights of inheritance. A father was forbidden to leave a *nothos* more than a small fixed amount. Since the bastard's mother had never been received into

---

[33] The *engue*, as it was contracted between *kurios* and suitor, made a kind of bond between them even in the absence of an actual marriage; thus Orestes, thinking he and Electra are both about to die, says to Pylades:

> You've lost your chance of a wedding night with this unfortunate girl
> Whom I contracted to you in my deep respect for your companionship.
> You are to find some other bed for the begetting of children;
> The marriage-bond between you and me exists no longer.
>
> Euripides *Orestes* 1078–1081

[34] MacDowell (1963).

[35] Patterson (1990).

[36] For the difference between kindred and descent group see Littman (1979).

[37] It seems that he did not present his daughters: Gould (1980), pp. 40–42.

the family (here represented by the phratry), he was not entitled to more than a token share of family resources.

The legitimate bride thus entered a new family; as she did this, however, she remained part of her old family. Given the emphasis in legitimate marriage on the *transfer* of the woman, it is at first sight surprising to learn that the bride remained a member of her natal family.[38] Her sons could inherit their maternal grandfather's property in the absence of heirs to her brothers, and in any case she usually brought some of that property with her in the form of a dowry. The woman's dowry, further, never belonged to the husband. Although he administered it during the marriage, it was held in trust for the sons. Eventually they shared in this way in the estate of their maternal grandfather. If a man "left children of several wives, their dowries were allotted to their respective sons before his estate was distributed among all his heirs ([Dem] 40.14)."[39] In case of divorce, or if the wife died childless (Isaeus 3.36), the husband was expected to return the dowry,[40] and he not infrequently was required by the marriage settlement to pledge some real property as security for it. The Greeks generally recognized that a large dowry, because it was a continuing obligation of the husband to the father-in-law, gave a wife considerable leverage against her husband. She could threaten to divorce him, taking with her what she had brought.[41] At least until the birth of children the woman, with the cooperation of her father or other *kurios*, could easily divorce her husband on her own initiative.[42] She would then return to the family of origin.

The vocabulary of Greek marriage implies that the transfer of the woman is only conditional. *Enguē* (or *enguēsis*) was a term also used for the transfer of a debtor to the custody of a person friendly to him and prepared to guarantee the debt. The active verb, *enguein*, was used of the creditor who surrendered control (and of the father); the middle, *enguasthai*, was used of the guarantor who took responsibility for the debt (and of the groom). Similarly, the verb used for the actual transfer of the woman, *ekdidonai*, is a verb proper to transfers that "reserved

[38] In myth this connection is often important. Meleager and Odysseus hunt with their maternal uncles, and we hear of fosterage by maternal kin: "Greek examples include Hippolytus, Theseus, Pyrrhos, and the sons of Periander." Seaford (1990), p. 167.

[39] Wolff (1944), p. 61.

[40] Thus we see that the bride's father intends the dowry to pass to his own grandchildren, and no one else.

[41] The absence of a dowry made the wife vulnerable in her relation to her husband. That is why Sostratus, the virtuous hero of Menander's Dyscolus who is marrying a dowerless girl, gives (at line 308) a *pistis*, a pledge of fealty, to reassure her kindred.

[42] Rosivach (1984).

a right for the transferer, as for example when a slave is put out to service with another (Xenophon *Poroi* 4.15f) or for questioning by torture (Isaevus 8.10, Demosthenes 29.14, 18, etc.) or in cases of apprenticeship.[43] The conditional nature of the transfer was explicit in the formula of marriage. The father gave the girl to the bridegroom with the words: "I entrust her to you for the cultivation of legitimate children" (Menander *Dyscolus* 842 + Gomme/Sandbach ad loc.). "The woman was . . . only lent out . . . for the purpose of bearing offspring."[44]

The bride, it turns out, could become a proper member of her new family only by retaining her connection with her old one. This apparent paradox disappears when we realize that, while companionate marriage is a relation between two persons, legitimate marriage is a relation between two patrilines.[45] The bride is the symbol and the vehicle of a connection between families. It is this connection that confers on her status and dignity. She is a free woman, an *eleuthera gunē*, not because she has freedom of action but because she is a link between two free men whose primary relation is not to her but to each other. The woman herself becomes the focus of attention only in the case of the courtship of a "loose woman"—such as Glykera. Men contracted companionate marriages, marriages whose raison d'être was love, only with women who were their social inferiors.[46] Companionate marriage actually was the proper locus of the sentiments we nowadays associate with marriage: compatibility, personal affection, sexual excitement. Yet from the Greek point of view it is a relationship characterized by inequality. Only legal marriage, in which the wife came under the husband's control, was a relation in which the parties were equally respectable. Once again, freedom turns on discipline.

Menander's plays mostly center on love and courtship. Therefore, his heroines are usually marginal women of some kind: orphans, aliens, citizen-women whose marriageability has been compromised by premarital pregnancy. Such women, precisely because they are not marriageable, are free to choose their sexual partners—and to abandon them if passion or interest lead them elsewhere. If, however, the play is to end with a real marriage, the marginality must turn out to have been an illusion: the orphan's parents turn up, the alien turns out to be a citizen, the premarital pregnancy turns out to be by the man who later became or is to become the woman's legal husband and the child is

[43] Wolff (1944), p. 47 and note 35.
[44] Ibid, p. 50.
[45] Thus Virginia Hunter (1993) makes the important point that the married woman's bond with her natal family, because it is an assertion of her father's claims, is further evidence for the strength of agnatic kinship in Athens.
[46] Patterson (1990).

therefore acknowledged and legitimate.[47] The woman, in other words, turns out to have a *kurios* who can properly convey her to a husband who wants her, and to whom she is faithful, insuring the legitimacy of his children. Glykera, for instance, is actually a citizen—in fact the older man giving advice in the scene quoted earlier is her father, although he doesn't know it yet. When the truth comes out, he will marry her properly to Polemon, to whom she will then belong. This is a happy ending.[48]

A free woman was supposed to marry and have children. Those who did not were said to grow old—*katagēraskein*—with connotations of wasting away; life was passing them by.[49] The primary responsibility of a *kurios* was to find a dowry and enable his ward to marry. One of the most important personal charities (*euergasiai*) of the rich man was the provision of dowries for indigent girls; this was a good deed parallel to that of ransoming a citizen out of slavery. The unmarried state was intolerable, and a woman who lost one husband would, at least if she was still young enough to bear children, normally marry another. Athenian marriages in fact were often dissolved, by death or divorce; it was then quite usual for the woman to marry again and to have children by the second marriage.[50] One reason the husband had to return a dowry in case of divorce was to make it available for remarriage. A husband might leave his wife by will to another man, and a dowry with her;[51] this is for the protection of the woman. In an Athenian context it is thought totally implausible that a woman whose brother had property (for a dowry) and who was herself "of an age" (that is, fairly young) should live alone, unmarried (Demosthenes 30.33).

This Greek notion of care for a woman is nowhere better represented than in the narrative of Isaeus 2, where the *kurioi* found they had to marry off one of their women more than once. Two brothers had the care of their sisters after their father's death; they married off the elder sister, after which Menecles, a friend of the father's, recently a widower, asked for the younger. They handed her over with the appropriate dowry, and then, having met their responsibilities, left town. On their return they found their younger sister still childless.

> Menecles came to us and, speaking of our sister in the highest terms, suggested his suspicions concerning his age and their childlessness. He said it

[47] Cf. Fantham (1975).

[48] On this whole sequence, see Konstan (1987).

[49] Demosthenes 45.74, Hyperides *Lycurgus.* 12 and 13, cf. Sophocles *Electra* 962, Plato *Laws* 774e, Isæus 2.7.

[50] Thompson (1972).

[51] Diogenes *Lærtius* 5.12; Demosthenes 27.5, 45.28; on this last see Demosthenes 36.28–30.

would be no fit reward for her virtues that she remain childless wasting in age with him. It was enough that he himself should be unfortunate. . . . So he asked us to grant him this favor, that she should be given to another with her own agreement. And we told him to seek her consent, and if she should consent we said we would do this. At first she would not hear of it, but as time went by she did finally consent. So we gave her to Elius of Sphettus, and Menecles gave the dowry to him . . . and to her the clothing she had brought with her and the jewelry which she had. (Isaeus 2.5–9)

To us this may well seem the story of a woman who is moved about from man to man to suit the men; it is clear, however, that the narrator intends in his narrative to display the highest degree of concern for the interests and feelings of his sister.[52] Even the fact that he never mentions her name is a sign of respect.[53]

This narrative, in fact, tells us something about what Athenian men thought their women needed to be happy. The advantages of marriage for the woman are not thought to be in her relations with her husband but in the marital condition itself, which properly includes children. What is important is not that she be married to a man who suits her, but that she be married to someone who will establish her in that condition. Among the Greeks living in Egypt, where the marriage contract was made between bride and groom, this point is explicit; the earliest we have of these, belonging to the age of Menander, provides that the husband shall provide the wife "with everything which is proper to a free woman."[54] Later contracts specify further: He shall not keep another household not under her control, for instance, and must provide her with a servant. Thomas Williams argues persuasively that in the time of Menander such provisions already formed part of the understandings entered into by the parties to the *enguē*.[55]

Isaeus 2 refers to "the clothing she had brought with her and the jewelry which she had." These things were generically called *himatia kai chrusia* and included cosmetic apparatus, especially mirrors; they were signs of the married state. They were generally wedding gifts. (We recall that Thrasonides thinks he has married Krateia because he has given her these things.) At Athens, where the prohibition of woman's property was absolute, such things could not belong to the woman, but any decent husband would allow her to keep them in case of divorce,

---

[52] A similar story, less creditable to the husband, is told in Demosthenes 47: in order to secure an inheritance a man divorces his wife, but cares for her by arranging marriage to another; "one may infer that in these cases it was normal to arrange a prompt remarriage" Cohn-Haft (1995), p. 9.

[53] Schaps (1977); Sommerstein (1980).

[54] Edgar (1952), pp. 2ff.

[55] Williams (1961).

or to dedicate them in a sanctuary, or to dispose of them in some other way if she wished. There is "no evidence of a husband actually keeping the trousseau itself, although he surely had a legal right to do so."[56] Outside Athens, where women could own property and receive the dowry (*proix*) as their own, these gifts belonged to the woman and might be valued as part of the dowry (cf. SIG^3 1215); they might then be called *emproika*.

These objects were presented at the *gamos*, the ritual wedding, which, in contrast to the *enguē*, had no status in law but was generally a far more impressive occasion: expensive, showy, and extending over several days. That Greek women had two weddings, in fact, reflects the ambiguous status of these "speaking signs." The *enguē* was a transfer of the woman to a new social location; the *gamos* was her transformation into a new social actor. The *enguē* is the political wedding, while the *gamos* is the personal wedding. The *enguē* is between males; the *gamos* is managed by women, by the mothers of the bride and groom, and by the *numpheutria*, the matron who presided over the ceremony. As wedding gifts were women's things, so weddings themselves were women's business.

The *enguē* was about property and property-lines; it focused on the new relation between father-in-law and son-in-law. The *gamos*, by contrast, was about sex—as from the personal point of view marriage is centrally about sex; the Greeks referred to marital cohabitation as *gamoi* in the plural, continuing sexuality. The legalistic name of the occasion is *ekdosis*, "handing over"; the groom, having acquired title at the *enguē*, now entered into possession. The Greeks generally called it the *gamos* because they understood it was a celebration of the moment of consummation and (assuming it was her first marriage) marked the sexual initiation of the bride, the crucial moment of her maturity.[57]

Wedding songs were congratulatory; the couple were called *makarioi* or *olbioi*, happy, and others might be congratulated also, for instance the father of the bride (cf. Euripides *Trojan Women* 324–325). Some archetypal wedding might be invoked: that of Zeus and Hera (Aristophanes *Birds* 1731–1742) or of Cadmos and Harmonia, of Peleus and Thetis (Euripides *Iphigeneia in Aulis* 1036–1079) or of Hector and Andromache (Sappho fr. 44 Voigt). Everyone involved in the wedding is thus raised to divine or heroic status; not only do the bride and groom reenact a prototypical marriage, but the youth who drives their car plays the role of Eros, the women who escort them to their wedding

[56] Schaps (1979), p. 11.

[57] While Greek women could and often did remarry, only their first wedding fits this description. There were indeed certain differences of custom at a remarriage, but these were not great. Nevertheless (as for us) the first wedding remained the ideal type.

chamber play the role of the Fates, and so on. The wedding is thus placed in sacred time; all participate in an eternal mythical order, in *kleos aphthiton*, immortal fame (Sappho fr. 44 Voigt line 4).

On the other hand, the praise of the couple was not always so dignified: "His is long and big, hers is a sweet fig," sing the chorus in the *Peace* (1349–1350). This mixture of apotheosis and bawdry catches the ambiguity of the wedding, which is an event both noble and absurd; Sappho (fr. 111 Voigt), by reflecting on the difficulty of getting a god-sized bridegroom into the house, manages to catch them both in one poem. The newlyweds are both exalted and debased. The bride is adorned only to be unveiled; she receives gifts and is herself treasured as an *agalma*,[58] an object symbolic of value, but at the same time she is about to be plowed and sown like an open field. Marriage is about love and sex, about the maintenance of a social ideal and about the release of animal instincts.

Like all initiatory rites the wedding creates the status that it defines through liminality, which involves a play of oppositions, touching the contrary condition. "They purify the defiled with more blood," says Heraclitus (B5 DK), "as if one who had walked in mud were to wash it off with mud." To the despair of the philosophers, dirt purifies and disorder orders. Marriage clarifies the meaning of male and female— and sometimes does so by reversing the roles. Thus Plutarch tells us (304e) that at Kos the bridegroom had to wear women's clothes to receive his bride, while at Argos (245f) the brides had to wear beards when they went to bed with their husbands.

The *gamos*, as it celebrates the consummation of the marriage, may be thought of as an acculturation of the sexual act. To bring nature into the cultural realm requires an excess of culture; the means to this are *truphē*, luxury, enjoyments typical of those who are (for the Greeks) excessively cultured, like Homer's Phaeacians; King Alcinous could be thinking of weddings when he says:

The feast is dear to us, the lyre and the dance,
Changes of clothes, and warm baths, and bed.

Homer *Odyssey* 8.248–249

The *gamos* is thus a hypercultural, "hyperborean"[59] occasion, characterized by dance and maiden song. But there can be (as among the Phaeacians) an undercurrent of savagery. The god invoked may be a river or those titanic figures the Tritopatores (Suidas s.v.). Worldwide we find traces of this ambiguity in wedding customs, moments of ribal-

[58] Vernant (1973), p. 60; cf. Aeschylus. *Ag.* 208, 7–41.
[59] See pp. 112–113.

dry, mockery, even violence, along with gift-exchange and enacted inducements to consent. We need not see these as survivals of some original form of marriage by purchase or by capture. I should rather say that rape, purchase, and seduction are all latent elements of that complex transaction between man and woman which is a civilized wedding.

Marital Happiness

"To permit a woman to grow old unmarried was, to the Athenians, the foulest thing that could be done to her," says David Schaps.[60] Schaps thus explains the institution of the epiclerate, whereby a girl left without brothers and therefore heiress of her father's property was married to her closest kin—who might even dissolve his own existing marriage to marry her; if he failed to claim her in marriage, the next claimant would get her and gain control of the property. Schaps points out that by Athenian law such a brotherless girl at her father's death passed into the custody of her nearest relative as *kurios*; this man therefore had for the moment the control of her property. If she married another it would pass to her husband as new *kurios*; her kinsman therefore would have had every interest in postponing her marriage. The solution was to require him to marry her himself. The woman was thereby assured a husband, and this was the primary consideration; that he would be a close kinsman made him at least prima facie suitable, even if often much older than she. He was legally required to sleep with her three times a month (Plutarch *Solon* 20.2–5). The married *epikleros*, further, was under the special protections of the Athenian courts, which (substituting for patrikin) made it relatively easy for her to obtain protection against any kind of abuse.

This may or may not be the correct explanation of the epiclerate. That the institution was not all about property is shown by the provision that a brotherless daughter of the thetic class, that is, one without any significant amount of property, was also the responsibility of her closest male kin. He had to marry her himself or provide a dowry— consistent with his means, not hers.[61] On the other hand, in the case of several sisters left thus, he was responsible for the marriage of only one of them. It looks as though the concern of the law is not so much with the welfare of the women as with the entitlement of the deceased to grandchildren, and this also seems to be the purpose of the laws cited in Plutarch *Solon* 20.

---

[60] Schaps (1979), p. 41.
[61] Demosthenes 43.54, Fantham (1975), p. 48.

In any case the epiclerate did assure the marriage of many fatherless, brotherless girls. It put them in charge of a household, the servants, the household accounts, and the production of fabrics—both consumption and production. By acquiring a house, she became (by this way of thinking) most herself.

If a free woman is under authority she is also, once married, *despoina*, the mistress. She is now an adult, a responsible person. The Greeks lived in nuclear households, each centering on a couple. It is this pattern that made marriage a serious matter for a woman—and also for a man, since it put his partner in charge of half of his life, the private half. In societies composed of extended families, by contrast, there is often no gap between childhood and womanhood; as soon as the girls reach puberty they marry, and the children are then raised by them along with the older women—mother-in-law, aunts—who run the house. For the Greeks, however, the life-stage of the *parthenos* (as we have already seen in Hesiod) was set apart, precious, ritualized, and (as we shall see) demarcated by initiations. Although girls married (by our standards) pretty young, puberty was not enough; they had to grow up. The life stage of maidenhood was their education to womanhood. Thus the idealization of the nubile girl turns out to be an aspect of the private-property society. Maidenhood is a stage where important competence is being prepared.

To be married is to have a sphere of authority, and also of privacy. The house confines a woman, but also shelters her. The speaker of Lysias 3 speaks (with pardonable exaggeration, no doubt) of his women as "leading such orderly lives that they were ashamed even when seen by their own relatives" (Lysias 3.6). A man's dinner is often a party, a *sumposion*, perhaps with some women guests (some of whom might be prostitutes, and all of whom were less than respectable); free women characteristically eat in seclusion, by themselves—probably also with their husband, if he has no guests. Certainly the free women visited one another, but they expected to be protected from men—except, of course, from the husband with whom they shared the marriage bed. In the course of nature a married woman expected to have children— indeed it was only at that point that she came to belong definitively to her husband rather than her father. Her children as they grew older would continue to have the run of the woman's quarters, where they would be under her command (Plato *Lysis* 208d). Eventually she would join with the mothers of their spouses to oversee their marriages.

A woman who was denied all these things was denied a life. The woman, conversely, who kept a citizen's house was free in the way in which it is appropriate for a citizen woman to be free. In order to be a wife, obviously, she had to have a husband, but that was not the point.

The Athenians speak of the marriages of their women in a curiously impersonal way. So long as they remain married it does not seem to matter if they remain married to the same person. A woman's happiness turned (or was thought to turn) on a social role, and as long as there was some man to provide her with property, to protect her dignity, and to father her children, she could continue to play that role—which in our sense was not so much the role of wife as of mother and matron. As for the man, he was free to seek companionship elsewhere, from women who were not free. Love and marriage in this society thus appear to be in contrastive distribution. Marriage was rather a form of friendship (Aristotle *Ethics* 1162a). In respectable circles among proper free citizens Hesiodic misogyny remained an acceptable ideology: That women, our link to nature, should be necessary to mankind could seem an affront to the dignity of a free man, as the ultimate restriction on his aspiration to become a fully cultural, which is to say political, creature. From a political point of view marriage is an institution whereby a man marries a father-in-law and acquires sons with two grandfathers; the reproductive function of women is from this point of view an unfortunate limitation on autonomous masculinity. As Euripides' Hippolytus says:

> Zeus, why do you make us share the world
> With these rotten-to-the-core women? If
> It was your will that mortal generations continue
> We shouldn't have had to manage that through women.
> We could have gone into your temples and made a deposit
> Of gold or iron or of some quantity of bronze
> And that way bought a generation of children, every one
> Worth what we paid for it. Then we could have lived
> Free men in our houses, without these females.

Euripides Hippolytus 615–624

Erotic passion for the Greeks is generally antipolitical; the chorus in the *Antigone*, observing an engaged couple, speaks to the disruptive power of Eros: "you drive astray the wits of even the just into injustice and damage" (791–792). No doubt, men sometimes did fall in love with their wives, but as far as our evidence goes this was looked upon (by men) as something vaguely unrespectable.[62] It may be, of course, that the women, from whom we hear so little, had a different view.

[62] Candaules' troubles begin when he falls in love with his wife (Hdt. I.8.1). When Socrates (Xenophon. *Symposium.* 8.3) speaks of Niceratus and his wife as in love with each other, he is, I think, teasing Niceratus. Most interesting in this connection is the fragmentary prologue, perhaps from Menander, first published as P. Antinoopolis 15; here a young husband, married only a few months, confesses that after marrying at his

Erotic Marriage

Ancient women were what nowadays is called a "muted group": present but frequently not accounted for. They did not thereby cease to exist or to have opinions. Women talked to each other; we should like to know more about that "sophisticated female talk" (*kompsa theleiōn epē*) to which Andromache refers. We can learn something from those authors—Euripides, Aristophanes—who liked to represent women and seem to have known something about them. The *Lysistrata* certainly represents marital passion, and on marital affection we have this fragment, quoted more than once in Hellenistic literature:

> When her husband is in trouble or sick, a woman
> Is the nicest thing—if the household is well-run;
> She soothes his anger, and when he is discouraged
> Changes his mood; even deception is nice when it's loving.
>
> Euripides Fr. 822 Nauck

Deduction suggests certain other points. Classical Greek literature, for instance, has left us no love stories: boy meets girl, boy gets girl. Such stories, however, are very close to the surface in Homer and become a staple of Hellenistic literature from Menander onward.[63] During the period of the independent city-states, when politics absorbed Greek males, they are not heard; Menander, however, is already able to bring them out in such perfection[64] that it seems probable they were told somewhere in the meantime—most likely by the women. And we have other evidence that women believed in the power of love.

The division of Greek society between male and female voices is represented in our richest pictorial source: Attic painted pottery. A good part of this was made for the symposium, a typically male, political occasion, which took place, indeed, within the house, but in the *andrōn*, the men's dining room, which was essentially a public place.

---

father's wish he conceived "proper passion" (δικαῖον ἥρων) for his wife; "enchanted" (δεθείς) by her "free nature" (ἐλευθέρῳ . . . ἤθει) and her unaffected way of living "as she was good to me I grew fond of her" (τὴν φιλοῦσαν ἤγαπαν). "We know of no other place in Greek literature where the three words ἔρως, φιλία, ἀγάπη recur at such short intervals, in each case referring to love between a man and a woman and indeed between a husband and wife." Barnes and Lloyd-Jones (1964), p. 28. It seems that the speaker has some difficulty in finding language for an uncommonly reported experience.

[63] For an expanded treatment of this point see Redfield (1995).

[64] Jarcho (1979) finds in his fifth-century sources a picture of the good marriage purely in "ethical" and "objective" terms; in Menander, however, he finds plenty of evidence for "passion" and "subjectivity." See also Rudd (1981), Lefkowitz (1983), Walcot (1987), and Brown (1993).

When sex appears on pottery made for these occasions it is either homosexual or rather coarsely pornographic.

Fine pottery not intended for the symposium, by contrast, is, for the most part, women's things: cosmetic boxes, water jugs for the bath, and so forth, evidently presented in many cases as wedding presents. Here the treatment of sex is delicate and indirect, often merely suggested by the representation of *kosmēsis*, the woman making herself beautiful. On this pottery Eros is everywhere.[65] These objects were not made by women but they were made for women and surely represent women's evaluation of Eros. Eros in this context is the woman's power to draw the man to her. A woman who felt that she was losing her husband might have recourse to a love charm intended to rekindle his *erōs*.[66] This would bring him back to her (in the Homeric phrase) *philotētēi kai eunēi*, "in friendship and bed," which we may paraphrase (since *philotēs* means many things) "the special kind of closeness which is sexual." Surely the women always knew—what becomes explicit only later— that sex is one of the things that makes the marriage work.

The locus classicus on marital happiness is *Odyssey* 6. 180–185, with its evocation of *homophrosunē*, marital unity of hearts and minds. Later the word is generalized to groups of any size, and in many contexts is practically a synonym for *homonoia*, political concord.[67] In Greek of the Hellenistic period—as the love stories resurface—it again becomes the word for married happiness.[68]

Plutarch says:

> Aphrodite is the great technician of *homophrosunē* and *philia* for men and women, since in bringing together their bodies under the influence of pleasure she also welds together their souls. (Plutarch *Moralia* 156c)

Here also we have an epic paradigm: the girdle of Aphrodite (cited by Plutarch *Moralia* 141bc, 143d). This is the emblem of the woman's sex-

---

[65] Calame (1996), p. 132.

[66] See Faraone (1999).

[67] In Antiphon—fr. 44e—*homophrosunē* is an inner condition of the person, inner peace.

[68] The TLG turns up more than seventy occurrences of the noun; of these a majority are political, but almost half refer to relations of personal intimacy, and a good proportion of these refer to the intimacy of marriage. Partly no doubt this reflects the continuing influence of the Odyssey; Odysseus' speech to Nausicaa is quoted by Aelius Aristides (who gives it a political application—24.7), by Plutarch (*Moralia* 770a), by Clement of Alexandria (*Stromateis* 2.23.143.1) and by Hierocles of Alexandria (apud Stobaeus 69.24). The word is, however, used in its marital sense often enough independent of this literary reference for us to see that it had entered the language; we find it in the Greek Anthology, for instance, in poems of the Hellenistic (GA 6.29) and Byzantine (GA 2, line 167) periods. *Homophrosunē* indeed still belongs to the Greek ideology of marriage, since the word appears in the Orthodox wedding service.

ual power; it has in it "love and desire and courtship, beguilement that steals the mind of even the steadiest person" (*Il.* 14.216–217). In the *Iliad* Hera borrows it in order to seduce her husband, but knowing this is wrong, she provides herself with a respectable excuse. She says she is going to see Okeanos and Tethys (her uncle and aunt), who looked after her when she was little; they have an unresolved quarrel (*akrita neikea*) and have not made love in a long time; if she can persuade them to make love she will earn their "eternal affection and respect" (*Il.* 14.210). So in Homer love and desire, so negatively evaluated in Hesiod, have a proper social use.

Certainly women were excluded from politics and therefore from power. It turns out, however, that this exclusion also conferred a power: hidden from the public, women became patrons of everything that cannot be made public, in particular of the secret sexual world. As the secret is close neighbor to the sacred, women, juridically reduced to negations, reappear as potent in the ritual sphere. They could not be magistrates but they could be priestesses; they could not sign contracts but they could manage rituals. Ritual appearance is paradoxical and often takes the form of invisibility. In women's rituals the women themselves are usually hidden or secluded—as typically at the Thesmophoria. But this is a well-advertised seclusion that incites masculine curiosity (as in Aristophanes' play about that festival). Thus in this paradoxical form—as custodians and representatives of all that may not be allowed to appear—women do after all appear before the public. To this paradox corresponds another: Women's ritual roles most often involve *service*, so that they appear in a sense humiliated—but since their service is of the god, they are also exalted. Thus the anonymous voice from the women's chorus of the *Lysistrata* qualifies herself (in a much discussed passage) as the perfection of Athenian womanhood:[69]

> I was just turned seven when I carried the secrets;
> Then I was the girl at the mill, when I was ten, for the Lady,
> And I shed the saffron robe and was a bear at the Brauronia.
> Finally I carried the basket, grown into a fine girl, wearing the
> garland of figs.
>
> <div align="right">Aristophanes <i>Lysistrata</i> 641–647</div>

We shall have more to say about these rituals; here it is enough to notice that at least two of them involve seclusion and at least three of them involve service, but all of them substantiate a claim to status. Through ritual service and concealment the woman grows into a cer-

---

[69] Sourvinou-Inwood (1971); Stinton (1976).

tain kind of public standing—as at marriage she is given away in a proper manner in order to be properly kept, to be linked in a new way to her patrikin, as mother of her father's grandchildren.

Marriage is for the woman both transfer and transformation. She is sent away from her father's house a maid and reappears as a wife. This is her fate and her achievement. She is both victim and beneficiary. Thus the marriage is both sacrifice and initiation.[70] This doubleness of marriage is represented in the doubleness of the wedding. As a transfer between males it creates a link between patrilines. As a transformation from girl to matron it makes a link between generations. From the juridical, which is to say the men's, point of view the *enguē* is the wedding. From the woman's point of view the wedding is the *gamos*, which may not be skipped. "That is not the custom," as a bride's mother says to her husband, "even if you think it trivial" (Euripides *Iphigeneia in Aulis* 734). In the wedding the bride makes a brilliant, if veiled, appearance, powerful as an object of desire. This passive power enables her to command a specific social role—subordinate, certainly, but not insignificant.

The Free Woman as Citizen

We began this chapter by pointing to a problem in Aristotle: that for him, free women are not citizens. We can now conclude with Aristotle's answer, implied (I suggest) in his rather opaque remark concerning a man's rule over his children and wife: "both are over free persons, but it is not the same sort of rule: the former is kingly, the latter, political" (*Politics* 1259a 40–b2). He goes on:

> The male is by nature more fit for leadership than the female (unless it somehow comes out unnaturally), and the elder and mature than the younger and immature. But in political offices mostly the ruler and ruled take turns (the idea is to be naturally equal and differ not at all); however when in office one seeks to be different in stance and language and honors. . . . The male is permanently related to the female in this manner. But the rule over children is kingly. The parent is ruler by affection and by seniority, which is the form of kingly office . . . for the king must differ in nature but be the same in race. (Aristotle *Politics* 1259b 2–15)

Aristotle here contrasts the relation of man and wife with the relation of parent and child; he says that parent and child differ in nature—that is, they are of the same nature and yet by nature different;

[70] This ambiguity can be a source of tragic irony—cf. Foley (1982).

the child is naturally just as capable of excellence as the parent, but in the nature of things the parent will always be elder, and always be parent. These differences provide a clear title to authority, at least while the child is immature, with a continuing claim based on continuing natural affection. Since Aristotle is making a contrast he would seem to imply that man and wife are not different in nature, or that in this case the difference is subtler. Aristotle then explains this subtlety by reference to the relation between ruler and ruled within the political order. Here both are citizens and in principle completely equal, yet they acquire a contingent inequality when one is in office and thus acquires a contingent title to authority over the other (this contingent inequality is reinforced by signs precisely because it is contingent). Aristotle says that in the case of man and wife this contingency is permanent—yet somehow, it seems, not based on a difference of nature. Yet he also says that the man is "by nature more fit for leadership" (*phusei hegemoni-koteron*). Why is this not the same sort of difference as that between parent and child, why is the husband not "kingly"? An answer is suggested by a passage in the *Ethics* where Aristotle repeats that the authority of parent over child is "kingly"—if exercised for the good of the child; otherwise it degenerates into tyranny. But

> [the community] of husband and wife turns out to be aristocratic. The man rules according to his worth, and in those matters where a man should rule. Such things as are fitting to a woman he turns over to her. If the man takes charge of everything it turns into an oligarchy—because he then does it contrary to his worth, and not for the best. (*Nicomachean Ethics* 1160b24–1161a1)

Whereas the king—like the tyrant—is ruler without qualification, the aristocrat rules only in a qualified sense. The king has authority; the aristocrat has a qualification to rule and rules only as he is qualified. Within marriage, similarly, responsibilities are distributed according to qualification. Masculinity is itself a qualification for authority. To be "more fit for leadership" in this context is a particular capacity, not a generalized superiority; it is a talent (a frequent meaning of *phusis* in Aristotle) expected of, although not always found in, males. It is not a status.

In a well-known sentence just after the passage from the *Politics* quoted earlier Aristotle says (1260a 12–14) that the slave has not the capacity for deliberation at all, the child has it, but immaturely, the female has it, but it is inoperative (*akuron*). A woman, in other words, can know what is best but she cannot enforce it in the form of orders or instructions (except, it goes without saying, in her own sphere, for instance to her own servants); that she should instruct a man is unwomanly: once again, "silence is an ornament for a woman" (*Politics* 1260a 31). Her acceptance of her husband's instructions, it would follow, is a recognition of his masculinity, an informed acceptance, silent but not blind, not an abandonment of her will to his superiority but based on a shared understanding and on her personal knowledge that his instructions are indeed for the best, or at least that it is best that he should be the one to give them. That is Andromache's view of marriage; this shared understanding is *homophrosunē*, even though Aristotle does not use the word. It is based on a mutual recognition by the couple of their difference—which (although Aristotle certainly does not say this!) is not so much a difference of sex as of gender. A qualification to rule is something the Greeks expect of males, that is, it is an aspect of generic maleness (socially constructed: that is why sometimes "it somehow comes out unnaturally"). In fact when Aristotle says "nature" in the phrase "by nature more fit for leadership," he actually evokes the (not infrequently disappointed) expectations of natural differences we have when we have put them to social use. It is not so much actual males but rather masculinity that is qualified to rule.

This is Aristotle's characteristically dispassionate and intellectual account of the bond between man and wife, of their asymmetrical mutuality. The woman is permanently in the position of a citizen who happens to be out of office and therefore respects the authority of the magistrate. She allows the man the trappings of authority—"stance and language and honors"—because they are proper to his role and to his performance of a function. In her own womanly way, however, she is his equal; it is not womanly to be passive, only to yield.

It follows that the authority of husband over wife is legitimate only by consent—not consent to each decision of the man's, but consent to the gender roles that provide a kind of constitutional order for the family. Ultimately, as we shall see, the woman's power in this paradoxical Greek universe is exercised in her consent to masculine authority.

In this way Artistotle resolves to his own satisfaction the paradoxical status within the *polis* of the wives of the citizens. Actually he does not so much solve the paradox as present it. Free women are full members of the city but excluded from political power; if they understand their nature they will, he implies, embrace this exclusion. The resulting tensions are surely predictable; on this point Aristotle has codified the bad conscience of the Greeks as to the Woman Question.

Three

The Theology of Consent

The Adornment of a Parthenos

When Pericles inaugurated his building program—of which the great display piece was the Parthenon—he met, we are told,[1] with a certain amount of moralistic resistance:

> Now is Greece abused with dreadful abuse and truly tyrannized, since the contributions she is forced to make for war are turned by us to the gilding and beautification of the city as if she were some woman making a shameless display (*alazōn*), as we deck her out with costly stones and idols (*agalmata*) and thousand-talent temples. (Plutarch *Pericles* 12.2)

This tells us that the Parthenon is a female thing; it is an adornment. Greek women (and to a certain extent older men) are meant to be adorned; young men are ideally stripped down—as they appear naked in sculpture by the convention of "heroic nudity." Sculptured *kouroi* were nude male figures; *korai*, their female counterparts, were draped with embroidered cloth and hung with jewelry—sometimes also carved on the stone, sometimes painted on, sometimes actually added in metal. Similarly Pericles adorned the city and then (according to Thucydides— 2.43.1) told the citizens that she should become an object of their erotic desire. Thus the building program made Athens (as it were) a female among cities. Thucydides (1.10.2) also remarks that the ruins of Athens would make you think her twice as powerful as she was. She was showy, *poikilos*, and deceptive, like Pandora—in contrast to minimally adorned Sparta.

The Parthenon was a kind of elaborate container or jewel box holding the chryselephantine statue of Athena by Pheidias. This statue was not a particularly sacred object; the ancient *xoanon*, the archaic wooden image of Athena, continued to reside in the Erechtheum, Athena's proper home (*Od.* 7.80–81). Pheidias's statue was a dedication to the goddess, who was honored by representing her in precious materials, in gold and ivory; in spending money on Athena, the Athenians brought out her feminine side. The Parthenon and its contents thus in

---

[1] Possible fifth-century sources for the quotation (Ion of Chios?) are discussed in Meiggs (1963), p. 42.

a way stood for the *chrusia kai himatia*, which were the wife's tokens of legitimate status.

For the Greeks a young woman is an *agalma*, a precious object in the house (Aeschylus *Agamemnon* 207); her jewelry is a token of the wealth of the house—as for many Greek families it must have represented a substantial portion of their savings. (Lysias—13.19—remembered with special bitterness that when the Thirty Tyrants came to murder his brother, they actually took the earrings from his wife's ears.) In the chryselephantine statue the adornment of this divine woman was collapsed into the representation of her by making her person, her flesh and clothing, of precious materials. It reminds one of those Greek wedding dresses of the Turkish period now shown in the Benaki Museum in Athens, where the breastplate of the dress is sewn with coins. Pheidias was commissioned to make a statue out of money—and Thucydides' Pericles tells the people that the gold has been made to be removable, so that it could serve as the final cash reserve of the state: forty gold talents (Thucydides 2.13.5).

The temple that held this statue, the adornment of an adornment, was by Greek standards enormous, and of superbly refined design, materials, and workmanship. Around the top it was further adorned with sculpture. The pediment on the east end, over the entrance to the *cella* where the statue stood, represented the birth of Athena; over the west end—which was the "back" of the building, and also the entrance to the *opisthodomos* where the public treasury of Athens was kept—was figured the contest between Athena and Poseidon. Poseidon has just brought forth the salt spring, Athena the olive tree; both are shown at the moment of their competitive realizations, as at the other end Athena was shown at the moment of her birth, already full-grown and fully armed.[2]

Just beneath the level of the pediments the building was ringed with a double ring of sculpture. The inner ring is the frieze, which is a scene of peace; the whole city, men and women, old and young, horses and sacrificial animals, join in procession toward the east end, where the gods and heroes, quietly at ease, flank a moment of ritual work, the folding of Athena's *peplos*. The outer ring is the metopes; these are scenes of war: on the east, gods and giants; on the west, Greeks and Amazons; on the north, Greeks and Trojans; on the south, lapiths and centaurs. A further consideration of the arrangement of these metopes may teach us something more about the ideology of women in the Greek state.

---

[2] See Robertson (1963).

It has been noticed[3] that the metopes on the ends of the building go with the pediments set over them. The birth of Athena, as we saw, is the event that secured the sovereignty of Zeus among the gods; the defeat of the giants by the gods imposed the collective sovereignty of the gods over the universe. These events are cosmic. The events at the west end, by contrast, are local; the goddess takes possession of the city, and below on the metopes the citizens repel an invader. The Amazons, we are told, had come from far away and had been defeated under the leadership of Theseus. The choice of the Amazons from among many mythical invaders seems, however, to have a further implication (providing we take the two sets of metopes as parallel): that gods are to giants as men are to women (giants are a disordering force opposed to legitimate order, and so, in the form of Amazons, are women).

The war with the Amazons was a commonplace of Athenian patriotic rhetoric; this legendary event was presented as the defense of civilized values against barbarous disorder.[4] Amazons refuse marriage and are out of control; as women who fight like men they invert a fundamental rule of civil society: that the man is raised for war, the woman for marriage.[5] In all this they are wild, titanic creatures like the giants; they must be defeated if society is to continue.[6]

The war with the Amazons was represented a second time in the Parthenon, on the outside of the shield belonging to the chryselephantine statue. On the *inside* of the same shield was a second battle of gods and giants; the pairing of the two battles, in other words, was stressed by redundancy.[7] It seems that the message is this: The subjection of women, like the conquest of the giants, is the imposition of cosmos on chaos, the acculturation of nature. Thus the *Theogony* was given plastic representation.

The giants were not actually annihilated but suppressed into Tartarus (*Theogony* 729–735). The Amazons were annihilated, but the women of whom they give a particular representation are still here. The dangers proposed by nature, in other words, are *normal dangers*, which must be continually confronted. Danger legitimates violence; thus we

---

[3] Tyrell (1984), p. 20.

[4] Snell (1960), p. 35.

[5] Vernant's rule; see chapter 2, note 33, in this volume. Detienne (1977 [1972]) compares the Amazons with the Lemnian women, and remarks: "if a girl should refuse marriage she finds herself to some extent with the alternative of war."

[6] On Amazons see Dubois (1982a), Merck (1978), and Tyrell (1984).

[7] The gods and giants appear (in a way) a third time on the Parthenon, since their battle was represented on the peplos which is itself represented (folded) at the center of the frieze. This double redundancy marks this image as the master-image of the set; it is indeed the cosmic prototype for the victory of order.

can see the metopes as meditations on the normal, legitimate use of violence, in the service of order.

The Parthenon—we remember—was built with the tribute of the Delian league formed to continue the war with Persia after Plateia. The Athenian appropriation of that tribute for the building program was part of the transformation of that league into the Athenian empire. Part of the legitimation of that transformation was a claim that the danger of the barbarians was a normal danger, not something defeated once and for all at Plateia and Eurymedon but a permanent threat requiring a permanent military establishment to confront it. The metopes of the Parthenon can be seen as representing the religious ideology of this military establishment—which was, of course, the Athenian empire: as Athens was in a peculiar sense the city of city-guarding Athena, so Athens (Athena's temple there says) was particularly qualified to defend civilization against barbarism. As Athens had faced the barbarians alone at Marathon (Herodotus 9 27.5) so (as the myth developed) Athens alone had faced the Amazons (Lysias 2.4–6; Isocrates 4.68–70).

Athens is thus represented as the proper leader in the violent resistance of cosmos against chaos. The choice of Amazons, barbarous women, as the legendary representatives of the barbarous threat equates women with barbarians as threats to the civil order; women, in a by now familiar formula, appear as the Other. The Amazons came from afar, but women (who might turn into maenads) are kept hidden within the house; they are an inner Other, and their suppression (the message seems to be) is a defense of an inner frontier, perhaps more important even than the outer frontier that divides us from those peoples other than ourselves.

All this is quite familiar in the by now extensive literature discussing Greek attitudes toward women. When we come to the north and south metopes, those on the sides of the building, the issues become more complicated. In the first place, these are not simply representations of war. The identification of two panels on the north side as representing Menelaus's recovery of Helen has led to the assumption that this whole set represented the sack of Troy, and this is probably correct, but those few panels that remain, at the two ends, show peaceful scenes.[8]

However, the Trojan war "belongs" in this set of representations; it

---

[8] These are mostly of persons talking, perhaps watching; two have been identified as the moon departing and the day arriving. The actual conquest of Troy may have been confined to the central panels; whereas the east and west sets on the end were only fourteen panels, the sides were thirty-two panels each, and it may well be that to devote each of these to a scene of violence would have been thought intolerably repetitious.

often occurs along with the battle against the Amazons and the war against Persia (specifically, at Marathon) among the scenes of Athenian excellence—for instance in the Athenian speech of self-praise before Plateia (Herodotus 9.27.1–5) and in the pictures on the Painted Porch (Pausanias 1.15). The Trojans also are prototypical Others, and as a panhellenic event the Trojan war is in a way intermediate between the cosmic scale of the gods and giants and the local scale of Theseus and the Amazons. The Trojans, however, are different from giants or Amazons because they are known to us from epic as people very like the Greeks, somewhat "Asiatic" perhaps (Priam's polygamous household is a non-Greek feature), but enemies (within the frame of the epic) more as a matter of historical contingency than structural necessity. It is true that the Trojans were identified with the Persians, as Xerxes was said to have sacrificed at Troy on his way to Greece (Herodotus 7.43), but it is also true that the hostility between Greeks and Persians, though by the fifth century it may have been thought permanent, could be attributed not to a structural opposition but to an accumulation of contingent disputes. Herodotus indeed in his introductory chapters (1.1–5) grounds the hostility of the peoples in a set of legendary disputes turning on claims to women. Certainly the Trojan war (as the north metopes remind us in their representation of Menelaus and Helen) was about a woman, and an unfaithful one at that. So between what we might call the giant-axis, the Other that must be expelled, confined at the edges, and the woman-axis, the Other that must be controlled, confined at the center, the Trojan War is as a theme somewhat indeterminate.

This brings us to the south metopes. Here panels on the two ends representing lapiths fighting centaurs frame some other subject in the middle.[9] The two panels that separate the centaurs from the central section, in sharp contrast to the wild struggles of the outer panels, are among the most reposeful. This defeats our expectation that the central panels represent an event in the process of being disrupted by the centaurs; in this case, we would expect disorder to ripple into them from the edges toward the center.[10] It seems rather that the scenes of

[9] As on the north (although much better preserved), only the panels at the ends survive, but we have Carrey's careful drawings of the central panels, made before the explosion of 1687, as well as a few fragments which generally confirm his evidence. From these we learn that on this side of the building (probably reversing the pattern of the other side), scenes of war at the ends framed scenes of peace in the middle. The twelve panels furthest to the left and the eleven furthest to the right contain each one centaur, in most cases carrying off a young woman. The central panels, numbers 13–21, are enigmatic and have never been satisfactorily interpreted. They vary between relatively energetic and relatively reposeful scenes.

[10] Fallen wine-jars on the centaur metopes identify the scene of the combat as a feast,

peace are demarcated, not shown to be subject to war but rather enclosed by it. They represent the ordered life threatened by disordering
force.

The battle with the centaurs, like the battle with the Amazons, was a
familiar theme of classic plastic art (it recurred in the Parthenon on
the sandals of the chryselephantine image) and, like the battle with the
Amazons, was a theme that originally belonged to Heracles (among
others) and had been at Athens transferred to Theseus. According to
this Athenian version, Theseus came to the wedding of Perithoos in
Thessaly—or perhaps the wedding was held in Attica. In any case the
centaurs were invited, got drunk, and began to carry off the women;[11]
the metopes represent the ensuing melee, in which Theseus distin-

---

probably a wedding; we naturally look for the bride of Perithoos. Probably she is the
veiled listening figure of #19; the veil should indicate a bride. In that case the woman
talking is probably the *numpheutria*, the matron who supervised the bride at the wedding.
I do not, however, believe that the whole set can be taken as representing the wedding in
the process of disruption—in particular any notion that the women in #21 have just
escaped the centaurs and taken sanctuary with the image is belied by their relaxed posture. (Contrast the women taking sanctuary on the Bassae frieze—Hofkes-Brukker and
Mallwitz [1975], pl. H4–524.)

Number 16 has been taken as part of the melee, but the struggling figures are both
human; why are two humans fighting in a battle between humans and centaurs? I suggest that the odd turn of the falling body implies not combat but wrestling, and originally the hands of the figures were joined; the standing figure has just thrown the falling
one. In that case the horseman on #15 may be not a warrior but a racer, and the two
panels represent peaceful athletics. I further suggest that the inclusion of the bride on
#19 is the asymmetrical element that makes this central section consist of nine panels
rather than eight, and that otherwise the panels are to be taken in pairs.

I suggest that the woman in #17 is holding a lyre in both hands because she has just
taken it from its peg and is about to play; in that case it may be that the man is holding a
flute, which he has just finished playing. In this case it may be that the women on #18
are not running but dancing, and the two panels represent music and dance.

Taking the outer pairs together, we may notice that numbers 13 and 14 represent men
and women together, while numbers 20 and 21 represent only women. The two women
on #20 are back-to-back; this pose is typical of Attic representations of housework, where
the women share a space but go about their separate tasks. The bare breasts shown on
#21 (these beautiful breasts are among the preserved fragments) would seem to place us
in the women's quarters; some ritual is being performed. In this case it is possible that
numbers 13 and 14 also represent the household, seen as a place where men and women
interact; the house is a woman's world where men are also at home. The smaller male
figure of #13 should be a child, and #14 surely represents preparation for or conclusion
of some ritual act.

By this reading the public agonistic sphere of athletics and music is enclosed in the
private sphere. This inversion would work to encapsulate these central scenes and demarcate them from the surrounding melee.

[11] Barron (1972) argues that the version that placed the melee at the actual wedding
(rather than later) was introduced by Polygnotos and Mikkon in their decoration of the
Theseion.

guished himself. Both centaurs and Amazons were represented in the Theseion (Pausanius 1.17.2–3).

The centaurs, like the Amazons, involve Theseus; as opposed to the cosmic and Panhellenic themes on the east and north sides, the metopes on the west and south sides illustrate local legends—in the sense that, even if similar stories were told elsewhere, these representations illustrate the local version, which involves the local hero. We may notice also that they both involve marriage. Theseus in some versions himself married an Amazon; in any case the Amazons were primarily defined by their antipathy to marriage. The centaurs, of course, got drunk at a wedding; they are represented stealing women. This is the *panos gamos*, the "panic marriage," which is rape.[12]

Theseus is not among the earth-born first kings, such as Cecrops, Codrus, Erechtheus, and Erichthonius. He was born of woman and came to Athens from elsewhere. He did not found the state; he perfected it. He is a kind of last king, and is often represented as the founder of the democracy. Here, however, he appears as an exponent of the arts of war, not peace, as master of legitimate violence, and in a sexual, not straightforwardly political, context, warring with centaurs and Amazons.

Centaurs and Amazons are alike in that both are monsters. Amazons, women who act like men, collapse the categorical distinction between women and men (and thus, in defiance of nature, make *particularly dangerous* warriors); centaurs, half-man, half-beast, collapse the difference between men and animals (in some early representations, where the forelegs as well as the upper body are human, the creature has *both sets* of genitals).[13] Monsters, in other words, are more excessive than either component.

Both centaurs and Amazons are excessive in their sexuality—but oppositely. Amazons refuse men (refuse to marry them, at any rate); centaurs rape women. One displays a power in being excessively sexual, the other in being insufficiently so—and since it is the role of men to propose, of women to consent, these may be seen as aspects of gender, as the characteristic error of each sex: to omit to ask, to refuse to say yes.

The subordination of women, in other words, is not slavery (if it is unjust it is some other kind of injustice) since it involves the woman's consent. Of course she is supposed to give it, but equally he is supposed to ask it. Centaurs are as much a threat to the civil order as

[12] Borgeaud (1979), pp. 115–135.
[13] Cf. Baur (1912), numbers 228, 238, 296, 313, etc.

Amazons, and marriage controls male sexuality as well as female. Centaurs and Amazons together represent a system.

Not that Greek males were by law or religion forbidden extramarital sex—at Corinth the proceeds of prostitution apparently went to a temple—but when a man took a wife "for the sake of legitimate children," male sexuality became political. Marriage, as we have seen, is a contract between males, but it is also a compact between a man and a woman, and in a society where the family was the primary mode of social and economic organization this compact was the foundation of the social order. In these terms, perhaps, we can understand why the central panels of the south metopes represent much more than a wedding, represent, it seems, something like a whole peaceful society: wild male sexuality is seen as a threat to social peace in general.

This may in turn help us to understand another place where the centaurs appear in plastic art: the west pediment of the temple of Zeus at Olympia. (This temple is slightly older than the Parthenon and was also built to enclose a chryselephantine statue by Pheidias.) The east pediment displays the contest of Oinomaos and Pelops; this seems an almost inevitable choice when we understand that this was the (main) legendary founding event of the Olympic games. *Oinomaos, we are told,*[14] *did not wish to give his daughter in marriage. He therefore challenged each of her suitors to a chariot race, gave them head starts, overtook them with his wonderful horses, and stabbed them from behind. Finally came Pelops to defeat him by some means or other (perhaps by bribing Oinomaos's groom). Oinomaos died and Pelops won Hippodameia. The chariot race at Olympia, where Pelops was buried and had his hero-cult, commemorated this event—and the women organized footraces in honor of Hippodameia.*

Oinomaos is a kind of male Amazon; he is a displacement into the father's role of Amazonlike Atalanta, who challenged her suitors to a footrace, gave them a head start, and then overtook them and stabbed them from behind. As Atalanta refused marriage, substituting for it murder, so on the same terms Oinomaos refuses marriage-exchange. We can thus understand[15] why the *west* pediment at Olympia displayed the battle of the lapiths and the centaurs: the two pediments offer another version of the Amazon/centaur contrast. The east pediment is dominated by the central figure of Zeus, whose justice is about to bring death to Oinomaos and deliver to Pelops his bride. The west pediment is similarly dominated by Apollo who, after all, had been known to play his lyre at weddings (*Iliad* 24.63–64).

[14] Pausanias 5.16.2–4; for the women's festival see Calame (1977), pp. 210–214.

[15] Pausanias is obviously puzzled to find the relevance of the west pediment; he suggests (5.10.8) that it has something to do with Theseus's descent from Pelops.

The Olympia pediments link marriage to feasting and to rule-governed athletics, two other modes of ordered social life. The links, however, are negative: the contest between Oinomaos and Pelops is unfair, murderous, and in the end properly won by treachery; the centaurs spoil the feast. In both cases things go wrong because women are too much desired; the centaurs can't keep their hands off them, Oinomaos can't let his go—in one version, because he wanted her for himself (Apollodorus *Epitome* 2.4–9, Scholiast to Euripides *Orestes* 990). Society, it seems, can carry on only if males can distance themselves enough from these tempting creatures to allow others to marry them. Woman, in other words, as daughter or stranger is dangerous because men like women *so much*. This danger requires to be moderated by the juridical order, where competition is governed by rules and cooperation is maintained by exchange of entertainment and of brides. The desire of the women to be properly married—to be asked for their consent and to be allowed to give it—is then in the service of the juridical order.

On the base he made for the chryselephantine state of Athena in the Parthenon, Pheidias set one further image: the adornment by all the gods of Pandora. This problematic bride suggests something problematic about the relations of Athena to the city. This choice is all the more striking in that Pandora was but rarely represented in the Classical—or any other—period. Possibly this adornment was meant to figure the adornment that is the Parthenon itself so that the gods correspond to the Athenians and Pandora to Athena. In any case, Pandora is an ironic completion of the whole design. Athena Poliouchos, "city-keeper," was for Greek males patroness of male authority; nevertheless she was among those who adorned Pandora, who is the emblem of the limits of male authority over nature, which requires birth from woman. That Athena adorned her reminds us that Pandora, for all the sorrows she brought with her, was a gift of the gods, and as such not to be refused. Thus (in part) is defined the human condition: Free men become so only in relation to free women.

I am not suggesting that Pheidias and his collaborators in designing the Olympia temple or the Parthenon intended a statement about love and marriage. They intended, surely, a statement about the divine power that holds the world together, and about the forces that make that power necessary and worthy of our worship. I am saying that for them sexuality was a leading example of those forces, and the acculturation of sexuality in marriage a leading proof of that power. Themes of sexuality and marriage turn up in this iconography because for the Greeks (as perhaps for everyone) the relation between the sexes is isomorphic to certain theological issues, and therefore a metaphor of these.

Peitho

Marriage, for the Greeks, is a civilised institution wherein women consent to sexuality. One Greek word for "consent" is *peithō*. The more frequent voice of the related denominative verb is the intransitive middle, which ranges in meaning from "obey" (consent objectively exhibited in the following of instructions) to "trust" (consent subjectively experienced as an inner yielding). The active is a transitive, meaning "cause to consent" and only secondarily "persuade"—since one can be said to *peithein* with bribes or threats.[16] Even though some offers can hardly be refused, *peitho* is regularly contrasted with *bia*, "compulsion," as (more legalistically) *hekōn*, "voluntary," is contrasted with *akōn*, "involuntary."

Peitho was a goddess and, as such, sometimes independently object of cult.[17] Most often Peitho is associated with Aphrodite, either as *epiklēsis*[18] or *paredros*.[19] In Aphrodite's temple at Megara, near the old image of the goddess called Praxis, "act," were two images by Praxiteles, one of Peitho and "another they call Paregoros, 'coaxing.'" Only at Argos is Peitho an *epiklēsis* not of Aphrodite but of Artemis, and in this case we hear that Hypermnestra, when she founded the cult of Artemis Peitho, also dedicated a statue of Aphrodite Nikephoros, "victory bringer" (Pausanias 11.21.1). At Athens the sanctuary of Aphrodite Pandemos, "of all the folk," was said to have been founded by Theseus; Pausanias (1.22.3) says that when Theseus had gathered together the city of Athens, "he established her for worship and also Peitho." These two were thus

---

[16] Buxton (1982), pp. 49–52.

[17] The study of Peitho was founded by Otto Jahn (1846). There have followed a number of encyclopedia articles: Pottier (1905) in Darenberg-Saglio, Weizsäcker (1909) in Roscher, Voigt (1937) in *RE*, Simon (1965) in *EAA*. All this material is reviewed by Buxton (1982).

There was a sanctuary of Peitho at Sikyon with a story connecting it with Apollo and Artemis (Pausanias 2.7.7–9). We have evidence for a priestess of Peitho at Mylasa and in Caria (*Bulletin de Correspondance Hellenique* V 1888 38–40) and for a sanctuary of Peitho on Thasos (*IG* XII.8.360, cf. suppl. 394). This inscription was evidently the horos of the sanctuary of Peitho at Thasos, near the agora. Pouilloux (1954), pp. 333–334, notes that the stone is lost and of uncertain date. The other item is Hellenistic. There seems to be no solid evidence for an independent cult of Peitho in the Classical period.

[18] Pharsalus (5th c.) *IG* IX.2.236; Lesbos (Hellenistic) *IG* XI1.2.73.

[19] A probably late-classic stone found near Cnidos (*Annual of the British School at Athens* 47 [1952] pp. 189–190) is inscribed to "Aphrodite Peitho" and surmounted by a relief of two female figures, evidently representing the two as separate persons. Pheidias included on the throne of Zeus at Olympia Aphrodite rising from the sea, greeted by Eros and crowned by Peitho. See the Pyxis by the Splancopt Painter, *ARV* 899 #144.

patrons of the synoikism.[20] The political implications of this point will be considered later.

Peitho is also closely associated with Aphrodite in the literary tradition—indeed sometimes the two seem almost interchangeable, as in the *Works and Days* (65–74), where Aphrodite is instructed to adorn Pandora but Peitho carries out the instruction. Sappho (fr. 200 Page) called Peitho the child of Aphrodite; Peitho is thus parallel with Eros, whom Sappho also called child of Aphrodite (fr. 198 Page). Pagenstecher calls Peitho "the female Eros."[21] Peitho and Eros are not, however, represented as a brother-and-sister pair. Eros is a boy, winged, and often a miniature figure; he is Aphrodite's messenger, the embodiment of her power to work at a distance, and often flies to crown the bride. Peitho is a mature figure, and wingless; she is Aphrodite's handmaiden, at her side. Both evidently symbolize love, but Eros in the aspect of *celeritas*, the vivid speed of erotic feeling, whereas Peitho in representation has a quality of *gravitas*, graceful and meditative. The two are surely complementary; so the allegoristic "Orphic" tradition called Hygieia, "health," the child of Eros and Peitho (Proclus ad *Timaeus* 3, 158e)—as it were, of Passion and Compassion.

Because Peitho has no special attributes her representations can be recognized with certainty only when the artist has labeled the figure.[22] The earliest example known to me is a skyphos in Boston signed by Makron (Boston 13.186; *ARV* p. 458): Paris leads away Helen; Aphrodite dresses Helen's hair, and Peitho stands close behind Aphrodite.[23]

Weizsäcker says that Peitho embodies the woman's yielding to the persuasive arts of the man. This fits well with her presence at the abduction of Helen,[24] for Helen is typically swept away, as in Sappho (fr.

[20] The alternative version, according to which the temple of Aphrodite Pandemos was built by Solon with profits from a public brothel (Nikander apud Harpocration s.v. Pandemos Aphrodite), evidently goes back to a comic source (Philemon apud Athenaeus 569d); it is a parody *aition*, like the accounts in Aristophanes of the origins of the Peloponnesian War.

[21] Pagenstecher (1911), p. 23.

[22] Richter (1945) proposes to recognize her in a seventh-century ivory.

[23] Similarly she appears on a neo-Attic relief in Naples (Baumeister, *Denkmäler* 1.708), which the art historians trace to an Attic original of the late fifth century (Ghali-Kahil [1955], p. 255); here Aphrodite is with Helen and Eros with Paris, while Peitho is represented as a smaller figure (illiterately labeled PiΥV) seated in the background, with a bird nestled under her hand. An original from the late fifth century is the name piece of the Heimarmene Painter; here Helen is sitting on Aphrodite's lap; to their right are Himeros (desire) with Eros, and to their left, Peitho holding a casket. To the far right, Heimarmene (fate) speaks to another female figure; to the far left, Nemesis lands on another figure, apparently labeled Tuche (fortune).

[24] Richter (1945) would add a skyphos fragment in New York (*ARV* 806) to the list of

16 Page): "she no longer remembered her child or her near-and-dear parents, but [Aphrodite?] led her astray." Gorgias took *The Defense of Helen* as his theme for a rhetorical showpiece because Helen is the typical victim of the power of the word; though persuasion is not force, he says, "yet its capacity is the same"—and therefore Helen, if she was seduced, was as guiltless as if she had been raped (82 DK 11.12).

The contrast—which is also uncomfortably a similarity—between rape and seduction helps to explain the association of Peitho with Pan, as on a fragment of a cup by the Codros Painter (*ARV* p. 1269, #6; *American Journal of Archaeology* cf. 1960 pl. 53 f. 2). Pan can symbolize rape; the *panos gamos*, the panic marriage, includes rape.[25] Pan and Peitho can represent complementary aspects of one event: An Attic aryballos (now evidently lost) (J. Millingen, *Ancient Unedited Monuments* [London, 1826], I pl. A.1) represents Peleus wrestling with Thetis, while Pan looks on, as does Aphrodite, with Peitho close behind her. Here rape turned to marriage when Peleus's mastery of Thetis led her to consent to be his bride; force and free consent are often both present in a sexual relation, as marriage ceremonies worldwide often combine some enactment of the abduction or seizure of the bride with a ritual of her yielding of herself.

Pan and Peitho are allegorically joined when they are called the parents of iunx (Schol. Pindar *4th Pyth.* 56). Iunx is the love-charm, an overpowering spell that invades the mind and thus forces the beloved to consent. The distinction between rape and seduction then disappears. Pindar symbolizes this paradox by calling the iunx "the whip of Peitho" (*4th Pyth.* 219); the whip is particularly associated with Pan.[26]

This association of erotic persuasion with violence may help us to understand two other scenes in which Peitho appears; both involve violence against women. On an oinochoe by the Heimarmene Painter in the Vatican (ARV p. 1173) Menelaus attacks Helen, who cowers by the Palladion; Aphrodite stands between them, and sends a winged Eros toward Menelaus, who has already dropped his sword. Peitho is on the other side of Menelaus and looks away from him. Peitho also appears on the name piece of the Meidias Painter (London E 224; ARV p. 1313 #5). Here she is included in the representation of the rape of the Leucippidae; she looks back, evidently in flight. Weizsäcker interpreted her detachment in both cases as emblematic of the fact that she has no proper role in an action ruled by violence. I would prefer to notice that

representations of the rape of Helen; the painting is by no means clear, but the inscriptions indicate that Peitho was here represented with Aphrodite.

[25] Borgeaud (1979), pp. 118–127.
[26] Ibid., pp. 185–191.

in both cases, as in the case of Peleus and Thetis, rape led to marriage (for Helen and Menelaus, remarriage); Peitho is thus emblematic of the consent that is to come.

Homer offers an instance in which rape led—or rather would have led, if all had gone well—to marriage: that of Achilles and Briseis. Achilles says that she is his *alochos*, his wife, and he loves her, "spearwon though she be," *douriktētēs per eōn* (*Il.* 9.336–343). Briseis says that Patroclus had pledged that Achilles would make her his wedded wife (*kouridiēs alochos*) when they returned to Phthia, where he would feast her marriage, *daisein de gamos* (*Il.* 19.298–299). This could not have made of Briseis a proper bride, taken by an agreement with her father or brothers; Achilles had killed them all, along with her first husband. She cannot become *mēnstes*, courted, or *poludoros*, won with many gifts.[27] The meaning of the projected wedding must therefore have to do simply with the relation between the parties, with the conversion of Briseis from captive to consenting bride. The ceremony would have recognized an epic version of what I called in the previous chapter "companionate marriage."

In either kind of marriage the consent of the woman is of the essence. Pindar provides a mythical paradigm in his account of the marriage of Apollo and Cyrene (*9th Pythian* 5–70). Apollo found this wild virgin sporting with beasts in the mountains; as a nymph, Cyrene is a sort of marriageable Artemis. He seized her and carried her off—yet Aphrodite welcomed them to the wedding chamber and "shed lovely *aidos* on their sweet bedding" (12). The sweetness of their union, it turns out, is founded in the fact that Apollo, for all his forcefulness, approached Cyrene in a spirit of reverence (*hosia*—36). Apollo asked Cheiron the wise centaur for advice in her courtship; Cheiron responds: "Hidden are wise Peitho's keys to legitimate loves" (39). (For *hieros* as "legitimate" see Plato *Republic* 458e, *Laws* 841d.) Apollo found the secret ways to gain her consent.

The critical moment in the classical wedding was the *anakalyptēria*, the formal unveiling of the bride to the groom, which probably took place in the midst of the wedding party; the word may be used to refer by metonomy to the wedding feast as a whole (Timaeus 566 FGH 122). The feast celebrated the consummation of the marriage; the gifts given then to the bride, also called *anakaluptēria*, were evidently understood as compensation for the surrender of her person.[28] Another name for

---

[27] For the equivalence of *kouridiēs* and *mnēstes* in normal marriage, see *Il.* 11.242–243.

[28] Cf. Pollux 3.36 on the *diaparthenia*. Another name for *anakalyptēria* was *opteria*, first-sight gifts (this term could also be used by a father receiving a child—Euripides *Ion* 1187).

these gifts was *prosphthengtēria*, direct-speech gifts. As the bridegroom presented them he spoke to the bride, no doubt often for the very first time. Pherecydes (Fr. 68 Schibli) preserves what was evidently the formula: "Wishing that my *gamoi* be with you, with this I show you your value (*timē*). Do you accept my greeting and be with me (*sunisthi*)?" She replied in some formula, but the papyrus breaks off at that point. It is, however, important that she said something. The *anakaluptēria* was the moment of consent.

The unveiling of the face—as in many wedding ceremonies world-wide—signifies the availability of the body. The most famous representation depicting the actual consummation is the metope from Selinunte—the bride unveils herself; she is alone with the groom and by this gesture gives herself to him. The ceremonial *anakalyptēria* was an anticipation of this moment (parallel to our "you may kiss the bride"). It is probably represented on a vase by the Phiale Painter in Boston.[29] Here the bride sits quietly with her head bent while an older woman, probably the *numpheutria*, stands behind her and lifts the veil; the groom sits across from her in a similar pose to hers, while Eros flies across to crown the bride with a *tainia*. Their union is thus represented as a moment of peaceably sanctioned consent. Only later in the wedding ceremony does the groom seize the bride by the wrist to lead her to her new home; in representations of this later phase the *numpheutria* often comes with her, still adjusting her veil.[30]

Of special interest in this connection is an Italian wall painting in the Terme Museum in Rome.[31] This is generally taken as derived from an Attic original of the classical period.[32] A woman adorned and crowned, holding a flower, is seated on a throne; Eros stands before her leaning against her scepter. Behind her stands another woman holding her veil over her head. These two women are usually taken as Aphrodite and Peitho; it has even been suggested that the source was the cult-group of these two goddesses in the temple of Aphrodite Pandemos at Athens (Preller-Robert, 1.508.3). Whatever the merit of this suggestion, it is worth noting that the figures closely echo the pose of the bride and *numpheutria* in the Phiale Painter's representation; it seems that we here have Aphrodite represented as a bride, unveiled by Peitho, who once again figures as the goddess of consent. (The strand of violence recurrent in the wedding material makes an oblique ap-

[29] Oakley (1982).

[30] Cf. ibid., note 16.

[31] Monumenti Inediti Pubblicati dall' Instituto di Corrispondenza Archeologica [Deutsches Archaeologisches Institut] Rome 1884–1885, vol. XII, pl. XXI, whence Weizäcker (1909), fig. 5

[32] Helbig (1913), vol. 2, pp. 208–209.

pearance here also, in a combat of armed men figured on the arm of the throne.) It would follow, inversely, that the *numpheutria*, the matron who in the actual wedding ceremony unveiled the bride, accompanied her in the wedding procession to her new home, and saw her to the wedding chamber, was the personification of Peitho, as the bride personated Aphrodite.[33]

Peitho is in any case one of the wedding divinities; Plutarch (264b) specifies five: Zeus Teleios, Hera Teleia, Aphrodite, Peitho, and then Artemis as patroness of children. Peitho is also patroness of prostitution; Pindar (fr. 122 Snell[3]) speaks of Aphrodite's prostitutes at Corinth as "handmaidens of Peitho" and Peitho could be the name of a prostitute.[34]

In the *Works and Days* (73) Pandora is adorned with necklaces by "the divine Charites and Lady Peitho." This raises the question of the relation between Peitho and the Charites, the Graces. Hermesianax (Pausanias 9.35.5) had made Peitho one of their number, but more often they are her companions (cf. Pindar fr. 123 Snell[3]). Cornutus (ND 24) says that Aphrodite shares her seats and altars with the Charites, and also with Peitho and Hermes, "since it is by persuasion and speech and favors that the beloved is seduced, [more than?] by the attractions of intercourse." Plutarch says:

> *Charis* . . . was the name given the yielding of the female to the male by the ancients. Thus Pindar says that Hephaistus was born to Hera "without *charites*" [that is, asexually]. And Sappho is speaking to a girl not yet of the age to be married when she says that "I could see you were a small child without *charis*." Heracles also is asked by someone: "did you accomplish *charites* by force or by persuading the girl?" (*Amatores* 571d)

Certainly the Greek verb *charizesthai* can mean, among other things, to grant sexual favors. Therefore Charis is closely related to Peitho as consent—even though, as we see in Plutarch's last quotation, favors taken by force can still be called *charites*. In any case, as Jahn says, "Peitho in precise meaning is however in contrast to Charis; the latter means originally 'yielding,' while Peitho signifies the power which *brings about* amicable yielding, so that . . . the two express different aspects of the same idea, aspects which are reunited in the third figure, Aphrodite."[35]

We cannot, however, thus explain the role of Peitho and the Charites

---

[33] Mangien (1936) notes that it was the special task of the *numpheutria* to adjust the bride's hair; Peitho is also represented more than once adjusting the bride's hair.

[34] Voigt (1937), p. 217—or the name of a ship; presumably the two share the quality of reliable responsiveness.

[35] Jahn (1846), p. 11.

in the adornment of Pandora; the point of Pandora is not her yielding but her overpowering attractions, and the gods make her person entrancing[36] as Hermes equips her with "lies and wheedling words and a thievish temper" (*Works and Days* 78). It seems that Weizsäcker's formula is only half the story; Peitho means the man's persuasion of the woman and also signifies the persuasive power of the woman's beguiling charms. Thus she appears in an epigram by Meleager:

> The triple Charites wove a triple crown
> For Zenophila, token of triple beauty.
> One on her flesh shed longing, one on her form
> Desire, one on her speech sweet-uttering words.
> Thrice-fold blessed, whose bed Aphrodite decked,
> Peitho her utterance, and her sweet beauty Eros.
>
>   A. P. 5.195

Peitho is similarly an emblem of the beloved's power in two early poetic fragments where the context is one of homosexual love: Pindar (fr. 123 Snell[3]) says that Peitho and Charis together reared the beloved. Ibycus (fr. 5 Bergk) says that the beloved is a "sprig of the Charites"—Aphrodite and Peitho reared him among the roses.

In both senses, as availability and as attractive power, the locus of Peitho (as of Charis) is the beloved. The verb appears in both the active and the middle voice; the role of the beloved is *peithein kai pithesthai*, to allure and to yield. This duplicity reflects an ambiguity in the erotic relation itself, an asymmetrical mutuality. It is the availability of the beloved that makes her so sweetly attractive, and the lover as he conquers is conquered; in yielding she has her way. Eros comes to crown her; to become the object of love is the perfection of the beloved's power, which is no less triumphant for being passive and receptive.

Courtship

Heterosexuality is a mediation of the most socially significant of differences: that between male and female. In marriage this mediation is socially instituted. The meaning of marriage, therefore, goes beyond animal pair-bonding; it is a relation proper to creatures with the power of speech. The social creation of this relation is through courtship.

Aphrodite is everywhere in nature, and we experience her power over us as a vulnerability to our nature, to a fate and a potency we

---

[36] For the necklace as a love charm, see Buxton (1982), p. 37.

share with the animals. In society, however, our nature acquires new meanings. When Aphrodite becomes a goddess not merely of sex but of marriage she therefore tends to be specified with *paredroi* that socialize her power. Peitho is with Hermes the most important of these. Plutarch wrote:

> The ancients placed Hermes beside Aphrodite, thinking that the pleasure of marriage most requires words, and also Peitho and the Charites, so that they would accomplish their wishes by mutual persuasion, not in battle and quarrels. (*Moralia* 138 c–d)

The Greek word for the social mediation of differences is *homophrosunē*, the union of hearts and minds. It is by no means a specifically sexual relation, yet the relation between husband and wife is the privileged case.[37]

The epic also has a word for the kind of speech proper to such a relation; it is *oaros*. *Oaros* is also not specifically sexual; Pindar uses it for his own songs (cf. LSJ sub voc.)—which can be as soothing as a warm bath (*4th Nemean* 4f). It can mean any kind of easy, relaxed speech (*Hymn to Hermes* 170) that inspires confidence and creates intimacy (*Hymn* 23.3), and that is guileless (Pindar *4th Nemean* 136–141). The typical uses of the term, however, are sexual, because such talk is seductive, and seduction is typically sexual. Aphrodite's girdle contains *oaristus parphasis* (*Il.* 14.216), soft talk that steals the mind, and she boasts of her *oarous kai mēteis*, sweet talk and wiles, with which she joined immortals to mortal women and subdued them to her will (*Hymn to Aphrodite* 249–251); her portion is "maidenly prattle (*oarous*) and smiles and deceits" (*Theogony* 205).

Hesiod says that the sixth day is bad for the birth of a girl; it is good for a boy, even though a boy born on this day (and here he adapts his earlier line concerning Hermes' gift to Pandora) will have a taste for "lies and wheedling words and secret dalliance (*oarismous*)" (*Works and Days* 789). This is also a good day for gelding young goats; it seems that the day is hostile to masculinity, and a boy born on this day will have certain feminine qualities. (A girl would presumably have them to excess, and be dangerous.) *Oaros*, which is an intimate kind of speech, is thus somehow feminine; women after all are at home only in the intimate private world. It is also speech proper to men who enter this world and who work to win the hearts of women. Thus Hector says there can be no intimate speech between himself and Achilles:

---

[37] For a fuller treatment see Redfield (1982); the next few paragraphs are reprinted from this essay.

There is no way now from an oak or a rock
To dally (*oarizemenai*) with him, like a maid and a youth,
A maid and a youth that dally with each other.

Iliad 22.125–127

Oaros is here the language of courtship; for Theocritus (#27) *oaristus* is a word for seduction. The verb can also be used for the intimate talk of man and wife (*Il.* 6.516).

Oaros, in other words, is a name for the rhetoric that is proper to Peitho. It is speech that softens boundaries and mediates oppositions. It has a kind of openness that is entangling; in its guilessness it is beguiling. This paradox reflects the paradox of Peitho: a yielding that is a kind of power. In terms of this characteristic paradox courtship can become a paradigm for relations in other social spheres, for instance in politics. Seductive rhetoric, when well–intentioned (as we would wish all seducers to be), can produce the special relation of *homophrosunē*— the more specifically political (and postepic) name for which is *homonoia*. We shall return to this last.

I have remarked that the classical Greeks lacked love stories; nevertheless courtship continued. Our evidence for the ideology of the institution must be drawn largely from the plastic arts, especially (as noted) the fine pottery given as wedding presents. Most useful for the present argument is work by the school of the Meidias Painter, since these artists had the habit of labeling their figures, many of which are allegorical personifications.

A typical example is a squat lekythos in the British Museum (London E697; ARV p. 1324 #45) probably from the hand of the master himself. Here we have six female figures and a winged boy, evidently Eros; the women are all labeled: Kleopatra, Eunomia, Paidia, Aphrodite, Peitho, and Eudaimonia. Aphrodite is seated at the center; she seems to speak to Eros, who is seated on her shoulder and bends his head to listen. At the right Eudaimonia (Prosperity) is picking fruit and has a tray with fruit in one hand; at the left Kleopatra (probably the bride; this name recurs for brides) holds a similar tray and in the other hand a garland. To her right Paidia (Playfulness) holds a similar garland outstretched between her two hands while Eunomia (Good Order) reaches around her as if to take it. Peitho is bent over some project of her own; it is a construction with a round base from which rise loops that seem to be of wicker, and braced with string; from these rise twigs or little branches. This is evidently the sacrificial basket, the so-called Opferkorb, which at the wedding held fruit. Here again Peitho appears as patroness of the ceremonial aspect of the marriage.

We have scores of small decorated objects by followers of the Meidias Painter, women's things, mostly pyxides, lefkanides, and squat lekythoi.

Inscriptions on many of them name figures of bewildering variety. A few have names of sea-nymphs, Oceanids or Nereids—Nesaie, Halie—but mostly the figures (overwhelmingly female) are allegorical of some aspect of marital happiness. Two pyxides are typical; one is in the British Museum (London E 775, *ARV* p. 1328 #92): Aphrodite rides in a chariot drawn by Pothos (Longing) and Hedylogos (Sweet Talk); around them revel Eunomia and Paidia, Eudaimonia and Himeros (Desire), Harmonia (Harmony), Kale (Beautiful), and Hygieia (Healthy). The other is in the Metropolitan (New York 09.221.40, *ARV* p. 1328 #99): Here Aphrodite is with Peitho and Hygieia, joined by Eudaimonia and Paidia, Aponia (Carefree) and Eukleia (Well Reputed).

The most surprising name in this group is, at first sight, Eunomia, since we know this as a political term. Eunomia is one of the Horai, daughter of Themis (Tradition) and sister of Dike (Right) and Eirene (Peace) (*Theogony* 901–903; Pindar *13th Olympian* 6–8). These names are all political terms. Eunomia was the ancient descriptive name for the Lycurgan organization of Sparta (Herodotus 1.65.2, Thucydides 1.18.1).[38] Solon borrowed the term as a name for his own political aims (Fr. 4.32 West).

Eunomia is thus not obviously erotic. We have seen, however, that erotic Peitho is often present when violence is to be followed by consent; it may therefore be relevant that Eunomia is the order that results when disorder is overcome. Both Herodotus and Thucydides stress that Sparta was the worst of governments before it became the best of governments. Eunomia seems to have something to do with repair.

Of all the allegorical names which appear on works from the school of the Meidias Painter, Eunomia is the most frequent.[39] Her presence, I suggest, signals the political significance of marriage, which we may approach by considering the political significance of Peitho.

Political Erotica

Peitho is of course also a political term, even when personified. As persuasion makes the difference between rape and seduction, so she also makes the difference between tyranny and legitimate authority (Xenophon *Memorabilia* 1.2.45). Themistocles in Herodotus (8.111.2) creates Peitho and Anagkaia (Necessity) as contrasting personifications; if you don't respond to one you'll face the other. Alcman (apud

[38] Tyrtaeus's poem describing the constitution was called *Eunomia* (Aristotle *Politics* 1306b 39).

[39] Hampe (1955) takes note of five, see *ARV* p. 1324 #45, p. 1326 #67, p. 1327 #85 and #87, p. 1328 #92; I add p. 1330 #8.

Plutarch 318a) said that Peitho, Eunomia, and Tyche (Fortune) were the children of Prometheia (Forethought). King Pelasgus, as he leaves the stage in Aeschylus's *Suppliants* (523) to address the Argive assembly, calls to his aid Peitho and Tyche Prakterios (Successful Fortune); he will succeed if he is persuasive. Pelasgus's invocation shows that Peitho is completely at home in the masculine world of *praxeis* (transactions) where men accomplish things by their ability to persuade their fellows.

On the other hand we remember that Praxis is also a name of Aphrodite and for the act of love (Euripides *Hippolytus* 1004). In her political appearances, Peitho often is connected with women's seductive power. In Menander's *Epitrepontes* (555 Sandbach) Habrotonus calls on Peitho to help make her case, and she is of course an appealing woman.[40] Lysistrata, about to employ literally naked sexual power, raises a glass to Peitho (Aristophanes *Lysistrata* 203). King Pelasgus similarly pursues an erotic cause: the right of the maidens to withhold their consent. These connections have a special mythical resonance at Argos, where the founding event was the marriage of Peitho to Argos, the eponymous hero (Schol. Euripides *Phoenissae* 1116) or to Phoroneus, the founding king (Schol. Euripides *Orestes* 1248). In either version it is evident that the legitimacy of the state originates in a legitimate mythical marriage. Peitho here becomes the original woman, or the quintessential female quality.

The final chorus of the *Suppliants* calls on Artemis as protector against forced marriage (1031–1032); the Argives have already decreed, as a precondition of marriage, that "respectful speech persuade" (*eiper eusebes pithoi logos,* 941). In the meantime the girls are to value chastity more than life itself (1013). Yet Aphrodite is also invoked:

> This our gracious composition neglects not Cypris
> For her power is closest to Zeus, with Hera,
> And the goddess of shifting wiles is honored in her hallowed works.
> There are present as partners with their mother
> Pothos, and she to whom nothing is denied,
> Beguiling Peitho.
> There is granted to Harmonia a share of Aphrodite
> And to the whispering pastimes of the Erotes.
>
> Aeschylus *Suppliants* 1034–1042

This, although two generations earlier, is almost a translation of the Meidias Painter into poetry: Aphrodite with her train of allegorical personifications. In its context the verse probably looks forward to the last play of the trilogy, the only surviving fragment of which (apud Ath-

---

[40] Cf. Buxton (1982), p. 44.

enaeus 600b) is a speech by Aphrodite praising the universal cosmic power of love. One possibility is that this final play dealt with the trial of Praxagora (who alone disobeyed Danaus's command to murder her husband) for disobedience—that is, for the crime of consenting to marriage—and her acquittal. If so, it is plausible that the trilogy ended with the establishment of the cult of Artemis Peitho at Argos (and the honoring of Aphrodite Nikephoros), as we meet them in Pausanias.

Herodotus says that the Danaids brought the Thesmophoria from Egypt (2.171.3) and it is possible that the institution of that ritual was also part of Aeschylus's play. But Herodotus also says (2.156.6) that Aeschylus, influenced by the Egyptians and parting company with all previous poets, made Artemis the daughter of Demeter, so it is also possible that the play somehow linked the Thesmophoria with Artemis Peitho. All this about Aeschylus's trilogy is to the last degree hypothetical, but it does seem clear from Pausanias that the cult of Artemis Peitho at Argos referred through its *aition* to the problem of marriage as presented in the story of the Danaids, and for that story Aeschylus remains a valid source.

The Danaids are a problem because they refuse to consent to marriage. King Pelasgus in Aeschylus (287–288) compares them to unarmed Amazons; they threaten not war but suicide (465), passive aggression. At the end of the story Praxagora escapes from her father's control and gives her husband her consent; as Aeschylus says in the *Prometheus* (853) "desire beguiled her." It seems most probable that Aphrodite's speech was given in Praxagora's defense.

At the trial of Praxagora love and politics interconnect, and Peitho, as an *epiklēsis* of the Artemis to whom Praxagora founded a sanctuary, takes on the multiple meanings of that interconnection. Praxagora had found the power of Peitho to persuade her judges, but it would seem that in the cult, Artemis Peitho should be an Artemis of Consent, and thus a patroness of marriage—if not a marriageable Artemis (like Cyrene) at least an Artemis of marriagability. She should, as it were, defend women against the centaurs among us by demanding consent as a precondition of marriage (as the Danaids demanded it); she would also, to extend the metaphor, defend society against the Amazons among us (those who like the Danaids withhold their consent) by assuring that consent will be given. Her cult would then place marriage in a political context (since its *aition* was a political event) and at the same time make of marriage, in which the threat of violence is replaced by the meeting of minds, a model for politics.

Peitho, in other words, can become political without ceasing to be sexual. When Athena appeals to the Furies in Aeschylus (*Eumenides* 885–886) she uses the vocabulary of courtship: "if you have any holy reverence for Peitho, for my tongue's soothing and beguilement" (*mei-ligma kai thelkterion*).[41] Similarly Eupolis (94 Kock) said of Pericles: "Some kind of Peitho sits upon his lips. He is enchanting, and alone among the public men leaves in his audience planted some kind of sting (*kentron*).[42] As Pericles called upon each citizen to become lover, *erastes*, of the city (Thucydides 2.43.1), so he made love to the citizen body.

As politics can be sexual, so sexuality can be political. The place of Eunomia in Aphrodite's circle is perhaps best understood through her link with Eukleia. Eunomia and Eukleia had a joint cult at Athens; their priestess, like the priestess of Peitho, had a special seat in the theater (*IG* iii 277).[43] Eukleia is a patroness of weddings, either as an *epiklsis* of Artemis or as an independent maiden:

> Eukleia most people use as a name for Artemis, and they honor her thus; some say she was daughter of Heracles and Mynto, daughter of Menoetius and sister of Patroclus; dying a *parthenos*, she has honors among the Locrians and Boeotians. There is an altar to her and an image set up in each marketplace, and there make prior sacrifice (*protelousin*) to her the women who are being married and the men who marry them. (Plutarch *Aristides* 20.6)[44]

Eukleia is the good repute of the happy couple, which is a sign of their respected place in the social fabric. Thus when the disguised Odysseus speaks of her fair fame (*kleos*), Penelope says that her *kleos* would be much greater and fairer if her husband would return to take charge of her life (*Odyssey* 19.127–128). She seems to agree with Pericles (Thucydides 11.45.2) that her *kleos* would be best if people heard

[41] For the sexuality of *meiligma*, compare Aeschylus *Agamemnon* 1439 and Mimnermus fr. 1.2: *kruptadiē, philotēs kai meilicha dora kai eunē*, "secret affection and soothing gifts and bed."

[42] For this as the sting or goad of love, see Euripides *Hippolytus* 39, 1303.

[43] Cf. Hampe (1955). Eunomia, like Peitho, is a ship name—*IG* ii ind. p. 85. Eukleia, like Peitho, is a name for a prostitute—Athenaios 583e. It seems that both are praised as reliably responsive.

[44] Plutarch has just finished telling us that buried in the precinct of Artemis Eukleia (at Potidaea) is Euchidas, who brought new fire from Delphi to purify the land after the battle of Potidaea. The reason for his connection with the nuptial goddess is not obvious. We may notice, however, that he has gone a long journey to the shrine of Delphian Apollo, who is also Hyperborean Apollo, so he is somehow linked to the Hyperborean Maidens at Delos, like him buried in the shrine of Artemis, which is the local site of the *proteleia*. His fate may also remind us of Cleobis and Biton (Herodotus I.31) who served the goddess Hera (and their mother), died in the temple, and were sent to Delphi in the form of statues. Also buried in a precinct of Artemis Eukleia (at Thebes) were Androcleia and Alcis, as Iphigeneia was buried in the precinct of Artemis at Brauron (see pp. 100 and 104). It seems that males who serve a god may receive the same honor as a self-sacrificing girl.

nothing about her. Odysseus, as we have seen, speaks to Nausicaa of the fame of those who achieve in marriage *homophrosunē*: It is grief to their enemies, joy to their friends, *mala t'ekluon autoi* "they hear it most themselves" (*Od.* 8.184)—which would seem to mean "they themselves best know their marriage to be worthy of fair repute," with the implication: "they do not need anyone else to tell them; they mostly pay attention to each other."

The Eukleia of marriage is thus an innerness; so also the Eunomia of marriage is an intimate, inward-turning order, which nevertheless mirrors the political order—as, from a religious or philosophical point of view, both may be taken to mirror the cosmic order. The best statement of this last point is in a late source, Polos the Pythagorean:

> In the cosmos this is the same that gives orders to the whole realm, forethought and harmony and justice and the mind of some god that thus keeps the accounts. In the city it is justly called peace and Eunomia. In the household it is of man and wife, their mutual meeting of minds (*homophrosuna*). (Stobaeus 3.9.51)

The Hellenistic theologian here formally and abstractly states a pattern that had probably long been informally present on the level of folk belief. Certainly the connection between the natural and the cultural order, between civil order and the fertility granted by cosmic forces, is as old as Homer and Hesiod (*Odyssey* 19.101–114; *Works and Days* 225–237). We find a similar link in a fifth-century description from Athens, probably originating in the sanctuary of Aphrodite *Pandemos* (and Peitho). Someone dedicates first fruits and makes certain requests, which are unfortunately incomplete:

>]doros set me up to Aphrodite as a first fruits gift.
> Lady, do you give in return abundance of good things,
> and those who unjustly speak false words and . . .
>
> Fourcart (1889), p. 160

It seems clear that here Aphrodite *Pandemos* is addressed as patron both of abundance and of fair dealing. Pausanias (1.22.3) mentions as associated with the sanctuary of Aphrodite Pandemos, perhaps included in or connected to it, a sanctuary of Demeter *Chloe* (of Greenery) and Gē Kourotrophos (Earth Nourisher of Youth). It is perhaps no accident that the theater seat of the priestess of Peitho was next to that of the priestess of Demeter *Kourotrophos* (*IG* iii.351 = ii.5131). *Kourotrophos* is also one of the names of Aphrodite. Some of the pictorial representations of Peitho suggest that she too had a kourotrophic function, for instance a squat lekythos in Kansas City by the Eretria Painter (*ARV* 1248 #8), on which the baby Kephalos and his mother are depicted in the company of Eunomia, Paidia, Peitho, and Antheia (Flow-ery), and a pelike in New York by the Meidias Painter (*ARV* 1313 #7), which shows, in the company of four Muses, Musaeus with his wife Deiope and his son Eumolpus, and also Aphrodite, Harmonia, Pothos, and Peitho. Perhaps a similar connection between sexual consent and fertility explains, on an Apulian crater in Leningrad (Stephani #350), depicting the sending of Triptolemus by Demeter, the presence of Aphrodite with two Horai, a satyr, Eros, and Peitho. Certainly marriage presents us with an evident link between social concord and natural fecundity. Peace, as we know, is *kourotrophos* (*Works and Days* 228); most kourotrophic is the peace brought about by Aphrodite *Peitho*, which is *homophrosunē*.

Political and Domestic Concord

The political name of *homophrosunē* is *homonoia*, which is defined by Aristotle:

> This is concord about practical matters, and about such as can be shared by the parties, or by all; for example the cities [experience *homonoia*] when it seems to all that the offices should be elected, or that there should be an alliance with the Lacedaemonians, or that Pittacus should rule and he him-self is willing. . . . Thus it turns out that political friendship (*philia*) is *homonoia*. (*Nicomachean Ethics* 1167a28–b3)

Pittacus was the typical Aisymnetes or mediator, one who purifies the state, especially after the murder of kindred:[45] *homonoia* is a condition in which communities transcend a latent conflict or overcome discord. And the term can be applied to families as well, as by Plato's Alcibiades (*Alcibiades I* 126e), who speaks of the friendship and *homonoia* that arise "when a father in friendship for his son is in *homonoia* with him, as is his mother, and brother with brother, and wife with husband." Similarly Lycurgus wrote: "when a wife is deprived of *homonoia* with her husband, the life that remains to her is unlivable" (apud *Stobaeus* 68.35). In the domestic sphere also we may believe that, as in Aristotle's political ex-amples, *homonoia* has to do with the resolution of underlying conflict by agreement about the joint relations of the community so consti-tuted, or about its very constitution.[46]

---

[45] For a fuller treatment, see Redfield (1990), p. 131.

[46] In Chariton's romance *Chaireas and Callirhoe*, set in the late fifth to early fourth centuries, the city of Miletus has a custom that bridegrooms receive their brides in the

This brings us back to Aristotle's claim that the rule of man over woman is "political" and modeled on that of the citizen in office over the citizen out of office. Because the analogy can be read in the other direction, the woman in turn provides a model for the citizen contingently under authority; *homophrosunē* provides a model for *homonoia*, for that political *philia* that is the health of cities.

> It would seem that *philia* maintains cities, and that the lawgiver aims at this even more than at justice. *Homonoia* seems something like *philia*, and it is at this that those most aim who drive out *stasis*, civil conflict, which is the enemy. For when we are friends we have no need of justice, while even the just have need of friendship, and the fullness of justice seems to *be* friendship. (*Nicomachean Ethics* 1155a22–28)

Here, as in the weddings material, we have reference to the strand of violence that underlies the bond. Concord must be the concern of the lawgiver because it is not spontaneous, because *stasis* is endemic. The natural condition of the parties is difference, and concord is achieved only by the mediation of differences. As in every instance of the mean this mediation is more than the calculation of a midpoint that splits the difference; a principle must be brought into play—or (in the traditional language) a god invoked.

One Greek name for the power of mediation is Peitho. In the general Greek understanding (although not in Aristotle, who excludes Eros from his understanding of politics), she is an erotic power. Hers is the power of the subordinate to beguile the ruler into a concern for the good of the ruled, and to secure a more perfect union by the graceful acceptance of authority. Peitho embodies the politics of sexuality, the possibility that sexual relations can go beyond power to justice and beyond justice to *philia*, to mutuality and the meeting of hearts and minds. So also she embraces the sexuality of politics, which makes of a community something more than the joint pursuit of private interests, which takes the city beyond negotiation to consent and a common understanding of the common good.

---

temple of *homonoia*. For the possibility that this is historically accurate, see Thériault (1996), pp. 138–141.

Part Two

THE LOCRIAN MAIDENS AT TROY

Four

The Locrian Maidens at Troy

The Symbol of a Community

In the course of the sack of Troy, we are told,[1] *the Lesser or Oilean Ajax, leader of the Locrians, attempted to carry off Cassandra, who had taken sanctuary in the temple of Athena and clung to Athena's image; in the struggle the image was pulled over. The Greek leaders met in council and determined to stone Ajax, but he saved himself by taking refuge in the temple of Athena.*[2] *Athena remained angry with the whole Greek army owing to Ajax's sacrilege and subjected them to various trials on their way homeward. Ajax himself was shipwrecked by storm near the rock of Gyraia;*[3] *he grasped hold of the rock and would have been saved "in spite of the anger of Athena" had he not boasted that he had escaped despite the gods; these words caused Poseidon to split the rock so that he drowned (Od. 3. 499–511). His companions recovered his body, buried it at Tremon on Delos, and made their way home. In the third year wasting and plague overtook Locris; the oracle at Delphi then told the Locrians that they must propitiate Athena at Ilion by sending two maidens chosen by lot, and that this must continue for a thousand years. The first chosen were named Cleopatra and Periboia. The maidens were taken to Troy by Locrian males, landed at night, then led into Ilion by secret ways, while the Trojan men came out to hunt them. If any Trojan succeeded in killing a maiden he was honored by his countrymen* (Lycophron 1172–1173); *the body was burned with fruitless wood and the ashes cast into the sea, from the hill of Traron. If, however, the maidens succeeded in reaching Athenas temple their lives were spared; they were then condemned to lifelong virginity in the service of the goddess. They swept and sprinkled the temple, wore*

---

[1] Leaf (1912), appendix C, prints the relevant passage from Lycophron with a selection of scholia and other relevant passages. For the myth I follow the *Iliou Persis* as summarized by Proclus (Allen, p. 108), for the ritual, the scholiast on Lycophron—unless particularly noted. A good recent review of this material is in Hughes (1991). Other discussions: Bethe, *RE* s.v. Homer III "Die Sage"; Bömer (1961), pp. 310–322; Fontenrose (1978); Gruppe (1921); Huxley (1966); Lippold, *RE* s.v. "Palladion"; Momigliano (1945); Vidal-Naquet (1975); Wilamowitz von Möllendorf (1883) and especially Graf (1978).

[2] The council was depicted on the Painted Porch: Pausanias 1.15.2.3.

[3] The festival of the Geraistria on Euboea, which included games in honor of Poseidon, probably commemorated this epic storm: see Schol. on Pindar *Ol.* 13.159b. Cf. Schumacher (1993), p. 65.

but a single shift and went barefoot, and could not approach the goddess or leave the temple except by night. When one died another was sent to replace her.

All this is very odd, nearly unparalleled. For one thing, it is a ritual that takes the celebrants overseas. Greek religion is rich in processions,[4] in movings of images and offerings from place to place, but these are generally confined to the territory of a particular state.[5] We do have the Athenian Delia, the annual festal voyage to Delos; this in turn commemorated the mythical tribute paid to Minos, when young people were sent to Crete as a kind of sacrifice—and that myth may remind us of the Locrian story. We know of the Delphic Stepterion;[6] held every eighth year, this required a group of young men to travel all the way to Tempe and back. Both the Delia and the Stepterion, however, involve major panhellenic sanctuaries, places that exist to have ritual connections with distant lands; it seems quite another thing to establish such a relation between Locris and Troy.

I know of only one ritual parallel for the hunting of women: Plutarch (*Greek Questions* 38) tells of a rite at Orchomenos in which the priest pursues the women of a particular family with a sword "and can kill any one he catches." There is a mythical parallel in the hunting of the Proitidai (Apollodorus *Library* 2.2.1–2). Without any real parallel in the Greek material is the lifelong virginity of the maidens.[7] We are familiar with this custom from the Roman Vestals[8]—and, of course, the Christian convent—but it is not Greek. Greek women were sometimes required to be chaste as a condition of religious service but this was a lifephase, proper to girls before marriage or to matrons after—usually long after—marriage. Just as the Greeks have no word for "maiden lady" or "old maid," so also they recognize no single vocation.

The whole thing, in fact, is so odd that we are led to ask whether

---

[4] "Les dieux font volontiers des promenades"; Gernet and Boulanger (1932), p. 310, with examples.

[5] Indeed, they usually play a role in defining the territory of the state, as argued in de Polignac (1984).

[6] Calame (1977), pp. 191–192.

[7] Parker (1983), p. 93: "Firm evidence for the 'virgin priestess for life' is very hard to find." He cites as "the only case I can find" Heracles' priestess at Thespiae (Pausanias 9.27.6) and also mentions as a relevant literary example Theonoe in Euripides' *Helen.*

The case of Thespiae is interesting; Pausanias tells us that this city was especially devoted to the god Eros, and had commissioned statues of him by both Lysippos and Praxiteles. He also tells us the *aition* of the ritual, which is a kind of inversion of the story of the Danaids: Heracles slept with the fifty daughters of Thespius on one night—with all of them except one; she refused, and in exchange was compelled to be his priestess all her life.

As for Theonoe, it seems clear that her special powers are somehow connected with her refusal of marriage; she is, however, both non-Greek and imaginary.

[8] These were vowed to virginity for thirty years, not forever—and apparently could marry at the end of their term, although no happy story is told about this.

anything like this ever happened. This question received a definitive affirmative answer early in this century by the publication of the so-called "Mädcheninschrift."[9]

The Locrians who take part in the Trojan War are from Opuntian Locris, a district across the straits from Euboea. The Mädcheninschrift is a third-century B.C. document found in Ozolian Locris, a district along the Corinthian Gulf. It provides that the Aianteioi, evidently the descendants of Oilean Ajax, and their city Naryx (in Opuntian Locris), shall receive very substantial privileges in exchange for sending the maidens (here called *korai*). The maidens are referred to in the dual, and provision is made for their expenses and adornment (*kosmos*). Clearly the Locrians did in historical times send maidens to Troy. Polybius (XII.5) tells us that they were originally chosen from the "Hundred Houses," the leading families of Locris.[10]

This evidence does not, however, require us to take the whole story as literally true. For one thing, the chronology is impossible. The site of Ilion was apparently uninhabited between Troy VIIB2 and Troy VIII—this is to say, roughly between 1100 and 750 B.C.[11] At that time the city of New Ilion was founded by Greek colonists, as part of the general occupation of the northern littoral of Asia Minor. The custom could, in principle, have begun any time after 750, although our earliest literary evidence for the Greek city there (unless *Iliad* 6 with its description of the temple of Athena be taken as evidence) is no earlier than 480 B.C., when Xerxes stopped to sacrifice to Athena at Troy (Herodotus VII. 42–43).[12] Our earliest evidence for the maidens comes from Aeneas Tacticus (31.24) a writer of the mid-fourth century; he refers to the custom as one of long standing, so that (although "long-standing" in such a writer need not be very long) we can perhaps place it back at least as far as the mid-fifth century. In what follows I shall consider the custom as it would have appeared in that time, comparing it with other customs that we know to have been current in the fifth century.

Second, we need not believe that in every generation two of the best Locrian families sacrificed daughters to lifelong degradation and virginity, or else early death and an ignominious funeral. Aeneas Tacticus

---

[9] First publication: Wilhelm (1911); cf. Leaf (1914–1916). Republished with revisions: *IG* 9.1.3 # 706, Buck, *Dialects* # 60, Schmitt, *Staatsverträge* # 472. Discussion and further revision: Bravo (1980).

[10] More precisely: he defines the "hundred houses" as those that sent the maidens.

[11] Huxley (1966).

[12] Demetrias of Skepsis (Strabo 13.1.40) denied that New Ilion was the heir of Troy; he believed that Troy had been utterly annihilated. Demetrias therefore denied the antiquity of the ritual of the maidens; he says it is not earlier than the time of the Persian rule. He is probably, like us, relying on Herodotus; Xerxes' visit was the earliest report he had of the existence of the temple.

(cited above) says that in all the years no maiden had ever been actually killed. It seems that they were greeted with a show of force but were not actually at risk. We have a parallel in the passage from Plutarch cited earlier: in his own time, Plutarch says, the priest at Orchomenus actually caught one of the women and killed her—with the result that the priesthood was taken from that family. The priest had committed the sin of literalism.

There is evidence, moreover, that the maidens did not actually serve for life, but that each pair was annually replaced by another pair.[13] The lifelong service seems to have been the "real"—that is, putatively original—version of the ritual, but not its actuality. A fifth-century observer would have been told that the girls were hunted because they were supposed to be killed—that on other occasions they had been killed—and that they were supposed to serve the goddess all their lives, being annually released only because another pair of maidens arrived to take up the obligation.[14]

We may therefore believe (and I shall be relying on this reconstruction) that in the fifth century B.C. (and perhaps earlier, and certainly later) the Locrians annually chose two well-born girls; these were adorned and brought to Troy, where they were greeted with a show of force; having got past this to the temple of Athena, they were stripped of their adornment and served the goddess for a year; at the end of this time they were replaced by another pair and returned to Locris, where (presumably) they became marriageable—indeed, more marriageable than before, their status having been enhanced by their ritual service.

The whole complex consists of three parts: a myth, and a ritual in two versions; one of these, that in which the maidens were dedicated to lifelong service, is itself mythical.

Toward Interpretation

Although the content is odd, this myth/ritual complex displays some familiar patterns. The myth has the characteristic shape of an *aition,* a

[13] Part of this evidence is indirect: A number of sources, including Servius, Strabo, and the Mädcheninschrift, presume the sending of maidens each year; if maidens had not been sent home each year they would have accumulated in "a sort of hieratic concentration camp . . . unless very many of the maidens were caught and killed" (Huxley [1966], p. 150). Aelian (quoted in Leaf [1912]) clearly says that the oracle instructed them to send two each year; he is speaking of a revival of the rite, but the revival would presumably imitate the original (Momigliano [1945]). Aelian also tells of the disasters which ensued when the rite was suspended, "their replacements not arriving."

[14] This relation between a symbolic actuality and an "original" literalness is in fact characteristic of Greek stories involving human sacrifice; see Brelich (1969b).

story that explains the origin of a ritual: First there is a transgression (the crime of Ajax), then there is a calamity (wasting and plague), an oracle is consulted, and as a result the ritual is instituted. The ritual, in turn, has the familiar shape of an initiation: There is an elaborate phase of separation (adornment, transport, and threat of violence) followed by a phase of liminality (degradation and service). Only the phase of reaggregation is masked in the myth—because in the mythical "original, real" version there is no reaggregation.[15] The ritual, further, involves seclusion and service, which are characteristic of women's ritual roles.

Some other patterns are in play. The ignominious funeral, particularly the burning of the body with fruitless wood (Tzetzes *Chiliades* 5.728ff), is an element in some reports concerning the treatment of *pharmakoi*, those persons driven out of the city on certain occasions carrying with them the impurities of the community.[16] Even if Tzetzes in his account of *pharmakoi* has introduced this detail by conflation with the rite of the Locrian maidens, which he goes on to describe, at the very least he has seen a parallel between the two rites. And he is correct. Fruitless wood had a specific use in Greek ritual, being used to burn monsters.[17] Its occurrence in the (mythical version of) the ritual tells us that the maidens are monsters—as were the *pharmakoi*; those unfortunates were chosen from the maimed and crippled, the lowest of the low.[18]

All this suggests that the ritual was a purification rite. However, the Locrian maidens, far from being the lowest of the low, were high-status *parthenoi* from the Hundred Houses, and *parthenoi* are in any case typically pure and valuable, particularly when sacrificed.[19] In one version of the Iphigeneia story, for instance, Agamemnon is forced to sacrifice her because he had vowed to the god the finest creature that should be born to him in the year in which, as it happened, she was born. The point is made more explicitly in a story from Orchomenus. *When, we are told,*[20] *there was about to be a battle between Orchomenus and the Thebans led by Heracles, there came to them an oracle saying that victory in war would be theirs if that one should be willing to die by his own hand who was most notable of the citizens. This was Antipoinus, but he was not inclined to die for the*

---

[15] For these patterns and the relation between them see Redfield (1990), pp. 119–124.
[16] See Bremmer (1983), and Hughes (1991), chapter 5, with bibliography in the notes.
[17] Graf (1978), p. 70.
[18] *Pharmakoi* were also, like the maidens, adorned before being degraded.
[19] Tzetzes (Schol. ad Lykophron 1141) calls the ritual a *thusia*, sacrifice; cf. Servius ad *Aeneiad* 1.41.
[20] Pausanias IX.17.1.

people; his daughters Anticleia and Alkis, however, consented. They thereupon killed themselves, and are buried in the sanctuary of Artemis Eukleia.

Evidently the only persons of higher status than Antipoinus (or at the least exchangeable for him) are his (presumably virgin) daughters.[21] They save their father and the state—as does Iphigeneia in Euripides' play—by consenting to self-sacrifice.

In part 1 we spoke of the wedding as the father's sacrifice of his daughter, and as requiring the bride's consent. In this sense the bride is a victim who consents to be sacrificed. The Locrian maidens, also, are something like brides. The names of the original pair, Periboea and Cleopatra, are bridal names.[22] The maidens were adorned, separated from their families, and made a night journey with a male escort, in principle never to return; in all this the ritual is like a Greek wedding. It is, however, a wedding in negative transformation. The girls are adorned only to be stripped of their adornment (the tradition emphasizes the humility of their service); they are not initiated into sexuality but dedicated to chastity.

However, as in the case of the occasions for seclusion and service mentioned in the *Lysistrata* (see above, p. 53), the ritual lowering of women can raise them in status. That is why I am assuming that when the maidens returned they were more marriageable than before. Only in the mythical version of the ritual were they actually sacrificed; in the actual version they went through an experience of sacrifice and came out the other side enriched. The two versions, in fact, represent the doubleness of the Greek wedding, as transfer (by and for males) and as transformation (of and for women), as sacrifice and initiation. All this suggests that the ritual is about marriage.

To this we may add three more points:

1. The maidens were sent in compensation for the crime of Ajax the Locrian. He had taken from the goddess one maiden; the Locrians therefore owed her two. (Twofold compensation is commonplace in Greek jurisprudence.) The ritual therefore is *with* women (who function as tokens with exchange value)[23] and also *about*

---

[21] His name means "adequate to be exchanged as a penalty"; their names are feminized versions of terms for masculine warlike prowess and honor. The paradox reappears in the name of the sanctuary, since the Eukleia there attributed to Artemis is cognate with the *kleos* won by men in heroic story, primarily in war—although, as we have seen, Eukleia is peculiar to women.

[22] Periboea, whose name evidently means "she for whom many cattle are given," is the name of a number of mythical brides; so is Cleopatra ("fame of the father") including Meleager's bride in the Iliad (9.556). See *RE* under these two names.

[23] Cf. *Il.* 23.700–703, where three women are worth one tripod.

women, and about their real value, since it compensates for a crime against a woman that is also a crime against a goddess.

2. The sending of the maidens was a collective act by the whole community.[24] The Maidens were not transferred to husbands, but to a temple, which is to say, to the goddess. Since they returned only when replaced, they were in effect immortal.[25] Athena had always two Locrian maidens to serve her. The ritual thereby represents the continuing relation of the Locrians to the goddess at Ilion; this is a relation of *normal danger*. Athena is always angry about Cassandra, always palliated by the sending of the maidens.[26] The ritual thus says something about the permanent condition of the community.

3. Although the ritual has the shape of an initiation, it is not truly initiatory because it involves only two maidens, not the whole age-class. Most Locrian girls became marriageable without it. It is at most an *exemplary initiation*. By this I mean a ritual for which a few are chosen out of an age-class to undergo a rite having something of the shape of an initiation. Other examples are at Athens the Delia and the Arrhephoria (to which we shall come later), also the ritual of Hera Akraia at Corinth.[27] This does not mean that these young people are initiated on behalf of others or that through them the whole cohort is initiated. I cannot be initiated for someone else any more than another can take a bath for me.[28] The point is rather that this ritual work is reserved for members of that age-class, and that those selected represent the cohort in the sense that the ritual represents something about the meaning of that age-class to the wider community. Such rituals tend to fit a pattern of sacrifice, specifically a *first-fruits* sacrifice. The Locrians give to the goddess two of their maidens in order the keep the rest—or in the actual ritual, the sacrifice is reduced to a year's postponement of marriage, so that this year's

[24] King Antigonus told the Locrians to choose the maidens by lot; in this way all the girls would momentarily be at the disposition of the goddess, since each would be possibly among those chosen. From the Mädcheninschrift we learn that this arrangement, if tried, was not continued; quite possibly it was too disruptive not to know in advance which girls would spend a year in Troy. The Mädcheninschrift can then be seen as a record of a reestablishment of the collective character of the sacrifice in a new form: The Locrians, by awarding the Aianteioi and the town of Naryx special privileges, as a collectivity pay for the maidens; thus the collectivity acquires title to the sacrifice.

[25] Vidal-Naquet (1975).

[26] We even have a story that at one time the ritual was suspended, and the Locrian women bore monsters.

[27] Brelich (1959).

[28] Although in the world of legal fictions almost anything is possible, even proxy marriage.

worth of nubile sexuality is given to the goddess. As in the familiar
first-fruits sacrifice of cattle and crops, the Locrians give to the goddess part of their cadre of brides in order to keep the rest and distribute them to husbands. They sacrifice the maidens in order to
appropriate their maidens.

This brief discussion should suffice to establish the complexity of the
ritual and to suggest that in this case—probably in most cases—it is
wrong to attribute *one* function to a ritual. Rituals are overdetermined
and survive because they are useful in many ways. The extended discussion that follows will attempt to enrich our understanding of that multiplicity by placing it in a context—actually, in two contexts. By comparison with other Greek rituals we shall further explore the themes set
out in the first part of this book, themes involving the social and theological status of Greek women. By placing the ritual in historical and
geographic context we shall begin to explore the meaning of "Locrian," and thereby establish some themes that will further serve us
when we come in later parts to the Locrians of the West. This part
therefore looks both back and forward; it makes a transition from
Greek women in general to the Locrian women in particular. We shall
begin with some comparative cases of maiden sacrifice and initiation.

The Self-Sacrifice of Maidens

Stories of the self-sacrifice of maidens are related to stories of the self-
sacrifice of kings and other high-status figures;[29] these figures are not
rejected by the society, like *pharmakoi*, but rather *internalize* the society
to such a degree that their death substitutes for the death (or danger
of death) of the group. Durkheim called this altruistic suicide. In them
the community dies that it may live. They are heroes.
   There is another story from Orchomenus:

> When Artemis took Orion from this world, his daughters Metioche and Men-
> ippe were reared by their mother; Athena taught them weaving and Aphro-
> dite gave them beauty. Then there was a plague and the people sent to
> Apollo, who told them to propitiate the gods of the underworld, whose wrath
> would cease if two *parthenoi* would be willing sacrifices. No maiden responded
> until a servant woman brought the oracle to the daughters of Orion at their
> loom. They determined to die for the citizens rather than leave this world
> struck down by the public disease; three times calling on the spirits of the
> underworld that they were willing sacrifices, they struck themselves with their

[29] Cf. Versnel (1981), p. 144; Bremmer (1983), p. 302.

shuttles and so died. Persephone and Hades taking pity removed their bodies from this world, and placed them in the sky as comets. And there is a notable sanctuary to them in Orchomenus, and each year the boys and girls bring there *meiligmata*, offerings of placation. And even now they are called the Coronidae Maidens. (Antoninus Liberalis *Metamorphoseon Synagoge* 25)[30]

This story provides no explanation of the name Coronidae, which seems to be derived from *coronē*, the crow. *Coronē* also suggests Coronea, whose emblem was the crow,[31] and this connection is probably more than coincidental. Coronea was the site of the temple of Athena Itonia, and of the Pamboeotia, a festival that drew celebrants from a distance (presumably from Orchomenos, as from other Boeotian communities) and involved feasting, dancing, and games.[32] Here there was a cult of Zeus Meilichios, which may remind us of the *meiligmata* received by the Coronidae at Orchomenus. Also at Coronea there was a maiden story:

Iodama, we are told,[33] *in service to the goddess, by night entered the precinct and Athena appeared to her; on the chiton of the goddess was the head of Medusa the gorgon. When Iodama beheld it she turned to stone. That is why a woman puts fire every day on the altar of Iodama and says three times in the Boeotian dialect: Iodama lives and asks for fire.*

A maiden who serves Athena at night must remind us of the Locrian maidens; in Iodama's case, however, the service becomes truly eternal as the girl in the *aition* becomes literally a monument, a stone maiden. As such she becomes the object of hero-cult. Humans die, gods live forever, heroes do both. This paradox is enacted in the cult when her votary with the ritual threefold cry proper to the dead[34] asserts that she is alive.

A *lekanē* in the British Museum[35] represents the Pamboeotia: A ritual procession of men, some of them in a mule-cart, approaches the altar of Athena, which blazes with fire. The men in the front are leading an ox to sacrifice. Before them a woman carries a tray of offerings on her head. We may be reminded of the Hyakinthia at Sparta, where the hero received an offering "before the sacrifice"; these on the tray must be the offerings to Iodama who "asks for fire." Hyakinthus had been loved by Apollo, and the god accidentally killed him when they were exercising together; they were then worshipped together in a joint fes-

---

[30] Cf. Ovid *Metamorphoses* 683–699.

[31] As we know from explanations of the name of her daughter-city, Messenian Corone: Pausanias IV.34.5.

[32] This festival is best known to us from the decorations on its characteristic pottery: Ure (1929).

[33] Pausanias IX.34.2.

[34] Aristophanes *Frogs* 1176 and Dover ad loc.

[35] Ure (1929).

tival—which, like the Pamboeotia, involved music and dancing.[36] Iodama was killed (and immortalized) by the goddess she served and in this form loved. As so often, the hero is one who perishes by getting too close to the god, and in perishing thus becomes immortal.[37]

Iodama's fate is parallel to that of Hyakinthus; at Athens there are maidens linked to Hyakinthus by their name: the Hyakinthides;[38] these also received heroic honors. *When, we are told,[39] a Boeotian army led by the Thracian Eumolpos was attacking Athens, king Erechtheus received an oracle that victory would be his if he sacrificed his daughters. Two of his daughters gave themselves for sacrifice, and so he won the day. Since the girls were sacrificed on the Hyakinthian hill they were called the Hyakinthides.*

The heroic honors of these girls are prescribed by Athena in the speech that concluded Euripides' *Erechtheus* (fr. 65 Austin—the story here is slightly different: One daughter offered herself for sacrifice, and the other two followed her by suicide). The girls are to be buried together and receive the name of Hyakinthides; their souls do not go into Hades but dwell in the *aithēr* (65–74) as the Hyades (107–108—cf. schol. Aratus 172). They are to have annual worship with sacrifice of cattle and maiden dances (78–80). At time of war they are to receive a special sober and fireless offering of honey mixed with water (81–86).

Also at Athens are the Leokorai, the daughters of Leos; these were three in number and killed themselves when the Delphic oracle said the state could not otherwise be saved from famine and plague (Aelian *Varia Historia* 12.28); their cult place is the Leokorion, in the Agora. Athenian Makaria also sacrificed herself, to defend the plain of Marathon from the Tyndaridae; she became a spring at that place.[40] Finally there is Aglaurus or Agraulus the daughter of Kekrops, who threw herself off the Acropolis as a voluntary sacrifice in order to save the city from invasion from Eleusis (Philochorus FGH 328 F 108—this story seems to involve the same legendary war as the story of the daughters of Erechtheus, the Hyakinthides). At the sanctuary of Aglaurus the ephebes swore their oath to defend the boundaries of Attica.[41] She had defended the boundaries and becomes their heroic patron.

All these Athenian stories are political; the maidens defend the health of the state or its territorial integrity. They are not warriors like the

---

[36] See pp. 295–302.

[37] The Daphne story has some of the same elements; cf. Dowden (1989), pp. 174–179.

[38] The link between the name of the Hyakinthides and Hyakinthus is in one story explicit: Hyakinthus moved from Sparta to Athens where his daughters, the Hyakinthides, were sacrificed (Apollonius *Library* 3.15.8.3).

[39] Phanodemus *FGH* 325 F 4.

[40] Hughes (1991), p. 226n.7.

[41] Merkelbach (1972).

Amazons—they do not kill; they die. If marriage is to the woman what war is to the man, self-sacrifice is a higher form of marriage in that it is the woman's way of dying for her country. Euripides, who had a special interest in virgin self-sacrifice,[42] makes this point repeatedly (*Erechtheus* fr. 50 Austin, ll. 22–31; *Heracleidae* 503–519; *Iphigeneia in Aulis* 1387–1390). To give oneself away is quintessentially feminine. These maidens are not forceful; they are powerful not in this world but in the next, in ritual, not in politics. They go directly to death and transfiguration; they become heroes, monuments, even stars. Their death is a transaction with the gods; whereas warriors protect their communities forcefully, by war, these protect their communities magically, through cult.

Hero worship has to do with the persistence of the dead, of exceptional personalities who die but do not go away. *Hērōs* can mean simply "ghost," one who is invisibly present.[43] Such persistence of the personality most often has to do with incomplete stories, with those who die too young (the *aōroi*),[44] and also with the dead who cannot depart because their work is not done or not recognized. Founders of cities become heroes, and lawgivers show the same tendency. Athletes become heroes, particularly if they have been disqualified or otherwise mistreated.[45] These people have all in one way or another been separated from society and not reintegrated; after death the power so demonstrated becomes a continuing element of community life.

The stories of the self-sacrificing maidens are incomplete because they consent not to arrive at the normal perfection of a woman, which, for the Greeks, is marriage. Those maidens who give themselves to death abandon marriage in favor of a higher perfection. In a sense they marry death—as does any maiden who dies before marriage—but because they give themselves to save the state, in another sense they marry the city.

The sacrifice of a maiden, from this point of view, is an inversion of the seduction of a maiden by a god. In the stories told by Hesiod in the *Catalogue of Women* we learned how the gods entered history through their sexual interest in Greek women and thus founded the first families of Greece. In the sacrifice stories, by contrast, the woman is *sent to* the god; she thereby loses her place as a link in the generations of men, replacing it with a transhistorical cult that belongs not to a specific bloodline but to the city as a whole. Through seduction the gods

---

[42] Studied by Schmitt (1921).

[43] *Republic* 558a.

[44] On these, see Johnston (1999).

[45] Fontenrose (1968).

produce something divine that is mortal, a hero; through self-sacrifice
the women produce something human that is immortal, a hero-cult.

When the gods seduced their women Greek society received power
from above, a force that ran through their veins and founded a bloodline. When the maidens sacrificed themselves they sent themselves
downward, to Hades, and the power received in return rose from below. H. S. Versnel in a study of Greek and Roman self-sacrifice stories
notes that the gods who receive the sacrifice are usually anonymous; if
they are named they are usually gods of the dead, as Makaria in Euripides is sacrificed to Persephone (*Heracleidae* 408).[46] He proposes that
the underlying theme of these self-sacrifice stories is that of squaring
our accounts with the dead. We do not deserve our health and safety,
and must pay something precious to be safe. The city will perish unless
the maidens die. The danger comes from the accumulated rancor of
the departed; in the sight of the ancestors we feel ourselves unworthy.
This danger, it seems, must be overcome; Hades must be transformed
into Meilichios, giver of prosperity. One way to achieve the transformation is to send a maiden down to death. Just as marriage is the mediation of male and female, so the sacrifice of a maiden is the mediation
of life and death.

This brings us back to Athens, and to the daughters of Erechtheus.
We are told by one source that they were sacrificed to Persephone
(Demaretes FGH 42 F 4). In another source (Hyginus 46) the sacrifice
is to Poseidon, father of the Thracian Eumolpus who was leading the
attack. It is not clear which version Euripides used. It is, however, clear
that Euripides saw the story as a replay of the contest between Athena
and Poseidon for the soil of Attica, the contest that was memorialized
on the west pediment of the Parthenon. Poseidon had struck the ground
with his trident and brought forth a salt spring; Athena brought forth
the olive tree that still lives on the Acropolis; thus she became patron
of the city. In the *Erechtheus* Poseidon's son Eumolpus comes against
Athena's city. Euripides' Praxithea, wife of Erechtheus, says that the
triumph of Athena is not to be undone; Eumolpus is not to triumph,
planting his trident in the ground in place of the olive (fr. 50 Austin ll.
46–49). Furthermore after the death of Eumolpus in Euripides' play it
seems that Erechtheus sinks into a chasm in the earth (fr. 65 Austin ll.
59–60, cf. *Ion* 281) and Poseidon shakes the city with earthquake (fr. 65
ll. 45–51). Athena intervenes and gives her final speech of disposition
for the Hyakinthides, and also for Poseidon. He is to acquire the *epiklēsis* of Erechtheus (fr. 65 Austin ll. 93–94, cf. Hesychius s.v. Erechtheus) and he and Erechtheus are to receive joint worship in the

[46] Versnel (1981).

Erechtheum. Praxithea is to become priestess of Athena (fr. 65 Austin ll. 95–97) and Eumolpus son of Eumolpus is to become priest of Eleusinian Demeter.

The end of the *Erechtheus* is thus a general festival of reconciliation whereby the enemy is incorporated under the patronage of city-keeping Athena. The ending of the play *Erechtheus* must remind us of the end of Aeschylus's *Eumenides*. The "sober sacrifices" offered at time of war to the daughters of Erechtheus (and to Dionysus—Philochorus *FGH* 328 F 12) remind us of the *nēphalia meiligmata*, sober placations, offered to the Eumenides (Aeschylus *Eumenides* 107), who received water and honey, no wine (Sophocles *Oedipus at Colonus* 481), and of the *meiligmata* offered to the Coronidae at Orchomenus. When there is a general settlement everyone sobers up, especially the gods.

The Eumenides at Athens become beneficent spirits when they consent to their new roles as guarantors of Athenian lawfulness; the question of their consent is the dramatic focus of the latter part of the play. Similarly in the case of maidens their sober consent to the sacrifice seems to be essential to a good result. In Aeschylus, Iphigeneia does not consent to be sacrificed and brings disaster on her slayer—as does Cassandra, another whose death is seen as an unwilling sacrifice.[47] Maidens cannot, after all, be treated as mere commodities or sacrificial victims; because they are "speaking signs" the settlement works only when they are consenting parties to it.

The daughters of Erechtheus become powerful underground; Euripides' Athena instructs that their sanctuary be kept locked lest some enemy gain access to these powers by surreptitious sacrifice and destroy the state (fr. 65 Austin ll. 87–89). They have not, in other words, been absolutely appropriated by the state, but retain enough independence to be potentially a danger to it. Similarly the Eumenides, powerful underground, turn their powers to a new purpose and thus secure peace and fertility—but nonetheless they are the same powers they always were, destructive of the transgressor.

All this taken together may give us some general understanding of the sacrifice of maidens. The voluntarily sacrificed maiden marries her fate; that is, her sacrifice is a heroization of her marriage. Instead of being kept within the network of marriage-exchange and of the generations she is sent outside this world and thus establishes a link between the society marriage-exchange sustains and that other world. That other world is fundamentally hostile to us; Hades, the chthonic Zeus, is as much our adversary as is the Olympian Zeus in the Prometheus story. Our health and security therefore depend upon some act of compensa-

---

[47] Loraux (1987), p. 81n.4.

tion on our part that can convert that hostility into protective energy. The power of the maiden, which is that of pure potentiality, of the unallocated resource, of fertility not yet called upon, can achieve this conversion, but as it is her power it must be her act. She must marry her heroism.

The Locrian maidens are a little like this; they, however, are not heroes. They do not receive a cult, they are a cult. What is immortal in the ritual (for a thousand years, at least) is not the particular maidens but the service maintained by maidens continually renewed. The triumph over time is therefore achieved not by the girls (who reenter society and find their place in this world) but by the community that sends them. The girls stand for the whole cohort of marriageable girls—and, since they are eternally renewed, for the eternal renewal of marriageable girls, eternal like the generation of leaves. What is heroized at Locris is not their self-sacrifice—or their marriage—but, through a first-fruits sacrifice, marriage itself as an institution.

Becoming a Maiden

So far we have discussed the ritual of the Locrian maidens as a rite of sacrifice. We now turn to an alternative model: that of initiation. From this perspective the point of the ritual is to transform the maidens from girls to brides—and since they represent the best of the cohort, to present a model or transformation to the whole cohort. In order to explore this notion we shall take as our model the best documented and most studied Greek rite initiatory of women: the Arkteia at Athens.[48] Here we have literary and also archaeological/art-historical evidence bearing on both the myth and the ritual. However, in spite of—or perhaps because of—this range of evidence the whole has proven difficult to integrate. It seems clear that some or all Athenian girls "were bears" at some point in their lives, that this ritual was prior to and somehow in the service of their marriage, and that it followed the typical scenario of an initiation: They were separated from society (segregated for some time in a sanctuary), underwent a liminal transformation (played the part of animals), and were reaggregated (became newly marriageable). The ritual has been extensively studied in these terms by Brelich.[49]

---

[48] On this myth-ritual complex see (besides items cited in later notes) Cole (1984b); Dowden (1989), pp. 9–47, Ghali-Kahil (1965); Linders (1972); Osborne (1985), pp. 154–172, Pearlman (1983); Sale (1975); Stinton (1976); Vernant (1985), pp. 15–30; and Walbank (1981).

[49] Brelich (1969a).

However, exactly how all this happened, and when, and why, and even where, has been difficult to establish.

At least three different sanctuaries were involved: the sanctuary of Artemis Mounichia in the Peiraeus, the sanctuary of Artemis Brauronia in the coastal deme of Brauron (about halfway between Marathon and Sounion), and the sanctuary of Artemis Brauronia on the Acropolis. All three of these have been excavated; little is left of the first and third,[50] but at Brauron, where parts of the buildings after their collapse sank into the marshy soil and were therefore preserved, much has been found and it has been possible even to rebuild one of the structures.

The sanctuary at Brauron was near the sea but not in sight of it, sheltered by a low rocky hill. It was entered from the inland side, toward Athens, over a bridge across local water.[51] In the midst of the precinct an empty space was bounded on the south by a temple, altar, and sacred enclosure; this latter was a cave (now collapsed) in the lowest level of the little rocky hill. The other three sides of the central space were bounded by the three wings of a stoa. The east wing was a simple stoa with a colonnade and continuous exterior wall (probably intended to receive dedications); the other two wings with colonnades also contained a series of rooms: six on the north, and four plus a passage between them on the west. These were dining rooms, each holding eleven couches; the couches and in many cases the stone tables beside them are preserved. Behind the north colonnade was a narrow open space, accessible by a gate at the east and west ends, and along the north side of this an even narrower colonnade (also probably for dedications). The whole is dated on stylistic grounds to 425–416; Bouras calls it the earliest known example of a horseshoe stoa.[52] It is, however, in some respects parallel to the U-shaped stoa at Locri, which in its earliest phase is considerable older (cf. p. 210).

Here were found an extensive set of inscriptions recording dedications to Artemis, mostly of fabrics. There are quite a number of marble votives in the form of plaques or statues; some of these represent children and a number of them represent whole families, approaching the Holy Family of Leto, Apollo, and Artemis with sacrificial animals. There were also found numerous small drinking cups of a characteristic shape, called *krateriskoi*; these were evidently ritual vessels, left in the sanctuary after use. Others have been found in Brauron's sister sanctuaries at Mounichia and on the Acropolis, at Halai (close to Brauron

---

[50] For Artemis Brauronia on the Acropolis see Wycherly (1978), p. 134n.44; for Artemis Mounichia see Palaiokrassa (1991).

[51] The description that follows is based primarily on Bouras (1967).

[52] Ibid.

and linked to it in myth) and at the sanctuary of Artemis Aristoboule, and one or two in the Agora[53] and at the cave of Pan at Eleusis.[54] On them are typically depictions of little girls, running or dancing, wearing a characteristic short garment or in a few cases naked. These are evidently the "bears," and they are most numerous at Brauron.

We cannot, however, deduce much about the rite from the sanctuary, since evidently quite a number of other things went on there as well. The majority of the marble dedications are for boys, but we hear nothing in the literary evidence of boys being bears. Evidently there was some other rite for male children. Euripides, in the etiology he provides for the sanctuary at the end of the *Iphigeneia in Aulis* (quoted below) refers to it as a sanctuary of Iphigeneia and says that she will receive gifts of fabrics in memory of those who die in childbirth. No archaeological evidence connects Iphigeneia with this place; the dedications of fabrics, in so far as they are identified by inscriptions, are to Artemis and in gratitude for *successful* childbirth. It is clear from the dining rooms that ritual meals took place here, but it is unclear who took part, and why. These couches are exceptionally short—1.77m— and seem more suitable to children than adults; quite possibly they were intended for the "bears." On the other hand, we do sometimes find short couches in places where they were evidently intended for adults.[55] Euripides (IT 1462) refers in an obscure phrase to the *semnai klimakes*, the "sacred steps" of Brauron. It is possible that *klimax* is here being used in its special sense of "bench in the theater" and that the low rocky hill served as a kind of natural grandstand. It certainly provides a fine view of the central space. Perhaps it served as a grandstand for athletic events, or else (or also) some kind of *mimēsis* or sacred representation took place here, possibly as part of the Arkteia. Ghali-Kahil has published three Attic vases from the third quarter of the fifth century.[56] Two are exceptionally fine *krateriskoi*. The first represents a woman supervising young girls, a woman with two baskets; there is a palm tree, and girls running. It seems to represent preparations for a race. On the second there are nude nubile runners with crowns, plus one nude little girl; by some palm trees is an animal that may be a bear. This might be a race as an element of a ritual. The third vase is more elaborate, and is not truly a *krateriskos*; on it can be seen Leto, Apollo, and Artemis with a deer, a man naked (at least from the waist up) and a woman clothed, both wearing bear masks or turning into bears. This

---

[53] Ghali-Kahil (1977), p. 88n.18.

[54] Sourvinou-Inwood (1988), p. 116.

[55] Bouras (1967), p. 75.

[56] Ghali-Kahil (1977).

might be a representation of some kind of *mimēsis*. On the other hand this vase may represent myth, not ritual.[57]

Our understanding of the ritual has been further confused by our earliest source for it, the sentence in the *Lysistrata* (already quoted): "In the tenth year I wore [or shed] the saffron robe and was a bear at the Brauronia." Because of this the initiatory ritual is by some scholars called the Brauronia. The proper term, however, for being initiated in this way is *arkteusai*.[58] The Brauronia was a penteteric festival conducted by the state *hieropoioi* (Aristotle *Ath. Pol.* 54.7); it involved a somewhat rowdy procession from Athens to Brauron (cf. Aristophanes *Peace* 872–876). If this were the only occasion on which girls were bears we cannot believe the flat statement of the scholiast on *Lysistrata* 645 that the law required Athenian girls to be bears before marriage: The number in a one-year cohort of the daughters of Athenian citizens can be guessed at as between 700 and 800; if these were all to be initiated at one penteteric festival, there would be a crowd of more than 3,000 little girls.

However, it should be noticed that the speaker in Aristophanes (a voice from the women's chorus) is claiming marks of distinction, and that the other three rituals she mentions were the privilege of certain select girls. I would suggest that the "be a bear" *at the Brauronia* was a special mark of distinction; most girls went through the rite on some less publicly significant occasion.

The dining rooms at Brauron may or may not have been built for the Arkteia; the enclosed space behind it looks like an exercise yard (for little girls) or a protected space for mysteries. But because the sanctuary was polyfunctional it is difficult to guess.

Here I propose a different approach to the ritual, starting from the myth, that is to say, from the stories that serve as its *aitia*. These fall into two groups, one connected with Mounichia, the other with Brauron. I tend to believe that the Arkteia began at Mounichia and was only later extended to Brauron; whether or not this belief is historically correct, this is indeed the most convenient order in which to "read" the *aitia*. I therefore begin with the Mounichia story.

At the time when the Piraeus was still an island, we are told,[59] *Mounichus established on its headlands the sanctuary of Artemis Mounichia. A she-bear came to frequent that place, and grew tame. One day a young girl teased the bear and was clawed or even blinded; the girl's brother(s) killed the bear. There was a famine or plague. The oracle said that the trouble would stop only when*

[57] So Sourvinou-Inwood (1988).

[58] Montepaone (1979), p. 351.

[59] Sources collected in Scanlon (1990).

someone sacrificed his daughter to Artemis. Embarus (or Barus) alone offered to do so, on condition that he and his descendants should hold lifelong the priesthood of the sanctuary. He then adorned his daughter and concealed her in the aduton, *the most secret part of the temple; he adorned a she-goat and, calling her his daughter, sacrificed her where she could not be seen. The plague or famine stopped. The people became suspicious, and Embarus told them to consult the oracle. The oracle said that the man who said he had sacrificed should in future do just as he had done. Embarus then revealed his secret, and the ritual was instituted: "because of this the girls do not shrink from being bears before marriage, in as much as they are making atonement for the matter of the beast"* (if that is the meaning of *ta tes thêrias*—Anec. Bekk. 1.144).[60]

Here we have again our familiar scenario: transgression, calamity, oracle, and institutionalization. The teasing and killing of the bear is a transgression; the catastrophic plague or famine is followed by an oracle that produces a demand for the sacrifice of maidens. What is founded here, however, is not a hero-cult commemorative of a sacrifice but rather a ritual whereby the sacrifice is avoided. The oracle requires to be interpreted by Embarus; a second oracle then endorses the interpretation. The writers on proverbs tell us that "I am Embarus" meant "clever" and also "demented"; I would suggest that it meant "intelligently demented," "crazy like a fox." Embarus pretended that he really couldn't tell the difference between a goat and his daughter, and in this way carried off the substitution.

The *aition* tells us that the ritual enacted at least the latter part of the *aition*; the oracle said that the man who had said he had sacrificed (and in every generation the priest was presented as the descendent of Embarus) should do as he had done. Evidently each priest did what Embarus had done, so that the ritual, at least at Mounichia, involved the adornment of a girl for sacrifice, her concealment in the *aduton*, and the substitution of a goat similarly adorned. Here again we have the theme of the transformation of sacrifice into initiation; the girl is threatened with death but survives to marry. The obscure expression "because of this the girls do not shrink from being bears" may imply that the earlier part of the *aition* was also enacted, and the girls played the part of the bear who was killed—so that they were pursued and mimetically put to death by the "brothers." In this case we have yet another parallel with the Locrian maidens: Maidens are hunted.

At Brauron the Arkteia became entangled with another story, that of Iphigeneia (told in Aeschylus's *Agamemnon*, in two plays of Euripides,

---

[60] Vernant (1982–1983), p. 452, calls attention to a parallel expression in the Scholiast on Theocritus 2.66.

and elsewhere). *Agamemnon, we are told, was (for one reason or another) obligated to sacrifice his daughter to Artemis. He therefore summoned her to Aulis (where the Greek army was gathered and becalmed) under pretense of giving her in marriage to Achilles. Instead he sacrificed her. Artemis, however, did not accept the sacrifice; at the last moment she substituted a deer as the victim and carried Iphigeneia away to the savage land of the Taurians, where she became priestess of a barbaric rite requiring the sacrifice of every foreign male.* Iphigeneia was thus transformed from victim into executioner, and since she was herself foreign she became potentially a killer of her own menfolk, of those who had tried to kill her. Her second situation was no solution, but merely a mirror image of the first.

Iphigeneia, indeed, eventually found herself in the position of being obligated to sacrifice her own brother, who passed that way as part of his attempt to purify himself of matricide. Clytemnestra had killed Agamemnon in revenge for the sacrifice of Iphigeneia; Orestes had executed Agamemnon's revenge on Clytemnestra, and Iphigeneia now found herself in the position of executing Clytemnestra's revenge on Orestes. However, at this point the cycle was broken; *Iphigeneia and Orestes escaped together, taking with them the statue of Taurian Artemis.* Thus brother and sister seem both to offend Artemis, she by leaving the priesthood, he by stealing the image. In fact, from the Greek point of view, all this is on behalf of Artemis, since *it results in the institution of a new rite of Artemis among the Greeks, at Halai on the Attic coast near Brauron.* In Euripides' play the goddess Athena prescribes the rite and turns the tale into an *aition:*

Whenever you come to god-built Athens
There is a place there by the farthest boundaries
Of Attica, facing Carystia's ridge;
It's sacred. My people name it Halae.
There you're to build a temple and set the image
Named for the Tauric land and for the toil
You endured in your wandering through Greece,
Stung by the Erinyes. Mortals will hymn her
In time to come, Artemis Tauropolus, the goddess.
Do you fix this custom: At the festival of the folk
As recompense for your slaughter let the sword be set
To a man's neck, and let the blood be drawn
For piety's sake, that the goddess have her honor.
You, Iphigeneia, by the sacred steps
Of Brauron, keep the keys there for this goddess.
Here they will bury you when you die, and robes
Of fine-wrought weft they'll sacrifice, a joy to you,

Which women leave in their houses when their lives
Are lost in childbirth.

Euripides IT. 1449–1467

The rite of the sanctuary at Halae, in other words, was like that of Spartan Orthia[61] (which sanctuary also claimed to possess the statue of Artemis Tauropolus): the drawing of blood was understood as a substitute for human sacrifice. The rite at Halae, however, did not substitute for an "original" version, but for a sacrifice that failed to occur in the *aition* (interpreting "your slaughter" as "your sacrifice by the Taurians"); when Iphigeneia rescued Orestes a debt was owed to Artemis, which the men of Attica annually paid. At both Halae and Sparta the ritual makes a connection between Greeks and barbarians—while at the same time marking the difference between them. When Artemis Tauropolus comes to either place she becomes relatively civilized.

Iphigeneia, the poet tells us, became the (first?) priestess at Brauron and was buried there. Halae and Brauron thus share an *aition* and are in a sense brother-and-sister sanctuaries, the former exposed on the seashore, the latter in a sheltered spot very near the shore, the two within easy walking distance of each other.[62]

On this evidence in Euripides (and Euphorion, who referred to the "seaside Brauron cenotaph of Iphigeneia"), the "collapsed cave" has been identified as the hero-tomb of Iphigeneia—although, as noted, there is no archeological or epigraphic evidence for this identification, or for the dedication to Iphigeneia of fabrics woven by women who had died in childbirth; it seems, however, that Euripides would not have spoilt his play by falsifying traditions about a sanctuary well-known to his audience. There is, as noted, ample evidence for the dedication at Brauron to Artemis of fabrics woven by women who had successfully delivered. It has been suggested that at Brauron Artemis was divided between her positive and negative identities; the positive aspects (*kourotrophus*, nurse of youth, and *eilethyia*, helper with childbirth) were ascribed to Artemis herself, while the negative aspects (slayer of women) were associated with Iphigeneia.[63] This suggestion is powerfully confirmed by a fragment of Hesiod (23a) that describes the sacrifice of Agamemnon's daughter (Hesiod calls her Iphimede) to Artemis as the ships depart for Troy; Hesiod says that the girl sacrificed was only an image, and that Artemis actually made her immortal with ambrosia: "now the race of mortals upon the earth calls her Artemis Enodia." Enodia was sometimes a name for a *paredra* or spouse of Zeus Meili-

[61] For more on this rite see Redfield (1990), pp. 128–129.
[62] On Halae see Graf (1979).
[63] Kondas (1967), p. 162.

chios; evidently it is a name for a goddess having to do with the dead.[64] It seems that at Brauron Iphigeneia had become a sort of chthonic Artemis, an "Artemis Meilichia," as it were. As the prototypical sacrificed maiden she had become the patroness of those for whom femininity entailed not generation and nurturance, but death.

We have some evidence for another function for Iphigeneia in the Thessalian cult of Artemis: It seems that there girls became "deer" and their prospective husbands had to pay a sort of ransom to recover them for marriage.[65] Here the adventures of Iphigeneia served as the scenario for an initiation ritual: She was threatened with death (separation), exchanged for/transformed into an animal (liminality), rescued by some kind of apotheosis or heroization (reintegration). So the girls were taken away, became deer, and were then rescued as part of a transformation, no longer *parthenoi* but brides.

This ritual seems to have been adapted to Attic Brauron—perhaps by Peisistratus, who was based in this part of Attica, and is plausibly responsible for the relocation or extension of the Arkteia from Mounichia to Brauron.[66]

The Attic story, we are told by the scholiast on Aristophanes (*Lys.* 645), held that *Iphigeneia was sacrificed not at Aulis but at Brauron, and that the animal substituted for her by Artemis was not a deer but a bear.* Iphigeneia's burial at Brauron was thus, from the point of view of this tradition, a kind of homecoming,[67] and the Arkteia at Brauron could refer to this bear (rather than the bear in the Mounichia story). Sourvinou-Inwood (1971), whose text I adopted in my translation, emended the text of Aristophanes so that it refers to "shedding" (rather than simply "wearing") the saffron robe at the Arkteia; her suggestion is founded on a reference in Aeschylus's *Oresteia* (*Ag.* 239) to Iphigeneia "shedding her saffron robe" at the moment of her sacrifice. This emendation in turn suggests that the girls performing the Arkteia may have worn saffron robes because they enacted some *mimēsis* of the sacrifice of Iphigeneia, and that (following the local tradition) the girl who enacted the sacrificial victim became at the moment of shedding the robe

---

[64] Enodia was typically an epiklesis of Hecate, who is a kind of chthonic Artemis (*RE* s.v. Enodia). Pausanias (I.43) is probably misquoting this line when he says that Hesiod asserted that Artemis transformed Iphigeneia into Hecate. Hecate has a special role in the *Theogony*, where she is a mighty mediator—see Boedeker (1983).

[65] Clement (1934).

[66] Angiolillo (1983). On the other hand, Brauron also had close connections with the Philaidae, (Montepaone [1979], p. 355), and another plausible suspect is Philaid Cimon, who well understood the politics of religious innovation.

[67] Euphorion, and before him Stesichorus, had actually made Iphigeneia an Athenian, child of Perseus by Helen—Pausanias II.22—see Wilamowitz von Möllendorf (1883).

(mimetically) a bear.[68] Here again, however, we wander into supposition.

It is in any case clear that Mounichia and Brauron, as they were linked by a common ritual, the Arkteia, were also linked by the bears that appear in their respective *aitia*. The two bears, however, have opposite functions; in the Brauron story the father's attempt to kill a daughter leads the goddess to substitute a sacrificial bear; in the Mounichia story the killing of a bear leads the goddess to demand the sacrifice of a daughter—for which the father substitutes a goat. (The victims actually sacrificed in Greek blood-sacrifice were almost without exception domesticated animals;[69] the only major exception known to me is the historically problematic rite of Artemis Laphria at Patras—Pausanias VII.18.11–13.) In both stories a girl is equivalent to a bear, and at both places the Athenian girls marked a stage in their maturity by becoming "bears."

The sources describe the rite as a precondition of marriage but do not present the girls as brides; they are transformed, not transferred, and there are no bridegroom figures in the stories. Both stories, in fact, are about fathers and brothers. The Iphigeneia story nearly comes full circle with the father's sacrifice of the daughter being repaid by the daughter's sacrifice of the son; instead brother and sister cooperate to break the cycle. This contrasts with the political solution in Aeschylus; Orestes' acquittal by the newly founded Areopagus. Both on the Areopagus and at Brauron a new institution results from and commemorates the breaking of a family curse—but at Brauron (as opposed to the Areopagus) the solution is reached entirely within the family. Iphigeneia lives forever in Brauron, as an eternal *parthenos*, the object of hero-cult. Iphigeneia in a way marries her brother, since her relation with him determines her fate and thus substitutes for marriage. After all her adventures she ends where she began, locked within her family; in this sense her story is unsuccessful. As we have seen, this fits her to be a heroine.

A heroine requires a ritual; this is the completion of her story. As so often, everything that had gone wrong in the myth was repaired by the ritual. The maidens who did penance for the bear of Artemis by a *mimēsis* of sacrifice and thus became marriageable also reenacted and survived the fate of Iphigeneia, the prototypical maiden who had been promised marriage, threatened with sacrifice, and replaced by Artemis's bear.

Iphigeneia became an eternal *parthenos* because ultimately nothing

---

[68] According to one tradition (Phanodemus apud Tzetzes ad Lycophron 183) Iphigeneia at the moment of her sacrifice was actually turned into a bear.

[69] J. Z. Smith (1987).

(within the code of significance defined by the story) happened to her; she was spared the role of victim and refused the role of executioner. In the end she returned to the place of her attempted sacrifice, where she died still untouched and as such became a monument. She made something heroic out of an unfinished woman's life. Perhaps the ideal dedications to her were those fabrics left unfinished by women who died giving birth.

In the Mounichia story, however, the family system is active. The brothers bring about the anger of the goddess, killing the bear who had disfigured their sister (and thus made her unmarriageable). A father (of a different maiden) repairs the situation, and thus institutes a ritual whereby maidens become marriageable. Embarus, who saves his daughter from sacrifice by finding a substitute, may be seen as the good father, in contrast to Agamemnon, who sacrifices his daughter and loses her when the goddess contrives a substitute. Both myths, however, tell us that the goddess does not want a maiden sacrificed; what she demands is a *mimēsis* of human sacrifice, through a substitute. Embarus was successful because he understood the god when no one else did, and thus avoided the sin of literalism. In order to carry the people with him into the new, correct situation, he had (if my interpretation of the proverb is correct) to pretend to take literally what he knew to be a fiction. Thus at Mounichia the basic scenario is doubled (there are two oracles)—with an overlap similar to what is called in baroque music "stretto." The death of the bear is the first transgression; it is followed by calamity and by an oracle that demands the sacrifice of a maiden—which in its turn is a new calamity. Embarus performs his sacrifice, and the oracle then tells the people that the final solution has *already been accomplished*, and needs only to be made permanent. Embarus has earned his priesthood; he understood that ritual like all *mimēsis* is an unreal reality; that is why it can be a mediator between realities.

The good father gives his daughter to a husband. Marriage can thus be seen as a positive mediation between two negative extremes: that of Agamemnon, who sacrificed his daughter (and was murdered by his wife), and that of, for example, Oinomaus, who killed his daughter's suitors (and was murdered by her husband) because (according to one version) he wanted to marry her himself. In marriage the father neither destroys his daughter nor keeps her; he entrusts her to another "for the procreation of legitimate children." The ritual tells us that this mediation is accomplished by entrusting the daughter to the goddess; in the Mounichia story, the girl who is saved is concealed in the *aduton* of the temple; in the Arkteia the girls became "bears"—that is to say, wild creatures under the protection of the goddess.

The girls at some point, it seems, put on and at some point took off saffron robes. A saffron robe is an emblem of mature sexuality. The fourth-century. marble statues of little girls found at the sanctuary (among the finest Greek representations of children) show them in long flowing robes; although they are obviously children, they have the knowing look of "little women." Probably their garments are the saffron robes. Sourvinou-Inwood has made a careful argument suggesting that the saffron robe was worn at a relatively early stage in the rite, and that the girls shed it and became naked as a preparation for their return to society in their new status.[70] If so, the sequence can be seen as a progress from culture toward nature. Mature sexuality in girls the age of the "bears" is premature and could be assumed only fictively, proleptically; their return to the wild can at this stage be seen as normal development.

The sacralization of the girls can be seen as an initiatory ceremony and at the same time remain parallel to the sacralization of the crops through the first-fruits sacrifice.[71] The girls have to be taken from their fathers; that is, they must be separated from their natural origin. Only a god is powerful enough to break the bonds of nature and convert the new crop of girls into consumable commodities. Once the girls have belonged to the god—for whatever period of segregation and transformation—they can be returned by the god to society as new creatures with a new kind of social potentiality.

The "bears" were little girls, five to ten years old.[72] Greek girls did not marry so early. The Arkteia, in fact, should not be seen as a part of the ritual of marriage, but rather as an initiation into marriageability, into the status of *parthenos*, or more precisely, into the life-stage that stands between babyhood and the menarche[73]—what we call the latency period. Healthy development at this stage is characterized by an inner freedom, a sense of the wild. The girls become a little wild because they are starting to find their powers. The *aitia* of the ritual are about difficult relations with fathers and brothers because it is a rite not of union with a husband but of separation from the family.

Athenian girls, in other words, for all their seclusion had an adoles-

[70] Sourvinou-Inwood (1988), pp. 131–134; cf. also Pearlman (1989).

[71] Didymos (apud Harpakration s.v. dekateuein) noted that Demosthenes used *dekateusai* for *arkteusai* because *dekateusai* "has become a general term for consecration, since it was the Greek custom to consecrate a tenth of crops to the gods." Demosthenes, in other words, interpreted the Arkteia as a first-fruits ceremony. Others thought *dekateusai* was employed because the girls were ten years old, but perhaps ten was the preferred age because it carried with it the idea of dedicating the tenth.

[72] So say the literary sources, and Sourvinou-Inwood (1988) in a careful analysis of the iconographic evidence finds this figure confirmed there.

[73] Sourvinou-Inwood (1988), p. 28.

cence. *Parthenos* is everywhere in Greece a liminal status, characteristically fascinating, precious, and vulnerable. *Parthenoi* are typically prizes, the focus of competition and courtship. As yet unallocated objects of desire, they belong to everyone and no one. Their role, further, is not to seek mates but to be sought; in the meantime they remain passively enticing and thus actively sustain the role. *Parthenoi* typically relate to each other competitively and cooperatively, racing and dancing. Their sexuality is also turned inward, as a more or less explicitly homosexual sentimentality. The rites of maidenhood do not accomplish any social work; they rather celebrate the glories of maidenhood— as in Alcman's *Maiden Song*, the girls sing each others' praises. In some places there were even contests of beauty.

The patroness of *parthenoi* is Artemis; she is eternally marriageable and always just out of reach. Once again, the gods are different from us; we are not gods, and they are everything we are not. What for us is a transient phase can remain for them an immutable essence. By their difference they remind us that we must accept our mortal destiny, wherein each phase implies an acceptance of the next—and the necessity to solve the problem of getting there. Artemis alone remains invulnerable, turning Actaeon from hunter into prey, hiding herself in the mire from Alpheius (Pausanias VI.22.9). The girls who are closest to her—Callisto, Cyrene, and so on—are all carried off. So also we find many stories of girls being raped or carried away from maiden dances— one actually local to Brauron, where the Pelasgians "ambushed Athenian women who were celebrating a rite to Artemis in Brauron" (Herodotus 6.138). These stories remind us that maidenhood, although a joyful time, is also a time of danger; the task of the maiden is to survive this phase intact, to "save herself," as we used to say, for marriage. Maidenhood is an extended phase of transition and, as such, shot with instabilities. From this point of view, we can see the crucial developmental phases of women as a large-scale enactment of our familiar initiatory scenario. First they are daughters; we have seen the Arkteia as a rite of separation that introduces them to the liminal status of *parthenoi*. The rite of reaggregation is then marriage, whereby women become wives. But since marriage itself is transitional the true reaggregation does not occur until successful childbirth—which brings them back to Brauron to dedicate fabrics to Artemis. Each of the boundary-rites recapitulates the scenario in little and has its own liminal phase. On the way to becoming *parthenoi*, Athenian women become bears;[74] on

---

[74] In Thessaly the girls were called "deer" and the prospective husband actually had to pay the goddess for his bride—Clement (1934). See Calame (1977), pp. 223–224 and 443.

the way to becoming wives (for which the Greek term—as a status, not a relationship—is simply *gunē*, the "unmarked" term for "woman") they become *numphai*, brides, in the wedding and as long as the wedding defines them—until pregnancy. Childbirth alone does not have to be ritualized, since nature has marked it so exquisitely, through the phases of pregnancy and into labor, which is itself liminal—culminating in the phase we call "transition."

Each of the boundary rites, further, could have its own rites of separation and reaggregation. In order to celebrate the Arkteia, Athenian girls entered and left a sanctuary. The rite of separation in the wedding is the *proteleia*, to which we shall come in the next section; the rite of reaggregation after marriage is the *epaulia* wherein the bride, on the morning after the wedding night, is sent her *phernē* or trousseau, the women's things that establish her in her new home. Finally the dedication to Artemis can be seen as a reaggregation after childbirth.

The developmental history of Greek women thus involved prolonged and internally differentiated liminality. No doubt this was true of men also, most obviously at Sparta, where the system was highly rationalized and the young men were taken through a long series of stages. At Athens male development was more informal, but we should remember that men did not reach full maturity until age thirty, when they became eligible for jury service and the council. Such postponement of maturity is both effect and cause of a specific representation of adulthood, a cultural understanding that the roles of man and woman are complex and challenging, and presuppose a careful education. It was primarily through the elaboration of the ritual sphere that the Greeks produced a population of a sophistication equal to the complex social life of the *polis*, and this was as true for the "passive citizenship" of women as for the active citizenship of men.[75]

---

[75] There is one additional point: Harpakration s.v. *arkteusai* adds a tantalizing item: "Lysias, in the speech for Phrynichus' daughter (if it is genuine): the consecration before marriage of maidens to Artemis Mounychia or Brauronia. Things contributing to the aforesaid are stated by (among others) Craterus in his *Decrees*. That the maidens who are being bears are called bears: Euripides' *Hypsipyle*, Aristophanes' *Lemniai* and *Lysistrata*." If this, in turn, is right, Craterus's compilation included a decree regulating the Arkteia. Unfortunately "Craterus" is an emendation; the manuscript says Cratinus, and it is possible that the reference is to an otherwise unknown comedy called *Psephismata*, "Decrees." (The elder Cratinus did write a play called *Nomoi*, "Laws.") I am inclined to think, however, that the emendation is supported by this statement in the sources: "The Athenians decreed (*epsephisanto*) that a maiden should not set up house with a husband if she had not been a bear for the goddess." The phrase *mē proteron sunoikizesthai andri* looks like something that could occur in a decree. (The Arkteia would not have been a precondition of the *enguēsis*—which, as we have seen, was legally the wedding—but of the actual marriage.)

Becoming a Bride

Greek marriage is a family affair, in both its juridical and ritual aspects; a marriage is a private contract, which is not licensed or recorded by the state, and it is a family festival, which needs no priest or special invocation of the gods beyond those usual at family meals. Only at one point did the wedding ceremony (optionally, and probably not everywhere) intersect with the civic religion of precinct and temple: Many Greek communities knew a rite called the *proteleia* whereby brides or couples as a preliminary to the *gamos* observed some ceremony in a sacred place. Often this involved the metonymic dedication of something close to the self, especially to the old childish self—a toy, for instance, or an ornament. Most often the dedication was a lock of hair, which is especially in the Greek tradition a familiar metonym of the self, of one's life; at this time of transition the self comes apart and part of oneself is left behind with the old life.

The divinities of the *proteleia* are always female; Pollux (3.38) says: Artemis, the Moirae, Hera Teleia. Elsewhere we also hear of Artemis (A.P. 6.276, 280), and of Hera (A.P. 6.133), also of Aphrodite (A.P. 6.207), of Athena (Statius *Theb.* 2 251–256), and of the nymphs (Plutarch *Narr. Amat.* 1, 772b). At Athens, to judge by the dedications, the *proteleia* sanctuary was the sanctuary of Nymphe, just outside the gates of the Acropolis.[76] At Sparta it was, most probably, the sanctuary of Alexandra at Amyklae.[77] The precinct of Hippolytus was also proper to the *proteleia* (Euripides *Hippolytus* 1425–1426); his gender is not really an exception to the rule, since this case involves an inversion: Hippolytus was the child of an Amazon, a woman who fought in a way appropriate to a man; he grew up as a man who refused sexuality in a way appropriate only to a young woman, and in fact he says he has a *parthenos psuchē*, a maiden spirit (ibid. 1006).[78] The other heroic sanctuaries known to have been places of the *proteleia* belong to (literal) *parthenoi*: Iphinoe at Megara (Pausanias 1.43.4), the Coronidae (see above, p. 92), and the Hyperborean Maidens at Delos (Herodotus 4.32–35). I now proceed to a discussion of this last as a further exploration of the ideology of marriage.

Herodotus says that no one seems to have any direct knowledge of

---

[76] See Wycherly (1978), pp. 197–200.

[77] See below, p. 294.

[78] As Zeitlin (1985), p. 110, notes, in this play "the *kouros* appropriates the role of *parthenos* . . . Hippolytus has, in fact, reversed the typical courting pattern, so that when he at last leaves the stage, the chorus of maidens lament that they will no longer be able to compete for his hand in marriage (1140–1141)."

the Hyperboreans, but that they are mentioned by the poets. The Delians, he says, have a lot to say about them; *Apollo and Artemis, they told
him, came from Hyperborea to Delos, bringing with them the Hyperborean
maidens, Arge and Opus, who are buried to the east of the sanctuary of Artemis.
The women of Delos gather to honor these with a hymn written by Olen, the
legendary hymn writer of Delos.*

*Later there came another pair of Hyperborean Maidens, Hyperoche and
Laodike, bringing offerings, and tribute to Eileithyia, goddess of childbirth, as
prescribed to achieve a quick delivery. There came with these five men as their
escorts, the so-called Perpherees; these have great honor among the Delians. These
maidens also died. The Hyperboreans took it amiss that they should be put in the
position of sending maidens and not getting them back; from that time, therefore, they carried the offerings only as far as their own border, where they turned
them over to their neighbors, whence, passed along from place to place, they
eventually arrive at Delos wrapped in wheat-straw.* At least that is the story
Herodotus was told, and offerings wrapped in wheat-straw, he says, certainly do arrive at Delos from somewhere. As for the maidens, they
were buried inside the sanctuary of Artemis, and the young couples
come to their tomb before marriage to dedicate locks of hair—the
woman's wrapped around a spindle, the man's around something green.[79]

Hyperborea is a legendary place; it is the back of beyond, literally
"back of the North Wind"; it is what the French call an *au delà*, another
world.[80] "Not by ship nor by going on foot," says Pindar, "could you find
the wonderful road to the Hyperboreans' gathering" (*Ol.* 10. 29–30).
You can't get there from here.

On the other hand, as is the way of other worlds, we do somehow
maintain contact. Pindar is about to tell us that Perseus went there.
Heracles brought the wild olive to Olympia from there (Pi. *Ol.* 3.13–
34). Apollo of Delphi goes back there for three months every winter.
Aristeas the wonder worker, who spent part of his life as a crow, wrote
about the place, although even he didn't claim to have been there
(Herodotus 6.16). The offerings wrapped in wheat-straw may or may
not come from there. The maidens certainly did come from there;

---

[79] Herodotus (IV.34) actually says that the girls dedicate their hair before marriage,
and *hosoi de paides*, also dedicate their hair. He could mean that the boys make their
dedication on some other occasion than marriage—for instance, at majority, and that
would in fact be the most natural meaning of the Greek. So perhaps the dedication at
marriage was made by the bride alone, not the couple. I have taken the dedication to be
by the couple because the *aition* seems to me so clearly to have to do with marriage, and
to be inappropriate to males coming to majority.

[80] Nagy (1990), p. 277n.15: "On the land of the Hyperboreans as a multiform analogous to Elysium, the Islands of the Blessed, the White Island, and so forth, cf. Hesiod F
150.21 MW, *Epigoni* F 3 Kinkel, scholia to Pindar *Pythian* 3.28, and so on."

their Hyperborean origin is the *aition* of the *proteleia* at Delos. This fact tells us that the rite is somehow about another world—which is, further, a land of the blessed; as Pindar describes Hyperborea:

> The Muse is not absent
> From their ways of life; everywhere dances of maidens,
> The cries of the lyre, the sounds of the flute are in motion;
> With golden laurel binding their hair they feast in gladness.
> Neither disease nor hateful age are mingled
> With that holy race; without toil or war
> They live escaping
> Avenging Nemesis.
>
> Pindar Pyth. 10.37–44

The Hyperboreans live at ease in nature and with each other, without age or sickness or struggle or conflict; their lives are given over to music, dance, feasting, and ornament. Their life, as Claude Calame points out,[81] is like that of the Golden Age and also like that of the gods, in that they wait for no special festival occasion, but sing and dance more or less continuously. As Pindar says: "the Muse is not absent," *Moisa d'ouk apodamei*, which might be translated "their Muse is never out of town." This means that maidens are particularly at home in Hyperborea, in the Golden Age world, since maidens are typically sheltered, know nothing of war, political conflict, or toil, and are (or always should be) young, beautiful, healthy, and adorned. Thus those who dance among the gods—the Graces and Hours along with Artemis on Olympus (*Homeric Hymn to Apollo* 186–206) and the Nereids under the sea (Bacchylides 17. 100–111)—are typically divine maidens.

Calame further suggests that every dance among mortals recreates the golden age—or, as we might say, is a bit of Hyperborea. By the same token every maiden is somewhat Hyperborean, and it is not surprising that those who come from Hyperborea are typically maidens, or that these were celebrated at Delos with hymns and rites—most probably, since Herodotus mentions a gathering of women, including dance.

On the other hand we should not forget that, according to Hesiod's story, it was the first and most perfect maiden, Pandora, who brought an end to the Golden Age and introduced age, disease, conflict, and toil. She was a beautiful snare, and Epimetheus was helpless, "but once he took her, when he had the evil fast, he knew it" (*Works and Days* 89). He thus anticipated the experience of the whole race; as Zeus says, she is the sort of evil "in which they would all take pleasure, welcoming in their spirits their proper evil" (ibid. 57–58). In all this, as I have argued

---

[81] Calame (1977), pp. 173–174.

above (see p. 24), Hesiod seems to be sketching a theme more than familiar from later European fiction: the woman's power to entrap the man into marriage. Courtship, which is a magic time, turns into the burdens and restrictions of married life. The *parthenos* is thus a contradictory figure; she embodies both the Golden Age and the Fall, the carefree life to which we aspire and the fact that, in seeking it, we incur instead toil and obligations. Nowhere do men feel this paradox more routinely than in their love of beautiful women. The Hyperborean maidens avoid this temptation to contradiction by being incomplete, by being unavailable. Therefore they can freely be adored, and are a source of power.

It is the incompleteness of the other world (like the incompleteness of the hero's life) that makes it a source of power. Other worlds define this world by selection and inversion. They have to be like the world we know or we would be at a loss to describe them. They are the opposite of our world, however, in that they transform a part into a whole. Our world, in the Greek proverb (Plato *Gorgias* 447), is characterized by the alternation of the battle and the feast; the other world can be all feasting or all battle, heaven or hell. The point of the other world is then to remind us that our lives cannot be like this. Once again, the gods are everything that we are not.

Thus the gods remind us of the limitations of our condition by their perfect enjoyment of what we know only as mixed blessings. They have not only life but immortality, not only health but agelessness. The immortal *parthenoi* include both Hestia and Artemis. These two seem to separate and embody diverse and even contradictory aspirations of the mortal *parthenos*. Hestia embodies the longing of the daughter to stay in her father's house, not to be "sold abroad, away from her paternal gods and those who bore her" (Sophocles Fr. 583.7–8). Artemis, by contrast, wild in the wilderness, embodies the aspiration to remain in a liminal position, neither daughter nor wife. In myth this condition can be immortalized; in ritual, as we saw, it can only be a transitional inversion. Real girls consort with Artemis only in order to return to the city as brides.

Ritual, in other words, can code a transition by reference to a series of eternalities; the gods provide a set of roles and masks that can be assumed and shed in sequence, or a set of patrons and companions whose spheres we may traverse. They stay where they are, but we change by moving from one to another. The gods thus provide a conceptual structure, a myth that can make the terms of a transition intelligible, and the ritualization of the transition is a mediation of structure and event.

A hero-cult like that of the Hyperborean maidens is more complicated because heroes both die and live forever. Their cult is centered on a tomb, to which a story, the *aition* of the cult, is attached. What became locally immortal, therefore, was the story, and the ritual derived its meaning from the meaning of the story. The Hyperborean maidens came to Delos as *parthenoi*, unmarried, but seeking the favor of Eileithuia, goddess of childbirth; in other words, their quest was the *proteleia* of their own marriage seen in its full implication. On Delos they died. This reminds us that the gap between Hyperborea and this world is wide, too wide to be crossed in both directions except by an actual god. The Hyperboreans came to realize this, and instead they send the wheat-straw offerings, which make a connection with Hyperborea and at the same time are tokens to us of our separation from it.[82]

This transaction is only in one direction; we cannot send anything to Hyperborea. On the other hand, the grave of the maidens is in a way a piece of Hyperborea; the young people of Delos can therefore make the journey in a modified form that enables them to return from Hyperborea to us.

The maidens are marked twice as eternally maiden—because they are Hyperborean and because they died before marriage. Because they are permanently liminal, incomplete, they possess a power of transformation. The ritual appropriates their power as a blessing.

The *proteleia* is a rite of separation from a status that is itself liminal, the status of *parthenos*. By the sacrifice of the hair the young people express their solidarity with these eternal *parthenoi*, die a little with these dead. It is a ritual of perpetual mourning. This relation with the hero is stated explicitly in the *Hippolytus*:

> The unyoked girls before their marriage
> Will shear their hair for you, and through long ages
> Yours will be the greatest harvest of mourning tears.
>
> Euripides *Hippolytus* 1425–1427

As in all mourning, the dead person is clung to and at the same time let go.[83]

The tokens, the spindle and the "something green" (a fresh-cut plant), seem to be proleptic and to represent the other side of the rite. Something green is surely an emblem of fertility, and thus represents sexual production (which requires the male, and is therefore part of his dedication), whereas the spindle represents that asexual mode of produc-

---

[82] In other words, the offerings mark an ambiguous relation with the other world, parallel to that marked by meat sacrifice after Prometheus's division of the sacrifice at Mecone; we join with the gods in commemorating our separation from them. See above, p. 21.

[83] On epic story as a perpetual mourning, see Nagy (1979).

tion that women can do on their own. Both dedications (like everything connected with the *gamos*) celebrate the bride. Taken together they represent the powers of her new status. By dedicating these votives to the Hyperborean maidens the new couples of Delos appropriate their heroic powers to these new powers.

The gods are brought to our assistance before marriage because marriage is dangerous. On our behalf against danger we call upon certain allies. The Hyperborean maidens, exiles from that golden land where there is no trouble or danger, were links to the sheltered and sheltering gods at home there, and brought a little of its safety to this troubled world of ours.

The Hyperborean maidens went (with male escorts) a great distance and died. Death and marriage are of course familiar metaphors for each other, and a long journey may be a metaphor for either.[84] The same triad is in play with the Locrian maidens; they are quasi brides who (with male escorts) go on a long journey and are threatened with death. Insofar as they replace one another and thus are always present in the temple they even achieve a kind of immortality—and agelessness, since by being annually replaced they are never any older. On closer examination, however, they turn out to be not parallel with the Hyperborean maidens, but their inversion—because moving in the opposite direction. Marriage is not only a departure but an arrival. The Hyperborean maidens come to what is to them another world and fail to marry. The Locrian maidens (from the point of view of the Locrians, whose ritual this is) travel into the world of the others only to return—not to burial and immortality, but to marriage and a secular mundane existence. Therefore their journey is parallel not to that of the Hyperborean maidens, but to that of the Delian young people who visit that sanctuary. Nevertheless it can still be true that the Locrian maidens embody the power of transformation—not, however, as a myth, but as a ritual. Theirs is a representative heroic *proteleia*.

Lévi-Strauss says somewhere that in myth untenable positions are taken in order to show that they are untenable. (This is one way of saying that the beginning of wisdom is to know that we are not gods.) He might have added that in ritual extreme positions are often taken to show that they are (if only barely) tenable. It is thereby demonstrated, a fortiori, that less extreme positions are completely tenable. If the monk can manage asceticism and celibacy, we can surely be content with monogamy and moderation. In these terms we can under-

---

[84] On this triad in modern Greece, see Danforth (1982), pp. 74–79. He reports that some of the same songs—involving journeys—are actually sung at some weddings and funerals, although in a different tone of voice!

stand the representative status of the Locrian maidens. The rite is like an initiation, but only this select pair are initiated. They are, as it were, cultural virtuosi; they enact in an extreme form the risky journey that is marriage. Their task, on behalf of the whole cohort of marriageable girls, is to confront these risks at their limit. By returning, the maidens annually reassure the Locrians that marriage, while involving all the risks of transfer and transformation, is completely possible. They may be taken to exemplify the passive strength of women.

Greek marriage was (with some exceptions) patrilocal; the wife came to her husband's house and joined her father-in-law's family. It is in this way that she takes a long journey, not usually in geographical but in social space. Marriage is also patrilineal; inheritance is through males and by males. The woman's role is to produce sons who will inherit her husband's name and property and through descent from him will inherit the status of citizen (as only males can). She keeps the house, but she keeps it for her sons, whose responsibility she will in old age become. Her daughters will pass away from her into other families.

From this point of view, then, women are commodities distributed through marriage-exchange, and also means of (sexual) production. The higher the standing of the household, the more important it becomes that the woman be acculturated to this role and undemanding, sexually or otherwise, on her own behalf. Every wife, however, is a potential Clytemnestra or Pandora, threatening to adulterate the stock or waste the resources of the house. Therefore women have to be kept under control. Women, in other words, are repressed in the interest of the private-property household. This is the *bourgeois* repression of women.

On the other hand it is also true that women, and high-status women especially, are expected to resist this repression. This resistance reflects a tension inherent in bourgeois marriage-exchange, which (as we have seen) is latently bilateral because the woman is a person with status of her own. The most desirable bride is precisely one with powerful kindred, men who care about her and will therefore assist her (and her husband's) offspring. Such a bride is probably her father's darling, and brings with her a large dowry, which (as we have seen) helps to secure her status and is a threat to her husband's. Such women may not be free agents but neither are they slaves; they have certain rights and dignities—and male kindred to enforce them. The position of the free woman is fundamentally contradictory.

A myth can describe the world; the point of a ritual, however, is also to do something about it. The Locrian maidens, by serving the god, came under her protection, and thus invoked the protection of the god for all brides. Furthermore by enacting in metaphor the contradictions of Greek marriage, they proved that those contradictions could be endured and overcome. They appear in the ritual as creatures both precious and dangerous, treasured and sent away, respected and exploited; these paradoxes can be contained by the ritual because they are placed in the paradoxical frame of sacred service, which both degrades and exhalts. Like the Spartan boys under the lash, the Locrian maidens proved themselves by their ability to endure the trials prescribed by the god—and by implication proved the power of their sex as a whole to endure as persons the rigors of marriage. Whereas the Hyperborean maidens die in a heroic myth, the Locrian maidens survive a heroic ritual.

This leads us toward another heroic ritual, which is also an exemplary initiation.

The Arrephoroi

In the midst of his description of the Athenian Acropolis, Pausanias makes a brief digression to allude to a story and to describe a ritual:

> Continuous with the temple of Athena is the temple of Pandrosus. She alone among her sisters was guiltless in the keeping of the deposit. What caused me the most to wonder—it is not generally known, but I describe what happens—there are two maidens who live not far from the Polias temple; the Athenians call them *arrephoroi*. These for a certain time live their lives with the goddess; when the festival comes around they do the following in the night: Bearing on their heads what the priestess of Athena gives them to carry (neither does she who gives it know what she gives, nor do they who bear it know)—there is an enclosure in the citadel not far from the so-called Aphrodite in the Gardens and through it a natural underground passage— through this the maidens go. Down there they leave their burden, and taking another they bring it wrapped up. And these they release from that time, and they bring other maidens to the Acropolis instead of them. (Pausanias I.27.2–3)

This ritual, which so impressed Pausanias and which seems to have shaken him into some very odd syntax, has been the object of prolonged modern controversy; everything about it is controversial, even its name.[85] Pausanias calls it an obscure ritual, and we have no other

---

[85] The ancient sources call the maidens *arrephoroi*, *errephoroi*, and *ersephoroi*, and derive their name from "secrets" (*arreta*) and from "dew" (*erse*)—*phoroi* transparently means "bearers." Robertson (1983) persuasively derives the name from the name of a particular type of basket, proper to this ritual; nevertheless the ancient derivations as folk ety-

description of it than his, but it was obviously important; we have already met it (see p. 53) as the first of the marks of ritual distinction cited in the *Lysistrata*, and it recurs in fourth-century literature (Menander wrote a play called *Arrephorus*) and in epigraphic evidence from the third century B.C. down to the time of Pausanias.[86] Like the ritual of the Locrian maidens, it really happened, and endured.

Limiting ourselves to Pausanias's evidence we can observe a number of striking parallels to the Locrian maidens. Here also there are two maidens secluded in the sanctuary of Athena; like the Locrian maidens, they serve for a year and then are replaced by another pair. These are not, however, nubile young women but rather little girls—from seven to eleven (*Et. Mag.* s.v. *arrephorein*). Nor is the service of these Athenian maidens far away; it is rather placed at the ritual center of the community. Like the Locrian maidens, however, they go on a journey by night, a journey that must have seemed long to little girls, and in company with a dangerous secret. In other words, they share with the Locrian maidens initiatory themes of seclusion, distance, and danger.[87] The key to the ritual, as we shall see, is the age of the girls and the location on the Acropolis. Therefore the points of difference with the Locrian maidens turn out in the end to be crucial. Nevertheless one ritual may help us understand the other.

Just before describing the Arrephoria, Pausanias alludes to a story he told some pages earlier (1.18.2)—a story that serves as a kind of *aition* of the ritual, although no ancient writer tells it in that connection: Erichthonius and the daughters of Cecrops.[88]

Hephaistus, we are told, *approached Athena sexually; she successfully resisted him but his seed fell on her thigh. She wiped it off with a bit of wool and threw it on the earth, which then gave birth to Erichthonius* (the name is interpreted as Son-of-wool-and-earth). *Athena placed Erichthonius in a basket and gave him to the daughters of Cecrops, telling them not to look inside. Two of them, Aglaurus and one of her sisters* (usually Herse) *disobeyed, and*

---

mologies are clues to the meaning of the ritual: a closed basket is indeed the symbol of a secret. Therefore I translated the line from the *Lysistrata*, "I was just turned seven when I carried the secrets." This particular secret, further, has much to do with dew—see Boedeker (1984).

[86] Citations in Robertson (1983), p. 242.

[87] The lexica (e.g. Harpokration s.v. *arrephorein*) tell us that the Arrephoroi (like the Locrian maidens) were chosen from the best families, and also that "If they wore gold, it became sacred"—that is, their jewelry was dedicated to the goddess at the end of their service. Here we have another parallel with the Locrian maidens: The Arrephoroi were adorned and despoiled of their adornment.

[88] Sources collected in Powell (1906), notes 1–27. Alan Shapiro (1995) shows from visual evidence that most of the story was already current in the fifth century, although he finds no representation of the suicide of the guilty sisters.

saw something monstrous involving snakes.[89] *They thereupon went mad and hurled themselves off the Acropolis to their deaths.* Aglaurus had a cult place on the Acropolis, as did the third daughter, Pandrosus.

This story is not a true *aition* since it contains no account of the instituting of the ritual; there is therefore no oracle in the story. Myth and ritual are here not linked as cause and effect, but rather by certain common themes: location in the Acropolis, the relation between Athena and a certain pair of girls who are called to serve her, a dangerous secret in a basket. It seems that these connections are too close to be casual, that (once again) the ritual makes right everything that went wrong in the myth. The little girls are entrusted with a basket which they do not open; therefore they do not fall from the Acropolis but go down safely by the steps, and return. This myth is related to the ritual, therefore, in the manner characteristic of an *aition*: In the ritual danger is normalized; every year the goddess makes her dangerous demand and every year she is safely served.

On the other hand the ritual does this piece of social work only by breaking with the myth in a crucial respect: whereas the daughters of Cecrops were mature *parthenoi*—in Euripides's *Ion* (495–502) they are spoken of as dancing on the Acropolis to the music of Pan—the Arrephoroi are little girls. If the upper age was indeed eleven it seems that they were supposed to be prepubescent, as we learn from the *Lysistrata* that their service preceded the Arkteia. They are called *parthenoi*, which breaks the rule that this term is used only for nubile girls, but it seems that the exception fits the rule in that while not *parthenoi* they were playing the role of *parthenoi* (the daughters of Cecrops)—but safely, because still under adult supervision and control. All this suggests that we should seek in this ritual, located in the sacred center of the city, a specific representation of the relation between sexuality and politics.

The ritual has the general shape of an initiation (the girls are secluded, survive an ordeal, and return enhanced) and Walter Burkert notes that in some sources we are told that, as well as accomplishing the ritual, they assisted in the weaving of the *peplos* for Athena—they were, in other words, introduced to the characteristic productive activity of the mature woman.[90] But it is hard to think of this as a exemplary initiation to womanhood, like that of the Locrian maidens; the girls are *too young.* I would suggest that this is precisely the point: The girls weave, as they imitate the daughters of Cecrops, playing at a maturity

---

[89] In some tellings, Athena is informed of their disobedience by a crow. Can there be some link with the Coronidae?

[90] Burkert (1966).

that is obviously still beyond them, and at which they can therefore safely play.

The story of the daughters of Cecrops is one of a group of stories about the "original" condition of Athens, stories that (considering they were all told in one community) seem to have been peculiarly unstable, involving a shifting and overlapping set of characters. Erichthonius and Erechtheus, for instance, are spoken of as father and son but as Nicole Loraux notes, Erichthonius hardly appears in legend (in the fifth century) except as an infant, while Erechtheus has no childhood and appears as a mature king.[91] No wonder that the two were sometimes taken as alternative names for the same person (cf. *Et. Mag.* s.v. Erechtheus). Erechtheus, in a story told in a bewildering variety of versions (and discussed earlier in our discussion of virgin sacrifice—p. 94) sacrificed one or more of his daughters in order to save the state from invasion. Aglaurus, who appears in the Arrephoria story as a victim of her own imprudence, appears as a virgin self-sacrifice in the story told earlier (p. 94), which made her patron of the Athenian ephebes; she is supposed to have thrown herself off the walls, thus volunteering for the very destruction that in the other story is visited on her and her sister by the anger of the god. In her self-sacrificial role her name is sometimes Agraulus.[92] She, like the other daughters of Cecrops, is a typical *parthenos*, but she is also wife of Ares (Suidas s.v. *Areios pagos*) while the Kerykes at Eleusis claimed to be descended from Aglaurus and Hermes (Pausanias 1.38.3). Others, however, said their ancestor was born of Hermes and Pandrosus (Schol. *Il.* 1.334; Pollux 8.103), and Herse was also said to have born a child to Hermes (Apollodorus 3.14.3) These variations indicate that this group of figures, rather than being stable personalities in a quasi-historical legendary past, functioned as personifications of underlying cultural structures, and as such were available to be shaped and reshaped—even renamed—in the shifting contexts of Athenian self-representation.

The underlying theme that unites these figures has to do with the relation between the people and the land. The birth of Erichthonius (to which we shall return) is the primary myth of Athenian autoch-

---

[91] Loraux (1981), pp. 46–47.

[92] Aglaurus apparently means "bright water," a name that matches those of her sisters; Pandrosus means "all-dewy" and Herse simply "dew." Agraulus means "sleeping in the open" and is thus appropriate to the ephebes who guarded the border districts in their military service—the association here could still be "dew," since those who sleep in the open are particularly threatened by the evening's dews and damps—a point made explicitly in Aeschylus *Agamemnon* 559–562 (I owe this reference to Leslie Kurke). Cf. Boedeker (1984), pp. 105, 107.

thony. The people of Athens, like the Arcadians,[93] claimed to be born of the soil that they still inhabited; whereas the legendary history of most Greek peoples told of conquest and displacement, these two peoples claimed to represent continuity and direct transmission from the origins. Otherwise the two are contrasted; the Arcadians never securely adopted the *polis* in its full political development and remained always somehow primitive,[94] whereas Athens claimed to be the *polis* par excellence; as Thucydides's Pericles says: "The same people ever inhabiting this territory by continuous transmission through the generations handed it down to the present time free through its excellence" (Thucydides 2.36.1).

This claim of kinship between people and land is made in Athenian myth several different ways, and thus redundantly and insistently. Cecrops, for example, is also autochthonus; he is represented as half-man, half-snake, and thus is halfway in the ground. Apollodorus (3.14.5–6) mentions two other autochthonous kings. And Erechtheus is also autochthonous:

> Him once Athena nurtured,
> The daughter of Zeus, and the grain-giving soil bore him,
> And she settled him in Athens, in her wealthy temple
> And there they propitiate him with bulls and rams,
> The young men of Athens as the years circle round.

Iliad 2.547–551

In the *Odyssey* (7.81) Athena lives in Erechtheus's house. He is her hero, and through him she, though Olympian, is located in Athens.

Pandrosus and Aglaurus also have their precincts on the acropolis. Their names, like that of their sister Herse, are associated with dew, which is the source of the fertility of the soil.[95] In the precinct of Pandrosus was the sacred olive tree (Apollodorus 3.14.1), which was the living symbol of Athenian agriculture and also of the life of the society in the nurturing presence of Athena (cf. Herodotus 8.55). The ephebic oath, which was taken in the precinct of Aglaurus, was an oath to defend the territory of the *polis*, and to protect the crops and fruit trees.[96]

Aglaurus is a character in a familiar folktale scenario: Two siblings fail the test; only the third succeeds. The test has to do with curiosity and with the fascination of the forbidden; it has in it the quality of the *dangerous game*, of the perils of teasing and testing. As such it is a symbol appropriate to adolescent initiations, since, as the psychologists tell

---

[93] Borgeaud (1979).
[94] Ibid.
[95] Boedeker (1984).
[96] See Merkelbach (1972).

us, teasing and testing is the age-appropriate and developmentally necessary, but disruptive, behavior characteristic of adolescents. Taking this
more general framework we can see that the opening of the basket has
a reflex in the Arkteia *aition*: There the girl teases the bear and (as in
the case of the daughters of Cecrops) what is intended as casual behavior, fun, turns into disaster.

In the *aition* of the Arkteia the girl is injured by a bear, but in the
ritual the girls become bears. They thus represent the girl as a latently
savage creature. This bear had been domesticated but became savage;
this represents well the adolescent who goes through a phase of savagery in the process of turning from a child, a kind of pet, into a mature
adult who must be treated as an equal. This phase of savagery has to do
with the onset of puberty. We may think of Aeschylus's fable, applied by
him to the unfaithful Helen: A lion cub raised in the house grew up to
savage her master (*Agamemnon* 716–737; in this play Artemis is specifically patron of young lions [140–141]—rather than bears). Helen is of
course the typical case of woman's sexuality as something dangerous.
Perhaps the most dangerous game, the pervasively latent savagery, is
sexuality itself.

The Arrephoroi correct the action of the daughters of Cecrops. They
also repeat the action of the Erichthonius story. They carry something
from Athena down toward the earth as Athena threw the wool upon
the earth, and they bring something back in a basket; these may be
taken to represent the seed and the infant. It is probably pointless to
speculate as to the contents of the basket, since the point of the ritual
is that the contents were secret; Pausanias says that not even the
priestess knew what they were. Whatever they were they seem to represent the nocturnal secrecy of sexuality and generation. The little girls
perform a sexual act, but as little girls they can perform it asexually and
safely. In this way they represent the ambiguity of the myth, which tells
us that the origin of the Athenian people is both sexual and asexual.

A myth of autochthony is a kind of inversion of hero-cult. The hero
appropriates the land by dying to it, and his (or her—we have already
met a number of female heroes) tomb becomes a monument to the
story. Thus the land acquires a personality, and the tomb of the hero is
a place where the people can carry on personal relations with their
land through gift and prayer to the patron of its security and fertility.

In the case of autochthony, by contrast, the land produces persons.
The myth legitimates appropriation by representing it as an inversion
of itself. In actuality, people occupy territory; they secure it by military
organization, and by the application of technique they cultivate it and
turn it to the purposes of culture. By the myth of autochthony, however, the people, and (more important) their cultural organization

(since the autochthon is a founder-king), are represented as natural products of the soil. Thus a historically contingent fact—the location of a culture—is represented as natural kinship; an event is transformed into a structure. The myth thus asserts an inalienable relation between the people and their land. Instead of the people owning the land, the land owns the people.

To be born of the land is proper to vegetables. Whereas the first-fruits sacrifice appropriates vegetables and other natural products by shifting them into the sphere of humanly usable things, the myth of autochthony asserts a kinship between the people and the crops, and thus shifts persons into the category of vegetables. This is really a sub-case of a broader rule: monstrous sexuality and generation through unnatural categories are a source of power. Even more generally, persons display their power over nature, their freedom from the constraints imposed by the lawfulness of nature, by their capacity to collapse and reshape the categories of nature.

The prototypical case of the consolidation of power through unnatural generation is (as we have seen) the birth of Athena. Zeus thus acquired a daughter who (paradoxically) is an eternal *parthenos* because completely unmarriageable—asexually produced and without sexuality. In Athena the contrast in paternal relations between Hestia and Artemis, between the loyal daughter who conceals herself by the hearth and the savage *parthenos* who ranges the wilds, is deleted: Athena, who is completely her father's creature, puts her aggression at his service, not as a solitary huntress but as a loyal warrior.

Zeus is the patron of the juridical order; Athena, as Walter Burkert says, is "everywhere the pre-eminent citadel and city goddess; often this is expressed by her epithets, *Polias, Poliouchos* . . . She manifests herself in the evocative image of the armed maiden, valiant and untouchable; to conquer a city is to loosen her veils."[97] Athena embodies the chastity of the city; she combines female prohibition with a male capacity to protect herself. Her asexual origin makes her completely a creature of culture; she was born from Zeus by a technical act. Sometimes Prometheus brings her to birth, sometimes Hephaistus—indeed in one version of the Erichthonius story Hephaistus approached her sexually because he had been promised her maidenhead as a reward for using his tools to separate her from her father (*Et. Mag.* s.v. *Erechtheus*, Schol. Plato *Timaeus* 426). Hephaistus, we remember, was also produced asexually—in a story that would exclude him from the birth of Athena, since he was supposed to be Hera's revenge for that event. In either case Hephaistus is clearly marked as a secondary figure, and Athena

[97] Burkert (1985), p. 140.

was destined to win their encounter; as the embodiment of the Juridical Order Militant she is Victory personified.

The Athenian claim to be the *polis* par excellence is founded on a claim to a special relation with Athena, a relation closer than that of any city with a god; as Solon says:

> Our city's share from Zeus will never be quite lost,
> Nor her link with the minds of the blessed gods, the immortals;
> So great is the mighty-spirited guard and daughter of
> Thunder, Pallas Athena, who holds her hands above.

Solon 3.1–4[98]

In the myth of Erichthonius, where the seed intended for Athena falls to the earth, which then produces a child for Athena to rear, this special relation is combined with autochthony in such a way that the Athenians could be descended from the earth and also could be "children of Athena."[99] The sexual conflict between those two monsters Athena and Hephaistus produces a monstrous birth that is a hideous secret and at the same time a "first king" who gives the Athenians title to their soil.

Arcadian autochthony, by contrast, is a vague generalized thing; "the black earth produced" Pelasgus, the first king (Asios apud Pausanias 8.1.4); there is no story about it. Similarly in the case of Eumelus, the "original" king of Patras, we are simply told that he was autochthonous (Pausanias 8.18.2). At Athens the story is elaborate and in it Athena is at once mother (she receives the seed), father (she casts the seed), and nurse (she receives the infant from the earth). While retaining her chastity she repeats the two-in-one parenthood whereby Zeus was her own mother and father both; as she belongs completely to the father, so Athens belongs completely to her.[100]

The Arrephoria, as the most recent commentators have clearly seen,[101] was the ritual of Athena's link with her people, which also embodied the link of the people with the land. In the myth everything went wrong; the father Hephaistus was no proper father—since his attempted rape was improper and in any case a failure; the mother earth was no proper mother, since Athena did not intend to implant the seed, but rather cast it from her in a gesture of disgust. The daughters of Cecrops similarly failed in the role of nurse, and so died. In gathering all these roles to

---

[98] On this passage see Herington (1963).

[99] Peradotto (1977) treats Erichthonios as a "mediator" between asexual and sexual production.

[100] This discussion owes much to the extensive analysis of these themes in Loraux (1981).

[101] Boedeker (1984), Zeitlin (1982), p. 104.

herself—so that the Athenians are triply "children of Athena"—the goddess also institutes a ritual whereby children become the vehicles of her link with the land. Thus the disasters of the myth instruct us in the meaning of the ritual. Athena's juridical authority commands a link between fathering Acropolis and mothering territory; the little girls act as the responsible nurses of this link, and the link nurtures the Athenians.

The little girls thus embody in ritual, as Athena embodies in myth, the fertile and nurturing chastity of the city. Their service is a sacrifice in that it requires the suppression of an impulse—in this case, the impulse of curiosity, which plays such a large role in the sexuality of children. They have learned their lesson from the daughters of Cecrops; they will not inquire too closely into the origins of Athens, into that primal scene that generated the Athenian state.

Political power everywhere traffics with mystery and has its secret agents; to the monopoly of violence corresponds the monopoly of certain kinds of information. In a premodern society this tends to mean mystery in the technical sense, the keeping of ritual secrets. In the Arrephoria the secret involves a monster: the snaky Erichthonius, born of the soil and of the spoilt sexuality of the gods. To the degree that all the Athenians are descended from him they are all monsters too; in keeping the basket closed they keep this secret from themselves. Perhaps the secret they are really keeping is the secret of power: that all juridical power is monstrous and founded on interference with the order of nature. Therefore the state, which is a supernatural being, the institutionalization of the moral order, must be maintained by sacrifice, whereby we overcome the nature in ourselves. From this it would follow that, at least from the Greek point of view, the most political sacrifice is the sacrifice of women; women, who both are and are not citizens, represent categorically the entanglement of culture with nature, and therefore represent the problem that the polity must solve by generating a supernatural power.

We have seen this problem already represented in the ambiguity of the Locrian maidens, who are both precious and impure, treasured and outcast. We may see it represented again in the two stories—both told within the same community as aspects of two simultaneously valid rituals—of the death of Aglaurus. In one story she is the voluntary sacrifice who hurls herself to her death in order to secure Athens against invasion, who survives in hero-cult, and to whom the ephebes dedicate their defense of Athenian boundaries and fertile territory. From this point of view her death is the self-sacrifice of first-fruits; she represents all those goods, dewy-fresh and burgeoning, that war intends to fence and protect. In the Arrephoria story, however, she fails to keep her distance from the monstrous birth at the core of this order, goes mad, and dies involuntarily. Rather than securing the structure she represents the weak point that must be continually repaired by ritual. The woman who must be repressed is really the nature that, while offering us nurture, also entangles us in mutability.

Culture maintains itself by securing nature to its uses, so that the land brings forth crops and the women bring forth sons like their fathers. By the same token, however, this same nature, which is never quite subject to cultural control, is within culture the systemic vulnerability of culture. Everything that is formed of matter has an inherent tendency to form-lessness—including society. This point may be coded in terms of plague and famine, in terms of the health of the people and the land. It may also be coded in terms of the social fate of women. Women are in a way the *point* of society; they are the custodians of home and family, of the hearth, of the gods, of everything worth dying for. At the same time women's sexuality may be identified (as by Hesiod) as culture's weak place. From this point of view the juridical suppression of women is that fundamental denial (and distortion) of nature which makes possible the moral order.

Greek men make the juridical order for themselves, and defend it with their lives; they also make it for some others, for their women, and these they must both defend and control. Men without women have not yet become cultural—or more exactly, their cultural life is unproblem-atic, like that of the Golden Age, and therefore only partial, not yet real. It follows that in this superbly androcentric society men only truly achieved culture by their relations with women. Therefore women were the preferred stakes—as sacrifice, votives, and bearers of initiatory power—in the primary rituals of acculturation. Women were impor-tant—which does not mean they were in charge. On the contrary: The celebration of women's roles in civic festivals was also an appropriation of women by men in defense of a masculine order. Women were the carriers of an order to which they did and did not belong.

From this point of view the ritual of the Locrian maidens can be seen as a transaction by which the Locrian males transmit certain messages to themselves: that their women are theirs to dispose of, and in that sense weak, and yet strong enough to endure an ordeal, and precious enough to be pleasing to the god. The Locrians are Leleges, born of the stones that Deucalion and Pyrrha threw over their shoulders; so they, too, are autochthonous. But their ritual does not seem to be a ritual of auto-chthony; it does not celebrate nature as a collective source. Rather it recognizes and respects nature as a collective problem, with which, how-ever, the Locrian collectivity has managed (after crime and punishment) to establish an adequate relation. At the same time, as we shall now see, the Locrians established a relation to history.

Locris and Ilion

First-fruits sacrifices are recurrent compensatory sacrifices because
fruits recur. The annual or occasional surplus is sent to the other world
in order to enable us to keep in this world a sufficiency of its goods.
The Locrians (at least in the "original" version) sacrifice surplus brides.
This sacrifice, further, as payment for the crime of Ajax is explicitly
compensatory. However the sacrifice is not to the dead (e.g., it is not to
Ajax[102] or Cassandra) or to the gods of the dead but to a particular
immortal, to Athena, the lady of the citadel, and it takes the form (in
the actual version) not of death but of service. Also, the Locrian maidens
were not sent away into another world; they were sent to a particular
place, which called itself Ilion. The ritual thus enacts a bond between
two communities, one of which is in a sense mythical. As a deposit that
creates and memorializes a bond, the maidens may be considered a
kind of votive.

The people who lived at Ilion in historical times were Greeks—indeed they may even have been Locrians, since the Aeolian colonists
here were supposed to have tarried in Locris (Strabo 13.1.3). They
were, however, playing the role of Trojans and claimed direct descent
from the Dardanids; they could show the temple of Athena mentioned
in *Iliad* 6, (Strabo 13.1.41). They could point out to the visitor the
tombs of Protesilaus, Paris, Memnon, Hector, Ajax, Achilles, Patroclus,
and Antilochus, and maintained a hero-cult of the last four (Strabo 13.
1.29–32). When in 480 Xerxes called to make his sacrifice, the magi
also poured libations to the heroes, and panic overtook the army (Herodotus 7.43). The Troad was in historic times a magic place, haunted
by heroic ghosts; the Greeks who lived there were custodians of a kind
of vast theme park or outdoor museum to the heroic past, to those
stories which, the poet tells us, will be told forever, since they have a
kleos aphthiton, an imperishable fame.

The journey of the maidens from Locris to Ilion was therefore a
journey not only in space but in time, a journey into the heroic past
that is placed somehow outside of time, *in illo tempore*, and is at the
same time the space of origins, of the ancestors.[103] By sending the
maidens the Locrians continued the heroic action of Ajax into historic
time; by the link between crime and recompense they established a

---

[102] Ajax might easily, despite for all his wrongdoing, have become entitled to sacrifice—
as in the case, to be explored later, of the hero of Temesa.

[103] Both Alexander and Caesar patronized the temple of Athena in Ilion; both, of
course, claimed to be descended from the defenders of heroic Troy: Caesar from
Aeneas, Alexander (on his mother's side) from Andromache.

relation between the mythical past and the continuing present. Annually maidens were sacrificed and rescued from sacrifice. Thus we can understand why the Locrian maidens did not themselves become an object of hero-cult. They are not heroes; they are for heroes. Hero-cult—in fact the prototypical hero-cult—already existed, at Troy; here many heroes were honored and heroes in general were evoked. The ritual of the maidens evidently enabled the Locrians to maintain their contact with them.

The heroic world was present to the fifth-century Locrians as to the Greeks in general in two forms: as heroic story and as an inheritance—in Locris particularly the inheritance of the Aianteioi, whose claim to special status in the society was founded on their claim to be descended from Ajax. Originally, Polybius (XII. 5) tells us, the maidens were drawn from the Hundred Houses, whose special distinction was therefore marked by this obligation. The Mädcheninschrift assigns the burden more specifically to the Aianteioi; it further provides that they are entitled to the special protection of the community, and also that they have in effect met their social obligations; they are not to be asked to pay taxes, or to raise horses for the cavalry, or to give their children as hostages. The sending of the maidens, in other words, is their whole social task. By either set of arrangements the burden is a mark of status. By going to Ilion the Locrians, that is, both recovered contact with the roots of their own social order, and reaffirmed it.

If every ritual is a symbol of a community, the community symbolized by the ritual of the Locrian Maidens is Locris. Ilion plays a passive role (with its people's complicity, no doubt); it is put to use. Indeed, since the Maidens were annually brought in against a show of force, Troy was annually re-conquered by the Locrians, who thus in penance for the historic crime of their leader annually re-enacted his violation of the temple. This paradox will concern us further at another time. Here I conclude the section with some account of the community of Locris.

Locris was unique among Greek communities in that it consisted of two discontinuous districts, divided by the territory of Phocis. The Locrians explained the division (plausibly enough) by asserting that at some time the Phocaeans had invaded their territory and appropriated all the best land, pushing them back into the mountains on both sides of the plain. Eastern, known as Opuntian or Epiknemidian Locris,[104] was a coastal strip about fifty miles long on the south side of the gulf of Euboea. The leading town was Opus, "metropolis of the right-lawed

[104] Strictly speaking, Opuntian and Epiknemidian Locris were two distinct—and even, at times, discontinuous (Fossey [1990], p. 7)—territories; the two names, however, are often conflated as if they were interchangeable; cf., e.g., Strabo 9.416.

Locrians" as the Thermopylae epigram recorded (Strabo 9.4.2); similarly Pindar tells us that Opus is kept safe by Themis and her daughter Eunomia (*Ol.* 9 14–16). Opus controlled the best harbor and most of the agricultural land. Opus was the birthplace of Patroclus (*Il.* 23.85) and even after Patroclus had gone into exile continued to be home of his father Menoitius (*Il.* 18.326—although at 11.770 Menoitius seems to be resident at Phthia). Opus was not, however, the ritual center; this was Naryx (cf. Virgil *Aeneid* 3.399), in the mountainous country on the other side of Mt. Knemis. Here was the home of Locrian Ajax (Diodorus 14.82.8) and (as we have seen) the Aianteioi.

Eastern Locris as a whole had in the fifth century B.C. some kind of federal organization, under an annual magistrate called the *archos* and a legislative body called the Thousand, meeting at Opus.[105] Since one thousand is given as the number of Locrians at Thermopylae (Diodorus 11.4.7), where they turned out in full force (Herodotus 7.203), this probably represents a hoplite franchise.[106]

Western, or Ozolian, Locris was a somewhat larger area, similarly mountainous, on the north coast of the Corinthian gulf. The leading town was Amphissa, which had special links with Aetolia[107] and in later years was not always classed as Locrian. Here there was a bronze image of Athena which Thoas had brought from Troy (Pausanias 10.38.5). Thucydides (3.101.1, 2; 102.1) mentions twelve other towns, each of which evidently had its own foreign policy—at least each made a separate decision on how to deal with the Spartan commander who was moving troops through their area. The ritual center of Ozolian Locris was at Physkeis, which (like Naryx) was deep in the mountains. Here there was an Achilleion[108] and also a temple of Athena Ilias.[109] Here, at least from the fourth century B.C., met the federal organization of the Ozolian Locrians.[110] It is not known if before this time these Locrians had a formal organization—indeed the evidence of Thucydides would seem to indicate that they did not—yet at times they seemed to be able to operate as a unit.[111] The two branches of the Locrians, further, seem to have been in easy contact with each other, and certainly cooperated

[105] Larsen (1968), pp. 52–55.

[106] Actually, Herodotus does not specify that the Locrians at Thermopylae were hoplites, but he includes them in a list of contingents, most of which he specifically calls hoplites.

[107] Lerat (1952a), p. 15.

[108] Evidently a sanctuary dedicated to Achilles—it is known only from an enigmatic inscription published by Klaffenbach (1935), p. 608.

[109] Lerat (1952a), pp. 156–158.

[110] Ibid., pp. 55–60.

[111] Larsen (1968), pp. 55–56.

in connection with the colony at Naupactus, on the extreme western border of Ozolian Locris.[112]

The (Opuntian) Locrians in Homer are light armed bowmen (*Il.* 13.714–718): Ajax, their leader, is a heroic spearman, but he does not fight with them any more, having joined his namesake, the Greater Ajax (*Il.* 13.701–705). Their role is to stand at a distance and harass the enemy with missiles. In historical times these tactics were characteristic of the Ozolian Locrians, who were of special importance to Athenian operations in that area during the Peloponnesian War precisely because they were light armed troops, equipped like the Aetolians against whom the Athenians were fighting (Thucydides 3.95.1, 3; 97.2). Their relatively informal gear and tactics were suited to the rough backcountry.

Thucydides mentions the Ozolian Locrians in a much-quoted passage on *lēisteia*.[113]

> The Greeks of the old time and the barbarians on the coastal mainland and the islands, when once they began to go about in ships back and forth, turned rather toward *lēisteia* . . . falling upon the cities that were without walls and spread out in villages they sacked them; they were not ashamed of this kind of thing, but it rather conferred credit. This is clear from some of the people of the mainland even now, who glory in this kind of action. Even up to the present day a large part of Greece is inhabited in the old style, the part around Ozolian Locris and Aetolia and Acarnania and the mainland in that direction. The bearing of arms continues among these mainland peoples because of the ancient *lēisteia*. (Thucydides 1.5)

Thucydides thinks of this as a backward part of the world where the social transformations associated with peaceful commerce and hoplite warfare have not yet occurred.

The Opuntian Locrians were able to send hoplites to Thermopylae, but their contribution to the forces at Artemisium was not triremes but the relatively primitive penteconters (Herodotus 8.1) and they contributed to the Peloponnesian War primarily as cavalry (Thucydides 2.9.2, 4.96.8). The Athenians, further, had to garrison an offshore island by Opus to prevent Opuntian *lēisteia* of Euboea (Thucydides 2.32). The Opuntians, in other words, seem not to be much in advance of their western cousins. In the fifth century both groups took part in the battle of Nemea: light armed Ozolians and Opuntian cavalry (Xenophon *Hellenica* 4.2.17).

Cavalry suggests an aristocratic society, like that of Thessaly; Polybius

---

[112] Ibid., p. 57.; cf. Tod # 24.
[113] On *lēisteia* see p. 177.

mentions the Hundred Houses as existing at a very early period, and it
may be more than a coincidence that the Athenians took one hundred
hostages "from the richest" in the mid-fifth century (Thucydides
1.108.3). Beyond this general impression there is not much to say; the
Locrians hardly have a history—indeed it is hardly an exaggeration to
say that they make as individuals no appearance in the historical record.[114] As a people the Locrians are thoroughly "back"—backcountry,
backward, and in the background.

The Locrians, says Lerat, were "always mere playthings of neighboring forces."[115] They submitted to Xerxes when he demanded earth and
water, and were therefore on the list of those who had submitted "not
under compulsion" (Herodotus 7.132). Nevertheless, when sent an ur-
gent message to reconsider they did send troops to the battle of Thermopylae, which was fought on their doorstep (Herodotus 7.203). After
the Persians turned the pass the Locrians submitted, joined the invasion of Attica (Herodotus 7.66), and fought for Mardonius at Plateia
(Herodotus 9.31). In the Peloponnesian War the Opuntians and the
Ozolians found themselves, at least for a time, on opposite sides—not,
evidently, as a result of any ideological differences, but owing to local
circumstances. The Locrians do not make much mark on history as
communities any more than as individuals; there is something insubstantial about them. The Spartans when asking for ships treat them
simply as an appendage of the Phocians (Thucydides 8.3.2).

The Locrians, like the Arcadians, were an "original" people—in fact
they descended from the stones sown by Deucalion and Pyrrha when
they came down from Parnassus as the sole survivors of the great flood.
(Pindar *Ol.* 9 42–55). Like the Arcadians they were an *ethnos*, which in
this context means a group of loosely connected towns that could be
called *poleis*, but which were not fully independent. Apparently no part
of Locris had been through the process of *sunoikismos*, the unification
of a territory around one juridical and ritual center, which made Eleusis and Marathon, for example, completely Athenian. Locrian political institutions were not therefore without complexity—indeed, as
Larsen points out,[116] they were in a way more complex than those of

[114] Alexandros Isios is a notable character in Polybius "with a reputation for competence and a good speaker" (17.3.1), and "the richest man in Greece" (21.26.9). Eusebius
(1.207) mentions a Locrian Olympic victor; Plutarch mentions a Locrian poet (*Greek
Questions* 15) and a Locrian doctor (*Anthony* 28.2); Pausanias (7.18.10) mentions sculp-
tors from Naupactos. This is about what I have been able to glean in the way of literary
references from Lerat's prosopography of Ozolian Locrians; I do not suppose that a
similar list of Opuntian Locrians would give a very different impression.

[115] Lerat (1952a), p. 39.

[116] Larsen (1968), p. 58.

classic city-state, since the Locrians were organized both on the level of the local community and on the level of the association of communities. Nevertheless it is also true that they were in a way primitive—in the respect that the Locrians had not gone as far as other Greek communities in securing to the state a monopoly of force. This point shows up not only in *lēisteia* but also in *sulē*, the Greek word for the seizure of goods under color of some legal right to them.[117] This is not theft but a form of legal self-help, not unknown even in sophisticated cities like Athens, but evidently much more characteristic of Locris. The Mädcheninschrift, for instance, grants immunity to *sulē*, and one of our earliest Locrian documents, the fifth-century treaty between Oeanthea and Chaleion (Tod #34), is extensively concerned with its regulation. Precisely because of their tentative organization the Locrians had to excel in negotiation among themselves; to them we owe some of our earliest political documents. Perhaps that is why Opus, their political center, could be called "well-lawed." Because they have a tendency to lawless behavior they have to be inventive of laws. We shall return to this paradox.[118]

In any case the heroic was at Locris a present actuality; in the classical period they were still in some respects a heroic society. The Locrians who appear in Homer are the Opuntians, but as we have seen the Ozolians are also provided with heroic tradition, whether through Thoas (in Homer the leader of the Aetolians—*Il.* 2.638–643) or more directly. We must be particularly interested in the temple of Athena Ilias at Physkeis, since it is hard to think that its cult was not connected with the sending of the maidens to Athena at Ilion. In fact the Mädcheninschrift may well have been set up there. In any event this text was found not in Opuntian but in Ozolian Locris; the agreement there recorded was made between Naryx, the town and people of Ajax (in Opuntian Locris), and the Locrians as a whole, both Opuntian and Ozolian. The ritual of the maidens, it seems, worked to unify the Locrians.

Perhaps it is significant that what these "well-lawed" Locrians had in common, what made them, in a sense, one community, was a crime; their hero is characterized by his bad behavior. Nor is this limited to Ajax; Patroclus, whom we know from the *Iliad* as mild and good, was, we remember, forced into exile from Opus when he killed another child in a quarrel (*Il.* 23.85–88); the Locrians actually maintained a hero-cult of Patroclus's victim (Strabo 9.4.2). Locrian Ajax's half-brother (his replacement as commander of the Locrians) similarly was

---

[117] See Bravo (1980).
[118] See p. 259.

in exile because of a homicide (*Il.* 13.695–697). These stories seem proper to a community where violence was endemic. The *aition* of the ritual of the Locrian maidens tells us that this ritual also is somehow about violence—specifically, sexual violence— and the risks of war.

The ritual theme of marriage also seems relevant to Locris, because where the state is weak the household must be relatively strong, capable of self-help, perhaps, and of that form of negative reciprocity with other households known as the vendetta, but also capable of those lasting bonds with other households produced by marriage-exchange. It seems to me likely that the unity of the whole of Locris was sufficient to permit general *epigamia*, so that any Locrian could marry any Locrian without penalty. If so the Locrian community was to an important extent unified by the exchange of brides—particularly at the top, for if there were only one hundred distinguished houses a young aristocrat would have needed pretty much the whole cohort of girls available in order to have anything like a choice. In sacralizing the cohort of brides the Locrians were then enlisting the support of the gods for a critical supporting system of their community. Also in making recompense for the heroic violence of Ajax, they were coming to terms with their endemic violence. The ritual thus seems twice embedded in the community, as cure for its ills and a celebration of its functioning. What begins with sex ends with politics.

From Ritual to Myth

While disentangling this ritual I have given it various generic labels, most frequently "exemplary initiation." As the ritual work of the children in the Arrhephoria said something about what the children of Athena meant to the Athenians, so the ritual at Ilion said something about what their maidens meant to the Locrians. Another way I have put this is to say that the maidens sacralized the whole cohort of brides. This reading led me to call the ritual a "first-fruits sacrifice"—and indeed, as we saw at Brauron, sacrifice and initiation overlap, as they overlapped in the reality of ancient marriage. This sacralization, however, is not the only function of the ritual; like most recurrent rituals it confronts a normal danger and defends against a communal anxiety. Since it defends by exclusion it has (as we saw) something in common with the rite of the *pharmakos*. The maidens are precious and dangerous—like Pandora. Violence is offered to these women and they respond with patient virginal service; theirs seems to be an amplification of the ambiguous status of the bride, and of women in general. A woman is an anxious object.

I am going to suggest, however, that the Trojan setting of the ritual tells us that wider issues are in play, that for the Locrians sexuality is only one aspect of that pervasive normal danger that nature is to culture, and that their fragile society could, in their eyes, be best defended by a recurrent assertion of the people's link with their (legendary) history.

This brings us back to the *aition* of this ritual: the story of the crime of Ajax. This is a story with three leading actors: warrior, maiden, and goddess. I conclude this chapter with some discussion of this narrative. We shall find in it independently expressed themes already explicit in the ritual: sexuality, the risks of war, and our ambigious relations with the gods. These themes will lead us into the uses of mythical history.

The Lady of the Citadel

Usually the *aition* of an epichoric ritual is an epichoric story; the crime of Ajax is Panhellenic. In fact it was one of the more frequently represented incidents of the fall of Troy[119]—on the Olympia bronzes, for instance, as early as the first quarter of the sixth century.[120] It was represented on the chest of Cypselus at Olympia (Pausanias 5.19.5) with the inscription "Ajax the Locrian drags Cassandra from Athena," and also painted by Paianaios among his decorations for the throne of Olympian Zeus (Pausanias 5.11.5). Polygnotus's paintings of the Lesche at Delphi included "Ajax holding a spear; he stands before the altar taking the oath concerning his crime against Cassandra" (Pausanias 10.26.3). (Cassandra also appeared in this painting—Lucian *Imagines* 7.) The incident chosen to represent the fall of Troy on the Stoa Poikile at Athens was the council of the kings concerning the crime of Ajax (Pausanias 1.15.2). Very probably this crime also appeared among the north metopes of the Parthenon, along with the recovery of Helen.[121] These two scenes, in fact, can be imagined as a kind of diptych; the theft of Helen began the Trojan War, so that her recovery closed a chapter; the crime of Ajax opened the next chapter, since it began the misfortunes of the Greeks, which formed the sequel, the Nostoi. Cassandra is thus like Helen a source of misfortune and a figure of power; both were objects of cult at Sparta (Pausanias 3.19.9, cf. Herodotus 6.61.3; Pausanias 3.19.6). Cassandra was worshipped there under the name of Alexandra, under which name she also had a cult at Leuctra (Pausanias 3.26.5).

[119] For a review of this material see Davreux (1942).
[120] Kunze (1950), pp. 160–161.
[121] Brommer (1967), p. 215.

The crime of Ajax was told in Arctinus's *Iliou Persis*. There is no trace of it in the *Iliad*. Cassandra appears in that poem only twice. In book 13 (361–382) she appears in one of those anecdotes introduced to add interest to the death of an otherwise unknown hero, in this case Othryoneus, of whom we are told that he had come to Troy asking Priam for the fairest of his daughters, Cassandra, without bridegift, undertaking to drive the Greeks from Troy.[122] Priam had promised her, but Idomeneus kills him and drags off his body with a mocking speech that asks if he would now like instead to discuss the marriage of the fairest of *Agamemnon's* daughters.[123]

In book 24 (697–706) Cassandra briefly appears on the scene; she is the first to come to meet Priam when he returns with Hector's body. Taking these two appearances together we can see in her a sketch of the typical *parthenos*: desirable, perhaps unobtainable, quite possibly dangerous. She is a great prize but her suitors die in their courtship,[124] and she remains within the family, loyal daughter and sister.

Her attacker, the Lesser or Oilean Ajax, appears in the Catalog of Ships (*Iliad* 2.527–530); he is small but excels all others with the spear. He does not fight with his troops, because they are light armed and harass the Trojans from a distance (*Iliad* 13.712–722). He rather fights next to his namesake, the Greater Ajax—and is rather in his shadow. The two make a contrasted pair. The Greater Ajax is large, slow, particularly effective at holding off attack; the Lesser is swift—*tachus Aias* is his formulaic name—and particularly good at running down and killing those who are trying to run away (*Iliad* 14.520–522). He kills Cleobulus when he is helpless in the dust and offering no resistance (*Iliad* 16.330–332) and he cuts off Imbrius's head and rolls it like a ball to Hector's feet (*Iliad* 13.202–205). In a poem where the mutilation of the dead is much more talked about than actual, this is the only place where anyone goes so far as to play with a piece of a corpse.[125]

In the funeral games of Patroclus, Oilean Ajax competes with Odysseus in the footrace. Ajax should surely defeat short-legged (*Iliad* 3.210–211) Odysseus, but Odysseus prays to Athena, who makes Ajax slip on a bit of dung. Ajax takes his second prize, protesting against

---

[122] Laodike is also "fairest" (*Il.* 3.124), but she is already married. A very similar story was told of Coroibos and Cassandra in the cyclic literature—cf. Pausanias 10.27.1.

[123] The fairest of Agamemnon's daughters was Iphigeneia—at least in the version that told of Agamemnon's ill-considered vow, she was the fairest thing born to him that year. This links Iphigeneia with Cassandra, the daughter as sacrifice with the daughter as prize.

[124] Moreau (1989).

[125] Agamemnon also makes a head roll (*Il.* 11.147) but it is less clear that this is done intentionally.

Athena's bias and spitting manure, and all the Achaeans laugh (*Iliad* 23.740–783). Earlier in the games, Ajax and Idomeneus quarrel about who is leading in the horse race, and Idomeneus denounces Ajax:

> Ajax, best at quarreling, evil-witted, in all other ways
> You fall short of the Achaeans, because your mind is savage.

> *Iliad* 23.483–484

Ajax is characteristically a hero of excess, cruel, quarrelsome, and somewhat out of control.

There is no sign that the author of the *Iliad* knew the story of the crime of Ajax (of course he knows many stories he does not use). Nevertheless we can say that the story is in a way latent in his poem, in the sense that Ajax and Cassandra are already characterized in a way proper to that story. They are the Marauding Male and the Perilous Female; put them together in the context of the fall of Troy and something of the sort "must" happen. We are reminded that these stories have a sort of life of their own: As the tradition elaborates plots it brings to the surface contrasts that are already there on the level of character—in this case, between the desirable, unobtainable *parthenos* and the hero without respect for limits.

The author of the *Odyssey* evidently did know the story of the crime of Ajax—at least to my mind there is a transparent allusion to it in book 4, when Proteus says that Ajax would have escaped death "in spite of the anger of Athena" (*Odyssey* 4.502)—if he had not boasted in a characteristically outrageous way that he had escaped against the will of the gods. It is of course possible to believe that the anger referred to here is Athena's general anger against all the Achaeans, but it seems beyond a coincidence that the phrase should be used particularly of Ajax.[126] Cassandra is mentioned in the *Odyssey* only in Agamemnon's account of his own death: Clytemnestra killed her, sprawled across the dying Agamemnon (*Odyssey* 11.421–423). Cassandra had presumably been allocated to Agamemnon because she was, as fairest of Priam's daughters, the pick of the spoil (like Chryseis after the sack of Thebe— *Iliad* 1.366–369) and fit prize for a king. Neither maiden, of course, brought Agamemnon any joy. The first brought down on him the

---

[126] Strabo—following Demetrios of Skepsis—denies that the crime of Ajax was known to the author of the *Odyssey*, but he is clearly arguing a case, not making a sober judgment. Actually, the fact that the story is not told in the *Odyssey* is an interesting aspect of the narrative strategy of that poem. The poet never tells us why Odysseus has such trouble even before he offended Poseidon by blinding the Cyclops, and when Odysseus in effect asks her for an explanation (*Odyssey* 13.318–323) Athena fails to provide it. Odysseus never finds out that Athena was angry at all the Greeks and contrived for them an evil return; it is somehow more effective to leave the whole matter obscure.

wrath of Apollo, the second the wrath of Clytemnestra. Both stories contain the theme of the maiden as dangerous prize; the story of the crime of Ajax "classically" develops this theme.

The theme of the dangerous prize clearly relates to the theme of the dangerous game; both, further, have an erotic color and relate to the theme of the poisoned gift, which is also likely to be erotic. One thinks of the poisoned robe Deianeira sent Heracles, thinking it a love-charm, or that other poisoned robe that Medea sent Creusa as a wedding present. The gifts of love turn poisoned when love goes wrong, and love itself becomes a poison when it cannot be fulfilled, as, for example, in the case of Phaedra.

By the fifth century, Cassandra as an unobtainable beauty has developed to the point that she has an unfortunate love affair of her own.[127] Apollo, we are told, sought her favors and gave her the gift of prophecy; when she after all refused him, he was unable to recall his gift, and so gave her a second: that her prophecies would never be believed. Her gift thus became, or was perceived to be, a form of madness; it was a poisoned gift.

Cassandra's error was in rejecting a god; as Paris says:

> They are not to be rejected, the glorious gifts of the gods
> Whatever they themselves give, and one does not choose them freely.
>
> *Iliad* 3.65–66

Paris is speaking here of his attractiveness to women, which brought to him Helen and all the destruction that came with her. Helen surely is (along with Pandora) the "classic" poisoned gift. Application of the same principle would have required Cassandra to accept the love of Apollo—and bear his child, since "the loves of the gods are not without issue." It is not that the woman of epic is required to accept any suitor that comes along. On the contrary, a woman of status should be properly married to a man who has gained her father's consent, and before marriage she is not to be "easy." "I would feel *nemesis*, moral outrage, about any girl who would behave that way," says Nausicaa (*Odyssey* 7.286–288). But a god is not in the same category because the love of a god does not make a girl unmarriageable. She rather comes under the god's protection, bears his child, and thus becomes more marriageable than before. To refuse the god is therefore to refuse marriage in general, like an Amazon; the love of the god is an ideal love, and a rejection of the god is a rejection of the idea of love, of marriage, and of fertility.

---

[127] The earliest source for this story, which Aeschylus may have invented, is *Agamemnon* 1202–1214—although in the *Cypria* she was already a prophetess.

Cassandra is thus one of those women who reject marriage, like Atalanta. They are, however, contrasting examples of the type: Atalanta resisted violently; she killed her suitors and escaped into the wild. Therefore eventually she is forced to marry (her story develops in a variety of directions, but this element in it is as old as Theognis—1294). Atalanta was a huntress like Artemis. Cassandra was shrinking, like Hestia; she was too feminine. She is allowed to keep her maidenhood,[128] but in her refusal to consent becomes a danger to self and others. Hers is a passive aggression; she becomes a passive Amazon, like the Danaids.

If Cassandra is a kind of Amazon, Ajax is a kind of centaur. Here again it is a matter of going too far. Men are (for the Greeks) properly aggressive, in their sexuality and in everything else; the quintessential masculine role is that of warrior, whereas the coward who shrinks back is womanish, becomes a woman. The warrior's aggression, furthermore, is on behalf of women. Like children, women cannot be violent themselves and therefore must rely on the violence of their men to protect them from the violence of others. By the same logic, women are properly among the spoils of war; if their men cannot protect them, they belong to the men who can seize them. Therefore Ajax was doing nothing wrong in attempting to seize Cassandra. He was not even (in most versions) collecting her for himself, but as an addition to the pool of spoils. His crime was not against her but against Athena; when he pulled at Cassandra, Cassandra clung to the statue so that it fell over. Actually Cassandra pulled the statue over, but the crime is attributed to Ajax because as a suppliant Cassandra was entitled to hold on to the statue. It follows that Ajax's crime was the direct result of Cassandra's absolute refusal to be appropriated.

Cassandra went too far and offended a god; a woman who will refuse a god will refuse anyone. Similarly a man who will put his hands on a goddess—or even her statue—will spare no one. Ajax went too far and offended a goddess. The crimes of Ajax and Cassandra are symmetrical

---

[128] Here again what counts is social status, not physical condition. In some versions of the crime of Ajax he actually took her physical virginity in the temple; in the Greek tradition this is a relatively superficial variation, since his real crime is against the god. Polygnotos's painting at Delphi showed Ajax taking an oath—perhaps that he had not physically abused her (Pausanias X.26.3). Such an oath would have been reassuring to Agamemnon, whose prize she became (cf. Agamemnon's oath to Achilles that he has not touched Briseis—*Il.* 9.133), but would not have cleared Ajax's accounts with Athena. In one version Cassandra went on to have twin sons by Agamemnon—infants slaughtered with her (Pausanias II.16.6). But she remains a *parthenos*, since she is never married. Lycophron, for whom the main point about Cassandra is her refusal of marriage, reports that in Daunia her sanctuary was a refuge for maidens who wished to refuse a bridegroom (1128–1140).

and constitute a system. From this point of view, we can see the whole story (as developed) as a representation of marriage gone wrong.

Marriage, from the Greek point of view, is surely an institution in which we acculturate the sexuality of men by making it political, in the service of the patriline; we accomplish this transformation by sacrificing virgins to it. For this sacrifice to be effective, however, it must be voluntary; the *parthenos* gives herself over to the institution of marriage and in recompense acquires the brilliant, almost heroic, role of bride. As a self-sacrifice, like Antikleia and Alkis, she dedicates herself to Eukleia, to good fame, and thereby sustains the state.

This in turn helps us to understand Locrian story as an *aition*. Once again, all that has gone wrong in the myth is put right in the ritual. The Locrian males play the part of Ajax against the resistance of the Trojans; annually they reconquer Troy. They play this part, however, in reverse; instead of taking a maiden away, they bring maidens to the goddess. This is a first-fruits sacrifice that compensates for the crime of Ajax; in the process it demonstrates the male power to dispose of women—a power that is (in the epic understanding) the inner meaning of war and that is here exercised through a fiction of war—employed not impiously but piously.

At the same time the Locrian maidens reenact the crime of Cassandra; they take refuge from marriage with the virgin goddess. But in the process they also correct Cassandra's error. Just as the Arrephoroi correct the error of the daughters of Cecrops (they do not open the basket) and the girls who play the daughters of Embarus correct the passion of Iphigeneia (they are not sacrificed), so the Locrian maidens take refuge only (in the actual version) to come out at the end of their year of service, and marry. They demonstrate that the modesty proper to a girl, hesitation at the brink of sexuality, can be proper to a life-stage, initiatory rather than pathological. The maidens enact a kind of ritual stylization and vast amplification of the demure sexuality of the bride. As so often, initiatory material forms a part of a ritual with wider meanings; in the ritual the maidens display their capacity to overcome the limitations asserted by the myth, to do something the heroic archetype could not do: make the transition from maiden to wife. In so doing, they become figures of power.

This ritual is one of a number in various places that involve characters known from epic; these were always available for hero-cult, certainly at Ilion, but also elsewhere, most notably at Sparta, where the people, lacking anything much in the way of visible Mycenean remains, built in the eighth century a kind of artificial Mycenean ruin at Therapnae to be the tomb and cult place of Menelaus and Helen, and at Amyclae also appropriated, in defiance of epic tradition, Agamemnon and Cassandra. They even had a shrine of Odysseus (Plutarch, *Greek Questions* 48). These epic heroes, whose stories are told forever, wherever Greek is understood, are a kind of paradigmatic set of figures of power usable in a generalized Greek ritual syntax. The peculiarity of the Locrian rite is its adversary relation with these heroes, signaled by the fact (a unique feature) that the rite actually takes place in Troy.

The native, who explains the system in terms of the system, explains this point by the fact that the crime of Ajax occurred at Troy. We, who stand outside the system, are entitled to ask why the Locrians should have included Troy in their ritual world, as part of a cult of Athena Ilias. We may begin to seek the answer in the ritual meaning of the Athena of Troy.

We begin with the *Iliad*. In book 6 the women make a sacrifice to Athena; this sacrifice has been within the poem extensively anticipated. Helenus, Hector's brother and the Trojan seer, suggests it (*Iliad* 6.73–101); first he tells Aeneas and Hector to restore order to the Trojan ranks, then he gives Hector particular instructions: He should tell their mother to gather the women in Athena's temple on the citadel, and they should place on Athena's knees the finest robe in their store, and make a vow to sacrifice twelve oxen if she will pity the women and children of Troy and will hold back Diomedes. Hector repeats this message to Hecuba, largely verbatim (*Iliad* 6.268–278); Hecuba sends her servants to gather the women and goes to her storeroom, where she draws from the back her largest and finest embroidered robe, Sidonian work brought by Paris on the same voyage on which he brought Helen, "and it shone like a star" (*Iliad* 6.295). Theano, the priestess of Athena, unlocks the temple, the women give the ritual cry raising their hands to the goddess, Theano places the robe on the knees of the goddess and prays for mercy—"and Lady Athena refused" (*Iliad* 6.311). That is the end of it; all this preparation comes to a half line of summary dismissal. Nor could we have expected anything else; we know that Athena does not favor the Trojans—indeed she and Hera, as the losers in the judgment of Paris, are the two most implacable enemies of Troy. The incident is part of the gathering fatality of book 6, which ends with anticipation of the death of Hector, his women mourning him while he still lives (*Iliad* 6.500).

Yet in a way the scene is a false trail, for Troy will not fall to Diomedes, whose greatest acts in the *Iliad* are already over by the time this scene occurs. Diomedes is driven back by the thunderbolt of Zeus in book 8 (133–134), and in book 11 Diomedes is wounded and retires from the field (399–400). None of this, of course, has anything much to do with Athena, but the fact that the prayer is unnecessary as well as unsuccessful adds irony to irony.

No other scene in the *Iliad* is set in the temple of a god, although we hear in passing of Apollo's temple at Troy (*Iliad* 7.83). Apollo is Troy's faithful defender, and he comes directly into the action; Troy's people do not have to deal with him through the indirect means of ritual. Athena's temple is important in the poem precisely because the relation of the Trojans with her is ambiguous, because the goddess who protects Troy is Troy's great enemy, patron of Odysseus, the inventor of the Trojan Horse, because in her temple the Trojans are trying to speak to a god who is actually elsewhere, on the other side.

The *Iliad* seems to have established Athena's temple as the main temple of Troy; the only temple we hear of in New Ilion is the temple of Athena (Herodotus 8.43, Strabo 13.26). Because Homer wrote about this temple, this is the temple visitors would ask to see. The statue shown there represented Athena standing (Strabo 13.41) and therefore could not have been identified with the statue in book 6; this latter must be seated, since the robe is placed on its knees.[129] The statue pulled over by Cassandra, however, must have been standing, and the statue at New Ilion was presumably shown as that statue. The cult there which the Locrian maidens served therefore inherited all the ambiguities that cluster around Athena in the *aition*. She helps bring about the fall of Troy and is offended by its sack; she is the god Ajax offends and the god with whom he takes refuge. By accepting Ajax as her suppliant, Athena in effect become a shield against her own anger and presents the Greeks with an insoluble problem: They could not punish Ajax and thus palliate Athena without at the same time committing sacrilege against her.

The statue pulled over by Cassandra was almost certainly meant to be the most famous standing statue of Athena, the Palladion. This statue had been made by Hephaistus and had fallen from heaven to become part of the sacra of the Dardanids. The safety of the city was invested in it; Dardanus had an oracle that the city would be safe as long as it held the sacra (Dionysius of Halicarnassus 1.68.2–69). Therefore the story was told, as early as the *Little Iliad* of Lesches, that Odysseus and Diomedes stole the Palladion from Troy and so made possible the city's fall (Allen, p. 107). On the other hand, it was also known as early as Homer that Aeneas at the end had rescued the Palladion from its secret hiding place and had taken it away with him. In order to reconcile these two stories, Arctinus told how the Trojans had been careful to make a copy and leave it out to be stolen (Dionysius of Halicarnassus

---

[129] Although some tried to solve this problem by emending or reinterpreting the text of Homer—Strabo 13.41.

1.69). Arctinus also, as we remember, told the story of the crime of Ajax; presumably he thought of the statue pulled over by Cassandra as yet another statue, a tradition (I am supposing) ignored at New Ilion in the fifth century. These contradictions are generated by the fact that the tradition uses one statue—one symbol—for a variety of functions, which are hard to reconcile within the frame of one naturalistic story. The Palladion is the secret strength of Troy, an imperishable element that therefore survives the fall of the city; smuggled out by Aeneas, it provides the seed of the successor kingdom. Or it is the secret weakness of Troy, the magical weak link that is mastered by the cunning intelligence of the fated conquerors. Or it is the virgin goddess with whom the virgin Cassandra takes refuge. In all three cases it is a symbol of protection that is ineffective. Whether the statue is stolen or preserved, Troy falls; in spite of the statue, Cassandra is dragged away.

The Palladion at the end of the Trojan story remains in Troy and also leaves in two directions, in the custody of the Trojan survivors and of the Greeks. In both directions it has further adventures and further multiplies itself. The Palladion was shown at Argos, where Diomedes had taken it after the sack (Pausanias 2.23.5). It was also shown at Sparta, with a story that explained how it had been stolen from Argos (Plutarch *Greek Questions* 48). And it was also shown in Athens, where it was explained that the statue had never reached Argos; various stories were told as to how it had come to Athens instead (*RE* s.v. Palladion I.5 Athen).

The statue rescued from Troy was supposed to have come to Siris, where another story was told of its failure to protect suppliants (Strabo 6.1.14). Strabo tells us that this statue was also supposed to be in Luceria and also in Lavinium. The most famous Palladion of all, of course, was that which was supposed to be in custody of the Vestals in Rome—although it was kept in such secrecy that there was a question as to whether it was actually there (Dionysius of Halicarnassus 2.66, Plutarch *Camillus* 20). Nevertheless its ghostly presence embodied the claim of Rome to be the heir of the Dardanids.

The Palladion is thus curiously insubstantial: It stands for protection and does not protect; it is a precious thing to be kept close and yet it wanders; everyone who has it has the only true copy, and must therefore recognize that all the others are false. The statue does not so much ensure the integrity of the citadel as embody the problematic of that integrity. The temple at Siris was called the temple of Athena Ilias. Whatever the true origin of this epiklesis, it was surely taken in historical times to mean that the cult there honored the Athena brought from Ilion. In Ozolian Locris, at Physkeis, there was (as we have seen) a temple of Athena Ilias; it has been thought that this also must have contained a Palladion[130] In consideration of the ritual of the Locrian maidens it seems to me more probable that this temple did *not* contain an image, or if it did, contained the only Palladion that declared itself to be a copy. The Locrian cult was a cult of an Athena still in Ilion. It remains to investigate the meaning of this link.

The spoils of Troy should be taken from Troy and established elsewhere; that is what one does with spoils. One example is in the *aition* of the cult of Dionysus Aisymnetes at Patras:[131] A statue of Dionysus concealed in a box, like the Palladion part of the sacra of the Dardanids and cursed by Cassandra, drove Eurypylus mad until he brought it to Patras, where the dangerous sacred object on its arrival was transformed from curse to blessing and ended the human sacrifice that had resulted from the crime of Comaitho, a priestess who had made love in the temple. In the Patras *aition*, too much sex is followed by too much repression; only the arrival of a new god from elsewhere can then reconcile the people with their god—and with their land, since Artemis Triclaria, the god with whom they make their peace, is god of the "original" inhabitants, which the people of Patras, even though they have displaced them, somehow continue to be. The result is something like a myth of autochthony; an incorrect sexual act takes place and then is overcome and the result is an inalienable link between the people and the land. Within the Patras cult this link is expressed in hero-cult—of the stranger Eurypylus and of an unidentified "local woman."

In the Locrian rite, by contrast, the people do not welcome the sacra to their land; rather they go to the sacra. The maidens are inflicted on the Trojans; they are defined as impure creatures and greeted as a poisoned gift. Once they reach the sanctuary, however, they are safe. They thus reenact not only the supplication of Cassandra, but also that of Ajax. The goddess of Troy makes the Trojans helpless to repel these helpless creatures. The normal fate of the Palladion is thus inverted; instead of being taken away it is appropriated by strangers where it is.

In the Locrian *aition* the goddess inhibited sex (since she accepted the supplication of Cassandra) and also inhibited repression (since she accepted the supplication of Ajax). The story is left completely unfinished: The maiden is never properly allocated, the hero never properly restrained (he dies as a result of a further outrageous act). The task of the ritual, from this point of view, is to finish the story by reenacting and correcting it, so that the maidens end up married, the males pious. This is the opposite of hero-cult, in which the hero's story is appropri-

---

[130] Lerat (1952b), p. 157.
[131] For a full treatment see Redfield 1990.

ated along with his bones; here the story, so far from embodying a power, sets a task. This difference may have to do with the fact that at Patras the *aition* defines the original problem as the excessive sexuality of a woman (since Comaitho, the priestess, is the one responsible for the temple) while the Locrian *aition* defines the original problem as the excessive sexuality of a man (since, however incorrect Cassandra's behavior, Ajax is the Locrian in the story).

Women characteristically remain at home and receive visitors; they may (like Comaitho at Patras) receive them too warmly. Men characteristically go off and have adventures; they may go too far. The Locrians sent their hero venturing to Troy and they never got him back. Nor was his one of the tombs that could be shown at the Troad in historical times; he did not die in Troy—which, next to getting home, is the second-best fate, as Odysseus says when he is threatened with shipwreck:

> If only I had died and met my fate
> On that day when the greatest number of bronze-tipped spears
> Of Trojans fell about me by the dead son of Peleus.
> Then I'd have had share of mourning, and the Achaeans had told my story
>   (*kleos*).
> Worst of all is to die at sea without funeral or memory.
>
> Odyssey 5.308–311

Odysseus of course survives; Oilean Ajax was the only leading hero to die at sea. (The stories say that many drowned in the storms Athena sent, but in fact all the other famous people made it ashore one way or another.) According to tradition (Schol. ad Lycophron 387, 397) Thetis brought back his corpse from the sea, salt-soaked and rotten, and it was buried on Delos—which, as a sacred island, is neutral territory. Probably there was some sort of heroon to him there, but the Locrians did not make this the focus of their cult; they chose rather the place where Ajax went wrong.[132]

---

[132] At this point it is worth noting that the scholiast preserves, as an alternative "true" version, a story in which Ajax is no criminal but completely a victim, first of society and then of nature; the gods play no part. That there is something authentic about this version is suggested by the ritual that it validates as an *aition*; this is like nothing else in the Greek material and therefore probably was actually celebrated by someone (where? when?):

> Locrian Ajax in the sack of Troy when Cassandra was fleeing into the temple and clinging to the Palladion of Athena dragged her away and there coupled with her; Athena being angry killed him on the sea with many others. That is what the many say, but the truth is like this: When she was escaping he dragged her from the temple and kept her as booty, just as the rest of the soldiers were

The Lesser Ajax can be thought of as a kind of failed Odysseus. Odysseus is precisely the hero who finishes things, however long it takes. Just as he defeats Ajax in the footrace, so there is a story that Odysseus had proposed to stone Ajax after his crime (Pausanias 10.31.1). The Lesser Ajax was, like the Greater, one of Odysseus's adversaries. Their stories have a parallelism; Odysseus also (already subject to Poseidon's anger) is shipwrecked and finds himself clutching a crag, but Athena gives him good sense and he knows to be pious, and he survives (*Odyssey* 5.424–450). So Odysseus, who also had been touched by the anger of Athena, recovers her favor. Of course, he is always good with women and knows when to stop.

The *Odyssey* is the perfect marriage story. The wife receives her visitors but (barely) not too warmly; the husband goes far but (barely) not too far to get back. Both are haunted by a fear that they will take one risk too many, that they will not be able to finish their story after all. Odysseus in disguise compliments Penelope on her story, her *kleos*

> keeping other women, as each had been quick enough to seize them. Agamemnon, enamored of her, conspired with Odysseus, and he made public accusation of Ajax that he had made love with this woman in the temple. The consequence was that she was taken by Agamemnon and that the general [i.e., Ajax] was hated by the irrational multitude and rabble. So he, considering the outrage against Achilles, how Briseis was taken from him, and further taking into account the unjust death of Palamedes and fearing that in some way they would kill him also by guile, embarking on his ship in stormy and unpropitious weather with contrary winds blowing was shipwrecked around Teos and Mykonos or Andros and Tenos; his ship was broken up on the rocks, and for a time the man, bravely swimming, was saved as far as the rock of Geraia. The waves, however, came upon him one upon another and a piece of the rock was broken off and so he was born back into the sea and drowned. All Locris learning the news for all time wore black and mourned the man and annually filling a hull with fine offerings and putting fire in it and setting a black sail without steering oar sent it into the open sea to be burnt as a sacrifice to the hero. (Scholiast on Lycophron 365)

It is probably unprofitable to speculate as to the source of this odd version, which must be late, since it both presumes and contradicts epic sources and also misunderstands the epic rules for the division of spoils. Perhaps there was a Hellenistic romance of the Lesser Ajax, and a ritual somewhere, one of those Antonine "revivals," to go with it. We note here only that it is a further transformation and exploration of the tradition. The ritual (which must remind us of the Viking funeral) is an inversion of hero-cult; instead of recognizing a relation with a hero captured by the soil it seeks to reestablish contact with a hero lost in the infinite ocean. The ambiguity of the hero is shifted; whereas the epic Ajax is situationally ambiguous (is Athena his patron or enemy?), this Ajax is ontologically ambiguous (is he or isn't he still out there somewhere?). Both rituals, this one and that of the Locrian maidens, open out on distance and share a theme of something unfinished (the judgment of Ajax or his funeral).

(*Odyssey* 19.108) and she answers that her *kleos* would be much greater and better if her husband would come home (*Odyssey* 19.127–128). And in fact Agamemnon says in Hades at the end of the poem:

> Her *kleos* will never perish
> Of her excellence, and the immortals will make for mortals
> A lovely song of Prudent Penelope.
>
> *Odyssey* 24.196–198

Everyone lives happily ever after, in song and story.

This is just what does not happen to Ajax; he neither dies nobly nor lives happily, and in a more radical sense also his story is incomplete, since its meaning is never clarified. As an unfinished story he is fit to generate a ritual.

For us, guided by Homer, the Lesser Ajax is a minor figure; he was, however, the hero of the Locrians, and they must have seen the Trojan story through him. From this point of view it does not appear so much a story of great deeds, *klea andrōn*, as of muddle. The Locrians are at Troy an insignificant people, since they fight only at the edges, from a distance; Ajax both is and is not their leader, since he does not fight with them. In the course of proper heroic behavior he accidentally commits a crime for which he is neither forgiven nor punished. Through their annual ritual the Locrians remained forever engaged in these ambiguities, finishing the unfinished.

The result is an inversion of an autochthony myth. The Locrians here define themselves, not by their origin from eternal nature, but by their continuing engagement in a (legendary) history. They did not have their hero, and they did not have their god either—that is, they had many gods, but this particular god, Athena Ilion, Lady of the Citadel, was elsewhere. The Locrians as a people defined themselves through their ritual in relation to this elsewhere.

The Trojan War, as a story that will be told forever, a *kleos aphthiton*, is in a sense eternal; a ritual originating at the fall of Troy has a universally understood starting point in eternity. The heroic age is another world, like the Golden Age or the land of the Hyperboreans, and like them is a "space of origins." Hesiod in fact made the heroic like both of these (*Works and Days* 166–173), since he speaks of the heroes as an earlier race that has utterly passed away, like the Age of Gold, and that nevertheless still persists beyond the edges of the world, like the Hyperboreans.

Nevertheless the heroic is another world in another sense. Other other worlds are perfect, characterized by peace, abundance, and ease; the heroic is a world of struggle, scarcity, and trials. Other other worlds are outside of history; the heroic is a schematized image of history. In other other worlds nothing ever happens; in the heroic world every-thing happened in its "classic" form.

The heroic, further, is still present in history in the form of survivals and descendants; it has left its mark on the landscape in the form of ruins, and its heirs continue as the Aianteioi continued at Naryx. The heroic is a symbol not of a cosmic order but of history, process, change. Through their ritual the Locrians continued their entanglement in this process. This ritual symbolized them as a community. They were all descended from those who (at a safe distance) had followed Ajax to Troy—and who now still owed the goddess reparation for his crime. In paying that price they remained one people.

The Uses of Heroic Story

Heroes—their women included—are close to the gods. This does not make them better people in human terms (the gods are not good in human terms) but rather means that they are characterized by excess. They are better only in the sense that they are beyond the law. Thus they put in question customary rules and law; heroic story sets its actors against the moral order, sets individual against society, action against structure, and thus clarifies our understanding of both.

Social structure has to do with the maintenance of limits, both inter-nal and external. External limits define the boundaries of the society; internal limits demarcate roles and persons in such a way as to main-tain proper relationships. One aspect of heroic story, that most popular with the writers of Attic tragedy, dealt with the breakdown of these internal relationships, with family murder, for instance, and incest. The two great epics, by contrast, focus primarily on the external definition of social groups and of humanity itself in relation to the Other. In the *Odyssey* the Other appears in the form of literal monsters (and also as an all-too-human threat to a realistically described household); in the *Iliad* Otherness is explored through that monstrous distortion of social action that is war.

In war those like ourselves, in a cosmic sense our brothers, become through the contingency of history an Other, the enemy; we must kill or be killed. In the process their property and their women become potential spoils. As war is a parody of entertainment—"come here and be greeted," the hero often says to his adversary on the battlefield—so also the siege becomes a parody of courtship. This involves a transfor-mation of norms that is appalling, even though comprehensible and possibly even just. The Trojans are transgressors; it is the theft of Helen that has put them and their women at risk. However, as crime legitimates war and war legitimates violence, social structure turns to anti-structure and generates danger. The appropriation of the Other is a dangerous act, since it involves going beyond limits and easily leads to further transgression. Who can observe limit and proportion while sacking a city or pursuing a maiden? If all is fair in love and war, that is because in war and in love we play for keeps and move out of the space where the rules apply. Love and war are thus the typical heroic adventures, and these stories engage us because we know that caught up in such adventures quite ordinary persons like ourselves may find themselves, like the heroes, faced with a reality that cares nothing for rules, and at risk.

In the story of the crime of Ajax themes of love and war are collapsed. Ajax went too far in the sack of the city; at the same time his crime was an attempt to appropriate a maiden. Yet Ajax's crime was really not against Cassandra but against the Palladion; this shifts the same collapse to a higher level. The Palladion is an image of a maiden, and Cassandra clung to it for security; it promised safety to the maiden and at the same time, as the Lady of the Citadel, symbolized the chastity of the city. The crime of Ajax therefore was not merely an incident of the sack of Troy, but a symbol of it, and his sexual crime was political.

The ambiguities of the story of the crime of Ajax mirror, as we have seen, profound ambiguities in the Homeric picture of the relation between city and goddess. It turns out that irony is of the essence. The Palladion can be seen more generally as an ironic symbol of the ambiguities involved in the appropriation of women and in the Greek attitude toward the woman in her role of wife.[133] As the Palladion guarantees the integrity of the city, so the woman guards the integrity of the house, yet she is only there because she had been brought from elsewhere. Her duties require her to be strong, yet she is culturally defined as weak; the house must rely on her faith yet distrust her as potentially faithless. She is both integrating center and weak point. All this can be seen in the history of the Palladion—which is, however, not a domestic but a political history. The question is, in which direction should this analogy be read? We can say that these political legends reflect underlying anxieties about marriage—or we can say that wives in the Greek tradition are made to bear deep-rooted Greek anxieties about the in-

---

[133] According to one tradition the Palladion was a wedding gift from Athena to Chryse at the time of her wedding to Pallas—Dionysius of Halicarnassus I.68–69, drawing on Satyros or Callimachus?

tegrity of all communities. The analogy is equally meaningful either way.

Every marriage from the man's point of view is an appropriation of the Other; it brings into the house a creature of another sex and a person of another family. Marriage is therefore fraught with danger, but only as the most intimately experienced example of the dangers of social organization in general. The Greek response to these dangers was the *polis*, which attempted to secure a plurality of formally equal households within developed juridical structures of male citizenship, founded on common subjection to a military organization. In Locris, however, the *polis* never arrived; it was permanently emergent. In these terms we can understand why the most famous ritual of this people should have involved them with a permanent effort to finish an unfinished heroic story; in this way they presented to themselves the risks of sexuality and war as normal danger. Their maidens played for them a dangerous game, and thereby made risk habitable. This was no easy thing; by the scale of the privileges granted to the Aianteioi and to Naryx by the Mädcheninschrift we can measure the burden carried by the maidens and their families. What was at stake, however, was nothing less than the health of the society, the success of life in the Locrian mode.

All this has been intended as a kind of ideological introduction, the collection of a mythical vocabulary, in order to speak of the famous Locrians, who were truly elsewhere, in the West. In many ways these western Locrians seem not derived from the old-world Locrians, but their opposite: If Locris was constantly open to process, Epizephyrian Locri presented itself as a closed and perfected state, the process of conscious design, defended against history. This defense was so successful that it is by now nearly impossible to discern how it worked, but there are persistent traces suggesting that the Epizephyrians had somehow adapted to their situation a "Locrian" understanding of the critical importance of the disposition of women and of the powers of the women so disposed. To these Locrians, the Locrians who inhabited the great Locrian *polis* by the cape of the West Wind, we now turn—after a substantial excursus.

EXCURSUS

Five

On Development

A Justification for This Chapter

Marx says: "Men do make their history, but they do not make it just as they please." This is not really different from Wölfflin's rule that "not all things are possible in all periods." History is made within a frame of constraints, some of which are themselves historically conditioned. There is no point in asking people to do the impossible, or to think things by them unthinkable. That we ourselves are the cause of the intellectual structures that constrain us remains a puzzle. As Louis Gernet remarked, there are some fields of action, for instance the legal and the economic, "whose intellectual nature it is possible to forget . . . man himself seems absent from them."[1] Yet they are entirely created by human action. The "objective conditions" of "concrete praxis" on which Marx is so insistent are ideal in the sense that they consist of ideas; "ownership of the means of production" requires a collective idea of "ownership" and, for that matter, of "production" (an activity becomes productive rather than a form of consumption because it is so classified) and even of "means" (which enter into the calculus only when perceived as scarce). These ideas have a history, as more obviously does the law—in fact these two sets of ideas overlap—and both appear most of the time to the individual actor simply as given, a kind of second nature, defining the possible and the desirable.

The present chapter sets out to describe some objective conditions of economic and social action in the classical Greek city-state, by contrast with previous conditions from which these emerged by an intelligible process. The description is on a level of generality that in the context of this book requires some justification. I am here and now working toward an account of the particularities of one peculiar Greek city-state: Epizephyrian Locri. The problem is that very little is known about that odd place. We do know, however, that it was a Greek city-state, and therefore what was true of them all was true of this one. I would go further and suggest that the peculiarities of Locri were a set of peculiar solutions to problems all the city-states experienced; in this sense Locri was both exceptional and paradigmatic, like Sparta. In or-

[1] Gernet (1981 [1968]), p. 73.

der to compare these two, as I intend, it is necessary to say something about the classical city-state in general; the comparison in turn intends to illuminate the more general situation of the city-state. We are working toward Locri, but Locri is as a topic interesting as a special instance of a generic type.[2]

On Interpretation: Class

Claude Lévi-Strauss speaks somewhere of the contrast between "cold" societies and "hot" societies. A cold society, he says, is like a wound-up watch: A certain amount of energy is stored in it at the beginning, and this energy gradually dissipates as it runs down. These are the societies that we, with our commitment to history, call "primitive"; they are the prehistoric societies, whose history is experienced (by themselves) only as cultural decay. A hot culture, by contrast, has a source of energy inside itself, like a steam engine; innovation is here experienced not as sheer loss but as a project of the society, an enactment of the culture, an exploration of new possibilities on an open historical frontier. This internal energy, says Lévi-Strauss, is class conflict: Once the socioeconomic conditions develop that make class conflict both possible and necessary, there is a decisive turn toward social history, toward, that is, the self-conscious making of history and remaking of society by itself. The state then becomes a work of art, self-consciously a response to the challenges set by class conflict.[3]

Lévi-Strauss is a past master of antinomies that conceal polarities; actual societies surely cannot be neatly categorized into one type or the other, nor is class conflict a phenomenon that is either pervasive or absent. Nevertheless his antinomy points to a difference, and I here adopt the language of Lévi-Strauss in order to propose four theses: (1) that during the period we call (for Greek history) "archaic," the lands bordering the Mediterranean made a decisive turn toward history, from cold to hot; (2) that this turn introduced as a novelty class relations, and that Greek development therefore is the arena wherein the idea of class conflict—and, to a large extent, its practice—entered our history; (3) that class conflict among the Greeks is to be understood in terms of particular economic institutions, specifically: private property, market-exchange, gradually pervasive monetization, and the development of an international price-setting market in agricultural commodities; and (4) that the Greek idea of the polity can be understood as a (still

---

[2] This chapter develops notions I launched in Redfield (1977–1978) and Redfield (1986), and occasionally reuses parts of these.

[3] This gives politics an aspect of Weberian "formal rationality"—cf. Murray (1990).

influential) solution to the problems of this specific type of class conflict.

These theses may seem to fly in the face of the evident conservatism which, while not universal to the Greeks, characterizes their political thought: Innovations were mostly resisted (to innovate, *neoterizein*, is a pejorative verb in Greek political discourse, with implications of violence) and when proposed were mostly justified as a return to the constitution of the fathers, the *patrios politeia*. The most influential (in the archaic period) constitution, that of Sparta, seems, indeed, to attempt to abolish history; every crisis there was met by a reassertion of the "original" idea, an insistence on being more Spartan. Yet the Spartan idea, we must notice, was conceived as originating in history, ascribed to a mortal inventor (guided, it is true, by oracles) in response to the challenge of a previous disorder. Indeed, as we have noticed,[4] *eunomia* in the Greek tradition invariably follows a phase of disorder that motivates it. The order of society, therefore, is not given as cosmic in origin, but is seen as a human achievement.

Greek development was a kind of first modernism, and ideas we are still using originate there; in some writers of late fifth- and early fourth-century Athens we recognize a tone that would not recur for millennia: disenchanted, secular, individualistic, concerned with cost-benefits and functional analysis. No sooner have we identified these similarities, however, than we are compelled to acknowledge the differences. Greek development was in critical respects premodern: Society was organized around issues of power, not prosperity, and the major players were motivated primarily by status, not profit. On the other hand, Greek development was anything but primitive: It prefigured the modern partly in that it was already a second urbanization, owing much to—although self-consciously opposing—the by now ancient urban civilizations of Egypt and the Near East. Whereas, however, those societies were hierarchical, Greek society was, at the top, egalitarian. The ruling concept was that of citizenship, which may be defined as the condition of a plurality of persons who have no legitimate superior, and who therefore can generate legitimate authority only by conferring it on one another, that is, by exchanging it. The citizen learned to rule by being ruled (*archein te kai archesthai*—Aristotle *Politics* 1277b).[5] Authority belonged to the office and not the man.

It is a thesis of this chapter that this type of polity introduced into our history class conflict as a process determinative of social structure.

---

[4] See p. 75.

[5] Aristotle quotes a proverb that is elsewhere attributed, in a different form, to Solon (D.L.1.60); see also above, chapter 2, note 3.

In order to explain and defend this thesis it will be necessary to explain my somewhat idiosyncratic definition of "class" and develop it, in the first place by the proposition that classes are defined by their conflict with each other. "Class" therefore is an inherently dualistic concept— although there may be more than one dyadic conflict going on in a given society, and there may be, in any situation of conflict, a third group of those who are not engaged in the conflict. This residuum, however, is not a class but rather the category of the classless.

Class conflict I here define as competition for scarce utilities between diverse social strata whose members are self-consciously defined in relation to one another by a specific and pervasive type of antagonism within a zero-sum system. Typical examples of class opposition are landlord/tenant, creditor/debtor, and employer/employee. Classes are created by their competition; class competition is thus distinct from competition and conflict between preexisting groups: distinct peoples, for instance, or natural categories such as men/women or young/old. In fact the relation between classes is always such that in principle it is possible for an individual to move from one to the other.[6] Class relations, in other words, are and are understood by the participants to be contingent, historically generated relations; class conflict therefore is not the cause of the decisive turn toward history but rather *is* that turn seen from the point of view of social structure. The understanding of social action in terms of class relations is the demystification of society.

Because class conflict involves competition for scarce resources it is an inherently "economic" phenomenon. Indeed it may be that class conflict is always about money. It is a nice question whether such conflict could be over resources symbolic rather than material in nature, that is, marks of status—over *timē*, in Greek terms, rather than *kerdos.* Certainly there is competition for *timē,* and it is scarce, in that within any society it forms a zero-sum system: As mine increases, yours decreases. Competition for honor, however, differs from economic competition because symbolic utilities are by nature not only evaluated but evaluative; they are not only worth possessing but mark their possessor as worthwhile. Therefore they lack the fungibility peculiar to money; the man of honor, for example, is not encouraged to surrender honor in one sphere in order to obtain a greater amount of honor in another. Certainly money can be spent to gain honor, but money-power is not in itself honorable; someone who wins the lottery is envied, not respected.

---

[6] This distinguishes class from race—whatever the facts of the matter, one's race is described as predetermined rather than achieved—although of course a class may be ideologically described as racially constituted precisely to make class mobility seem unthinkable.

Money is pure economic power; a money economy relativizes the values of all commodities with a price, and puts them at the disposal of anyone who commands the price. We can claim not what we deserve but what we can afford. The development of a money economy to some degree separates power from status; this involves the disengagement of the economy as a separated sphere of social life. This disengagement entails the demystification of some aspects of social life; action in the economic sphere is characterized by cost-benefit analysis and short-term rationality. We tend here to assume that we know what we mean by happiness and that our only problem is to pursue it. Money, in fact, *is* that demystification; the money economy, therefore, is the fated arena of class conflict.

By this definition, note, money is prior, often long prior, to currency. A category of transactions can be said to be monetized when these are typically undertaken not within the constraints of reciprocity but as a matter of personal gain-seeking and risk. This social change, however it occurs, is the monetization of the economy; the whole meaning of the transaction is then profit and loss.

Since, however, we are speaking not of the modern but of its prefiguration we must remind ourselves that money economies vary in their institutional structure; in particular the type we call capitalistic is proper only to industrial and postindustrial societies. Surely the ancients possessed capital in the sense that they saved and put those savings to work to accumulate further resources, but in the sense that capital implies a proletariat—an available force of free labor—capital is a modern development. The agricultural labor of the Greek city-state was either proprietary or servile—in most Greek communities farming was done by the families, *autourgoi*, who owned or leased the farms, assisted by a few slaves. Craftsmen were organized in workshops—once again, operated by the owners working with slave labor—so that what was sold was not labor but the laborer and his products. There was a certain amount of free labor and it was available at a price, but there was not the kind of labor market that would have enabled the ancients to compute an unemployment rate. Nor was investment understood as a precondition of employment. The key institution of the developing archaic and classical economy in fact was not capital but private property, particularly private property in land.

The *polis*, the emerging form of Greek life, embodied ideas both political and socioeconomic linked by the concept of *autarkeia*, self-sufficiency. The citizen was to be self-sufficient in his own person, through his health and physical training, and self-sufficient politically, confronting his fellow citizens without subservience or deference. Such a persona was to be secured by economic self-sufficiency, the possession of a livelihood. Ideally at least, the full citizen of a Greek state was supposed to be the proprietor of a domain, his *klēros*, which supported his family (including the slaves) by employing their labor, and which was his little kingdom. The *klēros* maintained the household and provided the householder with the resources—military equipment and the time to train for its use—that were the precondition of full political status. Just as the citizen has no juridical superior, so his property is held not in fealty to any overlord, but as his share of a community of peers.[7]

No doubt property in this sense was always an ideal, which came into existence gradually and imperfectly, always immersed in a structure of real inequalities and dependencies. Nevertheless it is an important idea. In order to say something about it, it is necessary to say something about what it is not, and about its relation to market exchange and to the most fundamental of exchange relations: reciprocity.

Reciprocity, Redistribution, Property, and Market Exchange

Reciprocity is the transfer of goods and services in terms of, and for the sake of, a bond between the parties; the transfer is motivated by the bond and at the same time serves to represent and reinforce it. I buy my godchild birthday presents because that is the sort of thing godparents do; at the same time I am making it true that her godparent is a significant person in her life. Reciprocity presumes a counterprestation—not necessarily an equal one, but a response proper to the bond. (In the example, a thank-you note is ample.) Between peers the proper response is equal, as in the exchange of dinner parties: "We owe them." Between unequals the equality is often looked for only on the level of the system, as a generalized reciprocity: I care for my children as I was cared for and as I expect them to care for theirs. (The notion that they owe me reciprocal care in my old age is a secondary one, by no means culturally universal.)

To the positive reciprocity of the gift contrasts the negative reciproc-

---

[7] Morris (1991), p. 26, states the link between property and politics as follows: "The polis was a complex hierarchical society built around the idea of citizenship. It was made up of hundreds or even thousands of independent peasant households, which neither paid impersonal dues to a centralised government, nor depended on the state for the means of life. In contrast with most equally complex societies of its day, the primary producers owned (in all the most important sense of that word) the means of production. The wealth of the polis elite and the finances of such centralised government as existed was not based primarily on direct exploitation of a peasantry through tax or rent. The equation of the polis with the whole citizen body, even if governmental functions were often reserved for a smaller group, marks it off from other ancient states."

ity of theft. Gifts are proper between friends, and make friends; thefts make enemies and are proper between enemies. The radical form of negative reciprocity is the vendetta, which takes life for life. Its mirror is marriage-exchange, a radical form of positive reciprocity that creates bonds understood not merely as friendship, but as kinship. Still today reciprocity remains fundamental in the family and other face-to-face interactions. Reciprocity, in fact, simply *is* society, conceived under the heading of exchange.

Political authority, a special case of inequality, is further character-ized by *redistribution*, a particular form of reciprocity in which goods and services are exchanged between core and margin. Goods come in—or, because the core is always higher, they come up—and then are passed down again, minus an amount extracted to maintain the higher status of the core. Such was the fundamental exchange structure of the first urbanism, the civilizations of palace and temple of the Near East—which the Greeks habitually contrasted with their own. There the peas-ants gave part of their produce to palace and temple, and palace and temple, after consuming some of it, passed the rest back in the form of emergency assistance and public services (including such "services" as conspicuous consumption and "protection"). In the process the goods mysteriously changed their meaning: What came in as a sign of the deference of the peasantry could be passed back as a sign of the gener-osity of the lord. This mystification is at the heart of redistribution. There is no such thing as negative redistribution, since redistribution, as it asserts and legitimates inequality, unites positive and negative rela-tions in a tense synthesis. Although redistribution can make a real con-tribution to welfare—for instance, by distributing risk—the point of redistribution is the social order that it displays, secures, and justifies.

Although redistribution is an essentially asymmetrical relation it obli-gates both parties. In a premodern society status creates wealth and wealth obligates generosity, which advertises status. Redistribution therefore buys social structure at a cost to the economic aspects of the system. Redistributive norms inhibit saving and reinvestment; the Pa-cific island chief, for instance, who is lucky at sea and lands a great catch of fish may be expected to give a series of lavish parties until his profits are pretty much gone. He cannot use his windfall to build more boats; that would be antisocial behavior.

Private property I here define as possessions released from redis-tributive restraints. The narrative that defines its ideology is Aesop's fable of the grasshopper and the ant. All summer the ant works and saves while the grasshopper sings; when winter comes the grasshopper comes shivering to the door of the ant. "All summer you sang," says the ant; "now you must dance." I am entitled to what is mine, says the ant; I am therefore entitled to deny it to others. The privacy of property is thus an ethic. It associates work with entitlement; wealth is discussed not in the language of ascribed status: I have what is proper to my role and station—but in the language of achieved status: I have what I have *earned.* But if wealth is not conceived as a consequence of status it no longer has to be employed exclusively or even primarily in the service of social status: It can become instrumental in economic competition with others, now defined as counterplayers similarly self-seeking. Furthermore, because wealth is no longer a consequence but rather a cause of status, the players are freed to concentrate on the pursuit of wealth in confidence that the status will follow. This ethical shift preconditioned the second urbanism as surely as the "Protestant ethic," the ethic of economic discipline (which is a real historical phenomenon, whether or not linked to Calvinist predestination or even truly Protestant), preconditioned modern industrialism. Not, let it be clear, that it was the *same* ethic; rather the property ethic had a similar place in the ideology of this different and earlier socioeconomic change, this prefiguring of modernization.

Private property is ethically linked to market exchange. Market exchange is founded on a bargain; therefore the parties meet as adversaries, each seeking profit at the expense of the other. In the Greek view, however, if both parties are fully rational and informed and the bargain is therefore a fair one, they come out even and "each has his own," as Aristotle says (*Ethics* 1132b15).[8] We would say that in the ideal bargain each acquires something more valuable to him than what he gives up; complementary marginal utilities make deals. But in either case, the transaction is thereby concluded. In gift exchange, by contrast, each ends up with something of the other; therefore each exchange motivates a further exchange. They are now in a sense one substance. Not that gift exchange need be irrational; the bond between the parties that it creates is something advantageous to one or both of them, and (more often than the natives like to admit) one or both parties seeks an advantage in terms of the value of the gifts. The difference is in the institutional relation between the parties. In gift exchange the exchange is (at least ideally) for the sake of the connection; in market exchange the connection is for the sake of the exchange. This shift is the "disembedding"[9] of the economy. Transactions do not accumulate in a web of social relations; instead each transaction opens a

---

[8] See the seminal (and controversial) discussion of this passage in Polanyi (1957).

[9] This term is of course a signal of the writer's debt to Karl Polanyi, a debt I make no effort to document in detail. Polanyi's first and best book is Polanyi (1944).

space to further transactions, and acquisition comes to be for the sake of acquisition.

Private property is institutionally linked to a tax structure that leaves the surplus in the hands of a plurality of private parties, rather than stockpiled at the center. The Greek states, like the Italian Renaissance cities, financed their important public activities through taxes on capital, in the Greek case either by a direct levy (the *eisphora*) or by assigning public works to individuals according to their wealth (the "liturgies"). In the interim between obligations and emergencies these resources, instead of being at the disposal of palace or temple, remained in the hands of free and independent households. These households were the *plousioi*, the rich; as Aristotle says, a city consists of "free men, and some who meet a property qualification, for there could not be a city entirely of poor men, any more than one of slaves" (Aristotle *Politics* 1283a17–19).[10] The wealth of the city was in the hands of its wealthy, who were in a position to use it to make more wealth—for themselves, and thus for the city. In the society thus emergent the rich confronted another new class, the liberated peasantry, now themselves become free and independent households as smallholders. The relation between these two classes now had to be negotiated. This change was the social-structural content of Greek development.

In order to form a view of the emergence of these new classes we now explore the difference between the *Odyssey* and the *Works and Days*; the two poems also well illustrate the contrast between the old and the emergent economies. Homer's view is retrospective, idealizing a coherent heroic past; Hesiod looks forward and instructs his audience in the conditions of their moral survival in the nascent Age of Iron.

Property in Homer and Hesiod

Homeric society is easy to describe because the epics put before us a detailed and on the whole convincing picture of social life. We need to remember, however, that "Homeric" is not a period of history but a type of poetry, and that the world the epics describe is partly imaginary. In large part this is a matter of deletions; certain things are not heroic. Heroes do not ride horses (except as a circus trick), do not eat fish (except when starving), do not die of wounds, use no iron weapons (although they have iron agricultural tools), cannot read and write, have no pottery. Relevant to our topic: Heroes do not trade, a point

---

[10] In such a city there would be no one to tax; that is why "if the many distribute the property of the few it is obvious that they destroy the city" (Aristotle *Politics* 1281a18–19).

that becomes explicit in the scornful speech of the young Phaeacian nobleman to the disguised stranger Odysseus:

> Stranger, you do not look like a man of any skill
> In games, in any of the varieties people have.
> You look rather like one who sticks close to the many-oared ship he goes about in,
> A commander of sailors and those who are traders
> Worrying about his wares and with an eye out for goods he can acquire in exchange
> And whatever profit he can snatch. You look like no athlete.
>
> *Od.* 8.159–164

This passage expresses contempt for trade in a well-developed commercial vocabulary, with words for trader (*prēktēr*), profit (*kerdos*), the wares one puts in the boat for sale (*phortos*, cf. *Od.* 14.296), and the wares one brings back on the return journey (*hodaia*, cf. *Od.* 15.445). The heroes may have nothing to do with trade, but the poet obviously knows a lot about it. Here, as elsewhere in Homer, aspects of life excluded from the epic are nevertheless included as part of the common knowledge of poet and audience.

Correlatively, an entire social stratum is excluded from the epics on the principle that only some kinds of people are interesting. In the *Iliad* the interesting people are the *promachoi*, the leading warriors who have names (even if we meet them only once, as they die), whose stories are worth telling (even if only in half a line); behind them is the anonymous mass, the *plēithus*, from which they emerge for their moment of glorious action, and into which they retire when hard pressed. This anonymous mass also forms the audience of the assemblies, including steersmen, oarsmen, and stewards (*Il.* 19.43–44), "not warlike or brave, never to be counted in war or in council" (*Il.* 2.200–201).

The same basic structure of society appears in the *Odyssey*, where the interesting people are the *basilēes*, the lords. *Basileus* in later Greek means "king" but in Homeric Greek the authority of the *basileus* need not imply sovereignty. The *basilēes* are those who are "scepter-bearing" (*Il.* 2.86), who participate in deliberation (cf. *Il.* 9.346), who enjoy marks of privilege (*Il.* 9.334, cf. 12.310–321). They are masters of large households. Some are more lordly—*basileuteros*—than others. The most lordly—*basileutatos*—in any community becomes its king; he can be called "the *basileus*." The word, however, means "king" only ambiguously. When Antinoos teases Telemachus, saying that Zeus might make him *basileus* of Ithaca, Telemachus replies: "it is no bad thing to be *basileus* . . . but there are other *basilēes* . . . some one of them can have it" (*Od.* 1.392–396). The king, in fact, is *primus inter pares*, as Alcinoos tells us:

There are twelve notable *basilēes* for all the folk
Who as rulers make determinations, and I myself am thirteenth.

Od. 8.390–391

The *Odyssey* is the story of Odysseus, who is *basileutatos* on Ithaca. His establishment is based on a large house in town, big enough to entertain (in the courtyard) the sons of most of the other *basilēes* of this and the neighboring islands. On Ithaca all the characters in the *Odyssey* who are not *basilēes* or members of their immediate families are slaves. The house is run by two senior house servants, Eurycleia and Eurynome. Odysseus's father, Laertes, had purchased Eurycleia "while still in her first youth . . . for a price of twenty oxen" (*Od.* 1.430–431). We are not told anything of Eurynome's origins; Telemachus does speak generally of the "servants (*dōmes*) whom Odysseus won for me by raiding" (*Od.* 1.398).

Attached to the property is a kind of home farm; this is where Laertes retires to console himself by working in the garden. This farm is worked by Dolius, whom Penelope had brought with her as part of her dowry (*Od.* 4.736) and his sons; another son, Melantheus, keeps goats, and a daughter, Melantho, does women's work in the great house. Then there is Eumaeus the swineherd; we hear the whole story of how he was born a prince, kidnapped by Phoenicians with the complicity of his Phoenician nurse, and carried to Ithaca, where Laertes purchased him (*Od.* 15.483). Finally there is Philoetius the herdsman; we hear nothing of his origins.

It looks as though the population of Ithaca consists of the *basilēes*, their families, and the slaves they have acquired by gift, theft, or purchase. This cannot, however, be the whole story. For one thing, we hear of *thētes*; in later Greek this means "hired hands." Evidently they are in contrast with the *dmōes*, who are more permanently attached to the great house. Taken together they are numerous; the *thētes te dmōes te*, hired men and bondsmen of Odysseus are said to be sufficient to man a ship without drawing on the general population of Ithaca (*Od.* 4.643–644). Furthermore the *dmōes* work dispersed over a considerable area; Telemachus says it would take a long time to visit them all, spread out as they are in various farmsteads across the agricultural area (*Od.* 16.309–320). It seems implausible that the basic agricultural productivity should all be in the hands of persons acquired by the present *basileus*; what happened to the previous generation? And what is to happen to these *dmōes*, and to their children? To the surviving children of Dolius, for example?

Eumaeus provides an answer to this question when he speaks of the normal outcome of personal servitude: The master, if he had stayed at home,

> Would have treated me very much as one of his own and given possession,
> The sort of thing a king of good spirit gives to his houseman (*oikeus*),
> A house and a *klēros* and a much-courted wife,
> When one has toiled for him much, and the god increases his work
> As he increases for me this work, where I am faithful.
> Thus the king would have benefited me much, if he had grown old here.
>
> *Od.* 14.62–67

Eumaeus, who came into the great house as a child and was brought up almost as a child of the house (*Od.* 15.363–365), is an *oikeus*, a houseman, a special case; his hope, however, had been to enter the mainstream as a smallholder dependent on the great house. Thus we can begin to picture the life and livelihood of the shadowy mass of persons who never reach the foreground in the heroic stories: They are small farmers, some of them, *dmōes*, dependent on great houses, others, *thētes*, formally more independent but available to the great house as wage laborers. In this society, further (as M. I. Finley saw),[11] the status of *dmōs* is higher than that of *thēs*, because the bond to the land, which is also a bond to a *basileus*, gives him a recognized and reasonably secure place in the social order. Eumaeus speaks of the loss of Anticleia, Odysseus's mother:

> The *dmōes* feel the lack very much
> Of talking face-to-face with the mistress, and getting the news,
> And eating and drinking something, and then taking something back
> To the country, the kind of thing that rejoices the heart of *dmōes*.
>
> *Od.* 15.376–379

The word for "farm," in Homer as in later Greek, is *klēros*, literally a "share" (or "lot," as in English). *Klēros* can mean in Homer a share of an inheritance (*Od.* 14.209) but seems already to have the more general sense of a share of the city's agricultural land. To hold a *klēros* is to have title to a place in the community. The *dmōes* who hold *klēroi* are dependent on some *basileus*; authority over their land can even be transferred by him to another, but the people go with the land. Thus Agamemnon offers to give Achilles seven villages, rich in flocks and cattle, which will "honor him like a god with gifts, and under his scepter carry out his shining judgments" (*Il.* 9.155–156). This is a redistributive system. Similarly (on a more modest scale) Alcinoos, addressing the *basilēes* dependent on himself, those who "drink the dark wine in my house, the mead of elders, and hear the bard" (*Od.* 13.8–9), tells them each to give a tripod to the departing Odysseus; "we in turn will make collections from the folk and pay ourselves back. It is hard to do

---

[11] Finley (1954), p. 58.

favors uncompensated" (*Od.* 13.14–15). Within the frame of redistribution, the smallholders are available to the *basilēes* as a tax base. On the other hand, their land is not absolutely at the lord's disposal. I would imagine that to evict such a family would (if not absolutely impossible) be savage behavior unworthy of a *basileus*. And the *basilēes*, for all their overbearing ways, know that if their behavior is sufficiently outrageous they may find the folk rising against them and casting them out (cf. *Od.* 16.424–430).

The worst of fates is to be *aklēros*, without land—or by an impossible hyperbole, to be *thēs* to an *aklēros*, a farmhand hired by a man without a farm (*Od.* 11.489–490). Conversely, people who are very rich are *poluklēroi* (*Od.* 14.211); they have in their demesne many *klēroi*, and thus have many *dmōes*. These *klēroi* belong, in different ways, both to the *dmōes* and to the *basileus*; the land is the link between them. It is twice-owned, by lord and serf.

The *Odyssey* gives us (in epic dress, with certain statable distortions and deletions) a recognizable picture of a premarket economy. Control of land and labor is talked of in the language of loyalty and obligation. Commodities circulate in restricted networks—in fact they can be roughly sorted according to the old triad of animal, vegetable, and mineral. Vegetable commodities belong to the subsistence sector; they seem to be produced by the *klēroi* for their own consumption. (That is why Odysseus's house needs a home farm.) Animal produce, by contrast, belongs to the *basileus* alone. (Philoetius thinks at one point of taking his herd elsewhere—but he would not become independent, he would take it to some other *basileus*; a herd unattached to a great house is unthinkable: *Od.* 20.218–223.) The flocks and herds are kept in the rough hill land that belongs to no one and is only marginally part of the community; here we meet Eumaeus, who thinks he has been there far too long. It seems that herding is not so much the work of a social stratum or caste as of a life-stage; Odysseus, disguised as a beggar, says that he is too old to keep beasts and obey the order of the overseer— *Od.* 17.20–21. We remember that Prince Paris was herding when asked to judge between the goddesses—as was Aeneas when Achilles almost caught him (*Il.* 20. 90–91, 188–190). Aeneas's father, Anchises, had also been herding when visited by Aphrodite (*Hymn to Aphrodite* 54– 55). This herding by princes is, I suspect, an epic transformation of a society in which herding was done by young men (like Melantheus) borrowed for a time from the families of the *dmōes*. Most of the meat so produced came into the great house, where it was consumed on festival occasions. Wool also came into the great house,[12] where it was worked

---

[12] This closely resembles the position argued by Morris (1987), pp. 178–179.

up into textiles by the women—apparently including girls (like Melantho) also borrowed from the families of the *dmōes*. The young people thus formed a disposable labor pool. After this period of service they (with, it seems, the advice and consent of the *basileus*) could marry and take over a *klēros*. Thus we can understand how population and productivity were kept in balance; marriages only occurred as land became available (as in rural Ireland and other farming communities). We also understand Odysseus's rage at the faithless serving girls: Their sexuality, like that of a daughter, is properly his to dispose.

In any case, animal produce circulates in a redistributive network, serving to signify and reinforce status. Mineral produce—metals and precious materials (also horses, which are the prestige good par excellence, and some exceptional fabrics)—circulate in reciprocity, through lordly gift exchange. These materials are associated with a special category of skilled workmen, the *dēmioergoi*, a term that also covers seers, physicians, and bards. All are employed by the *basilēes*—as are heralds—but are not their dependents. Their special skills allow them to move from community to community, since their skills are welcome everywhere (*Od.* 17.382–386). They form the nucleus of a specifically urban population, and are the human armature on which could be accumulated a panhellenic culture.

None of these social categories is a class, since their relation is represented by themselves to themselves as cooperative, not competitive. The economy altogether in the *Odyssey* is represented as what Clifford Geertz calls a "cultural system," with that characteristic collapse of fact and value whereby the natives assure themselves that things are as they are supposed to be. Commodities, along with authority, are a sign of social status; conversely the status thus signified constitutes a claim to authority and commodities. Consumption legitimates itself by being conspicuous. The *basileus* is entitled to claim more because he is a *basileus*; conversely, his success in enforcing this demand proves that he is and ought to be a *basileus*. At the same time he is subject to *noblesse oblige*; in making his claims, the *basileus* implicitly promises to acknowledge the counterclaims of those who acknowledge him.

When we come to the *Works and Days*, however, we are in a very different world. The *basilēes* are still present; Hesiod calls them *dōrophagoi*, "gift-eating" (*Works and Days* 39, 263, cf. 221), echoing Achilles' epithet for Agamemnon: "people-eating" (*dēmoboros—Iliad* 1.231). The *basilēes* also retain their control over land, but it is here indirect, through their power to settle disputes. Hesiod[13] has had a dispute with

---

[13] By "Hesiod" I mean the persona asserted in the poem; for the purposes of this

his brother Perses over the division of their *klēros* and Perses got the better of it, "greatly glorifying the *basilēes*" (*Works and Days* 38). That is not the right way to gain wealth, however (according to Hesiod); the right way is to work:

> From work men become rich in flocks and wealthy,
> And by working they are much dearer to the immortals.
> Work is no shame; idleness is shame.
> If you work, soon the idle man will envy you
> As you grow rich, and on riches attend excellence and glory.
> Whatever your luck, working is better.
>
> *Works and Days* 308–314

Work is a kind of piety; it brings a response from the gods—and reinforced by other kinds of piety, it makes it certain that "you will buy other people's *klēros*, not they yours" (*Works and Days* 341).[14] Land, in other words, is in Hesiod alienable, and it seems probable that this fact conditions his entire ethical stance.

Distrust pervades the *Works and Days*: "even when laughing with your brother bring a witness" (*Works and Days* 371). The ideal is self-sufficiency:

> What lies in the house never troubles a man;
> Better what is at home, since harm is out of doors.
> It is good to take from what is at hand, and a sorrow to the heart
> To have need of what is absent; I bid you think on it.
>
> *Works and Days* 363–368

Nothing is trustworthy except the capacity of the land to respond to labor.

> Should each season
> In turn bring increase, there is no fear that afterward in want
> You'll beg at the houses of others and accomplish nothing.
> So you came to me just now. But I'll give you nothing
> Nor add a measure. Work, fool Perses,
> Work, that is what the gods marked out for mankind.
>
> *Works and Days* 394–398

Hesiod here plays ant to Perses' grasshopper; work not only brings wealth, it legitimates it. Help is neither offered nor expected.

---

argument it makes no difference whether the poem retails literal autobiographical fact or is the work of some imaginative poet, a Corinthian Bacchiad, for example.

[14] For a good review of the controversy surrounding this line see Càssola (1965).

Hesiod does have a few things to say about good relations with one's neighbors (*Works and Days* 341–351) but even they are unreliable:

Keep all the equipment ready in your own house
Lest you ask another, and he refuse it, and you waver
And the season be going by, and your work suffer.

Works and Days 407–409

Next to nothing is to be expected of kindred or the wider community.

The *Works and Days* is a celebration of the isolated life of the small-holder. The only thing that troubles Hesiod about his isolation is that it is incomplete. The self-sufficiency of the farmer is threatened by his involvement with others—politically, through his vulnerability to disputes and to those with the power to settle them, and economically, through his involvement with the market. Indeed the market, with its bargaining, seems for Hesiod to be in the same category as litigation, with its bribery and perjury.

The market appears in Hesiod only in the form of overseas trade in agricultural commodities; Hesiod says he knows nothing about this (*Works and Days* 649), yet he is ready with some seventy lines of counsel concerning it, ending with advice not to put the whole harvest into ships: "leave the greater part, and load as cargo the lesser" (*Works and Days* 690). Hesiod, it seems, can actually imagine farming entirely for export, although he is against it. Agriculture, in other words, is potentially monetized.

The *Works and Days* is suffused with the tensions that have forever characterized the peasantry: An economic aspiration to self-sufficiency is compromised by involvements with the market, and a political fear of dispossession is induced or at the least exacerbated by the peasant's inability fully to insulate his property from higher authorities. The peasantry, in fact, is as a class defined by the ambiguity of its relations with the town, with an urban world that is alien, feared, distrusted, and yet an ineradicable aspect of their lives.[15]

[15] The working definition of *peasant* employed in this paragraph is that mentioned (although not endorsed) by Anthony Leeds: one engaged in "small-scale, largely family enterprise, involving limited but, nevertheless, significant involvement in a money economy," Leeds (1977), p. 228. I realize that I have already used the term *peasant* to apply to the resident farmers represented in the *Odyssey*, although (as a piece of epic archaism) they are supposed to have practically no involvement with a money economy. I tend to agree with Leeds (1977), p. 228, that "the concept 'peasant' has no precision whatsoever. It is used with different attributes in different situations, and in fact, is more or less uniquely defined in each ethnographic case. It is used to cover a multiplicity of forms of production, social organization, jural orders, and ideologies. It is used ethnocentrically and temporocentrally. Clearly the term represents a total muddle and a permeating lack

The *Works and Days* is a profoundly antipolitical poem; it may seem strange that it should have become one of the ethical classics of the Greeks. Yet from another point of view the *Works and Days* is a founding document of the *polis*. As government conceived to be of, by, and for *klēros*-holding citizens, the Greek city-state remained politically as well as economically founded on the smallholders; these worked its soil, manned its army, and constituted the mass of the citizens, the archaic and classic *plēithus* or *dēmos*.

Victor Davis Hanson, himself a fifth-generation California fruit farmer, has written eloquently of Greek "intensive agriculture," identifying six farming practices that are already to be seen in the *Odyssey*, may have been quite novel at that time, and characterized Greek rural life during the next four hundred years. They are "homestead residence, irrigation [to which we should add drainage, on Greek evidence even more important], slave labor, diversified crops, the incorporation of marginal ground, localized food processing and storage."[16] Hanson uses his knowledge of the techniques of farming to fill out our general sense that the Greeks were for their time exceptionally gifted farmers. He also emphasizes the extent to which these emerging smallholders (he calls them a "new 'class' of man"—p. 88) gained control of their operations. Because (or better, to the extent that) they lived in the midst of their lands they acquired a domain with a perimeter, in contrast to the scattered land-rights of an open-field system. To the extent that their crops were diversified they were less subject to the vagaries of the weather; to the extent that they opened up marginal ground they had available an open frontier guaranteeing them returns on intensive labor. To the extent that they managed their own irrigation and drainage (rather than relying on central administration) they were involved as equal players in negotiating rights and claims with their neighbors. As they learned to process and store flour, oil, and wine themselves they became independent of redistributive institutions based on the palace. As they acquired slaves they undertook to train and manage their own labor. Hanson might have added that chattel slavery helped to perpetuate the family farm through the generations because it provided a flexibility that enabled the smallholder to rear a smaller family; he could work with a slave or two while his son was growing (Hesiod tells him to

---

of theoretically useful distinctions. It is essentially a folk term adopted into social science without the necessary scientific refinement for appropriate scientific use. Indeed, the term has basically no scientic validity at all." From this point onward I shall abjure the term *peasant*; I shall be using *smallholder* as a translation of the Greek *autourgos*.

[16] Hanson (1995), p. 50.

have only one, or at most two: *Works and Days* 376–377), then sell off the slaves when the boy was grown, avoiding dividing the estate.

Yet in none of these aspects is the smallholder truly self-sufficient. Slaves are available because somewhere armed men are capturing them, transporting them, and offering them for sale. Farmhouses can be dispersed only if someone is protecting the territory; otherwise the farmers will huddle together—preferably on a rock somewhere high above the agricultural land—in expectation of raiders. Dispersed processing and storage also imply the security of the farmstead. Irrigation and drainage involve investment in the hope of long-term reward; so does the development of marginal land, since under Greek conditions this usually meant planting olives, which take years to bear. And the diversification of crops, if it is to be tailored to the most effective use of the land rather than the family's pattern of consumption, presumes some kind of exchange of agricultural produce outside the boundaries of the farm, and (for maximum efficiency) outside the boundaries of the community.

Thucydides, who may have been the first to think deeply about these things, lays out the issue in two sentences.

> It is obvious that what is now called Hellas was in old times not securely settled, but back then there were shifts of population; the various inhabitants were quite ready to leave behind their own lands under pressure from those who at any given time were stronger. There was no trade, nor did they have secure commerce one with another by land or by sea; each group made such use of their resources as enabled them to live, not accumulating any surplus of possessions nor planting the land with trees, since they had no way of knowing when some other was going to come and—lacking in walls as they were—take it all away, so supposing that they could get hold of a minimum day-by-day livelihood anywhere, it was not hard to dispossess them, and for that reason they were not strong in the size of their cities nor in the rest of their material equipment. (Thucydides 1.2)

A farming community, if it is to thrive, requires a boundary that is closed to thieves and open to peaceful commerce. Infrastructural support could be provided only by the state. Surely the country sustained the city, but the reverse was also the case, and this fact provided the basis for conflict between them. Hanson seems to think of these early polities as associations of the smallholders for their mutual benefit, but in fact the elites of the premarket economy continued their political domination into the new order, transforming themselves, in the process, into a new class.

Private property in land meant the liberation of the smallholders. They were no longer the dependents of the great houses; the product of their work was their own. On the other hand, as Hesiod lets us know, they remained subordinate and largely powerless. In fact in an important respect they were more powerless than before. They had lost their claims on the surplus, at least insofar as that agricultural surplus remained in the storerooms of the great houses; in bad years nothing stood between them and hunger but the savings they themselves had managed to accumulate in better times. Not even their property was secure. The kind of property we call private belongs to those whose title is recognized by the community, and if the *basilēes*, acting in their capacity as judges, withdrew that recognition the smallholder was threatened with dispossession. That threat was the more realistic in that the eviction or enslavement would be represented, not as the arbitrary personal act of the overlord, but as a kind of righteousness, the application of a rule.

The smallholders were thus doubly motivated to increase the productivity of their land through prudent effort: If they did well enough they could buy land with the proceeds; if they did badly they might lose everything. Private property of smallholdings (as opposed to alternatives tried by other Mediterranean societies: serfdom with sharecropping, large estates worked by gangs of slaves, rack-renting on short leases) ensured maximum per-acre yields; for this reason (among others) it remained the fundamental socioeconomic institution of the city-state as long as the city-state endured. It ensured those high yields by making farming (and Hesiod has much to say about this) into an anxious business.

That the smallholder had to achieve the productivity of the soil in order to maintain his status was, however, only one aspect of a pervasive shift in the relation between wealth and status. In the society portrayed in the *Odyssey* wealth follows status: A man's adventures might lead his status to shift—Eumaeus was born a prince, raised a slave, finally "like brother to Telemachus"—but at each stage the distributional norms provide the material resources appropriate to that station in life. Entertainment of the stranger is such a tense issue partly because his status must be adjudicated in order to see how he is to be entertained: as a *basileus*, a craftsman, a beggar? He cannot buy his way in.

In the emerging society of the archaic age, however, the relation between status and wealth begins to be reversed, so that wealth becomes a source of status. This transformation and its discontents are a frequent theme of Greek poetry, for instance in the fragment ascribed to both Theognis and Solon:

> Many bad men are rich, and good men poor,
> But we with them will not exchange

Wealth for excellence (*aretē*), since that is ever stable,
  While different people at different times have possessions.

Solon 6 = Theognis 315–318

Similarly Theognis says: "For the mass of people there is only one *aretē*, to be rich" (Theognis 699–700). In other words, the glitter of wealth threatens to eclipse all other forms of social appearance, and thus deprive traditional *aretē* of the social support it needs to survive.

There is, furthermore, a moral danger here; the pursuit of wealth is the appetite that gains increase by what it feeds on, and it literally drives men crazy. The following verses are also attributed to both Theognis and Solon:

Of wealth there is no limit plainly marked for man;
  Those of us who now have the richest life
Seek twice as much; who could satiate them all?
  You know that profits come to mortals from immortals
And from profits delusion (*atē*) next appears; Zeus sends it
  In punishment; different people at different times have it.

Solon 1.71–76 = Theognis 227–232

As the economy comes to be "disembedded" there is a relaxation of those social controls which had molded the distribution of material resources to reinforce social structure. You never know your luck, life is unfair, and enough is never enough. The society is heating up; this disembedding, which is another name for monetization, is the critical factor in the change from a cool society to a hot one. Another name for this change is the origin of private property.

To say that private property developed between Homer and Hesiod would be a radical oversimplification. We have no knowledge of the relative chronology of the poems; even if Hesiod is later, the difference between the two poets is not primarily chronological. The point of view of the *Odyssey* is centrist; it celebrates the benign power of the good king. The *Works and Days* places its implicit author far from the seats of power, perched up in Askra, marginal land on the edge of Boeotia "bad in winter, harsh in summer, never good" (*Works and Days* 640). It may well be that independent smallholders first developed on such marginal territory, as population expanded and worse land came under cultivation.[17] But by the late archaic period private property had be-

---

[17] That is, it may well be that those who planted land that had previously been waste or pasture acquired some kind of title to it—since previously it had belonged to no one. Later Greece knew this kind of property as empheutic tenture—cf. Nilsson (1954–1955) for a suggestion of an early origin for the institution.

come (except in some very backward areas, such as Crete) the normal institution for all agriculture. The difference between property in Homer and property in Hesiod reflects, through a schematic contrast, a real change. And this was a change that affected all sectors in the society, not agriculture only or the smallholders only. Equally it involved the rich and trade.

The most difficult and most discussed question in the study of early Greek development, however, is the question of the relation of trade to the agrarian economy and to the class structure there emerging. To this question we now turn.

How Development Happened

The first precondition of development is underdevelopment. In our story this precondition is provided by the Greek dark ages. After the fall of the Mycenean palaces, between 1200 and 1150 B.C., the Greeks experienced a catastrophic collapse. There were many fewer people and those who remained were much less well provided. This condition of impoverished depopulation lasted about three hundred years; it is not until the middle geometric period, about 850, that we begin to see some signs of revival. About one hundred years later, at the beginning of the late geometric period, there is a population surge—in Attica conservatively estimated at threefold in fifty years, and evident elsewhere in Greece as well.[18]

Population is the leading indicator of economic development. The economy consists of nature as humanly appropriated; more people mean more consumption and make possible more production and a larger economy. So a first question is: How did this sudden increase occur?

People, first of all, have to eat, so it is generally understood that the basis of development is new agricultural productivity. On the other hand, it is also understood that the pressure of increasing population leads to increased agricultural productivity: People are now motivated to invent, borrow, or revive more productive techniques, to put into use marginal land, to organize their societies in order to increase per-acre and per-capita production. Demand and supply interact through a feedback loop. Also production motivates population in another sense: People set out to rear more children when there is more for those children to do. Even in those countries where it seems to the outsider that the birthrate is much too high, families are usually having children

---

[18] The evidence is reviewed in Tandy (1997), pp. 19–30.

not by accident but because they believe the children's labor will shelter the parents in their old age.

In such cases, on the other hand, typical of the third world, increases of population and productivity are insufficient to constitute development. Otherwise the Nile delta would long since have taken off. Population and agriculture there merely keep pace, so that the soil supports a steadily growing number of paupers. In modern times at least, this situation is typical of colonial and quasi-colonial areas, of that "periphery" that is established by the "core" as a "zone of extraction," where there is a tendency toward "monoculture" conducted on behalf of the core's "accumulation of surplus"[19]—the situation, in short, of the typical banana republic. This example reminds us that development usually occurs through interaction between different communities quite asymmetrically related, and that the production of resources is one thing, their appropriation something else. By the fifth century, Greek development seems to have produced something of the sort among the indigenes on the north coast of the Black Sea, where barbarian peoples produced wheat for Greek consumption (Herodotus 4.17.2). But the Greeks themselves, however peripheral they may have appeared to the established civilization of the East, in their own development managed to play the role of the core.

That the Greeks enjoyed a long and spectacular period of development is obvious. In 750 B.C. they were one of hundreds of peoples scattered about the Mediterranean, confined to a small area extending from the Ionian islands on the west of the Peloponnese to the Anatolian coast on the east of the Aegean, no further north than Thessaly, and south as far as Crete and east to Cyprus. Furthermore even in this area they were "Balkanized," sharing the district with pockets of other "Pelasgian" peoples. They were illiterate, living and worshipping in mud-and-wattle huts; they had no common institutions or sanctuaries and even their most pervasive pottery style, which we call middle geometric, was common only to the central part of the Greek district. Four hundred years later, by contrast, there were Greek cities scattered all around the Aegean, monopolizing the seacoastal areas up into and including the Black Sea, in Libya, most of Sicily, and the greater part of southern Italy, also in southern France. Greek lands were thickly settled; their cities were well laid out, set with stone temples, theaters, gymnasia, and public buildings. These cities were joined with one another and with their neighbors—who increasingly were imitating their art and to some degree their way of life—by habitual commerce, including tourism; the Greeks, further, now enjoyed together common

---

[19] These terms are drawn from Wallerstein (1979).

sanctuaries ornamented by their great plastic artists, also games, also a common written literature. They never came to political unity but they became, in their own eyes and to a remarkable degree in the eyes even of those others who eventually conquered them, *the* pattern of civilization.

I doubt that anything in 750 would have enabled an observer to predict this development. One might rather have expected that the multiform civilization of the Middle East, which for millennia had been forming and reforming itself in a series of gradually expanding empires, would eventually take over the Mediterranean. In the Mediterranean itself the Phoenicians were in 750 ahead of the Greeks in commerce, and probably in urban institutions; the Etruscans (at the end of the phase we call Villanovan) were at least their equals in overall standard of life. The Etruscans and the Phoenicians were the two peoples with whom the Greeks competed for control of the sea and of the littoral, but both of these had reached the furthest limits of their expansion by the end of the sixth century, and both were by that time increasingly imitating the Greeks. Greek development, in other words, can be measured by success against competition in Hellenic expansion and in Hellenization. The Greeks found the resources not merely to put themselves on the map but to dominate it.

It is possible that what set the Greeks apart from the beginning was the range of their appropriative energy, as represented, for instance, by Odysseus as observer and reporter:

> There is a shaggy island strung out by the harbor
> Of the land of the Cyclopes, not near, not far off
> Wooded. On it numberless goats have grown,
> Feral. They are not driven along any human track
> Nor do hunters go after them, who through the brush
> Would take the trouble to get across the crags of the mountains.
> It is not possessed by shepherds nor by plowmen
> But unsown unplowed all its days
> Is widowed of men, and feeds the bleating goats.
> The Cyclopes have not ships with ruddled sides
> Nor do they have the craft of carpenter, men who could make
> Well-benched ships, which would arrive each place
> Going about the cities of mankind, all those cities
> Where men go visiting each other in ships on the sea.
> Such as these would make of this island their proper settlement.
> It's not at all bad, but bears all things in season.
> There are meadows along the seaside banks
> Well watered and soft. The grapes would grow in abundance.

There is smooth plowland. Very thick would be the crop always
They would reap in season, for the topsoil runs down deep.
There is a bay fit for a harbor, where there's no need of cables
Nor to throw out anchors nor tie up the prow;
Just drag the ship up on the sore and wait until
The sailors are ready and the winds begin to blow.
Right at the head of the bay there flows clear water
A spring under the crag. Poplars grow round it.
There we sailed . . .

Od. 9.116–142

Odysseus speaks as a seafaring farmer, and his speech displays a number of pervasive Greek attitudes. He looks at the land with a farmer's eye and sees it going to waste. He is patronizing toward those primitives who have no use of the sea. From his point of view the whole district is more or less uninhabited, since there is no one there except the Cyclopes, and they have no agriculture, only herding. The land needs Greek settlers; they would develop it agriculturally—and he assumes that they would have ships, not only to bring them there, but as an ongoing part of life.

The Greeks borrowed much; their special gift seems to have been that of synthesis. The Greeks, following the Phoenicians, very early produced long-distance voyagers and risk-takers, far more than the Etruscans, whose trade tended to be overland and whose naval adventures were confined to their own waters. In the archaic period Greeks also became metal workers to rival the Phoenicians, but at the same time they were always (as were the Etruscans) an agricultural people, which the Phoenicians were not. Early Phoenician settlements were coastal trading stations; the hinterland of Carthage, for instance, was not agriculturally developed until the fifth century, by which time the Carthaginians were pretty thoroughly Hellenized. Possibly it was the combination of seafaring and agriculture that gave the Greeks their comparative advantage in the development of the Mediterranean.

We do, however, need to notice that seafaring preceded agricultural development. Up to 850 we have very little non-Greek material from Greek sites, almost no Greek material from non-Greek sites, and no reason to believe that any of this material was transported by Greeks. After that date we begin to be able to trace Greek, especially Euboean, travel to the Near East and the West. Travel is not, however, coterminous with trade; in order to imagine how development happened we need to place trade in the cultural context in which it developed. This brings us back to Homer—who, as we saw, as an aspect of epic archaism excludes Greek trade, but describes the heroic form of venturing that preceded it.

When Odysseus is planning with Penelope the restoration of his possessions he says:

> Much I myself will gain by raiding (*lēïssomai*), other things
> The Achaeans will give, until they have refilled our stores.
>
> *Od.* 23.357–358

Odysseus mentions the two ways in which the great houses of the *Odyssey* provide themselves with wealth: They receive it as "gifts" from their subordinates, and they steal it—from elsewhere. This type of theft is called *lēïsteia* and the thieves *lēïstēres* or *lēïstai*. These words have no good English translation; *piracy* carries an unfortunate suggestion of the Spanish Main, as we usually restrict it to those who prey on shipping. *Lēïstēres*, by contrast, are seaborn adventurers who land various places—to raid, and for other purposes. The closest (not exactly English) word is *viking*. Like the Icelanders who would "go a-viking," *lēïstēres* are young men who furnish and man a ship together and go off and see what they can find, most often to steal. More than anything they are kidnappers, seizing the helpless and selling them into slavery.

Lēïstēres in the epic are always foreigners: Phoenicians, Taphians, Etruscans. Nevertheless Odysseus, posing as a Cretan in one of his lying tales, gives (without using the word) a sense of the activity:

> I had no taste for work
> Nor the increase of the house that rears fine children
> But my taste was ever for ships fitted with oars,
> Battles, polished missiles and arrows,
> Baneful things, that for others are full of pain
> But were to my taste, and god somehow made them suit me—
> Since different people take delight in different works.
> Before the sons of the Achaeans went to Troy
> Nine times I commanded men and swift ships
> Against alien peoples, and I achieved much—
> From which I took the first share I wanted, and then
> Allocated much. Quickly my house increased, so then
> I became dread and respected among all the Cretans.
>
> *Od.* 14.222–234

The ambiguities of language in this passage represent the ambiguities of the poet's attitude toward any source of wealth other than agriculture. Odysseus says that he had no taste for work (*ergon*) and then says that raiding was the work (*ergon*) that suited him; he says that his raiding increased his house (*oikos ophelleto*) and yet says that he had no taste for the increase of the house (*oikōpheliē*) "that rears fine children." These ambiguities correspond to the marginal position of the persona here adopted: an illegitimate son, cut out of the inheritance but nevertheless, because of his personal valor, able to marry into "people rich in *klēroi*" (*Od.* 14.211), but now, after the misfortunes of a further voyage, a vagrant. The riches of such a person are only ambiguously his, because uncertainly related to the soil, which is true wealth. In fact all the spoil of his earlier raiding in the end accrued to his father-in-law; his valor has profited only his wife's family, secure on its agricultural base.

Lēisteia is inherently risky and opportunistic; *lēistēres* "wander, staking their lives, bringing harm to alien peoples" (*Od.* 3.73–74 = 9.254–255). On his last voyage, the "Cretan" Odysseus relates, he and his companions set off for Egypt. He does not say what they intended to do there, only that he told his men to stay quiet while he sent out scouts. His men, however, invaded the Egyptian farmland, looting, killing, and kidnapping women and children; the Egyptians responded in force, killing some of his men and enslaving others. He himself, however, successfully supplicated the king of the Egyptians, who received him as a guest. Seven years he spent in Egypt, and "collected much property from the men of Egypt, for they all gave it" (*Od.* 14.285–286). He then accepted the invitation of a deceitful Phoenician who entertained him for some time in Phoenicia and then took him along to Libya with the secret intention of selling him into slavery. On the way they were wrecked; our narrator ended up in Thesprotia where the king took him in, gave him clothes, and sent him along in a passing Thesprotian boat bound for Doulichia with instructions to deliver him to the king there. These sailors, however, decided to sell him as a slave; they stripped him and tied him up. He managed to get untied and escaped. That is his story.

Obviously a great variety of things can happen to *lēistēres*: riches, death, slavery, entertainment. Its opportunities can even include, or be created by, market exchange—as the Phoenicians in Eumaeus's life story had used the opportunity produced by a year spent selling trinkets on the shore to seduce a local slave girl (herself a kidnapping victim) and kidnap the king's son (*Od.* 15.415–475). This kind of gypsy trading does not constitute commerce in any sense useful to the understanding of development. Indeed, as Thucydides well understood, below a certain level of social organization commerce inhibits the development of commerce: "once they began to go about back and forth in ships they turned to *lēisteia*" (Thucydides 1.5.1). Wealth of any kind stimulates theft; the thieves then use the resources so accumulated to steal more rather than to produce more.

For a long time the contact of the eastern Mediterranean with the West seems to have been largely of this kind; in the absence of textual evidence it is hard to tell, because material remains at best tell us that people from one place have visited another, not what they did there. Nor is there a clean distinction between piracy and commerce; the young Phaeacian calls the profits of the trader *harpalea*, "snatched." In those times it was not safe to travel for any purpose except as part of a band of armed men, and force available for defensive purposes could easily go over to the attack. The epic, however, understands the difference between viking and trade; *lēistēres* "wander wantonly" (*mapsadiōs*), "not on business" (*ou kata prēxin*)[20] (*Od.* 3.72 = 9.253). *Prēxis* by contrast is less random; it is a mode of enterprise planned with some rational expectation of advantageous result secured with determined means in particular places. The beginnings of exploration of the West *kata prēxin* probably belong to the ninth century B.C., probably involved the Phoenicians, and probably centered on Sardinia. There the Phoenicians seem to have been joined by Greeks from Euboea, sometime very early in the eighth century. Slightly later, ports of call in Etruria were added, and rapidly they became the primary interest of the western trade.[21]

By 750 B.C. there was an established Greek trade route linking by sea Etruria and the Near East. The Near Eastern end was at Al Mina on the Syrian coast, a predominantly Semitic emporion which seems to have had some Greek population by 800 B.C. The western end of this route was anchored by Pithekoussai on the island of Ischia in the bay of Naples. Both of these communities served for transit of goods; we also have archaeological evidence for the smelting of Etruscan iron on Pithekoussai. The areas that they served were beyond them, as far east as Urartia by Lake Van in southern Armenia, and at least as far west as Etruria. The trade route united two areas well-fitted to trade with one another: Etruria was a source of metal, especially iron, chronically in demand in the Near East; the Near East, in turn, provided luxury goods to Etruria, which thereby entered upon its orientalizing period.[22]

Once the link is made between two substantial areas with complementary demands the result is rapid development; it is a little like clos-

---

[20] In later Greek, a *prēxis* is a transaction—usually, but not necessarily, monetary. The word, in any case, has implications of fixed purpose and definite understanding.

[21] This story is told, and argued with extensive references to the supporting bibliographies, in Ridgway (1992) and in Tandy (1997).

[22] The evidence is most recently reviewed in Ridgway (1992), and also in Coldstream (1994); Popham (1994); Ridgway (1994); Snodgrass (1994).

ing an electrical circuit. Trade, *prēxis*, now became a livelihood for certain individuals who were in a position to take advantage of the new opportunities, mostly Phoenician and Euboean Greeks, with some scattering (on the evidence of the pottery) of Syrians and Rhodians. By the last half of the eighth century Pithekoussai had grown to a population of between four and six thousand, predominantly Greek but with a substantial Semitic element, and the women mostly Italian.[23] It was something of a boom town and had the look of a mining community (even though the actual mines were hundreds of miles away, on Elba and elsewhere): cosmopolitan, egalitarian, and (insofar as it lacked a substantial agricultural base) impermanent. By 700 B.C. Pithekoussai was a ghost town; the currents of trade had shifted and the population moved away, in some part to the mainland, to Cumae, which became the long-term Greek center in Campania.

The long-distance middleman trade between Etruria and the Near East powered the heroic period of Greek development, which was also the period from which we inherit Greek heroic poetry. From the beginning, however, this trade in metals and luxury goods was paralleled by another type. As early as 800 B.C. Corinthian transport jars were reaching Otranto, at the southern tip of Apulia;[24] they can hardly have contained anything but Greek agricultural produce. Otranto was never a Greek community. Therefore these jars are evidence for the beginnings of international trade in Greek agricultural commodities.[25]

The exchange of agricultural commodities no doubt originated in inequalities of local production;[26] the Mediterranean is all microclimates and throughout its history has been subject to localized droughts. When, on the other hand, a district had a good year it produced a surplus which could be disposed of advantageously elsewhere. This seems to be the kind of trade envisaged by the *Works and Days*. Hesiod says nothing about what the seafaring farmer will bring home in exchange for his crops; he calls it only *kerdos*, "gain." Presumably the starving districts had to part with some of their hoarded valuables, usually in the form of metals.

[23] Ridgway (1992), pp. 67, 102.

[24] D'Andria (1979); D'Andria (1984).

[25] For a discussion of these two types of trade—focused, however, on the first type—see Will (1973); Mele (1979) distinguishes *prēxis*, long-distance trade in metals carried on as a primary activity (probably by those elite figures who commanded the resources to undertake it), from what he calls *ergon* trade, the type described by Hesiod, which is worked into the farmer's year as a subordinate activity. In the long run, however, Greek trade turned out to be institutionally a development of early *prēxis*, but with the cargoes provided by Hesiod and his ilk.

[26] Cf. Rackham (1990), pp. 106–107.

The arrival of Corinthian produce as far away as Italy suggests, however, a different pattern with long-term implications. Here comes into play Greek intensive agriculture, particularly of the vine and the olive; Greek soils and climates were far better suited to these crops than to the staple grains the Greeks consumed. The Salentine, the hinterland of Otranto, is (although no Kansas) an open, reasonably fertile territory, comparatively well suited to grain. An exchange relation between these two territories immediately increased the value of Italian wheat—now worth Greek wine and oil, luxury goods in this part of the world—and at the same time increased the de facto productivity of Greek farms; acreage that had grown wheat for four people could now produce wine and oil worth bread for, say, eight. Even when the cost of the exchange had been paid there remained for the Greek farmer a substantially higher return, measured in staples.

Greek intensive agriculture, therefore, was not only a technology and a set of skills. It was a social organization in two senses: private ownership of the smallholding motivated these skills and techniques, and an international network made it possible for Greek farmers to make the most effective use of the soil, growing for their own consumption when possible, but for the market when preferable. The exchange of "wine for grain" (Aristotle *Politics* 1257a27) became the typical form of Greek commerce; while most districts continued to aspire to autarky the level of such exchange became sufficient by the sixth century to generate an infrastructure—warehouses, law courts, reliably available loans. Certain communities—most notably, Aegina—lived primarily by the carrying trade.[27] By that time the Greeks had made contact with Egypt and the southern Ukraine; these are beyond the southern and northern limits of the olive, and these markets gave new value to Greek oil.

Oil, in fact, was the export commodity par excellence; when Solon barred exports, we are told, he exempted oil (Plutarch *Solon* 24.1). Olive oil as a cash crop is post-Homeric; in Homer the olive is one fruit tree in a garden among others, and its oil is for external use only.[28] As olives were planted up the Greek hillsides the oil no doubt found an increasing home market and was put to a greater variety of uses, but the market for oil was primarily overseas. By the fifth century some Greek communities—most notably, Athens—imported the greater part of their wheat, and oil probably paid for much of this.

Whereas the long-distance trade in metals might involve Greeks only as middlemen, trade in agricultural commodities involved them as primary producers and changed the pattern of production. The first was

[27] Figueira (1981).
[28] Mele (1979), p. 75.

an alternative to agriculture that could make a few families rich; the second involved the monetization of agriculture itself and changed the character of riches. The surplus accumulated in the great houses was no longer dissipated in display or held against future consumption within the community; it was salable, which is to say, transformable into luxury goods, which could be saved and also turned into resources for further development. In the Greek economy such resources were mobilized not so much by direct investment through ownership of an enterprise as by lending to the entrepreneurs. The social power of the rich was exercised as creditors.

This transformation of riches entailed the transformation of the rich. Their task in the new order was to finance the infrastructure and bankroll the exchange network that made Greek agriculture successful. Surely in Greek cities generally the elite families were known as landholders, but even the largest holdings were fairly small, not more than five times the size of a smallholding. Real property remained the most reliable and reputable, the foundation of fortune and status, but there simply was not room in these communities for great estates (except perhaps in Thessaly). Most of the wealth of these families was held in precious metals. The whole mythology of Greek wealth turns on this kind of mobile and fungible resource: We hear, for instance, how the Alcmaeonidae at Athens founded their fortunes when an ancestor so amused Croesus that Croesus literally showered him with gold; later the family, in exile from their lands and city, had the resources to rebuild the temple at Delphi in marble instead of (as contracted) ordinary stone. Resources of this kind could be invested in the high-risk, high-profit sectors, particularly maritime trade and mining, and they were available for overseas development.

Long-term economic development is founded on reliable opportunities for reinvestment, so that new productivity becomes in turn the basis for newer productivity. That is how development happens. Given the agricultural base of the Greek economy, such reinvestment had to be primarily in agriculture. To some extent it could take the form of "improvements": drainage, roads, terracing (although, oddly enough, there is no literary evidence for terracing in the archaic or classical period).[29] The most important form of agricultural reinvestment, however, was colonization, which provided a livelihood for "extra sons" through an inheritance pattern whereby one son got the land and an-

---

[29] Rackham (1990), p. 103. There is a Greek word for a rough stone wall, *haimasia*, and mentions of building these are often taken as references to terracing, but a *haimasia* can also be an enclosure wall.

other some movable property,[30] enough to serve as a stake in a new community or in an established community receiving new citizens. For four hundred years the Greek frontier was open; the world said to the young what the laws said to Socrates: "Perhaps you want to go off to a colony if we and the city do not suit you" (Plato *Crito* 51d). The steady growth of the Hellenic world over this period can be understood as steady reinvestment in that intensive Mediterranean agriculture which the Greeks were the first to master, the culture of the vine and olive, and steady development of the exchange relations that made it profitable. In the colonial areas those relations were often between a Greek coast and an indigenous interior, involving the exchange of Greek agricultural produce for wool, meat, timber, pitch, and other commodities that were cheaply produced by the indigenes and that the Greek coastal cities were then often able to export. Colonization—which included the steady generation of subcolonies by existing colonies—completes the schema that made Greek development work: Intensive agriculture produced the commodities whose value was enhanced through international exchange, and the new wealth so generated was reinvested in intensive agriculture through extensions of Greek agricultural settlement. Thus more people produced more goods, which produced more people, which produced more production.

Colonies and Citizenship

The colonies provide our best evidence for the Greek idea of citizenship; they were founded *ep' isēi kai homoiēi*, on a basis of equal shares and equivalent status.[31] This ideal was inscribed on the landscape by the geometric land survey for which we have direct evidence at Metapontum, in Thessaly, and in the Crimea,[32] and indirect evidence as early as Megara Hyblaea, one of the very first Sicilian colonies. Colonial land evidently was normally laid out in rectangular parcels, each about fifty plethra (about ten acres), the conventional size of a family farm;[33]

---

[30] The mythical paradigm for this solution was the arrangement (which proved unviable) between the sons of Oedipus, as the story was told in Hellanicus (*FGH* 4 fr. 98); this version was already in Stesichorus, if the Lille Stesichorus (see ll. 20–24) is authentic. See also Cameron (1968).

[31] For a monographic treatment of this topic see Asheri (1966).

[32] For bibliography see Jameson (1990), p. 173n.4; add Pericika (1970) and Adamesteanu (1974).

[33] Burford-Cooper (1974).

these parcels were then distributed by lot to the citizens—whether original or reinforcements.[34]

A distribution of land, of course, does not imply equality of citizenship. Homer tells us that when Nausithoos founded Phaeacia he "divided the fields" (*Od.* 6.10) but this community, as we have seen, was hierarchical and redistributive. A contrasting case is that of the territories of the United States of America where, after a geometric survey, the land was allocated to individuals on application to the government and sold at a token price. Here the best land went to the first-comers; the land could be sold at a fixed per-acre price because the value of the land appreciated as it was settled, so that eventually there were buyers for the least attractive parcels. Such a system rewards entrepreneurs and (given the overall failure of the various Homestead Acts) makes land into a speculative commodity.

In Greek colonial settlements, however, the whole body of the settlers arrived, in principle at least, together;[35] as soon as the "god Kleros" (Plato *Laws* 741b) had placed them on the land they began to function as citizens. As smallholders they were not tied to the land, but the land tied them to the city; such a citizen owns land not as an investment but as (however acquired) his birthright, his livelihood. Karl Marx states this ideology as follows:

> The community—as a state—is, on the one hand, the relationship of these free and equal private proprietors to each other, their combination against an outside world—and at the same time their safeguard. The community is based on the fact that its members consist of working owners of land, small peasant cultivators; but in the same measure the independence of the latter consists in their mutual relation as members of the community. . . . To be a member of the community remains the precondition for the appropriation of land, but in his capacity as a member of the community the individual is a private proprietor. . . . We have here the precondition for *property* in land—i.e., for the relation of the working subject to the natural conditions of his labor as belonging to him. But this "belonging" is mediated through his existence as a member of the state—hence through a *precondition* which is regarded as divine, etc. . . . The precondition for the continued existence of the community is the maintenance of equality among its free self-sustaining peasants, and their individual labor as the condition of the continued exis-

---

[34] Cyrene provides an example of the latter: Herodotus (IV.159) tells us that the colony remained small until the third generation, when the city under Battus the Lucky sent out a call for *epoikoi*, additional settlers, who were promised a *gēs anadasmos*, a distribution of land.

[35] Delphi warned the Cyrene *epoikoi* that those who came late would miss the distribution.

tence of their property. Their relations to the natural conditions of labor are those of proprietors; but personal labor must continuously establish these conditions as real conditions and as objective elements of the personality of the individual, of his personal labor.[36]

Marx here explains the political implications of the *Works and Days*: The labor of the smallholder was not merely a livelihood but also a claim to the land and (since land is conceived as a share of the common territory) to membership in the group. This claim, in practice, was doubled by military service, which was also proprietary: As the smallholders owned their tools, the hoplites owned their arms. The city-state thus appears as a territory that was appropriated by individuals distributed over it, and defended collectively by the same persons ranged at its borders. It is urban only in the sense that its citizens gather also at the center for peaceful collective purposes: politics and ritual.

Marx, who is here concerned with the difference between property in antiquity and real property in the bourgeois order, describes the city-state as essentially classless. Marx in fact describes not the actual but the ideal shape of these communities, an "original" condition of property that the colonies attempted to recover at the moment of foundation, through the initial distribution.

If Marx missed the reality of class in the city-state it is perhaps because, like most later writers on the ancient economy, he conceived class conflict in terms of the propertied versus the unpropertied, the bourgeoisie versus the proletariat; in the ancient city, by contrast, class conflict was within the category of the propertied. Secondarily Marx recognizes conflict between different types of property, a trading interest, for example, versus a landed interest. The Marxist tendency in classical history has typically attempted to identify conflicts of this latter type. However, conflict as we actually encounter it in our evidence is nearly always in terms of agrarian questions, that is, in terms of the maintenance of the smallholding and the protection of the smallholder. The paradox of property among the Greeks (and in Rome also, as it developed—hence the Gracchi) is this: Smallholding was the basis of Greek development and the smallholder, as producer and warrior, the fundamental form of the citizen, yet smallholding was always a fragile institution.

Nor was this fragility in any direct sense the result of trade and the new wealth thereby generated. The relation of international trade to Greek development is, as I have tried to show, subtle and complex, so

---

[36] This is from Marx's notes headed *Formen die der Kapitalistischen Production vorhergehen*; the passage as here translated may be found in *Pre-capitalistic Economic Formations*, ed. E. J. Hobsbawm, trans. J. Cohen, London: Lawrence and Wishart, 1964, 72–73.

complex that both those who have minimized its importance and those who have exaggerated it have found plenty of material for their arguments. Trade perfected Greek intensive agriculture, making possible increased yields and lowering risk. Trade explored the world and made the colonies possible. Trade generated new wealth for reinvestment, and trade changed the meaning of wealth so that this wealth was available, not dissipated through redistribution. Trade, in fact, was in all probability the catalyst that, in the somehow peculiarly favorable conditions of the Greek late geometric period, produced in that society private property. And yet (perhaps because market exchange never became for the Greeks a truly reputable form of behavior) there never developed among the citizens a specific commercial interest. Indeed it has often been remarked that—in Athens, at least, the only commercial state for which we have a substantial amount of evidence—the citizens preferred to leave much of the commercial activity in the hands of resident aliens.

There is no question that the Greeks themselves conceived class conflict as conflict between rich citizens and poor citizens, that they conceived of the poor as nevertheless propertied, and of the rich as very rich. Yet it is unclear in what these riches, in the absence of large estates, actually consisted or how they were employed. How was this wealth acquired and held profitably? Certainly some of it was employed in mining, which was the capital-intensive (counting slaves as rapidly depreciated capital) and high-profit industry of antiquity. Probably much wealth was employed, somehow, in financing the international trade in agricultural commodities. Finally the rich, while they had to pay taxes, were also able to hold office, and no doubt often made a substantial return on their opportunities in the political sphere. But all this is rather conjectural. What we do hear about is agricultural debt.

Max Weber has given perhaps the most useful, because most universal, statement of the social power of wealth in a monetized economy:

> It is the most elemental economic fact that the way in which the disposition over material property is distributed among a plurality of people, meeting competitively in the market for purposes of exchange, in itself creates specific life-chances. According to the law of marginal utility . . . this mode of distribution monopolizes the opportunity for profitable deals for all those who, provided with goods, do not necessarily have to exchange them. . . . This mode of distribution gives to the propertied a monopoly on the possibility of transferring property from the sphere of use as a "fortune" to the sphere of "capital goods"; that is, it gives them the entrepreneurial function and all chances to share directly or indirectly in the returns on capital. . . .

"Property" and "lack of property" are, therefore, the basic categories of all class situations.[37]

Weber's language is somewhat problematic; he appears to be saying that the propertied have a monopoly on property. In fact this apparent tautology captures the ambiguity of the Greek situation: Class conflict could take place within the category of the propertied because it was a conflict between two social meanings of property, between the small-holders, whose property was a livelihood, and the "propertied" families, whose resources enabled them to finance the livelihood of others.

The patterns of Greek credit most extensively studied have been in international trade; within the commercial sector the creditors funded development in a way not utterly different from the ways in which capitalists fund industrialism, and very similar to the styles of credit typical of early modern trade, of Renaissance Florence or Venice. Even in relation to this last case, however, there is an important difference: Early modern trade turned mostly on the exchange of raw materials for processed goods—especially wool for textiles—so that the early modern city was primarily a community of craftsmen. Greek commerce turned primarily on the exchange of specialized agricultural produce for staples, and was therefore agricultural at both ends. Much Greek lending was to the Greek agricultural producers, and in this sector lending seldom financed new productivity; rather the smallholders had to borrow when the land failed to sustain them, to make up the shortfall of a bad season. In lending of this type "capital goods" display their naked social power.

The development of private property, in fact, was equivalent to the monetization of the economy. The smallholders now related to the rich not as their asymmetrically related social partners, but in terms of a relation defined by commodities and their value. When the smallholder ran short he had to come to those who still controlled the surplus; their interaction, however, was on a new basis. The ant in actuality does not turn the grasshopper away; she rather proposes to tide her over by lending her a winter store—at a rate of interest, of course. The security the creditor took was the livelihood of the debtor, his land and/or (unless such loans had been made illegal) his person. The smallholder who borrowed when times were bad was in effect selling next year's crop at a reduced price, and therefore the next year he had to do better than usual just to get even. Agricultural debt by nature

---

[37] From *Wirtschaft und Gesellschaft*, part 3, chapter 4. The passage quoted may be found as translated in *From Max Weber*, ed. Gerth and Mills, New York: Oxford University Press 1946, 181–182.

accumulates, leading to the dispossession and even the enslavement of
the smallholders—a process best documented for Athens just before
the reforms of Solon.[38] Thus the capacity to lend showed itself a social
power. It was this social power that constituted the primary class division within Greek society: the division between a creditor class and a
debtor class.

As more and more of the productive base became concentrated in
the hands of the creditor class, however, the political base of that class
would contract, until the debtors found their savior in a lawgiver or,
more often, a tyrant. Throughout the history of the city-states the economic demand that focused social unrest and popular revolution was
always for the cancellation of agricultural debt and the redistribution
of the land. Thus the very economic success of the creditors could lead
them into political disaster; their piecemeal dispossession of the smallholders could lead to revolution and to their own catastrophic dispossession as a class. The classes in their antipathy needed to work out
some way to live with each other.

Private property was thus the socioeconomic basis of the Greek political order, and also a persisting threat to that order; that paradox reflects the doubleness of real property in a monetized economy, where
land is both a livelihood and a commodity—if not for sale, at least
available as security for debt. Private property gave institutional form to
the bond between the citizen and the land, and thus placed him in the
community through a mythologically resonant link between nature and
culture; at the same time private property set citizen against citizen as
profitable investment created social power for some and threatened
others.

The Politics of Class Conflict

As development of the *polis* was a kind of first modernization, so also the
plousioi, the propertied, were a kind of first bourgeoisie, a class defined
by money and its social power. The city-state, however, was not parallel to
that of the medieval burg, whose propertied elite called themselves
"bourgeoisie" in self-differentiation from the aristocracy. In the classical
period the Greek rich were landholders, often with inherited ritual
privileges; many claimed heroic lineage and were in that sense aristocrats. On the other hand, their wealth was not based on ground rents
(although they might well have a tenant or two on their farmland) nor

---

[38] Probably a parallel development motivated the *palintokia* at Megara: Figueira (1985),
pp. 147–148.

did they control large numbers of agricultural workers. Their power was visibly exercised as political power; the political arena was both the sphere in which they pursued their interest and the sphere in which they collectively maintained the constitutional structure that made that pursuit of interest possible in a nondestructive form.

The paradox of property, in fact, is the archaic version of the "contradictions of capitalism"; the creditor class in this respect formally resembled the capitalistic bourgeoisie. In its own way the creditor class also was a class in competition with itself, which faced the necessity of regulating the conditions of its own competition. The most elegant statement of this contradiction is also the earliest extensive prose document in Greek political thought: the debate of the Persian conspirators in Herodotus (3.80–82).

In spite of Herodotus's protestations to the contrary, this debate in its origins can have been no more Persian than are Montesquieu's *Persian Letters*; its concepts are entirely Greek. Otanes opens the debate by praising democracy, which he describes simply as the self-government of the community by its members; "I move that we set aside monarchy and support the masses, for in their multitude is the whole." Megabyzus introduces the distinction of the classes, and describes it as absurd that the inferior multitude should govern their superiors; "let us therefore, selecting a company of the best men, entrust power to them, and we ourselves shall be among them." Darius then settles the matter with an assertion of the necessity of monarchy, based on the impossibility of any other regime. "In an oligarchy where many pursue excellence in public affairs, powerful private hatreds are likely to happen"; therefore they fall into faction, and from faction into murder, making necessary a monarch. Furthermore "if the people rule it is impossible that there not be corruption (*kakotēs*). When there is corruption in public affairs there are not hatreds among the corrupt, but powerful friendships. The corrupt conspire together to manage public affairs. Things go on like this until someone becomes patron of the people and puts a stop to them. From this he is admired by the people, and through this admiration turns into monarch. So in this case also he makes it obvious that monarchy is the best."

The diagnosis is not far from that of Theognis and Solon one and even two centuries earlier: "it is precisely the excesses of an oligarchy that lead to *stasis*."[39]

Cyrnus, this city is pregnant, and I fear lest it bear a man
    To be corrector of our insolent corruption.

[39] Nagy (1985), p. 44; Nagy quotes the Persian debate in his discussion of the Theognis passage, and cites relevant diction from Solon.

The citizens here are still sensible, but their leaders
  Are set on course to fall into great corruption.
Never, Cyrnus, did good men destroy a city
  But when insolence begins to please the corrupt
And they destroy the people and give judgment to the unjust
  For the sake of their own profit and power
Do not expect that city to remain calm for long
  Even if now it lies in deep peace—
When all these things become dear to the corrupt,
  Profit coming along with public corruption.
That is how civil war happens, and murder of kindred,
  And monarchies. May such never please our city.

Theognis 39–52

Because there is no limit to gain, says Theognis, because those who live for it respect no limits, they fall to violence among themselves and provoke the citizens to support a "corrector" to suppress them; either way the result is some kind of monarchy.

It is true that class difference in the Persian debate is presented not in economic but in ethical terms; the claim of the few to rule is founded not on their property but on their wisdom. "How could the people know anything, since they were never taught and have nothing noble proper to them, but rush forward falling on affairs without sense, like a river in flood?" Wisdom and property are, however, for the Greeks forever correlated—not so much because the wise acquire property (as in Ben Franklin) as because the management of property is a rough school of wisdom. The most extended statement of this point is in Xenophon, in the form of a Socratic dialogue (Xenophon *Memorabilia* 3.4). Socrates meets Nicomachides, an old soldier who has been passed over in the election for general in favor of Antisthenes "who knows nothing except making money." Well, says Socrates, that's not so bad, if he can provide the troops with supplies.

"Merchants also," says Nicomachides, "can make money, but that's no reason to make them generals."

Socrates replies by observing that Antisthenes loves victory; his choruses always win their contest. "Wherever a person is in charge, if he can see what is required and is able to provide it he will be a good administrator (*prostatēs*) whether he is in charge of a household or a city or an army." Socrates goes on to develop an elaborate parallel between the task of the householder and the general: Both must manage their subordinates effectively, must be able to seek the additional help they need, must be careful and energetic; both have enemies and must be utterly committed to defeating them. "So, Nicomachides, do not despise men who run large households (*hoi oikinomikoi andres*). The care of private business differs only in scale from public, and otherwise is pretty much the same." The class line, like all cultural phenomena, was therefore self-reinforcing—not only ideologically (the rich are the sort of people who ought to rule because rule ought to be given to that sort of people) but also empirically: They were actually, *en gros*, the most competent group.

Because the practical management of everyday life, both public and private, was everywhere concentrated in the hands of those who owned large households, every Greek city-state was more or less an oligarchy; the propertied families, because they monopolized disposable resources, provided the government with its tax base; at the same time, because of their privileged education and life experience, they provided the administration with a pool of somewhat qualified office-holders. They were the political heirs of the archaic *basilēes*; indeed in most cases they must have been the same families.

The Persian debate assumes that the same class is de facto in power under either oligarchy or democracy. In the former they display the weakness of a class in competition with itself, struggling for resources; in the latter they steal resources from the people, the ostensible sovereign, and conspire against their common class adversary. In either case they turn out to be the collective enemy of the community principle as stated by Otanes: "in the multitude is the whole." Therefore although they are the only class capable of power, they are unable as a class to hold power, and (this is the real point of the debate) politics is impossible. Darius concludes that the only workable regime is monarchy, which in the Greek cities bore the name of tyranny.

For the Greeks tyranny is never a legitimate regime;[40] it represents a failure to establish any regime on a legitimate basis (although the tyrant must rely on the same governing class as every other regime; we should therefore not be surprised when we find—as we do—that the same families hold office under the tyranny as before and after it). The Persian debate is therefore a particularly elegant (if consciously paradoxical) statement of the contradictions of the city-state. The constitutional ideal of Otanes is shown to deny the reality of classes, and the reality of classes is then asserted to falsify that ideal. Darius then gives an accurate if schematic account of the two ways things go wrong. Struggles within the governing class may lead to the power of a faction, the kind of factional tyranny the Greeks called a *dunasteia* (cf. Thucydides 3.62.4; Aristotle *Politics* 1292b), or their power may be over-

---

[40] Although the Greeks did recognize as legitimate a dictator—the so-called *aisumnetēs*—under certain circumstances.

thrown by a populist leader, usually with slogans of cancellation of debts and redistribution of the land; the result (in the archaic period at least) was a period of tyranny. Darius's account is so plausible that we are left puzzled by the fact that in the city-states constitutional government was ever made to work—sometimes even for prolonged periods. We are left, in fact, with the questions: How is it that, as development proceeded, new wealth was not once again, as in the older civilizations, collected at the center and managed in the interest of hierarchy? What made the politics of citizenship work?

The Politics of Class Relations

On the evidence of Homer, the political structure of the city-state was in place before development happened, and long before it received any formal codification; the politics of status set the mold for the emerging politics of class. The fundamental political institution of the Greeks, the *agorē*, the general meeting, is already commonplace in Homer; everyone comes but only a few may speak: the same who are foremost in battle and in domestic life, the *promachoi*, the *basilēes*. The others are there as an audience. These few speakers are the same who meet also by themselves, in an institution already called the *boulē*, the council; an *agorē* is in effect a council meeting conducted in public. The speakers generally address one another; sometimes they (as the actors say) "cheat," playing their remarks partly to the audience, but seldom do they formally address the crowd. The audience functions like any audience: they applaud, cheer, boo, and (at the worst) riot. They take no part in debate; the exceptional Thersites is introduced to prove this rule.

Because the audience in the Homeric assembly does not vote it might seem powerless; in fact it is essential. What takes place in public space has public meaning; by locating their debates in what Hannah Arendt called "the space of appearance" the *basilēes* subject themselves to the evaluation of the folk. The ultimate standard of appeal in Homer is *themis*, that which is "done" or "established" (ultimate in the sense that one cannot say: "this thing is *themis* but wrong"); the *agorē* is where *themis* is determined. *Themis* "opens and closes the *agorai* of men"; in the center of the Greek camp at Troy there is *agorē* and *themis*. Themis is a goddess, the wife of Zeus and his counselor; the voice of the people is the voice of this divinity. *Vox populi vox dei*. That voice is heard as the audience responds to the speakers—who in the assembly address one another without hierarchy, as peers; it is *themis* to dispute the word of your commander in the *agorē*. The *agorē* thus adumbrates the institution of citizenship.

This fundamental structure, relating actors to each other and to an audience, remained at the core of the Greek understanding of politics throughout the archaic and classical periods. It would be anachronistic to call it "theatrical" since the theater derived from the political arena rather than vice versa. More generally we can say that the Greeks were a live-performance culture. Nothing for them had public validity unless it had taken place before the whole body of the community—or at least an audience that could be taken to be that whole body, like the Athenian juries. Those who appeared in this public space, however, whatever the written rule might say, were a select few; without this status distinction the *agorē* could not have worked. Athenian assemblies, for example, where major issues of state were openly and contentiously discussed, were large crowds; once a month at least the quorum was set at six thousand. Quick arithmetic tells us that if one person in ten had something to say and speeches were held to five minutes, the assembly would last fifty hours. In fact the one time in literature when an unscheduled speaker does attempt to speak from the floor (at the beginning of Aristophanes' *Acharnians*) the chair calls the police and has him thrown out. We know nothing about how the calendar of speakers for the Athenian assembly was set, but somehow it was done, and done by people who knew who was supposed to be heard on a given issue.

It is not that democratic institutions were meaningless; on the contrary, as the moral power of the folk was rationalized through the counting of votes, through the creation of a council chosen by lot and thus representative of the mass, through the creation of popular law courts, the context of life (at Athens at least) changed radically. It is only that the fundamentally oligarchic character of society was assumed by these political institutions as their necessary precondition. Democracy was a form of government in which the ruling class conducted their disputes in public, and gave the public the power of mediation. In this way the archaic quasi bourgeoisie resolved the contradictions of archaic quasi capitalism; to the degree that their competition was translated from the economic sphere into the political arena they were able to compete and maintain the conditions of their competition by competing before an audience of free citizens which could limit and legitimate the outcome. Therefore the free smallholders were necessary to the few not only economically—as the creators of base productivity— but also politically.

Nevertheless this necessity does not in itself explain the viability of the system, since it was based on a sociological absurdity ("admitted foolishness" as Alcibiades calls it—Thucydides 6.89.6): The lower sort of people had power over the higher sort. This absurdity was workable only because of an ambiguity represented by the ambiguity of the word *dēmos*: the whole community, or else a part excluding the notables. As a part the many were unfit to govern, but as the representative of the whole, the vehicle of community standards, they were. Theirs was, however, a moral authority only; as persons they were subordinate but as a collective consciousness they were fit to evaluate their betters.

Moral authority, however, is in itself not strong. It was all too easy for the actors on the stage, like Agamemnon and the suitors in Homer, to ignore the mediation of the audience and to pursue their private interests to the point where they could be resisted only by violence—Darius's first form of dysfunction. Or else they could conspire to conceal their acts from the public and divide the spoil among themselves until one of their number, insufficiently gratified by their joint corruption, undertook the interests of the people as his own, as Cleisthenes took "the *dēmos* into his faction," and thereby "gained personal power over his own class"—Darius's second form of dysfunction. Such a one would be a tyrant or, more legitimately, a *prostatēs tou dēmou*, a "patron of the people." In either case constitutional government in the Greek sense was at risk. In other words, the social preconditions of the Greek political order were not sustainable by the operation of that order in itself; they had to be maintained by joint action on the social level.

That this was possible to the Greeks has much to do with their political self-consciousness; they were well aware of the problem of class and of the effects of the market and the paradox of property, and inventive in their attempts to manage these. In fact attempts to manage this paradox are thematic in four hundred years of Greek social legislation, both actual and utopian. Thus, for instance, we can understand the recurrent attempts to regulate consumption through sumptuary legislation, laws limiting expenditures on, say, weddings and funerals; these sought to mitigate inequality by forbidding the display of wealth, understanding that display provokes *phthonos*—that corrosive envy of the successful so pervasive in Greece as the ethical correlate of economic competition. Furthermore economic competition in a peaceable community was informally mitigated by the habit of generosity among those who could afford to be generous—both to each other and to their inferiors. The Greek term for this latter is *euergesia*; a poor family would have wealthy connections—a patron, almost; this is one of the meanings of *prostatēs*—to whom they could turn when they needed a dowry for a daughter or to ransom one of their own taken prisoner of war. In return for such benefactions, members of the poor family these served the wealthy family in certain ways, most particularly by providing political support. Parallel to these benefactions to private individuals were

the so-called liturgies, the funding of public services—particularly theatrical performances and other rituals, and military units—by persons
of wealth. Such liturgies, while compulsory, included a voluntary element; law-court speakers often claim to have spent on such a project
far more than the law required, and they seek for this largesse the favor
of the people in return. Thus the class line becomes a basis for cooperation. The basic principle is already stated in a fragment of Democritus:

> When the powerful endure to spend on behalf of those who have nothing, to
> serve and favor them, in this way immediately springs up pity, an end to
> isolation, the existence of comrades and mutual assistance and concord
> among the citizens and other good things such as no one would be able to
> number. (Democritus Fr. B 255 DK)

Through *euergesiai* and liturgies a private fortune was re-embedded
in the social fabric; Xenophon's Socrates, speaking to Critobulus (ad-
mittedly one hundred times as rich as himself) paradoxically describes
this re-embedding as a sort of dispossession of the rich:

> My own resources, he said, are sufficient to provide me with what is enough
> for me, while when I consider the role you have assumed and your reputa-
> tion I doubt whether yours would be sufficient even if it were three times as
> great. . . . In the first place, you must sacrifice often and grandly; otherwise I
> think neither gods nor men will endure it. Then you must entertain many
> foreigners, and these magnificently. Then you must feast your fellow citizens
> and benefit them, or you will lack allies. Furthermore I notice that the city
> even now requires you to pay large sums, in support of the cavalry and the
> choruses and the gymnasia, also presidencies (*prostateis*); if there is a war I
> know they will assign you triremes and taxes on capital such as you will find
> difficult to meet. And if they decide you have fallen short in any way I know
> that the Athenians will punish you just as if you had deprived them of some-
> thing of their own by stealing it. (Xenophon *Oeconomicus* 2.5)

Property at Athens is private but it also belongs to the state.

Because the rich are members of the community, the community has
certain—rather indefinite—claims on their riches. These claims, however, are often seen as illegitimate, as the attempt of the poor to steal
from the rich their riches by political means, under cover of law. That
is the point of the little conversation on the meaning of law preserved
in Xenophon's *Memorabilia* (1.2.40–46). Alcibiades asks Pericles if it is
not lawless for the tyrant to make people do things against their will,
and for the few rich to join in an oligarchy which governs the people
against their will. Pericles agrees. "And when the whole multitude gains
power over the moneyed few, and writes a rule without persuading

them, this would be force rather than law?" Pericles, the great demo-crat, has no answer to this question. It seems that the membership of the rich in the community was somewhat tentative, and that the assign-ment of their riches to the community interest was often seen as a continuation of class war by other means.

The rich, therefore, as they seek to maintain the smallholders as a class, seek also to keep them and their demands at a distance. Aristotle remarks:

> The best populace (*dēmos*) is agricultural, so that it is possible to create a democracy where the multitude lives by farming or herding. Because their fortunes are modest they are kept busy, so they cannot attend the assembly very often. Because they do not have the necessities they pass their time in farm work and do not desire other people's goods, but prefer agricultural work to politics or officeholding—providing that the profits of office are kept small. Most people aim at gain rather than honor. (Aristotle *Politics* 1318b10–18)[41]

Aristotle, in contrast to Marx, places the smallholder in a clearly de-fined context of class relations. Aristotle writes from the point of view of the propertied townsman, for whom the ideal ordinary citizen is the Hesiodic farmer who keeps his distance from the political center and utterly devotes himself to the productivity of his land. It is then possible to grant political rights to the mass of citizens, because the mass will not care to exercise them. This is the paradox of the emerging Greek peasantry: They were politically empowered in theory (which is impor-tant) but not much in practice (which is also important). So we can see how the *Works and Days* came to be an ethical classic of the Greeks, quoted by the heirs of the very *basilēes* Hesiod despises. Hesiod and his fellows, as Hesiod makes it clear, are part of the city in the sense that they have access to the *agorē*, the arena of political dispute—but they will be well advised (by Hesiod) to keep out of it.

A democracy, Aristotle implies, presumes the existence of small farmers more interested in gain than honor, and of a compact urban stratum more interested in honor than in gain—because insulated from the struggle for existence by affluence—a governing class, in fact. A stable democracy, it seems, presumes inequality; the city consists (in princi-ple) of free smallholders, but is managed (in practice) by the urban rich. These alone could underwrite the exchange network and provide a tax base; the town was the place where production was financed and

---

[41] Cf. Aristotle *Politics* 1297b6–8: "The poor are content to keep the peace even when they have no share in offices (*timai*) so long as they suffer no outrage (*hubris*) and their property is not taken."

where public services were provided—out of contributions by the rich. It is the town and its money that provides the means of public life, and in this sense the moneyed are the only genuine public men.

But this public power tended to result in the concentration within the same circle of all material property as well. Therefore efforts to embed riches within the polity were supplemented by legislative efforts to limit the most socially destructive effect of economic competition, namely, the progressive concentration of real property in the hands of a restricted circle of owners. Aristotle in the *Politics* notes a number of projects and legislative acts intended to stabilize smallholdings, *klēroi*, as the only secure basis for a stable society.

> The inequality of wealth has a great effect on the political community, and many of the ancients evidently recognized this; there are, for instance, the laws of Solon; others have a law which forbids one from owning just as much land as he might wish; similarly the laws may forbid one from selling property (as among the Locrians there is a law that one may not sell unless he can show some obvious misfortune which has overtaken him); the law is still to maintain the ancient *klēiroi*. (Aristotle *Politics* 1266b14–21)

> With regard to maintaining a farming population some of the laws in force in many places in ancient times have a general usefulness, either that one was absolutely forbidden to own land beyond a certain amount, or at least within an area a specified distance from the citadel and the city. In fact in antiquity, at least, it was actually the law that in many cities one could not sell the first *klēiroi*. Then there is the law they attribute to Oxylus,[42] which has much the same effect: that there is some portion of anybody's holding against which he may not borrow. (Aristotle *Politics* 1319a6–14)

The proliferation of these projects—even if some of them were somewhat effective—shows that in some fundamental sense the paradox of private property was insoluble.

In the context of these legislative efforts we can better understand the legislated distribution of real property characteristic of the colonies. In the colonies, as we have seen, the ideal of citizenship was inscribed on the land in the form of equal *klēroi*. This distribution of property is the "correct" economic basis for the city-state. However, everything we know about the colonies tells us that they suffered very much the same social and political vicissitudes as the mother cities: civil conflict, tyranny, redistribution of the land. The colonies therefore as they exemplify agrarian legislation with particular clarity also dem-

---

[42] Oxylus was the legendary founder of Elis; to attribute a law regulating mortgages to him is for us an obvious anachronism, but presumably served the Elians to fix the law as immemorial.

onstrate its ineffectiveness. The equality of citizens, after all, could not be secured by the initial equality of *klēroi*; some brought with them more money than others, and these became a creditor class as soon as the need for lending arose—which is to say, as soon as the settlers had had some actual experience of agriculture. If some of these colonies were more stable than others (and Aristotle, in the passage quoted, cites a Locrian law, probably from Epizephyrian Locri, one of the most stable colonies), that is not because they were more equal in the beginning, but because they took somewhat effective steps to maintain stability as they went along—and in this also they were no different than the stable cities of the homeland.

The contribution of the colonies was different from this: The utopian promise of the frontier, even if it could not be kept, gave hope of a fresh start for persons and communities. (Not for nothing is "Novus Ordo Sæclorum" inscribed upon the Great Seal of the United States.) Also in practical terms the colonies provided a safety valve for increasingly heated Greek development. Social "heat" in this context can be given a simple definition: It is the presence of more visibly qualified persons than there are places for them to occupy in the exercise of their qualifications.[43] The safety valve creates new places. In terms of the family farm, these qualified persons are the "extra" sons; they are raised to farm but there are no farms for them. The same principle, however, applies to superior strata, and we can see that the colonies provided an outlet for "extra" leaders, for such as Dorieus of Sparta and Miltiades the Elder of Athens, sent away to exercise their leadership elsewhere because there was no comfortable use for them where they were. It may be that this contribution of the colonies to stability explains a discontinuity in Greek social conflict. As Alexander Fuks has pointed out there is an early phase of social conflict, in the seventh and particularly in the early sixth centuries.[44] This seems to have been the period when the contradictions of the city-state were confronted and, to a degree, resolved; at any rate from the time of the Seven Sages (c. 580 B.C.) we seem to have (starting later in Athens than elsewhere) relative social peace. Starting with the Peloponnesian War and continuing into the fourth century discord recommences—perhaps because the inadequacies of the earlier solutions only became obvious as the frontier began to close, heightening class tension.

In any case, all solutions to the social problems of the city-state were at best tentative, since the opposition of classes was built into its socio-

---

[43] This is a fundamental notion in Fried (1967), developed in relation to early Greek evidence by Tandy (1997), pp. 89–90.

[44] Fuks (1984), p. 12.

economic foundation. Everywhere the city-state was "two cities," of the rich and the poor, "ever plotting against each other" (Plato *Republic* 551d). Since this social reality, although it might be ameliorated by social legislation, could not be made to go away, it had everywhere to be addressed on the political level.[45] A successful polity was one that accepted this conflict and worked with it constitutionally in a effective way. No Greek democracy ever attempted to eliminate inequality; the aim of democracy, like that of every Greek constitution, was to manage relations between the classes—in the democratic case, by making the people the arbiters of conflicts within the governing class and thereby giving the members of that class a motive to behave, or at least to appear to behave, in the public interest.

When the interaction of the classes broke down the result was a tyranny—either the seizure of power by some members of the privileged class, as in the tyranny of the Thirty at Athens, or the seizure of power by some member of that class who, having developed a popular political base, could use it to suppress his fellows. Archaic tyrannies were generally of the latter type. They contributed, furthermore, to the constitutional development of the Greek cities; the tyrant, on behalf of his popular constituency, found himself asserting the community principle, and when at length the governing class regained constitutional power they found themselves further embedded in the principle thus asserted.

Tyranny, in fact, was in the archaic period (except in Dorian Sicily) a one-time event; whereas Darius describes what should be a cycle of recurrence, actual tyrannies lasted at most two generations and then did not recur. The tyrannies seem to have been critical phases in the political education of the Greeks, and in that sense necessary to the creation of constitutional government. They educated the governing class to their need of the smallholders in both political and economic terms: Oligarchy and democracy both could thrive only when the rich remained on decent terms with the poor. We may suspect, in fact, that most of the institutions I have described for the "re-embedding" of wealth arose after a tyranny, or (as in the case of Solon's laws) in fear of one.

Two of the great Greek cities notably avoided tyranny and this form of political education: Sparta and Epizephyrian Locri. These were also the cities thought to have been shaped by legendary, prehistoric, "original" lawgivers: Lycurgus and Zaleucus. Both were societies that took shape early; both, I suspect, aspired to avoid history through an almost ritualized social order; both, I suggest, sought not to regulate and nor-

---

[45] Cf. de Ste. Croix (1954).

malize class relations like other cities, but to avoid class competition altogether. About Sparta we know a good deal, about Locri, much less; I shall, however, proceed to suggest that from what we know of Sparta we can make some intelligent guesses about what Locri must have been.

Before we proceed to a description of Locri and to the comparison of these two polities it may be well, however, to summarize the theses stated in this chapter: (1) Greek economic development was coextensive with the development of private property, monetization of the economy, and market exchange; (2) Greek constitutional practice aimed everywhere, although by diverse means, to solve the social problem thus generated of conflict within the category of the propertied between a creditor and a debtor class; (3) everywhere this problem turned on the "agrarian question," which arose from the tendency of agricultural property to become concentrated in a progressively contracting circle of the propertied, as the smallholders became dispossessed through the accumulation of agricultural debt and parallel encumbrances upon the land. On the economic level the problem was that of putting money at the service of property without making property subject to the power of money; on the political level the problem was that of restraining the avarice produced among the rich by the pressure of their competition with one another, a competition that threatened with a loss of class status anyone who did not effectively exploit the economic opportunities which that status provided.

Part Three

EPIZEPHYRIAN LOCRI

Six

Epizephyrian Locri

LOCRI has been the object of extensive attention; Maria Parra's bibliography, which runs only through 1989 (BTCGI vol. 9, pp. 214–249), includes well over six hundred items with at least six each year since the mid-1950s, and the stream has not slackened since. In 1976 the annual Convegno at Taranto was devoted to the city (Locri Epizefirii 1977), with important papers by Musti, Torelli, and others; there is an excellent guide to the site and antiquarium[1] (now officially a museum) and a number of chapters on Locri in various general works on Magna Grecia. Nevertheless, there has been no complete, synthetic account of the evidence since Oldfather's idiosyncratic, not to say eccentric, article for Pauly-Wissowa (*RE*). Nor is such an account intended here. The reader, however, as a preface to the more hypothetical inquiry that follows after, does deserve some account of what is actually known about Locri and what evidence we have on which to build. In each section of this book I have attempted to begin from what is more or less certain, and only after stating this have gone on to work my way into possible implications of those facts. In this spirit I now present a geographical/historical account followed by a review of the archaeology of the place; this is to serve as a foundation for the cultural explorations of later chapters. The general reader may find what follows a bit heavy with detail; students of this material, of course, will see this as a mere rough sketch.

Locri in History

The city of the Locrians-by-Zephyrion stood on the Italian coast at the far southern end of the Adriatic—almost exactly in the latitude of Messina, in fact, but separated from the straits by the Aspromonte, a massif that rises some two thousand meters to form the toe of the Italian boot. All along the Adriatic side the hills run down to the sea, although somewhat less steeply here than elsewhere; ancient Locri stretched back from the coast and then up along a low rise between two gravel-bedded intermittent rivers, a rise which divided at the top into three

---

[1] Costamagna and Sabbione (1990).

low peaks, 140–150 meters above sea level. On the northernmost of these peaks was a small temple of Athena, evidently Athena Poliouchos; on the other two were two small independent fortresses (Livy 24.6.14–17). There was no acropolis as such.

The town straddled the ancient coastal road, and was thereby divided into two parts: a lower town on the flatter land between the road and the sea, laid out in regular blocks and in classical times densely settled, and an upper town (largely archaeologically unexplored), which may have included a substantial amount of open space. The enclosed area was 2.4 square kilometers (Foti 1977).

Along this coast, as throughout the West, the Greek colonists had occupied the shore, displacing the indigenes inward and upward. Locri controlled the coastline from her border with Caulonia on the north (probably the river Sagra) to the Halex (or, at some periods, to the Caicinos), which divided her from Rhegion. Not one of these rivers has been securely identified, but it is evident that the Locrian coast extended at least fifty to sixty kilometers. The extent of Greek penetration of the interior is, in the absence of a thorough archaeological survey, unclear. Nevertheless, it seems that Locri commanded a substantial territory; there is evidence for a rural Greek population as early as the mid-sixth century[2] The town, to judge by its extent, contained at least twenty to thirty thousand inhabitants; we can suppose at least as many free rural inhabitants. This means that Locri was what the Greeks called a *muriandros polis*, a city to be reckoned with, large enough to have (at least notionally) ten thousand adult male citizens. (The notional citizen-body of Athens, the largest Greek city—or in some periods second largest, after Syracuse—was thirty thousand.) Locri was in fact one of the five great cities of Greek Italy, along with Taras, Croton, Rhegion, and Cumae (Sybaris and its successor city Thurii, during their intermittent periods of prosperity, made a sixth).

Cumae played almost no part in Greek history; its relations were with the other Italian communities, particularly Etruria. It was from Cumae that, initially, the Etruscans and through them the Romans acquired Greek letters and many other things Greek. From the Greek point of view, however, the bay of Naples was a backwater, not on the road to anywhere; Greek commerce in this part of the world was in the hands of the Phocaean cities, primarily Massalia (modern Marseilles) and to some extent Velia. Taras, Croton, Rhegion, and Sybaris/Thurii, by contrast with Cumae, regularly appear in the Greek historical record, dominating between them the southern Adriatic coast of Italy. They have a rich history of competition and alliance. Locri is strikingly absent from

[2] Sabbione (1976a), pp. 368–370.

that history.[3] There are stories about the origins of the colony, to which we shall return. These are largely legendary. Then we hear nothing of the place until the Battle of the Sagra, where, we are told, the greatly inferior forces of Locri some time in the late sixth century totally defeated the enormous and arrogant army of Croton. That battle cannot be securely dated within fifty years, and whatever its historical reality it comes to us surrounded by legends. The archaeological material from Locri places the Greeks here from the mid-seventh century but (except for the Sagra) Locri has no part in the historical record before 494 B.C., when the Samians who had escaped from the Aegean after their defeat by the Persians at Lade took temporary refuge there (Herodotus 6.23.1). At this time Locri seems to have been on good terms with Rhegion, since it is Rhegion that intervenes to help the Samians to their final refuge, but by 477 B.C. Locri and Rhegion are at war; we have dedications at Olympia of Locrian spoils by both Rhegion and Messena from this period.[4] Messena and Rhegion were at that time ruled by Anaxilas and his son Cleophron;[5] Hieron of Syracuse intervened to protect Locri.[6] From this time until the mid-fourth century Locri appears as dependent on Syracuse, particularly on her tyrants.

During the Peloponnesian war Locri was the faithful ally of Syracuse, finally sending ships to fight Athens in Aegean waters (T. 8.91.2). When after the war Dionysius the Elder took power at Syracuse he used Locri as his Italian base, rewarding the city with a good share of the Italian territories he conquered (Diodorus 14.106.3, 107.2–3). He also married a Locrian woman, who bore his heir, Dionysus the Younger. This latter, after losing power in Syracuse, retired to Locri with catastrophic political results there. I shall have more to say about all this later.

In the third century, as the Italian peninsula began to be swept by warring peoples, Locri was at war with the Brettii (Nossis A.P. 6.132). Later the city passed back and forth between Pyrrhus and the Romans, as still later during the Punic wars she passed between the Romans and the Carthaginians. Her standing remained high enough to induce the Romans to repay, with interest, the treasures Scipio's legate had stolen from the sanctuary of Persephone (Livy 31.12.1–5), and in the time of Polybius she was still an independent city with pride in the peculiarity of her traditions.

The Locrians, indeed, were not like the others. Partly this difference

---

[3] Sources for Locrian history are conveniently collected by Niutta (1977).

[4] SEG 24 (1969), 304, 305, 311, 312—republished by Niutti (1977), p. 334.

[5] *Schol. Pindar 2nd Py.* 38, printed in Niutti (1977), p. 308.

[6] This event was narrated by Epicharmus (Fr. 98 Kaibel), the early classic Syracusan writer of comedies (*Schol. Pindar 1st Py.* 99 A), printed in Niutti (1977), p. 308.

appears in their absence from the historical narrative; theirs was a city that apparently was content, when possible, to have no history. Pindar (*10th Ol.* 19–20) says: "Calliope is their concern, and brazen Ares." Calliope we can understand; Locri had a place in the history of music. Xenocrates of Locri invented the "Locrian harmony" (*Schol. 10th Ol.* 19–20). Ares seems more dubious. Surely they were warriors, but their wars, so far as we hear of them, were primarily defensive. There was even a story about this, linking Locri to the greatest poet of the Greek West:

> Stesichorus told the Locrians that they must not be offensive (*hybristai*) so that their cicadas would not sing on the ground. (Aristotle *Rhetoric* 1395a)

This sentence requires some explication. Cicadas sit on trees to do their singing; a country where cicadas sat on the ground to sing would be a country with no trees at all, that is to say, a country laid waste, particularly by war. So the warning tells the Locrians that if they go on the offensive they will be laid waste.

The cicada has a special status at Locri; *along the river,* we are told,[7] *that marks the boundary between Locri and Rhegion, the cicadas sing on the Locrian bank, but not on the other.* This is supplemented by another story:[8] *When Euonymus of Locri competed in lyre-playing against Ariston of Rhegion at the Pythian games, Euonymus was victor with the help of a cicada who replaced the note of a broken string.* The cicada is thus a symbol of Locrian musicality, and also of the difference between Locri and Rhegion. It seems likely, therefore, that Stesichorus's advice was directed particularly against offensive behavior toward Rhegion.

Stesichorus puts us back in the sixth century, somewhere near the time of Locri's legendary victory over the Crotoniate aggressors at the Sagra.[9] Probably the story was told in that context: The Locrians were warned not to allow their defensive success against the powerful city to the north to make them overconfident and aggressive against the powerful city to their south.

That warning was heeded; for their defense against Rhegion, as we have seen, they turned to Hieron of Syracuse. Pindar sang of this in an ode addressed to Hieron:

You, son of Deinomenes
The Zephyrian Locrian maiden

---

[7] Pausanias 6.6.4.

[8] For sources see Niutta (1977), p. 267.

[9] The advice was also attributed to Dionysius of Syracuse—presumably the Elder (Demetrius *On Style* 99)—perhaps knowingly adapted as a threat against Rhegion (Cordiano 1988).

Before her house invokes
From the insoluble toils of war
Through your power gazing in safety.

Pindar 2nd Py. 34–38

Locrian reliance on Syracuse and her tyrants can be seen as a peace-able strategy, a kind of Finlandization: Locri found protection at the cost of abandoning an independent foreign policy. In so doing Locri, warriors and all, adopted a feminine role, precious and in need of protection, precisely symbolized by Pindar's apprehensive maiden.

Historical insignificance is a "Locrian" trait and links the western Locrians with their putative homeland, old-world Locris: backcountry, backward, and in the background. In the old world, however, where the Locrians were a prepolitical *ethnos*, this insignificance had been dictated by geography and social organization; in the West, where the Locrians had built a great *polis*, it appears as the result of a conscious choice. We shall return to this difference in the context of our inquiry into the relations between Locri and Locris.

The Archaeology

The archaeological exploration of Locri begins, as on so many west-Greek sites, with the work of Paolo Orsi, who, beginning in 1890, de-voted nine campaigns to the place. Orsi was primarily interested in the cemeteries (including the non-Greek cemeteries in the area) and the sanctuaries; working with his characteristic focused energy he found more than all later excavators put together. He traced the line of the walls, described the overall topography of the city, and in the Lucifero cemetery dug more than 1,600 graves. He never gave any of this work definitive publication, but we have his extensive preliminary reports.

Because the deities proper to the various sanctuaries were initially (and in some cases still are) unidentified, the sites are known by the names of the farms on which they were found. Thus we say that Orsi investigated the "Marasà temple" (of which some remains were still above ground). This was the first known Ionic temple in the West, and is still the most important of the three known examples of the order there.[10] Beneath it was an archaic temple with a different orientation. This latter, after some further excavation, was published by de Fran-ciscis (1979).

Orsi also found the Casa Marafioti temple, now thought to be that of Olympian Zeus, the small temple of Athena at the top of the city, and

---

[10] Gullini (1980).

just below it the Mannella sanctuary, which turned out to be the Lo-crian sanctuary of Persephone. This sanctuary was, in Hellenistic times at least, the special pride of the city; a number of stories were told of its great riches and of the miracles with which the god protected them (Livy 29.18.3–18). After this literary buildup the actual site turned out to be unexpectedly modest. Orsi found no temple, but a small square building which he identified as a treasury, although it contained no treasures. He did find a remarkable deposit of dedicatory material. At some time in the mid-fifth century the sanctuary had been cleared and (setting aside the objects of intrinsic value—nothing of precious metal was included) the accumulated dedications had been carefully broken and buried—not indiscriminately, but layered, by types. The bottom layer consisted of figurines with some pottery; the next layer up con-sisted of many thousand fragments of the now famous *pinakes*, the char-acteristic Locrian terra-cotta plaques. The top layer was of pottery. The whole filled to a depth of several meters a trench thirty meters long and from five to seven meters wide—several hundred cubic meters of dedicatory material, going back to the late seventh century. This mate-rial is in Reggio; it has never been published.

In the second phase of excavation, in the 1940s, the leading figure was Paulo Arias. Whereas Orsi had investigated the city along the line of its northeastern wall, Arias worked mostly along a line beginning more or less at the center of this wall and extending at right angles to it into the city, across the "Piano Caruso." Here he found a Hellenistic aqueduct and, nearby, the theater. Dug into the escarpment of the plateau that forms the Piano Caruso he found an important cave sanc-tuary of the nymphs (now reburied); this material has been restudied in Costabile (1991a and 1991b).

In the 1950s further work at Locri was carried out by the Scuola Nazionale di Archeologia; during this period the "U-shaped stoa"—the oldest and most mysterious sacred structure in Locri—was investigated. This work is still unpublished; we have only the preliminary reports of Elisa Lissi (Caronna) (1961). In 1958 a substantial portion of the third-century archive of the temple of Olympian Zeus, inscribed on metal tablets, was found by one of the local farmers and, with the help of an anonymous tip, recovered by the state. This material was published by A. de Franciscis (1972); it was later the subject of a major conference (*Le tavole di Locri*, 1977) and of a collection of articles, edited by Cos-tabile (1992b).

These tablets are only the most important of numerous casual finds; since the late nineteenth century sporadic material has continually come to the surface, most of it dispersed through various illicit chan-nels. An important private collection was formed from this material in

the last century, the Collezione Scaglione. More recent finds make
their way into the world market. There are those who believe that the
famous Riace bronzes (like the tablets, recovered as the result of anonymous information) come from Locri.

Since the late 1960s Locri has been the project of the University of
Turin, under the direction of Marcella Barra Bagnasco. For more than
twenty years these investigators have been working along the sea front
in the area known as Centocamere, in the vicinity of the U-shaped stoa.
Most of this area is occupied by late-classic and Hellenistic houses; they
also found, in association with the U-shaped stoa, a sacred building
dedicated to Aphrodite, later replaced by an exceptionally elaborate
house. These excavations have been very well published by Barra Bagnasco (1977–1992).

Still awaiting publication are the finds from the Parapezza region,
close to the Marasà temple but just outside the wall. Here have been
found four distinct votive deposits, as well as a curious altar with tubes
going into the ground. On the strength of a terra-cotta of a woman
carrying a piglet, this has been identified as the site of a Thesmophi-
orion, set aside for women's worship of Demeter.[11] Such sanctuaries
existed all over the Greek world; it is particularly striking to find it at
Locri, however, because the Locrians in their greatest sanctuary (as we
shall see) worshipped Persephone not as Demeter's daughter but independent of the divine mother. The identification of the Thesmophor-
ion shows that Demeter also had her cult at Locri, but independent of
her daughter.[12]

This is a great deal of archaeology; Locri is actually the most thoroughly investigated of the west-Greek cities. At the same time this archaeological work feels frustratingly incomplete, perhaps because it answers so few of our questions. Much of the city remains unexplored;
the political center has never been found. Since the site has not been
built over since late antiquity (a distinction it shares, among the major
west-Greek cities, only with Sybaris/Thurii, where the remains are buried
under a thick layer of gravel, were very difficult to find, and once found
proved to be a couple of meters below the water table) much of the
material must remain more or less intact and temptingly available,
awaiting only permits and resources to explore it. However it is probable that most of the questions that excavation has failed to answer

---

[11] Lattanzi (1990).

[12] Whereas at Athens the two were so closely identified that they are often spoken of in
the dual, as tō theō, in the Greek West Persephone's cult is frequently independent of her
mother's. Diodorus (5.4.5–7) describes a Sicilian festival of Persephone in the spring,
complemented by a festival of Demeter in the fall.

would be unanswered by further excavation. It would be at least as useful to give proper publication to Orsi's material.

What Excavation Tells Us

The earliest Greek objects from Locri are Corinthian aryballoi dating to the first quarter of the seventh century; these however, as they may well have been acquired by the pre-Greek inhabitants, do not in themselves constitute evidence for Greek settlement. For this the earliest good evidence belongs to the second quarter of the century. The Monaci, the earliest Greek cemetery, found some distance from the shore where the ground begins to rise along the ancient arterial road, contains some material from the seventh century. Probably the first nucleus of settlement was nearby, quite possibly on the Piano Caruso, where some early houses were explored by Arias (1947) and dated by him to the mid-seventh century. From this phase of Locri we have no public buildings.

The earliest[13] substantial building known from Locri is down by the shore: the "U-shaped stoa," one of the most enigmatic monuments in Greece. When some time in the earlier part of the sixth century. the sea front of the city was defined by a wall, this wall had to make a indentation in order to leave the U-shaped stoa outside it. The first phase therefore is earlier than the wall and probably dates from the later seventh century. It consisted of two rows of six rooms each, 4.9 by 6.8 meters, facing each other across a space more than 40 meters wide. In the mid-sixth century these rows were extended by five more rooms on each side, making two rows of eleven.[14] These rooms have the off-center doorways characteristic of Greek dining rooms and are perfectly recognizable as such[15]—seven-couch dining rooms, in fact. Each row was fronted by a roofed portico which finished at the seaward end in a smaller room, perhaps for storage. The ends of the two rows were joined by enclosing walls with a gate in the wall on the seaward side, so that the dining rooms form the two sides of a square, about sixty meters to a side, that is, 3,600 square meters; the enclosed open space between the porches is about 2,200 square meters. Gullini (1980), p. 199, argues persuasively that between the first and second phase the unit of measurement shifted; the first phase is one hundred Doric feet square, the second phase one hundred by two hundred Ionic feet.

---

[13] Taking Gullini's later date for the first Marasà temple—see p. 215 below.

[14] For this dating of the two phases see Barra Bagnasco (1977a), pp. 46–49. Cf. Gullini (1980), pp. 111–127.

[15] Rolley (1977).

Within this open space, over the course of some two hundred years (from the mid sixth century to the mid-fourth century), were dug little pits, varying in size from 0.4 meters wide and deep to 2.5 meters wide and deep (mostly at the smaller end of the range). The excavators found 371 of these. The contents of these pits were fragments of pottery (always broken, sometimes with the name of the dedicator scratched on it), terra-cotta images (similarly broken) especially of reclining male figures, and burnt animal bones: mostly cattle, goats, sheep, and pigs, but also dogs, cats, chickens, and pigeons. The material from each pit was chronologically homogeneous. The pits are fairly evenly scattered and do not impinge on one another; therefore they were probably marked, in wood or some other perishable material.

This enclosed space with little interments scattered across it looks like nothing so much as a Tophet, the characteristic Punic cemetery set aside for sacrificed children. The U-shaped stoa is indeed a "cemetery for sacred material"[16] and as such is unparalleled. Typologically the building resembles Brauron, where the rows of dining rooms (although those are nine-couch dining rooms) similarly look out on an enclosed court—although at Brauron the two rows are at right angles to one another. At Locri, by contrast, they face each other symmetrically, and as that symmetry was carried over from the first to the second phase it may well be significant. We may note that, over the life span of the ritual, 371 pits comes to roughly two a year, quite possibly one representing each side. Few of the pits are large enough to hold the material from eleven dining rooms; some kind of selectivity must have been exercised. It looks as though each pit contains the equipment and remains from a single dinner.

Athenaeus (234c–235e) collects a set of classical texts, including several inscriptions, in which the word *parasitos* (later pejorative, like the English *parasite*) means "one taking part in a ritual meal on behalf of the public."[17] Possibly the banquet burials reflect such representative dining; ten groups on each side, and an eleventh with a special status, obligated to dedicate its tableware. Ten suggests a division of one hundred, as in the Hundred Houses, or one thousand, as in the Locrian assembly of the Thousand. As for the symmetry of the two sides, the obvious explanation is some kind of moiety system, but we have no evidence for this; as far as we know classical Locri was divided into three tribes, like Sparta. Conceivably the principle was sex-difference: a men's side and a women's side.

---

[16] Lissi (Caronna) (1961), p. 113.

[17] This material is reviewed by Schmitt-Pantel (1992); she also refers to a possibly parallel inscription of the seventh century from Tiryns.

Aphrodite's name appears on the material, and it seems clear that the ritual was for her. This connects the U-shaped stoa with the temple of Aphrodite that went up less than fifty meters distant in the late sixth century (when the U-shaped stoa may have been already a century old). This is a long rectangular building consisting of three rooms in a row, two of them about four meters square, the third about four meters by three meters. There was no peristyle.[18] There is a little porch attached to this smaller room on the end of the building; it therefore seems that the entrance was at this end (the remains are so poor that it is not possible to be definite about the doorways). An inscribed statue base within informs us that this building belonged to Aphrodite; near the building stood an altar.

This is an unusual type of structure, closely paralleled only in Sicily, where six are known.[19] All date from the sixth century. The critical feature, unusual in a temple without peristyle, is the third room. Assuming that the rooms communicated with each other and there was only one entrance, we have a structure consisting of pronaos, naos, and adyton—that is to say, an entry space, a sacred chamber, and another chamber beyond it. The closest parallel is the three-roomed temple at Monte Iato, also dedicated to Aphrodite.[20] In that case the entry space was initially demarcated not by a partition wall, but by a pair of columns only; the adyton, however, was walled off from the naos.

The Locri Aphrodite temple was later remodeled by adding a third room on the side, larger than the naos. It may be that the entrance was relocated at this time. In any case, the remodeling produced a ground plan that is apparently unique. It is worth noting that the Monte Iato Aphrodite temple was also remodeled, in this case by constructing a small room inside the naos. This produced another unique ground plan.

None of this is actually unexpected. We have so little material relating to the worship of Aphrodite that we do not know what to expect. Aphrodite's few temples do not conform to any particular pattern either in plan or location. Aphrodite's temple at Corinth was at the top of Acrocorinth, high above the city she protected; the statue was armed, as was Aphrodite at Sparta (both apparently under the influence of the

---

[18] Romeo (1989), p. 49, suggests that closed buildings without perisyles, particularly in association with *bothroi*, were proper to the worship of chthonic deities—including Aphrodite.

[19] Isler (1984), p. 54. In at least one of these the third room was accessible from the outside, rather than through the building; it therefore was an opisthodomos rather than an adyton. Isler also lists four three-room buildings from other places, but none of these, upon examination, turns out to be a close match to the Locrian building.

[20] Ibid.

Near Eastern Astarte). The most famous representation of Aphrodite, by Praxiteles, was in the sanctuary at Cnidos; she was Aphrodite Euploia, protector of ships, and her sanctuary was placed on a terrace above the harbor. The complex includes a *tholos*, a round building, which the first excavator took to be the temple of Aphrodite. The sanctuary of Aphrodite at Paestum[21] included a room-sized circular space demarcated by a low wall; this was, however, concealed within a square room so as not to be visible from the outside, a pattern duplicated only by the "heroon" at Olympia and a sixth-century structure at Sabucina in Italy. Concealment at Paestum was further assured by a porch masking the entrance door, very like the porch on the Locrian building.

Evidently the temples of Aphrodite among the Greeks were a tissue of anomalies, so it does not say much to say that the Locrian instance is unparalleled. Nevertheless, it is unparalleled: We are confronted with a complex consisting of an open space defined by facing lines of dining rooms, used also for ritual disposal of the remains of (evidently ritual) meals; nearby is a temple of Aphrodite with image and altar. The following points should be significant.

1. The entire complex was extramural—like the sanctuary of Aphrodite at Paestum—and the adjustment of the line of the seawall should indicate that this location was part of the meaning of the sanctuary.

2. The combination of masking porch without and adyton within (if indeed the third room was an adyton and not an opisthodomos) suggests that the ritual involved concealment. Here again there is a parallel at Paestum, where there was some kind of "mysterious activities within."[22]

3. That the U-shaped stoa was the earliest substantial sacred building of the Locrians (and preceded Aphrodite's temple) implies that ritual feasts dedicated to Aphrodite were peculiarly important to the city. At Paestum also, however, we have "ample evidence . . . for sacrifice and dining."[23]

4. The material buried in the little pits might tell us much if it were ever published. Even on the basis of the preliminary report, however, it is possible to say two things:

A. These things have been systematically broken and carefully buried; this procedure is characteristic, not of sacrificial remains

[21] Pedley (1990), pp. 129–162.
[22] Ibid., p. 136.
[23] Ibid., p. 150.

(which are normally thrown on a discard heap in the sacred area where they accumulate, as on the intermediate terrace below the sanctuary of Aphrodite in Cnidos, or in the Corinthian Isthmia sanctuary, or by the archaic temple at Kommos) but of dedications when a sanctuary is cleared. Objects thus dedicated belong to the god and therefore must be made unfit for human use and reverently deposited. Apparently in the U-shaped stoa the utensils and remains of certain ritual feasts (two of twenty-two perhaps) were held to belong to the god. The ritual may have been like that of the *theoxenia*— except that there the god attended as a guest, while in this case it looks as though the god acted as host. Everything happens as if the communicants had been to a feast in some other world from which they could bring nothing back.

B. The appearance of dog and cat bones, even though they form only a small proportion of the total, is unusual enough to be significant. Dogs were linked to Hecate and sacrificed to her; she is an underworld goddess. Cat bones (along with dog bones) are found in the *bothroi*[24] at the sanctuary on the Sele, and apparently nowhere else. Such *bothroi* are characteristically used to receive offerings intended for dead heroes and for the gods of the dead. It seems probable that the ritual of Aphrodite at Locri linked her in some way with the underworld—that she was, in fact, a chthonic Aphrodite, perhaps Aphrodite Meilichia, attested for Metapontum and for Epidaurus.[25]

That is about as much about Aphrodite as the archaeology can tell us. We shall return to these themes, however, when we come to consider the representations of Aphrodite in Locrian art.

We may also note in passing an early sixth-century graffito to Cybele,[26] by far the earliest evidence for her cult in the West, anomalous and unexplained—another Locrian singularity.

We now turn to the Marasà; this by contrast was an intramural sanctuary. This is the best studied and most adequately published of the Locrian sanctuaries; here, however, the god worshipped is still unidentified. The architectural sequence is pretty clear, although the absolute dates are contested. The earliest structure here was a small rectangular building with a porch on the east end; this was probably the first tem-

---

[24] The excavator called the burials at the U-shaped stoa *bothroi*; since *bothros* means "little pit" this is unexceptionable and at the same time confusing—because *bothros* in the archaeological literature usually means a pit dug for the reception of sacrifices and intended for repeated use.

[25] Pugliese Caratelli (1989b).

[26] Guarducci (1970).

ple. It was of mud brick on a base of sandstone blocks; the walls were ornamented on the outside with terra-cotta plaques. The tile roof was supported by the walls and by a row of wooden columns on stone bases which ran down the center of the building, dividing it into two naves. De Franciscis dates this building to c. 675, Gullini to c. 600, both on stylistic grounds; the later date, which makes it roughly contemporary with the first phase of the U-shaped stoa, seems more plausible in terms of the overall development of the city. The earlier date would make this temple two or three generations earlier than any other public building known from Locri.

Some time in the sixth century this temple was provided with a peristyle—evidently in wood, since no column fragments remain. De Franciscis dates this event to the late seventh century, contemporary with the first phase of the U-shaped stoa, while Gullini dates it as contemporary with the second phase, c. 550, shortly before the sea-front wall and portal, which belong to the same level. (Gullini [1980], p. 38, also argues that the peristyle was built in the Ionic order, primarily on the ground that by this date the time had passed when a Doric peristyle could be built in wood, and also on grounds of the proportions of the ground plan.)

These alternative chronologies represent competing attempts to place this structure in a historical context. 550 is a late date for a wooden peristyle, but Gullini accepts this date because he sees the development of the Marasà as integrally related to what we might call the Ionian rediscovery of the West. In order to explain this point it is necessary to say something about the development of the western colonies over time.

The earliest western colonies were founded (in the eighth century) from the Peloponnese (and Megara) and to some extent by the Euboeans, who had long made a cultural specialty of the extended sea voyage. By 700 the Euboeans had been replaced in that role by the Corinthians, whose pottery in the seventh century dominates the Near Eastern emporion at Al Mina as well as every western site. Much Corinthian pottery was exported as containers for other luxury goods— perfumes and lotions, mainly, for which there was a ready market among the now Hellenizing barbarians. Under the tyrannical regime that took over Corinth in the mid-seventh century the city continued her colonial policy, concentrating now on control of the sea route between Corinth and her chief western colonies: Corcyra and Syracuse. In the later seventh century and early sixth century Corinth therefore colonized a number of old-world coastal sites adjoining this sea route.[27]

[27] Best studied in Graham (1964).

Initiative in the sending of Greek colonists out to further frontiers now passed to Miletus, and a new frontier was opened to the north, on the Black Sea and its approaches.

The seventh century as a whole is in the West a period of consolidation. Gela was founded early in the century (688 is the traditional date), just about the time of our first solid evidence for Greek inhabitants at Locri. After Gela no colony was founded from old-world Greece until Massalia, c. 600. For most of a century the West was left alone, and it will have been in this century that it developed its separate culture. When the next wave of settlers arrived they found established Greek communities with established ways.

This next wave came from new places: The cities of the Anatolian coast, and later of the off-shore islands, had begun to feel the pressure of the Near Eastern monarchies, first of Lydia, then of Persia. Phocis, having inherited the maritime vocation of geometric Euboea, led the way; refugees from other cities followed. Acragas was founded in 580; Metapontum and Cyrene greatly expanded their populations with new settlers. Most of these people were Ionians, and increasingly in the sixth century we see Ionian influence on western bronzes, terra-cottas, even in temples built in the Doric order. One such is the Marafioti temple at Locri (now generally held to be the temple of Olympian Zeus). This was a large building and (to judge by such poor fragments as remain) an odd one, lacking a peristyle, with wooden supporting members masked in stone and terra-cotta. Orsi (1911a) describes it as mixed Doric/Ionic.[28]

The first half of the sixth century was a period of development at Locri: Nearby indigenous settlements disappear at this time, representing the absorption of the local population, and it is in this period that the Locrian subcolonies across the peninsula, Medma, Metauros, and Hipponion, first provide solid evidence of Greek habitation. In the mid-sixth century, also, Locri was provided with a rational street plan.[29] The sea-front wall was built, the U-shaped stoa extended, and (if we follow Gullini) the first Ionic temple was built in the Marasà sanctuary. The Ionians, it seems, had arrived in Locri.

By the end of the sixth century the Persians has taken over the Ionian mainland and Ionian influence meant mainly the influence of Samos, where Polycrates from 540 to 522 maintained the last brilliant independent Ionian state. From there Pythagoras the sculptor came to

---

[28] This temple had one feature unique to Locri: Instead of triglyphs on the frieze it had pentaglyphs. Evidently by the mid-sixth century. Locri was already prepared to innovate. (A frieze depicted on a *pinax* has tetraglyphs.)

[29] Foti (1977), p. 356.

Rhegion, and Pythagoras the philosopher to Croton; from there came the settlers of Dicaearchia, the new colony on the bay of Naples. Samos also seems to have had a special relation with Croton. Locri does not seem to have had any connection of this kind with a particular east-Greek city, as Sybaris had with Mytilene (Herodotus 6.21) or Taras with Cnidos (Herodotus 3.138.2), but when after the final defeat of the Ionian rebellion at Lade the Samians resolved, along with certain Milesian exiles, to leave for the West, the city that first received them was Locri (Herodotus 6.23). Locri may also have been the main center from which Ionian styles were transmitted to the West.[30] It seems probable that the Samian refugees of the early fifth century included master builders from the island, or that the West received them later in the century—especially as in the classical period there was no work for them on Samos: "not a single new building went up [in the sanctuary of Hera] and imported votives are almost entirely lacking during this time."[31]

Certainly when in the second quarter of the fifth century the Marasà sanctuary received a new temple, reoriented to the late archaic street plan, it was an Ionic temple patterned after late archaic Samian Ionic. The influence of Polycrates' Heraion on the classical Marasà temple was already noticed by Orsi[32] and has been further traced by Gullini.[33] To judge by the remaining fragments this Locrian temple was Ionic of unusual quality, unusual enough to suggest refugee craftsmen. It was certainly made of imported stone (an indication of Locrian prosperity), a limestone superior to anything found in the Locrian area, quarried near Syracuse.

By this time, Locri was firmly in the Syracusan sphere. The earliest connection of which we hear is a casual mention in Athenaeus (542a)—in a section on gardens—of a garden at Hipponion belonging to the tyrant Gelon; this would seem to imply some connection between Sicily[34] and this Locrian outpost by the end of the sixth century. We have even earlier archaeological evidence of close Sicilian connections: In the foundations of Locrian houses have been found substantial quantities of volcanic rock deriving from the area below Etna. The earliest use of this material dates from the late sixth century. These rocks evidently crossed the water as ships' ballast, and are thus evidence for substantial exchange of bulk commodities between Locri and this part

[30] De Franciscis (1979), p. 115; cf. Gullini (1988), p. 349.
[31] Kyrieleis (1993), p. 129.
[32] Orsi (1890), p. 255.
[33] Gullini (1980), pp. 92–95. That the Marasà temple was laid out in Samian feet was apparently already asserted by Dörpfeld: Dunbabin (1948), p. 296n.2.
[34] Gelon was tyrant of Gela, and only at the end of his career tyrant of Syracuse.

of Sicily.[35] In the same area, at Francavilla di Sicilia, halfway up the Randazzo valley along the north side of Etna, a chance discovery of made in 1980 revealed a set of *pinakes* of the early fifth-century Locrian type, a fragment or two from Locri, most locally manufactured.[36] They are evidence that this Sicilian district—which is actually very close to Locri—was part of the Locrian cultural area at this time. Quite possibly it was inhabited by Locrians transplanted to it by Hieron of Syracuse, who was patron of Locri around the turn of the century.[37]

The early fifth century was the golden age of Locrian art; it gave us the *pinakes* and the Ludovisi Throne and most of the other works of art to be discussed in part 4. This was also the period during which Locri seems to have been most involved with contacts between Athens and Etruria. During the second quarter of the fifth century much Attic pottery was exported; more pieces are known for this period from Etruria than from Athens, with substantial numbers elsewhere in Italy and Sicily. Locri was clearly involved in this traffic; more than forty Athenian painters from this period are represented in the Locrian evidence (although not by their best work), and these forty between them accounted for about two-thirds of the fine Attic pottery of this period.[38] Almost 60 percent of the Attic vase fragments found at Locri date from the period between 475 and 450.

Locri is the place where the sea route to eastern Sicily divides from that through the straits to the Tyrrhenian; as such it was a convenient stopping place on either voyage. This need not, however, have made of Locri a commercial city. We have no evidence for substantial port installations, and the seawall dating from the mid-sixth century (which probably was not intended as a fortification)[39] was most likely put there (as a prelude to the general replanning of the city) to separate the city from the sea—subjectively, as well as objectively. Outside this wall were built and rebuilt down the centuries a series of little shops and storage spaces.[40] This area was never crowded; when one building went out of use it was not replaced but was allowed to collapse while another was

[35] Francesco and Frisatto (1986).
[36] These are discussed on pp. 347–348.
[37] As suggest by Torelli, in Settis (1988), p. 610.
[38] All these figures are from Giudice (1989).
[39] It is wide and low and does not look like a fortification wall—nor is there any good evidence for early walls surrounding the city to which it could have connected. Barra Bagnasco (1977a), p. 33, calls it a retaining wall, but the ground is pretty flat there—there is little for so massive a wall to retain.
[40] Barra Bagnasco (1977b), p. 380, remarks that these buildings were clearly not inhabited. She suggests that they may have served for storage connected with cult.

built next to it.[41] These few structures seem to have been adequate to Locri's involvement with long-distance commerce.[42] It seems that Locri entertained her numerous visitors outside the wall.[43] This is consistent with another striking fact: Locrian art did not travel.[44] Locrian workshops were in the early fifth century an important influence on the coroplasts of Catania, Gela, Selinus, and Himera[45]—that is to say, in the farthest reaches of Greek Sicily—but less than a handful of pieces produced in Locri have been found in these cities. Evidently visitors were

[41] As a result the structures in this extramural area are in chronological order from east to west: Barra Bagnasco (1977a), p. 8.

[42] Giudice (1989), p. 104, suggests that the Locrians maintained Cape Zephyrion as their "international port" and appositely quotes Aristotle *Politics* 1327a as to the advantages of such an arrangement. It is indeed possible that the remains of a substantial port are concealed under the gravel deposited on the site by the river; it seems strange, however, that no ancient author mentions it.

[43] Cf. Torelli (1979), p. 99.

[44] On this point see D'Agostino (1973), p. 227. Terra-cottas of course do not travel much anyway, but it is striking that the Locrian *pinakes*, which are of high quality and stylistically unmistakable, are hardly found outside the Locrian area. D'Agostino, speaking of the high quality and considerable quantity of Locrian bronzes found at Locri, remarks that given the very incomplete publication of material from the surrounding area it is hard to be sure, but it looks as though Locrian bronzes did not travel—in contrast (I suppose) to bronzes from other sources, for instance Taras and Posidonia.
There is one important exception, a terra-cotta statuette in the Orsi Museum in Syracuse (Bonacasa [1990] 280–281). This piece represents Persephone enthroned, holding her familiar attributes of *patera* and *larnax*. Standing on her lap is a small winged male holding out a crown—surely identified by the crown as Eros. This piece has been identified—presumably by the clay, which looks very Locrian—as made in Locri. At something over fifth centimeters high, it is one of the largest surviving Locrian non-architectural terra-cottas.
There should be some special reason for the presence of this exceptional piece in the Camarina cemetery. Displayed in the same case (Bonacasa [1990] 282–283) is another exceptional piece from the same cemetery: an enthroned deity identified by the label as "Aphrodite/Persephone of the Locri/Medma type"—in this case the origin of the piece has evidently not been determined, but typologically it belongs to the Locrian culture area. One feature, however, has no parallel: The deity shelters with her robe a much smaller adult figure who stands by her knee, plausibly identified as signifying the heroized dead.
These two pieces—Persephone with Eros, Persephone/Aphrodite sheltering the dead soul—surely carry forward Locrian ideas; this in turn suggests that their owners were drawn, not so much to Locrian art, as to Locrian religion—not that they could enter Locrian cult as participants, for if they were straightforwardly converts we would expect to find closer parallels to these items in the Locrian material. Rather I would suggest that they had acquired these pieces with some hope of thereby sharing in the promise of Locrian eschatology. The exception thereby proves the rule: Locrian art did not travel outside the Locrian culture area—except, rarely, as a vehicle of Locrian culture.

[45] Uhlenbrock (1989), p. 22.

allowed to admire but not able to acquire them.[46] This is consistent with the notion that Locri was intentionally a closed community.

Classical Locri, in fact, gives a paradoxical impression; she is a sophisticated community, in touch with a wide range of tendencies, and yet closed off unto herself. She was influential, but did not exploit her influence. Quite possibly exactly this paradox was at the core of the Locrian civic project, which is to say, of Locrian culture. I conclude this section by saying something about what we know of this from the plastic arts material—Locrian work, and some imports, buried as grave goods and dedications.

Our source for Locrian grave goods in the late archaic and classical periods is the Lucifero cemetery. This stretches out northeast of the city, about three hundred meters from the sea. Here Orsi dug 1,675 graves, making this one of the best explored cemeteries in the West; of these he published a mere 162 in his preliminary reports—Orsi (1911b); Orsi (1912); Orsi (1913); Orsi (1917)—selecting those that seemed to him most interesting in construction or contents.[47]

Graves are highly motivated assemblages; each is a kind of message, making a statement as much by what it omits as by what it includes. These messages, because they are intended for no one in particular, in a sense are meant for us. To spend time with Orsi's reports is to encounter the Locrians by the most direct channel now open between us and them. I shall recurrently refer to this material in later sections.

Even during the richest period of the cemetery the overall impression is one of modest simplicity, although they are rich in bronzes. Inhumations predominate, although one burial in ten is a cremation. Graves for inhumations were dug into the sand, sometimes lined with clay, occasionally (mostly in the last phase) lined with bricks, topped with roof tiles or built as enclosures out of tile. Only one stone sarcophagus of the type frequent elsewhere in West Greece is reported (#648); Orsi (1917), p. 458, mentions one other. Tombs were extremely crowded and often disturbed one another. Above-ground markers were evidently

[46] Without piece-by-piece analysis of the clay it is not possible to distinguish with certainty works imported from the Locrian area from those imitative of its styles, but it rather looks as though actual imports are much more frequently from Medma rather than Locri. Probably Medma was less rigidly closed to strangers.

[47] Cerchiai (1988), who in the cellars of the Reggio Museum reviewed the excavated material along with Orsi's notebooks, tells us that a few graves date from the early sixth century; Orsi, however, published none before mid-sixth century. The great majority of the graves Orsi published belong to Cerchiai's Phase II: mid-sixth to mid-fifth century. In Phase III, which extends into the mid-fourth century, offerings become sparse and plain, often consisting of nothing more than a clay lamp; although Orsi dug many of these graves he seldom thought them worth publishing. In other words, the 10 percent he did publish are far from a random sample.

the exception, and of modest proportions; only five small fragments were found (Orsi [1917], p. 159). The funeral rite evidently often involved the use and abandonment in and around the tomb of large pottery vessels;[48] much of this is Attic pottery but it is of very poor quality compared to the Attic pottery employed in Etruscan funerals (Orsi [1917], p. 155). Locrian grave furnishings are scant in comparison with the Greek cemeteries of Sicily. There is almost nothing in precious metal; one woman (#23) was buried with a small gold perfume bottle, and a baby (#355) had a little heart-shaped gold pendant around its neck. There are a few silver rings, but most are of bronze.

Evidently Locrian males did not make much of grave goods. Many of the most elaborately constructed graves are altogether without furnishings (e.g., numbers 399, 453 bis, 649); it may be that these are late, from the period when grave furnishings are in any case sparse—but we should observe that this later period was not one of poverty for the Locrians; it simply seemed to them improper to bury valuable objects with their dead. For the earlier period there is some indication of an inverse correlation between social status and the richness of graves. Children are often buried with a quantity of things. Orsi makes no effort to determine sex from skeletal remains, but he does tell us that one of the objects most commonly found in a Locrian tomb was a strigl, the blade used by a Greek athlete to scrape off the oil with which he covered himself after exercise. Very few of these graves are individually reported by Orsi, presumably because they contained little else. One or two other masculine items turn up in his reports: A jumper's hand weight was found in a cremation (#944) associated with fragments of a knife and nothing more; one grave (#642) contained a collection of agricultural equipment. But it seems that most of the graves published by Orsi were graves of children and women, and that is because such graves were more likely to contain an array of objects. Certainly most of the published objects from the Lucifero are toys (dolls, balls, miniature pots and pans) and women's things: spindles, needle cases, tweezers, ointment boxes, perfume jars, and above all mirrors.

It is the prevalence of women's things among Locrian grave goods and dedications that most gives us the sense of the importance of women at Locri. This need not, again, mean that they were powerful or of high status; it does mean, however, that a woman's life was furnished with, and womanhood manifested in, objects of craft and art. The Locrians in at least this sense paid attention to their women.

This brings us to the dedications from the great deposit in the Man-

[48] Arias (*GTCGI* c.v. "Locri" II.), however, thinks that all this material had been buried in tombs and became scattered as a result of overburials

nella sanctuary, Here women's things are even more prevalent; while
there are a few male objects—including weapons inscribed to the goddess—this was evidently a sanctuary frequented mostly by women. Like
the sanctuary of Aphrodite it was extramural—high and hidden, however, as opposed to low and exposed. From dedications inscribed to the
goddess it is known to have been the sanctuary of Persephone. Representations of Aphrodite, however, also occur on some dedications; this
raises the question of the relation between Aphrodite and Persephone
at Locri. That question will turn out to be at the core of Locrian culture, and must be reserved for the closing chapters of this book.

When I speak of Locrian culture I refer mainly to the classical period, which began there with the beginning of the fifth century (the
pinakes began to be produced in about 490). The civic and religious life
of this period comprised at least the two known intramural sanctuaries,
the Marasà and the Marafioti, and also the two extramural sanctuaries,
that of Aphrodite and Persephone. These latter two, furthermore, seem
to have been linked and as between them they defined the urban space,
seem also in some sense to have defined the boundaries of Locrian life.

The classical period at Locri lasted until the middle of the fourth
century, when Dionysius the Younger, exiled tyrant of Syracuse, came
there. For the Locrians his arrival was a seismic event, which has left
its enigmatic traces in the archaeology. It was at this time that the
U-shaped stoa passed out of use; the Temple of Aphrodite was actually
demolished and replaced by a secular building—the so-called House of
the Lions, a luxurious house which looks remarkably like a residence
fit for a tyrant.[49] Possibly Dionysius demonstrated his hybristic power
and wealth by actually moving into the precinct of the goddess.

In any case it was most probably at this time that dedicatory rituals
having to do with marriage shifted from the Sanctuary of Persephone
to the Cave of the Nymphs beneath the Piano Caruso, where they were
linked to the cult of the hero Euthymus.[50] At this time, also, the
Locrians began to issue coinage. The cultural conditions of their life
had evidently been transformed. This is another topic that will be further investigated later.

For the moment we can say that the archaeology enables us to trace
the curve of Locrian development. The place begins very modestly in
the late seventh century, continuously develops through the sixth century, is shaped by the reception of Ionian culture in the mid-sixth cen-

---

[49] Barra Bagnasco (1994) presents evidence that the cult of Adonis was celebrated in
this house. This notion in no way conflicts with mine, especially given that (as she notes)
the elder Dionysius wrote a tragedy on Adonis.

[50] Costabile (1991b), p. 228.

tury, reaches a peak of creativity in the early fifth century, holds its place until the mid-fourth century, and undergoes massive cultural change at that time. Whereas the literary tradition (as we shall see) links Locri with Sparta, the archaeology shows Ionian influences of the sixth century linking Locri with Samos—a place itself closely linked to Sparta. John Barron has even spoken of a "Samian, Spartan, Locrian triangle,"[51] and we shall return to this notion. We can also see that the Locrians were from the beginning unlike the others, and continued to be so throughout their development—until something happened that made this no longer possible.

The Economic Base

One of the many mysteries about Epizephyrian Locri has to do with its location. The literary tradition tells us that the first site chosen by the Locrian colonists was at Cape Zephyrion, usually identified with Capo Bruzzano, about twenty kilometers south of Locri (cf. Niutta [1977], p. 260). Here, before the river silted it up, was the only natural harbor on this coast (Sabbione [1982]). It seems the natural spot for a "protocolonial" foundation:[52] the shift from a community of adventurers to a regular agricultural settlement, further, often involved a shift of site. The relation between Cape Zephyrion and Locri would then be analogous to the relation between Pitheccousae and Cumae, or Satyrion and Taras, or between Berezan and Olbia. In the case of Cape Zephyrion, however, we have no archaeological confirmation. If the first settlement was actually there we find it fairly easy to see why they began where they began, harder to understand why they moved where they moved.

All the other major Greek cities of Italy are where they are for obvious reasons: Rhegion commands the Straits of Messina, Taras is on an island at the mouth of an immense harbor, Croton is a high promontory sheltering two ports and looks across to the fertile plain around Crimisa, Cumae is on a ridge commanding the Campanian plain; Sybaris/Thurii are in the richest agricultural plain south of Naples. Locri is not advantageously placed from the point of view of either commerce or agriculture. Certainly the surrounding territory is today laid out in farms, and it must have been similarly farmed in antiquity. Locri in Hellenistic times was noted for the export of pitch (Strabo 6.1.9) derived from the pines of the Sila, but this can never have been an important source of public wealth, and cannot have motivated the

[51] Personal communication.
[52] For this term, see p. 255.

choice of location. The simple answer is probably that Locri was the last of the great Italian Greek cities to be founded, and the best sites on the Tyrrhenian were already taken. On a relatively featureless coast the Locrians chose the ridge that already, slightly further inland, held the chief aboriginal center (at Janchina—cf. Sabbione [1977], p. 364). The spot seems to be relatively defensible, and that may have been attraction enough.

The best agricultural land is across the mountain, on the Tyrrhenian side—particularly the plain between Metauros (Goia Tauro) and Medma (Rosarno), which today is filled with groves of extraordinarily large olive trees. The ancients most admired the land further to the north near Hipponion; Strabo (6.1.5) tells us that "the surrounding countryside is so rich in meadows and flowers that they believe the maiden came here from Sicily for her flower picking." The easiest overland crossing to the Tyrrhenian side is along the Torbido, to the north of Locri. Possibly the city itself was placed so as to be roughly midway between the harbor at Cape Zephyrion and this overland crossing, but this is speculative. We are told that Medma and Metauros were Locrian colonies, as was the fortress city of Hipponion (later Vibo Valentia) high above the Tyrrhenian to their north. The archaeological material from these sites clearly places them in the Locrian cultural area throughout their history,[53] and Locri herself begins to develop at about the time of their foundation, roughly the mid-sixth century. It may be that Locri lived by controlling these satellite communities, but the political relations are undocumented and unclear (cf. Musti [1977], pp. 108–120); on one of the few occasions when there is something in the literary record Locri is actually at war with her Tyrrhenian colonies (Thucydides 5.4.3).

We do have some evidence for the progressive appropriation of the interior; Janchina, the aboriginal settlement immediately inland from Locri, was eliminated at the time of the foundation of the city; the aboriginal settlements at Stefanelli and San Stefano survived until the sixth century (Sabbione [1982]). On the Tyrrhenian side of the mountain the indigenous community at Torre Galli continued through the sixth century (de la Genière [1964]). That these communities so long retained indigenous culture within the Locrian territory is probably an indication that they served the uses of the Locrians as agricultural labor[54]—whether through sharecropping (like the Spartan helots) for individual Locrian landlords, or being taxed by the Locrian state. In

---

[53] From Metauros there is actually some pre-Locrian material; the place evidently became Locrian about the time Medma was founded.

[54] Musti (1977), pp. 60–63; Osanna (1992), p. 207.

any case they were progressively Hellenized until in the fifth century their separate culture disappears altogether—which means that they were gradually transformed from a dominated people into a subordinate social stratum.

Surely the Locrian economy was based on the familiar Greek agriculture of the vine and the olive, with some cultivation of cereals; surely there was also exchange of this produce for the products of the mountain districts inhabited by the aborigines, particularly cheese, meat, and wool, and also timber (and pitch). It is relatively easy to imagine how this agricultural base could have maintained in comfort an oligarchy of a few hundred families; it is harder to think how it provided support for an urban population of twenty or thirty thousand.

Certainly Locri was not purely agricultural; the city was on the sea, possessed a navy, and was involved in commerce. The question is (again): How active was this involvement? Giudice (1989) has shown reason to believe that from the last quarter of the sixth century Locri was the favored stopping place on a voyage from mainland Greece to the West. The Athenian potters who were being exported to those districts are consistently represented at Locri, indicating that the traders left an item or two from their cargoes as they stopped there. This did not, however, make Locri herself a major market. The small quantity and relatively poor quality of imported craft work found at Locri (compare, for instance, the Attic pottery in Locrian tombs with that found at Syracuse, Acragas, or even Camarina) suggests that the leading families of Locri were not well provided with money. Furthermore, that Locri was a major craft-work center, at least in bronze and terra-cotta, but that her products (as noted above) seem not to have traveled outside of the Locrian cultural area, suggests an insulation of Locri from the money economy: The pattern of distribution suggests that these goods never reached the market and never had a money price. They were produced, suggests Bruno D'Agostino, by craftsmen working as dependents of a few great families; those few items that found their way abroad may have been presented as guest gifts.[55] This interesting suggestion implies that as late as the fifth century B.C.—a time when cities such as Athens and Corinth had already experienced centuries of commercial development—Locri maintained a largely nonmonetized economy.

This notion receives a certain amount of support from the literary record. The Aristotelian *Constitution* of Locri, for example, noted: "there is no retail trade among them, but the farmer sells his own

[55] D'Agostino (1973), p. 227.

produce."[56] Without retail traders, as Socrates notes in the *Republic* (371c–d), an effective market in agricultural commodities is impossible. Probably this lost work is also the source of another fragment attributed to Aristotle (apud Athenaeus 272a) that the Locrians forbade the possession of purchased slaves.[57] (See also Polybius 12.9.6.) I have already in the last chapter quoted Aristotle:

> The laws [sometimes] forbid the sale of [real] property (*ousia*), and among the Locrians there is a law against selling it, unless [the seller] can point to some evident misfortune that has befallen him. (Aristotle *Politics* 1266b)

The implication of this language is that the seller had to appeal to some political or judicial body and show cause why he should be permitted to sell land; such an arrangement implies something different from private property in the full sense. The landowner held property as a member of the group and could not dispose of it without the consent of the group.

There is some evidence for a law of Zaleucus forbidding contracts for debt (Zenobius 5.4). Then we have the fact that Locri, like Sparta, refused to have a currency. Locri issued no coinage until the fourth century, some two hundred years after other western cities began to coin. Coinage and monetization are in principle independent—one does not have to issue coins to use money, and coins can be issued by a community where money is little in use—but the refusal to coin looks like some kind of refusal of economic development.

Polybius (12.16.10) speaks of a lawmaking assembly of the Thousand. Probably this was the whole body of Locrian full citizens—who therefore formed a narrow oligarchy.[58] I would imagine that Locri was in the classical period what Max Weber calls a "consumer city," where a few great families drew wealth into the city in virtue of their claims on the land and labor of the rural population, claims realized as prestations of produce and other things of value conceived as tithes, traditional gifts to the overlord, and so on—and that these great families then informally redistributed this wealth to an urban population, engaged in service occupations, small crafts, and petty commerce (for the butcher's trade see d'Errico and Moigne [1985]), and socially orga-

---

[56] Heracleides Lembus *De constitutionibus* 60.

[57] Unless Aristotle was there speaking of old-world Locris.

[58] Emily Mackil (n.d.) observes that both Rhegion (Heracleides Ponticus fr. 25) and Croton (Iamblichus V.P. 35 257 and 260) had assemblies of One Thousand, and that Rhegion (like old-world Locris—Thucydides 1.108) gave one hundred hostages (Diodorus Siculus 14.106.3). She therefore suggests that the institution of the Thousand had been imitated from Locri by these cities, and in at least one case the institution of the Hundred Houses as well.

nized as client or dependent families of the great houses. An economy of this type, as D'Agostino observes,[59] is not incapable of development; indeed as wealth develops at the top, surplus agricultural labor will be drawn into urban occupations. But such an economy will be somewhat sheltered from the sort of class conflict characteristic of more rationalized, monetized societies.

This picture of Locrian society is not based on direct evidence and in that sense is imaginative, but it is consistent with what else we know of Locri and her avoidance of history. It seems that Locri, like Sparta, was a city that resisted development.

[59] D'Agostino (1973), p. 227.

Plate 1: Dedications from the Locrian Cave of the Nymphs, Museo Nazionale di Reggio. Photograph by Leonard von Matt, Buochs/Switzerland, © by NZN Buchverlag, Zurich/Switzerland 1962, 1967. Reproduction with friendly permission of the publishers.

Plate 2: Locrian perfume burner, Museo Nazionale di Reggio.

Plate 3: Locrian perfume burner, detail: bottom. Photograph by Leonard von Matt, Buochs/ Switzerland, © by NZN Buchverlag, Zurich/ Switzerland 1962, 1967. Reproduction with friendly permission of the publishers.

Plate 4: Locrian perfume burner, detail: top, Museo Nazionale di Reggio.

Plate 5: Ludovisi Throne, front, Museo Nazionale, Rome. Photograph by permission of the Museum of Antiquities, University of Saskatchewan.

Plate 6: Ludovisi Throne, left side. Photograph by permission of the Museum of Antiquities, University of Saskatchewan.

Plate 7: Ludovisi Throne, right side. Photograph by permission of the Museum of Antiquities, University of Saskatchewan.

Plate 8: Boston Throne, front, Boston Museum of Fine Arts. Courtesy, Museum of Fine Arts, Boston. Reproduced with permission. © 2000 Museum of Fine Arts, Boston. All rights reserved.

Plate 9: Boston Throne, left side. Courtesy, Museum of Fine Arts, Boston. Reproduced with permission. © 2000 Museum of Fine Arts, Boston. All rights reserved.

Plate 10: Boston Throne, right side. Courtesy, Museum of Fine Arts, Boston. Reproduced with permission. © 2000 Museum of Fine Arts, Boston. All rights reserved.

Plate 11: *Pinax* type 8/29. P 3. Originally published in Prückner, H. (1968). *Die Lokrischen Tönreliefs*. Mainz am Rhein. Reproduced by permission.

Plate 12: *Pinax* type 2/22 P 57. Originally published in Prückner, H. (1968). *Die Lokrischen Tönreliefs.* Mainz am Rhein. Reproduced by permission.

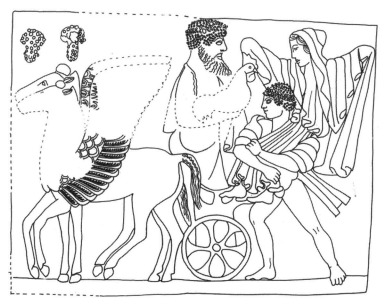

Plate 13 *Pinax* type 2/30 P 83, Museo Nazionale di Reggio. Originally published in Lissi (Caronna), E., C. Sabbione, et al., eds. (1999). *I pinakes di Locri Epizefiri.* Rome, Società Magna Grecia.

Plate 14: *Pinax* type 2/10 P 68. Photograph by Leonard von Matt, Buochs/
Switzerland, © by NZN Buchverlag, Zurich/Switzerland 1962, 1967.
Reproduction with friendly permission of the publishers.

Plate 15: *Pinax* type 7/3 P 3. Photograph by Leonard von Matt, Buochs/
Switzerland, © by NZN Buchverlag, Zurich/Switzerland 1962, 1967.
Reproduction with friendly permission of the publishers.

Plate 16: *Pinax* type 3/6
P 2. Originally pub-
lished in Prückner, H.
(1968). *Die Lokrischen
Tönreliefs.* Mainz am
Rhein. Reproduced by
permission.

Plate 17: *Pinax* type
5/2 P 14. Photo-
graph by Leonard
von Matt, Buochs/
Switzerland, © by
NZN Buchverlag,
Zurich/Switzerland
1962, 1967. Repro-
duction with
friendly permission
of the publishers.

Plate 18: *Pinax* type 10/1 P 1. Originally published in Prückner, H. (1968). *Die Lokrischen Tönreliefs.* Mainz am Rhein. Reproduced by permission.

Plate 19 *Pinax* type 10/2 P 4. Originally published in Prückner, H. (1968). *Die Lokrischen Tönreliefs.* Mainz am Rhein. Reproduced by permission.

Plate 20: *Pinax* type 8/31 P 86. Photograph by Leonard von Matt, Buochs/Switzerland, © by NZN Buchverlag, Zurich/Switzerland 1962, 1967. Reproduction with friendly permission of the publishers.

Plate 21: *Pinax* type 5/19 P 31. Photograph by Leonard von Matt, Buochs/Switzerland, © by NZN Buchverlag, Zurich/Switzerland 1962, 1967. Reproduction with friendly permission of the publishers.

Plate 22: *Pinax* type 5/3 P 16. Photograph by Leonard von Matt, Buochs/Switzerland, © by NZN Buchverlag, Zurich/Switzerland 1962, 1967. Reproduction with friendly permission of the publishers.

Plate 23: Chrysaphe relief from Sparta, Berlin. Originally published in Blümel, C. (1940). *Griechische Skulpturen des sechsten und fünften j. v. c.* Berlin/Leipzig, Verlag für Kunstwissenschaft.

Plate 24: *Pinax* type 4/3 P 45. Originally published in Prückner, H. (1968). *Die Lokrischen Tönreliefs.* Mainz am Rhein. Reproduced by permission.

Plate 25: *Pinax* type 10/11 P 50, Museo Nazionale di Reggio.

Plate 26: Spartan cup from Samos. Originally published in Stibbe, C.M. *Lakonische Vasenmaler* Amsterdam/London, North Holland.

Plate 27: Locrian terra-cotta, Museo Nazionale di Reggio. Originally published in Arias, P. (1947) "Locri (Piani Caruso) Scavi di case antiche" Notizie . . . Scavi 72 (vol. 1) pp. 165–171.

Seven

Locrian Culture: Locri, Locris, Sparta (and Crete)

On Interpretation: Stories

One way of explaining something, perhaps the best, certainly throughout history the most popular way, is to tell a story about it. Most of
stories we have from the early Greeks are explanations: how it is that
the universe persists, how we know that the rules by which society lives
are the right rules, why it is that in a certain town on a certain day each
year certain things are proper. Most of these stories are set in story
time—either in mythical time, the time before any time of which we
know anything, or in that once upon a time that could be any time at
all. Because they are in story time they cannot be historically true. But
some stories tell of particular, even rather recent times: the time, for
instance, of a remembered grandfather. Such stories tend to get into
our histories—which does not make them historical. The point of
these stories still is not to tell us how it was, but rather why it is. Narrative histories of Athens, for instance, generally begin with the conspiracy of Cylon in 626 B.C., because that is the earliest dated event in
Athenian history. Our sources do not tell us this story, however, as an
event in Athenian history but as an explanation of how it was that two
centuries later the family of the Alcmaeonidae was hostile to tyranny,
high-handed in politics, and under a curse.

   We make history out of these stories by stringing them together into
chronological order and by asking if they are true. We have been doing
this since Thucydides. Since these stories most often quite obviously
follow a story logic unconstrained by plodding quotidian reality, we can
see that they are in large part untrue, but we look for the "kernel of
truth"—as if truth were a nourishing fragment wrapped in a thick husk
of fiction, or perhaps the irritant that causes the culture to secrete the
pearl of folklore. This inquiry of ours misrepresents the story and is
likely to produce a poor result. Not but what there can be some truth
in the story, but in the absence of independent evidence this truth is
unlikely to identify itself, and the attempt to discern it on grounds of
sheer plausibility, as Thucydides does in his opening chapters, tells us
much more about the historian than about the past. Also while picking
apart the story in the service of this enterprise we tend to lose its inner

structure. The story of Cylon may or may not tell us about political conflict in the Athenian seventh century; it certainly tells us something about the powerfully ambiguous standing of the Alcmaeonidae, taken locally to include Cleisthenes, Pericles, and Alcibiades. In the story the family is represented *both* as the savior of the state and as a god-hated threat to its health.

Stories can be true to the past, but they are always completely true to their present. Even if we have the past exactly right we still have to imagine it in order to tell it as a story, and in this sense every story is a work of the imagination. Furthermore, truth is a relatively weak motivation. Even if the story is completely true we still have to ask why it is being told here and now, and the answer to that question is likely to be the most interesting truth in the story.

Nevertheless, historians have been trying to turn explanatory stories into true history at least since the mid-fifth century B.C., when Herodotus's western contemporary, Antiochus of Syracuse, went about collecting and selecting "from the ancient tales the most believable and the plainest" (59 FGH 2). Most of the stories the people of the West told Antiochus were stories of the origins of peoples and the foundation of cities—at least the fragments we have of him contain virtually nothing else. Foundation stories are explanations of cities—and since the founder, the *oikistēs*, received heroic honors, they also belong to that subtype of explanation we call an *aition*, the narrative explanation of a ritual.[1]

Usually there is nothing else for a long time after the foundation of a city—except other foundation stories: The first event in the history of Syracuse is the foundation of her subcolony Akrae; the first event in the history of Zancle is the foundation of Mylae.

Occasionally the foundation is followed by another story narrating what we may call a *heroic event*, nearly always a moment when the very existence of the community is at risk and it is rescued—in effect refounded. In such an event the community again defines itself. In the Spartan stories the foundation story is the return of the Heracleidae, wherein the Dorians conquer the Peloponnese; it explains the relation of the Spartans to their land, to the valley of the Eurotas. Later comes the story of the Messenian Wars; this explains the relation of the Spartans to their labor, to the helots.

---

[1] Quite possibly the heroic honors of the founder included at least in some cases an annual celebration, perhaps with games (characteristic of hero-cult), and these were counted, so that colonial foundations dated their years *ab urbe condita* or its Greek equivalent: This would explain why the traditional dates of foundation as they appear, for instance, in the opening pages of Thucydides' sixth book stand up pretty well when confronted by the archaeological evidence. But this is sheer speculation.

In the Locrian narrative, after the foundation (to which we come later), the heroic event is the battle of the Sagra, the insecurely datable battle (somewhere between 550 and 510) whereby Locri secured its autonomous existence through defeating the overwhelming forces of Croton, the large city to their north. This battle became part of the language in the expression "truer than the Sagra" (more or less: "you'd better believe it"). Also many miracle stories were told about it—for instance, that the result of the battle mysteriously became known on the same day at the Olympic games, or perhaps at Sparta, or perhaps simultaneously at Sparta, Corinth, and Athens.[2]

Heroic events define the community: America was founded on Plymouth rock, and by the Declaration of Independence, and on the field of Gettysburg. Since all these events signify the same community, all have the same meaning, although with variations. Because heroic events are reaffirmations they enable a group to read its long history as one of cultural continuity: Magna Carta signifies the liberties of Englishmen, and so does the Glorious Revolution. The French somehow have the same revolution over and over again. In fact one way to understand culture is as a persisting set of structures that cause the histories of particular peoples to repeat themselves, or at least to be so interpreted by the natives. Culture shapes events, but even more it shapes the interpretation of events. It will follow that the culture is more evident in the narration than in the actual event it narrates, and that one way, perhaps the best way, to understand a people's culture is to listen to their stories.

As an example, let us take the case of Helike. One night during the winter of 373–372 B.C. an earthquake and tidal wave shook the city of Helike—up to that time one of the most important cities in Achaea—into the sea. This was no myth; it was one of the most destructive earthquakes in the history of an area noted for destructive earthquakes. The loss of life must have been enormous, and four hundred years later the ruins were still visible under the water. The event had a special theological significance, because earthquakes are sent by Poseidon and Helike had for centuries been especially noted for its piety toward Poseidon (*Il.* 8.203). In these terms the event generated stories—that the people of Helike had murdered suppliants, for instance (Pausanias 7.25). Others linked the event to a story (which may even be true) that Helike had rejected and sacrilegiously interfered with a sacred embassy from Ionia (Diodorus Siculus 15.49). There is also a Locrian story concerning this event, linking it to events in Oiantheia, a town in Ozolian Locris:

[2] See Niutta (1977), p. 268.

Themisto was daughter of Crithon of Oiantheia. Philon, the son of the tyrant Phricodemus, fell in love with her. The tyrant asked for the daughter in marriage. The father refused. The tyrant, seizing the sons of Crithon, threw them to hungry beasts before the eyes of their mother and father, and seizing the girl he celebrated the marriage. Themisto, who had given her consent under duress, concealed a sword under her little shirt and when the bridegroom was asleep in the wedding chamber she leaned over him and cheerfully cut his throat, so that the murder victim had no chance to cry out. Leaving all this unrevealed by night she got back down to the ocean, found a boat, encountered a favorable wind, drew up the anchor, and putting to sea alone sailed to Helike, a city in Achaea, where there was a holy sanctuary of Poseidon. She took refuge there as a suppliant. Phricodemus sent his other son, Herakon, brother of the murder victim, to ask for the girl from the people of Helike. And they actually handed her over, but when they put out to sea a great storm drove their vessel into Rhion in Achaea; while they were anchored here two ships showed up from Arcanania, which place was hostile to the tyrant. These grappled with their vessel and took them under tow to Acarnania. When the assembly of Acarnania heard what had been done they took pity on the girl and, binding Herakon, turned him over to her. The tyrant sent her an embassy on behalf of his son; she sent back the message that if he would turn over her parents she would give his son back. He trusted her and sent her parents. The Acarnanians brutally tortured Herakon anyway and killed him. As for Phricodemus, a few days later the citizens did away with him. The inhabitants of Helike shortly afterward were swept into the sea, and their city with them, as a result of an earthquake and tidal wave. This was thought to be the wrathful act of Poseidon, because they had handed over a suppliant of his, a maiden. (Polyaenus 8.46)

The story has to be horrible enough justify an earthquake. The atrocities are so great that destruction properly falls on the whole community that cooperated with the perpetrator, as well as on the tyrant himself and his family. Whether the tyrant ever existed is another question; his name (it means "he makes the people shiver") suggests that he is invented. The kernel of truth here is the earthquake; everything else serves to integrate the event within some frame of collective representation such that the earthquake becomes intelligible. The earthquake, however, is not what makes the story meaningful.

The story of Themisto has something in common with the story of Aristides the Locrian, to which we come later;[3] in both, the father who refuses to give the tyrant his daughter loses his sons. The story of Aristides, however, is told from the point of view of the father, and stresses

[3] See p. 282.

his stoic psychic resistance. This story is told from the point of view of the girl; she is a figure of power. Themisto is brave and competent and ruthless and lucky. She has the weather on her side; she can sail a ship and cut a throat and strike a bargain—which she does not have to keep. In the end she gets back her parents and gets her revenge as well. She is extremely appealing and very dangerous. The story tells us that those who deal impiously with a Locrian maiden bring on themselves destruction on a cosmic scale. This, it seems, is how history happens among the Locrians. Whenever we enter the domain of Locrian stories we must be prepared for the extraordinary; these people did not explain themselves to themselves with Thucydidean materialism. And we must be prepared for some remarkable maidens.

Euthymus and the Hero of Temesa

As another sample of the storymaking process, let us take the case of Temesa.[4] Temesa was a real place (even though its location is now uncertain), somewhere north of Hipponion on the Tyrrhenian Sea. We have coins from there that link the place to Croton, probably in the first years of the fifth century; later it seems to be independent.[5] Strabo had been there and had heard the *aition* of a local sanctuary:

> Nearby is the heroon of Temesa, shaded with wild olive, belonging to Polites, one of the companions of Odysseus; he was treacherously slain by the barbarians and became a harsh curse to them, so that the inhabitants of the place made a tithe to him according to an oracle—and it is a proverb of unpleasant things, people say "the hero of Temesa lies by them." When the Epizephyrian Locrians took the place the story goes that Euthymus the boxer went down against him and defeated him in battle and compelled him to spare the local people their tithes. (Strabo VI.1.5)

The story of the hero of Temesa is the only evidence we have that Locri ever controlled the place—and perhaps Locri did not. There was, however, some political change about the mid-fifth century, and it seems that this event was, at the time or later, represented as the conquest of a local spirit by a Locrian champion.[6]

[4] For the state of the question on Temesa, see Maddoli (1982).

[5] Dunbabin (1948), p. 367. Stazio (1982) pp. 100–101, sums up the evidence from coinage as follows: from the end of the sixth century to the mid-fifth, Temesa is closely dependent on Croton; around the middle of the century the place gradually acquires autonomy.

[6] For a thorough review of the sources, literature, and issues relating to this matter, see Costabile (1991a).

Euthymus was a real person; he was the Olympic victor in boxing in 484 B.C. In the next Olympics he was defeated by Theagenes of Thasos, whose proper event was the pancration; Theagenes was then made to pay a fine to Euthymus on the ground that he had entered the boxing only out of spite. Theagenes stayed out of boxing in the next two Olympics, and Euthymus won the event in them both. Pausanias (6.6), who tells us all this, had seen and admired the statue of Euthymus in the precinct at Olympia, the work of Pythagoras of Samos (later of Rhegion). The base of this statue was found in 1878;[7] it is inscribed:

> Euthymus the Locrian son of Astykles thrice at Olympia I won
> And he set this image for mortals to behold
> Euthymus the Locrian from Zephyrion dedicated it
> Pythagoras the Samian made it.

Euthymus, like some other Olympic victors (especially those who had been disqualified or in some other way unfortunately treated),[8] was heroized. Pliny (*Natural History* 7.47) tells us that Euthymus became, indeed, a hero in his own time; from Callimachus Pliny had learned that the statues of Euthymus at Locri and Olympia were struck by lightning on the same day, and that the oracle when consulted said that sacrifices should be made to him; this began, says Pliny, in his lifetime and continued after his death. Pausanias adds that while he was called son of Astykles his real father was the river Caicinus (Pausanias 6.6.4), also that he lived to a great age and escaped death, "departing from mankind in some other manner" (Pausanias 6.6.10). We learn from Aelian (quoted below) that his final mortal act was a plunge into the Caicinus. Costabile (1991a), (p. 211 and note 37) plausibly suggests, by parallelism with an anecdote in Suetonius (*de Rhetoribus*, s.v. M. Epi-

---

[7] Frazer (1898), vol. 4, p. 22, quotes the inscription, and adds: "An examination of the stone shows that the words *tēnde brotois esoran* were carved by another and less skillful hand than the rest of the inscription, and that the word *anethēke* is an addition made to the original inscription by the same less skillful hand. Hence it is supposed that the statue was originally dedicated, not by Euthymus himself, but by someone else whose name was mentioned in the second line, and that for some reason this name was struck out and the inscription altered into its present form. This explains the awkwardness of making Euthymus speak in the first person in the first line and in the third person in the second line. Messrs. Dittenberger and Purgold suppose that the statue was set up not by Euthymus himself, but by his native city Locri; that the original inscription recorded this fact; and that the Eleans, offended at any state besides their own presuming to award such an honor, caused the inscription to be altered in such a way as to make it appear that the statue had been erected by Euthymus himself." Costabile (1991a) pp. 212–213, suggests that the inscription was rewritten after Euthymus's apotheosis, and that the reference to mortals who look on is intended to suggest that he himself is immortal.

[8] Fontenrose (1968).

dius) that his apotheosis happened at that moment and that he himself became a river god.

Here again we have archaeological confirmation; Paolo Arias in 1941[9] found at Locri, in the Cave of the Nymphs also known as the Caruso sanctuary, a terra-cotta plaque in high relief, at the top three female heads (evidently nymphs), below in profile a bull with a young, beard-less man's head, facing an altar and inscribed EUTHY[mou hi]E[ra], "sacred to Euthymus."[10] A number of others have been found since.[11] A bull with a man's head must be a river god; usually, however, these are represented as old and bearded. Euthymus, although he lived to a good age, seems to have recovered his youth as an immortal.[12] There are also from Locri a number of somewhat similar plaques, with the three female heads along the top, where the bull has the head of an older bearded male and appears half concealed by a doorway from which he looks out.[13] These represent either Achelous (father of all the rivers, and everywhere in Greece worshipped in conjunction with the nymphs) or else Euthymus's father-in-religion, the Caicinus.

Pausanias includes in his account of Euthymus the story of the conquest of Temesa:

Odysseus in his wanderings after the sack of Ilion was carried, we are told, by the winds into various cities of Italy and Sicily; he came to Temesa also with his ships. There one of his sailors got drunk and forced a maiden; in revenge the natives stoned him to death for his crime. Odysseus took no special account of this loss but sailed away; the spirit (*daimōn*) of the person who had been stoned then missed no chance wantonly to kill the people of Temesa, young and old, until, when they were ready to leave Italy altogether, the Pythia would not let them go, but told them to appease the hero by setting aside a precinct and building a temple, and to give him each year the fairest of the maidens of Temesa as his wife. Once they began fulfilling the instructions of the god they suffered no further terror from the spirit. But Euthymus—he came to Temesa, and (as it happened) just at the time of the customary observance for the spirit—found out what was going on among them and wanted to be in the temple and see the maiden come in. When he saw her he felt first pity, and second actually fell in love with her. And the girl swore to marry him if he saved her. Euthymus then readied himself and awaited the entry of the spirit. In the fight he was victorious; the hero, in as

[9] Arias (1941).

[10] This reading of the inscription was established by Costabile (1991a), p. 200.

[11] Costabile (1991a), p. 200.

[12] Mele (1983) notes that Aelian (*Varia Historia* 2.33) describes the eponymous river of Acragas as similarly represented.

[13] Costabile (1991a), pp. 221–226.

much as it was driven from the land, disappeared, sinking into the sea. Euthymus got a brilliant wedding and the people there were henceforward liberated from the spirit. (Pausanias 6.6.7–10)

The Suda (s.v. Euthymus) adds the name of the *daimōn*: Alybas. Strabo had given the name of the hero as Polites. Polites in the *Odyssey* (18.304) is the companion of Odysseus who takes the lead in falling victim to Circe's charms, who is, in other words, incautiously attracted. Circe turned him into a pig; the people of Temesa turned him into Alybas, a name that seems to mean "withered" or "skeleton" (LSJ ad voc.). In other words, he became a terrifying figure, the most hostile kind of ghost. By the time Strabo got there, however, he was again called at his heroon "Polites"; evidently Euthymus's victory was not seen as ejecting the hero but as transforming him into a benevolent hero. He "disappeared . . . into the sea" only in his hostile form; Euthymus canceled not Polites, but the consequences of the crime of the people of Temesa.

The general scenario resembles the *aition* of Artemis Triclaria at Patras.[14] As in that story, there is a crime that must be expiated by the sacrifice of the marriageable young; an outsider intervenes to cancel the sacrifice and to transform hostility into beneficence. In some other respects this story resembles those colonization stories—that of Massalia, for instance—in which the outsider obtains a place for himself and his people by gaining the hand of a princess. The story, in other words, asserts a Locrian claim to Temesa in two forms: The Locrian hero is stronger than the local hero, and the Locrian obtains a local maiden. The result, as in the Patras story, is a refoundation of the community.[15]

This particular version of a foundation story is, moreover, quite Locrian. Allowing for transformations, there are certain parallels with the *aition* of the Locrian maidens at Troy. Both stories begin when an intruder, a Greek veteran of the Trojan War, rapes a maiden. A rapist should be stoned to death, but in neither case is this a solution; Locrian Ajax escapes stoning (so that the anger of the goddess fell on his people) while this rapist suffers it, so that his own anger falls on those who stoned him. The people of Temesa, like the Locrians, consult the oracle, which tells them to sacrifice annually the fairest maiden—not to serve the god as a slave, as at Troy, but to serve the hero as wife. This, like the sacrificed year of the maidens at Troy, is a first-fruits

[14] Discussed at length in Redfield (1990).
[15] Mele (1983), p. 873, says the story describes "un rito di transizione da *parthenos* a legittima sposa che, in quanto vissuto sullo sfondo di un contrasto tra l'animalità del demone, ferino e notturno, e la tranquillità della communita liberata, è contemporaneamente un rito di rifondazione della comunità stessa."

sacrifice, in this case a kind of *droit de seigneur.* "In the morning," says the commentator on Callimachus (*Diegeseis* 5.5–15), telling the same story, "her parents received her back, no longer a maiden but a wife."[16] These girls were presumably used up, no longer marriageable (or Euthymus would not have been so moved to pity)—but Euthymus, by cheating the monster of his victim, thereby acquires a particularly valuable wife—just as the Locrian maidens, on their return, were (we have supposed) particularly valuable brides. Both stories therefore involve the transformation of sacrificial victim into desirable wife.

Such parallels are evidence of shared culture, of the Locrian character of Epizephyrian Locri. The parallels are not, however, equally evident in all versions; Aelian tells a version in which the maiden does not appear.[17]

This brings us to another foundation story, placed this time not in the West, but in old-world, Ozolian Locris:

By the base of Parnassus southward there is a mountain which is called Cirphis-by-Crisa, and in it there is a very large cave in which there lived a large and supernatural beast, and it they call Lamia, or some call it Sybaris. This beast used to go out every day and seize from the fields the beasts and the people. The Delphians were already considering migration and asked the oracle to which country they should go, but the god signaled to them a solution for their misfortunes, if they were willing of their own free will to place in the cave one youth of the citizens. And they did what the god had told them. They drew lots and it fell upon Alkyon, the son of Diomos and

---

[16] Note that a similar story was told of Dionysius the Younger at Locri—see below, p. 285.

[17] "Euthymus of the Italian Locrians was a fine boxer; he was so confident in the strength of his body as to become extremely bold. The Locrians show an extremely large rock which he moved and placed before his doorway. Also he stopped the hero in Temesa from taking tributes from the inhabitants. He went into his sanctuary, which was barred to most people, and struggled with him, and compelled him to pay back more than he had pillaged. That is how the proverb circulated, about those who make profits which are not to their benefit, that the hero in Temesa will come to them. They say that this same Euthymus descending into the river Caicinus—which is by the city of the Locrians—vanished" (Aelian *Var. Hist.* VIII.18)

Here, as in Strabo, we learn that the hero of Temesa had entered into the language. The story was familiar. There is no point in asking which is the original version. All the versions are motivated. The culture represents itself in the play of variants; as it is told and retold the story progressively reveals the underlying archetypes and collective representations. Another element of Locrian tradition to enter the language as a proverb was the "Locrian Ox" as a proverbial expression "for things that are cheap. . . . The Locrians were once without an ox for public sacrifice, and so stuck together bits of wood with cucumbers in the form of an ox, and thus served the god" (Zenobius V.5). Economy suits either old-world or Italian Locrians (a similar story is also told of an Athenian—Zenobius V.22).

Meganeira, his father's only child and as fine in his looks as in the character of his soul. And the priests crowning Alkyon led him into the cave of Sybaris—and then as fate would have it there arrived from Couretis Eurybatus, child of Euphemus, descended from the river Axios, young and noble, and he encountered the boy as he was being led in. Love-struck, he inquired for what reason they proceeded, and thought it outrageous not to defend the child so far as he could, rather than see him die a pitiable death. Seizing the crown from Alkyon and putting it on his own head he told them to lead him in instead of the boy. Once the priests had brought him up to the cave he rushed in and seized Sybaris from her lair, dragged her into the open and hurled her down the rocks. She hurtled down and broke her skull at the base of Crisa, and so wounded disappeared, but from that rock broke forth a spring, and the natives call it Sybaris. From this spring the Locrians founded in Italy the city of Sybaris. (Antonius Liberalis *Metamorphoseon Synagoge* 8)

Again, the parallels are striking, this time with Euthymus and the hero of Temesa. The monster torments the people until they consider migration; the oracle instructs them instead to institute a human sacrifice. They offer the fairest; the young warrior, descended from a river, falls in love with the victim and overcomes the monster, causing it to disappear. The result is a political change, in this case a new foundation. The most obvious difference, the shift of the love interest from heterosexual to homosexual, is probably motivated by the fact that this story is pinned to Sybaris, who by her name must be female: her hostile sexuality thus requires a male victim—whose rescuer, however, must remain male in order to be a warrior.

It would not have occurred to us, however, to link directly the maidens at Troy with the Sybaris story; we require the Euthymus story as an intermediary link. The Euthymus story could have borrowed content from the maidens at Troy and then have shaped the Sybaris story or the transmission could have been reversed; in either case we have evidence of the cultural connections working in both directions.

This is not the usual story about the foundation of Sybaris; usually the colony is held to have originated in Achaea, actually in Helike (the city destroyed by the earthquake) on the other side of the Corinthian Gulf, and the spring Sybaris was placed on that side (Strabo 252, 386). It is somewhat astonishing to find the Locrians claiming the foundation of Sybaris,[18] and even more astonishing to find them claiming Delphi for their territory. Nor is it possible to provide a plausible date for the origin of any of these stories. It is enough for our purposes to

[18] Mele (1983), pp. 868–869, notes two other traces of a Locrian claim to Sybaris: The Latin grammarian Solinus (2.10) says that the founder of Sybaris was the son of the Locrian Ajax; Pseudo-Skymnus refers to Zaleucus as the lawgiver of Sybaris.

observe that the Sybaris story is a typically Locrian story: The foundation of a city is linked to the dangers of sexuality and the purificatory
power of love.

The Sparta of the West

Domenico Musti observes that the socioeconomic peculiarities of Epizephyrian Locri remind one of Sparta; the city "is in a way the Sparta of
the West."[19] The ancients recognized the parallels. Pausanias (3.3.1)
actually asserted that Locri (along with Croton) was a Spartan foundation. This notion has been defended in modern times,[20] and Blomquist
in his analysis of the Locrian dialect[21] notes that the closest links are
with Sparta, Messenia, and Heracleia (itself a subfoundation of the
Spartan colony Taras); that the colony originated in old-world Locris
he holds to be definitely excluded. I know of no archaeological evidence for links between Locri and old-world Locris; there are, by contrast, a number of iconographic features in Locrian art—for example,
the representation of an enthroned couple belonging to the underworld, approached by worshippers, and the motif of a horseman sustained by a winged figure (see n. 25 below)—that are evidently Spartan.[22] Nevertheless the Epizephyrian Locrians insisted on their old-world
Locrian origins, asserting the links with Sparta in other ways. Their
foundation story, for instance, attributes the origin of the city to
Locrian involvement with Sparta: *At the time of the Messenian War*, we are
told,[23] *the Locrians came to help the Spartans. Because their men folk were
absent the women took up with the serfs. Some of these women with their consorts
were sent out to found the colony of the Locrians in Italy.* We shall come back
to this story; here we note only that the foundation of Locri is attributed to Locrian involvement with the Spartans.
    Similarly one of the miracle stories about the Battle of the Sagra

[19] Musti (1979), p. 9.
[20] Malkin (1994), p. 63n.62, cites an unpublished manuscript by L. Moscati Castel-
nuovo "on the Spartan origins of Croton and Lokroi"; he concludes, "the case, in general, is circumstantial, and the sources are late."
[21] Blomquist (1975); Blomquist (1978).
[22] Rolley (1982), pp. 39–40, notes that Spartan stylistic influence is strong in all the
Greek cities on the Adriatic coast of Italy from the early sixth century onward, and that
the influence of Taras has been much overrated; the iconographic links with Sparta,
however, remain peculiarly Locrian.
[23] This story was told by Aristotle, evidently in his *Constitution of Locri*, now lost. Timaeus, in a passage now also lost, denied its truth. The story can be reconstructed from
Polybius (12.5) who supported Aristotle against Timaeus. See pp. 264–265.

involves Sparta. It is in Diodorus Siculus (3.32).[24] *The Locrians,* we are told, *threatened by Croton, sent to Sparta for help. The Spartans, hearing of the power of Croton, put the Locrians off with a promise to lend them the Dioscuri as their allies. The Locrians accepted the omen and spread for the gods a couch on their ship when returning from Sparta. The result was the miraculous victory at the Sagra.*

The victory is thus represented as achieved by a *theoxenia,* an entertainment of the gods—a rite proper to the Dioscuri (who are also typically saviors). That this story of the Sagra was canonical at Locri we know from Strabo (6.1.10), who found on the banks of the Sagra altars to the Dioscuri, and also from the acroteria of the Marasà temple at Locri, which represent the Dioscuri dismounting from horses borne by sea-creatures—evidently coming across the ocean to rescue the Locrians.[25]

Origin and heroic moment, the foundation story and the story of the Dioscuri at the Sagra, state a single message: without Sparta, Epizephyrian Locri would not exist.[26] On the cultural level, however, Locri is not represented as dependent on Sparta, but as her peer. The Locrian lawgiver Zaleucus—who shares some odd traits with Spartan Lycurgus, for instance that of having one eye (Aristotle Fr. 61 Rose[27])— is along with Lycurgus called pupil of the Cretan Thales, who himself is called companion of a Locrian Onomacritus, "who was the first to be ingenious in lawgiving." (Aristotle, who tells this story—*Politics* 1274a— tags it as chronologically impossible.) Another Locrian influence on Sparta is asserted through the story that Xenocrates the Locrian was

---

[24] Cf. Photius apud *alēthesteron* . . . , Justin 20.2, Cicero *Nat. Deorum* 2.2.6, 3.5.13. On this anecdote see Compernolle (1969); Sordi (1972); Giangiulio (1983).

[25] On this architectural motif—fairly frequent in the West—see Szeliga (1982). Peculiar to the Locrian type is the support of the horses by a sea-creature, with evident allusion to the story of the Sagra. Pausanias (3.18.14) reports that the motif of the Dioscuri supported by monsters (in the Spartan case, by sphinxes) was already on the Amyklae Throne, a work of the sixth century. De la Genière (1986), p. 405, comments that the Locrians not only sought help from Sparta; when the time came to thank them, they borrowed from Sparta the mode of their representation. See also de la Genière (1985); both these articles include good discussions of links between Locri and Sparta.

[26] There is in Herodotus another story that Sparta later helped Croton when that city, abandoning its hopes of Locri, turned the other way to conquer Sybaris (Herodotus 5.44–45); Sparta, however, is all over the folk history of the West. That story, also, was not canonical at Croton: Herodotus says it was told not there but by the Sybarites. Also this latter story is told in terms of practical help (the colonial expedition of Dorieus of Sparta paused to help Croton eliminate Sybaris). The link between Locri and Sparta, by contrast, is asserted on the level of myth and of divine intervention.

[27] Cf. Piccirilli (1978), p. 925.

among those who took part in the second reform of Spartan music and instituted the *gumnopaidia* ([Plutarch] *de Musica* 9, *Moralia* 1134c).[28]

All these stories are tokens of a folk perception of a kinship between these two cities, a kinship that existed on a more significant level in that both were paradigms of civic legality, of *eunomia*—the Locrian name for which was probably *atrekeia* (Pindar *Ol.* 10.13). Both were exceptionally stable societies, in some respects culturally secretive, in the classical period without coinage or literature, but cities where music and ritual were cultivated. These two cities seem, in their different ways, to have secured their political institutions by embedding them in a peculiar local culture—which is to say, a peculiar education. Both cities seem to have set themselves to shape their citizen class in such a way as to eliminate or at least repress the contradictions created elsewhere by development.

The most important link between Sparta and Locri, then, is on the constitutional level—not that either imitates the other, but that their political development was in certain critical respects parallel. Even the claim of the Epizephyrians to be Locrian turns out on examination to make them like the Spartans, in the sense that (as I shall argue in the next sections) it is parallel to the Spartan claim to have derived her civil order from Crete.

Locri and the Locrians

One of the many odd things about this odd city is that she never had a name. We call her Locri—as opposed to Locris, the territory of the old-world Locrians—because her people called themselves *hoi Lokroi*, the Locrians; their city was called *hē polis tōn Lokrōn*, the city of the Locrians—or, to avoid ambiguity, "of the Italian Locrians," or "of the Locrians by Zephyrion." While other Greeks were named after their cities—the Athenians after Athens, the Corinthians after Corinth—the city of these Locrians was named after her people, who were thereby identified as one branch of the Locrian people, parallel with "the [old-world] Locrians by Cnemis," or "the Locrians of Ozolis."

Those other Locrians, however, lived in named communities and were named after their communities—they were called Opuntians or Naupactians, as well as Epicnemidian Locrians from Opus, or Ozolian Locrians from Naupactus. Furthermore the old-world pattern was re-

---

[28] See Gigante (1982), pp. 588–589. Oldfather (1908) notes that the Locrian name of Persephone, *Pēriphona*, is close to the Spartan version, *Pēriphoneia*.

peated in the West by the secondary Epizephyrian communities on the
Tyrrhenian coast. We have a seventh-century inscription: "Demarchus
son of Philotes, a Locrian, one of those by Zephyrion, from Hipponion" (Dunbabin [1948], p. 165). Here Locrian is the genus, Epizephyrian the species, and Hipponion the particular community. We
also have an inscribed shield from Olympia, dating probably from the
late sixth century, which reads: "the Hipponeis dedicated [this spoil
taken] from the Crotonians, also the Medmaei and the Locrians [dedi-
cated it]" (SEG XI 1211). Hipponion, Medma, and the city we know as
Epizephyrian Locri were allies against Croton—naturally, since they
were all Locrians. The people of Hipponion, however, are here named
after Hipponion, and the people of Medma after Medma; the people
of their mother city are "Locrians" *tout court*. Evidently they were the
Locrians par excellence. Certainly they were the important Locrians;
we may suspect that in the classical period the Epizephyrians were most
often the makers of Locrian manners, so that the old-world Locrians
found themselves taking the Epizephyrians as their model. This great
nameless city, although she called herself their colony, had in other
words become in a way the metropolis of all the Locrians. She did not
have a name because she was in the paradoxical position of a *polis*
insistent on being an *ethnos*.

The claim of the Epizephyrians to be originally Locrian is unsup-
ported by evidence of dialect, archaeology, or any single cultural peculiarity ascribable to such an origin, or of diffusion in either direction.[29]
It is supported only by legendary history which comes to us from the
classical period and later. Such stories are told because they have a use;
we are entitled to ask what use the Locrian connection had for the
Epizephyrians.

The Greeks have transmitted to us an ideal picture of a colonial
foundation as the collective act of a city-state. Some individual, the
oikistēs, would be assigned by his city (often as a punishment) and instructed (often by Delphi) to take a band of young men out to the
frontier and found a new and independent city that was yet somehow
notionally a replica of the metropolis—in its dialect, its *nomoi*, and especially its cults. In this way, we are told, Corinth founded Syracuse and
Corcyra, Sparta founded Taras, Thera founded Cyrene, Paros founded
Thasos, Miletus founded Olbia, and so on. There must have been some
truth to this ideal picture; only the collective act of an already organized group would have made possible the division of the new town
into equal allotments—as at Megara Hyblaea, possibly the earliest colo-

[29] But see Landi (1967).

nial foundation in Sicily. The settlers of Megara Hyblaea did not just drift in; they were from the beginning able to take collective possession of the territory and divide it rationally amongst themselves.

Not all early colonization, however, followed this pattern. The West was first opened up in middle geometric II (800–750) by Euboean sailors, traders and *lēistai*. Such communities are sometimes called "protocolonial"; their populace was relatively individualistic and entrepreneurial. Of both Zancle (later Messena) and Corcyra we hear that Eretrian *lēistai* had to be expelled before a proper community could be established. In Pithekoussai we have a well-documented protocolonial site, which, as we have seen, briefly boomed and then faded.[30] Emporio on Chios and Zagora on Andros seem to have had a similar history in the Aegean. Naxos in Sicily may have originally been a similarly informal foundation (we can call these "trading" colonies, but they are more generally communities of adventurers); when the Greeks here began to exploit the territory through agriculture the center shifted inland to Leontini.

The Italian colonies (except for Taras) seem all to have been of this relatively informal kind. "Some of them had mixed populations and may have had more than one foundation. There were other settlements which never reached the form of a *polis*. It appears that . . . there were in south Italy many colonial ventures which just grew."[31] Only later did these communities assimilate their histories to those of the planned settlements, providing themselves retrospectively with stories about *oikistai*, Delphic oracles, and so on.[32]

Sybaris and Croton, the early cities between Locri and Taras, are both called Achaean, that is, derived from the Greeks on the south side of the Corinthian gulf, across from Ozolian Locris. The *oikistes* of Sybaris, we are told (Strabo 6.1.13), was Is, from Helike (as we saw), the capital of the Achaean federation; on the other hand, a substantial part of the colony was supposed to have been derived from Troezen, east of the isthmus of Corinth (Aristotle *Politics* 1309a29).[33] The *oikistes* of Croton was said to be Myskellos, from the obscure community of Rhypes. In neither case is there evidence of continuing links between colony

---

[30] See p. 180.

[31] Dunbabin (1948), p. 23.

[32] For a suggestion that the "Achaean" colonies came to claim their ethnic identity only in the course of the sixth-century conflict with Dorian Taras, see Morgan and Hall (1996). For evidence that Epizephyrian Locri derived from "a mixture of Greeks from different areas of the mother country" see Blomquist (1978), p. 124.

[33] The folktale of Lamia/Sybaris (see p. 249) ascribes the foundation of Sybaris to mainland Locrians.

and mother city; the connections of both Croton and Sybaris in histori-cal times are with Ionia.[34] It appears that the foundation stories were meant to clarify the identity of these cities by giving them a definite origin, an origin which, however, was not made to require any continu-ing connection.

In the case of Locri, Strabo (6.1.7) tells us that the *oikistes* was named Euanthes. This should give us pause, for Euanthes is the name of a son of Dionysus who was the heroic eponym of Oiantheia (also called Eu-antheia) in Ozolian Locris—that is, Euanthes was a legendary founda-tion-figure in old-world Locris, a figure from the prehistoric time of origins. In other words, at Epizephyrian Locri history was made to reca-pitulate myth by a reinsertion of the "original" (metropolitan) founder into the historical (colonial) narrative. Everything else about the foun-dation is controversial. Strabo (6.1.7) tells us that Ephorus held that the colony derived from Opuntian Locris, but as Strabo gives us this information he flatly contradicts it, claiming the colony for the Ozolian Locrians. Aristotle, Timaeus, and Polybius (as we shall see) across the centuries conducted a quarrel about the foundation legend.

Polybius in the course of this controversy tells us (XII.9.3.) that Tim-aeus claimed to have been shown during his visit to old-world Locris "a written agreement, still in force, with this opening clause: 'as to parents in relation to their children'; in addition there were provisions whereby each party would have an established standing in the polity of the other (*politeian huparchein hekaterois par' hekaterois*)." This document (whether or not it was a forgery) surely existed; it is probably significant that Timaeus found it in old-world Locris. Such symmetrical privileges would in historical times have been advantageous primarily to the old-world Locrians. Old-world Locris was backcountry with little to offer the visi-tor, whereas western Locri was a great city and a cultural center. Indeed the controversy between Timaeus and Polybius (to which we shall re-turn) is as sharp as it is largely, I suspect, because Timaeus, who spent his working life in Athens even though he was born in the West, con-sulted old-world Locrian sources which tended (in their own interest) to assert close relations between the two communities, while Polybius talked to the Italian Locrians, who rather insisted that the connection was founded on a separation. "There were no treaties made with the old-world Locrians, nor do [the Epizephyrians] say there were," Po-lybius (12.6.1) says flatly.

---

[34] For Sybaris and Miletus see Herodotus 6.21; Croton is linked with Samos through Pythagoras (who is said to have left Samos for Croton to escape the tyrant Polycrates) and Democedes (who is said to have left Croton to practice medicine in Polycrates' household).

It is characteristic of Locrians of all kinds to live in more than one place, to relate to more than one center, and to maintain various complex relations with one another. Exactly these characteristics mark the people of old-world Locris as an *ethnos*. The old-world Locrians seem, by the document shown Timaeus, to have insisted on their political connections with the Italian branch; the Epizephyrians, by contrast, tended (as we have seen) to assert their connections with Sparta, the prototypical *polis*. The Epizephyrians thereby (correctly) asserted their integrity as a *polis*—a dignity which Locrians had achieved only on the western frontier.[35]

Nevertheless the Epizephyrians indubitably called themselves Locrian; this seems to have been for them not an acknowledgment of current connections but a claim to a peculiar origin. Such a claim involves a cultural self-definition. The Epizephyrian Locrians called themselves by an ethnic name because they defined themselves primarily in terms of the peculiar manner of their life, what the Greeks call *ēthea*, *nomoi* and *diaita*. The content of the peculiarity remains to be specified. One place to look is to the points of commonality between old-world Locris and western Locri.

The Well-Lawed City

We do have one bit of material where the legendary histories of old-world Locris and western Locri are united: the alternative explanations of the phrase *Locrōn sunthēma*, "the agreement of the Locrians":

> The proverb is applied to those who falsify. For the Locrians betrayed the agreements with the Peloponnesians and joined the Heracleidae. It disregards the chronology. Others take it as that they cheated the Sicilians by double meanings. (Zenobius 4.97)

In other words (Zenobius's note is extremely curtailed), there were two stories: One explained the phrase in terms of old-world Locrian involvement with the heroic foundation of Sparta (yet the phrase, in defiance of the chronology, was applied to the Epizephyrians), and another story referred the phrase to the colonial foundation of Epizephyrian Locri. As with "Euanthes," the heroic original history of the old-world Locrians is doubled in the colonial legends of the West.[36]

---

[35] So also the "Locrian" story of the Sagra—which ascribed the victory to Locrian Ajax, hero of the mainland Locrians—was told at Croton, not Locri (Pausanias 3.19.11); the version told at Locri ascribed the victory to the gods of Sparta (see p. 252).

[36] The involvement of the mainland Locrians in the story of the return of the Her-

However no source actually tells us the story that linked the old-world Locrians to the Heracleidae. We do have the colonial story of Locrian falsehood; it is told by Polyaenus:

> The Locrians in Italy made a treaty with the Sicels, putting heads of garlic on their shoulders under their cloaks and having earth inserted under their feet in their sandals, swore that they would preserve the constitutional arrangements for their security so long as they trod this earth and bore their heads on their shoulders. The Sicels trusted this oath but the Locrians broke it one day later, in as much as they no longer trod on the same earth nor wore their heads on their shoulders. (Polyaenus *Strategemata* 6.22)[37]

This story represents the Locrians as naively duplicitous, manipulators of the literal.[38] Their art is like that of Autolycus, Odysseus's maternal grandfather, who excelled all men "in stealing and with the oath" (*Od.* 19.396)—presumably not by breaking his oath, but by swearing in ambiguous and deceptive terms. This is the capacity of *mētis*, crafty intelligence. Another story of Locrian *mētis* is among the legends of the Sagra (Justin 20.3.1): *Croton sent to the oracle asking for victory in the battle; the oracle replied that battles are won not so much with arms as with vows. Croton therefore vowed one tenth of the spoil to the god. The Locrians, hearing of this, vowed to the god one-ninth—and therefore won the battle.*[39]

That this story was canonical at Locri we learn from the third-century archive of Olympian Zeus: Locri, uniquely among Greek cities, set aside one-ninth (or in some cases one-ninetieth) rather than one-tenth (or one-hundredth) as in other Greek cities. The story must have been told as the *aition* of this odd custom. The two stories refer respectively to the foundation of the city and to her heroic moment: The city was originally secured, and her safety achieved at the Sagra, by her crafty intelligence, her *mētis*.

There is one more explanation of the proverb:

> The Locrians their agreements: For the Epizephyrian Locrians, we are told, Zaleucus became a lawgiver; he made it a law that there should be no contract of indebtedness. As a consequence many renounced their agreements, and the proverb came to be used of those who use falsehoods. Zenobius V.4

---

acleidae links the Locrians to the heroic history of Sparta, just as the foundation story of Locri links the legendary history of Epizephyrian Locri to the legendary history of Sparta. There is a third explanation which links the phrase to a law of Zaleucus forbidding contracts for debt; this might be derived from similar stories about Solon's cancellation of debts, but might also be the correct explanation of the phrase—see p. 226.

[37] Polybius (12.6) was also told this story by his Locrian informants.

[38] A very similar story is told in Herodotus: 4.201.2.

[39] This story is told in the same sources, and discussed by the same scholars, as those cited in note 23 above.

Zaleucus was the legendary lawgiver of the Epizephyrians; he is said to have established the first Greek written law code. He is a figure of justice and it may seem odd that he is given as a source for the Locrian reputation for duplicity, but in fact there is an ambiguity in lawgiving: Reform, even as it establishes a new order, breaks an old one; as a manipulation of the social system it provides opportunities for the manipulative.[40] Very similar stories were told of Solon's cancellations of debt (Plutarch *Solon* 15.6).

Lawmaking is an assertion of the power of reason over tradition, and as such is morally dubious in a way characteristic of *mētis*. *Mētis* is an unruly capacity, unrespectful of limits, tending toward lawlessness. Lawlessness, as we have seen, was endemic in old-world Locris and in her myths. Yet at the same time (as we have seen—cf. p. 133) Opus, the political center of old-world Locris, is called "well-lawed" in the Thermopylae epigram, later echoed by Pindar. To be well-lawed is also a trait of the Epizephyrians; indeed, they were noted for their conservative lawfulness. Thus we read in Plutarch:

> The authorities of Locri did well: When someone returning from a trip abroad asked, "What's new?" they had him punished. (Plutarch *de Curiositate* 8)

The story is told in a slightly different form by Diodorus (8.23.4), who concludes: "so tireless were they about justice." Justice, for these Locrians, seems to involve the abolition of novelty, which is to say, the abolition of history.

Particularly there were to be no innovations in the law. Demosthenes tells it:

> I want to explain to you, gentlemen of the jury, how they make laws in Locri, for it will do you no harm to hear an example, especially that provided by a well-lawed city. There they are so sure that the long-established laws should be obeyed and ancestral usage protected, that laws should not be made to suit the wishes and evasions of criminals, that if someone wants to pass a new law he must propose his law with his head in a noose; if the law is found fine and serviceable, its author lives and goes free; otherwise he dies because they tighten the noose. So they are not so bold as to pass new laws; rather they strictly adhere to the old ones. In the course of many years, gentlemen of the jury, they have passed, we are told, exactly one new law. They had there a law that if someone knocked out an eye he must submit to having his own eye knocked out; they allowed no compensation in money. We are told that someone had an enemy with only one eye, and threatened to knock out this

---

[40] In this respect—as in others—foundations and refoundations of Greek cities recapitulate Greek cosmological origins—cf. Detienne and Vernant (1991 [1974]), especially chs. 3 and 4.

one. The one-eyed man took this threat very badly and thought his life would be hardly worth living in such a condition, and so, we are told, he made so bold as to introduce a law that if someone knocked out the eye of a man with but one eye he should submit to having both his eyes knocked out, so that they might both endure equal misfortune. And we are told that this is the only law the Locrians have passed in more than two hundred years. (Demosthenes 24.139–141)

This story is what the Greeks call an *ainos,* a fable or cautionary tale; it tells us that for the Athenians of the fourth century, Locri was a fabulous place, legendary for its lawfulness, for *eunomia,* like Sparta and Crete.[41] Plato (*Laws* 638a–b) speaks of Locri as having a reputation for the greatest *eunomia* in that part of the world, and this claim is repeated in the *Timaeus* (20a). Strabo (6.1.8) says "for the longest time they experienced *eunomia,* until Dionysius [to whom we shall come later] . . . treated them in the most lawless manner of anyone."

The Epizephyrians, like the Spartans, ascribed their constitution to a local lawgiver; Spartan Lycurgus matched Locrian Zaleucus.[42] One of the laws of Lycurgus was that no law should be written down, whereas Zaleucus was famous as the composer of the first written code; they are, however, both "original" lawgivers. Zaleucus is no less mythical than Lycurgus—indeed, Timaeus of Tauromenium denied his existence altogether (Cicero *Ad. Att.* 6.1.18; *De Leg.* 2.15). Aristotle (Fr. 548 Rose) in his *Constitution of the Locrians* told his story:

The city of the Locrians was in great disorder (tarachē); *they therefore turned to the oracle, who told them to impose laws on themselves. Then there appeared a shepherd named Zaleucus who was able to provide the city with many admirable laws; when he was interrogated as to where he had got them, he said that Athena came to him in a dream. Therefore he received his freedom and became their lawgiver.*

Delphi is involved here as in the Lycurgus story; otherwise the story reminds us of the story Hesiod tells of himself in the *Theogony,* where he says he was a shepherd inspired by the Muses. Zaleucus is inspired by Athena, and like Hesiod he comes in from the wild, from the shepherd's world out beyond the edges of civil society. Since the city is sick the remedy must come from outside it, from god and from nature, that is to say, from the prehistoric.

The constitution of Locri, like that of Sparta, presents itself as a work of art. It comes from a simple person on the margin and is in this sense primitive, but at the same time it is inspired, god-given. As such it is perfect and immune to development. It provides (in principle, if not in

---

[41] The three are grouped together, along with Athens, by Aelian *Var. Hist.* 2.22.

[42] On these patterns see Szegedy-Maszak (1978).

practice) the secure frame that insulates the city from history. Immunity to history is possible only by the recovery of what lies before history.

The original, prepolitical condition of the Locrians (as of the Spartans—Thucydides 1.18) was one of lawlessness; having become lawful they had perhaps not lost their original nature. The Epizephyrians shared with the Spartans and the old-world Locrians an ambiguity of lawfulness and lawlessness. This ambiguity is also characteristic of the Age of Cronos or of Hesiod's prior ages; both lawfulness and lawlessness are "primitive." Therefore they are both proper to the "original" peoples. The old-world Locrians were the Leleges, the people created by Deucaulion and Pyrrha from the stones (Strab. 7.7.3). They live in an original manner, in the style prevalent before the invention of justice and injustice. They are "well-lawed" in the sense that they are not corrupt; at the same time they can be violent—and perhaps crafty—in the heroic, uncorrupted manner. In asserting their link to the mainland, the Epizephyrians in turn seem to have asserted their own share of both craft and violence.

In its ambiguity the Epizephyrian link with Locris is parallel to the Spartan link to Crete. Crete is typically classed with Sparta; Socrates liked to call them both "well-lawed" (Plato *Crito* 52e), and in Plato's last book a Spartan and a Cretan join with the Athenian Stranger to write the Laws. The great mythical judges, Minos and Radamanthys, are Cretan. In fact some of the earliest surviving Greek written law does come from Crete, most notably the Gortyn code. The Spartan laws are supposed to have derived from those of Crete (Herodotus 1.65). Yet as everyone knows, all Cretans are liars, and Aristotle looks on Crete as a place so anarchic that it might as well not have a government (Aristotle *Politics* 1272b).

Sparta also, prototypically well-lawed, displays an undercurrent of lawlessness. Lawlessness was built into Spartans' education; they learned as children to steal and hide, and in the *krupteia*, the elite cadet corps, they learned to live off the land and secretly murder the helots. Vidal-Naquet told us that the *krupteia* displayed the inversion characteristic of initiations: the young Spartans who were about to be accepted into the collective discipline of the phalanx lived for a certain time dispersed and unregulated.[43] But the ambiguity is more complex than that, since Sparta lived as a warrior community and the warrior's condition is inherently ambiguous, demanding perfect discipline within the army, but exhibiting unbridled violence and deception toward the enemy. An army must learn to live off the land. Thus as all Cretans were liars, all

---

[43] Vidal-Naquet (1986 [1981]), pp. 112–113.

Spartans were thieves. Xenophon, asking a Spartan officer to steal a hilltop for him, reminds him that Spartans are trained to steal: "now is your chance to show off your education" (Xenophon *Anabasis* 4.6.15). The war of some against some is to a degree a reversion to the most primitive condition of things, the war of all against all. Spartan discipline at its best—or in its own idealization—was animated by a strong current of primitive ruthlessness.

This ruthlessness was given social-structural meaning at home in the Spartan repression of the helots—by the *krupteia* certainly, and also by other means. The ephors annually declared war on the helots (Aristotle Fr. 538 Rose), so that the propertied class existed in a state of continual war with its own labor force. At Sparta, theft was property.

In Crete also this ruthlessness seems to have been straightforwardly expressed; the locus classicus is the so-called Scolion of Hybrias, apparently an authentic archaic document:

> I have the wealth of a great spear and sword
> And a fine shield, defense of the body.
> With these I plow, with these I reap,
> With these I tread the wine from the grapes
> With these I am named master of the serfs.
> They dare not to hold the spear and sword
> Nor the fine shield, defense of the body.
> All cowering at my knee bend down, calling
> Me their master and great lord (*basileus*).

Athenaeus 695e–696a

Crete was a model for Sparta in that Crete was a heroic society, ruled by a warrior caste, and characterized by certain specific institutions, particularly the *sussitiai*, the dining-societies, which brought together initiated high-status males. These heroic institutions were at Sparta "re-institutionalized" (to borrow a nonce-word from M. I. Finley[44]) and made part of a coherent system of life, a kind of working utopia. Finley's notion of reinstitutionalization captures the ambiguity of Sparta's relation with her (putatively Cretan) sources: The Spartan way of life was conceived as a work of art that at the same time had the vitality of the time of origins, so that primitivist Sparta was, as it were, postcivilized. Thus Thucydides (1.6) lays out the development of civil society in three stages: After the primitive stage of *lēisteia* and the habitual wearing of arms (still current in old-world Locris), the Athenians were the first to introduce the more delicate and luxurious manners characteristic of the Ionians. Then the Spartans were the first to adopt public

---

[44] Finley (1981 [1968]).

nakedness, moderation in dress, and an equalization of the lifestyle of the propertied with that of the many. The Spartans, that is, led the way forward by readopting something like the primitive simplicity.

I would suggest that a similar relation existed between Locri and old-world Locris, even though the specific links are harder to trace. Old-world Locris was still to some degree a heroic society, and could well serve the Epizephyrians as their access to uncorrupted political energy. We cannot, however, trace specific social-structural features to the link—with one exception, which is explicit in our sources: Locris and Epizephyrian Locri were both communities where maidens were important. This likeness will turn out also to be definitive of the Epizephyrian similarity to, and difference from, Sparta.

The Women of Sparta and Locri

Sparta and Locri were both cities where the status of free women made their women different from other Greek women. In Sparta women were not confined to the house, doing wool-work; they exercised like the men (Xenophon *Lac. Pol.* 1.4; Pollux 7.55; Plutarch *Lycurgus* 14.2–3) and showed their thighs (Plutarch *Comparison of Lycurgus and Numa* 3.3–4, citing various poets). There is some evidence that the women of Locri also exercised.[45] The implications, however, seem to have been different. The women of Sparta were noted for their *anesis*, their license; Plato's Athenian stranger refers to this as a familiar reproach (*Laws* 637c). As early as Alcman's maidens, who run like horses in dreams, the Spartan women appear vivid and physical. But whereas the physical training of the Spartan men subjected them to discipline, the training of the Spartan women made them unruly. The story went that Lycurgus attempted to subject them to the laws, "but when they put up resistance, he backed off" (Aristotle *Politics* 1270a). The Spartan women are thus seen as adversaries of the law, wild, not properly part of the polity.

The Locrians—in their foundation story (see above, p. 251)—told of women out of control: Locri was founded by women unfaithful to their husbands. However these wild women became at Locri vehicles of legit-

---

[45] This evidence consists of (1) strigils (used to scrape down the body after exercise) found in some Locrian women's graves, and (2) a large red-figure vessel found in the Lucifero cemetery, decorated by the "Locri Painter" (380–360) now in Reggio; this depicts a young woman clad only in a brief garment very like those worn by female figures on Spartan mirror-bases a couple of centuries older. She faces a naked young man who leans on a lance. The space, which is defined by two pillars surmounted by amphorae, might be a palaistra.

imacy. The story comes to us indirectly, through Polybius's polemic against Timaeus. Timaeus, in his lost *History*, had denied the foundation story told in Aristotle's also lost work; Polybius claims to know better:

> It happens that I have many times visited the city of the Locrians and have been of essential use to them. They were let off the Iberian expedition through me, and also the expedition to Dalmatia, to which they should have made a naval contribution on the basis of their treaty with the Romans. . . . And they have responded to me with every sort of honor and good will; therefore I should rather wish to praise the Locrians than otherwise. Nevertheless I do not hesitate to say and to write that the story transmitted by Aristotle concerning the colony turns out to be more true than that told by Timaeus. I well know that the people there agree that the tale of the colony transmitted to them from their fathers is that which Aristotle has told, and not Timaeus, and for this they offer the following supporting evidence:
>
> First: All inherited marks of status (*endoxa*) among them pass through women, not through men, as for example they customarily consider well-born the men of the so-called Hundred Houses. These Hundred Houses were those distinguished among the Locrians even before the colony set out, from which the Locrians in accordance with the oracle were to choose by lot the maidens sent to Troy. Some of these women took part in the colonial movement, and their descendants are still now called well-born and men of the Hundred Houses.
>
> Furthermore there is a traditional story about the woman called the bowl bearer (*phialēphoros*), which tells us that on the occasion when they expelled from this part of Italy the Sicels—indigenes led in their sacrifices by a child belonging to the most reputable and well-born families—they themselves, adopting quite a number of Sicel customs because they had nothing from their forefathers (*dia to mēden autois patrion huparchein*) kept this also from the indigenes, but made this correction, so that they did not make one of their boys the bowl bearer, but a maiden, because good birth is through women. (Polybius 12.5)

Polybius's report is not, of course, good evidence for what happened in the seventh century, at the time of the foundation, but it is good evidence for certain elements of the peculiar cultural system that existed there in his day, which was surely seen in his day as immemorial, and which may well actually have been of considerable antiquity.

Polybius tells us that the Locrians recognized some form of matriliny—not, evidently, inheritance of property exclusively through the female line (which he would surely have mentioned, had it existed), but inheritance exclusively through females of certain tokens of good birth, presumably ritual privileges. Matriliny of this or any kind is otherwise undocumented for Greek communities, even those of old-world Locris,[46] and was probably a unique institution of the Epizephyrians.

Second, Polybius tells us that since (according to the foundation legend) the colony did not include any males who were legitimately Locrian, the Locrians had no forefathers. Therefore they derived much of their ritual from the indigenes whom they displaced—transforming it, however, in the process, so as to present the ritual primacy of women. The primacy of women thus places Locri between two peoples: the people of Locris and the Sicel indigenes. The Epizephyrians explained that they had been expelled by the one and had expelled the other; nevertheless they were linked to both. The rituals of the Epizephyrian women, by this logic, would represent both their connections with and their differences from both their claimed cultural sources. The *phialēphoros* is not doing something brought from the motherland, but (in transformation motivated by the Epizephrians' special relation with the motherland) she is not Sicel either. She can be taken as emblematic of Epizephyrian uniqueness.

Third, Polybius implies that the sending of the Locrian maidens to Troy was regarded by the Epizephyrians as a ritual definitive of Locrian social structure (even though the Epizephyrians almost certainly never took part in it); they mentioned the maidens of Locris in the course of explaining that status at Locri was transmitted through women. It follows that the special legitimacy transmitted to the Epizephyrians by their women was the special legitimacy of those who in old-world Locris took part in that ritual. The sending of the maidens to Troy, as we have seen, was a ritual dramatizing the importance of *parthenoi* in civil society. Therefore the ritual primacy of a certain *parthenos* at Epizephyrian Locri (the *phialēphoros*), while not derived from the mainland, on another level reflects a "Locrian" trait. There is something ethnically Locrian, in old-world Greece or in Italy, about a focal interest in marriageable girls. I am about to argue, circuitously and at some length, that this focus reflects the special importance of marriage in their society.

We have no literary confirmation of Polybius's report.[47] We do have an odd story connecting Italian music with the control of women:

---

[46] Pindar's *11th Ol.* 63–64 refers in a mainland Locrian mythical context to naming after the maternal grandfather; this, however, is no more evidence of matriliny than is the naming of Odysseus by his maternal grandfather.

[47] Nossis, the Hellenistic Locrian poetess, does, however, celebrate her matriline in A.P. 6.265. Cerchiai (1982) notes that in the Lucifero cemetery two of the three family grave-groups reported cluster around an exceptionally well furnished woman's grave; the woman seems to be the notable ancestor whose grave attracted others to her.

Aristoxenus the musician [and associate of Aristotle] in his life of Telestes, whom he encountered in Italy, says that at this same moment there occurred events, one of which was the strange thing that happened concerning women. There were ecstasies that took place of such a kind that sometimes while they were sitting at dinner they responded as if someone had called them, and then they jumped up uncontrolled and ran out of the city. The Locrians and the Rheggians consulted the oracle concerning recovery from these events; the god said to sing springtime paeans for fifty days. And that is why there are so many writers of paeans in Italy. (Apollonius *History of Miracles* 40)

Here is a story in which Locri and Rhegion, so far from being musical competitors, share a problem with a musical solution. Apollonian songs of healing and purification overcome the Dionysiac frenzy of women who rush from the city, and in the process these cities make a permanent contribution to the stock of civilization.

Our best evidence, however, for the Locrian focus on marriage and the marriageable girl, and for the presence of this focus already in the classical period, is the preeminence of women's things and of representations of women and the woman's world in Locrian art: sculpture, terra-cottas, and small bronzes. The greater part of my extended argument, therefore, will consist of a series of iconographic studies.

These studies, however, are a set of later chapters. For the moment let us return to Sparta and her women. I shall argue in the next section that the status of Spartan women was a consequence of the peculiar Spartan solution to the problem of private property. I shall then be in a position to suggest that the (differently) peculiar status of women at Locri was also the consequence of their (different) solution to the problem of property.

Women and Property at Sparta

The Spartan origin myth told of the god-given conquest of the valley of the Eurotas.

The son of Cronos himself, husband of fair-crowned Hera,
    Zeus, gave this city to the sons of Heracles
Joined with whom, leaving windy Erineos
    We came here to the broad island of Pelops.

Tyrtaeus Fr. 2 Diehl

The Spartan state is thus conceived as an occupying army, whose claim to the territory is force of arms. Whether there is any kernel of truth to this narrative remains debatable;[48] from the point of view of the present analysis it is perhaps more relevant to point out that this legend describes Sparta as if it were a colony. (Pindar—7th *Isth.* 13–20—actually calls Sparta a "Dorian colony," *apoikian*, established by "Pythian oracles.") The western colonial city-states were similarly god-given to the degree that they were guided by oracles, and all were established at least in part by force of arms. They originated as armed camps set up in more or less hostile territory; the risks of foundation imposed on the settlers a high degree of solidarity. This memory of dangers survived and surmounted formed the moral basis for an "aristocracy of the first arrived," of the descendants of those who had pledged their lives to the state and to each other.

The Spartans, in their quest for solidarity, seem to have applied the experience of the frontier—among other things, in the Carneia, where the moment of arrival was ritualized. The citizens celebrating this festival at Sparta carried models of the rafts that had borne the original expedition across the Corinthian Gulf (*Anec. Bekk.* 305.31; Hesychius s.v. *stemmatiaion*) and slept out, like settlers before the building of houses.

Ritual, further, was reinforced by Spartan self-interpretation of history: The Spartans interpreted in terms of their founding experience the long war that ended with the siege of the Messenians on Mount Ithome. The conquest of Messenia was a sort of internal colonization; the land was given, as Tyrtaeus says

> To our king, loved-by-the-gods Theopompus,
> Through whom we took Messenia with its broad lands
> Messenia good to plow, good to sow.
>
> Tyrtaeus Fr. 4 Diehl 1–3

Tyrtaeus also told the Spartans that if the force of their arms did not continue to triumph they would be forced into new exile as refugees:

> It is noble to die when one falls in the front battle line
> As a brave man fighting for his fatherland;
> To leave one's own city and fertile fields
> To go begging is more painful than anything,
> Wandering abroad with one's own mother and old father
> With little children and with wedded wife.
> He comes among them as an enemy, wherever he goes
> Yielding to want and hateful poverty

---

[48] The best review of the debate remains that in Cartledge (1979). For a review of the issue with reference to more recent publications, concluding (*contra* Cartledge) that "the people regarded themselves as new arrivals because they remembered something true" see Malkin (1994), pp. 43–45.

And shames his race, and degrades his heroic appearance;
  Every kind of dishonor and disgrace attends him.
Given that when a man wanders thus he lacks all season,
  All modesty, and leaves no descendants,
Heartfelt let us battle for this land and our children;
  Let us die no longer hoarding our lives.

Tyrtaeus Fr. 6 Diehl

The Spartans were thus perpetually threatened with dispossession and perpetually engaged in the conquest of their territory. Their whole polity was a kind of ritualization of the original act of conquest.

In a number of districts Greek colonists had acquired, along with the territory, control of an aboriginal population—the Kallikyrioi at Syracuse, the Bythinians at Byzantium, the Mariandynoi at Heracleia Pontica. These peoples were "between freedom and slavery" (Pollux 3.83); they were not chattel slaves since they retained their social organization and could not be dispossessed from their land, but were regarded as a population which, having once surrendered in battle, had forever lost its political and economic liberty. This was also the usual Greek account of the helots at Sparta; once again Spartan society mimics a colony. In some respects this model was an unfortunate one; ancient writers saw clearly enough that as an internal enemy the helots were the great weakness of the Spartan state (Plato *Laws* 776cff, Aristotle *Politics* 1269a36–39). The military organization of Spartan society, whereby the whole citizen body was kept, as it were, perpetually mobilized, was justified by the need to suppress the helots. However, no effort was ever made to normalize the position of the helots or to integrate them within Lacedaemonian society as a peasant class of the Cretan or Thessalian type; on the contrary, the relation between the Spartans and the helots was itself ritualized in the perpetual war and the *krupteia*. It seems the Spartans actually valued the hostility of the helots—as in the proud boast that at Sparta "the free man is most free and the slave most a slave" (Critias 81B37 DK); the constant threat (and not infrequent actuality) of revolt was thought by the Spartans not too high a price to pay for their military organization and the social solidarity it sustained. It seems that the hostility of the helots was for the sake of Spartan social structure, rather than the other way round.

Spartan civil society was a huge military school, militaristic without being particularly aggressive—indeed it was notoriously difficult to get the Spartans to go to war (cf. Thucydides 1.70.2–4). Much of their collective life was invested in games and in rituals, especially those involving dancing. Their militarism was turned inward, as a mode of social solidarity, through compulsory membership in male dining groups, the *sussitiai*, patterned on army mess-groups. Thereby the Spartans used the military system to enforce collective values of cooperation and conformity. They also asserted a specific attitude toward property, focused not on its acquisition and use but on its security—property, as it were, in its collective mode, as the jointly defended territory of the *possessores*.

Sparta, however, was for all that a private-property state—however the facts may have been misrepresented by Hellenistic reporters who wished to make of it a working utopia.[49] Taxation there was handled in the conventional manner through the *eisphora*, an assessment on capital (Aristotle *Politics* 1271b13–16); citizens sometimes owed debts to the state (Herodotus 6.59). It seems clear that the basic economic unit at Sparta as elsewhere in Greece was the *oikos*, a household ideally, and usually, centered on a married couple, owning land and personal servants, transmitting property by inheritance. Some were born rich, some poor; furthermore wealth could be increased or lost. Herodotus can speak of Spartans who were "in their origin well born and had attained the first category in possessions" (Herodotus 7.134, cf. Thucydides 5.15.1); Aristotle says that Sparta was as much as any oligarchy two cities, one of the rich, one of the poor: "all have not equal possessions and are not similarly superior people, *agathoi andres*" (Aristotle *Politics* 1316b9–10). Power tended to belong to a few wealthy families—which, as M. I. Finley notes,[50] is the implication of Aristotle's observation that election to the *gerousia*, the senate, is *dunasteutikēn*, "managed by a clique" (Aristotle *Politics* 1306a18). Most important, there was a minimum property qualification for active citizenship, and those whose wealth fell below this line lost their rights as citizens. Status thus followed wealth; Sparta was therefore in contrast to a genuinely archaic society, like that of Crete, where wealth to some degree followed status (Aristotle *Politics* 1271a26–37).

There are some indications that the Spartan *eunomia*, their characteristic social and political organization, was a response to stress produced by the development of private property. It was a sixth-century Spartan who said "money makes the man" (Alcaeus Fr. 360 Voigt, quoting "Aristodemus . . . in Sparta"). Tyrtaeus recorded demands for the distribution of land (ap. Aristotle *Politics* 1307a1–2)—the familiar prelude to tyranny. Both Herodotus and Thucydides, as we have noted, assert that Spartan reform followed a period of disorder—but as we have also noted, this assertion is conventional and perhaps need not be

[49] This position is well argued by Finley (1981 [1968]).
[50] Ibid., p. 34.

given much weight.[51] Be that as it may, the Spartans did avoid the experience of tyranny in the archaic period (Thucydides 1.18 calls them *aiei aturanneutos*); they achieved their early, rigid, successful solution to the problems of the private-property society by developing to an extreme themes we find elsewhere in Greek social reform: diffusion of authority and limitation of consumption. Sparta thereby became the oddest and at the same time the prototypical city-state, everywhere praised and nowhere imitated, as Xenophon remarks. (Xenophon *Lac. Pol.* 10.8).

The political arrangements of Sparta involved the division of authority without any provision for mediating conflicts within it. There were two kings, each of whom served as a check on the other (Plato *Laws* 691d); the elected officials, the Ephors, served as a check on the kings, and vice versa (each party annually swore to uphold the authority of the other—Xenophon *Lac. Pol.* 15.7); the *gerousia*, the senate of elders whose members served for life, was the legislative body but at the same time its acts had to be approved by the assembly of citizens, whose approval was presumed. Such arrangements require an extraordinary degree of consensus; every disagreement within the government is a constitutional crisis. The political structure therefore presumed the solidarity and conformity produced by Spartan social arrangements and idealized in Spartan culture. The controlling metaphor was that of a functioning organism, with the unmediated cohesion of the parts:

> She is not walled with words, this Lacon city,
> But when fresh war may fall upon the troops
> Counsel rules and the hand completes the act.

Ion of Chios Fr. 63 Nauck

In other words, the Spartans had no need to discuss or explain; they all know what they were supposed to do, and this common knowledge constituted the state.

Spartan conformity was produced by a universal (for the citizens) education—the *agōgē*, "upbringing" or "coming out"[52]—whereby every Spartan male passed through identical experiences. This education started early, at age seven. Young and old, the Spartans were divided into small identical groups, in each of which the same norms were enforced. Each *sussition*, says Persaeus (ap. Athenaeus 140f), was "a little polity." The Spartans were uniquely loyal to the state because for them the state possessed the kind of moral authority that elsewhere

---

[51] Cf. p. 75.

[52] The word is also used for the ceremony that leads the bride from her natal home into the new husband's house, and for the love-charm that is to bring its object into the arms of her seducer. Faraone (1999). The *agōgē* similarly separated the Spartan boy from his home and brought him into another intimate community.

belonged to the family. Every elder male stood as parent to the younger men (cf. Xenophon *Lac. Pol.* 2.10, 6.1). Each of the small groups, further, was competitive; in games, rituals, and warfare the Spartan males were constantly testing who could be most Spartan. The losers— those who failed to conform—were subject to continual penalties. Xenophon's account of the fate of the coward may be taken to describe the fate of deviance in general:

> In Lacedaemon anyone would be ashamed to take the coward into his tent, or to exercise with him at the wrestling ground. Often when they choose up to play ball such a one finds himself without a place, and in the dance he is sent down to the most disgraceful position, and in the roads he must give way, and where they sit must give his seat even to younger men, and must keep the girls who are related to him at home, and endure their complaints on his cowardice, and must see his hearth left wifeless and must pay the fine for that as well; he must not walk about cheerfully or imitate the blameless— or else he must endure the blows of his betters. (*Lac. Pol.* 9.4–5)

This is a society focused on penalties, not rewards; the result was a typical personality: cautious, hard-bodied, ascetic, miserly, and laconic. The Spartans were tough and self-contained, but not individualistic; their adherence to the law seems integral with their fear of the disapproval of their fellows; obedient as they were, they found it hard to take orders from anyone but another Spartan. Their virtues did not travel; as the Athenians say, "each of you when he goes abroad uses neither his own customs nor those customary in the rest of Greece" (Thucydides 1.77.6). The emphasis on solidarity left them morally walled within their own community; all strangers were in principle enemies (cf. Thucydides 2.39.1). Furthermore as we meet them—in Thucydides especially—the Spartans seem liable to uncontrollable bursts of temper. Possibly this has something to do with the rupture in their development represented by their entrance to the *agōgē*, their transfer at age seven to an all-male world—especially since, given the absence of their fathers and brothers in the same world, they would have been raised until that age almost entirely by women.

The conclusion of the paragraph from Xenophon quoted above reminds us that Spartan citizens, like Greek citizens everywhere, were members of—ideally, heads of—*oikoi*, familial households linked by marriage-exchange. The Spartans did not eliminate these households; they rather saw to it that the men were often absent from them. They passed much of their time in an all-male sphere of disciplined competition to which property was largely irrelevant. Although the Spartan householders were, as we saw, propertied, to an important extent they were insulated from the economic sphere. To *what* extent exactly is

unclear, this being another place where Sparta was adopted by the uto-
pians and described as the philosophers would have had them be. Xenophon, for instance, says flatly that Spartans were forbidden to make
(*Lac. Pol.* 7.2) or possess (*Lac. Pol.* 7.6) money; in the same essay, however, he says that in his own day Spartans had come to flaunt their gold
(*Lac. Pol.* 14.3). Thucydides (5.34.2) makes it clear that in the fifth
century Spartans were permitted to buy and sell.

They do seem, however, to have been forbidden to ply a trade (Plutarch *Lycurgus* 24.2–3).[53] To this extent they were shielded from the
market. They were a rentier class, free to accumulate the returns from
their property but not, it seems, to seek to increase those returns. The
rents paid by the helots were fixed and could not be increased (Myron
of Priene ap. Athenaeus 657d; Plutarch *Inst. Sp.* 41.239c). Neither
could they be driven off the land (Ephorus 70 *FGH* 117); helots could
be murdered more or less arbitrarily but they could not be evicted. The
Spartans thus adapted to conditions of private property the kind of
double ownership I have reconstructed for the Homeric situation:[54] the
estate, in a sense, belonged to its helots, or (to put this another way)
the Spartiate owner owned something in which land and labor were
indissolubly bonded together.

Sparta was thus a private-property society in which, up to a point,
property could seem irrelevant. As long as the estates of the Spartiate
produced enough income to sustain his membership in the *sussition* he
feasted among his peers on a basis of equality—feasted, indeed, in a
kind of recovery of the Golden Age; his livelihood arrived as if by magic,
without labor of his own or labor that had to concern him. The kings,
with their special links to the divine, played the role of the gods at the
feast.[55]

The asceticism of the Spartans also served—not, indeed, to eliminate, but—to make invisible economic inequality. As Aristotle says:

> Many say that [the Spartan constitution] is democratic because their organi-
> zation has many democratic features, for example first of all the nourish-
> ment of children (for the sons of the rich are nourished like the sons of the
> poor, and they are educated in a manner within reach of the children of the
> poor) and it is the same when they come of age, and when they are men it is

[53] This Hellenistic anecdote, which tells us that Spartans were forbidden to practice a
trade but permitted to make money (although, says the anecdote, they had no motive to
do so), is not in itself of great historical weight. It is supported, however, by Herodotus's
comment that the Spartans were like the Egyptians in that their warriors had no other
occupation.

[54] Cf. pp. 163–165.

[55] I owe this point to Marshall Sahlins.

in the same manner—there is no visible distinction between rich and poor—their nourishment is the same for all in the *sussitia*, and the clothing of the rich is such as the poorest man could manage to procure. (Aristotle *Politics* 1294b19–29)

Thus (in the language of Plutarch) "avarice (*pleonexia*) was legislated out of existence" (*Lycurgus* 9.1), or as Xenophon puts it:

What interest could wealth have for them there, where he ordered it so that they would contribute equally to the necessities of life, and carry on their lives all alike, so that no one would be eager for money for the sake of enjoyment? (Xenophon *Lac. Pol.* 7.3)

In their disciplined, even ritualized, mode of life the Spartans might seem to have repealed history and to have thrown off the evils of the Age of Iron: *ponos* and *kerdos*. The philolakon (pro-Spartan) Critias, in his fifth-century idealization of their life, described it (like the Greek picture of the happy afterlife) as a continuous genteel symposium. Thalia sustained Eunomia.

The youth of Lacedaemon drink so much
   As brings their hearts to cheerful hope,
To common genial speech and moderate laughter.
   This much of drink improves the body,
The mind, possessions. It nurtures love
   And also sleep, of toil the harbor,
And Health, the goddess who grants greatest joy,
   And Piety's neighbor, Self-restraint.

Critias Fr. 6 Diels

In this picture the Spartans have achieved a purely cultural, which is to say godlike, existence, insulated from nature and all the ills the flesh is heir to. It is to be noted that like a genteel symposium (and like the Golden Age, for that matter), their society achieves this cultural perfection at the cost of excluding women.

The Spartans were for the Greeks a political object-lesson because their society was more political than the others: They had shifted to the side of the political order certain critical aspects of social life, particularly the education of boys and the sociability of adult males. Their society remained nonetheless divided between public and private, and at Sparta precisely because their society was more political this division was more sharply felt than elsewhere. The dream of an all-male godlike society had its limits; at home the Spartan found private wealth and women. The Spartan thus became a double man, as avarice was driven underground. "They made each man's door-sill the limit of his personal freedom" (Dionysius of Halicarnassus 20.13.2); discipline and uniformity could be the rule out of doors, but at the price of concealed license. Sparta is surely the source of Socrates' picture of the timocratic man in the *Republic*:

> Such men will be avid for wealth, and savagely in the dark will prize gold and silver, in as much as they possess storerooms and private treasuries where they can deposit such things in hiding; they will further have the enclosures of their houses as (if you will allow the expression) private nests, where they can spend their money on their wives and on anyone they like—and their expenses will be great.
>
> Quite true, he said.
>
> So also they will be miserly with their wealth, in that they prize it, but do not possess it openly; they will be ready to spend the property of others through their avidity, secretly harvesting their pleasures, like runaway children truants from the law, inasmuch as they have not been educated through consent but under compulsion and have disregarded the true Muse—the Muse of reason and philosophy. (Plato *Republic* 548b–c)

For Socrates Sparta represents the inadequacy of a political order imposed by external discipline rather than shared ideas, and the mark of this inadequacy is the existence of private households there. The Spartans restricted public consumption but not private possession; they restrained the exercise of the passions but not the passions themselves. Theirs was a society not purified but repressed.

Aristotle is clear (as Plato hints) that the leading symptom of what was wrong with Sparta was the position of women there:

> [The women] live intemperately with all kinds of intemperance and luxuriously, so that by necessity in such a regime wealth is valued, especially given that they are ruled by women. . . . There is much management by the women in their government. What difference does it make whether women rule or the rulers are ruled by women? (Aristotle *Politics* 1269b 22–33)

What was truly repressed at Sparta was, on the ethical level, avarice, and on the political level, inequality—repressed by the fiction that all Spartans were equal, competitive only in their selfless devotion to the state. The Spartan, however, was a double man, one thing among his peers, something else at home with his women. Women thus became the vehicle of the repressed.

The Women of Sparta

When Aristophanes wants to give us a typical Spartan woman he shows us Lampito (the bearer of a noble Spartan name); she is displayed primarily as a magnificent physical specimen; she could throttle a bull and has superb breasts (*Lysistrata* 80–84). Spartan women are fit to breed heroes—and to rear them; they seem to have been specially in demand as nurses. They are superb animals.

This physical exuberance had another aspect. The prototypical Spartan woman was Helen, and she remained their patron (Herodotus 6.6l; Aristophanes *Lysistrata* 155). A cult of Helen will have celebrated the demonic power of Eros against the bonds of civility. The sexual license of the Spartan women is part of the tradition about them. In historical times Alcibiades played the part of Paris and seduced a Spartan queen (Plutarch *Alcibiades* 23.7) There is some (scattered and opaque) evidence that Spartan women were allowed certain sexual freedoms even within the bounds of legitimacy—that they could have, under certain circumstances, more than one husband. Their physicality is represented as relatively unsubdued by the cultural and juridical order. Their purported refusal of the law is in a way a refusal to become Greek; they appear as barbarians within the gates, with familiar barbarian qualities: an intemperate taste for luxuries, fierceness without real courage, an unlimited passion for wealth.

Aristotle says:

> The fact that the women are handled badly, as was said before, not only produces an internal disorder in the constitution, taken itself by itself, but also contributes to avarice (*philochrēmatia*). (Aristotle *Politics* 1270a 11–15)

We, if we wish to see the Spartan women as a sign of failure on the part of the lawgiver, might rather say that in transferring male energies to the public sphere of war and politics the Spartan men had lost control of their households, which were most of the time left to women and small children (cf. Plutarch *Lycurgus* 14.1, *Lac. Apoth.* 242c). Excluded from *philotimia*, public ambition, the women were left alone to their spontaneous *philochrēmatia* (cf. Plato *Laws* 806a–c). But we might rather want to see the indiscipline of the women as after all part of the Spartan solution: The men had transferred to the woman all the qualities that they did not permit themselves to display in public. The women, they told the world, demanded money, enjoyments, and advantageous marriages; if they themselves sometimes sought these things, it was only because the women made them do it.

In any case the peculiar position of women at Sparta was integrally an aspect of the constitution there. Overall, Spartan constitutional arrangements can be read as a political effort to inhibit the social effects of private property and minimize class conflict. This effort peculiarly affected the position of women because women were for the Greeks the unpolitical sex, their interests, if not their persons, confined (ideally) to the household. As the carriers of household values they were also vehicles for the transfer of property between patrilines and across the generations. As such, they became at Sparta the locus of certain systemic weaknesses.

The Spartan solution was certainly outstandingly successful for centuries, yet in the long run it displayed an essential weakness: Property became concentrated in the hands of an increasingly constricted circle of families, to such a degree that more and more Spartans lost control of the minimum resources needed to maintain their citizenship. Aristotle places the blame squarely on private property, that is, that political status followed wealth:

> The common dining-groups (called *phiditia*) were not well institutionalized by him who established them first. The groups should have been maintained from common resources, as in Crete. Among the Lacedaemonians each must contribute, and some have become very poor so that they are not able to pay even this expense, with a consequence opposite to the intention of the lawgiver. He wanted the dining-groups to be democratic, but they become quite undemocratic, institutionalized in this form. For the very poor do not find it easy to take part, and this is the traditional criterion of the constitution: that anyone who cannot pay this levy does not take part in it. (Aristotle *Politics* 1271a27–33)

Those whose property sank below the minimum level became *hupomeiones*, "lesser people"; this seems to have been a loss of status from which it was difficult to recover. The result was what the Greeks called *oliganthropia*, "shortage of personnel," which means not a loss of population but a restriction of the circle of effective citizens.[56] *Oliganthropia* was a progressive disease; we trace it through the decline in the number of hoplites, since at Sparta the hoplite was the full citizen. At Plateia Sparta turned out eight thousand hoplites; by the end of the Peloponnesian War the number was down to three thousand. By Aristotle's time there were a thousand, and when the crisis finally broke during the reigns of Agis IV and Cleomenes III, there were not more than seven hundred citizens, of whom one hundred owned nearly all the land.[57] Constitutional government could not survive on such a narrow base; revolution came to Sparta with the familiar calls for the cancellation of debts and redistribution of land, and their King Cleomenes III, claiming to restore the laws of Lycurgus, killed the other king and became (in effect) the first Spartan tyrant.

As their numbers decreased the Spartan citizens had increasingly be-

[56] Asheri (1966).
[57] Fuks (1984); Cartledge (1979), pp. 280–281.

come an officer class, commanding armies made up of liberated helots, *perioikoi* (the free but disenfranchised general population of Laconia) and *hupomeiones*. From a military point of view this solution seems to have been reasonably effective but politically it was a disaster. The military organization was no longer doing the sociopolitical job it had been designed to do. It had been intended to maintain the solidarity of a body of men sufficiently large to represent itself to itself as the community of Sparta; once this body fell below critical mass it revealed itself as a class, oppressive of the community.[58] As such the remaining land-holders were politically vulnerable—and, indeed, Cleomenes III dispossessed them *en bloc*.

The concentration of property, in turn, Aristotle blames on the effects of competitive marriage-exchange:

> One might make some further criticisms with respect to the inequalities of property. It has come about that some of them possess a great deal of property, others very little. That is why the land has come into the hands of a few. Here also the law arranges things badly. To buy, or to sell what one has, it makes ignoble (*ou kalon*), and rightly does so, but it has given the power to give and to devise to anyone who wishes to do so. Yet this has to turn out the same way as the other. There belongs to the women nearly two-fifths of the whole territory, the heiresses[59] having become numerous, and because the dowries have been large. It would have been better to have none or to fix them at something small and moderate. As it is, one can give an heiress to whomsoever one wishes, and if one dies intestate, the heir, whoever he may be, can give her to whomsoever he wishes. And so although the country could support fifteen hundred knights and thirty thousand hoplites they are not even one thousand in number. (Aristotle *Politics* 1270a 15–31)

Marriage-exchange is like market exchange governed by the law of marginal utility; those who bring most to the bargaining table are in the best position to make advantageous marriages. As Spartan males increased the size of dowries—at Sparta actually the property of the wife—in order to obtain rich husbands for their daughters and sisters, property slowly—because this sort of transaction is governed by the rhythm of the generations—came into the hands of a few families; as a secondary effect the women became major property owners.[60] There-

---

[58] See Kinadon's early-fourth-century revolutionary plot (Xenophon *Hellenica* 3.3.8): Out of four thousand persons in the assembly only some forty were Spartiates, which is to say, full citizens—and all the rest, helots, neodameis, hupomeiones, and perioeci, "would be only too glad to eat the Spartiates raw."

[59] Aristotle says *epiklēroi*, but he evidently misunderstands the Spartan situation with respect to female inheritance: cf. Cartledge (1981) pp. 97–98.

[60] Hodkinson (1989) gives reason to believe that in the fifth century there was at

fore an observer could see the major socioeconomic weakness of the Spartan state as the position of women there; women were valued— able to claim their share of values—and were conduits of value, in that the negotiation of the exchange of women became a focus of economic competition across the highest stratum of the society. Because, at the same time, this type of competition, although pervasive, was discreditable, women were politically devalued and excluded, able to exert their real influence only deviously. Once again, it was supposed to be all their fault: The Spartans claimed that they were trying to live as public-spirited warriors, but because of the influence of their women, they failed.

When the Locrian polity failed, however, it was different; failure came through women, but everyone understood that the fault lay with the Locrian men.

Dionysius the Younger at Locri

Property and women were the locus of the systemic weakness that led to the collapse of the Spartan constitution, and also at Locri; Aristotle points the parallel:

> Furthermore because all aristocratic regimes are oligarchic the notables take more than their share, as for example in Lacedaemon the properties came into the hands of a few. And the notables have more ability to do whatever they wish, and to form marriage alliances with whomsoever they wish, through which the city of the Locrians was destroyed by their marriage alliance with Dionysius, which would not have happened in a democracy or in a well-regulated aristocracy. (Aristotle *Politics* 1307a34–40)

The decay of Sparta was a slow process; it reached its crisis finally in the mid-third century, with the assassination of Agis IV and the tyranny of Cleomenes III, but Aristotle most of a century earlier could already see the crisis coming. At Locri, by contrast, breakdown arrived without warning, in the mid-fourth century, with the arrival of Dionysius the Younger of Syracuse. He was able to come there because his father,

---

Sparta increasing resort to other marriage patterns that tended to concentrate wealth. Here again the women might be held responsible: As he remarks (p. 112), "It was greater economic differentiation which led to the changes in marriage practices [listed earlier as "homogamy, close-kin marriage, wife-borrowing, uterine half-sibling marriage, and polyandry"] which increased female influence; and for the benefit of their children women probably supported these new practices which themselves fueled the growth of economic differentiation."

Dionysius the Elder, had been allowed by the Locrians to marry a Locrian maiden. The Locrian constitution, it seems, was sustained by the
closed circle of aristocratic marriages; when that circle was broken the
constitution fell. How this happened is a long story, which I shall proceed to relate.

Epizephyrian Locri, as we have seen,[61] was reliant on the protection
of Syracuse at least as early as 492 B.C., when the city was sheltered
from Rhegion by the intervention of Hieron; his brother and successor,
Thrasybulus, when exiled from Syracuse, took refuge in Locri (Diodorus Siculus 11.68.4). Locri was at this time an independent state
friendly to the Syracusan tyranny, and so she remained. The connection persisted through the fifth-century interlude of (more or less)
constitutional government at Syracuse; Locri was a faithful ally throughout the period of the Peloponnesian War and the great Athenian Expedition.[62] There is no record of practical help from Locri during the
siege,[63] but she was among the cities that sent ships to the Aegean
afterward, when the Syracusans under Hermocrates came to repay Sparta
for her help (Thucydides 8.91.2). Nor did Locri change her allegiance
during the tyranny of Dionysius the Elder. Her importance to Syracuse
in fact increased. The great Carthaginian sack of Sicily—probably the
greatest military disaster to befall any group of Greek cities during the
classical period—brought Dionysius the Elder to power in Syracuse in
406; constitutional government, always weak there, could not survive
the crisis. The external situation of Syracuse also changed. The whole
western part of the island from Selinunte to Camarina was depopu-
lated; Greek refugees streamed into the areas on the east coast under
direct Syracusan protection, and into Italy (Diodorus Siculus 13.91.1,
95.3, 111.5). This demographic shift, which changed the shape of the
Greek West—at least until Timoleon's time—greatly increased the
population of Syracuse and at the same time turned the attention of
the city from western Sicily toward Italy, where there were still Greeks
to govern. This turn gave a new importance to the Syracusan alliance
with Locri, their main Italian base. The Locrians ceased to be merely
passive recipients of Syracusan protection and became active participants in Dionysius's enterprises. They are the most likely source for the
Italian troops that fought in the battle of Gela in 405,[64] and may well
have contributed more troops to Syracusan operations in 397–396 and

---

[61] Cf. pp. 205–207.

[62] Cf. Musti (1977), p. 91.

[63] A papyrus fragment—577 FGH 2—gives her a brief and inglorious part in resistance
to the first Sicilian expedition, 427–425 B.C.

[64] Caven (1990), p. 62.

387.[65] From their territory Dionysius launched his attack on Rhegion in 390 (Diodorus Siculus 14.100.2—Dionysius of Halicarnassus 20.7 says the Locrians invited him). In return for their loyal support Dionysius increasingly offered material rewards: He resettled Messena with Locrians from Locri and Medma in 395 (Diodorus Siculus 14.78.5), leveled Caulonia and gave its territory to Locri in 389 (Diodorus Siculus 14.106.3) along with the neighboring town of Skulletion (modern Squillace) (Strabo 6.1.10), and in the same manner gave the territory of Hipponium to Locri in 388 (Diodorus Siculus 14.107.2).

Dionysius sought to secure his Locrian base by means of a dynastic marriage. This is in the manner of the Sicilian tyrants. The marriages of the Deinomenids had normally been dynastic in two senses: They served to secure alliances supportive of the power of the dynasty, and they were endogamous or restricted within a sharply limited exchange network.[66] Hieron married a daughter of Anaxilas, tyrant of Rhegion, at a time when he was seeking to secure the alliance of that city.[67]

Dionysius sought to found his own dynasty. He was particularly reliant on his brothers—although Plato (*7th. Ep.* 332a) notes that they were unreliable. Leptines served as Dionysius's *nauarchos* or admiral—the number-two position in the tyranny—until he showed too much independence and was exiled; Dionysius then replaced him with another brother, Thearides (Diodorus Siculus 14.48, 102). Later he recalled Leptines and married him to one of his own daughters (Diodorus Siculus 15.7.4)—an endogamous marriage typical of the Sicilian tyrants.

Dionysius's own first marriage, in 406, was to the daughter of Hermocrates, the hero of the resistance to Athens, who had been his patron in his early career;[68] at the same time he gave his sister to Polyzelus, the brother of Hermocrates' wife (Diodorus Siculus 13.96.3). Dionysius made these marriages, says Diodorus, "wishing to acquire kinship with a notable household and make it secure with relation to the tyranny." And in Polyzelus he did indeed acquire a brother-in-law who was still serving as his subordinate commander in 387 (Xenophon *Hellenica* 5.1.26) although they quarreled in the end.

The tyrant's first wife, the daughter of Hermocrates, lived only until the next year, when rioters in Syracuse sacked Dionysius's house and "seizing his wife used her so abusively as to ensure that Dionysius's anger would be deep and lasting, considering his revenge for her the surest pledge (*pistis*) of their mutual partnership in the attack" (Di-

---

[65] Cf. Musti (1977), p. 97.
[66] Cf. Gernet (1968 [1954]).
[67] See p. 282.
[68] Caven (1990), pp. 42–43.

odorus Siculus 13.112.4).[69] The woman died, Plutarch (*Dion* 3.1) says, by suicide.

Such a rape may be seen as the negative inversion of a dynastic marriage: It uses a woman not to forge an alliance but to launch a vendetta. As in heroic times, so at Syracuse friendship and enmity are coded in the gift and theft of women. The woman's suicide reminds us that this is not a game played with tokens, but entails real human suffering.

Dionysius won the ensuing civil war, but remained unmarried for the next seven years; in 398 he contracted the marriage that determined the future of his dynasty. Plutarch tells the story:

> Once Dionysius had recovered and secured his power, he married again, two women at the same time, one from Locri, Doris by name, and a local woman, Aristomache, daughter of Hipparinus, who was a leading man in Syracuse and had shared the office with Dionysius when he had first been chosen general with full powers. It is said that he married both on one and the same day and that no one ever found out which marriage was consummated first, and that afterward he divided his time equally between them; it was his habit to dine with them together, and at night he slept with them by turns. (Plutarch *Dion* 3.2)

While there were various circumstances at various times and places whereby a Greek might have more than one wife, this joint arrangement is unique in the annals of Greek marriage.[70] It is as if Dionysius had taken one wife who happened nevertheless to be two different people. It seems that he intended to inscribe on the marriage bed his determination to make Sicily and Italy one realm. Both wives were taken with all possible pomp: For Aristomache he sent a chariot drawn by four white horses, for Doris, the first of his new giant warships, the quinquereme, decorated with gold and silver (Diodorus Siculus 14.44.7–8). He gave the city a series of feasts, and people remembered that his tyranny became milder at this time (Diodorus Siculus 14.45.1).

Dionysius's Syracusan marriage followed a familiar pattern: By it he secured his connection to an important family that had supported him in the past.[71] The Locrian marriage was much more of an issue, as we learn from two other stories told about it. Here is the first:

> *Dionysius*, we are told, *in need of children to secure his rule, sent to the*

---

[69] On a *pistis* as a crime committed in common to secure the solidarity of a conspiratorial group, see Hatzfeld (1940), pp. 164, 186.

[70] We do not have to believe Plutach's details to be stunned by the concept embodied in his narrative. Dionysius certainly married two woman at more or less the same time and treated them both as legitimate wives.

[71] For Hipparinus and Dionysus see also Aristotle *Politics* 1306a1.

people of Rhegion for a marriageable girl of the citizen body. The citizens met and determined to reply that they would give him none but the daughter of the public executioner (Diodorus Siculus 14.44.5, 107.3).

This story, which seems to be placed after the death of Dionysius's first wife and before his double marriage, is inherently improbable: It asserts that Dionysius asked the city of Rhegion to send him any one of their marriageable girls (Diodorus refers to "one of the *politikoi parthenoi*"). Even the courtships of tyrants were not conducted thus; it was necessary to ask for a particular girl and deal with her father. Probably this story was told at Rhegion, where they remembered Hieron's marriage with the daughter of Anaxilas. That was a dynastic marriage that failed; Anaxilas's sons, who inherited the tyranny, were never drawn into the orbit of their brother-in-law. A century later the lines had hardened and Rhegion was the frontline state in the resistance to Syracusan expansion. Their resistance is coded in this narrative, wherein they tell how they humiliated Dionysius and implicitly contrast themselves with the Locrians.

The other story is told in Plutarch:

> With great vehemence Aristides the Locrian, one of Plato's companions, when Dionysius the Elder asked for one of his daughters to wife, said he would sooner see the girl a corpse than married to the tyrant. Soon thereafter Dionysius killed Aristides' children and asked him in insolence (*pros hubrin*) if he had still the same opinion about his daughters' wedding; he then replied that he grieved for what had happened, but he had not changed his mind about his answer. (Plutarch *Timoleon* 13.9–10)

For a Locrian maiden, marriage to the tyrant is a fate worse than death.

This story seems to come from Academic circles, since it is ascribed to one of Plato's *hetairoi*; its dramatic date must be during or after Plato's first visit to Syracuse c. 388, the only time Plato could have acquired a western companion during the reign of the elder Dionysius.

It was on this visit that Plato met Dion, whom he was much later to describe as "a quick study especially of my discourse, to which his response was penetrating and powerful, more than any other young person I ever met, and he was ready to spend the rest of his life differently from the other Italians and Sicilians, inclined as he was to virtue (*aretē*) rather than to pleasure and the rest of luxury" (*7th Ep.* 327a–b). Dion became Plato's friend—perhaps even his lover (cf. *A. P.* 7.99)—and the link between the Academy and Syracuse. Plato might well have taught some Locrians also on this first visit to Syracuse; their local culture, with its distrust of luxury, would certainly have appealed to him more than Sicilian manners.[72]

---

[72] We do have one other story of the connection between Socratic philosophers and

Dion's circle, however, had more reason than philosophy to decry Dionysius's Locrian marriage: Dionysius's other, Syracusan, wife was Dion's sister. From the point of view of Dion and his people—which is to say, from the Syracusan side of Dionysius's power—Dionysius's Locrian marriage meant the introduction of a foreign element into the community; their hostility to this event is expressed in yet another story (which, like the others, might even be true!):

> The fact was, the people of Syracuse wished the local wife to have more than the foreign one. However, since that one was the first to become pregnant she had the fundamental advantage of the eldest son of Dionysius's line on her side to counterbalance her origin. Aristomache for a long time remained childless in her marriage to Dionysius, hard as she tried to get pregnant by him; Dionysius in fact accused the mother of his Locrian wife of using drugs against Aristomache and killed her. (Plutarch *Dion* 3.3)

We can read this accusation as a kind of displacement; Doris herself is perceived as a poisonous substance within the body politic.

From the Locrian point of view, correlatively, Dionysius's Locrian marriage introduced a foreign element into *Locri*. It took place in two steps: Dionysius first applied to the Locrian government for the right of *epigamia*, the right to contract a marriage with a woman of the citizen body (Diodorus Siculus 14.44.6), and then paid court to Doris, "daughter of Xenetus, the most notable (*endoxotatos*) citizen of that time." Xenetus gave his consent. By these two steps, in the language of Aristotle, "the state was destroyed."

Because legitimacy at Locri was transmitted through women,[73] Doris's children were born legitimate Locrians—in fact they were by birth legitimate members of two communities. Evidently this is why Dionysius applied to the Locrians for the right of *epigamia*; if his intention had been merely to make his children by Doris citizens of Syracuse, he would have handled his marriage with her the way the Greeks generally handled marriages between local men and foreign women: They were as legitimate as the laws of the father's community said they were—and given Dionysius's role at Syracuse, the law there was pretty much whatever he said it was. Clearly his aim was to have children who would be both Syracusan and Locrian; in the event, one of these was his heir. The unity of Sicily and Italy was embodied in the person of Dionysius the Younger.

Aristotle takes this event as an example of the fact that in an oligarchy "the notables" can "do whatever they wish"; he ascribes the mar-

---

certain Locrians (Aeschines Socraticus *FP6.* II 69, p. 415; Aristippus *FP6.* II 70, p. 415). One of Plato's letters also mentions a "feast for Locrian young men" given by the younger Dionysius, where the question of philosophy arose (*Ep. 8* 390a).

[73] This is the implication of Polybius's phrase *ta dia progonōn endoxa.*

riage, therefore, to Xenetus, with the compliance of the community, "which would not have happened in a well-regulated aristocracy." A well-regulated aristocracy, in other words, would not have granted *epigamia*. The attractions of the marriage for Xenetus seem obvious; not every daughter's courtship involves a gold- and silver-trimmed quinquereme. The motives of the community are less clear; Dionysius the Elder, however, was the most powerful man of his time, potent to reward and punish the cities of the West.

As we investigate the nature of the disaster that came to Locri we must note first that the damage for a long time remained latent. So long as the tyranny could maintain itself in Syracuse Locri remained untouched. If Dionysius the Elder intended his son to be a Locrian he seems to have meant this as a backup identity, available in time of trouble—as it turned out to be.

Dionysius the Elder certainly did his best to transmit to his son an intact dynastic establishment; he proceeded to knit together the two halves of his double family by a set of intermarriages. The two daughters of Syracusan Aristomache, Arete and Sophrosyne ("Virtue" and "Moderation") were married to the two sons of Locrian Doris, Thearides and Dionysius the Younger. (Most Greek cities permitted such marriages, between children of the same father but different mothers, as not incestuous.) After Thearides' death Arete was married to Aristomache's brother, her uncle Dion. The tyrant's brother Leptines, after his recall from exile, married Doris's daughter Dicaeosyne ("Justice").[74]

Upon his father's death, Dionysius the Younger inherited the tyranny, and Dion, who had been his father's trusted minister[75] and who was now both the tyrant's step-uncle and brother-in-law, stepped forward to become his leading advisor. Dion evidently held the office of *nauarchos* or admiral,[76] which, as we have seen, Dionysius the Elder had given to his brothers. Dion, in other words, was playing the role of Dionysius the Younger's elder brother. He undertook Dionysius's education, gave him some of Plato's dialogues to read (Plutarch *Dion* 11), and proposed to introduce him to philosophy. At Dion's instigation Dionysius induced Plato to come to Syracuse. At this point the court split; Dion's adversaries, who accused him of aiming to acquire the tyranny himself or on behalf of his nephews (the sons of Aristomache) called to lead them Philistius, who had been a collaborator of Leptines, and who was a historian in the manner of Thucydides.[77] A struggle for the soul of Dionysius thus commenced, a struggle between philosophi-

---

[74] Caven (1990), p. 243 with note 31.

[75] Ibid., p. 211.

[76] This seems to be the implication of the language in Plutarch *Dion* 7.1.

[77] Orsi (1994), p. 16n.10.

cal idealism and historical materialism. Whether in spite of Plato's efforts or because of them, Dion was soon overmatched and exiled; Plato never succeeded in persuading Dionysius to recall him. Finally (after Dionysius stopped sending him his rents) Dion returned in arms. After a prolonged struggle Dionysius, even though he still retained control of the island citadel of Ortygia, felt compelled to withdraw from Syracuse, leaving the island in the hands of his son. Like the Deinomenid Thrasybulus before him, he went to Locri; unlike Thrasybulus, however, he arrived not as an exile but as a Locrian.

We have several stories about the Locrian period of Dionysius the Younger. The first is from Justin's epitome of Pompeius Trogus, a second century A.D. (or later) condensation of a first-century B.C. historical narrative, itself a compilation from various sources:

> Dionysius . . . afraid to stand a siege in the fortress, ran away secretly, with all his royal apparatus. Accepted in exile by the Locrians as his allies, with the understanding that he would rule legally, he occupied the acropolis and behaved with his usual savagery. He ordered the wives of the principal men to be seized and raped, maidens before their marriage he abducted and after he had raped them returned them to their husbands-to-be, and the most notable men he either drove from the city or ordered killed, and their property he appropriated.
>
> Later when he lacked an excuse for plunder he got round the whole city with an artful device. When the Locrians had been hard pressed in war by Leophron, tyrant of Rhegion, they had vowed, should they be victorious, that on the day of Aphrodite's festival they would prostitute their maidens. This vow was let to lapse; when their war with the Lucanians was going badly Dionysius called them into assembly and urged that they send their wives and daughters, adorned as lavishly as possible, to the temple of Aphrodite, and that one hundred of these, chosen by lot, should carry out the vow of the people: For religion's sake they would spend one month in the brothel, all the men having taken an oath that they would not touch a single one of them. Lest there should be damage to maidens who in this way made good to the city its vow, he made a decree: No maiden should marry until these had found husbands. As his plan was accepted, having regard as it did for the modesty of the maidens and for their religious fervor, all the women eagerly adorned gathered in the temple of Aphrodite. Dionysius then sent in soldiers and despoiled them, taking the jewelry of the matrons as his booty. He killed the husbands of some—the richer among them—and tortured others to reveal their husbands' money. With such devices he ruled for six years; then expelled by a conspiracy of the Locrians he returned to Sicily. There, where all felt secure after a long interval of peace, he by treachery recovered Syracuse. (Justin 21.2–3)

The next is in Strabo, one of his brief notes on the place:

These are generally believed to have been the first to employ written laws. For the longest time they had good government (*eunomēthentas*), but Dionysius when he was expelled from Syracuse used them more lawlessly than anyone; he had prior sex with girls dressed for marriage, slipping into their chamber, and collecting the nubile girls he would let loose at the symposia doves with their feathers clipped and make the girls circle around naked; some also wearing sandals that did not match, one high, the other low, were made to chase the pigeons for the sake of indecency. However, he paid the penalty when he went back to Syracuse, resuming his rule: The Locrians tore down his fortress and set themselves free and got control of his wife and children. Two were daughters, along with the younger of the sons. (The elder son, Apollocrates, shared command with his father in his restoration.) Although Dionysius begged and pleaded in his own person and the Tarentines pleaded on his behalf, that they surrender the persons of his family on any terms they liked, the Locrians did not give them back, but stood a siege and the laying-waste of their territory, and poured out upon the daughters the extreme of their wrath. First prostituting them they strangled them, then burning their bodies they ground the bones and cast them out to sea. (Strabo 6.1.8)

The third account is from Athenaeus; the authors he quotes both wrote in the third century B.C.[78] These therefore are the texts closest in time to the event:

Concerning the luxury (*truphē*) of Dionysius the Younger, tyrant of Sicily, Satyrus the peripatetic giving the history in his *Lives* says that he filled up at his house thirty-couch rooms with feasters. And Clearchus in the fourth book of his *Lives* writes as follows:

Dionysius son of Dionysius becoming of all Sicily the avenging spirit (*alastōr*) coming to the city of the Locrians which was his mother-city (for Doris his mother was Locrian by birth), spreading the largest room in the city with thyme and roses, sent for the Locrian maidens by turns. And naked among them naked he did not skip any obscenity as he rolled about on the floor. So it happened that not much later the victims [masculine in the Greek] of his outrages getting his wife and children into their hands—standing them in the street—they molested them to the point of outrage. Once they were glutted with outrage, running needles under the nails of their hands they killed them. When they were dead they ground up their bones in mortars and cutting the rest of them into butcher's meat they pronounced a curse on those who did

---

[78] The passage Athenaeus quotes from Clearchus is clearly the source of Aelian *Var. Hist.* 9.8; this latter adds nothing to our sources. The same stories were also known to Plutarch: *Timoleon* 13.10 and *Moralia* 821d.

not taste them. The reason they ground up their flesh in keeping with this impious curse was that this food might be eaten as they baked their bread. The leftovers they threw out to sea. As for Dionysius himself, in the end he spent his life as a begging priest, pitiably waving his tambourine. So be careful of so-called luxury—it can ruin your life—and understand that outrage brings destruction on all parties. (Athenaeus 541c–e)

The word I have translated "outrage" in this last selection is *hubris*; it is a quality characteristic of tyrants, and is also the name for specific illegal acts—assault, and also rape in the sense of forcible sex. Greek has no specific term for this last.[79] It is clear, however, that the main theme here is the violation of women.

It is hard to know what to make of these stories. It is perhaps not obvious how odd, in a Greek context, they are. Greek cannibalism is unparalleled; the only thing close is the story of the ritual in the precinct of Lycaon, where, we are told, a bit of human flesh was included in the sacrifice; he who ate that bit became a werewolf.[80] The systematic torture of women is similarly hard to parallel from Greek sources.[81] There is not even an exact parallel for substitution of violence against a man's woman for revenge upon the man himself[82]—although a man's woman might be killed along with him, as Cassandra was killed with Agamemnon.

Those who have been interested in the "real history" of Locri[83] have mostly focused on Justin, on his account of Dionysius's seizure of the acropolis and his mention of a war with the Lucanians (certainly active in those parts at this time); they have puzzled over the chronology (Justin says that Dionysius ruled for six years, but he seems to have been ten years in the city) and over the question as to whether he was expelled, as Justin says, or whether the reaction followed his return to Syracuse, as in Strabo's version.

There has also been consideration of Justin's (that is to say, Pompeius Trogus's) sources. It is usually assumed that he is following Timaeus of Tauromenium (in histories of the Greek West, Timaeus is usually assumed to be the source when no other source is cited). However

---

[79] The word often translated "rape"—as in the Rape of Europa—is *harpagē*, which means "kidnapping."

[80] Borgeaud (1979) pp. 62–63; no human remains were found in the excavation of the sanctuary; in the case of cannibalism, as in the case of human sacrifice, the fantasy seems to have served the Greeks for the deed.

[81] Athenaeus (596f) mentions Leaina, the courtesan beloved of Harmodius, who after his attempted coup died stalwart under torture.

[82] Athenaeus (609b), citing Theopompus, says that after Agesilaus of Sparta drove his enemy Lysandridas into exile, the Spartan killed Lysandridas's mother and aunt.

[83] E.g., Meloni (1951).

the author who most evidently followed Timaeus—Diodorus Siculus—
has nothing at all to say about Dionysius at Locri; possibly Timaeus had
nothing to say about it either. In fact Justin need not have been reliant
on sources of any kind; his account in large part consists of common-
places about the tyrant: "he changes inherited lawful ways and forces
women and executes without trial" (Herodotus 3.80.5).

Actually, aside from Justin's narrative there is no good evidence that
Dionysius ever was tyrant at Locri.[84] Justin says that the Locrians accepted him "with the understanding that he would rule legally," but it
is hard to see why they would have taken him as any kind of ruler. That
he was Doris's son did not give him any claim on sovereignty, only a
place among the leading citizens. Nor did Locri really have the sort of
acropolis a tyrant and his retinue could occupy; the top of the city
divides into three small hilltops, with a temple of Athena on the northernmost, and small fortifications on the other two. Locri had long been
a Syracusan base and no doubt some mercenary troops loyal to Dionysius were stationed there (Strabo speaks of his *phroura*, his fortress);
perhaps these troops occupied the hilltops. This would have made him
an odd sort of citizen—and, as it seems, an uncomfortable one. We
need not assume, however, that during Dionysius's six- or ten-year residence at Locri he was tyrant of the place. In fact it is difficult to form
any sort of plausible picture of what did happen, and at this point it is
probably impossible to find out.

We can, however, say that these stories (aside from Justin's common-
places) focus on the violation of women, on crime and retribution, on
impurity and purification. Furthermore, they have the look of local
stories. There is something quintessentially Locrian in conceiving the
safety and destruction of the city as embodied in the purity and impurity of maidens. I suggest that these stories record through the transformations of folk narrative the Locrian experience of Dionysius the Younger.
Dionysius came to Locri as a foreigner who was nevertheless a citizen.
This was evidently experienced as the introduction of impurity; if "dirt
is matter out of place," Dionysius the Younger, the product of the wrong
marriage, was wrongly Locrian and as such a kind of social filth. Therefore the permission of *epigamia* to Dionysius the Elder (which Aristotle
calls the result of arrogant self-indulgence by an out-of-control oligarchy) produced a kind of monster and was felt to imply the defilement
of all the Locrian women. Perhaps Dionysius did some of the things of

---

[84] The Athenian Stranger in Plato's *Laws* (638b) says that "greater cities defeat lesser
cities in battle and enslave them, as Syracuse did Locri"; possibly he is thinking of Dionysius the Younger, but probably not. In any case there is no known battle between
these two cities at any period.

which he is accused, perhaps not; in any case the real violation was committed on the body politic. Such impurity could only be purged by the defilement and destruction (at least in thought, perhaps in fact) of the alien element.

Violence against women is a Locrian theme, as in the myth and ritual of the Locrian maidens at Troy: Ajax violates Cassandra and in retaliation the maidens are menaced with death by the people of Ilion. In the Euthymus story also, the violence of the hero occurs in two places, in the original rape and in the forcible marriage of the maidens given the hero in recompense for his lynching. Women are in these stories the vehicles of impurity and of purification; the violation of women is redressed not by the punishment of the violator but by the degradation of compensatory women.

Still in all these stories the Locrians are, at least superficially or in some formal sense, protective of their maidens; violence comes from the others, from the intruder and the aliens. Ajax, it is true, was a Locrian, but for his original rape the Locrians paid one thousand years of atonement.

In the stories around Dionysius, by contrast, the Locrians themselves commit the violence; they prostitute, defile, torture, and eat Dionysius's women. We can feel the tradition reaching for some form that would be extreme enough to express the fear and self-loathing of the Locrians. "Self-loathing" because, as Aristotle makes clear, Dionysius the Younger was, in his very existence, *their fault*. The women of Dionysius then become the *pharmakoi* whereby the impurity that was Dionysius's presence is expelled from the state. Their remains are then cast into the sea (as in the "original" version of the Locrian maidens at Troy). This last detail is the only one that appears in all the versions of Epizephyrian revenge—in Strabo, in Clearchus, and also twice in Plutarch (*Timoleon* 13; *Moralia* 821b); it must represent the inner meaning of the stories. The women become *katharmoi, lumata*; the Locrians, having consumed them, vomit them out. Thus the state is purified.

There is not much use in looking for a kernel of truth in these ugly stories; they rather tell us something about the Locrian *mentalité*. As always with things Locrian, maidens and marriage are important; in this western version the critical sustaining structure is the closed circle of marriage-exchange, and the destructive element is a tyrant's marriage-in. Beyond this point we are reduced to conjecture. On the general principle that some theory is always better than none, I shall now propose a social-structural explanation, suggesting that the peculiar type of matriliny practiced at Locri served to protect the propertied class from the concentration of property and its attendant social evils. This theory will keep my promise to find out how the Epizephyrian

Locrians found through women a solution to the problem of property—a solution parallel to and opposite to the Spartan solution.

Double Descent

We hear from Polybius that "all inherited marks of status (*endoxa*) among [the Epizephyrians] pass through women, not through men." Polybius's language implies that (by contrast) the inheritance of property was in the normal Greek manner primarily patrilineal; it would follow that Locri enjoyed a double descent system—that is, wealth was transmitted through males, marks of status (claims to "good birth" and the privileges that confirm them) through females. The bride brought her status with her into her husband's house and conferred it on all its members. Therefore, to the extent that status was independent of wealth, sons (so long as they were unmarried) acquired status from their mothers; husbands acquired status from their wives. In order to make this system lucid we need only assume that property was not in any important sense transmitted through females at all: in case there were no sons, property passed to collateral males (the daughters nevertheless remaining marriageable because of their status) and brides brought with them no dowries except the *himatia kai chrusa*, the trousseau (itself a sign of status). The status brought into the patriline by the bride would pass out of it in the next generation, with the marriages of her daughters. Fathers would attempt to use their daughters' status to attract wealthy sons-in-law, and their sons' wealth to attract high-status daughters-in-law. Because each marriage would constitute an exchange of wealth for status, wealth would not become concentrated in a restricted circle of patrilines; the high-status matrilines would in each generation tend to attract wealth, and as the matrilines would be constantly moving from patriline to patriline, this attraction would move with them and keep the wealth circulating between families.

This is a lot to make out of one phrase in Polybius, and it is of course only a hypothesis. It is offered as a possible explanation of the way in which marriage-exchange could sustain the polity. Note that this hypothetical system would function only as long as the circle of marriages remained closed; in that case a finite amount of status would circulate within the system, keeping wealth in symmetrical circulation. Conversely the society would need to remain economically closed (as Epizephyrian Locri seems to have been) so that the amount of wealth circulating would also remain more or less fixed.

Dionysius the Elder married the daughter of "Xenetus, the most notable (*endoxotatos*) citizen of that time." By this hypothesis Xenetus had this status from his wife, who transmitted it to her daughter Doris. Therefore the unmarried (at least in Locrian terms: i.e., unmarried to any Locrian) Dionysius the Younger arrived at Locri as one of its highest-status males, and at the same time brought with him wealth beyond the dreams of avarice, Syracusan gold. The shock to the system was evidently seismic, and in some way permanently transformed the state. Dionysius the Younger marked an epoch in Locrian history; after him the state had to be reconstructed, the constitution was transformed, and the Locrians began to coin money.[85] It seems that the circle of marriages could be closed no longer. Locrian cooperation with Syracuse had protected and sustained the state as long as the Locrians could maintain a distance; they could not, however, merge with Syracuse, even in the person of her tyrant, without enduring a fate worse than death.

The Legend of Locri and the Legend of Taras

Throughout the classical period Locri was dependent on Syracuse; we have, however, no stories that celebrate this fact. Disordered and tyrannical, Syracuse is the opposite of Locri; possibly this opposition was the best ground for their alliance. Be that as it may, it made them an odd couple, with ideological problems. The Locrians were all the more motivated to insist on their similarity and mythical links with Sparta, the scourge of tyrants. This brings us to the links between the Locrian foundation story and the story of the foundation of Sparta's only acknowledged western colony: Taras.

The Taras story appears in two versions. The older version was in Antiochus, and is, in fact the longest surviving fragment of that author:

> When the Messenian War happened, those of the Lacedaemonians who did not join in the expedition were adjudged slaves and called Helots, while all those who became youths (*paides*) were called Partheniai and adjudged without civic rights. They not accepting this (for they were many) plotted against the [Spartiate] people. Perceiving this [the Spartiates] quietly sent along certain persons who by means of a pretense of friendship would report to them the manner of the plot. One of these was Phalanthus, who actually was thought to be their main patron, but was not absolutely happy with those named to the council. It was agreed that at the Hyacinthia when the contest at Amyclae was reaching its conclusion, when Phalanthus put on his skin cap, they would make the attempt. Spartiates were recognizable by their hair Since they reported secretly the agreements of Phalanthus's circle, and the

---

[85] Cf. pp. 222 and 311, also Musti (1977), pp. 103–105.

contest was taking place, the herald came forward and proclaimed that Phalanthus should not put on his cap. So they perceived that information had
been laid about the plot; some then ran away while others became suppliants. Instructing them to be of good heart they handed them over to custody,
and sent Phalanthus to the god about a colony. The oracle came:

> I give you Satyrion that the rich country of Taras
> Be your home and you be a sorrow to the Iapygians.

So the Partheniai went with Phalanthus, and the barbarians and the Cretans
who held the place accepted them. (555 FGH 13)

The obscurities of this narrative make us less regretful that we have
lost Antiochus, but it is not entirely his fault; the story is complicated.
The Partheniai have an ambiguous position; they are sent away as hostile to the state, but at the same time they are to be a Spartan colony
and are to recapitulate Spartan experience: As the Spartans dominated
the Peloponnese the Partheniai are to dominate Iapygia. Phalanthus,
who plays the part of *oikistēs*, has a similarly ambiguous role in the
story: he is not originally one of the conspirators (evidently he is himself a full Spartan) but is sent to infiltrate them. Nevertheless, he acquires the position of their patron—but does not fully agree with
them. Therefore he is assigned to take them somewhere they had no
wish to go.

The role of the Italian natives is similarly ambiguous; they welcome
the colony that the god has sent to vex them, and they are not really
barbarians at all, but Greeks from Crete (arrived in heroic times, as
Strabo, perhaps following Antiochus, goes on to explain). Strabo also
tells us that the Iapygians, the indigenes whom the colonists found in
control of the territory, were actually Cretans (see Athenaeus 523a)
taking their name from Iapynx, a son of Daedalus and a Cretan woman
(Strabo 6.3.2), These Cretans had ended up there as a result of King
Minos's failed effort to recover the escaping Daedalus. Herodotus remarks that these same Cretans became Messapian Iapygians and later
inflicted on Taras and her allies the greatest slaughter ever endured
by Greeks (7,170). As Cretans they belong to Minos, identified by the
Greeks as their prototypical lawgiver, but at the same time they are
the Greeks' worst enemies.[86]

---

[86] There is a similar ambiguity in the Spartan relation to Crete: Lycurgus visited Crete,
found Spartan colonists observing local laws ascribed to Minos, and took them as his
model (Aristotle *Politics* 1271b). Here again the Spartans appear as colonists, acquiring
their laws from the natives, and then instructing the mother city.
   Aristotle also tells us (according to Jacoby [ad 577 *FGH* 13] he is following Antiochus)
that the *sussition* was an ancient institution found in Crete, but at a much earlier date in

All these ambiguities are typical of foundation stories, and seem to reflect the problem of making one city into two, so that colony both is and is not something new. The colonists are typically rejected by the mother city—there is something wrong with them, or their departure is in some other way unhappily necessary—while at the same time upon their arrival in the new territory they are seen as a branch of the motherland, an honorable extension of her sphere.

So it is not unusual that the Partheniae are sent away because something is wrong with them, but just what is it? The story is unclear. Perhaps we should start with the peculiar account of the origin of the helots, here not ascribed to conquest but to cowardice: those who joined the war became Spartans, those who chose not to join became serfs. The Partheniae were, however, intermediate: "all those who [something] during the expedition were called Partheniae." (The word is never applied in Greek to any other group of persons, but is close to Parthenioi, which in Homer means sons of unmarried women.) The "[something]" I have put in brackets represents a textual problem. The received reading is *hoisois paides egenonto*, which is normal Greek for "those who had children." This makes no sense. It would seem to mean that those citizens to whom children were born during the war lost their citizenship—or, by a possible vagary of syntax, that children born during the war were deprived of citizen rights. But what is supposed to be wrong with having children—or with being born—during a war? The obvious answer is that they were children of non-Spartan fathers, perhaps of helots, as in the Locrian foundation story, but it seems strange that if Antiochus meant this he did not say so.[87]

The alternative reading is *hosoi paides egenonto*. This is certainly not normal Greek, and as the more difficult reading has some claim to be original; it is hard to imagine an editor putting it in. It has been interpreted to mean (like the other reading) "those born," but the normal Greek for this is *hosoi egenonto*. The phrase should rather mean "all those who became *paides*"—and I suggest it meant exactly that. The

---

Italy, where it had been introduced by King Italos when he transformed the people from nomads to farmers, and is still observed by some of them. Italy here means the district to the south of Iapygia, roughly the modern Calabria (whereas Iapygia is roughly the modern Apulia). It is striking that the legendary influences move in both directions: Crete may have shaped Iapygia, or Italy may have instructed Crete. In any case there is some link between Spartan institutions and an original or native society—just as the Epizephyrians drew their institutions, or some of them, from the natives.

[87] This was certainly Aristotle's version in the *Politeiai* (Fr. 611.57 Rose); probably this was the best he could make of Antiochus's text. In the *Politics*, however, he says that the *Partheniae* were descended from the *homoioi*; here he seems to be using Ephorus's version, to which we shall come below.

paides at Sparta were a definite age-class, the eighteen-year-olds; in Doric communities generally *pais* is used where Greeks elsewhere use *ephebos*, for the youth on the verge of manhood. Antiochus then would mean that when the Spartans went off to war they left behind the women and children; the boys who grew to manhood during the war were called Partheniae because, like the children of unmarried women, they belonged to their mothers. Having been reared by women they could not be men.

While the Partheniae were exclusively men (stories of the earliest colonies—except Locri—tell us that the colonies were founded by men, who presumably found their wives among the indigenes), the Spartan woman by all interpretations play a key role in their story. The women of Sparta—at least in the festival, as we shall see—also had some role at Amyclae, the setting of the story. On the Amyclaean altar of Apollo, along with much else, were figured Aphrodite, Athena, and Artemis carrying to heaven Hyakinthus and his sister Polyboea, who had died a *parthenos* (Pausanias 3.19.4). We have no other information about Polyboea; she seems, however, to belong to a category by now familiar to us: the virgin heroines who become patrons of nubile girls and their marriages. It is interesting that she was represented here, because Apollo, the god of young men, nowhere plays a role in the initiation or marriage of young girls. Near Amyclae was also the sanctuary of Alexandra, which seems by the dedications there found to have been the *proteleia* sanctuary of Sparta, the place where Spartan brides went to seek the protection of the god before their wedding.

There is also evidence of a goddess at Amyclae; Callimachus (*Aitiai* Fr. 75) speaks of the Amyclaeon as a place where Artemis might be found "weaving rushes"; this suggests that Artemis also played some role at the sanctuary, perhaps associated with a rite involving dining or sleeping on the ground, on rush mats. Sleeping on the ground is a familiar aspect of initiatory rites.

Furthermore we know that at Cnidos, thought by the Spartans to be a Spartan colony, there was a cult of Artemis Hyacinthotrophus which in Hellenistic times, at least, included a penteteric festival with games and musical contests.[88] Games and musical events were characteristic of the annual Spartan Hyacinthia, which (as we shall see) was an initiatory festival. It seems that at Cnidos Artemis had a role in the nurture of young males. Pugliese Caratelli has seen grounds for placing a similar cult in Taras.[89] If such a cult existed in both these places, it probably derived from the common source of these two communities, Sparta,

---

[88] Pugliese Caratelli (1987).
[89] Pugliese Caratelli (1989a).

and therefore existed at Amyclae also. This would give a different explanation of the name *Partheniae*, which would then mean, not "bastards" but "belonging to the *parthenos*, to courotrophic Artemis."

Courotrophic goddesses characteristically care for small children of both sexes—for children, in fact, during the life stage in which their sex is relatively unimportant and they belong to their mothers. By this interpretation the Partheniae were so called because they could not advance beyond Artemis Hyacinthotrophus, who was linked to their mothers and sisters, into the initiatory care of Apollo Hyacinthus, linked to their fathers and brothers. In other words, what was wrong with the Partheniae is that, because of the Messenian War, they had not been initiated.

We need not rely on the particulars of this interpretation in order to make obvious the parallel with the Epizephyrian foundation story: In both stories certain damaged persons, intermediate between slave and free, become the colony. In the Locrian story, however, the colony results from misalliances between the slaves and the free, and the damage results from a failure of marriage; in the Spartan story (by this interpretation) the colonists are those who lacked the chance to choose freedom or slavery, and the damage is the failure of initiation. This interpretation of Antiochus, in turn, helps us to understand why the story is set at the Hyacinthia: This was the initiatory ritual that the Partheniae lacked.

A Digression on the Hyacinthia and Amyclae

Athenaeus quotes from Didymus Grammaticus's summary of Polycrates a somewhat garbled, or at least overly compressed, description of the Hyacinthia:

> The Laconians celebrate the festival of the Hyacinthia over three days; because of the mourning which takes place for Hyacinthus they do not wear crowns at the dinner nor do they serve bread nor hand out cakes and all that goes with them; neither do they sing the paean to the god nor introduce anything else of that sort, the kind of thing they have in their other festivals; they have dinner in a very disciplined manner and then depart. On the middle day of the three there is an elaborate show and a large and interesting gathering. Boys in belted tunics play the lyre and sing to the flute while running the gamut of chords with the plectrum in anapestic rhythm, and in high-pitched voices sing to the god. Others pass through the theater on caparisoned horses. Then numerous choruses of youths pass through and sing one of the local songs, and mingled with them are dancers doing old-fashioned figures matched to the flute music and song. Of the maidens, some

are carried by on wicker carts expensively fitted out, while others join the procession racing multi-horse chariots, and the whole city is caught up in the excitement and delight of the performance. They sacrifice in quantity on this day and the citizens entertain all their acquaintance and their own slaves also. No one is absent from the sacrifice; instead the whole city gets to be emptied by the show. (Athenaeus 139d–f)

Polycrates is evidently taking us through the three days of the festival: The first belonged to mourning, the second to spectacle, the third to sacrifice and entertainment. The name of this third day was *Copis*, Cleaver; Athenaeus has a description of it from Polemon:

> First they set up tents by the god, in these they make pallets out of brushwood and spread carpets over them, and there feast together not only our local people, but any strangers who are in town. (Athenaeus 138f)

The *Copis* was thus an inversion of one of the most characteristic Spartan institutions, the *xenelasia* or expulsion of strangers. On this day the stranger was welcome—and by another inversion, the slave was entertained. These inversions suggest a new-year's festival, like the Cronia at Athens, when the masters served the slaves at a dinner held in the fields. A day of mourning is also appropriate to the new year. Rituals of renewal often proceed by creating an intermission, fasting or otherwise interrupting the flow of life, then by breaking down social structure and starting over, as it were from scratch; the tents and the feasting on carpets (rather than couches) seem also intended to suggest the primitive condition.

The Hyacinthia, with its procession, races, musical competitions, and entertainment of strangers, also reminds us of the Dionysia at Athens, and the ancients evidently saw the parallel: The Peace of Nicias was to be annually reaffirmed by the parties at the Dionysia and the Hyacinthia—and put up at the Amyclaeon, clearly conceived as an urban central place equivalent to the acropolis at Athens (Thucydides 5.23.4). The Hyacinthia, however, was more complex than the Dionysia, in that it honored both a god and a hero. *Hyakinthus, we are told, was loved by Apollo, who however accidentally struck him with a discus while they were exercising together and killed him; the eponymous flower sprang from his blood.* In some versions *Hyakinthus was also loved by the West Wind, who in jealousy blew on Apollo's discus so that it struck the boy.* In any case he was buried at Amyclae where the Hyacinthia was held; the festival, like so much herocult, was a recurrent funeral, with mourning followed by a procession, competition, and then feasting.[90]

---

[90] All of these elements are found in the funeral of Patroclus in *Iliad* 23, and in classi-

Pausanias (3.19.1) reports that Hyacinthus was buried within the altar at the base of Apollo's image at the Amyclaeon and that there was a little door through which were passed offerings to him. The construction here, the so-called throne of Bathycles dating from the sixth century, was altogether odd. It consisted of a one-story enclosure adorned with statues and friezes (mostly scenes involving women or monsters), and within this an altar, similarly adorned. From this altar rose the roughly made image of the god, a bronze pillar some sixty feet high, equipped with helmeted head and arms holding bow and spear.

The myth of Hyacinthus, the youth loved to death by the god, should be the *aition* of a boys' initiation. Like the unmarried virgins who become heroines because they do not survive the perils of being a *parthenos* to become women, so Hyacinthus did not survive the perils of late boyhood—including those of being the love object of an older male—to become a man. By initiation, as we have seen, these perils are survived; what goes wrong in the myth is put right in the ritual.

We are in any case fairly safe to call the Hyacinthia an initiation: Because the Spartan community was so focused on creating that unnatural creature, the Spartan, most Spartan rituals have some initiatory element. In order to understand what relation such an aspect of the Hyacinthia could have had to the colonial enterprise, however, we need to consider the relation between Sparta and Amyclae.

Classical Sparta was not walled nor did it have the look of a city; it was a cluster of four villages spread out to the south of the hill on which stood the temple of Athena of the Brazen House. Amyclae was the fifth village, or *oba*, of Sparta, and it was clearly different from the others—in the first place spatially; it stood some kilometers away and was reached by a sacred way. The Amyclaeon has the look of one of those external sanctuaries so frequent in Greek cities, a place set apart, where the city goes on special occasions.

Pausanias (3.10.1) says that during the Corinthian war when the day of the Hyacinthia came round King Agesilaus sent home the Amyclaeans, "so that they could perform the established rites for Hyacinthus and Apollo." This tells us that the Hyacinthia was in some sense a local festival, the responsibility of the men of that village—who, it seems, on these three days entertained the Spartans.

About the history of Amyclae we have two stories. One was in Ephorus:

---

cal times musical and athletic competitions are frequent elements of recurrent heroic funerals—among them the great Panhellenic competitive festivals: Olympia at the tomb of Pelops, the Isthmia at the tomb of Palaemon, Nemea at the tomb of Opheltes. Even the Pythian games had their tomb: that of the monster Python, slain (like Hyacinthus) by Apollo.

When the Heracleidae got control of Laconia, Eurysthenes and Procles divided the country into six parts and established towns. One part, Amyclae, they kept apart and gave it to the man[91] who had betrayed to them Laconia and persuaded the people then in control of it to depart with the Achaeans into Ionia. (70 *FGH* 117)

This is obviously a very abbreviated summary of the story, but it seems that in this version Laconia was betrayed from within to the Dorians, and that the betrayer was rewarded with Amyclae. He alone, therefore, remained when the other Achaeans departed—or else, which seems a more plausible story, he and his people remained at Amyclae, protected from eviction by their collaboration with the invader. If we think of Sparta as a kind of colony, Amyclae is the place of contact between the Dorians and the indigenes.[92]

Pausanias tells a different (if not necessarily contradictory) story, placed in the reign of King Telecles, eighth generation from Eurysthenes and (by this account) third generation after the laws of Lycurgus.

During this reign the Lacedaemonian cities, victorious in war over the perioeci, destroyed Amyclae and Pharis and Geranthras which the Achaeans were holding. Of these, the men of Pharis and Geranthrae in terror of the attack of the Dorians agreed to withdraw from the Peloponnese under treaty. The men of Amyclae they could not get rid of out of hand; rather they endured a long war and showed themselves in action not inglorious. The Dorians make this plain by the trophy they set up against the men of Amyclae, that what happened then remains for them most worthy of note. (Pausanias 3.2.6)

---

[91] 70 *FGH* 118 tells us that his name was Philonomus.

[92] Conon, who was apparently an orator of the age of the Antonines (26 *FGH*) told a story (fr. 1.36) which began: "Philonomus the Spartiate betraying Lacedaemon to the Dorians got as a gift Amyklae, which he settled from Imbros and Lemnos." The settlers of Amyklae in this version were neither indigenes nor Spartans. The identification of Philonomus as both a Spartan and a traitor would seem to make him a Spartan who pretended to join with the indigenes and then betrayed them—which would make him an ambiguous figure not so different from Phalanthus in the Taras story. Conon's narrative, however, was not really about Philonomus but about ejection of these Amyklae settlers three generations later, and through them the Spartan colonization of Melos and Gortyn. This story follows the pattern of the Taras story in a broader sense: In both, persons who have some claim, but an insufficient claim, to be Spartans are ejected to a colony, which thereby becomes a Spartan colony; everything happens as if the colonists can become Spartan only by leaving Sparta. A third example is the Thera story told in Herodotus 4.145–149—which, by the way, gives yet another account of the Aegidae at Sparta.

This story is consistent with Ephorus if in fact Ephorus said that Amyclae after the conquest continued to be occupied by Achaeans; in any case Amyclae appears in this story as the Achaean city par excellence, the last and most worthy opponent of the Dorians in the valley of the Eurotas. Whereas in the Ephorus story the people of Amyclae (whether or not indigenous) were (at least temporarily) incorporated, in the Pausanias story they are overcome. The taking of Amyclae is thus an heroic event of the same type as—and inserted between—the Return of the Heracleidae and the Messenian Wars; like these, it is a founding moment of the city, the moment when, by the acquisition of its fifth village, it became complete. Yet this completion involves an ambiguity since Amyclae is apart from the others, has a local character (the Hyacinthia is a local festival), and in some sense belongs to, or for a longer time belonged to, the indigenes.

In Mycenaean times, the archaeology tells us, Amyclae was a population center, and the presence nearby of a beehive tomb (in a district on the whole lacking visible Mycenaean remains)[93] will have signaled to the archaic Spartans that there were people there in heroic times, which is to say (for them), before the Return of the Heracleidae. Amyclae, in other words, was the original pre-Spartan Sparta.[94] It would seem that the Amyclaeon and the Hyacinthia are where they are because they have something to do with origins and with indigenes—and perhaps also with the problem of relation to the land.

The story in Pausanias, or something much like it, was already in Pindar. In the Seventh Isthmian he begins his praise of Thebes by asking which of her heroic moments gives the greatest joy:

> Or was it when you put on its feet (lit: "a straight ankle") the Doric colony of the Lacedaemonians, and the Aegidae your kinsmen took Amyclae by Pythian oracles? (Pindar *Isthmian* 7.17–21)

The scholia on this passage are worth quoting complete, as they give a good idea of the welter of alternative versions that constituted the folk history of the Greeks:

> "Doric colony": The Heracleidae had an oracle from the god to take with them the Aegidae, and thus they would take control of the Peloponnese. These were by descent Phlegraei, a kinship-group in Aegina. They, accepting

---

[93] The actual Mycenaean center seems to have been at Pellana, thirty kilometers from Sparta: Spyropoulos (1998).

[94] Huxley (1962), p. 18, remarks that "Mycenean votive offerings . . . in association with Protogeometric material" permit the "inference that Amyklae did not become Dorian until long after the arrival of the Dorians in Laconia." This assumes a literal Dorian invasion, and even if the inference establishes a fact, there is no reason to believe that the Spartans would have known it. The beehive tomb they certainly knew.

[the Aegidae] according to the Pythian oracle, were not disappointed of their hopes, and once they had got control of the Peloponnese they settled the Aegidae in Thebes as resident aliens. But some say the Aegidae were Athenian by descent, and some that they were a kinship-group in Thebes, and that they came from there as allies against Lacedaemon and took control; some, however, that certain persons in Lacedaemon bear this name from a certain Aegeus of Thebes, who they say cooperated with the Heracleidae in the establishment of Laconia. Some write their name "Argeidae" because Argeia was the given name of the wife of Aristodemus, the descendent of the Heracleidae whose children were those Procles and Eurysthenes who possessed Laconia.

The meaning is: when you arranged it that the Dorian return of the Heracleidae be established on a secure base—because your descendants the Aegidae took Amyclae by the oracles of Pythian Apollo.

Another: He would not here be talking about the Athenian Aegidae; the topic is Thebes. And there are Aegidae a brotherhood in Thebes, some of whom came into Sparta to assist the Lacedaemonians in their war against Amyclae; Timomachus acted as their leader, who was the first to set in order for the Lacedaemonians all that has to do with war, and was by them found worthy of great honors. And at the Hyacinthia his bronze breastplate is displayed (the Thebans call this "arms"): Aristotle relates this in his *Constitution of the Lacedaemonians*. Some say Pindar does not here bring to mind the war with Amyclae nor the Aegidae under Timomachus, but those others who came with the Heracleidae on their return to the Peloponnese, whose leaders were Aristomachus son of Cleas and Cleas son of Hyllus. Actually there came on that occasion from Thebes Aegidae along with the Athenians. The Aegidae at Thebes are Athenian by descent. Since there were two expeditions of the brotherhood of the Aegidae from Thebes to Sparta, it would be a job to work out which one Pindar here brings to mind. Maybe it's the second one? Because Aristotle says that when the Laconians were at war with Amyclae, because they had an oracle to take the Aegidae as their allies, they set out to travel to Athens. They broke their journey in Thebes, where the brotherhood of Aegidae were holding a feast and invited them. After dinner they heard the priest pray that the gods should give good things to the Aegidae; remembering the oracle, they took from thence their ally. (Scholia Vetera in Pindaro ad *Isthm.* 7.18)

Evidently there were Aegidae at both Athens and Thebes, and there were stories about Aegidae involved both with the Return of the Heracleidae and the later conquest of Amyclae, and there were various efforts to put these things together—one of which, by changing their name to Argeidae, sought to eliminate the extra-Spartan element altogether. It would be hard to locate a kernel of truth here. Most interesting in the present context, perhaps, is the statement quoted from Aristotle that the breastplate of Timomachus was held up at the Hyacinthia. It seems that the Hyacinthia celebrated, along with much else, the conquest of Amyclae. This makes the Hyacinthia cognate with the Carneia; the Carneia (as we have seen) celebrated the Return of the Heracleidae; the Hyacinthia celebrated the second foundation of the state, the conquest of Amyclae.

Because the Spartan state ritualized the original conquest as a continuing structure, because the Spartans were continually at war with their agricultural labor force, because the Spartans aimed to created a purely cultural society insulated from economic concerns—freed, that is, from the labor and scarcity that arise in our adversary relation to nature—because of all these things the Spartans had a problem with their relation to the land. The land was theirs before they were the land's. Apollo of Delphi granted them the valley of the Eurotas (so their tradition told them) and by conquest they acquired it; Apollo then granted them Messenia and another conquest. In the course of this second conquest, in Antiochus's story, their relation to the land was finally defined: Those who refused to fight were forever bound to the land, while those who fought acquired title both to the land and to the labor of the others. The Partheniae, an undefined group, could be Spartan only by exclusion from Sparta, to take title in the name of Sparta to Italian soil and the finest harbor in Italy.

In the middle of this folk history, between the first and the second conquest, comes the acquisition of Amyclae, the second foundation of Sparta, commemorated by the founding of the Hyacinthia. In the ritual system, I would suggest, the Carneia celebrated the Spartans' title to the territory, the Hyacinthia their connection to the soil. By the incorporation or appropriation of this indigenous center the Spartans obliterated the claims of their indigenous predecessors and came to belong to the land. The monument itself seems to transmit this message: the god in the form of a tall bronze column planted upright in the earth, literally staking Apollo's claim to this space, and in the altar at its foot the young hero incorporated in the earth. The Spartans gave him offerings and observed for him an annual mourning, followed by funereal contests. Hero myth, as I have already observed, is the opposite of a myth of autochthony: The citizens are not linked to the soil by a claim to have arisen from it, but by their solidarity with a peer and predecessor who has died into it. Participation in the Hyacinthia was, I suspect, for the Spartan *paides*, the newly qualified youth, the initiation that gave them this legitimate link with the soil.

Therefore the conspiracy of the Partheniae was set for the Hyacinthia, because the Hyacinthia was the festival where the legitimate Spartans enjoyed precisely that which was denied to the Partheniae. As a signal Phalanthus was to put on his cap, perhaps because the cap conceals the hair, and long hair was the mark of the initiated Spartan male: They combed it out before battle (Herodotus 7.209). By this sign, then, the rejected were to identify their victims and annihilate those fully accepted at Sparta.[95] Instead they were forestalled and sent to be accepted elsewhere, in Taras, where (we learn from Polybius—8.28) they had their own tomb of Hyacinthus and sanctuary of Apollo Hyacinthus.[96] Elsewhere they became the complete men they could not be at Sparta.

Legitimacy and Sexuality at Sparta and Locri

There are two other stories concerning Phalanthus and the Partheniae. One is in Diodorus:

> The Epeunactae had prearranged with Phalanthus that they would rise in revolt in the main square whenever he would draw down over his forehead his cap, along with his arms. But someone gave information to the ephors of what was to happen. Whereas most of them thought it best to kill Phalanthus, Agathiadas who had been his lover said that if they did so they would rouse a huge revolt in Sparta; if they were then victorious theirs would be a hollow victory, whereas if they were defeated it would be the utter ruin of their fatherland. His advice was that the herald should command that Phalanthus leave his cap as it was. When this happened the Partheniae gave up the attempt and moved toward reconciliation.

[95] Making a comparison with the Roman rite of manumission, Pugliese Caratelli instead suggests that the gesture of putting on the hat was intended, not to cover the hair, but to claim the status of free citizen. Pugliese Caratelli (1990), p. 131.

[96] Malkin (1994) observes that "almost all the traditions concerning eighth-century Spartan colonization [including Melos and Gortyn] in some way involve Amyklae, either through explicit mention in the foundation story, or by inference from place-names and cults." He further suggests (p. 113), "the integration of Amyklae (or perhaps just of its aristocrats and their followers) into Sparta led to the export of those Amyklaians who, for whatever reason, proved not assimilable. These may have taken part in certain Spartan colonizing enterprises not as refugees but by way of a political compromise whereby they became 'Spartan colonists' led by Spartan founders. . . . There may have been two 'waves' of Amyklaians—one in the mid-eighth century, eastward to the Aegean, and the other toward the end of it, westward to Taras."

Once again this seems to me to take the legends too literally. The stories about Amyklae in my reading are stories that code an ambiguity in the relation between the Spartans and their land, and it is this ambiguity that makes colonization subjectively possible, which is to say, intelligible. Because Amyklae is understood to exist ambiguously between Spartan and indigenous status, it is possible for there to be communities that are Spartan and yet (inasmuch as they are elsewhere) are not.

The Epeunactae sent emissaries to Delphi who asked if the god would give them the land of Sikyon. He replied:

> Fine is that between Corinth and Sikyon
> But you could not live there not if you were solid bronze.
> Consider Satyrion and the shining water of Taras
> And the leftward harbor where the goat the salt swell
> Enjoys, dampening the end of his gray beard.
> There create Taras, entering Satyrion.

They could make nothing of this when they heard it, so he spoke more plainly:

> I gave you Satyrion and the fat land of Taras
> To live there and be trouble for the Iapygians.
>
> Diodorus Siculus 8.21

This seems to be a Hellenistic version; it keeps some of the picturesque detail, the cap and the herald's command, and adds a love interest and some rhetoric. It mentions Partheniae but also Epeunactae, apparently equating the two. Epeunactae are explained to us by Theopompus:

> When many Lacedaemonians died in the war against the Messenians those who remained were concerned lest it become evident to their enemies that they were depopulated; therefore they made certain of the helots to mount onto each mattress of the departed. These they later made citizens and called them "epeunactae" (lit: "up-on-the-bed people") because they had been placed on the mattresses instead of the departed. (Theopompus 115 *FGH* 171)

Theopompus's story can be reconciled with Diodorus if we assume that at a later date the Epeunactae, feeling somehow disadvantaged, launched a revolt, possibly joining with the Partheniae, possibly in a separate revolt which was later confused with theirs. Such conjectures are, however, contrary to the spirit of this material, which asks that we treat the stories as different variants of one plot, rather than separate events that need to be interconnected. More relevant to our argument is the fact that Theopompus's story is very close to Aristotle's (and Polybius's) Locrian story: In both, the slaves mate with the wives of citizens as a result of the Messenian War. There is, however, a crucial difference: Here these unions occur on the initiative of the Spartan males, and the slaves become citizens in the old city, not founders of a new one. Both stories are about anomalous marriage, but in Theopompus the men are in charge and the result is normalized, whereas in

Aristotle the women are in charge and the result is the creation of a new community.

This brings us to the other Partheniae story, the one in Ephorus:

> The Lacedaemonians were at war with the Messenians, who had killed their king Telecles when he came among them to a sacrifice, and they swore not to come home again until they had taken Messenia or had all died. They left as garrison of the city for the time of the expedition the youngest and the oldest of the citizens. Later in the tenth year of the war the wives of the Lacedaemonians met and sent some of their number to their husbands in order to complain, that they were not fighting on an equal basis with the Messenians. Those stayed at home and were making babies, while the Lacedaemonians had left their wives widowed during their expedition in enemy territory; so that the fatherland was in danger of underpopulation. In order both to keep their oath and to attend to their wives' message they sent from the army the most vigorous, the youngest—whom they knew had taken no part in the oath, since they had come with those of age as mere children. The instructions they gave them were to all couple with all the maidens, thinking this way there would be more childbearing. That is what happened, and the sons were named Partheniae. Messenia was taken after they had fought for nineteen years, as Tyrtaeus says:

> > For it they fought nineteen years
> > Fruitlessly ever, maintaining an enduring spirit
> > The spearmen fathers of our fathers.
> > In the twentieth year [the Messenians] left their fertile lands
> > And fled from the great mountain peaks of Ithome.

> They distributed Messenia, and coming back home did not treat the Partheniae in like manner as the others, on the grounds that they were not born in wedlock. So they conspired with the helots against the Lacedaemonians and agreed to raise as a signal in the market a Laconian cap, whenever it was time for the attempt. Some of the helots gave information, and [the Lacedaemonians] judged it would be hard to offer direct resistance: [The conspirators] were numerous and of one mind, holding one another as brothers. So they [merely] instructed those who were about to raise the sign to leave the main square. These therefore knew they had been informed upon and held back from action; [the Lacedaemonians] persuaded them through their fathers to go out to a colony. And if they were able to get a place that suited them, they should stay; otherwise they would allocate to them the fifth part of Messenia when they came back. Those who were sent out came upon the Achaeans at war with the barbarians and taking a share in their dangers founded Taras. (70 *FGH* 216)

This story has its own confusions: The youngest, in particular, appear both as a home guard and as the childish escort of the grown males in the field. It shares little with the Antiochus story except the name Partheniae and the fact of the foundation of Taras by some sort of Spartans; also the cap makes an appearance, not however, on anyone's head, and the tactful device used to avoid confrontation with the conspirators is similar. Otherwise the Partheniae in this version are more like the Epeunactae in Diodorus, in that they are purposely produced to make up the numbers of the Spartans; however, in Ephorus's version they are not in the end permitted to serve that purpose. The Spartans seem to blame them for the very promiscuity which they had themselves prescribed: the instructions, after all, were not that the young men should contract instant marriages with the maidens or even seek out a partner, but rather that all should couple with all. I would suggest that the key to the story lies in this promiscuity.

It was part of the Greek image of the Spartans that they procreated children (within the citizen body) relatively promiscuously, that they shared their wives (Xenophon *Lac. Pol.* 1.7–9; Plutarch *Lycurgus* 15; Polybius 12.6b.8).[97] This is one of the features that makes Spartan life (to Greek eyes) look relatively tribal or primitive. The Spartans seem to tend toward the customs of those hardy savages described in Herodotus, who share their wives freely, or even copulate openly, like cattle (Herodotus 1.203; 3.107; 4.180.3).[98] In the light of this point about Spartans, I would suggest, Ephorus or his sources created their story, interpreting "Partheniae" as equivalent to "parthenioi" and therefore having something to do with illegitimate birth, here understood (as in Plato's *Republic*) as the deletion of marriage in the service of the community. The Partheniae (or perhaps the Partheniae and their helot fellow-conspirators) according the Ephorus, held "one another as brothers." This makes them like the Agathyrsoi in Herodotus, who "make generally available copulation with their women, so that they should all be each other's brothers" (Herodotus 4.104). They have one generalized mother and one generalized father.

The link with Herodotus suggests a more general point: The peoples in Herodotus are, as I have argued elsewhere, divided by him between the hard peoples, primitive and savage, and the soft peoples, over-developed and devious.[99] Soft peoples are characterized by luxury, the

[97] The evidence is briefly reviewed in Cartledge (1981), pp. 102–104.
[98] Rosellini and Said (1978) review this material.
[99] Herodotus (9.122) says that soft countries make soft peoples; he nowhere speaks explicitly of a contrast with hard peoples, but the contrast is implicit in that sentence.

division of labor, and complexity of *nomoi,* especially in the field of religion; hard peoples are simple, harsh, and fierce. Among soft peoples market exchange proliferates; hard peoples rely on gift and theft, the heroic modes of exchange. Soft peoples centralize resources through taxation, build monuments, are literate and organized; their politics tends toward tyranny. Hard peoples have relatively weak political organizations and tend toward anarchy.[100] By placing the Greeks as the mediating synthesis of these extremes, Herodotus is enabled to present Greece as the model civilization, in contrast to the undercivilized peoples of the North and West, and the "overcivilized" peoples of Egypt and the Near East.

The underlying categorical contrast is already in Homer, revealed by the patterned alternation of the adventures of Odysseus between the savage cannibals, who attempt to annihilate and consume him (use him as a natural resource), and the seductive creatures who attempt to transform him so that he will have no wish or ability to leave (radically acculturate him).[101] This second category includes, obviously, the lotus-eaters, but most notably the nymphs Circe and Calypso: The former attempts to make him a beast, the latter, an immortal.

These powerful, independent females have no *kurioi,* no men in charge of them, and in this way remind us of Glykera and her sisters, the independent, glamorous, somewhat unrespectable heroines of New Comedy. When outside of a myth we meet a woman unencumbered with a *kurios* she is most often an *hetaira,* one who lives by selling herself. This is relevant to the fact that in Herodotus (and in some other Greek authors) certain Near Eastern societies are characterized by the prostitution of free women—most notably Babylon, where it is a ritual obligation (Herodotus 1.199: "the most shameful of their laws"), and in Lydia, where the girls in this way earn their dowries (Herodotus 1.93.4: "they themselves sell themselves"). The free woman, the woman available only by legitimate marriage contracted between her suitor and her *kurios,* is for Herodotus typical only of the Greeks. The other peoples fail of this civilized norm in one of two directions: Among primitives women are generally available, like a free good in nature appropriated at will by the men; in the overcivilized societies they become a commodity, available by market exchange, and in charge of their own sexuality. In the hard societies women are nobody's and so everybody's property; in the soft societies they belong to themselves. Only the Greeks (it is silently implied) have perfected the civilized family, where the women belong to the men.

[100] The last four sentences are drawn from Redfield (1985), p. 109.
[101] This pattern is discussed more fully in Redfield (1983).

In Ephorus's story of the foundation of Taras the Spartans promiscuously share their women; this places Sparta on the side of the hard peoples—as we should expect: Sparta generally tends toward the harsh and the primitive.[102] I would further suggest that we can best understand the stories that tell us that there was or might have been prostitution of free women at Locri[103] in the light of the underlying categorical contrast: Locri is placed on the side of the soft peoples. In Sparta the women exercised, were shared, became at times a threat to the public order; they became something like Amazons. At Locri (I have hypothesized) the women were the bearers of legitimacy, vehicles of status, objects of unique value; that they were objects of competition suggested to the Greek mind that they could take control of their own sexuality for profit or pleasure, like the nymphs. And it is even possible that they really did; after all, the only example Athenaeus gives us of the "sultry . . . so-called Locrian" songs, "adulterous in spirit through and through," is in the voice of a married woman pleading with her lover:

> What's happening with you? Don't betray us, I beg you.
> Before he comes, get up, otherwise he'll do
> To you great harm, and to me, poor creature that I am!
> It's already day. Don't you see the light through the window?
>
> Athenaeus 697b–c

This has the look of a folk song; that it speaks informally and realistically of love would suggest a postclassic date, but there is every reason to believe that the folk tradition kept alive themes excluded from the high art of the classical period. It is a woman who speaks, and probably women sang it.[104] The familiarity to us of these themes should not obscure for us how unusual this piece is by Greek standards: It treats an adulterous relationship from the woman's point of view. In tone it may be compared with another unusual piece: the oinochoe by the Souvarov Painter, Berlin 2414 (*ARV* p. 1208, #41). This is the only item in Sutton's collection (Sutton 1981) that represents explicit lovemaking sentimentally—soft-core, as it were—and with the woman taking the initiative, and on top. It was of course made in Athens, but it was found in Locri.

---

[102] For Herodotus's links between the Spartans and those typically hard people, the Scythians, see Munson (2001).

[103] See appendix.

[104] Greek women are often represented singing while at work, weaving or grinding meal, and also as enjoying music (as when Socrates—Plato *Symposium* 176e—suggests that the flute girl be dismissed to the women's quarters).

Part Four

FOUR ICONOGRAPHIC ESSAYS

Eight

Nymphs

I HAVE SAID that the link between Aphrodite and Persephone—what Gunther Zuntz[1] called "the enigma of a union of the goddesses of love and death"—is at the center of the problem of Locrian culture. In terms of myth and ritual this link is in the Locrian choice of Persephone as the goddess of the *proteleia* and (to this degree) patroness of the wedding (which was everywhere in some degree under the patronage of Aphrodite). In terms of ritual institutions this link can be stated as the relation between the Mannella sanctuary and the U-shaped stoa—not that these two need have shared any ritual, but that the things that went on in these two locations, as they found a place in the collective life of a single community, were part of a single ritual system. In the mid-fourth century four things happened to the Locrians: (1) Dionysius the Younger came among them briefly and catastrophically, (2) the temple of Aphrodite was demolished, (3) burial deposits ceased in the U-shaped stoa, and (4) the Cave of the Nymphs came into frequent use, probably replacing the Mannella as the chief *proteleia* sanctuary. I am working on the hypothesis that these four events are connected, and that they are signs of the transformation of the ritual system, a transformation in which the link between Aphrodite and Persephone came to be no longer operative.

Such evidence as we have for the meaning of these events is largely derived from works of art in marble, bronze, and terra-cotta, and to these we now turn. Plastic representations are notoriously difficult (or all too easy!) to interpret, but I abjure methodology, at least initially; perhaps it is enough to remind the reader that all the objects to be discussed were used in rituals, and that they therefore are both representations and instruments: They say something to a audience, and they enabled certain persons to do certain things.

I begin, in an inversion of the chronological order, with the Cave of the Nymphs. The objects found here are readily paralleled from other fourth-century Greek communities. It seems that after Dionysius the Younger, the Locrians became more like the others. As this material is less specifically Locrian it can serve also as a general introduction to women's dedications.

[1] Zuntz (1971), p. 164.

Naked Dolls

When Paolo Orsi opened the great deposit in the Mannella sanctuary he was astonished by one type of dedication[2]—of which he found, be it said, only a few examples, dating from the mid-fifth century, the period just before the sanctuary was cleared. These were terra-cotta nude figurines of seated women, with their hands along their thighs and the legs missing below the knees. Their nudity astonished Orsi; the Greeks did not represent the nude female figure in sculpture before the late fifth century, and although such representations in other materials are by no means unknown, in 1909 they were still thought anomalous.

Since Orsi's original find, a substantial collection of these small nudes have turned up in many places, including Locri, where Orsi himself found a number in the Lucifero cemetery; others have been found in the houses near the seawall.[3] The most substantial set was found in the Cave of the Nymphs (see plate 1), explored by Arias and republished by Costabile and others.[4] These Locrian examples date from the mid-fifth century to the mid-second century. Elsewhere examples have been found as late as the first century. Most of them have been found in the Greek West, with a large group from Lipari (on display in the museum there). Some have been found in the Italian towns of Capua and Egnathia; a substantial group was found in Cyrene.[5] From a grave in Athens comes an isolated late-fifth-century example accompanied by a clay throne.[6] Other examples come from Aegina, Thebes, and Corinth. Larger groups—and most of the examples from the later period—come from Anatolia. Many of these have the hands arranged differently, and are holding an offering.[7] A group found in Troy has been studied by Thompson; a group from Morgantina is well studied by Bell.[8] The Locrian set is studied by Leone.[9] A variety of subtypes are illustrated in Winter, *Terracotten* (165–168).

Their hair is elaborately done, and most often they wear a *polos*, the round headgear characteristic of divinities. Earrings are usually indicated, and sometimes some other jewelry. Usually they have nothing else on at all. They are sitting, head forward and chin slightly down,

---

[2] "Una strana apparizione," Orsi (1909), p. 419.
[3] Molli Boffa (1977).
[4] Leone (1991).
[5] Ibid., p. 124.
[6] Higgins (1954), pp. 186–187, pl. 91, 702–703.
[7] Leone (1991), pp. 124–125.
[8] Thompson (1963); Bell (1981).
[9] Leone (1991).

arms extended along their thighs with the hands turned inward, in a version of the pose we have learned to recognize as proper to the *anakaluptēria*.[10] As their legs are cut off below the knee it appears, when they are placed on a flat surface, that their legs extend down through the plane of the surface; in most cases the curve below the knee is sufficient to prevent setting them quite flat. Probably they were intended to be set on some kind of stand or shelf. A few clay thrones suitable for this purpose were found in the Caruso cave, although these are too small for most of the figurines we have; also found there were a couple of clay footstools. A few figures found elsewhere are accompanied by clay thrones. Probably the figurines were in most cases placed on thrones made of wood, which has not survived, with garments long enough to conceal the absence of feet.

Orsi (without comment) called those he found "hierodoules," as if they were representations of sacred prostitutes, and this name has become commonplace for the type. However there is nothing in particular to connect them with this putative institution,[11] nor (with the exception of Locri) are they typically found in the places with which that institution has been connected (only one in Corinth, none in Cyprus). Typologically they most resemble *dolls*. Sometimes the arms are articulated in a manner familiar for Greek dolls; not infrequently they end at the elbow in a flat surface with a hole in it, evidently meant for fitting on forearms made in some other material. We have representations of Greek children playing with very similar figures.[12] The examples from the Lucifero cemetery were found in children's graves.[13] Bell (1981, note 167) observes that the Italian graves in which others were found were "apparently all of young girls."

Sometimes the figure and the throne were made in one piece, as a single moldmade object. In this subtype the figures are invariably clothed, in fact elaborately draped. In other words, the complete object includes clothing. Probably the nudity of most figures is a false lead: They were (like Barbie) made naked so that they could be dressed,[14] the terra-cotta body being only one part of an assemblage completed by cloth garments and a wooden stand. Sometimes the clothing was painted on,[15] and this is consistent with the rather sketchy anatomy

---

[10] Cf. p. 70.

[11] See the appendix.

[12] Elderkin (1930) with references to Conze (1900).

[13] Examples were found in nine graves; of these at least seven are graves of children: Leone (1991), pp. 249–250, notes 102 and 103.

[14] Cf. Kastriotis (1909).

[15] One example on Lipari (tomb 2124) retains enough paint to show how the clothing was painted on.

(many lack navels, and none have nipples), which somewhat resembles Barbie. More often, it seems probable, the clothing was made separately; this seems particularly obvious in the case of the dolls with articulated arms. Where the forearms are missing it looks as though the forearms and the clothing were made in one piece and attached together. In the case of the figures seated with their hands along their thighs, the clothing could have been a cloth tube slipped over the head, with openings along the sides to display the hands. The whole then had to be assembled on its throne or stand, a rather delicate piece of doll-play.

The *polos* marks these figures as divine beings. This does not exclude their being dolls; there seems to have been no rule forbidding children to play with images of gods. It is usually assumed that the examples found in graves and houses were children's toys. Most of these figures, however, are found in sanctuaries, where they were evidently left as dedications. Greek children, as they grew up, certainly did sometimes dedicate their toys in a sanctuary; part of the childish life, a metonym of the life phase, is given away to the god as the god grants passage to adulthood. Timareta's epigram is often quoted[16] in this connection (the dedication is to Artemis Limnatis):

> Timareta before marriage gives her drum, her lovely
>   Ball, her hairnet guardian of her locks,
> And her dolls, Limnatis, girls for a girl (*koras korai*), as is fitting,
>   And her dolls' girl-clothes (*endumata*) to Artemis
> Child of Leto: So do you hold out your hand to Timaretus's child
>   Holding it steady, and keep her piety piously.
>
>   A.P. VI. 280

Probably most of these figures, however, were intended from the beginning as dedications; in other words, the same type of figure could be used in play and in worship. Worship itself in this form at least is a kind of playing with the god. In order to explore this point it is necessary to say something about the uses of representation.

On Interpretation: Representation

Greek girls did not play with baby dolls; their dolls were all (like Barbie) proleptic images of the big girls they were growing up to be. To dress these dolls and move them around was to use the doll as a way of practicing to be a *parthenos*; this is the kind of activity referred to by Aristotle when he says that we humans do our first learning by *mimēsis*.

---

[16] Leone (1991), p. 252n.175.

By dressing and arranging a doll the girl made a working model of mature womanhood, just as a boy might make a model of the ship or wagon that would become his task in adult life (Aristophanes *Clouds* 878–880). These seated dolls in particular, to the degree that their pose evokes the *anakaluptēria*, seem to prepare the girl for the wedding, for the moment of her consent. They are something like bridal dolls (still a popular type). To dress and arrange such a doll on her throne was an anticipation of *kosmēsis*, the adornment that formed such an important part of the preparations for marriage.

A common noun meaning "doll" is *korē*, which also means "girl" or "daughter" and also means a young-girl goddess, usually Demeter's daughter, Persephone—although in the epigram just quoted the term is used for Leto's daughter, Artemis. Dolls are "girls"; they are (says the epigram) given to a "girl"; the poet thereby shows that he understands the play of representation. The doll represents the goddess, the goddess is goddess of girlhood; as the girl Artemis is claimed as goddess of the girl Timareta (and thus represents her) the doll represents them both. By dedicating her doll the girl honors Artemis with a representation of Artemis (not specifically—the image need not have any attributes of Artemis, it represents only Artemis's girlishness); at the same time, Timereta places in the care of the goddess her own girlhood by placing in her sanctuary a representation of it. If worship is an exchange the representation succeeds in both directions: Timereta gives the goddess something and by the same act secures the divine response.

The logic of representation is metaphorical; the representation, like the metaphor, both is and is not the thing represented. "You, Cecily, are [not] a pink rose" and "ceci n'est pas une pipe." The gods also are representations, at least to the extent that they represent some abstraction: Aphrodite is sexuality, and Ares is war. They are not so much metaphors as symbols, which is to say, concrete universals. Hestia and Artemis are contrasting representations of the virgin daughter. From this point of view an image of a god is a representation of a representation.

Ritual also is representational, at least to the extent that it recovers an archtypical event. Every blood sacrifice reenacts the feast at Mecone, where Prometheus set the gods against us. The girls who played the bear for Artemis were enacting patterns transmitted also through myth. These archetypes are also representations: The sacrifice story places us between culture and nature, made as we are of natural meat and consumers as we have learned to be of cultural meat; to play the bear is to enact in a ritualized form a specific transitional life-stage. Ritual *mimēsis* therefore invokes the universal through the play of particular representations.

At the Greek wedding, also, archetypal prototypes were invoked:

Hector and Andromache or Peleus and Thetis or Cadmus and Harmonia. Every bride, also, is Pandora: adorned and presented, a lovely
dangerous gift. Pandora, we remember, was also a doll, an artifact,
formed from clay, dressed and bejeweled. These little clay figures,
dressed and posed in a posture of bridal submission, are also (in a
sense) Pandoras. If, as I suspect, they were most commonly dedicated
as part of the *proteleia*, the prenuptial rite, they are representations of a
representation of the woman's transition that is marriage.

The logic of dedications, however, is metonymic. A dedication is not
primarily a sacrifice—a sharing of goods with the god or a gift to the
god in the interest of a countergift—but rather a sharing of the self
with the god. Dedications speak not to the establishment of common
interest but of common meaning. They are not exchange but communication. Therefore they often employ something metonymic of the
dedicator: the hair, or a garment, or a tool, or a toy. "I leave a part of
myself behind with you," says the dedicator; "therefore you will always
be with me."

When the dedication includes an image we have representational
metonymy. The dedicator says to the god: I give you an image of myself
(as an ideal type—for example, the little images of worshippers carrying their sacrificial offerings); thus I am yours. Or I give you an image
of yourself; thus a version of you is from me and you are mine. Best of
all: I give you an image of me representing you; thus, as we are metaphorically one in the ritual, so we become one in the dedication
through mutual metonymy.

Another common noun in Greek meaning "doll" is *numphē*, which
also means "bride" and also "nymph." The immortal, sexually available
girl who haunts the streams and springs metaphorically represents,
through a mythological transformation, the young woman as she is sexually initiated. Since the (first) wedding (the ideal type of the wedding) is or is by the Greeks supposed to be the occasion of the sexual
initiation of the bride, bridal dolls were appropriate dedications to the
nymphs—even though nymphs are anything but bridal.

Men are in charge of the bride; she is transferred from man to man.
Nymphs, by contrast, are loose and aggressive, *deinai theai*, dread goddesses, as Theocritus calls them. Being "seized by the nymphs" (*numph-
oleptos*) can drive a man mad, although it may also inspire him to poetry or prophesy; the nymphs also snatch people out of the world,
possibly to a higher plane, to heroic immortality.[17] As such the nymphs
are opposite to those prototypical brides, such as Thetis or Persephone, who are snatched; nymphs rather do the snatching. To dedicate a

---

[17] Borgeaud (1979), pp. 159–162.

bridal doll in the Cave of the Nymphs is a kind of oxymoron, which might also be a mediation: The bride places her submission to marriage under the protection of symbols of woman's power.

The earliest Locrian examples of our seated dolls were found in the sanctuary of Persephone, to which we soon turn. Most of them, however, were found in the Cave of the Nymphs, mixed in with images of Pan, of a three-headed stele of the nymphs (probably a cult image), of silenoi, erotes, maenads, river-gods, and heroes—the whole *fronde* of the wild minor divinities. That this sanctuary—like the Mannella sanctuary, just outside the limit of the city—came into active use in the mid-fourth century, after Dionysius the Younger, is probably a sign of the breakup of the aristocratic order at Locri. Pan and the nymphs are divinities of the people, not despised by the better sort, certainly, but generally available. Theirs is in fact a religion of availability. The focus here is not on structure but on process, not on social roles (as in Olympian cult) but on personal emotion. The nymphs become important elsewhere as the Hellenistic age opens and the common sensibility shifts from tragedy to romance. At that moment in Locri something specifically Locrian was lost. We now go back in time in search of the authentic Locrian strain.

Nine

The Tortoise and the Knucklebone

ONE of the most remarkable objects found in the Lucifero cemetery is a square iron rod with bronze decorations, one and one-quarter meters from end to end. (See plate 2.) This object is no great masterpiece; it is folk art, chiefly interesting for its iconography. It was found by Paulo Orsi in 1912[1] and was published by Carmelo Turano (1961) in *Kokalos*, the house journal of the Reggio Museum, where it now resides.

This object was found in grave #739—evidently by its contents (which include a mirror, an incense jar, and a jewelry box) the grave of a woman, although Orsi does not say so. The body, and the one in the grave next to it (#737, another woman), were laid in the opposite direction from nearly everyone else in this cemetery; evidently there was something extraordinary about the woman who owned this item, or about her family. The grave and the object, by both style and context, can be dated to the early years of the fifth century B.C.

The base of the rod is supported by a bronze male figure, nude, standing quietly with weight evenly balanced on a small square base, right arm raised with palm out, left hand lowered palm down. (See plate 3.) The top is surmounted by a clothed female figure standing in a similar posture, left hand holding her garment in a familiar gesture, right hand outstretched palm up, holding a fruit, evidently a pomegranate. Fixed to her head is a square piece with a hole through it, evidently intended as a bracket. She is standing on a knucklebone (see plate 4).

The iron rod is divided into sections by four bronze rings. From these protrude bronze branches or fronds, ending variously: at the bottom, serpent heads, above these heads of geese, then flower buds, evidently of the lotus, and finally serpent heads again.

Orsi took this to be a candelabrum, and it is typologically similar to candelabra of a slightly later period, especially Etruscan. However, there would be no convenient way to fit this with tapers or lamps. The base is not large enough for it to stand alone on the floor; on the other hand, the fact that is *has* a base indicates that it was not intended to hang from the ceiling. It seems that it was a kind of staff, intended to

---

[1] Orsi (1912).

be supported by the hand while resting on the ground. It was found, in fact, in the hand of the woman it was buried with; she had her right hand clasped around the female figure at the top. Turano calls it an incense burner; he suggests that the bracket is for the dish that held the incense, and that this was made separate and attached with a pin because over time it would burn through and have to be replaced. This may well be right. However, in my view the most striking *functional* point about this object is that it was meant to be carried in the hand.

This is not the only object meant for the hand to be found in the Lucifero cemetery. There are at least two other ornamented staffs, although these are smaller and less elaborate. Both are entirely of bronze, made in one piece, in fact, including the floral ornamentation. Objects like these must have had some ceremonial purpose.

We have considerable evidence for Locrian ceremonial from the *pinakes*, the clay tablets made for dedication in the sanctuary of Persephone. Zancani's group 5 consists of representations of ritual processions, and a number of these include incense burners. On type 5/5 P 18 the boy at the front of the procession is carrying a small pinecone-topped incense burner. On type 5/6 P 19 the incense burner is larger, standing on the ground, and topped by a rooster. On both types a woman is carrying a bowl and a stick—probably a spurge for lustration—in her hand. So we have incense burners, we have one carried in a procession, and we have a woman who carries objects in a procession; altogether we can say—even though we cannot illustrate this object from any pictorial source—that a incense burner carried in a woman's hand in procession would not be out of place at Locri.

Goose heads are an ornamental motif also familiar from the *pinakes*; the goddess Persephone commonly sits on a throne with a goose-head back.[2] This may puzzle us, since the goose is Aphrodite's bird; on Attic pottery she is sometimes represented riding on one. However, we are precisely in search of the local links between Aphrodite and Persephone. At Locri, both were evidently goddesses of marriage—and the goose seems particularly linked to marriage. Already in Homer, in Penelope's dream in *Odyssey* 19, we have the wife represented as a mistress of geese. As for the lotus, when represented as an actual flower and not reduced to a floral element, it virtually always carries an erotic message.[3] The serpents also may seem to us phallic in implication and obviously erotic, but the Greeks do not seem to have made this association.[4] Serpents for them are fundamentally chthonic, associated with

---

[2] This throne appears on the greater number of the types in Zancani's group 8.

[3] Koch-Harnack (1989), pp. 72–89.

[4] In one version of the Tiresias story he was transformed into a woman when he acci-

autochthony and the underworld. The autochthonus First Kings of Attica were represented as serpents from the waist down; Pheidias
included Erichthonius as a giant serpent in his statue group for the
Parthenon. Serpents appear as an emblem on Spartan hero-cult dedications. As for Locrian art, I know of no other representation of a
serpent. We shall return to this problem.

For the present let us focus on the two figures at the top and the
bottom of the staff. These are stylistically influenced by Ionic sources,
like so much west-Greek art of the period. In their architectonic function they most resemble the bronze figures which, throughout the late
archaic and the classical periods, serve as handles to bronze mirrors of
the so-called "caryatid" type, or to the kind of flat dish called a *patera*.
Handles of this type are found all over the Greek world, especially in
the Peloponnese and in the West.

The mirror is an object proper to the woman's world, necessary to
kosmēsis and often the central focus of representations of *kosmēsis*: The
woman holds a mirror or a servant holds a mirror for her. Evidently the
mirror is a metonymic symbol of the woman's adorned body. A representation of the woman's body would then be a particularly appropriate adornment of such an object, stressing the link between signifier
and signified: The mirror is used to adorn the woman, and the woman
adorns the mirror.

Fine bronze mirrors are particularly frequent at Locri; Orsi called
the Lucifero "the cemetery of the mirrors."[5] Some kind of mirror is to
be found in roughly two-thirds of the adult women's graves Orsi found
worth reporting, many quite elaborate. Mirrors are also found among
the Mannella dedications, but these tend to be less elaborate. My idea
is that an elite Locrian girl would receive at her marriage an elaborate
mirror which was the emblem of her mature womanhood, which she
kept with her through life, and which was normally buried with her.
The equivalent symbolic grave good for males is the strigil, found in a
similar proportion of men's graves.[6] The strigil was evidently the symbol
of *askēsis* and of the male body, trained and stripped. *Askēsis* and *kosmēsis* are understood by the natives to be the cultural procedures by
which sex is transmuted into what we call gender; training makes a
man manly, and adornment makes a woman womanly. Therefore the
strigil and the mirror are symbols of sexual identity.

The caryatid figure that sustains the mirror further specifies this sym-

---

dentally saw serpents coupling; this tells us that the eroticism of serpents is dangerous,
not that they symbolize eroticism.

[5] Orsi (1911b), p. 22.

[6] Two Italian graves (at Pantanello), however, contain both strigil and mirror—Carter
(1998), p. 584n.72—and a few women's grave at Locri contain strigils. These neat oppositions always turn out the be (at most) valid on the "emic," not the "etic," level.

bol. It represents the adorned woman as she shows herself to the world; most often she adjusts her garment with the left hand and holds forth the right in token of worship or communication. This symbolic complex can then be further specified by some of the other symbols that cluster on mirrors: sirens, or winged erotes, which in their different ways signify the woman's sexual power, or the hare pursued by dogs, which represents the woman as the object of pursuit.

In a fair proportion of cases the caryatid figure that supports the mirror is standing on some sort of creature; this creature must be a further symbolic specification. In two or three cases the creature is a lion and once a frog, but most often if a caryatid mirror base is standing on a creature, that creature is a tortoise. There are a dozen or so of these.

The tortoise evidently is properly underfoot; the Greek word for tortoise, *chelonē*, also means "footstool" (Hesychius s.v.). Evidently footstools were sometimes made in the form of tortoises. The figure on top of our object, however, which otherwise looks very like a mirror base, is standing not on a tortoise but a knucklebone. Such an arrangement is unparalleled among caryatid figures.[7] My contention is that the meaning of the knucklebone here is that it is *instead of a tortoise*. The tortoise and the knucklebone are in many ways parallel, are alternative signs on coins for instance, and appear sometimes as elements of an emblematic series. There is, for instance, in the Agora Museum in Athens more than one set of weights in which one value is signed with a tortoise, another with a knucklebone.[8] It would seem that their opposition is a little like that of the king and the jack in a deck of cards.

To pursue this analogy: The leading honor cards in our familiar deck are a couple, the king and the queen. The male outranks the female. The jack, however, ranks behind them both; his differentiating features—whether they are taken to be age, or class, or both—are sufficient to outweigh his status as a male. All this reminds us that cultural categories are at work to give stability to the arrangement of these emblems, which are collectively represented as a *system*. We shall be looking for similar categorical contrasts between the tortoise and the knucklebone.[9]

---

[7] We do have a statue-base from Olympia in the form of a knucklebone; probably it supported a personification of Kairos—Kurke (1999), p. 293 and n.94.

[8] Cf. ibid., p. 294n.99: the full Attic set (in descending order of weight) was knucklebone, amphora, tortoise, dolphin, and crescent.

In the Delphi museum there are figures of the "temple boy" type holding under their hands various things, including both tortoise and knucklebone: École française d'Athènes (1991), p. 256.

[9] In what follows I treat the land tortoise and the sea turtle together, as the Greeks seem to have found them ideologically interchangeable. The best-known iconic use of

The Tortoise

The chryselephantine statue of Aphrodite by Pheidias at Elis had her standing with one foot on a tortoise (Pausanias 6.25.1). This motif occurs in at least four surviving works of sculpture,[10] probably in all by derivation from the Pheidian original; the most important of these is the Aphrodite from Doura-Europus (LIMC #334). Franz Cumont, in his publication of this last,[11] provides evidence that the association of Aphrodite with the tortoise preceded Pheidias. Plutarch (*Moralia* 142d; cf. 381e) explains the symbolism: *oikouria*, housekeeping and silence. The praise of silence is probably Plutarch's own contribution, but the link between the tortoise and housekeeping is in Aesop's fable (#108) that tells how all the animals were invited to the wedding of Zeus; the tortoise alone failed to appear. When asked why, she replied: "East west, home's best (*oikos philos, oikos aristos*)." Zeus then punished her by requiring her to take her house with her everywhere.[12] The fable is undatable, but the link with housekeeping—in the literal sense of keeping within the house—is already in the *Homeric Hymn to Hermes* (36), where Hermes greets the tortoise with the proverb "Better to stay at home; there is harm out of doors" (Cf. *Works and Days* 365).[13]

Aphrodite is linked with the tortoise in the story of the courtesan Laïs, who having become excessively popular with the men of Thessaly was beaten to death by the Thessalian women with the "wooden tortoises" in the sanctuary of Aphrodite (Athenaeus 589a, cf. Schol. Aristophanes *Plutus* 179). Possibly the word is used here merely as a common noun for "footstool";[14] even so, the word choice would be significant. More probably wooden tortoises, or wooden tortoise footstools, were familiar dedications in this sanctuary of Aphrodite. Given the association of the tortoise with the home, they would be appropriate weapons in the hands of wives defending their marriages against the sexual interloper.

The tortoise then, as Marylin Arthur (Katz) has argued,[15] is a symbol of the chaste wife, of the woman who keeps to the house and remains

---

the turtle, for instance, is on the coins of Aegina; at the beginning of the fourth century, however, the type unaccountably shifts over to the land tortoise.

[10] Settis (1966), pp. 9–10.
[11] Cumont (1924).
[12] Cf. Servius ad *Aeneid* 505.
[13] This use of the proverb is of course one of Hermes' ironies; he takes the tortoise into his house in order to turn her out of her house and make her dead shell into the living voice of the lyre.
[14] But see Settis (1966), p. 29.
[15] Arthur (Katz) (1980–1981).

enclosed in the woman's world. Weddings, we may note, were (along with funerals and certain festivals) among the few occasions on which Greek women were expected to leave the house and appear in public. The tortoise in Aesop's fable therefore displayed an excess of what is otherwise a virtue in a woman: the refusal to cross her own threshold. The shell, which is in a sense a prison (it is a punishment) also signifies the womanly (if occasionally excessive) determination of the good woman to remain in the comfort and safety of her own space.

This said, however, we must come to terms with the fact that on two of the Locrian caryatid mirrors with tortoises the figure standing on the tortoise is male.[16] This brings us to a more general point about caryatid mirrors, which is also a point about the west-Greek area. On east-Greek and Peloponnesian mirrors the female figure is sometimes nude or nearly so; on west-Greek mirrors (with a couple of exceptions from Syracuse directly influenced by Sparta) nude females are nonexistent. In the East, male caryatid figures are extremely rare (and one of these is a clothed older man); in the West, including Locri, about half the mirror caryatids are male, always young, almost boyish, and invariably nude.[17] In other words, the west-Greek mirrors present a systemic contrast between male and female, extending to mirrors the familiar contrast between *askēsis* and *kosmēsis. Both* are proper to mirrors, the most typically female of objects; it follows that the young male body is itself a symbol of womanhood.

This conclusion may sound less paradoxical if restated: The mirror (especially if it is a wedding gift) is a symbol of the mature woman's life, which belongs in a house kept by a couple—from the woman's point of view, by a woman and her husband. In these representations the woman is in a position of centrality, as the significant center of attention—as her own face is indeed returned to her by the mirror as the focus of her attention. The young nude males in early caryatid mirrors have their arms raised in a gesture of adoration that supports the mirror; later, they take a half-step in the ephebic pose perfected by Polycleitus. The females, by contrast, have a more enclosed body line; they make a limited gesture from a body that is centered and calm; their gaze is straight before them. As between the two, the males are represented as more available, the females as more powerful.

Such are the two figures at the top and bottom of our object. The

[16] Congdon (1981), pp. 234, 238; in the British Museum there is a patera handle (bronze #567, c. 460), quite possibly Locrian, of a youth standing on a tortoise

[17] Here again there is one exception: The mirror base found in Lucifero grave #622, (mid-fifth century) wrapped in a cloak, is (by the treatment of the hips) almost certainly male. This figure is in every way anomalous—by its drapery, and especially by the right hand, which emerges from the cloak at the top.

woman is on top, the male supports the object. They are, I submit, a representation of the couple from the woman's point of view. It remains to ask what can be meant by setting the woman on a knucklebone[18] instead of a tortoise.

The Knucklebone

Hermes in the *Homeric Hymn* calls the tortoise an *athurma*, a toy, and we do find little clay tortoises that may be toys. I know of one representation of a child playing with a live tortoise on a leash.[19] There was a game called *Chelchelōnē*, "tortortoise" or simply "tortoise," mentioned by Corinna.[20] This is a further parallel between the tortoise and the knucklebone, because if a tortoise is something one can play with or play at, a knucklebone is *primarily* a plaything. Knucklebones are toys children liked to accumulate in quantity, like marbles. They were cheap and easily available, a minimal gift for a child (cf. Aristophanes *Wasps* 291–299). Some of the games played with them were like marbles, others like dice, others like jacks.

Furthermore, they are (like the tortoise) associated with Hermes. Our main source for games played with knucklebones is a scholiastic note on Plato's *Lysis*, where the boys are playing at knucklebones because it is the festival of Hermes. The knucklebone, like the tortoise, is also associated with Aphrodite; the most powerful throw, the equivalent of double-sixes, bore the name "Aphrodite."

Knucklebones, according to Herodotus (1.94), are among the games invented by the Lydians. Like everything Lydian they are associated with *truphē*, luxury. Like everything that has to do with luxury they carry with them associations of violence. Patroclus in Homer, we remember, had to go into exile as a child because he killed another little boy in a quarrel over knucklebones (*Il.* 23.82–83). Philocles, dedicating his toys to Hermes, says he was "completely crazy" (*poll' epemēnato*) about knucklebones. There is also a proverb that "boys are to be cheated with knucklebones, men with oaths." It is attributed to Polycrates (Plutarch *Lysander* 8), Lysander (Plutarch *Moralia* 229a), Dionysius (ibid. 330f) and Philip (Aelian VH.vii.12). All these are tyrannical figures. Another such associated with knucklebones is Alcibiades; Socrates reminds him that while a boy he was enraged when cheated at knucklebones (Plato

---

[18] The classic treatment of the knucklebone is Hampe (1951). For a more recent discussion with full bibliographic references see Kurke (1999), pp. 287–295.

[19] Keller (1913), vol. II, p. 259, fig. 98.

[20] Arthur (Katz) (1980–1981).

Alcibiades Major 110), and there is an anecdote about his crazy behavior while playing the game (Plutarch *Alcibiades* 2).[21]

The tyrant, as Plato tells us (*Republic* 573d), has his own inner tyrant, who is Eros. Knucklebones are erotic—as Anacreon (Fr. 53 Page) says: They are the "craziness and turmoil of Eros." A fifth-century oversized model of a knucklebone in pottery in the Metropolitan has painted on it Eros playing the lyre (New York 40.11.22; ARV² 965). The Erotes play at knucklebones (*Greek Anthology* XII.46); Eros plays at knucklebones with Ganymede in Lucian (*Dialogues of the Gods* 4); also Zeus, Ganymede's lover, plays with him at knucklebones (Lucian *Dialogues of the Gods* 5). They are exciting toys.

Knucklebones were a game for children; a grown man puts them away (cf. Justin 38.9.9, where a prince is sent knuckebones as a gesture of contempt, much as the French king sends tennis balls to the young Henry Vth in Shakespeare's play). They are, however, proper to grownup girls, *parthenoi*. The Graces, who are close to Aphrodite, as Pausanias says (6.24.6–7), were represented with flowers and with a knucklebone, which "belongs to youths and maidens, whose grace is in no way faded from age; their toy is the knucklebone." Polygnotus painted the daughters of Pandarus, the favorites of Aphrodite, playing at knucklebones (Pausanias 10.30.2). We have many representations of girls playing knucklebones.[22] Knucklebones is surely the game being played by Aphrodite and Pan on the well-known mirror in the British Museum.

The games proper to *parthenoi*, maidens, are ball and knucklebones. The ball was a love charm, sent rolling toward the chosen beloved, as in Anacreaon apud Athenaeus 599c. Knucklebones were particularly a love *gift*. Gloria Ferrari (Pinney) and others have argued that the long bags that often appear in courtship scenes on Attic vases, which have been taken for purses, are in fact the characteristic bags used to hold a set of knucklebones.[23]

Courtship involves toys because, more generally, courtship involves regression. In seeking to love and be loved we go back to the place where we found love in the first place, to childhood. Thus the movement toward mature sexuality involves, paradoxically, a movement in the opposite direction, a denial of our adult selves. As lovers we become childlike partly because the love of children is everywhere acceptable. Thus games may serve, as we say, "to break the ice" between the sexes; because they are rule-determined they permit an interaction that will not go too far, too fast; because they are childish they return us to

---

[21] For quarrels over knucklebones, see Hermann (1979).

[22] E.g. terra-cotta D 161 in the British Museum (Hellenistic).

[23] See Ferrari (Pinney) (2002), pp. 14–16, with additional bibliography.

the relatively safe asexual world of children, with its ready display of affection. Thus we tend to classify as children those with whom we wish to be intimate, call them "baby" and so on. An Attic word for "beloved" was *ta paidika*, which may be translated "my toys." We play at love, at least in the beginning, or love plays with us, as Meleager has it:

> Still a baby on his mother's lap in the light of dawn,
> playing at knucklebones he lost at dice my spirit, Eros did.

P. A. 7.47

Knucklebones are violent and aphrodisiac. They are, in Victor Turner's terms, antistructural. In the game of chance the order of things is at risk, open to instant reordering. Knucklebones are thus proper to festivals of reversal—to the Skira, for instance, in which women took men's roles. In Troezen, in another kind of reversal, the masters treated the servants to a meal and played at knucklebones with them (Athenaeus 639c).[24] These are New Year's festivals, characterized by an outburst of abundance and equality—which nevertheless, as H. S. Versnel tells us, cannot last,

> because it carries the seed of real social anomie and anarchy. It is a dangerous game, just as was the dice-playing allowed to the slaves; on this day the relationships are open, the dice are thrown and there is a possibility that it is not the master but the slave who will win. This is equality no longer, it is the world turned upside down. (Versnel [1987], p. 141)

I quote this language here because I find that courtship is something like a New Year's festival. In both, the world is renewed by the breaking of boundaries and the reversal of roles. Courtship involves reversal (for the Greeks) because it was the woman's moment of power. As she stood ready to leave her father's house and yet was not yet allocated to another, she had the potency of all potentialities. If she was not entirely a free agent she was at least a prize, the center of interest and the fulcrum for a restructuring of relationships.

Courtship is a dangerous game; the stakes are the future. This is no less the case if the person to whom court must actually be paid is not the girl but the girl's father. In either case the suitor puts at risk himself and his unborn children. As I said of Locrian Ajax: Who can observe limit and proportion while sacking a city or pursuing a maiden? All is fair in love and war. The knucklebone, that exciting toy, carries with it all the maddening lure of the crossing of boundaries.

The tortoise, as we have seen, represents the woman's place, the place she finds when courtship is successful and she is placed, made

---

[24] Cf. Versnel (1987), p. 130; Schumacher (1993), p. 65.

"perfect" (*teleios*) as the Greeks say. The knucklebone by contrast represents the moment of displacement. The knucklebone represents courtship, the tortoise, marriage. To use again a distinction made familiar by Dumézil: The tortoise (like Peitho) represents love in the aspect of *gravitas*, the knucklebone (like Eros) in the aspect of *celeritas*. Or perhaps is would be more useful again to employ the old scholastic distinction between *natura naturata* and *natura naturans*.[25] The tortoise represents woman's "natural" place in the social order; the knucklebone represents the displacement that gets her there.

That knucklebones represent new love and the transforming power of sexuality may explain (somewhat paradoxically) their presence in cemeteries. Knucklebones, real ones and imitations in a variety of materials, are of course found in a variety of contexts, for instance as dedications in sanctuaries (including the Mannella).[26] (We also find clay and metal tortoises as dedications.)[27] There is a giant archaic bronze knucklebone from Claros, half a meter long, inscribed as a dedication. On the other hand, real knucklebones, which were cheap and available, might serve as a kind of minimal dedication; the floor of the Corycian cave above Delphi is virtually paved with them. It seems that visitors to the sanctuary might climb up to the cave and throw in a knucklebone or two, as we throw coins in a fountain.

We do have some evidence for the use of knucklebones for divination in sanctuaries,[28] and it has been thought that this explains their presence in temples (and in the Corycian cave). It seems equally possible that they belong in sacred space because the playing of a game was part of a ritual. I would tend to interpret in this sense the representations we come across on coins of (sometimes naked!) girls playing at knucklebones before a statue of Artemis.[29] Artemis is the patroness of girls' initiations, and knucklebones, as they belong to courtship, should also belong to initiation.

Funereal Knucklebones and Mirrors

The place we most often find knucklebones, however, is in graves (where we also find some tortoises)[30] and in no Greek cemetery in such num-

---

[25] See p. 25.
[26] 2,620 knucklebones are reported from the sanctuary of Meilichios at Selinus: Picard (1943), #376.
[27] Settis (1966), p. 30.
[28] Kurke (1999), p. 289n.94.
[29] Hogarth et al. (1908), pp. 190–192.
[30] Settis (1966), p. 89.

bers as in the Lucifero cemetery in Locri. These are not buried like grave goods, as if they were the possession of the deceased, but are strewn over the body, especially around the feet (another parallel with the tortoise), and sometimes scattered over the lid of the sarcophagus. Sometimes they occur in considerable numbers. I have identified thirteen graves in Orsi's reports containing more than one hundred knucklebones;[31] ten of these are certainly women's graves (including the reversed-burial companion-grave to the one in which our perfume burner was found), and the other three probably are. It seems that knucklebones are particularly appropriate to the graves of women. We can in fact add them to the long list of items found in women's graves which are connected with love and marriage—mirrors, for instance. Knucklebones and mirrors are exceptionally frequent in the Locrian cemetery because women were important to that city.

These knucklebones in graves may be linked to the much studied parallel between the wedding and the funeral, a parallel that is worldwide but particularly striking among the Greeks—made explicit, however, mostly in the case of women.[32] When a woman dies—particularly if she dies unmarried—she is said to marry death, and her funeral is instead of a wedding.[33] It may then mark the ritual appropriately that the body is strewn with knucklebones, a typical love gift. "Sweets to the sweet, Ophelia," says Shakespeare's Queen Gertrude, "I thought thy bride-bed to have decked, sweet maid, and not have strewed thy grave."

This is turn suggests an explanation for one of the most remarkable graves in the Lucifero, #348. This is one of the very rare Greek graves in which a couple is buried together.[34] Around their bodies, down the left side of one and up the left side of the other, was laid a stream of knucklebones, more than fourteen hundred in all. I see this as the residue of some great moral disaster—perhaps a murder-suicide—and the use of this great mass of knucklebones as an effort to purify the unhappy dead, as if they were buried in flowers.

Hermes in the *Hymn to Hermes* calls the tortoise "a defense against evil spells"; probably knucklebones also were apotropaic. That would

---

[31] Grave numbers 587, 632, 709, 737, 826, 828, 849, 865, 922, 932, 1013, 1308, 1490; to this list must be added the double grave #348 discussed below.

[32] Occasionally also for men: See Euripides *Hercules Furens* 476–484.

[33] For a thorough review of this theme, in the plastic arts and in tragedy, see Rehm (1996).

[34] For a review of these, see Hughes (1991). In cemeteries such as the Fusco at Syracuse, where sarcophagi were sometimes reused—or in a cemetery such as that of Megara Hyblaea, where such reuse was absolutely commonplace, it did sometimes happen that the remains of husband and wife ended up together, but this is not the same as a joint burial.

explain why we so often find them pierced, so that they could be worn like beads. Perhaps they were hung around the necks of babies to keep them from the evil eye, just as the sign of the phallus is so used around the Mediterranean today. In fact everything sexual is apotropaic. This has to do with the link between purity and process. We purify with primary substances, fire and water; to these the Greeks added flour and wool, the matter of cultural life taken just halfway in the transition from nature to culture. In a pinch Odysseus could use oak leaves. In general we purify with agents of process and with matter in process. This tells us that impurity is an excess of structure. It is order gone sour; to purify we need to introduce some fresh air, some new life, reopen the process. The knucklebone, a love toy, can be the sign of such a renewed life.

Sexuality is a structuring force; it binds together the couple into a stable unit. At the same time it is the destabilizing force that uncouples and recouples its wayward victims. The process feels its way toward a structure, and the structure cries out for a process to create it. Courtship is under the sign of deception, capture, and transience; marriage is under the sign of trust, mutuality, and permanence. The two are linked by the wedding, which is the completion of a courtship and the foundation of a family.

Our object links two figures into a couple, and was probably employed in wedding processions to spread abroad the odor of incense. Incense sexualizes space; in a marital context it is a token of the woman's availability. The rest of the object is consistent with this reading of the couple: The woman is on top; geese and flowers speak of her grace and authority. Furthermore, she is standing on a knucklebone, the token of her destabilizing restructuring power. All this seems to me to make the object very Locrian. Probably it belonged to a Locrian matron who had made a cultural specialty of the role of *numpheutria*. We can believe that at Locri, where weddings were important, a trusted *numpheutria* would have been an exceptional person, exceptional enough to receive a mark of her difference in the manner of her burial.

On differences in burials we have very little documentary information. There is, however, the often-cited classical *horos* (boundary-marker) from Cumae, "It is religiously unlawful (*ou themis*) to bury here one who has not been made Bacchic." In this one case, at least, initiation made a difference to burial. Carter, the excavator of the countryside back of Metapontum, makes explicit reference to this item in his discussion of a peculiar set of burials in a necropolis there.[35] These are fosse graves, ten in number, decorated with white plaster applied to the

[35] Carter (1998), p. 67.

wall of the grave—or actually to the body: In some cases it is evident that the shroud was covered with a thin layer of plaster. These graves are not spatially segregated; they are scattered through the cemetery singly and in twos, and occur within family groups. None are earlier than the mid-fifth century or later than the second quarter of the fourth century, with the majority concentrated in a single generation: 405–385. There are two males, one evidently a foreigner, the other a very old man, two children, one of whom was probably male, and six women. Two of the graves contain mirrors; four pieces of painted pottery were found in these graves, and each includes a representation of someone, a woman or an Eros, holding a mirror.

This cemetery in the hinterland of Metapontum contains the highest concentration of mirrors of any Greek cemetery—slightly higher, on a percentage basis, than the Lucifero.[36] These two are the only Greek cemeteries in which mirrors are at all frequent. Mirrors and representations of mirrors are particularly frequent in the Metapontine white-plaster graves. Carter wishes to see in these mirrors evidence of an Orphic connection; the mirror, he says, "played a central role in Orphic beliefs" because it was one of the toys, according to one Orphic theogony, that the Titans gave to Dionysus prior to tearing him apart. Carter further notes that of the other two areas where large numbers of mirrors are found—the Scythian cemeteries near Olbia, and Etruria—one at least, Scythia, has known Orphic connections.[37] Actually Etruria also has such connections, since we are told that the Bacchic rites—initially restricted to women—were introduced to Rome from there. But rather than linking the mirror to initiatory and ecstatic ritual through one detail of the theogonic material, I would prefer to see the link as established through the connection between initiation and marriage, a link supported for later Italy by the Villa of the Mysteries fresco which—in one reading of it at least—represents the initiation of the bride. We may see here a representation of the ritual introduced from Etruria. Certainly Etruscan art is remarkable for its emphasis on married couples.

This is not the place for a discussion of the Villa of the Mysteries—which is, after all, centuries later than the Locrian material we have in hand. It is enough to notice that it suggests the possibility that the wedding, which is a transformation of the woman, from some eschatological perspective could transform her *forever*, so that the same ritual was initiatory in terms of social status and in terms of hopes for a happy afterlife. Such a wedding would be technically a heroization of the

---

[36] Ibid., p. 184.
[37] See below, p. 397.

bride. Marriage for the Greeks is a *telos*, a completion of the woman; those who die unwed marry death because they can now achieve completion only in this way. But those who are wed, at least in some communities perhaps, arrive in the next world as completed beings, like those initiated in mysteries.

With the suggestion that Locrian marriage was of this kind we can now proceed to an interpretation of the serpents on our perfume burner, beginning with the observation that in the Orphic material serpents are sometime erotic. In at least one Orphic theogony, Zeus and Demeter turn into snakes to produce Persephone, and Zeus again becomes a serpent to mate with Persephone (West [1983], pp. 73–74). Olympias, the mother of Alexander the Great, was found in bed with a serpent; she certainly had Orphic connections and may even have been reenacting this theogonic prototype.[38] If serpents come up from the earth they can in this way of thinking bring new life with them.

From the eschatological perspective we call Orphic, a chthonic symbol can be erotic because life and death are continuous: "life is death and death is life" in the frequently quoted formula. Euripides used this paradox, probably twice (Frs. 638 and 833), was quoted by Plato (*Gorgias* 492e) and twice mocked for it by Aristophanes in the *Frogs* (1082, 1478). That it did not originate with him is clear from the ivory tablets from Olbia; these have inscribed on them oppositions characteristic of the Orphics—except that life and death are not so much opposed as reversable: that tablet reads "LIFE—DEATH—LIFE."[39] If life and death are one, the powers of death are the powers of life and the next world can be the source of new growth and vitality in this one. So the serpent could join the goose and the lotus as an emblem of sexual power.

All of this suggests that our perfume burner may be taken to code a particular eschatological understanding of the wedding, an understanding with connections elsewhere, possibly in Metapontum, certainly in Etruria. It remains to explore further the proposed eschatological perspective.

[38] Plutarch *Alexander* 2–3.
[39] Vinogradoff (1991).

Ten

The Ludovisi and Boston Thrones

THE great treasure of the Terme Museum in Rome is a piece that was found in the gardens of the Villa Ludovisi in the late eighteenth century; it was called a throne because no one knew what it was, and it has been called the Ludovisi Throne ever since. It is one of the great masterpieces of classical art, more specifically of the Severe Style, which is to say that it belongs to the early years of the fifth century. The sculpture fills three sides of a block of Parian marble, which tapers up toward the long side. This side (the front, that is) represents three standing figures; the heads of two of these are missing as the top of the block has been sheared off (see plate 5). On each of the two sides is a seated figure. All are female, and about half life size. Both the origin of this work and its subject matter continue to excite a certain amount of controversy, but there is by now a general consensus that it originated in Epizephyrian Locri,[1] and that the front side represents the birth of Aphrodite. Without further argument I shall here take both points as settled.

Aphrodite is represented as a young nubile girl; her garment clings to her and reveals her body. She rises between two female figures, the one on the left wearing a peplos, that on the right dressed in a chiton. These women are standing on a pebble beach. Aphrodite is partly shielded by a cloth they hold between them before her, her body facing forward, her head turned toward the left. Her ear partly protrudes through her hair. She rises weightlessly, captured but not supported by the women who bend over her. Her lips open as she takes her first breath. The cloth held before her is conventional in birth scenes; it is in effect a receiving blanket. The placing of the cloth is unusual, and as it conceals the lower part of Aphrodite's body, it may be intended to be taken to conceal Ouranos's member, from which Aphodite (in Hesiod) originates. Such a figurative elision would be consistent with the restrained manner of the whole representation. The scene is focused, tense, inward-turning; the figures pay no heed to us. They are wrapped up in each other. The birth of Aphrodite is represented, as Erika Simon says, not as a miracle but as a mystery.[2]

---

[1] Best argued by Ashmole (1922).
[2] Simon (1959), p. 18.

There has been much discussion of the identity of the two female figures who receive Aphrodite. Are they Horae? (In the second *Homeric Hymn to Aphrodite* the Horae receive the newborn Aphrodite and dress her.) Are they Moirai? (Pausanias 1.19.1 tells us that an inscription in the Athenian sanctuary of Aphrodite in the Gardens called Aphrodite the eldest of the Moirai.) If they were Horae we should expect there to be three of them, and if they are Fates, Aphrodite is surely represented not as the eldest but as the youngest. Zancani Montuoro (1964), p. 395, suggests that the welcoming figures are Peitho and Charis; these welcome Aphrodite on a Pyxis from the Penthesilea Workshop (Beazley *ARV*, p. 899, #144) along with Zeus, Hera, and Eros—although on this piece Eros does the actual welcoming along with a female figure (holding out a cloth); the label of this latter as Charis is a reconstruction. Peitho is here to the side.

None of these parallels are clear enough to enable us to name the figures on the Ludovisi Throne. Two points, however, seem worth making.

1. This is the only known ancient representation of the birth of Aphrodite in which no male figure occurs (except for a *pinax*, type 10/3 P 13, also a Locrian representation). Usually she is welcomed by Eros or Hermes, or watched by Pan, or otherwise accompanied.

2. The presence of two female figures framing the goddess creates a triangle of femininity. In myth powerful males come singly or in pairs, *sun te du' erchomenō*, "two going together" to use Socrates' favorite Homeric quotation, but females are almost always a triad: the Horae, the Fates, the Graces. Not infrequently three must be reduced to two if they are to be overcome, as we have already seen with the daughters of Proetus (three are pursued, but only two are married) and the daughters of Cecrops (three dance together, but two throw themselves from the Acropolis). Powerful females may be three in one person, as Hecate is called three-bodied, and as the nymphs are often represented on votive plaques as a kind of conjoined triplets. Pausanias (8.32.2, 9.16.3) tells us that in two different sanctuaries Aphrodite was represented as three persons. The Ludovisi Throne, whatever else it may be, is a representation of female power.

Turning to the figures on the sides: One is a nude, actually the earliest known female nude in Greek monumental sculpture, a ripe, lovingly presented figure naked except for a snood covering her hair (see plate 6). She is playing a double flute, and is evidently a flute girl, which is to say, a prostitute. She is comfortably placed on a soft cushion.

On the other side is a young woman fully dressed, indeed tightly wrapped, in a garment that comes down to her toes and is wound up over her head and ears (see plate 7). She sits on a slightly stiffer folded cushion, evidently a mattress, and is intently engaged in the act of placing some incense in a incense burner. Evidently, in contrast to the flute girl, she is a young wife perfuming her bedchamber.

These two women represent, as it were, sacred and profane love: The available woman is contrasted with the free woman whose sexuality is confined to marriage. Given the primary contrast, it is to be noted that the secondary features tend to make these women more alike than different. The naked whore is not in an abandoned posture (as such flute girls usually are when pictured on Attic pottery) but reclines with her legs crossed and her attention turned inward. She is focused on the flute and on her music. The tempting outlines of the wife's body, on the other hand, are quite traceable through the cloth that wraps (not drapes) her, and (if we interpret correctly the meaning of the incense) she is the one with sex on her mind. These two women, in other words, are sisters under the skin. The Ludovisi Throne, it seems, is a celebration of women's sexuality and its power.

The Ludovisi Throne has a companion piece. A few years after its finding there appeared in the stock of an art dealer in Rome an object of virtually the same size and shape, in identical marble, and a similar composition: three figures on the front (the top is in this case intact) and two seated figures on the sides. It now belongs to the Boston Museum of Fine Arts and goes by the name of the Boston Throne. The dealer had a completely plausible story of its provenance—very near the find spot of the Ludovisi Throne[3]—but the piece is so odd that it immediately excited suspicion (even though forgers usually try to produce something that looks familiar, not shockingly unfamilar). Furthermore it is clearly not by the same hand as the Ludovisi Throne and is not nearly as good. Suspicion of its authenticity continues. However, those art historians and others who have been specially concerned with Locrian work—Ashmole, for instance, Sourvinou-Inwood, Simon, and Zancani Montuoro[4]—have generally accepted it as an ancient piece. The most probable explanation, in my view, is that of Gullini: the Boston Throne is a Roman copy.[5] When, some five centuries after their creation, some Roman determined to remove these works from Locri and install them in the Gardens of Sallust—perhaps in connection with the nearby sanctuary of Venus Erigena, which was patronized by

[3] Nash (1959).

[4] Zancani authenticated the Boston Throne—which she had seen and indeed climbed upon—in a personal communication. She pointed out that there are rope marks on the top; it had evidently at some time been used as a well head. Furthermore the head of the old woman is like that on a *pinax* which had not been discovered at the time the piece appeared.

[5] Gullini (1982).

the Caesars—he found that the original of the Boston Throne, having been on the weather side of the monument (or for some other reason) was in poor condition; he therefore commissioned a copy of it in the same marble as the original. This would explain why it is less good; also it would explain why the Ludovisi Throne, as we have it, was clearly made to fit into a bracket, while on the Boston Throne the bracket in the form of a volute is worked in one piece with the figures.

It follows (assuming it is a close copy, which as a replacement it would be) that we can interpret the iconography of the Boston Throne as if it were the original.

At the center of the long side (i.e., the front) stands a winged youth, naked, with a slightly *méchant* smile playing on his lips (see plate 8). He holds up a balance. The actual beam of the balance was evidently added in metal, and is lost, but the two pans are clearly represented, and in each there is a tiny naked figure suspended by his hands tied up over his head, only his toes touching the pan. The pan to the left is down; the figure here is stiffly upright and full face; the other pan is up, and here the figure is in profile and bends his knee. Two women sit facing this weighing scene from either side. They are identically dressed in chiton, mantle, and sandals. The woman on the left sits on a thick folded cushion, her posture is open and relaxed, she holds up her left hand with the palm to us in a gesture of pleasure; her right hand is relaxed at her side. The woman on the right may or may not be sitting on something; if so the drapery conceals it. Her posture is closed and tense. Her right hand is raised and her forehead rests on it in a gesture of mourning; her left hand is clenched under her cloak.

Here again there have been various efforts at identification: Thetis and Eos (Simon 1959), Aphrodite and Persephone (Sourvinou-Inwood 1974a); once again the identifications are speculative and probably unnecessary. Interpretation can best proceed by starting from what seems fairly certain and exploring the implications.

The weighing in the center is generally recognized to be modeled on a *psychostasia*, a weighing of souls. More than once in the *Iliad* Zeus, as he looks down on combat, raises his scales to determine which warrior will live and which will die; the *kēres* or death-spirits of the two heroes are in the pans. The scales of life and death appear later on Attic vases, where, however, they are held by Hermes; in the scales are little winged figures representing the souls. The duel in these cases is usually between Achilles and Memnon, and is sometimes watched from the sides by their respective mothers, Thetis and Eos. Thetis rejoices and Eos mourns.[6] In both the epic and pictorial versions the pan that goes

---

[6] Sourvinou-Inwood (1974a) p. 127n.14. We have (in the Reggio museum) a Locrian *arula* representing a duel of warriors watched from the sides by two women; there is no

down belongs to the warrior that dies; on the Boston Throne, however, the lower pan provokes the gesture of pleasure. It would seem that this reversal, immediately obvious to any viewer familiar with the type, might be the key to the significance of the whole.

On the bottom corners of the front relief are two small objects: to the left a fish, to the right a pomegranate. These are repeated around the corners under the seated figures, as if to insist that there is a connection between front and sides. The seated figure to the left, with the fish, is an old woman; she is not grotesque but she is aged and defeated: Her legs are pressed together, her eyes are down, the corners of her mouth droop, as do her shoulders (see plate 9). She is seated on the bare ground. Some part of the stone is missing here, but Erika Simon has convincingly suggested that originally she had before her a wool basket, and that she is a spinner.[7] On the other side, with the pomegranate, is a beautiful youth wearing nothing except sandals—and perhaps a crown, which may have been added in metal (see plate 10). He is playing the lyre and sitting on a wineskin. To be seated on a wineskin appears in Attic vase paintings in connection with dissipated enjoyment, usually enjoyed by a satyr.

If we take the weighing on the model of the *psychostasia* as dividing life from death, one interpretation would go as follows:[8] The two figures on the pans are souls; they are hung by their hands because this is a way of picturing prisoners[9] and they are portrayed as prisoners because in the Orphic tradition the body was the soul's prison and life an incarceration. The pan to the left obtains life, as is shown by the gesture of pleasure; nevertheless the pan is down because after all it belongs to the loser. The figure around the corner explains the sense in which this is so: She is a Fate, specifically Clotho, the spinner of our vicissitudes. Life consigns us to her untender mercies. Death, on the other hand, which is received with mourning, *really* carries us to the joys of the afterlife, feasting and music; that is what the youth with the lyre is there to tell us. The jarring discontinuity represented by this "really" is shown on the monument by a linkage of opposites: The joyful young woman seated on a cushion is joined by the fish to a laboring old woman seated on the ground; the mourning woman, not seated on any visible cushion, is joined by the pomegranate to the joyful youth seated on a wineskin. By this reading the message of the Boston

---

weighing scene on this one, but it does place the duel-with-watching-women type at Locri.

[7] Simon (1959), p. 69.

[8] This interpretation is in general (although not in detail) that of Sourvinou-Inwood (1974a).

[9] Ibid., p. 131n.48.

Throne is that life is death and death is life. Exactly this, as we have seen, was the Orphic good news in its most reduced phrasing.[10]

The Orphic tendency was generally individualistic; it set out to save persons, not communities. Even when mysteries were maintained by the public (Eleusis being the leading instance) they promised not better public life but a better personal fate. Mystic initiation and ecstatic release might be enjoyed by a crowd but they did not build a society. There is little evidence for Orphic communities; the Orpheotelestai, the Orphic initiators, were freelance wanderers (Plutarch *Moralia* 224e; Plato *Republic* 364b–c). Even the ecstatic choruses of Euripides' *Cretans* and *Bacchae* tend to speak in the first person singular.

But in the West and on the north coast of the Black Sea, Orphism seems to have achieved a certain public status; the boundary-marker from Cumae quoted above was a public document. For Locri we have Aristotle's testimony in his *Constitution of the Locrians* that "it is not their way to weep over the dead; rather, when they conduct a funeral, they feast" (fr. 611.60 Rose). Death, for them, was, it seems, a happy event, or at least they were so instructed, and Aristotle reported this fact as an element of the local political order. This is documentary evidence for the establishment of Orphic belief; at Locri Orphism took a political turn.[11]

In Aristotle's *Politics* (1274a), further, we hear of "Onomacritus the Locrian," who came to Crete "pursuing the prophetic art" and thereby became indirectly a source for the laws of both Lycurgus and Zaleucus. There was an Orphic theogony that circulated under the name of Onomacritus: Pausanias quotes it four times (1.22.7; 8.35.5; 8.37.5; 9.35.5), informing us, among other things, that Onomacritus was the first to connect the Titans with Dionysiac ritual (*orgia*) by making them the agents of Dionysus's sufferings. This work was also known to Sextus Empiricus (Kern test. 191). Possibly Aristotle when he speaks of Onomacritus the Locrian thinks of him as the author of this theogony. Aristotle's flat statement that the story about Zaleucus and Lycurgus is "in defiance of the chronology" shows, further, that he has in mind a particular datable Onomacritus who appeared elsewhere in the historical record known to him. Possibly this was the Onomacritus who, according to Herodotus (8.6), was thrown out of Athens by the tyrant Hipparchus for forging an oracle in the name of Musaeus (even though

---

[10] Herodotus (5.4.2) ascribes to the Thracians a parallel reversal: They mourn for a birth and rejoice at a death (that is, they produce the reaction which, according to the Boston Throne—as here interpreted—would be the "right" reaction). For other suggestions that death is superior to life see Herodotus 1.31.3 (Solon) and 7.46.4 (Artabanus), also Hesiod fr. 377 Merkelback-West and Theognis 425–428.

[11] Musti (1984), p. 77.

Herodotus calls this one an Athenian). Alternatively, if there were two called Onomacritus, it is still possible that the theogony was attributed to the Locrian. Therefore it is quite possible that in the fourth-century "Onomacritus the Locrian" was a recognized figure of the Orphic tradition.

The most notable Orphic document from the Locrian area is the Hipponion tablet. This is an inscribed sheet of gold; it was found in a young girl's grave, folded on her breast. She was wearing a gold ring on the fourth finger of her left hand.[12] By now we possess a score of these "tablets," various in date and place, giving instructions for obtaining a better life in the next world; this one remains, however, the earliest in date and one of the fullest in text. It is written in rough hexameters: A translation (from the text presented by Guarducci [1985]) follows:

> This is the work of memory. Whenever one is on the point of death
> By the well-built hall of death to the right there is a spring
> By it standing a white cypress
> There come the souls of the dead to cool themselves
> Do not go nearly close by that spring
> Further on you will find from the lake of Memory
> Cool water flowing out. Guards are set over it
> These will ask you with crafty mind
> What you seek in the dark of hateful Hades
> Say: Son of Earth am I and starry Heaven
> I am parched with thirst and I perish. Give me swiftly
> Cool water flowing from the lake of Memory
> And then they will pity you ruled by the underworld King
> And then they will give you to drink from the lake of Memory
> And then also once you have drunk you will go a great journey
> Such as the other initiates and bacchics walk the sacred way in fame.

These "tablets" are our best source for personal Orphism, for the beliefs and hopes of those who subscribed to this eschatology. This is not the place to review the corpus; they repeat phrases from one an-

---

[12] This ring is now in the Hipponion museum. It is half-round, like a modern wedding ring (and unlike most ancient rings). However, wedding (or betrothal) rings were not Greek, although there is some evidence for Roman betrothal rings—Pliny HN 33.4.12; Testullian *Apology* 6.4. Williams and Ogden (1994) includes (#79) a half-round ring signed with a flying Eros and inscribed *chaire*; this certainly looks like a love gift.

Several women in the Villa of the Mysteries fresco wear rings on the fourth finger of their left hand—which finger the ancients already thought had a direct link to the heart (Pliny HN 33.6.25). We do have evidence that the initiates from Samothrace wore iron rings, and it is possible that these also are tokens of initiation. (Cf. Burkert [1993], pp. 187–188.) Possibly the custom of the betrothal ring is derived from that of the initiatory ring.

other and seem to go back to a couple of archetypes, yet no two are the same—and not one is complete: The Hipponion tablet, as Guarducci has cogently argued,[13] is missing something between the first and second lines, something like: "writing on gold learn well these instructions." In their repetitions they reflect a remarkable degree of continuity—over a period of seven hundred years, given that the latest examples are from the third century A.D. The degree of variation, however, shows that this was language handed along from generation to generation, without an enduring written source to which each generation could refer. They vary, for instance, on the most critical point, the location of the correct spring: The Hipponion tablet places it to the right of the palace while on the Petelia tablet it is to the left; on the Cretan tablets it is marked by the white cypress, while on the Hipponion, Petelia, and Pharsalus tablets this tree marks the wrong spring. One hopes no souls ever actually had to rely on these directions!

Given that the form of religiosity here attested lasted a long time, and over a very large area, we know remarkably little about it, or about its relation to the established, state-sponsored mysteries, particularly those of Eleusis. One critical difference seems to be this: At Eleusis something was shown, and the salvific power of the rite lay in this experience: "Blessed (*olbios*) he who has looked upon (*opōpen*) these things" says the *Homeric Hymn to Demeter* (480); "blessed whoever seeing (*idōn*) these things goes beneath the earth" says Pindar Fr. 137 (Snell); "thrice blessed those among mortals who having gazed upon (*derchthentes*) these rites go to Hades" says Sophocles (Fr. 753 N). Aristotle says that at the Mysteries something is not *learned*, but rather *experienced*. The tablets, by contrast, are under the sign of Memory; they contain information to be learned and remembered, information which precisely will enable them to avoid forgetfulness. Those who are saved are those who can carry the word in their minds from one life to the next, and since memory is frail they are supported by the written tablet as an *aide-mémoire*.

Orphism was a religion of the written word. Theseus in Euripides, not understanding Hippolytus's religiosity very well, mocks him with stereotypes, saying: "take Orpheus as your lord, and become Bacchic with the smoke of many writings" (Euripides *Hippolytus* 953–955). Demosthenes, mocking Aeschines, says, "when you reached manhood you helped your mother celebrate her rites by reading the books and managing the rest of the apparatus" (Demosthenes 18.259). Many of these books were evidently theogonies, often written under the name of Orpheus; others may have been texts of instruction and consolation from

---

[13] Guarducci (1985), pp. 390–392.

which the tablets derived their language. None of these texts, however, achieved canonical status; it seems clear that Orphic texts, like the tablets, were constantly being rewritten with attendant variation. Although they are written they vary like orally transmitted texts. That is (again) because Orphism belonged essentially to the realm of personal religion, of private adherence to charismatic teachers. As such it never became established; indeed it generally fell short of respectability. Such Athenian references to Orphic doctrine and practice as we have uniformly present them as at best *outré*, most likely ridiculous.

An Orphic *polis*, therefore, seems to be a contradiction in terms, and the Boston Throne, if it is indeed an Orphic public monument, partakes of this contradiction. From certain points of view, however (as we have seen) contradiction is the stuff of social life, since society's moral reach ever exceeds its grasp and all social organization requires an accommodation of opposing values. Normally we take this fact for granted as "the way things go" and accept the contradiction in a relaxed spirit. Contradiction only becomes manifest as such when a problem is solved in an unfamiliar way. And (as we have seen) there is much about Locri that is unfamiliar. The "political turn" of Locrian Orphism can only be understood in terms of their cultural system as a whole.

We might advance a step in this direction by considering the Ludovisi Throne and the Boston Throne together, as the two halves of a single monument. It seems that the originals would have been facing in opposite directions, either as the ends of an altar or as some sort of balustrade around a small square structure or cavity. With this deployment the meaning of the whole would be revealed only to the viewer who walked all the way around; it consists of ten figures (not counting the small prisoners on the pans of the scale). The figures on the sides would face each other: the spinner [A] (with wool-basket, if Simon's reconstruction of the missing piece is right) facing the matron [B] with perfume-burner, the girl [C] with flute facing the boy [D] with lyre. Each of these side figures is defined by an object; each is intent on a task. The ears of the flute girl and the lyre player are virtually identical (these are the only two figures whose ears show, except for the newborn Aphrodite, whose ear is partly visible); they could be brother and sister.[14]

The four side figures taken as the four corners of a square can then be taken as representing the four most significant social-structural dif-

[14] There is a *pinax* type—1/20 P 133—that represents two sirens, one playing the double flute, the other the lyre, thus illustrating the fraternity of these two instruments, as well as their other-worldly aspect.

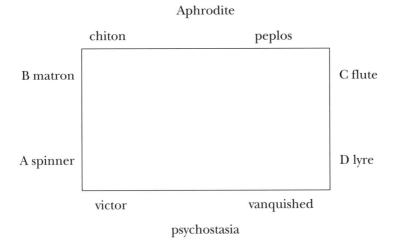

ferences in Greek society. The flute player and the matron [C and B] represent the contrast between unfree and free; the matron and the spinner [B and A] between young and old; the flute player and the lyre player [C and D] between female and male, and the spinner and the lyre player [A and D] between the living and the dead.

Furthermore these figures are united by a play of oppositions arranged as a permutation. A and B are clothed; C and D are naked. A and D have the hair revealed; B and C have the hair concealed. B and D are sandalled; A and C are barefoot. That these oppositions are intentional seems to be the simplest explanation of the odd fact that the lyre player [D] is wearing nothing but sandals; that was the only way to make the permutation come out.

A permutation of oppositions is a formal device that asserts the symmetrical unity of a complex assemblage. The Ludovisi Throne asserts the seductive power of women; the Boston Throne asserts a joyful eschatology. Taken together they assert a link between these two things, between love and death.

This link is reinforced by the play of oppositions in the cushions on which the side figures are sitting. The matron [B] is sitting on a relatively stiff mattress; the flute girl [C] on a relatively soft cushion. Facing the matron is the spinner [A], who is sitting on no cushion at all; facing the flute girl is the lyre player [D], who is sitting on a wineskin, which is (in a sense) more of a cushion than a cushion, being associated with self-indulgence. So moving from B to A we move from hard to harder, and moving from C to D, from soft to softer; the contrast that is asserted in the realm of love—marital sex versus recreational

sex—is asserted even more strongly in the cosmic realm: the toils of
life versus eternal bliss. While the figures emblematic of the first contrast are more like one another than we should expect—the matron
[B] and the flute girl [C] are sisters—the figures emblematic of the
second contrast are the two most thoroughly contrasted: the spinner
[A] is old, female, and at labor, while the lyre player [D] is young,
male, and at ease. The point of the play of oppositions seems to be the
amplification of a contrast, and the monument as a whole seems to be
constructed like one of Socrates' complex proportions, intended to
lead us from a difference we do understand (appearance and reality,
say) to a difference we do not yet understand (becoming and being,
for instance). The proportion here can be stated as follows: MARRIAGE:
SEX::LIFE:AFTERLIFE.

By this I do not mean to imply that the joys of the next life are
imagined as specifically sexual—although this possibility is not to be
excluded; it is cross-culturally an element of many images of eternal
bliss, for instance the Norse and the Muslim. I mean rather that the
matron and flute-girl, both of whom are portrayed as sexual and desirable, represent a contrast between joy trammeled—embedded in the
toils and complications of ordinary life—and joy untrammeled, experienced with the abandon and release of music. This is a "Hyperborean"
picture of the afterlife as a gentle, playful, enjoyable eternity. The canonical Greek representation of this condition shows the happy dead
feasting, reclining with cup in hand.

Any concrete representation of eternal bliss is easily mocked, as
Plato's Adeimantus mocks those who represent the next life as a symposium of the pious, reclining crowned and continually drinking, "supposing the fairest wages of virtue to be an everlasting drunk" (*Republic*
363d). But how are we to talk about bliss? The answer to this question
lies in the answer to another: Why should we want to?

I suppose no one knows anything about any afterlife; it is "that undis-
covered country," the "great perhaps," as Rabelais called it. We do know
a great deal, however, about eternity because we know what meanings
are to us eternal, no longer subject to contingency. We then talk about
the afterlife as a way of talking about what is eternal in this life, of
saying what it is that we value in this world. We shall see our loved ones
again there, and we know this because we experience our bond with
them as immutable. The wicked shall be punished there; we know this
because we know that what they have done is irremediable, and not to
be justified or covered over by their worldly success. When we speak of
eternal bliss we are talking of real happiness, of the fulfillments that,
however briefly experienced, stand for us as permanent realities.

In the epics immortality is a matter of eternal fame. The hero does something "for men to come to inquire about"; he (and in the *Odyssey* also she) becomes the protagonist of a story that will be told forever. Most often the story tells of some exploit on the battlefield, and also in later Greek texts battle is a place where men are transfigured into monuments, where they come to deserve eternal memory. But the notion is also generalized into the making of history in general; Diotima in Plato's *Symposium* speaks of the immortality of the sages and lawgivers and inventors, of Solon and Pythagoras and Anacharsis (who according to one story invented the potter's wheel). Such people are heroes and might even receive hero-cult, like the epic heroes who were honored in local sanctuaries here and there; thus Lycurgus, the lawgiver of Sparta, was the object of hero-cult, and so was Leonidas, the hero of Thermopylae. The founders of cities normally became heroes with their graves in the marketplace and an annual festival; this honor might be accorded great benefactors of the city, as in the fifth century B.C. the people of Amphipolis named the Spartan Brasidas their second founder and buried him in the marketplace. Victors in the games also shone with heroic brilliance; Pindar calls it the "god-given *aiglē*," the "gleam." Victors did sometimes literally become heroes in their own time, and were honored with hero-cult—as in the case of Euthymus at Locri.[15]

Heroism, in other words, is immortality; the hero persists in memory and often in the concrete form of a local ghost who is powerful and must be propitiated. The gulf between mortal and immortal is unbridgeable, yet heroes manage to be both. So not all deaths are the same. Achilles in the *Iliad* says that he has two *kēres*, two personal fates; if he returns home he will have a long life and marriage, without fame; if he stays in Troy his return will be lost, but his fame will be immortal (*Il.* 9.412–416).

The prototypical heroism, then, is a particular kind of death, what J.-P. Vernant calls *la belle mort*, the noble death: that of a young man at the peak of his powers, whose very corpse is beautiful.[16] "To a young man it is altogether fitting," says Priam in the *Iliad* (22.71–73), "when he is slain by the sword . . . all things are fine for him, though he is dead, whatever is laid bare" The hero is the perfection of manhood, even in death; his typical monument in archaic times is the *kouros*, the life-size or larger naked young male figure, striding forward on his statue-base.

There is, however, an opposing Greek image of immortality, corresponding to the proverbial Greek opposition between the battle and the feast, an image of immortality not as continuing potency—in mem-

---

[15] Cf. p. 246.
[16] Vernant (1988).

ory, in cult—but as continuing enjoyment. That image is of the feasting dead with wine and lyre. This is the image of immortality enjoyed by the lyre player on the Boston Throne. It is an image of antiheroic enjoyment, as Priam speaks of the unheroic sons left him after Hector's death: "dancers, outstanding at tapping their feet in the chorus" (*Il.* 24.261). But it has its proponents among the poets. Mimnermus of Colophon, who had perhaps more to say about pleasure than any of the lyric poets, even adapts Achilles' myth of the two *kēres*:

> The dark *kēres* stand ready:
> The one holding at the limit harsh old age,
> The other, death. Brief is of youth
> The fruit, so long as the sun shines upon the earth;
> But when one has passed the limit of the season
> It is better straightway to die than to live.
>
> Mimnermus Fr. 2 Diehl

If youth alone is blissful, eternal bliss must be eternal youth. But of all youthful enjoyments the most enjoyable (although perhaps least suitable for representation) are the works of Aphrodite. Mimnermus again:

> What is life, what is pleasure, without golden Aphrodite?
> May I die, when these things no longer stir me:
> Secret affection, and presents of reconciliation, and bed.
> Such are the flowers of youth that are to be seized
> By men and by women. But when the pain comes on
> Of old age it makes a man both ugly and base.
>
> Mimnermus Fr. 1 Diehl

Life without love is no life; eternal life, if it is indeed happiness, must be a life of love. It follows that in love and courtship we have our best intimations of immortality—or, to put this another way, the people who see the afterlife as a sphere of love will be those who have found in love the essential meaning of life.

The Ludovisi Throne and the Boston Throne, taken as a single complex monument, can be read as coding that message. The birth of Aphrodite refers to the origins of all life; the *psychostasia* to the fate of life in this mortal coil, and the possibility of release. The likeness between the young matron and the flute player affirms the sexuality of marriage, its fundamental natural energy. The contrast between the young matron and the spinner, the *nymphē* and the *graus*, reminds us that in this life we catch our moments of bliss as we pass through toil to decrepitude. The contrast between the spinner and the lyre player reminds us of the contrast between mortal toil and eternal bliss; the link between the flute player and the lyre player asserts that naked enjoyment, under the sign of music, is our best image of eternal bliss and our best foretaste of it in this life. The whole complex can be read as a public monument representing certain fundamental convictions whereby the Locrians maintained the validity of the personal promise contained in the Hipponion tablet.

Eleven

The Locrian *Pinakes*

THE three preceding chapters have attempted to establish a context in which to interpret the most important surviving Locrian material: the *pinakes*. These are rectangular terra-cotta plaques about the size of sheets of typing paper; although they vary somewhat in size, the longer dimension does not exceed 30 centimeters. They are 0.5 to 2 centimeters thick. They bear representations in low relief ranging from single animals or objects—a rooster, a decorated box—to complex scenes involving a number of figures, sometimes with indications of natural or architectural setting, interior or exterior. They were made in multiple copies from molds. Surviving traces show that they were originally whitewashed and painted; details—a hydria, detailing on a door—were sometimes added in paint. Each plaque is furnished with a small hole at the top (or more often two), evidently for a string that could serve as a hanger; clearly the plaques from the deposit had previously been hung by the worshippers about the sanctuary of the Mannella as dedications. Since there seem to have been no substantial buildings in this sanctuary, they were probably hung on trees. The workmanship is refined and the level of artistry generally high. They were produced throughout the first half of the fifth century, with the peak of production toward the middle of the period; while the individual hands have yet to be identified, the number of artists involved was not large, perhaps a dozen, give or take. The clay is local, and the molds were sometimes recut while in use by the same hands that had made them originally; the artists therefore were Locrian, by residence if not by origin.

Pinax is a generic term for a plaque, particularly a plaque bearing a representation in low relief; dedications of this type are found in many sanctuaries. The Locrian *pinakes*, however, were in style and content peculiar to the western Locrians. The vast majority come from the Mannella sanctuary. A few fragments have been found elswhere in the city, and one comes from a nearby rural site. A certain number of examples have been found in the Locrian communities on the Tyrrhenian side, Medma and Hipponion; some of these were locally produced. One fragment turned up just beyond the Locrian frontier, in

Caulonia.[1] Only two fragments—out of some six thousand—have been found outside the Locrian culture area; these are both of the same type.[2]

The Francavilla *Pinakes*

To these we must add *pinakes* of the Locrian type found quite recently in a deposit of votives at Francavilla di Sicilia, well up the Alcantara valley behind Naxos, on the north slope of Mount Etna. These have received so far only preliminary publication, but are well discussed in Spigo (1982); they can also be studied as displayed in the Orsi Museum in Syracuse.

The Francavilla deposit included at least one fragment from Locri, but most were locally produced. The excavator distinguishes nineteen types (hereafter F 1–19) of which twelve (F 3–14) closely resemble known Locrian types; however, not one of these is identical with its Locrian relative. Of the anomalous types, F 1 (a young woman moves to the right, dancing or fleeing) dates to the sixth century; it is both chronologically and iconographically isolated, and for our purposes can be ignored. F 2 (which looks much like a Locrian Hades with Persephone) is dated to the first quarter of the fifth century and may well be an import from Medma. The other types form a chronologically compact group belonging to the decades 480–460, contemporary with the height of production of *pinakes* at Locri.

The only completely novel type, F 16, represents a couple about to board a ship where a woman stands holding the tiller; this is probably the abduction of Helen by Paris, with Aphrodite at the helm. The story of Helen is an abduction story; the coroplasts drew freely from the Greek repertoire stories illustrating their pervasive themes. Similarly at Locri there are two rare types showing the abduction of Europa by Zeus (10/4 P 127; 10/5 P 128).

Then there are three types (F 17, 18, and 19) that are stylistically atypical of the published Locrian material.[3] These represent heads in profile, either a woman alone or with a crowned male behind her; the heads fill the frame. These Francavilla types are probably all by the

---

[1] For further details as to the provenance and current location of the fragments, see Rubinich (1999), p. 14.

[2] Prückner (1968), p. 130n.7.

[3] Spigo (1982), however, reports that similar types are represented on a couple of Locrian fragments not classified by Zancani.

same artist; the woman has a characteristic long chin.[4] They are particularly fine. They also fall ideologically within the range of the Locrian *pinakes*: They celebrate a woman or a couple and as such would be appropriate wedding dedications.

Two of the Francavilla types—F 17 and F18—resemble Locrian types displaying ritual processions, but with elements not found on the Locrian equivalents: the torch and the sacrificial piglet. Both of these are proper to the Thesmophoria, which at Locri, as we have seen,[5] was kept separate from the worship of Persephone, for which the Locrian *pinakes* were intended. So it seems that the Francavilla *pinakes* represent a community that shared in Locrian culture but was artistically and even religiously somewhat independent, "a kind of parallel universe in relation to Locri."[6]

Toward Interpetation

So far I have been stating more or less generally agreed facts about the *pinakes*. Beyond this point everything is speculation and controversy. Speculation has long been made the more erratic and controversy exacerbated by the lack of a definitive publication.[7]

---

[4] A not dissimilar long chin appears on the roughly contemporary tondo from Melos, now in Athens (#3990), which similarly displays a head in profile filling the frame.

[5] See p. 209.

[6] Spigo (1982), p. 303.

[7] The modern history of the *pinakes* is, in outline, as follows. A few fragments had come to light before the turn of the twentieth century and made their way into private collections or museums. By 1906 the local peasants had located the main deposit and set about removing the fragments; a local collector saw to it that these were not dispersed and eventually passed most of them on to the Italian national museum system. Paulo Orsi then proceeded to the excavation of the site in the campaigns of 1908 and 1909, turning up the great deposit with its layer of fragmentary *pinakes*. Almost all the material found in 1906–1908, along with further material excavated by Arias, found its way eventually to the museum in Reggio, where a selection is now on display, the rest being held in storage. Some few fragments are still in Locri.

In 1933, two years before his death, Paulo Orsi turned the Reggio collection of *pinakes* over to Paula Zancani Montuoro, who published her first paper on them in 1935. By 1964 she had published nine more—not that the *pinakes* alone kept her occupied; she continued her brilliant career as excavator, conservator, and editor. In her last twenty years nothing more was heard from her on the subject of the *pinakes*; she refused to attend the Convegno di Studi sulla Magna Grecia at Taranto in 1976, which was primarily devoted to Locri. She did not publish the *pinakes*, and so long as they were in her care no one else could publish them. She did, however, create for the museum in Reggio a display representing the range of types; it became possible to study the *pinakes* by going

Interpretation has (broadly) followed three paths: eschatological, mythological, and ritual. The first interpreters, including Orsi, saw the *pinakes* as representations of the fate of the soul, its life beyond the grave, a tendency continued by Gianelli (1963). Zancani Montuoro, who received the *pinakes* as a legacy from Orsi, began in this direction but quickly recanted; she has seen the *pinakes* primarily as representing episodes in the local myth of Persephone, her capture and marriage. Prückner (1968) sees them primarily as representing Locrian rituals, particularly rituals associated with sacred prostitution, which he conceives as an established and pervasive institution there.[8] (Torelli [1976] continues this tendency.) Thus type 8/29 P 30 (see plate 11), which represents a seated female confronted by two standing figures, a small female and a larger armed male behind her, can be seen as representing (a) the judgment of the soul before Persephone, (b) Persephone honored after her marriage by other divinities, or (c) a Locrian father dedicating his daughter to Aphrodite for her period of prostitution.

Obviously these three approaches are not always mutually exclusive, and Christine Sourvinou-Inwood (1973 and 1978), whose interpretations I find the most plausible overall, has sketched a synthesis, seeing mythology, for instance, as evoked in, and evocative of, a ritual context. Erika Simon (1977) has proposed a new start, taking account of the fact that these plaques are dedications, and beginning with what we know about the generic iconography of dedicatory plaques. Unfortunately the *pinakes* are in so many respects exceptional that it is hard to

---

to the museum, and otherwise with the help of such descriptions, photographs, and drawings as happen to have appeared here and there.

In the mid-1960s Helmut Prückner, a degree candidate at Heidelberg, undertook to publish as his doctoral dissertation the fragments of *pinakes* held at Heidelberg; this is actually the third-largest group, after those in Reggio and Locri. While working on this dissertation, he spent enough time in Reggio to review the fragments held in storage there—evidently with considerable assistance from Zancani, who was then deeply offended by his eventual publication (personal communication). His book (Prückner 1968) attempts nothing less than a general interpretation of the *pinakes*. His interpretations have not been well received. Nevertheless we owe him a great debt; he in effect published the *pinakes* (although very incompletely illustrated); he gave a complete catalogue with a type-by-type description and he also, through cross-reference, in effect published Zancani's catalogue, making it possible for the first time to refer to all types by the numbers she had for them. His commentary contains much useful detail. For all its eccentricities, Prückner's book has been, and will continue to be until the definitive publication is complete, essential for a study of the *pinakes*.

As I was finishing the present volume, the first part of the definitive publication became available: Lissa Caronna et al. (1999). It publishes only Zancani's groups 1 and 2, a little more than 40 percent of all the fragments.

[8] On this issue, see appendix.

be sure that what we know of iconography elsewhere applies to them. We can be sure, however, that they were dedications, and we can reflect on the ritual and social context of dedication.

On Interpretation: Representations

Dedication and sacrifice are rites that create a bond between worshipper and god. In sacrifice this bond results when the worshipper feeds the god—either *simpliciter*, as in holocaustic sacrifice or the gift of cakes and wine, or, more frequently among the Greeks, through commensiality, when worshipper and god share a meal and thus become one substance. First fruits, the tithe of spoil, and the libation of wine are other examples of sharing with the god.

A dedication was something left behind by the worshipper in a sacred space as the property of the god. First fruits and the spoils of battle could be dedicated; here the sphere of dedication overlaps with that of sacrifice. More often a dedication was a token of the worshipper, sometimes a mere token; in some archaic sanctuaries we find large rough fieldstones that were inscribed to the god and deposited. In this case the bond between man and god is formed simply by the effort of dedicating. More often, as we have seen, the token is a metonym of the worshipper; a lock of hair, or some intimately owned object; a tool, a toy, a weapon, a trinket. Often as a part of a rite of passage some token of the old life is left with the god; the old life thus both dies and becomes immortal.

Dedications need not, however, be specifically linked with the worshipper; any item of value will serve. In this context value is in contrast to utility. Items suitable for dedication are much the same as those which in the epics are suitable for prizes, circulate in gift exchange, and are treasured as *keimelia*: metal vessels and tripods, embroidered fabrics, arms and armor. These items, even if they could be useful, are generally reserved from use; the tripod has "never known fire," the arms are never again to be used in battle—just as in our own culture one does not visit a gift shop to buy an object for daily use. These objects are *agalmata*, made to be reserved to admiration, like the objects in a museum.

One important category of dedications has no parallel in epic gift exchange: representations. In all Greek shrines—at Olympia as early as the early geometric—we find a bewildering array of representations: statuettes in metal and clay, plaques, models, figurines, even (as time goes by) life-size or over-life-size sculptures. The array is bewildering because the relevance of the representation is unclear. Sometimes the god is represented, sometimes the worshipper; many figures could be either or neither. What are we to make, for instance, of the *korai*, those sculptures of adorned maidens found in such numbers on the Athenian Acropolis? When we find a *korē* (to take two of the earliest) inscribed:

> Nikandra dedicated me to the far-shooter pourer of arrows, daughter (*korē*) of Deinodikos of Naxos, standing out from the rest, sister of Deinomenes and now wife of Phraxos (*IG* XII.5, 2, p. xxiv)

it is natural to take the image as representing the worshipper (who calls herself a *korē*); when we find a very similar statue inscribed:

> Timonax son of Theodorus dedicated me to Artemis when he first held the priesthood (Richter [1968], p. 26)

we rather tend to take the image as representing the goddess. Perhaps we are wrong in both cases and the image "represents" the act of dedication itself—in the sense of being an object suitable to a dedication. After all, a *korē* could be dedicated by a man to Apollo (Richter [1968], pp. 26–27).

What is dedicated is first and foremost the value of the object—otherwise we would not find (for instance) a *korē* with the following inscription:

> Nearchus the potter [?] dedicated this work as first fruits to Athena. Antenor made it, the son of Eumaros, the beautiful thing [*agalma*—this last word is restored, as is "potter"]. (Richter [1968], p. 70)

Nearchus the potter (if this indeed be he) does not dedicate one of his own pots. He takes part of the profit from pot making and buys or commissions from Antenor a magnificent statue fit to adorn the sanctuary. The statue certainly does not represent either Nearchos or Athena; neither need it represent an idealized worshipper or divine servant. It is a beautiful object. No doubt it helps that adorned maidens are among the typically beautiful things; therefore representations of maidens are typically beautiful representations. But the statue is primarily of value—to us, to the god—not as a representation of something fine, but as a fine representation.

Similarly we need not think that the geometric horses found at Olympia—some of them grouped into teams—must be the dedications of horsemen; a horse, like a maiden, is a typically beautiful thing, and just as horses in Homer can be given as gifts, so representations of horses make gifts to the gods. Here again our own gift shops provide an interesting analogy: We do not ask for the significance of a china shepherdess or porcelain dog. These things are bric-a-brac, intended for display—on a shelf, as it happens, rather than in a sanctuary, but the principle is the same.

This is not to say that the representation is unmotivated: A horse could be a particularly appropriate choice for a horseman, and a female statue may even be inscribed: "I am ——oche, who also made the dedication to Hera" (Richter [1968], p. 49). It is only that the primary purpose of the representation is not to send a message or make a record or magically to create a substitute for the thing represented; its function is not instrumental but aesthetic; it should not mean but be. The object represented, and the ideal links of that object to the dedicator and the god, are elements in the aesthetic success of the dedicatory act; a good dedication is both beautiful and apt, as well as appropriately expensive.

Locrian Dedications

It follows from this general understanding of ancient dedications that the value of the *pinakes*—in both senses, their artistic quality and their price—is part of their meaning. They are works of fine art—indeed the best are extraordinarily beautiful—but since they were produced in multiple copies in a cheap material they were modestly priced objects, within the means (presumably) of most Locrians. Furthermore they are all about the same size and were probably priced more or less the same—in contrast to terra-cotta dedications found in other sanctuaries, which were produced in very different sizes to fit the pocketbook and fervor of diverse worshippers. To present a *pinax*, it seems, was something like lighting a candle to the Madonna—a modest act in which the rich came down to the level of the humble. This leveling down is consistent with what else we know of Locrian society, and may be considered an aspect of Locrian *atrekeia*.

In general the objects found on the Mannella were modest things, in clay or bronze, not precious metals. If this was indeed the sanctuary famous in Hellenistic times for its riches we must believe that the more glittering dedications were kept out when the sanctuary was cleared—as was indeed the usual practice. The objects found on the Mannella, further, are predominantly women's things: mirrors, perfume jars, dolls, ornamented boxes. It would seem that the sanctuary was mostly frequented by women. In the case of the *pinakes* this feminine tendency is so strong that one is tempted to presume that they were dedicated exclusively by women.[9] The figures are predominantly female, often

---

[9] There is one type of *pinax* found only at Hipponion (Ianelli and Ammendolia

women alone, sometimes with a male or two; there is only one type (8/38, P 129) that bears a male figure with no female, and this type exists in only one example. Also, the *pinakes* bring us into a woman's world: women adorning themselves, bathing, picking fruit, handling fabrics, in a setting rich in furniture, basketry, chests, boxes, ornaments. Presumably these plaques were made by men—we have no evidence for Greek plastic arts by women, excepting fabrics—but they surely try to represent the world as these men thought these women saw it.

The *pinakes* were made at Locri for dedication there and in other Locrian sanctuaries; they did not travel. In general there is no evidence that outsiders came to this sanctuary; such imports as have been found there—Corinthian perfume jars, Attic transport vases—are objects that most probably came to the sanctuary in Locrian hands. Probably the cult of the Mannella was conducted by and for Locrians alone; this would be consistent with what else we know of the "closed" quality of Locrian society. The life of Locrian women, presumably like other Greek women secluded, took place in an enclosure within an enclosure; it is part of the fascination of the *pinakes* that they seem to take us right into this hidden world.

The *pinakes* are not meant to be a sequence, like a set of Byzantine mosaics or the panels on a Romanesque church door; they were not made to be read in any particular order. On the other hand, they are an array; Zancani distinguished 178 types—as well as 28 variants, molds that were recut while in use. This variety has to be motivated—in contrast, for example, to those sanctuaries where we find thousands of nearly identical figurines. Those figurines really were like the candles of the Madonna; the dedication was a generic act, and its special meaning to the dedicator remained invisible. The Locrian women, by contrast, visibly chose a particular type and in this way asserted something particular about their relation with the god.

Obviously all these two hundred-some types were not available at once, nor were they designed in relation to each other; they do not in this sense form a set. But they were created within a relatively brief period of time by a small group of artists aware of each other, for a small and cohesive clientele. In this sense they are a unity. The closest modern example is perhaps a rack of postcards or greeting cards. The impulse to buy a card usually precedes the choice of card, and since they are all of the same price the choice is made on other grounds;

[2000], p. 120), which represents a young man being crowned by an Eros, and offering a dove to a female, probably a goddess. This type would seem to be suitable for offering by a man, and suggests that at Hippionion men did sometimes offer *pinakes*.

nevertheless it can take time to choose just the right card from the rack. The array as a whole represents a diffuse judgment, over time, by the makers of these cards as to the images likely to prove meaningful to the sort of people likely to buy them for the sort of purpose they are likely to serve. The semiotics of such an array must be a subtle matter, but questions are askable, even if difficult (or in a particular case, perhaps, impossible) to answer.

Types: Abductions

Let us begin with type 2/22 P 57 (see plate 12). A bearded male wearing a short cloak is driving a four-horse team of winged horses hitched to a light chariot; he holds the reins in his right hand and looks intently forward. His left arm is around a maiden, elegantly dressed with her hair carefully adorned. She turns back to gaze behind him and fling up her arms, palms out, in a familiar Greek gesture of distress; he holds his left hand cupped under her breast in an equally familiar gesture of rape. The right hand of the maiden and the cloak of the man break through the inner frame of the composition, adding to a sense of explosive motion.

This is virtually the only type concerning which there is agreement among all the interpreters: it represents the rape of Persephone by Hades. The immortal horses, the golden car, the moment of seizure, and the outcry of the maiden are all in the *Homeric Hymn to Demeter* (16–21). This further is the only type that has been found outside the Locrian cultural area; one example was found in the sanctuary in Selinunte, another in a grave in Syracuse. This type is an "orthodox" representation, immediately meaningful to Greeks in general and to us.[10]

Scenes of the abduction of a maiden dominate the *pinakes*, accounting for some thirty-three types, about one-sixth of the total,[11] and one-third of the examples. These types, in other words, were both numerous and relatively popular. None of the other "abduction" types, however, are in the same sense "orthodox." On only three of them is the abductor bearded, and on two of these (2/18 P 59; 2/19 P 58) he carries the maiden, who is relatively small, on his back or shoulder as he drives the car. On the last type with a bearded abductor (2/24 P 84) the two figures are the same size, Hades again has his hand under

---

[10] Representations of the rape of Persephone on Attic pottery are rare, but of a neck amphora by the Oionokles painter (*ARV* 647.21) Beazley remarks: "This is not the only occurrence [of Pluto pursuing Persephone] in Attic art of the fifth century, since the rape of Persephone is represented on the Skyphos from Eleusis."

[11] Prückner (1968), p. 68.

Persephone's breast—but she does not struggle; she stands facing calmly forward, as does he. Her head breaks through the inner panel, but this emphasizes her stature, not motion. The scene is so calm that Prückner did not even classify it as an abduction.[12]

In all the other abduction scenes the abductor is a beardless young man, naked except for a short cloak, never actually driving the chariot but rather stepping into or standing next to it. These types were far more popular than those where the abductor is bearded. There is much variation. Sometimes the abduction takes place in the presence of a group of other maidens (2/3 P 79). One type includes Hermes leading the horses (2/28 P 75) and another a flute player (2/29 P 76). The horses are sometimes wingless. On one type (2/30 P 83; see plate 13), Hades is present looking on; the maiden here is heavily veiled with her hands covered, the youth is crowned with myrtle, and the chariot has a six-spoke, instead of a four-spoke, wheel. I have not succeeded in interpreting this puzzling and anomalous type.

Most striking in general is the variation in the amount of struggle portrayed. Prückner distinguishes three groups.[13] In one group the maiden flings out her arms as in the "orthodox" type; she either looks back or straight at us. There is a spilt flower basket in the field. In another group she holds out only one arm and holds something in the other hand—usually a cock, sometimes a ball, once a basket full of flowers; she looks her abductor in the face—except in the type including Hades (2/30 P 83); here she looks at Hades. In the third group the maiden puts up no resistance at all; she looks calmly ahead while standing in the chariot, and in one case even takes the reins (2/17 P 81) or the youth leads her to her place *cheir epi karpoi*, hand on wrist. On another type (2/25 P 85) the upper body of the youth is naked; he is crowned with myrtle and holds the reins in one hand as he steps toward the chariot, while with his other arm he embraces the maiden already peacefully standing in the chariot, holding a flower basket.

The first explanation of these "young abductor" types (Quagliati [1908]) was eschatological: The youth was Thanatos and the maiden the Soul. Such allegorical representation was soon seen to be out of period for the early fifth century and was set aside in favor of mythological hypotheses. Perhaps the Locrians had a local story telling of the rape of some maiden by some local hero (Prückner [1968]); per-

---

[12] The scene is even more consensual on the closely parallel F2 (early fifth century, possibly from Medma), where the driver of the chariot is bearded, the horses are wingless, he does not have his hand on her breast, and she stands calmly next to him holding her veil in the familiar bridal gesture. This looks like a picture of an ordinary mortal wedding, except for the "heroic" chariot (as opposed to the mule cart).

[13] Prückner (1968), pp. 70–72.

haps the maiden was a (no doubt adopted) daughter of Persephone and Hades, so that the abduction was not *to* the underworld but *from* it—type 2/30 P83 therefore representing the seizure of the maiden from her father's house (Simon [1977]).

These interpretations fail to explain (1) why the maiden with the young abductor is marked with the attributes of Persephone—the flower basket and especially the cock; these are the same attributes that occur when she appears with bearded Hades; and (2) why the beardless abductor is never represented as an established husband; when the maiden is represented enthroned with a spouse that spouse is always bearded Hades. These objections, however, do not hold against Zancani's interpretation; she asserts that in a local Locrian version Persephone after her abduction by Hades withdrew and had to be brought back to him by another—and that type 2/30 P83 actually represents the delivery of the maiden to Hades.[14] The maiden would therefore be Persephone herself in all cases, and it would also be explained why the "young abductor" disappears; his part in the story is done.

However, the abductor's pose in 2/30 P83 is identical with his pose on many types on which he is clearly carrying away the maiden, not delivering her. Furthermore on some types he is clearly her initial abductor (e.g., 2/2 P 60, where he carries her off as she appeals to a group of maidens, or 2/3 P 79—the most popular of any *pinax*-type, accounting for more than 10 percent of all the fragments[15]—where she goes with him peacefully, leaving behind a triad of gesticulating girls). Leaving aside, further, the fact that it introduces an unparalleled and undocumented version of the story, this interpretation succeeds no better than the other in explaining the range of variation in the types: Why are there two types of abductors? This variation, it is to be noted, varies independently of other variables; the maiden, whether with Hades or the youth, is sometimes resistant, sometimes compliant; the horses are sometimes wingless, and wingless horses can occur when she resists (2/5 P 62, 2/7 P 63) or when she does not (2/17 P 81)—although always with a "young abductor"; bearded Hades' horses are always winged.[16]

The problem of the abduction types is the presence of the young abductor; he is the noncanonical element. That the two types appear

[14] Zancani Montuoro (1954a).

[15] Cardosa (1999), p. 210n.1.

[16] Marinatos (2003) sees "two distinct types" of abduction scenes on the *pinakes*, and identifies one type with sexual initiation, the other with marriage. The number of independent iconographic variables makes it, however, impossible to divide them cleanly into two groups, and suggests rather a range of responses to a single event: the sexual intitiation of the woman which is marriage.

together is a second problem but does not help us toward a solution of the first.[17] Sourvinou-Inwood (1973) makes a new start and notes that the iconography of the "abduction" *pinakes* is partially drawn from a repertoire elsewhere used to represent marriage. The typical marriage procession on painted pottery shows the couple standing together in the chariot, but the name piece of the Peleus Painter (ARV2 1038 #1) shows Peleus stepping up behind a Thetis who stands very like the maiden on type 2/17 (P 81). Hermes (2/28 P 75) and the flute player (2/29 P 76) are both typical elements of wedding representations. Prückner notes the gesture of hand on wrist (2/1 P 82); this is proper for leading off the bride. We may add that the ball, recurrent on the *pinakes*, is an element of wedding iconography elsewhere, at least on some Apulian vases. Perhaps most significant: At least one Attic representation of the departure of the wedding party[18] shows the bride being lifted into the chariot. And in Greek representations of marriage not directly linked to myth the bridegroom is generally represented (even though so many grooms were older men) as a beardless young man.

We have seen that the dialectic of persuasion and force is integral to the Greek conception of heterosexuality; the grasping of the bride by the wrist and the lifting of her into the car were (like our lifting of her over the threshold) gestures of capture, which was thereby enacted as one aspect of the marriage. Marriage, I have said, was both a transfer and a transformation, both the exercise of man's power over woman and an exercise of woman's power over man, creating a relation actualized only by the woman's consent, whereby she achieved full womanhood. I am suggesting that the variation of treatment on the *pinakes* responds to these ambiguities. No doubt some brides felt more abducted than others. The bride could picture herself as Persephone in the *Homeric Hymn to Demeter*: torn from her mother and by her father consigned to the power of a bridegroom who carried her off to another world careless of her wishes. At the opposite extreme, the marriage could be represented as the cooperative relation with a bridegroom of a bride who herself guides his quite mundane horses (2/17 P 81). The most popular types at Locri (e.g., 2/10 P 68; see plate 14) place her somewhere in between; she is literally swept off her feet and throws out one arm with a startled gesture, but with the other hand cradles her

[17] Roberta Schenal Pileggi (in Lissi Caronna [1999], pp. 877–891) reviews previous theories of 2/30 P 83 and (in a footnote) adds one more: On the basis of the possibility that some fragments bearing a grapevine, attributed by Zancani to another type, actually belong to this one, she suggests that the bearded figure is not Hades but Dionysus, present as a spectator at the abduction. She makes no comment on the implications.

[18] Sourvinou-Inwood (1973), n.52.

attribute and looks into her lover's face in a gesture of intimacy and consent.

This reading of the *pinakes* does not exclude the possibility that they reflect some local variant mythology; we know, after all, that the Locrians had in Euthymus a young hero who rescues a maiden, and we have plenty of stories elsewhere involving the abduction of maidens: Boreas and Orytheia, for instance, and the abduction of Basile from Hades by Echelos (Kekulé [1905]). But we do not know enough about this sort of iconography to be sure that the "young abductor" must be a specific personality with a story, rather than merely a generic representation of the bridegroom. Furthermore, even if we should come upon the local Locrian epic that explained the pictures, the persistence and use of the story in wedding dedications would have to be motivated. What would it mean that Locrian maidens associated themselves with an abducted (or rescued) girl?

Nor is eschatological relevance excluded; Persephone does, after all, figure on the *pinakes* and Persephone's story everywhere unites themes of love and death. These themes will require further consideration. Nothing, however, requires literal reference to a *hieros logos*. It must be significant, for example, that—however the abductor is represented—the spouse, in scenes where the couple is enthroned, is always represented as the bearded Hades. This means that when marriage is represented as a transfer, the male agent may be young and lovable, a figure of *celeritas*; when marriage is represented as a transformation, he is always older, a figure of *gravitas*. Both can be representations of a bridegroom, since the bridegroom has both aspects. The transfer of the bride is achieved by the transient process of courtship; by her transformation she "dwindles into a wife" and settles into the honorable condition of marriage.

Whatever their mythological reference and eschatological resonance, it is clear that the *pinakes* represent marriage. As Torelli (1976, p. 160) says, they "are evidently focused on a single social and conceptual moment, that of the wedding, with all its ideological, symbolic, mythic, and ritual implications." They were, further, women's dedications, and they evidently represent marriage from the woman's point of view. Many of them seem to have literal reference to these women's weddings—although since the west-Greek festivals in honor of Persephone seem themselves to have centered on the events of her wedding to Hades,[19] we can in no case exclude the possibility that these representa-

---

[19] Nilsson (1906), pp. 356–359, with sources quoted in the notes, identifies these rituals as Anthesphoria (picking of flowers—a ritual or custom attested for Hipponion),

tions illustrate the ritual enactment of the mythical prototype of the human wedding.

Types: Wedding Rituals

This brings us to type 7/3 P 3 (see plate 15), a relatively rare type— known from fragments of at least three examples[20] but not completely preserved. The center of the composition is a cart drawn by two mules toward the left. Seated on a cushion in the cart is a (fragmentarily preserved) woman: There may or may not have been another figure sitting next to her. In front of the team walks a young man with his left hand held low, the fingers in a fist, while the right hand is held straight up from a bent elbow, fingers together and the palm flat sideways toward the viewer. Over the team flies a winged robed female, gesturing forward with her right hand. Behind the cart walks a matronly figure, her garment looped over her head, carrying in her left hand a pointed-bottomed vessel with a rimmed neck and in her right a plain rod.

The closest parallel to the mule cart is on the late-sixth-century frieze from the temple of San Biaggio at Metapontum, now in the antiquarium there. Here there are no ancillary figures. The mules and the cart are, however, very similar, and the figures are preserved; they are a male with a whip and a female holding her veil in a gesture characteristic of Greek brides. It would seem highly probable that both these scenes represent weddings, and more specifically the journey from the house of the bride's father to her new home with the groom.

The winged figure closely resembles, as Zancani Montuoro (1954b, p. 43) notes, the Nike or Winged Victory who flies over the chariot team on many Sicilian coins, particularly those of Syracuse. Nike, goddess of victory, is a familiar figure in Greek wedding iconography. The figure on the *pinax*, however, is not holding the wreath of victory or anything else; in the absence of an attribute we cannot be sure that she is not meant to be, for instance, Iris. Torelli (1976, p. 161) even proposes Peitho, although as we have seen Peitho is never winged. Here again we cannot exclude the possibility that the figure is meant to be nameless and has a generic meaning; it is at any rate clear that her function—like, for instance, the winged Eros above the wedding car on the pyxis reproduced by Lorimer (1903, pl. l)—is to mark the magic of

---

Theogamia (divine marriage), and Anakalypteria (unveiling). They may have been phases of a single ritual.

[20] Zancani Montuoro (1954b), p. 30.

the moment, the Greek word for which is *aiglē*. I would be tempted to call her Aglaia, except that I know of no representations of the Graces singly, or with wings.

If the winged figure adds a dimension of magic, the wheel of the cart (identical to the wheel on the Metapontum relief) points in the opposite direction. This is the crossbarred wheel, as opposed to the wheel with spokes extending from hub to rim. It may be, as Lorimer (1903) says, that the crossbarred wheel, because it was easier to make, survived in country districts even when it had been replaced for most purposes by the spoked wheel; it may also be, as Zancani Montuoro (1954b) asserts, that its archaism gave it a special ritual status. Certainly we do find it in representations of both weddings and funerals. Its appearance here marks the occasion of a mortal, mundane wedding; the divine and heroic weddings that are much more frequent on painted pottery employ as their vehicle the heroic chariot with spoked wheel—and in this resemble the "abduction" *pinakes*.

Elements from type 7/3 P 3 recur on other types. The winged figure occupies one entire *pinax* type (10/8 P 125). The matron with vessel and rod recurs on many types. We are about to meet again the gesture of the youth in a different context. Wedding iconography, in other words, is pervasive on the *pinakes*. Since Greek women were defined by the institution of marriage, such themes could be appropriately evoked at any time in a woman's life; nevertheless the most plausible occasion for most of these dedications is at some stage in the wedding process, when the bride—and the couple—had a special need to establish a link with the god.

This brings us to 3/6 P 2 (see plate 16), the type that more certainly than any other represents "a *real scene* of ritual *realistically represented*."[21] This type is relatively rare but exists in at least five examples,[22] and at least once in its history of production was renewed by making a new mold from an example.[23] A young couple, the woman in the foreground, stand at an altar before a temple. The doors of the temple are open and within can be seen a pair of divinities. On the side of the altar is represented a representation, evidently a relief, of a satyr copulating with a deer.

The young woman is dressed in a chiton and himation, the latter thrown loosely around her shoulders and over her long hair, which hangs down her back. Her head is held straight—so straight that she seems to lean backward slightly. Her gesture is very similar to that of

[21] Zancani-Montuoro (1940), p. 214; her emphasis.
[22] Ibid., p. 205.
[23] Ibid., p. 206.

the youth on 7/3 P 3 (the wedding procession) although the hands are closer together: The left hand is held tightly closed (the thumb can here be seen to be outside the fingers) while the right hand is held up, fingers together, palm sideways. Her gesture is close to that which has been identified as a gesture of urgency accompanying prayer (Deubner [1943]). She gives an overall impression of energy, of intense response.

The young man, crowned with myrtle,[24] pours with his left hand a libation from a jug onto the altar; his right hand is held out a little way from the body, fingers somewhat spread, as if to feel the heat of the altar flame. His head is somewhat bent, his gaze toward the altar. He acts, she reacts; he attends to the ritual while she attends to the god. It seems, in other words, that he accomplishes some ritual act for her. Evidently we have here a representation of the *proteleia*, that visit to the sanctuary which was in many communities a customary preliminary to the wedding.[25]

This hypothesis finds some confirmation when we learn from Prückner that there exists a variant (his type 2A—evidently not known to Zancani in 1940) in which the youth is absent (being replaced by an object, probably a mirror). Further study has revealed that this is an independent type that was produced before 3/6 P 2,[26] so that the bridegroom there was something of an afterthought. We remember that the *proteleia* was a ritual that involved either the couple or the bride alone.

The representation within the representation, the satyr coupling with the deer, is both striking and unusual. Satyrs are frequently represented with deer, sometimes in poses that suggest carnal intentions (*ABV* 559 #501; *ARV* 73 #28), but the only close parallel to this literal representation cited by Zancani Montuoro (1940, n. 18) is a Euboean vase (her fig. 5). Since that piece has never been completely published I cannot say if there are other images on the vase that would help us understand it. Here on the *pinax* I would suggest that we have a parallel to the association of Peitho with Pan in stories where violence was followed by consent. Bestiality indeed is for the Greeks one form of panic sexuality; Pan typically "treads the goats."[27] We have observed that any representation of a mediation tends to include some allusion to the underlying strand of violence in the relation; the satyr would then appear on type 3/6 P 2 as an emblem of that savage sexuality which is included and at the same time overcome in marriage.

---

[24] This is Prückner's interpretation of the wreath, which is certainly some broad-leaved plant.

[25] Cf. p. 111.

[26] Marina Rubinich in Caronna (1999), p. 20.

[27] Borgeaud (1979), pp. 83, 123.

This theme has a parallel within the *pinakes*, on type 5/2 P 14 (see plate 17). There a folded cloth is placed in (or possibly removed from) a chest by a young woman; nearby are other furniture and implements. On the chest there is another representation within the representation: two panels are divided by a tetraglyph. On the left is represented Athena slaying a fallen warrior, probably the giant Enkelados. The other represents a couple: The man walks toward the woman, holding her right wrist with his right hand; she turns back toward him and with her left hand holds her garment by the side of her head; once again, this is a gesture characteristic of brides.

The tetraglyph is another unusual motif—indeed so far as I know it is unparalleled outside Locri (where the temple of Zeus included pentaglyphs). The Doric frieze anomalously included in the Ionic temple represented on type 3/6 P 2 (the *proteleia*) consists of an alternation of blank metopes and tetraglyphs. It is tempting to think with Prückner (1968, p. 40) that on the actual building the frieze bore figured metopes, that they were represented blank on the *pinakes* because the figures would have been too small to see, and that the scenes on the chest on type 5/2 P 14 are actually drawn from the building represented on 3/6 P 2. (Prückner offers parallels for both scenes from actual metopes elsewhere.) In any case the context of 5/2 P 14 is marital; in fact it probably represents a moment in the preparations for the actual wedding. The right-hand scene on the chest represents a seduction or more probably a wedding.[28] The left-hand scene—Athena killing the giant—is then in extreme contrast to marriage, and represents a couple in the most asexual relation: The virgin goddess has become a warrior and dominates the male. The specific themes are different, but we can say of this scene as of the representation of the satyr with the deer that its relevance to marriage is to identify the violence that should remain latent.

But if the scene on the altar on 3/6 P 2 is an allusion (by opposition) to marriage it would follow that the altar was intended especially for the wedding libation. Of course it is more than possible that the artist of the *pinax* took the liberty of decorating the altar as he thought appropriate to the scene he was representing, and that the actual altar was different. Nevertheless the point holds and it seems plausible to follow Zancani in thinking that type 3/6 P 2 represents a typical Lo-

---

[28] Prückner says that it represents an abduction, but type 1/23 P 136, which he cites as a parallel, instead shows the difference; on the latter type, in which the representation on the chest—in this case with only one scene on it—fills the entire *pinax*, the man again seizes the woman's right wrist, but in this case she pulls away and he leans back; Quagliati (1908), fig. 64.

crian couple looking much as they would have for the actual ceremony—indeed that 3/6 P 2 is a representation of the very occasion on
which the *pinakes*, or most of them, were dedicated: Couples came to
the Mannella sanctuary because it was the place of the Locrian *proteleia*.

This reading of 3/6 P 2 provokes a reconsideration of the implication of the myrtle wreath worn by the bridegroom. We have met this
type of crown before, on "young abductor" types 2/25 P 85 and 2/30 P
83. (The type of crown has been confirmed by me from the fragments
in Reggio.) Myrtle crowns were probably typical of weddings; the myrtle was certainly sacred to the Roman Venus (Daremberg-Saglio, I,
p. 525; Chirassi [1968], p. 22) and on the name piece of the Peleus
Painter (cited above) Peleus leans back to receive a myrtle crown from
Aphrodite. Quite probably Locrian bridegrooms wore them. But this
would suggest that the "young abductor" is not a mythological figure at
all, but a representation of the mortal bridegroom; the moment we see
as an abduction would then be a moment in the wedding ceremony
when the bride was lifted into the wedding car in a ritual of abduction.[29]

But what about the winged horses? The flute player on 2/29 P 76
may be proper to a mortal wedding, but the Hermes on 2/28 P 75
places us firmly in a realm of mythology—or does he? If a winged
figure can fly over the wedding cart, why cannot Hermes, visible to the
eye of art if not to the participants, take part in a mortal wedding? Why
is it that the horses are not always winged? Are the wings to be taken
metaphorically? And yet, as we have observed, the maiden on the abduction scenes is often marked by an attribute of Persephone, and the
vehicle is not the mundane wedding cart but the heroic light chariot
with spoked wheels, just the type driven by Hades on 2/22 P 57, the
"canonical" type.

The truth is that the artists of the *pinakes* do not seem to have made
much of an effort clearly to distinguish their mundane from their
mythological representations. Perhaps the confusion is part of the
point. What is represented, after all, is either a ritual or a myth, and
these are both already representations. The bride is lifted into the
chariot, Persephone is carried off from the meadow, and these two
events signify a common reality, the social fact of patrilocality. The dedication, which points out in these ritual and mythical moments the
common reality behind them, has no need to distinguish them. Is the
"young abductor" a typical bridegroom or a legendary hero? Does it
matter? There is something heroic about every bridegroom; therefore
to be the typical bridegroom is precisely to be that sort of hero.

Every representation, since it idealizes (in the sense of presenting

---

[29] So Sourvinou-Inwood (1973).

not the thing but an idea of it) has something divine about it. A geometric bronze horse is obviously not a horse, but it has in it the spirit of
the horse. Every god is a representation; Persephone is the representative bride just as Leto is the representative mother and Hera the representative wife. Conversely in the ritual the worshipper represents the
god; every bride becomes Persephone. The *korē*, as we have seen, can
represent either god or worshipper—or neither; it "really" represents
some third thing, the idea they have in common, the ideal adorned
parthenos. Similarly we can expect that on the *pinakes* the line between
myth and ritual will be blurred. If worshipper and god are distinct on
type 3/6 P 2, the *proteleia*—mortals at the altar, gods within the temple—this is because the theme of this type, alone among the *pinakes*, is
the relation of living mortals to immortal gods.

This brings us to the question: What gods are these within the temple? The male god—who stands in front—is naked except for a short
cloak around his shoulders; he carries a plate of the type called mesomphalos, which signifies the reception of offerings, and wears a wide hat.
This last item identifies him[30] as Hermes. The goddess wears a long,
severe peplos and carries an attribute—which is unfortunately effaced
on the only surviving fragment that includes the hand. Prückner (1968,
p. 18) is, however, surely right to say that the position of her fingers
indicates that she held a flower.

Hermes appears elsewhere with a goddess. Type 10/1 P 1 (see plate
18) shows us Hermes naked except for a short cloak around his shoulder, carrying the caduceus and wearing a wide hat. He faces a female
wearing a peplos and cloak with long hair down her back; she is holding a flower, probably a rose, and there stands on her arm a little
winged boy carrying a lyre in his left hand, and with his right gesturing
toward Hermes. Between them stands a thymaterion, an incense burner.

Hermes appears again with a goddess on type 10/2 P 4 (see plate
19). Here the woman wearing a peplos stands in a light chariot; with
her right hand she holds the reins, with her left adjusts her garment at
about the level of her waist. She looks back at Hermes, who steps up
behind her. The chariot is drawn by two small winged figures: a female
in front holding a dove, and a male behind her (his wings do not
actually show; it is possible that he is flying without them) holding a
perfume jar. Hermes is naked except for a short cloak; he again wears
the wide hat but this time it is provided with wings, and he has on
winged boots.

Pagenstecher (1911) seems to have been the first to compare this
type with a type of terra-cotta relief from Taras, of which several examples survive in the Taranto museum. This shows a female, himation up

---

[30] Pace Zancani Montuoro (1940), p. 217.

over the back of her head, in a light chariot drawn across the waves by two winged figures—not, in this case, notably smaller than she is. One is a clothed female and looks straight forward, the other, a naked male, turns back to offer the woman in the car something, probably a piece of fruit.

There is a companion type, which in more than one instance formed the opposite side of the same clay arula or household altar.[31] A woman is seated to the left on a bed piled with blankets and cushions; she holds her veiling himation away from her head in the characteristic bridal gesture. At her feet sits on a low ornate bench a small female figure holding her shoes. Next to the bed stand a hydria and a cylindrical basket. To the right stands a female in peplos and himation; she looks toward the other and sends to her with a gesture of her right hand a little naked Eros, winged and holding a *tainia*, the type of ribbon used to adorn the hair.

These Tarentine reliefs are a half-century or so later than the *pinakes* with which we are comparing them; nevertheless they can help us interpret Locrian iconography. There can be little question that the woman seated on the bed is a bride preparing for the bride bed; her removal of her shoes is a token of disrobing and the hydra is a token of the bride bath. The other female must be Aphrodite sending Eros to adorn the bride with a *tainia*. The scene, in other words, represents the acquisition of sexual power by the bride. It is hard to imagine a more reassuring object in the bridal chamber; on it from time to time the young wife would sacrifice a pinch of incense to her personal gods—and thus perfume her chamber.

Simon (1959), on the strength of the fact that the chariot is partly immersed, takes the representation as of Aphrodite's birth from the waves; Zancani Montuoro (1968) thinks that the fabrics are represented as wet and even dripping. If so the relation between the two sides is like the relation between the main scene and the side panels on the Ludovisi throne: The birth of Aphrodite is juxtaposed with the sphere of her activity. It may be, however, that she is represented merely as journeying; Aphrodite's homes are characteristically islands (Cyprus, Cythera) and thus her journeys are over water. So perhaps she is seen as on her way to the bride. The identity of the winged couple who draw her chariot remains obscure; what is certain is that Aphrodite's car drawn by a couple, rather than two winged males, is a west-Greek, probably Locrian type.[32] Aphrodite's car on the Tarentine arula thus corresponds to the car drawn by a winged pair on type 10/2 P 4 (Hermes, Aprodite, and the chariot).

---

[31] Wuilleumier (1935) p. 433—for illustrations see his pl. XLI, 5 and 6.
[32] Zancani Montuoro (1968).

Type 10/2 P 4 cannot represent a birth of Aphrodite because Aphrodite there looks back toward Hermes: Figures entering the world invariably look forward or upward. This Aphrodite must then be going on a journey, perhaps to the new bride. If the new bride is conceived as Persephone, Hermes would be present in his role as *psychopompos*, conductor between the worlds of life and death. If she is conceived as the mortal bride, Hermes would prepare for his role as conductor from the maternal to the paternal home; in other words he would be here as an emblem of the wedding.

Type 10/1 P 1 (Hermes facing Aphrodite) would in any case represent an earlier stage in the story: Hermes comes to summon Aphrodite to the journey. She there bears Eros on her arm as the emblem of the sexual power she is to bestow. (The representation is not so literal that she would have to be shown carrying him at every stage.) This does not explain why Eros is holding a lyre—but the lyre has specific connections with certain views of the happy afterlife—as on the Boston Throne.[33] And the end of the journey would be on type 10/12 P 56, where two female figures stand toe to toe (Prückner [1968], pl. 11.3) while one presents to the other a small standing winged Eros (Quagliati [1908], fig. 42). In other words, we have now identified three types of *pinax* that portray Aphrodite's active role in the consecration of the bride.

All this would suggest—which we might well have guessed anyway, even without this material from other representations—that in the little temple on type 3/6 P 2 (the *proteleia*) the goddess with Hermes is Aphrodite. We have plenty of material for the joint cult of these two; confining myself to the epigraphic material I note instances from Cnidos, and Priene.[34] This last is particularly interesting in that the dedication is made by an *agoranomos*; normally such dedications at Priene were made to Hermes alone, but here to Hermes and Aphrodite together. We remember the political aspect of Peitho;[35] it looks as if Plutarch (*Moralia* 138c) was not wrong to link Hermes and Peitho.

In any case we have no difficulty in associating Aphrodite and Hermes with the wedding ceremony. The fourth day of the month, which was particularly fit for a wedding (*Works and Days* 800) was sacred to Aphrodite and Hermes (Proclus ad loc. cit.) or to Hermaphrodite (Theophrastus *Characters* 16), who seems to have started as a combination of Hermes and Aphrodite, but in Roman times was recognized as

---

[33] The lyre is an attribute not uncommonly given to the heroized dead (Neutsch 1961b).

[34] Hiller von Gärtringen (1906), p. 35, #183; Paris and Holleaux (1885), p. 78, # 8; Kaibel (1878), p. 317, # 783.

[35] See p. 66.

their child (Ovid *Metamorphoses*), as Cicero recognized Mercury and Venus as the parents of Love (*De Natura Deorum* 111.23.60). Hermes and Aphrodite are both involved with marriages not (pace Prückner) because they themselves are a couple but because their functions are both needed.

We therefore (to return to type 3/6 P 2) need not be puzzled by a representation of the *proteleia* as taking place at a sanctuary of Aphrodite and Hermes. The question is this: What has this cult to do with the cult of Persephone? Here it is worth noticing that Pausanias (8.31.6) reports from Megalopolis a sanctuary of Aphrodite that had in it wooden (which is to say archaizing) statues of both Aphrodite and Hermes; this sanctuary was within the sanctuary of the Great Goddesses (Demeter and her daughter). At Samos (Buschor 1957) there was within the precinct of Hera a temple, evidently only a small building, with a statue of Hermes, and another small temple of Aphrodite containing her image along with an image of Hermes. (This last is particularly significant in the present context because of the many links between Samos and Locri.) It would seem that type 3/6 P 2 represents just such a small temple at Locri, possibly within the precinct of Persephone—although Orsi found no trace of such a structure in the Mannella. Or the artist could have created an imaginary temple in order to make clear the gods receiving the libation.

We can imagine that the precincts at Megalopolis and on Samos, sacred to goddesses, were much visited by women (although the Heraion at Samos, one of the first of the great sanctuaries to be elaborated and achieve something like Panhellenic status, was much more than a women's place). A sanctuary included within a sanctuary suggests a subordinate rite; I would suggest that in all three places—Megalopolis, Samos, and Locri—an altar of Aphrodite with Hermes was set aside for the *proteleia*. A sacrifice at a subordinate shrine would put the marriage under the patronage of the great goddess whose sanctuary it was (Hera at Samos, the Great Goddesses at Megalopolis) while at the same time putting the couple in contact with the particular gods whose help was needed to carry through the wedding.

Types: Persephone Enthroned

At Locri and only at Locri we find a joint cult of Aphrodite and Persephone.[36] We are entitled to ask the meaning of this juxtaposition.

---

[36] Pugliese Caratelli (1990) refers several times to a parallel at Cnidos, but I find nothing in Iris Love's preliminary reports to justify this assertion.

We may begin by observing that Megalopolis and Samos are in a way the problem. Neither Demeter nor Hera is particularly appropriate as patron of the institution of marriage. Demeter looks on at the wedding from the point of view of the mother of the bride, for whom the transfer of the bride is pure loss; Hera stands for the rights of the wife (and as such is an effective emblem of sovereignty) but her marriage with Zeus is infertile, full of quarrels, and constantly dishonored by Zeus's infidelities. Normally, as we have seen,[37] the *proteleia* is made to Artemis or to some Artemis-like maiden; in such cases the bride makes contact with the eternal maiden to take farewell of her maidenhood (as when she gives it to a river) and seems to look back with her own sense of loss. Persephone becomes a bride when she is carried off from the world of the living; it might seem that she too experiences marriage as a loss of all that makes life worthwhile. By this reading we might see Persephone as the perfect type of the Hyperborean maidens as we find them on Delos: the maiden who leaves maidenhood only for death.

The *pinakes*, however, give a very different picture. They are full of life: ritual processions; packing and unpacking of boxes; women bathing, making up, picking fruit, tending roosters, playing flutes. In contrast to the "orthodox" version, further, the Locrian version of the Persephone story is most obviously characterized by two absences: Demeter does not appear, and Persephone does not come back.[38] Instead she is represented as transformed to regal status in the underworld. The second most popular group of *pinax* types—next to scenes of abduction—were those which represented the goddess enthroned (Zancani's group 8, types 8/1–8/44). Sometimes she is alone, sometimes with a consort (but he is never represented by himself); sometimes she is greeted by gods who stand before her with their attributes, and sometimes there are other figures, who may be mortal worshippers. The one continuing representation, however, which runs through this entire group and gives it its character, is Persephone seated on her throne, usually holding one or more attributes.

For more than a millennium the enthroned figure (often facing standing worshippers) had been in the eastern Mediterranean a symbol of divine sovereignty. It seems clear that Persephone's story, which be-

[37] See p. 111.

[38] Demeter's presence has been argued on one type—10/6 P 124 (cf. Prückner [1968]). But even if Prückner's interpretation of this scene is correct—he derives it from the text of the *Hymn to Demeter*—the existence of one *pinax* reflecting an "orthodox" version would hardly affect the main point, which is that the *pinakes* as a whole reflect an "unorthodox" version. Similarly, one rare type represents Europa and the Bull—another abduction story; this does not make that story in any particular sense Locrian, or link the Locrians to Crete (pace Torelli [1976].

gins (as elsewhere) with her abduction, ends at Locri with her secure installation as queen of the dead, honored by and among the gods. She is transformed from Kore, the beautiful helpless maiden, to Persephone (Periphona, to use her Locrian name), who appears in Greek mythology from Homer (*Od.*, 11.633–635) onward as a figure of dark power, not the prey of Hades but its sovereign. The question of the *pinakes* can then be restated thus: What could be meant by a representation of marriage through this story of death and transfiguration?

Persephone marries death. In *proteleia* stories of the Hyperborean maiden type, the link between marriage and death is expressed as a substitution; here it appears as a condensation. In those stories death mirrors only the negative aspect of marriage, as a departure; the ritual then repairs the myth (the Delian girls, unlike the Hyperboreans, survive their marriage). At Locri the ritual apparently rather recapitulated the myth: The Locrian bride became a representation of Persephone, as this world represented the other. This shift was possible at Locri because death and marriage were there both positively evaluated, both understood as translations to a better life. This is the "Orphic" aspect of the *pinakes*.

Often we cannot tell on the *pinakes* whether the representation is of this world or the next; both are women's worlds of house and garden, furniture, dishes, basketry, and fabrics. Hell is a city very like Seville. Persephone survives the abduction to achieve a new life, both honored and comfortable.

These representations thus use the myth of Persephone to catch both the terror of marriage—the dislocation of transfer from father to husband—and its triumph, the transformation of the bride into the matron, sovereign of her domestic dominion. The two groups of types that mirror this duality—Persephone abducted, Persephone enthroned—in fact constitute between them the great majority of surviving *pinakes*.

Types: Presentation to Persephone

This reading of the *pinakes* allows us to go back to the earliest interpretation of them as representations of the fate of the soul, without losing the more recent interpretations that see them as representations of myth and ritual relevant to marriage. The two readings need not be taken as mutually exclusive; an analogical reading allows these two sets of themes not merely to coexist but to interpenetrate. Such analogies are particularly possible in a Greek city because of the many parallels that the Greeks accepted between wedding and funeral.[39] The myrtle was a bridal wreath, but it also grew on tombs.[40] Or take the great highly wrought door that appears on a number of *pinax* types, framing the royal couple enthroned or the maiden who adorns herself; it is important enough as a separable symbol to have a type to itself: 7/4 P 137. Is this the door to the wedding chamber or to the tomb? Both in Greek are called *thalamos*.

In her first paper (which she later disowned), Zancani still adhered to the party of eschatology.[41] This paper is on type 8/29 P 30, the type I chose early in this chapter to exemplify diverse analyses. The type is known from fragments of more than six examples,[42] probably of more than a dozen; the mold was recut more than once, altering fine points of detailing. (One of these recuts was more radical, either eliminating the small female figure in the center or relocating her.) The type represents a female, surely Persephone, seated on a thin cushion on an elaborate throne with side panels representing sphinxes. Her hair is carefully arranged inside a headband or wreath and hangs down her back. She is rather formally clothed in a peplos and mantle which covers her arms down to the forearm; she sits in a pose of calm dignity. In her right hand she holds, face up, a shallow dish, evidently the *phialē mesomphalos* typically associated with figures of the dead or the gods of the dead receiving offerings. From her left hand rises an elaborate floral stylization, looking like metalwork or the decorations on marble architectural elements. (A very similar design is in fact to be found on the statue base represented on 3/6 P 2.) At the top there is a flower, a rose or lotus, very like that held by Aphrodite on type 10/1 P 1 (Aphrodite facing Hermes).

Facing her, so close as to brush her knees with her garment, stands a smaller figure, probably, by the delicacy of the features and clothing, a girl not yet arrived at puberty. This figure is wrapped in a cloak which leaves her head uncovered but covers her left hand; with her right hand she deposits in the phiale a rough-textured sphere. She looks the goddess in the face, and on some examples her finger touches a frond from the floral ornament.

Behind her stands a warrior, fully armed (except that, like everyone on the *pinakes* except Hermes, he is barefoot); he wears greaves, carries a shield, and has a helmet pushed up to reveal his face. With his right hand he holds up a cock in a gesture of offering.

[39] See p. 328.
[40] Chirassi (1968), pp. 22–23.
[41] Zancani Montuoro (1935).
[42] Ibid., p. 196.

The identification of this armed figure as Ares has made it possible to assimilate this type to Zancani's group 8: various gods before enthroned Persephone—or, more frequently, before Persephone and Hades enthroned together.

Presumably *pinakes* of this general type enabled worshippers to associate with their worship of Persephone in her precinct some other god especially meaningful to themselves. The gods so represented are: Hermes, Dionysus, the Dioscuri, Apollo, Athena, and Triptolemus. All are readily recognizable, and all, with the exception of the last (one fragment) are known to have been objects of cult at Locri. Often there is associated with the god a female figure carrying a gift—a ball, a box, a perfume flask, a cock. Presumably this figure represents the worshipper herself, who is thus shown joining with some god in worship of Persephone.

To include Ares among the gods so represented seems odd; Ares is not a god who in the normal way received the worship of the Greeks. As he is hated by the gods in Homer, so he is as a rule neglected by mankind; we do hear of some altars, temples, and images of Ares (not many), but I know of no evidence of personal piety toward him. A Greek warrior would pray to Athena or Apollo—or even Dionysus, who had his warlike aspect. Nor is there any evidence for a cult of Ares at Locri.[43] That a Locrian maiden should appeal to Ares in her dedication to Persephone seems in the last degree anomalous.

Zancani Montuoro (1935) originally interpreted the scene as the judgment of the soul before Persephone. In this context she pointed out that elsewhere certain specifically chthonic attributes are sometimes associated with Ares, namely the torch and the cock, also that Pausanias mentions a temple of Ares in the precinct of Demeter at Hermione (11.35.10) along with temples of Chthonia and Clymeneus, underworld deities. Zancani also draws attention to the Homeric *Hymn to Ares* (often thought "Orphic") where the god, so far from being the savage outlaw of Homer, is seen as a protector of justice against violence and is implored to send peace. Zancani later withdrew her general interpretation (although she retained the identification of the armed figure with Ares). I should here like to revive it, with the support of two items. The first is a cantharus from Nola by the Amphitrite Painter now in the British Museum (*ARV2* 832 #37). Here we have to the left a female enthroned, identified by her crown as a queen, enveloped in a cloak which is over her head and covers her hands. The back of her throne is decorated with a bird's head exactly like the

---

[43] Pindar *10th Olympian* 14–15 is no more evidence for a cult of Ares than for a cult of Calliope.

throne on the *pinax*, and she is surely Persephone. Before her stands a naked bearded man; the wheel to the right identifies him as Ixion. His left wrist is held by Hermes, clearly identified by his attributes; his right wrist is held by an armed man, barefoot like the armed man on the *pinax*. Quite evidently we have here Ixion come to judgment. Hermes is present as conductor of souls; the other figure might be Kratos or Bia, infernal servants; he has been identified as Ares, but if so he is a chthonic Ares (like Ares at Hermione). One thinks of the *phulax*, the guard on the Hipponion tablet—and this latter is my second item. I propose an identification of the armed man on the *pinax* with the *phulax* on the tablet; in this case the *pinax* represents the last stage of the "great journey" whose first stage is described on the tablet. The soul there is told to appeal to the guard, who then acts as guide to Persephone's throne.[44]

The maiden on the *pinax* offers a sphere. Zancani originally took this as a celestial sphere or a symbol of the cosmic egg—a suggestion taken up and developed by Otto Brendel (1936). It seems simpler to see it merely as an emblem of maidenhood. The *sphaira* is already associated with maidens in the *Odyssey*, where Nausicaa, resembling Artemis among her nymphs, plays at ball with her girls (*Od.* 6.99–109). Groups of nymphs may be represented playing ball; the Arrephoroi had set aside for them on the Acropolis a play-yard called *sphaistrion* ([Plut.] X orat. IV, p. 839c). The ball, like other toys, was typically dedicated by the maiden about to be married, as in the epigram of Timareta, quoted above;[45] clay balls are found among the dedications of the Mannella sanctuary.[46] It would seem probable that here the soul of the dead maiden dedicates to immortal Persephone the same toy that the living maiden, had she lived to marry, would have dedicated in the terrestrial sanctuary of Persephone.[47] It would seem, in other words, that here as elsewhere the reception of the unmarried girl among the dead is seen as a substitute for her marriage, and an image of it.

In this connection I would like to suggest one further interpretation: that the floral ornament is meant as a plastic representation of perfume. I know of no iconographic parallel; Empedocles, however, refers to *muroi daidaleodmoi* (DK 128), using for perfume an epithet proper to plastic arts. Women often hold floral sprays or emblems, but in this case a close examination of Persephone's hand[48] shows that she is not

[44] A later tablet—Zuntz's (1971) A 2—makes the explicit claim (l. 6) "now I have come as a suppliant before pure Persephone."

[45] See p. 314; cf. Prückner (1968), n.371.

[46] Zancani Montuoro (1935), p. 208.

[47] Sourvinou-Inwood (1978).

[48] Zancani Montuoro (1935), fig. 1.

holding the ornament; rather it rises from her partially open hand. The tendril that touches the finger of the girl as she drops the ball is also represented as extended more in the manner of vapor than anything solid. Perfume I take to be an emblem of mature sexuality (as on the Ludovisi Throne); here the sharing of the perfume with a girl who dedicates a token of maidenhood may be taken as representative of an initiation to womanhood.

It is tempting to take 8/29 P 30 as intended for dedication on behalf of girls who, on the "Hyperborean" model, had died before marriage and were therefore eternal maidens, or married only to Hades. But we have no way to be sure that *pinax* types represented with this kind of literalness the occasion of their dedication. Equally plausibly we might think that this type would be chosen by those who, like the young girl buried with the Hipponion tablet, had received "Orphic" instruction concerning the *phulax* and the journey to Persephone. In any case the analogy between marriage and death, which is the core of the Persephone story, presumably pervaded every aspect of her cult; therefore it is quite plausible to believe that a girl could dedicate on the occasion of her marriage a *pinax* representing the reception of a maiden's spirit into Hades. The *pinakes*, in other words, are evidence for the relation between certain themes in Locrian wedding ideology—between capture and transfiguration, for instance, and between sacrifice and empowerment—but this relation to Locrian life is one of whole to whole, in the sense that the whole system of themes was (one must assume) generally meaningful to the Locrians; it will be much more difficult to establish particular relationships of part to part.

Types: Invitations to Ritual

Perfume recurs on the *pinakes* in the form of the thymaterion, the incense burner (usually on a long stem as on the Ludovisi Throne) which appears on a number of types—for instance, 8/31 P 86 (see plate 20), where it stands by the throne of the royal couple Hades and Persephone. The ball also recurs on quite a number of types; on 8/25 P 112 and 8/26 P 113 Dionysus appears with a worshipper before the enthroned Persephone; the worshipper holds cock and ball. On type 8/20 P 107, by contrast, the offerings have already changed hands; Dionysus is here without any worshipper before the enthroned couple; Hades holds the ball and Persephone the cock.

Then there are types 5/19 P 31, 5/20 P 32, and 5/21 P 33. Here we have two women facing one another. We can take 5/19 P 31 (see plate 21) as typical of the group. Here the woman to the right is seated on an armless chair with a birdshead back, a more modest version of the throne we have been seeing on the types just discussed. She wears a layered flowing garment and a mantle which comes up over the top of her head but leaves her ears exposed; we have seen this style on 8/31 P 86 (Persephone and Hades enthroned). It flows down over her elbows but without the tight wrapping characteristic of the enthroned Persephone. Altogether her pose is relatively informal. She holds in her left hand a curiously shaped vessel, evidently of metal, with a pointed base. With her right hand she lets drop, or possibly reaches for, a plain rod which floats in the field as if in midair.

The standing woman on the left, dressed in a peplos without mantle, holds in her right hand a ball, in her left a cock (in type 5/20 P 32 the left hand holds out a sleeve full of fruit or flowers). These offerings are like those on types 8/25 P 112 and 8/26 P 113; it therefore seems natural to take the scene as another representation of a worshipper before Persephone. These types, however, lack the hieratic quality of group 8.[49] The scene is rather given a certain domesticity by the ewer and flat vessels (probably baskets) hung on the wall, and by the *kibotos*, chest on legs, which stands between the figures with a folded cloth on top of it, and on top of the cloth, a box.

Beneath the *kibotos* there is a creature: a goose (5/19 P 31), a hen (5/20 P 32), a siren (5/21 P 33).[50] The siren would seem to place us firmly in the other world, and establishes a tension with the generally informal and domesticated tone of these representations. Once again the line between this world and the next is blurred. This ambiguity, I am again suggesting, goes to the heart of the meaning of the *pinakes*.

We have met the pointed vessel and rod before: in the hands of the woman (in a costume very like that on type 5/19 P 31) who follows the wedding procession on 7/3 P 3. This woman with rod and vessel appears elsewhere: for instance, on type 5/3 P 16 (see plate 22), where she walks in front of four maidens who in single file carry a peplos (the opening for the neck is visible) wound around and among them. She appears again on a whole group, of which we may take 5/6 P 19 as typical: Here she follows a maiden who carries a folded fabric on her head; between them is a thymaterion topped by a rooster. In other words, she is a figure with ritual responsibilities. The vessel and rod she carries suggest lustration, and the transporting of the cloth suggests some ritual involving it—possibly a bridal ritual (so Zancani Montuoro [1960]) or an offering to a god (so Prückner [1968]).

Types 5/19 P 31, 5/20 P 32, and 5/21 P 33 therefore represent ei-

---

[49] As remarked by Sourvinou-Inwood (1978).
[50] I know of no illustration that shows this last and rely on Prückner here.

ther a soul approaching Persephone in a setting less formal than that of an enthronement, or a maiden making some offering as part of a this-world ritual, probably having to do with marriage. If the latter, the woman with the mantle over her head is probably the *numpheutria*, the matron responsible for the conduct of the wedding.[51] If the former, it would seem that the girl is asking that Persephone herself perform the office of *numpheutria*—a role I have elsewhere identified with Peitho.[52]

The ambiguity of the representation may seem less strange when one considers that each of those transactions is in a way a representation of the other. A maiden who brings her offering in order to set in motion some ritual, in that she does something sacred, approaches the god. Conversely we represent in the person of the gods the ideal types and defining ideas of our cultural forms. Persephone is goddess of marriage because she is the representative bride, and once she has become the representative matron she can guide the marriages of others. The bride, further, enters a new life; this also can be read in either direction. We may think of marriage as a prefiguration of death—or we can understand death by extrapolating from our experience of the passages from life to life in this life. Analogies are about both sameness and difference, and every analogy is readable in both directions.

The Representation of the Dead

To die is to become a representation—by which I mean that the dead person survives as an idea, a name, and a presence in the memory of the living. The concrete embodiment of such survival is the ghost, for instance the Homeric psyche which, when it appears in dreams or elsewhere, is an image of the person and "looks wonderfully like him" (*Il.* 23.107).

Every god, as a representation, is the concrete embodiment of an idea, and as such, like all ideas, immortal. Every death, as it transforms the person into an idea, is a transfiguration. The hero both dies and also lives forever; he is a mortal god. But so are we all, since we are all mortal to ourselves and yet survive with the others.

Death also is a life stage—or at least that is what culture makes of it; the funeral is an initiation. The dead person becomes one of the eternal ancestors, which is a kind of deification. But then every initiation is a kind of deification, in that it transforms the person in society into an embodiment of the ideal of that transformation. Every girl as she mar-

---

[51] Type 7/1 P 42 represents the preparation of the marriage bed, a task we know to have been elsewhere proper to the *numpheutria*.

[52] Cf. p. 71.

ries becomes the typical bride; every youth as he completes his training and takes the oath becomes the typical warrior. It is only the next step to say that she becomes Persephone, he, Apollo.

If every initiation is a deification it follows that initiations are privileged occasions of contact between mortal and god; the powers released in initiations may be turned to a variety of social purposes.[53] In more secular language we could say that these rituals establish a relation between the actuality of social life and its ideal forms. The whole occasion consists of a play of representations; the mortal represents the god in the ritual and the god in the myth represents what the mortal is become. It is as a reflection of this fundamental theological epistemology that representations of all kinds become a privileged group of dedications—because, if to establish contact with the god is to become a representation, then, by inversion, every representation, because it is an idealization, establishes contact with the gods. If the representation is of god or worshipper—and it need not be—then we have a representation of a representation in an elaboration of the play of representations.

Death is the greatest of life stages, and the greatest of initiations is the funeral. No wonder the plastic representations used for tomb markers are so often indistinguishable from dedications. The most obvious examples are the *kouroi* and *korai*. I have said that as dedications these sculptures were primarily objects of value. As tomb markers they surely represent the dead person, but to represent the dead in this idealized form is in a way to assert that the dead have become objects of value—particularly through death in battle or, for a woman, death at the age of marriageability. These youthful dead are in a way sacrifices; they become immortal as they are carried off to the ideal. The co-occurrence of the two great life changes, adulthood and death, has doubled the charge on their initiation and has made them into monuments.

Another group of monuments, more relevant to the *pinakes*, are those which present enthroned figures holding attributes. These have been interpreted as grave markers, or else as dedications to heroes; they are found in many places; Blümel (1963) lists among the earliest a probably Parian relief from the mid-sixth century of an enthroned male figure, holding (most probably) three ears of corn, and another circa 520 from Thasos which presents an enthroned woman, seated on a cushion, barefoot, with a dove in her left hand and another object, perhaps a flower, in her right. These and others like them are the most direct iconographic source for the *pinakes* of Zancani's group 8. Most

---

[53] Cf. Redfield (1990).

relevant, in consideration of the many close relations between Sparta and Locri, are the examples from Sparta; here and here only in old-world Greece we find the representation of an enthroned *couple*.

These Spartan reliefs are archaic, some possibly as early as the seventh century, more likely all dating from the sixth century. They are in a rough popular style, not unlike the earliest metopes from the Heraion by the Sele, but executed with less finesse. Tod and Wace (1906) review seven archaic Spartan reliefs representing enthroned couples. The most famous is the Chrysaphe relief (see plate 23), which may be taken as typical of the set. An ornamented throne, with lions-feet legs and a back ending in a palmette, contains two enthroned figures. The male, who is nearer to us, turns towards us. His hair is trained in four long braids which fall across his shoulders and back; he is wearing a heavy garment, which is apparently draped across his body (it leaves the left shoulder, the shoulder closest to us, bare), and sandals. In his left hand he holds a large cantharus; his right hand is held out above this with the palm flat toward us, as if in a gesture of greeting. The female figure behind him holds up with her left hand her mantle beside her face in a familiar bridal gesture. In her right hand she holds a pomegranate.

Behind the throne, stretched out along the whole length of the back with its head thrust over the top, is a serpent. Beneath the cantharus are two tiny figures—less than knee-high to the enthroned couple—bearing offerings; the man has a cock in his right hand, the woman a stylized flower. Each has something else in the left hand, probably fruit.

The serpent places us in the underworld. The difference of scale of the figures should be the difference between gods and mortals. Evidently we have here a representation of the gods of the dead or the heroized dead approached by worshippers with appropriate offerings.

But which are they? Are the enthroned figures on the Chrysaphe relief dead, approached by their surviving relatives? Athenian funeral lekythoi often represent the dead man watching while women come to decorate his tomb. The long hair of the enthroned male here would seem to identify him as a Spartan. The problem is with the representation of the dead as a couple. To my knowledge the Greeks never (as the Etruscans did, and as we do) set up joint monuments for a married couple; a gravestone (or sepulchral inscription) was for one person. It would seem then that this is not a gravestone, and that the enthroned pair are the gods of the underworld, Hades and Persephone (or the same figures by other names); we remember that the *theoi meilichioi* were often a couple, chthonic Zeus and his consort.

But if the enthroned pair cannot be the dead person, the small figures approaching them cannot be that person either, since there are two of them also. Therefore they must be mortal worshippers. But if the gods of the dead are worth worshipping there must be something worthwhile about death; these gods are represented as happy (the cantharus, particularly associated with Dionysus, is an emblem of enjoyment), which in turn suggests the proposition that death is or could be a happy condition. Furthermore (and this is the link to the *pinakes*) the happiness of the gods of the dead has to do with the fact that they are a couple. This is the link between death and marriage.

The story of Persephone, represented on the Locrian *pinakes*, pictures marriage as death. The archaic Spartans (whose representations are echoed by the iconograpy on the *pinakes*) died, evidently, into an existence under the sign of marriage. The honored state of death is represented in both places by the enthroned couple. The analogy between life and death, further, works in both directions, since death, like marriage, is a *telos*, a perfection of the person. Gravestones and dedications in general are caught in the web of this double analogy, whereby the funeral is an initiation, and every initiation a death and rebirth. It is not that the two worlds are fully isomorphic; only those moments in this life which perfect the person, which rescue us from time, which achieve for a moment the ideal, foretell the eternal life to come. Such moments are appropriate for representation; such representations will float uncertainly between this world and the next.

In these terms we can understand the representations of the family groups on Attic tombstones.[54] Sometimes one figure is clearly meant to stand for the deceased; in other cases it is not so obvious. Often the dead and the living are represented together. The scene does not represent a particular moment of interaction but rather an enduring relation which defines the parties, in death as in life. It represents the perfection of the deceased, the enduring existence of a personality perfected in its relations.

Similarly we can understand the representations on tombstones of the adornment of women.[55] We have, for instance, Attic grave reliefs on which a seated woman is approached by a girl holding a box or something else; two south Italian tombstones show very similar scenes.[56] The Italian scenes include the motif of the mirror, which is characteristic of the *pinakes* group 6; these latter show a maiden with a mirror adorning herself, most often with a handmaiden, once also with Eros (6/4 P 41). On the tombstones the women are framed by the outlines of a *naiskos*;

---

[54] See Friis Johansen (1951).

[55] The parallels with the *pinakes* are particularly striking here, although the tombstones known to me are too late to be cited as iconographic sources for the *pinakes*.

[56] Pagenstecher (1911), pl. Xa, b, c; pl. IXa, c.

that is, they are placed in a little building like a temple, which seems to represent the tomb. On the *pinakes* this motif is absent; instead we have in the background the elaborate door—which, as I noted, ambiguously represents the tomb and the bridal chamber.

Much of the detail in these scenes—gestures, garments, objects—can be matched on the Attic weddings material, particularly scenes on vases by the school of the Meidias painter and others, representing the adornment of the bride. If we ask why such a scene should be put on a tombstone, the short answer, perhaps, is that the Greeks adorned women in order to turn them into monuments. At the moment of her marriage the woman is represented as her ideal self; this representation is called in Greek her *kosmos*. The adornment is the actualization of an eternal order, the revelation of an essence. It is as such an ideal form that she transcends her particularity; as such she is immortal and deserves to be represented to the memory.

The Locrian maidens who dedicated group 6 *pinakes* may have thought of them as representing the adornment of Persephone for her bridal, either in myth or ritual, or they may have thought of them as representations of their own adornment; in either case they dedicated them to Persephone, most probably on the occasion of their own weddings. They thereby sanctified the wedding by revealing its essence as an enactment and a representation of an eternal pattern. And thereby they also sanctified the marriage, seen from the woman's point of view as the transfiguration of the bride.

The most frequent types of *pinakes*, as we have seen, are those representing the abduction of the maiden; the next most frequent type are those representing the enthroned woman or couple. The third largest group are those which represent (evidently) some kind of ritual—indeed it is not an exaggeration to say that all of the remaining types may be taken to represent a ritual or metonymically to allude to such a representation. These objects were dedicated as a ritual act, and they represent the meaning of their own use.

These "third group" *pinakes* in large part form an iconographic bridge between the major themes of the set: abduction and enthronement. They document, in other words, the acts that accomplished the transformation from maiden to matron.

I shall not attempt here a detailed analysis of these types; for our purposes it is enough to notice that certain motifs recur, in a variety of combinations. There is, for example, the lustral vessel with rod—usually in the hands of a matronly figure, sometimes in the hands of a maiden. Much is made of the handling of fabrics; these go in and out of ornamented boxes, are seen laid by, are carried folded or unfolded. There are scenes of the adornment of maidens, and others that seem to suggest or represent bathing (3/1 P 138, 6/1 P 44). On one type (7/1 P 42) a bed is being prepared. The easiest interpretation of all this material (and this has indeed consistently been Zancani's view) is that we have here phases of wedding ritual (Zancani calls it the mythical wedding of Persephone); we know that Greek weddings involved fabrics, bathing, adornment, and of course the wedding bed. Confirmatory is the fact that these types represent women alone, or sometimes with a boy in their company; Greek weddings were conducted by women, but sometimes also involved a boy.

Then there are the scenes that evidently involve something offered. The ball, as we have seen, is frequently carried or presented (sometimes it is just there as an attribute); many plaques picture roosters, often as an attribute, but sometimes as loose fowl. On six types (1/11–14, 16–17, P 140–145) the representation consists of the rooster alone; on one (1/15 P 146) we find a hen with chicks. The rooster seems generally in Greece to have been the modest blood sacrifice offered by private persons; it is easy to believe that the sacrifice of a rooster was an aspect of the Locrian *proteleia*. Finally there are scenes of women picking fruit or flowers; these also are proper to the wedding.

Most striking is type 4/3 P 45 (see plate 24). To the left is a tree with leaves, flowers, and fruit. A maiden picks flowers from it; some are in her sleeve, others in a calathos. To the right, somewhat more elaborately dressed, is a young woman seated on a natural mound or rock. She is gazing downward at the flowers she holds, not looking about her or at the maiden. The closest Attic parallel to her pose is on the name piece of the Lyandros Painter (ARV2 835.1): On the interior of this white-ground kylix is depicted a woman seated on a delicately ornamented throne, by her a thymaterion; two erotes fly to crown her with a wreath and *tainia* while she contemplates a flower crown. This last seems to be a sign that she is in love (Aristophanes *Thesmophoriazusae* 400–401) as she is obviously blessed with the powers of the beloved. So on type 4/3 P 45 a friend or servant gathers flowers with which to crown the maiden, who herself seems lost in thought. This contemplative moment reminds us that in their representation of marriage the *pinakes* depict not only the transformation of women but the happiness of women.

Thus we come to type 10/11 P 50 (see plate 25).[57] To the left is a fruit tree; before it stand a *klinē* and a small table. On the cushions recline a youth and a maiden. The youth is to the right, propped on

---

[57] I know of no published drawing or photograph of this type. I reproduce not a scientific reconstruction but a rough drawing by Biff Atlass (whom I thank) based on fragments on display in Reggio.

his left arm. His upper body is naked; a cloak thrown over his arm covers his lower body. His left hand holds a cup; his right hand, resting on his upper thigh, is concealed by the maiden. She half sits, half lies at the foot of the *klinē*. She leans back against several cushions and her legs hang down. She is dressed in a chiton with a cloak thrown around her lower body. She plays the double flute. Both look toward the tree, which spreads its branches over their heads. A small Eros scrambles up the trunk and holds out a fruit. A second flies over their head, hands stretched downward (the contents of the hands are lost). Both of these turn toward the maiden.

The man's pose and costume are those proper to a symposium. Therefore it seems natural to identify the woman as a flute girl/prostitute: It is an axiom of much modern scholarship that free Greek women took no part in the symposium, that it was a masculine occasion where masculine values were asserted, where women were present only to serve the men. Clearly this is not literally a symposium, since (as the word implies) that requires a plurality of men drinking together, and here there is only one. But for those who believe in ritual prostitution at Locri (see appendix), this *pinax* represents the employment for that institution of the decor of the symposium: the feasting male is about to enjoy the free girl who plays the flute for him. That she is quite respectably dressed would then be consistent with her anomalous social position: prostitute for a day, and *parthenos* afterward.

There exists, however, a close parallel to type 10/11 P 50, a generation or two older: It was found on Samos and originated in Sparta (and thus belongs to the Locri/Samos/Sparta triangle) and no one has ever asserted that ritual prostitution was an institution in either of those places. This item is a fragmentary cup by the Arkesilas Painter, and represents a symposium being held in the open air (see plate 26). A bearded man reclines to the right, looking left; his upper body appears to be naked. He holds a flat cup in either hand; there is a ribbon in his long hair that hangs down. To our left a woman reclines against a double cushion. She wears a bordered chiton and a soft conical hat, colored purple by the painter. Her hair strays down her back and shoulder. She is playing the double flute. Above them, across the top of the scene, is a row of pomegranates, hanging down like a fringe. There flies toward the couple an Eros; he holds in his right hand the fruit and flower of the pomegranate, and with his left reaches out to touch the lips of the flute player. There is also at least one other reclining couple, similar although without the winged figure.

On the exterior of the cup (Diehl [1964], fig. 31b) there are figured pomegranate trees, with roosters around them (another subject that recurs on the *pinakes*); one of these is being picked up by a bearded man with long hair in a long garment which enfolds him from shoulder to ankle.

Their long hair identifies the men as Spartans. This is one of a number of Laconian II cups representing symposia. The others are more conventional—that is to say, more like those we know from Attic pottery; the feast is placed indoors, for instance. There is one other female flute player crowned by Eros; otherwise the figures are male. It seems likely that this pottery was made for use at symposia, perhaps the symposia represented on the cups. Pipili, who first suggested Spartan banquets in honor of Artemis Orthia, now prefers to see represented here a Samian ritual banquet in honor of Hera. In support of this interpretation she cites a group of Attic black-figure vases from the Heraion on Samos, most of them unpublished, "decorated with rich symposia with men and women."[58]

Men and women at symposia are not necessarily prostitutes and their clients. There were Greek ritual occasions when men and free women feasted together—weddings, certainly, and probably funerals. The seating arrangements on such occasions are unclear, and probably varied. Such ceremonial feasts were not technically symposia, but symposia were not the only occasions on which men ate and drank reclining. One Hellenistic source suggests that one normal arrangement when husband and wife dined together was for the husband to recline while the wife sat on a chair by his feet (Lucian *Lucius* 2). Exactly this pose is from the fourth century onward one of the most familiar types of funeral relief. Sometimes on the funeral reliefs the woman (like the woman on 10/11 P 50) is seated on the couch itself, toward the foot. These women are generally taken to represent the wives of the deceased;[59] they certainly do not look at all like prostitutes. On the well-known cup of the Codros Painter in the British Museum (*ARV* 1269.3) the gods, arranged in married couples (Zeus and Hera, Poseidon and Amphitrite, Hades and Persephone, Dionysus and Ariadne, and also Ares and Aphrodite), adopt the same pose.[60]

Symposiastic enjoyment was for the Greeks—at least from the late fifth century onward—the most familiar representation of eternal bliss.[61] Hence the little terra-cottas of reclining figures; these are found everywhere: in tombs, in temples, in private houses, even in the *bothroi* of the

---

[58] Pipili (1995), p. 90.

[59] Denster (1982), p. 564.

[60] On a black-figure Dinos with stand in the British Museum signed by Sophilos as painter the guests arrive for the wedding of Peleus and Thetis, a mixed group of gods and goddesses; three couples (Zeus and Hera, Poseidon and Amphitrite, Ares and Aphrodite) arrive in separate chariots. Surely they would have expected to sit together?

[61] Denster (1982).

U-shaped stoa. Normally these figures are male, but sometimes, especially in the West, they are female.[62] Bell (1981, numbers 85–95) presents a group from Morgantina. Letta (1971, p. 257) presents some from Metapontum. Others are included in the material from Catania given preliminary publication by Rizza (1960, p. 256). Thus it appears that the symposiastic pose could also represent the eternal happiness of women.

From Locri we have a terra-cotta of the couple reclining together (see plate 27). Actually the woman is represented as sitting, in the sense that her feet dangle over the edge of the couch, but she is not sitting primly like the seated women on the later funerary reliefs. Here the couple lean into each other in a pose of domesticated intimacy.[63] Assuming that the symposiastic pose represents the happy dead, this Locrian object anticipates the relief representations of men and women feasting together and further develops the archaic representations of the happy dead as a couple, shifted now from the *thronos* to the *klinē*. Putorti (1929) argues that these Locrian representations are actually one source for Etruscan representations of couples.

Symposiastic enjoyment was also of course a fact of everyday life. There is thus a further question: Do these women reflect customary dining of women with men on certain occasions, and if so, on what occasions? For the Etruscans we are able to answer the first question in the affirmative with some confidence, since in connection with Etruscan tomb paintings of symposia enjoyed by quite respectable-looking couples (the "Tomb of the Leopard" in Tarquinia, among others) we have Aristotle's assertion (from his book *Etruscan Customs*) that "the Etruscans recline with their woman under the same blanket" (fr. 607 Rose).[64] For Greek cities literary evidence seems to be lacking, but it is tempting to think that something of this kind occurred in the U-shaped stoa[65]—although since dining rooms were provided there, type 10/11 P 50, a feast in the open air, cannot be a literal representation. But it is tempting to think that a feast for Aphrodite Meilichia might have brought

---

[62] Actually the earliest of all Greek representations of a reclining figure, that on the Geneleos monument (from late archaic Samos—a place which, as we have seen, had great influence on the Greek West) is female.

[63] The closest parallels to this pose are probably provided by the couples included in late-archaic groups from Cyprus: Denster (1982), figs. 128 and 132. In the Locri museum there is a fragmentary terra-cotta of the early fourth century. (Costamagna and Sabbione [1990], fig. 175) which represents a reclining bearded male, and leaning against him a female in polos (a goddess?) holding a standing child.

[64] Compare the late archaic Etruscan basin handle in the British Museum (bronze #562) of a couple reclining together, also the early classic votive group (bronze #498) of a man embracing a woman.

[65] Nilsson (1906), p. 375, mentions a festival of Aphrodite on Aegina celebrated with a banquet.

together men and flute-playing free women, and concluded with a dedication of the dinnerware in a *bothros*.

I proposed earlier an understanding of the Ludovisi Throne whereby the likeness between the *hetaira* and the young wife makes a point about the sexuality of wives. The reclining flute player on 10/11 P 50 shares her instrument with the *hetaira* from the Ludovisi Throne, but she is clothed like the wife. The flute is the instrument of passion and can madden, but it also plays a more sedate role; in its only other appearance on the *pinakes* (3/5 P 53) it is played soberly, before a little temple, evidently as a part of some ritual. I would suggest that the woman on 10/11 P 50 combines the two figures on the Ludovisi Throne, that she represents a sexual wife, and that the *pinax* is a representation of marital happiness. In a cultural context in which marriage is interpreted in eschatological terms it makes relatively little difference whether the scene is placed in this world or the next. In either case marriage is the true, the erotic, paradise.

This concludes my account of the *pinakes*. It has not been complete. Many types have been alluded to only in passing. I have not at all attempted to deal with the "baby in a basket" types (Zancani's type 9, P 5–11); I do not think it possible securely to link these to mythology, but am ready to accept Sourvinou-Inwood's (1978) suggestion that they must reflect a kourotrophic use of the sanctuary.[66] I have not attempted any explanation of type 8/38 P 129 which represents a solitary male figure on foot preceding his horse. I have mentioned only incidentally type 10/4 P 127, which apparently represents Europa and the bull. The *pinakes*, as I said, are not a closed set but an array; we can expect a range of variation that escapes our analysis. It does seem to me clear that the array as a whole has to do with the secular and sacred aspects of woman's life and woman's love, and that taken together these terracottas present us with an ideology of marriage as the central—indeed the cosmically binding—social institution.

Conclusion

This interpretation of the *pinakes* has had three aspects. First, I see the abduction and enthronement scenes as representations of the initiatory content of the wedding, from transfer to transformation. In this I relate the *pinakes* to the pervasive Greek understanding of marriage, its fundamental ambiguity—but with a degree of symmetry between the

---

[66] Francavilla types F10, F11, and especially F 12 should help in the interpretation of group 9.

two aspects which marks the Locrians apart by their explicit celebration of the honorable condition of the married woman.

Second, I have evoked an "Orphic" ideological context for these representations. Here again I see a Locrian use of pervasive Greek themes, particularly the parallel between wedding and funeral, and the notion of the bride of death. In the context of an eschatology of hope, however, these themes are reevaluated; as death becomes heroization and eternal happiness, so marital happiness becomes the this-world heroization of the couple, and especially of the bride.

Third, I have attempted to explore the notion that the couple stands— for the Greeks in general, and especially for the Locrians—as a symbol or instance of perfection, that this accounts for the tendency of Greek underworld powers to be represented as couples, and also provides the basis for an ideology of marriage peculiarly elaborated at Locri. Probably it is worth enunciating the obvious: that all this tells us nothing about the subjective success of Locrian marriages, the actual level of contentment, cooperation, or communication between couples there. What we rather see—or glimpse, through a glass darkly—is an ideological use of sexual complementarity as a principle that can provide cosmic validation for a social order, for a closed oligarchy conceived as kept stable through the circulation of valued brides.

It is in terms of this proposed ideology that I offer Locri as a possible third alternative to Athens and Sparta. At Athens the emphasis in the classical period was on the citizen and the collectivity of citizens, the *dēmos*, with women present as their wives and daughters, and the ritual order foregrounded collective events, parades and theatricals. At Sparta the emphasis was on the perfection of the Spartan males, and the ritual order foregrounded rites of male initiation, with women beside them as a kind of imperfect males. At Locri we know little of the ritual order; however, the only public rite for which we have direct evidence, that conducted at the U-shaped stoa, focused on small-group enjoyment and in this sense foregrounded the private sphere.

It remains to consider the relation of the Locrians to that counter-cultural tendency which in its Hellenistic developments asserted the primacy of the private sphere over public life: I mean philosophy. It is possible that in the U-shaped stoa we have an anticipation of Epicurus's garden.

EPILOGUE

Twelve

Pythagoras at the Locrian Frontier

WE begin with an anecdote quoted from a fourth-century B.C. source in the third-century A.D. neo-Pythagorean literature concerning the fate of Pythagoras after the massacre of his companions at Croton:

> Dicaearchus and the best sources say that Pythagoras survived the coup. . . . When the Friends had been overpowered, Pythagoras at first sought safe haven at Caulonia, and from there turned toward Locri. When the Locrians learned of this they sent certain elders to the frontier of their country. These met him and said: "We, Pythagoras, hear that you are a man both wise and able (*sophos kai deinos*). But since we find no fault with our own laws, we for our part will try to stand by our established order. Therefore go somewhere else, taking from us anything you might need."
>
> Since he was dismissed from the city of the Locrians in the manner described, he sailed to Taras. There he had an experience similar to that in Croton and so came to Metapontum. Everywhere, in fact, there were great public disorders, which even now they remember and narrate in those parts of the world, calling them "the anti-Pythagorean movement." (Porphyry *Life of Pythagoras* 56)

This concluding chapter is to be an explication of this anecdote. Once again, the actuality of the event need not, for our purposes, come into question; the anecdote states a relation between Locri and the prototypical philosopher, and thus is suggestive of the relation between the Locrian civic order and philosophy. The Locrians, we are told, spared themselves the anti-Pythagorean disorders because they, uniquely, refused to admit him in the first place. Their relation with the prototypical philosopher is stated both as a closeness (they respect Pythagoras and offer to assist him) and a distance (they keep him out). It is this ambiguous relation that our explication will seek to recover.

Hitherto we have compared Locri with Sparta in terms of similarity and difference. Sparta and Locri we saw as the two archaic model states, admired for their political stability by others if hardly imitated. Whereas, however, Sparta (at least in its visible aspect) founded its stability on male solidarity and the public sphere, which is to say, war, Locri founded its solidarity (insofar as we can deduce from hardly visible indications) on the mediation of sexual difference and on the private sphere, which is to say, marriage. We shall return to this contrast.

This difference, in turn, generated a parallelism between the Spartan relation to Crete and the Epizephyrian relation to old-world Locris. The Spartans found in Crete an archaic source and model for the solidarity of the warrior band; the Epizephyrians adopted a Locrian identity in that they found in Locris a model and source for a social order centering on marriage and on the value of the marriageable maiden. In both cases the developed city-state claimed both to continue a primitive (and therefore powerful) social form, and also to re-form it as the basis of a perfected society.

We now turn to the relation between Locri and philosophy, beginning with the observation that this relation also in its ambiguity involves a parallel with Sparta. Sparta was the preferred city of the philosophers, who (in late fifth-century Athens at least) often appeared in the company of the *philolakōn*, the lover of Sparta, longhaired and with ears broken from boxing (cf. Aristophanes *Birds* 1281ff: *elakōnomanoun . . . esokratoun*). The first systematic descriptions of Sparta, almost unrelievedly adulatory, issued from the Socratic circle, from Critias and Xenophon. In the Pythagorean tradition, also, we have the reference to Sparta as a political model in the fragments attributed by Stobaeus to Archytas of Taras, and quite possibly actually by him.

At the same time Sparta was well known to be the least philosophical, or at any rate the least intellectual, of societies. This point often lurks in Plato's mild irony, for instance when the Laws point out to Socrates that he liked to talk of the *eunomia* of Crete and Sparta but never wanted to live there (Plato *Crito* 52e), or where Socrates teases Hippias at length about the lack of interest shown by the Spartans in the new education; evidently they said to Hippias, much as the Locrian elders explained it to Pythagoras, that "it is not their inherited tradition to change their laws, nor to educate their sons differently from the received way" (Plato *Hippias Major* 284b). In the *Protagoras* (342a–343c) Socrates' irony takes the form of a comic fantasy: The Spartans (and the Cretans) only pretend to be stupid and actually philosophize in secret; their philosophy, however, issues only in proverbs! And we have seen above[1] that Sparta appears in the *Republic* as the timocratic state, lacking the true philosophical Muse.

Sparta could not be philosophical because she reached definitive form early, before philosophy, and remained conservative in intention—if less so in practice—thereafter. Such societies cannot welcome inquiries that put existing institutions in question, and since any inquiry might do so they must resist inquiry in general. Nevertheless, because Sparta did self-consciously achieve some kind of definitive

[1] Cf. p. 274.

form she provided a necessary point of reference when the philosophers inquired into the form of the city-state. Even Aristotle, no great admirer of Sparta, remarks: "Only in the city of the Lacedaemonians— or perhaps in a few others also—has the lawgiver paid attention to the rearing and habits of life of the people. In most cities the law is totally unconcerned with these things, and each lives as he pleases, like the Cyclopes legislating each for his own children and wife" (Aristotle *Nicomachean Ethics* 1180a; cf. *Politics* 1337a). Elsewhere (*Politics* 1333b) Aristotle makes it plain that the Spartans have mistaken the human Good; nevertheless they are, for him, one of those rare communities that, like the philosophical community, allow themselves to be collectively guided by *some* view of what is best for man.

Timaeus of Locri

Locri also appears in the philosophic literature, in the person of Plato's Timaeus. Socrates introduces him thus:

> Timaeus here, citizen of the best-lawed city—that is, Italian Locris—in property and birth second to none that is there, having taken his share of the greatest offices and honors of that city, has also in my judgment come to the highest peak of philosophy. (Plato *Timaeus* 20a)

The scholiast tells us that this Timaeus was a Pythagorean, and there are two persons named Timaeus in Iamblichus's catalogue of Pythagoreans, one ascribed to Croton, the other to Paros, perhaps a mistake for Locri.[2] On the other hand, this catalogue also includes Empedocles of Acragas, Parmenides of Velia, Zaleucus of Locri, and Abaris of Hyperborea. The Pythagoreans were capable of any amount of retrospective recruitment, and the narrator of Plato's great cosmological myth was surely irresistible to them. Plato nowhere calls Timaeus a Pythagorean. Socrates in the dialogue makes reference to "the tribe (*genos*) of your persuasion (*hexis*) who partake by nature and nurture of both [theory and practice] (Plato *Timaeus* 19e). The *hexis* has been taken to be that of the Pythagoreans, but it is clear from the context that Socrates is so qualifying all three of his interlocutors. That Hermocrates of Syracuse (most probably the famous statesman of that name)[3] was a

---

[2] "In the catalogue of Pythagoreans given by Iamblichus (*Vit. Pyth.* 267) his name does not occur as a Locrian, but there is a Timaeus among the Parians, who are mentioned just before the Locrians, and it thus seems probable, as Diels has suggested (*D-K* i. 345) that the name has gotten into the wrong line." Taylor (1928) #381, p. 17.

[3] Ibid., p. 14.

Pythagorean is implausible; that Critias (almost certainly the grand-father of the infamous oligarch)[4] was a Pythagorean is impossible.[5]

There is nothing particularly Pythagorean about the doctrines attrib-uted to Timaeus; they seem to be a typical Platonic medley. Plato of course took from the Pythagoreans what he wanted, as from everyone else.

So far as I can tell there is nothing particularly Locrian about Tim-aeus either, and I am left to wonder—fruitlessly—why, as narrator of his prose theogony, Plato chose or invented a Locrian. We do, however, learn something important from this dialogue: Timaeus is later quali-fied as "advanced in astronomy, and one who has made it his business to understand all nature" (Plato *Timaeus* 27a). It seems clear that at Locri a respectable citizen could be steeped in (to employ Walter Bur-kert's[6] distinction) both "lore" and "science." In this important respect Locri evidently stood in sharp contrast with Sparta.

All this raises some general questions about the standing of lore and science in the Greek West. In order to provide some context for these questions I will permit myself a rather schematic and much too rapid history of Greek intellectual development in the sixth and fifth cen-turies.

Sophoi and *Philosophoi*

Until the early sixth century all named Greek intellectuals are poets. About 580, however, we begin to hear of men called *sophoi*—not exactly poets,[7] nor furnished with any particular skill, with medicine, say, or architecture, but simply *sophoi*, which is to say, wise, or intelligent, intel-lectually well provided. There is a defining anecdote about them:

There mysteriously appeared, we are told, *a tripod (or sometimes a gold cup)*

[4] Ibid., p. 23.

[5] Ibid., p. 49, suggests that the "offices" held by Timaeus were held by him c. 476 B.C. during a period when (Taylor suggests) Locri was controlled by the Pythagoreans; he also suggests that Pindar's reference in his ode of that year (11th Olympian) to the Locrians as a *stratos akrosophos* is an allusion to their Pythagoreanism. However, Locri is notably absent from the various lists of cities supposed to have been ruled or reformed by the Pythagoreans, and it would be difficult to fit a period of such Pythagorean influence into Locrian history; throughout the fifth century the Locrians were closely dependent on Syracuse. Taylor seems to assume that no other kind of *sophia* could have existed in the West.

[6] Burkert (1970).

[7] Martin (1993) points out that poems are attributed to most of the sages—although, except in the case of Solon these are lost or survive only in a few fragments. Perhaps it would be more accurate to say that the sages are not known to us from their poetry—as "Theognis" and "Archilochus" and "Sappho" are bodies of verse and nothing else.

which was inscribed "for the wisest" (Tōi Sophōtatōi) or for some other reason had to be given to the wisest man. Therefore it was given to Thales of Miletus, who however passed it on to another he thought wiser than himself, perhaps Bias of Priene, who then passed to another, say Cleobulus of Lindos, who then passed it to Pittacus of Mytelene; from him it went (perhaps) to Chilon of Sparta, and from there to Periander of Corinth, who gave it to Solon of Athens. Sometimes Solon is the last, sometimes he gives it back to Thales; in either case the last holder dedicates it to the god at Delphi.

The story may not be older than the fourth century, and the names vary; the oldest list of seven (which, however, makes no mention of the tripod) is in the *Protagoras* passage about Spartan philosophy cited above; that list excludes Periander in favor of Myson of Chen. (Socrates evidently rejects the notion that a tyrant could be *sophos*; he prefers to include one whose specific claim to inclusion seems to be that he is otherwise unknown and from an utterly obscure village.) Later lists vary widely. The only names that seem to be on every list are Thales and Solon.[8] Altogether Diogenes Laertius (1.40–41) lists twenty-two names that appeared on one or another list of the Seven.

Irrespective of the particular names and details, the message of the anecdote is clear. It is a version of the story of the apple of discord (which was inscribed: *tēi kallistēi*, "for the fairest [female]"). The Seven thus turn out to be wiser than the gods who came to the wedding of Peleus and Thetis; they do not contend for the title of wisest, they yield it, and ultimately yield it where it belongs, to the god. "God alone is wise," as Socrates says, reflecting on his own experience with the god of Delphi, " . . . this one among you is wisest who . . . has understood that in truth he is worth nothing in respect to wisdom" (Plato *Apology* 23a–b).

The Seven *Sophoi* are, by tradition, both wise and modest. Characteristically they produce proverbs, mostly fairly obvious sentiments: "measure is best," or "practice is everything." Thales is said to have studied the heavens and predicted an eclipse, but otherwise they are not much involved with science. As Dicaearchus said, "they were no philosophers nor even wise, but intelligent and lawgivers" (Fr. 30 Wehrli). Generally they are political figures: Periander was a tyrant, Pittacus an *aisymnetēs*, Solon a lawgiver, Chilon an ephor and perhaps reformer of the Spartan constitution. Thales and Bias are said to have given sage political advice. The Seven are generally a list of centrist figures: rulers, leaders, and counselors of sovereign assemblies.

But along with these there are some personae of a different color:

---

[8] For a collection of sources and review of the variants see Barkowski *RE* s.v. "Sieben Weise."

Epimenides of Crete, for instance, who slept in a cave for fifty-seven years, and who later wrote a Theogony and purified the city of Athens; Acousilaus, who composed prose *Geneologies* commencing with the origin of the universe (a work he claimed to have found written on bronze plates discovered by his father while digging in the yard—DK 73 Fr. A2); Pherecydes of Syros, of whom many wonderful stories are told: how the taste of well water told him there would soon be an earthquake, how he had foreknowledge of the sinking of a ship and the subjection of Messenia.[9] Pherecydes is supposed to have introduced into Greece the notion of metempsychosis.[10] If so he is the original source for a doctrine that we encounter in various forms in Plato's myths, in mystical passages in Pindar, in Empedocles, in relation to Epimenides (Diogenes Laertius 1.114), and most of all in the traditions concerning Pythagoras.[11] Pythagoras, indeed, is said to have been the pupil of Pherecydes (Frs. 2, 7, 42, etc. Schibli), to have attended him in his last illness and to have celebrated his funeral (Frs. 11, 28–30 Schibli); the miracles of Pherecydes as told by Theopompus were told by Andron in his book *The Tripod* (evidently a work centering on the anecdote of the Seven Sages) as the wonderful acts of Pythagoras (Fr. 22 Schibli). Epimenides, Acousilaus, Pherecydes, and Pythagoras all appear on one or another list of Seven Sages, along with those completely legendary figures Linus and Orpheus. Louis Gernet, in his seminal article on "The Origins of Greek Philosophy," mentions some other names:

> If the philosopher . . . desires to create a "school"—that is, establish the equivalent of a confraternity—it is by his singular deeds of boldness that he qualifies as a founder. Here we are speaking of men like Abaris, Aristeas, Epimenides, Hermotimus—and others, to whom we might add Pherecydes, who is also a philosopher of sorts. These men practiced purification and divination; but theological and cosmological teachings also were attributed to them. Moreover, even in the legends, they have some connection with Pythagoras. (Gernet [1981], p. 357)

Abaris, possibly a Hyperborean, carried his arrow over all the earth without eating (Herodotus 4.36). Aristeas of Proconessus died and his body vanished; he then traveled with Apollo toward Hyperborea, and on his return to life six years later composed an epic, the *Arimaspea*, in which he told of his wonderful adventures (Herodotus 4.13–15). Hermotimus of Clazomenae had the power to leave his body and wander

---

[9] Schibli (1990), pp. 5–6.
[10] Ibid., pp. 104–127.
[11] E.g., Aristotle *de Anima* 407b.

in spirit through the world, learning its secrets; later this same soul inhabited Pythagoras (*RE* s.v. "Hermotimus").

These stories tell us that as Greek intellectual life became prosaic it divided into two strands, between a centrist, commonplace, largely commonsensical group[12] represented by the Seven Sages and another type which we may call countercultural. These latter are figures with some kind of more-than-human wisdom, visionaries, wonder workers. The most important of them is Pythagoras.

Pythagoras the Orphic

For Pythagoras we have some contemporary witnesses. Xenophanes mocked his belief in the transmigration of souls, saying that Pythagoras recognized a howling puppy as a dead friend: "I knew him by his voice" (11 B 7 DK). Heracleitus said: "Pythagoras son of Mnesarchus practiced inquiry more than any other person, and selecting out these writings made it his own wisdom, learnedness (*polumathiē*), malign skill" (12 B 129 DK),[13] and "Learnedness does not teach understanding (*nous*)—or it would have taught Hesiod and Pythagoras, and also Xenophanes and Hecataeus" (12 B 40 DK). These last are an interesting list. Hecataeus wrote geneologies, rather like those of Acousilaus. Xenophanes wrote a poem, *On Nature*, describing the play of the elements and the one God who rules all and knows all. Probably the Hesiod Heracleitus has in mind is the Hesiod of the *Theogony*. It seems that Heracleitus groups together four theogonic writers. Ion of Chios tells us that Pythagoras wrote poems that he ascribed to Orpheus; such poems should be theogonic. It seems that Heracleitus is scoffing, not at learning in general, but at those who claimed to be able to describe the cosmos and its origins.

That Pythagoras wrote poems that he ascribed to Orpheus places him among the Orphics. This last term, it should be clear, is not to be taken to imply any kind of sect or organized movement; "Orphic" rather names a tendency, not so different from the contemporary tendency we call "New Age." Tendencies express themselves in various, even contrasting ways, although the plain man tends to lump the whole

---

[12] Although Thales is said to have been so rapt in his study of the stars that he fell into a well, he also used his *sophia* (we are told) to make himself wealthy, and in any case his relation with the stars is empirical, not magical; he predicted an eclipse, he did not cause one.

[13] Diels classes this among the "suspect" fragments; the text is probably unsound at the best. Some editors drop the words: "selecting . . . writings."

uncritically together. Thus Theseus in the *Hippolytus* thinks that Hippolytus's show of piety and of purity of life makes him an Orphic:

> Are you some special person who consorts
> With gods? You're virtuous, immaculate of evil?
> You'll not prevail upon me with your boasts
> Using your gods to fuddle my good sense.
> Go preen yourself, and in vegetable fashion
> Showcase your diet; acknowledge your lord Orpheus
> Inebriate by the smoke of all those prized writings.
>
> Euripides *Hippolytus* 947–954

The books the Orphics carried seem to have been competing theogonies—often attributed to Orpheus (sometimes Musaeus and possibly Linus). These books were prized by those who lived the "Orphic life"—which might involve vegetarianism (Plato *Laws* 782c). The books prescribed rituals; Socrates in the *Republic* (364e) refers to a "babble of books of Orpheus and Musaeus . . . by dint of which they traffic in sacrifices." Euripides' word I translated above as "inebriate" is *baccheue*, which implies Dionysiac excitement; these rituals seem to have been linked to those of Dionysus. Nevertheless Theseus makes it clear by his tone that he is not thinking of the established worship of Dionysus; the sort of ritual he has in mind is (to draw another distinction from Burkert) a matter of "craft" rather than "sect";[14] it is the affair of what was by the fourth century called the *Orpheotelestēs*, the itinerant holy man, the *agurtis* or *mantis* "who comes to the houses of the rich and convinces them that he has acquired such potency from the gods for his sacrifices and charms, that if his host or some ancestor is guilty of any crime it can be healed in the midst of pleasures and festival" (Plato *Republic* 364b–c).

By Orphic rituals, in other words, we refer to privately organized initiatory rites. They belong to the sphere of Greek personal religion. Dario Sabatucci has in fact powerfully argued that classical society, which privileged the political order, necessarily marginalized a religion of this type as hostile to public life.[15] We are then left with the question of the Eleusinian Mysteries (which seem in their origins to be more or less contemporary with the Seven Sages and their countercultural cousins, i.e., in the early sixth century). These after all were also "Orphic" in the sense that they were said to have been founded by Orpheus ([Euripides] *Rhesus* 943–944) and they also promised their initiates a better fate in the next life. And Eleusis was unquestionably the

---

[14] Burkert (1982).
[15] Sabatucci (1979).

scene of an established public cult; in fact by the fifth century the Eleusinian tithe had become an element in Athenian cultural politics (cf. Meiggs and Lewis #73, and Isocrates 4.31). There was certainly nothing disreputable or antipolitical about Eleusinian initiation.

On the other hand, the Mysteries were to a striking degree dangerous—not that it was dangerous to be initiated, but danger lay in possession of the secrets and in their revelation. Aeschylus was at risk for revealing them accidentally, Diagoras was exiled for revealing them intentionally, and Alcibiades was condemned to death for his illicit celebration of the rite in the presence of noninitiates. The Great Goddess was not to be trifled with. In the corpus of Lysias we come upon the story of some unknown malefactor who

> tied his horse to the knocker of the sanctuary in order to dedicate it, and then during the night took it away. This man died the most hateful of all deaths, starvation. Although many excellent things were set before him on the table he found the stink of the bread and the meal most foul, and he was not able to eat. Many of you have heard this story as the Hierophant told it. ([Lysias] 6.1)

The atmosphere of personal danger surrounding the Mysteries is possibly evidence of the subjective difficulty of integrating them into the order of public experience.

Be that as it may, privately conducted rites certainly remained unintegrated. As such they tended to make themselves ridiculous—and they were ridiculed. The Scythians, Herodotus tells us, tolerated the Hellenization of their king Skyles until he went so far as to "inebriate" himself in Dionysiac initiation (Herodotus 4.78). From the anecdote of King Leotychidas (Plutarch *Moralia* 224e) through Democritus (Fr. 297 DK) to Demosthenes' well-known account of Aeschines and his mother (Demosthenes 18.259–260) and the just-quoted passage in Plato's *Republic* we find Orphic initiatory rites treated with cheerful contempt, as also their threats of next-world punishment and promises of next-world bliss. As an author of Orphic verses, Pythagoras of Samos was, it seems, in his early life linked to this kind of eschatological religion, notable, even sometimes notorious, but socially marginalized and politically excluded.

Orphic Politics

In midlife, somewhere in the last quarter of the sixth century, Pythagoras left Samos in old-world Greece and went to Croton in southern Italy. At this point he seems, from the point of view of the homeland, to have dropped out of sight. Some time in the 420s, however, about a century later, Italian exiles calling themselves Pythagoreans began to appear in old-world Greece. Some settled in Thebes, where one of them became the tutor of the young Epaminondas; others formed a kind of refugee community in Phlius, on the north edge of Arcadia. Not one of these could have been personally acquainted with the great man, but they told his story: how Pythagoras had become by his teaching influential in Croton and the master of a school which through the mutual understanding of its members came to dominate political life there, how numerous cities had come under the influence of the school, how Pythagoras had led Croton against the tyrant of Sybaris and how that great city had been eradicated by Croton, how the refusal of the Pythagoreans to distribute the territory of Sybaris as private property had led to a backlash of resistance to the Pythagoreans, culminating in the burning of the house of Milo of Croton, Pythagoras's leading disciple, how some died in these disorders and the rest were dispersed into exile. Sometimes Pythagoras was one of those who died; more often, as in the anecdote that opens this chapter, he was among the exiles, dying finally in Metapontum. We hear of continuing disorders, of an arbitration by Taras, Metapontum, and Caulonia that arranged the expulsion of the Pythagoreans and the confiscation of their property, and a later return of the exiles (Iamblichus *Life of Pythagoras* 262–263). Later we hear that some of them gathered in Rhegion, and later still that all were exiled from the West except Archytas of Taras. These Pythagorean exiles in old-world Greece were known to Aristoxenus as "the last of the Pythagoreans" and their story formed the basis of his *Life of Pythagoras*, which, in turn—along with other Peripatetic works, by Heracleides Ponticus, for example, and by Dicaearchus—became the main source for all later accounts.

Not that the story they told was necessarily reliable; refugee stories seldom are. Herodotus, who knew what Pythagoreans were (Herodotus 2.81) and who knew the West well, says nothing about Pythagoreans there; he mentions Milo without reference to Pythagoras (Herodotus 3.137). He also has a different story to tell concerning the conquest of Sybaris by Croton—actually two different stories, neither of which involves Pythagoras (Herodotus 5.44–45). It is dangerous to argue *ex silentio*, but in this case the silence of Herodotus is deafening.

Nevertheless on the important general point—that these Pythagoreans were somehow involved in politics—there must have been some truth to the story; their refugee status was itself their evidence. They had been expelled. Somehow in the West the Pythagoreans had turned from harmless eccentrics to a public menace; at the same time they came to form a society that could survive the founder for several gener-

ations. In the West Pythagoras's teaching was institutionalized, and became political.

This is in retrospect predictable, because in the West political authority had long had a religious aspect. The priesthood of Demeter
and Kore was hereditary in the family line of Gelon and his brother
Hieron, tyrants of Gela and later of Syracuse. We are told, indeed, that
their possession of the sacred objects was the original source of the
fortunes of the family (Herodotus 7.153). Pindar in one of his "Orphic" passages (and all of these, so far as we know, come from poems
addressed to Sicilian tyrants) refers to another charismatic source of
authority, the myth of the "twice-born":

> Those from whom Persephone accepts atonement (*poinē*) for the ancient
>   grief—
> The souls of these in the ninth year she restores
> Again to the sun above.
> From these come splendid kings, and such men grow
> Swift in their strength and wisdom.
> In time to come these shall be called
> Sacred heroes among mankind.
>
> apud Plato *Meno* 81b–c

Here the archaic view of heroes is extended and to a degree inverted:
Heroic status after death results from heroic activity in life, as before,
but heroic activity itself results from the after-death adventures of the
soul before heroic life. The king, the athlete, the sage, these come into
the world trailing clouds of glory.

The wise are akin to kings. In the West philosophy was political. Parmenides wrote the laws of Velia (Plutarch *Moralia* 1126a). Of Empedocles many stories were told as to his political activity, even that he had
been offered (and refused) a royal throne (Diogenes Laertius 8.63–
67). Perhaps it was in the spirit of this same intellectualized politics
that Pericles, when he refounded Sybaris as Thurii, commissioned Protagoras to write the laws. Later Dionysius the Younger of Syracuse had
pretensions to philosophy; he was also priest of Cybele, whose rites he
continued to perform after his dispossession from the tyranny.

The intersection of the sacred and the political in the West (and in
the North as well: Vinogradoff [1991] has proposed a similar intersection between Orphism and tyranny in Olbia) has to do (I would suggest) with the conditions of political experience on the frontier. An
open frontier is always an anxious place; the people who have come
there have to some degree lost contact with the society they have left
behind, and there is always the question whether this home is only
temporary; they might be moving on. The Greek colonies generally

tried to mandate tradition and continuity by asserting that they originated in a mother city whose customs and cults they continued. In fact colonial populations were always to some degree at least heterogeneous, derived from various old-world communities and incorporating some elements derived from the indigenes. Furthermore the frontier was a place of real danger; probably more colonial foundations died in the attempt than survived. The settlers were under pressure to come to terms with each other and invent a society. The result, I would suggest, was a rage for order, for quick, simplified solutions. To borrow some terms from Max Weber: Where traditional authority is weak it must be supplemented by other types, both rational and charismatic.

Traditional authority legitimates itself by reference to the self-justifying cultural systems in which it is embedded: I am entitled to authority, it says, because I am generous, and I am entitled to the resources that enable me to be generous because they are the prerogative of authority. Rational authority legitimates itself as the means to a desired end: If you want the public services, it says, you'll have to pay for them and pay somebody like me to administer them. Charismatic authority bypasses the problem of legitimation altogether by asserting that it is already solved: I am here, it says, because God put me here, and what's yours is mine because God wants you to give it to me.

Charismatic authority derives from the invisible, and therefore it is invulnerable to empirical criticism. The frontier, which is a horizon of the unexplored, stimulates empirical inquiry and rational solutions to explicit problems—but at the same time brings us up against the limits of reason. Charismatic revelation then fills the gaps. The two complement each other. The frontier is notoriously the world of plain talk and ingenious inventions; it is also the proper home of sects, cracks, visionaries, and utopian projects.

In the Greek West early intellectual development displays just such a combination of rationality and revelation—for instance in Parmenides, who founded dialectic on a visionary journey of the spirit. An even clearer case is Empedocles, who wrote a rational book—the *Phusika*, in which he sketched the system of nature—and a charismatic book, the *Katharmoi*.[16] The most perfect synthesis, however, was that of Pythagoras, combining mathematics, music, and miracles.

The Pythagoreans remained the dominant political philosophers in the Greek West from the late sixth century, when the founder arrived in Croton, down to the mid-fourth century, when Archytas served (unconstitutionally) seven times as general at Taras and (apparently) col-

---

[16] If, indeed, they were two books rather than two aspects of a single book—cf. Martin and Primavesi (1999), pp. 114–119.

laborated with Dion of Syracuse and Plato of Athens in an ill-fated attempt to convert the younger Dionysius into a philosopher king. Indeed Alfonso Mele (1982) has made a plausible argument that *hē megalē Hellas*, the phrase we translate as *Magna Graecia* and Great Greece, was originally the Pythagoreans' own name for their political project: the creation of a purified Greek society in the West. This is not the place to tell that story. We are focused here, instead, on the exclusion of Locri from it.

To some extent this exclusion was quite possibly both cause and effect of the close relations of Locri with Syracuse. Syracuse (as Plato found to his cost) was a city superbly unsuited to philosophic discipline; it was the prototypical materialistic state, passionately devoted to money and power. We have, however, seen that Locri's relation with Syracuse was ambiguous, at best one of complementarity, not similarity. The Locrians, who like the Pythagoreans attempted moderation in the spheres of money and power, seem like them to have been hospitable to lore and science—but to some alternative to the Pythagorean type.

In the preceding section of this book I called this alternative "Orphic," and laid out the evidence for it: the Hipponium tablet, Aristotle's remark in his *Constitution of the Locrians* that bereaved Locrians do not mourn but feast, the Boston Throne (as here interpreted), *pinax* type 8/29 P 30 (ditto), the serpents on the perfume-burner. I make no claim that these ambiguous fragments "prove" the character of religion of Locri; I do suggest, however, that they might lead us to a plausible understanding of a city that apparently celebrated in some relation to each other cults of Aphrodite and Persephone.

The Fate of the Soul

Archaic Greek religion, as far as we can tell, recognized the survival of the dead in terms of their continuing reality to others: as a kind of living memory—insubstantial wraiths in Hades—and in the earth as heroic potencies. The Mysteries, whether established or "Orphic," by contrast focused on the fate of the soul as experienced by the person; they promised an afterlife, or rebirth, or some combination thereof. At one end of the scale were the Pythagoreans, who seem to have been the most worldly of the sects; for them, it seems, immortality consisted of a series of lives in this world, and life was perfected by worldly circumspection:

> They did nothing unplanned or unreviewed, but in the morning laid out the project for what to do, and in the evening took account of how they had managed it—which along with consideration trained the memory; similarly

if some of their fellows in this way of life should tell them to meet him at a certain place, there they would wait for him until he should come, day or night, so here was another example that the Pythagoreans were accustomed to remember what they had said and to say nothing casually, and their obligations extended unto death. And at the final hour he told them they should not blaspheme, but as if setting out on a journey take the omens in pious silence, as they would when setting out across the Adriatic. (Iamblichus *Life of Pythagoras* 256–257)

This disciplined serenity made of the Pythagoreans the Calvinists of the ancient world. Most of all they trained the memory:

They particularly valued the memory and devoted themselves to its care and exercise. . . . A Pythagorean would not rise from his bed before he had called to mind the events of the previous day. . . . He tried to recover in thought what he had first said or heard or instructed to his household when he first got up, and what second, and what third. . . . And then when he went out whom he met first and whom second, and what talk there was first and what second and third, and it was the same story with everything else, because he tried to bring to mind the whole day, and he eagerly attempted the disciplined recollection of everything, just how each thing had happened. And if he had plenty of time as he woke up he might try to recover the events of the day before that in the same manner. (Iamblichus *Life of Pythagoras* 165)

It seems likely that the ultimate purpose of this training of the memory was to enable the adept to remember his previous lives, or failing that, to carry with him into the next life memories of this one. Pythagoras certainly remembered his previous lives, and there was a legend that explained this:

Heracleides Ponticus says that Pythagoras told this of himself: that he once had been born as Aithalides and was counted a son of Hermes. Hermes offered to grant for him any wish except immortality. He asked that in life and death he should keep the memory of events. During his life he therefore remembered everything, and when he died he preserved the same recollection. Later on he lived as Euphorbus and was wounded by Menelaus. And Euphorbus told how he had been Aithalides and of his gift from Hermes and the circulation of his soul, how it had circulated about and had been in so many plants and animals and what his soul underwent in Hades and what the remaining souls endure. When Euphorbus died he transferred his soul to Hermotimus, who himself wanting to give some proof went to Branchis and entering the temple of Apollo pointed out the shield of Euphorbus which Menelaus had dedicated there . . . all rotted away, nothing left but the ivory emblem. When Hermotimus died he became Pyrrhus of Delos, a fisherman.

And he remembered everything, how he had been first Aithalides, then Euphorbus, then Hermotimus, then Pyrrhus. When Pyrrhus died he became Pythagoras and remembered everything as it is told here. (Diogenes Laertius 8.4)

If by the training of his memory the adept could acquire this power of the master's, his experience and education could accumulate from life to life, and eventually it might be possible to approach perfection here in this world—in fact, to become godlike. Aristotle reports that one of the secrets imparted to the Pythagorean adepts was this: There are three kinds of persons: mortals, immortals, and those like Pythagoras. Pythagoras himself, in other words, was intermediate between gods and men, and those who made themselves like him could form a godlike society. This evolutionary prospect made of the Pythagoreans educators and politicians. Their project was not merely the enlightenment of a few but also, under that enlightened leadership, the perfection of all.

In Sicilian circles, most brilliantly represented by Empedocles, man, by contrast, was represented not as in progress but rather as fallen; reincarnation then could be a step toward the recovery of an original perfection. Empedocles told how he himself had once been a god, but had been cast out of heaven, apparently for shedding blood; he had been compelled to start over again as a bush, the laurel. From this lowly beginning he had been reborn as a fish, the dolphin, a bird, the eagle, and a beast, the lion; finally he had become human as a last step toward heaven. He was able to advance from this life because he kept himself pure of bloodshed and ate no meat.[17] The intermediacy that for Pythagoras is stable becomes for Empedocles dynamic, a stage of purification. As a "last born" he is a superior figure, not unlike Pindar's "twice born" who have succeeded in clearing their accounts with the goddess of death.

Borrowing another distinction from Max Weber, we may call Empedocles an emissary prophet and Pythagoras an exemplary prophet. The emissary prophet (Weber's example is Jesus) brings the good news to a fallen society that there is after all a way to redemption. Believe in me, he says, and ye shall all be changed. The exemplary prophet (Weber's example is the Buddha) achieves perfection himself and thus sets before us a path to perfection and a model for imitation. Empedocles said: I am so far above you that you must listen to me. Pythagoras said: I am the way, be like me; he created a way of life, what the Greeks called a *bios*, that could be lived by anyone. The Pythagoreans stressed

---

[17] It is unknown how he explained the purity of those predatory carnivores the eagle and the lion.

askēsis, disciplined training; Empedocles stressed *katharsis*, purification. The Pythagoreans aimed to perfect this world; they did not reject ordinary morality and established religion, but added to them additional rules and a refined understanding. Empedocles, by contrast, through his rejection of blood sacrifice demanded "the reversal of all traditional religion"[18] and thereby promised a way out of this mortal coil, entry into divine and eternal life. Their attitudes to this life are opposite, but each in his own way makes extreme demands upon the life we live here and now.

When we come to imagine the relation of Locrian religion to these two models, which between them dominated the other cities of the West, it seems plausible to begin with the Hipponion tablet. This unquestionably involves the fate of the soul; it is a set of instructions for reaching the destination proper to the "initiates and bacchics." There is in this tablet (and its successors, the so-called[19] "B type") no reference to virtue, no claim to have lived well or purely in preparation for the moment of death; it seems to be enough to have learned to drink from the right spring and to speak the correct words to its guardian.[20] This strand of Greek eschatology does not demand discipline or strenuous purification; it promises salvation through privileged information, *mustikoi logoi*. The words of the tablet have the same power as the things seen at Eleusis; both work of themselves and make all the difference:

> Happy he who has seen these things among men on earth;
> But the uninitiate of these sacred things, the person with no share of them
> Has not a like portion among those who have perished into the broad
> darkness.

Homeric Hymn to Demeter 480–482

We have no record of any established initiatory sanctuary in the West parallel to Eleusis; most probably the Hipponion tablet (along with the ring worn by the girl it was buried with) is a token of some private initiation. My notion is that such private initiations were sufficiently respectable and expected at Locri that an eschatology of this type suffused Locrian society, at least at the elite level. In the service of this hypothesis I have suggested links between the Hipponion tablet, the Boston Throne, and *pinax* type 8/29 P 30. The best argument in favor of such an hypothesis, however, is the general character of Locrian

---

[18] Zuntz (1971), p. 258.

[19] Ibid., p. 355.

[20] On this point we may contrast the "type A" (Zuntz 1971) tablets, which typically make for the dead claims of purity and sometimes refer (like Pindar—ibid., p. 313) to the payment of a *poinē*, an atonement. These "type A" tablets seem much closer to the Empedoclean idea: A life of purification gives claims to an afterlife among the gods.

society so far as we have been able to discern it through the evidence available to us.

Orphic Locri

Locri, as we have seen, was a closed society; neither Locrian art nor Locrian women were available to outsiders. I am hypothetically suggesting that this closure was sustained by the Locrians' sense that they were special people, a circle of the elect—like the Eleusinian initiates in the *Frogs*: "we alone have the sun and its sacred light, all we who are initiate and have kept the ways of piety" (Aristophanes *Frogs* 454–458).

The mystic eschatology is an eschatology of joy; it promises that in the next life the initiate will be *eudaimōn, olbios, makarios*; will dance, play, and feast. What we know of the Eleusinian initiates suggests that this promise made little difference in the quality of their lives; they kept it by them as (perhaps) a personal hope, but no more. The hope was personal because the Mysteries did not constitute a community. Although there was a bond between those who had been initiated together, there was no community of initiates. The Eleusinian Mysteries were open to all Greeks; although the sanctuary was the pride of Athens, there was nothing peculiarly Athenian about being initiated.

A promise of joy like that of the Mysteries might mean something very different in a society where it made the difference between us and the others, so that it meant not merely: I am among the saved, but: *We* are the saved. The hope of joy then defines the character of the society; beliefs so reinforced by social interaction come to seem much more reliable. It then becomes possible to see this life as a life of joy in foretaste of the life to come. It seems that if the Pythagoreans were the Calvinists of the ancient world, the Locrians were something like those Anabaptists who believed that they were already saved and might as well enjoy it now. That, at least, is my hypothesis.

Such a hypothesis accounts for both the Locrian rejection of Pythagoras and their respect for him: By all means, they seem to say, give direction to those who need it; as for us, we are already arrived.

This hypothesis is, furthermore, a generalization of the proposal made in the last chapter that the Locrians looked on marriage as the heroization of the bride, so that the analogy between marriage and death can be read in either direction: marital happiness as a foretaste of eternal bliss, and salvation as eternal marital happiness. To die in the faith is to enjoy a happy afterlife just as to marry is to live happily ever after. I now generalize this hypothesis to suggest that the Locrians (at least on the elite level) conceived the meaning of their society in terms of the reversibility of life and death, that (ideally, at least) they lived their social lives at least in large part in anticipation of a better life, and that in this limited sense they approximated a community of Orphics.

Orphic Marriage

I further suggest that this hypothesis is consistent with the relatively elevated position of women in Locrian society, and with Locrian emphasis on marriage as a key social institution. Death is the great leveler, and eschatology extends this equalization into this world. At Eleusis even slaves could be initiated and share the promise of equal joys to come. However, eschatology need not have affected the status order at Locri if, as I suppose, initiation there was the privilege of an elite. The equalization would have been *within* the elite, between the sexes—as in Greek society in general we observe that women, virtually annihilated in politics, reassert themselves in ritual.

Marriage, furthermore, has a central place in Orphic ideology, not only because the Orphic tendency is antipolitical and reasserts against politics the values of social life, but also because Orphic theology centers on the mediation of difference. The Pythagorean variant asserted marital values straightforwardly, by requiring that men be faithful to their wives. To some extent this is no more than an aspect of Pythagorean *askēsis* and the control of the appetites.[21] But "male" and "female" figure on the list of Pythagorean oppositions (along with such pairs as "one" and "many," square" and "oblong," etc.) and marriage appears in Pythagorean numerology: Three is the number of marriage. Before Pythagoras, Pherecydes described the creation as a wedding gift; the papyrus fragment (Schibli 1990 Fr. 68—already quoted)[22] tells how Zas, the Orphic Zeus, marries Chthonie, whose name invokes the earth; he gives her a house and servants and possessions and as her *anakalupteria* embroiders for her a robe which is the heavens and the earth. The material world is thus the *kosmos* of the primeval bride. That Pherecydes described the cosmos as the marriage of form and matter is evidence that he saw marriage as the privileged paradigm for the mediation of opposites.

The most relevant cosmogonic reference, however, may be Sicilian, not Pherecydes but Empedocles. Empedocles' physics described the world and all its creatures as consisting of various combinations of the four elements; these in turn are kept in differentiation from each other

---

[21] For a careful review of this topic see Gaca (2000).
[22] Cf. p. 70.

by a principle of difference, variously called *neikos* (quarrel), *eris* (strife), and *kotos* (rancor), but recurrently brought together by *philotēs* (affection). This latter is under the sign of Aphrodite, whose power is great throughout the cosmos and at every level of organization, from the molecular to the macrocosmic. For mankind the rule of Aphrodite was the Golden Age before the Olympian patriarchal gods introduced blood sacrifice and war:

> For them War was no god, nor was the Clamor of battle
> Nor Zeus the king nor Cronos nor Poseidon,
> But Queen Aphrodite. . . .
> Her they worshipped with pious images
> With drawings of animals and fine-wrought perfumes
> With sacrifice of purest myrrh and fragrant cypress,
> Casting forth on the soil libations of blond honey.
> Their altar was not flooded with the unmixed gore of bulls
> Rather that was then the greatest filth for mankind:
> To rip out the life and then eat the excellent limbs.
>
> Empedocles Fr. 129 DK

Empedocles thus reverses the trend of the Hesiodic theogony: Whereas there the Olympian gods find a universe in flux and bring it to order, here the Olympians introduce violence into a peacefully integrated cosmos. The principle of integration—Aphrodite, *philotēs*—persists, but it no longer rules the universe, nor shapes social life as expressed in the mode of sacrifice.

When we return to Locri from Pythagoras and Empedocles we can, it seems, see the great prophetic cosmology of Empedocles domesticated and brought down to earth. The Locrians aimed not to save the world but to build a little world for themselves. This point may give us a further understanding of the link between these oddly contrasted long-term allies, Locri and Syracuse. The *philotēs* which in Sicily was only a mythical memory and a millennial aspiration was at Locri (ideally, at least) a present fact; what haunted the Sicilians as an impossible dream, an antistructural countercultural alternative, was at Locri cultivated on the level of the everyday—but only for the Locrians, whose sanctuaries and whose brides were unavailable to others. In uniting the powers of love and death the Locrians achieved (in this limited sense) a working utopia, an out-of-reach model—like Sparta, admired but unattainable.

We do not have to think that the Locrians abjured blood sacrifice and the eating of meat to hypothesize that they aspired to a community ruled by *philotēs*. In fact the contrast between the Empedoclean and Hesiodic theogonies makes possible yet another statement of the contrast between Locri and Sparta. The Spartans had been given their land by Zeus and were guided by his prophet, Apollo; their class dominance was founded on *bia*, force, and their internal organization was primarily a military organization, the solidarity of the warrior band. They were all similar (except for the kings) differentiated only by their success or failure in the pervasive competition to be the best conformist. Their most important rituals were thus the recurrent initiations that served to differentiate the citizen males from those others whose labor and deference they appropriated. The women were formally excluded from all this; nevertheless the free women reasserted their status by a life made parallel with that of the males—in exercise, freedom from labor, the accumulation of property and political influence (in spite of their exclusion from legitimate power).

The Locrian foundation story, by contrast, asserted that their city had been founded by free women under the power of Aphrodite and by the servile males over whom they had exercised that power. The power of Aphrodite, at its best, produces *philotēs*, expressed politically as *homophrosunē* and *homonoia*; these do not have to be enforced, as in the Spartan case, by solidarity against an external threat, but are rather inward-looking and maintained by complementarity and exchange. The unifying principle of the rule of Aphrodite, therefore, is not similarity but difference and the mediation of difference. Such a principle would shift the emphasis from the political to the social level.

The Locrian elite, like the Spartan elite, was closed; all those families who would ever belong to it already belonged to it, and therefore could assert that they were the "natural" elite, with a gift for superiority. Such elites rule by a self-validating demand for deference taking the form of claims on labor and its produce, accompanied by a sense of noblesse oblige and a parade of generosity. We can imagine that at Locri the class structure was maintained by "traditional relations" approximating to gift exchange of commodities between the elite and their subordinates.

Certainly Locri had an army and her men were warriors; most probably private property was transmitted, as elsewhere, through the patriline. The Locrian elite, however, seems to have included the women as the vessels of ritual privileges. This form of inclusion, I have suggested, made of each marriage exchange a double transfer of wealth and status. Therefore the most significant exchanges within the elite would not have been of commodities, but of women. We can thus understand why, in contrast to Sparta, where all major rituals approximated initiations, at Locri the most important rituals could have been the weddings. Aphrodite joined with Persephone, the one as agent, the other as exemplar, in achieving and celebrating the power and transformation of the bride.

Concluding Unscientific Postscript

Let as pause to imagine Timaeus of Locri, not just as Plato for his own purposes imagined him, but as he might actually have been. He is a cultivated man, versed in the science and cosmology that is all about him, well acquainted with the poems of Parmenides and Empedocles as well as other lesser works of which we know nothing, conversant with the medical schools of the West and with the Pythagoreans. He is also a political man, as are all males of his class in his city. Furthermore he is an initiate, as confident of bliss as any reasonable man ever can be confident. He is an Orphic, in other words, and a philosopher, but unlike other philosophers (except, perhaps, Parmenides) and other Orphics, he has a home where he is completely at home. He has a wife with whom he shares his gods—and perhaps also his learning (we hear quite a bit about women Pythagoreans)—and more important, he lives within a network of kindred by blood and by marriage who also share with him their gods and their rituals. He travels, certainly—to Syracuse, often, to old-world Greece when occasion arises; possibly he has even been to Egypt or Syria. But he is not in search there of the secret of a better life; he does not aim to improve the world to which he comes nor does he aspire to perfect the city to which he returns. It is already saved as he is. For him lore and science can be enjoyed purely theoretically, without practical or political dynamism; they justify themselves for him in the joy of sheer knowing and the sharing of knowledge. Like the philosopher celebrated by Socrates in the *Republic* he "is content if he can live his life here pure of injustice and impious acts and change it for another life, when he does, with good hope, gently and serenely." Unlike that philosopher, however, he (to adapt Socrates' next sentence) "has come upon a civic order fitting to himself . . . and in it he himself reaches his full development and along with his personal interests saves those of the community" (Plato *Republic* 496d–497a). Oddly enough (and quite contrary to Socrates' expectation), the result is that he lives and dies in obscurity.

We know very little of that great city Epizephyrian Locri because, I think, the Locrians thought themselves culturally *autarkēs*, self-sufficient. In principle, at least, they had what they needed. I do not wish to imply that this place was the earthly paradise or the isles of the blessed, only that it aspired to that model. As Sparta aspired to the Golden Age, to the original condition of mankind, so Locri aspired to a life anticipating that good hope, perpetual peace, Hesychia, who, as Epicharmus the Sicilian (Fr. 101 Kaibel) says, "is a pretty lady and lives next door to Sophrosyne." Obviously there was conflict at Locri, crime and misery and injustice, nor was the city free from war—even with her Locrian neighbors who shared her mode of life. Yet paradoxically enough this city deserves our respect precisely because she took so little care to obtain it. When all the other great Greek cities were deeply engaged in making history—which is to say, in the struggle for power—the Locrians seem to have been content to settle for happiness.

Ritual Prostitution at Locri

THE evidence for ritual prostitution as a Locrian institution is a few sentences from Justin, part of a longer passage quoted earlier:

> When the Locrians had been hard pressed in war by Leophron tyrant of Rhegion they had vowed, should they be victorious, that on the day of Aphrodite's festival they would prostitute their maidens. This vow was let to lapse; when their war with the Lucanians was going badly Dionysius called them into assembly and urged that they send their wives and daughters, adorned as lavishly as possible, to the temple of Aphrodite, and that one hundred of these, chosen by lot, should carry out the vow of the people: for religion's sake they would spend one month in the brothel, all the men having taken an oath that they would not touch a single one of them. Lest there should be damage to maidens who in this way made good to the city its vow he made a decree: no maiden should marry until these had found husbands.

It is important to notice the context of this statement—it is one of a series of more or less fantastic stories about the outrages committed by Dionysius—and it is also important to notice exactly what it says. According to Justin in the second century A.D.—according, actually, to Pompeius Trogus, whose work he is summarizing—it was believed in the fourth century at Locri that in the early fifth century they had made a vow to prostitute their maidens as an exceptional and emergency measure. Justin does not say that on either occasion the vow was carried into effect; indeed Dionysius in his narration evokes it only to trick the Locrian women into appearing in public wearing their jewelry, so that he can steal it from them. On the earlier occasion the Locrians were rescued from Rhegion by Hieron of Syracuse, and Justin's ambiguous language "hoc voto intermisso" is usually taken to mean that the vow was never carried out because it was, after all, not needed. Nevertheless this passage has frequently been cited as evidence that ritual prostitution was an established institution at Locri.

Next, it is important to be clear what we mean by ritual prostitution. We have considerable evidence from Athenaeus (quoting Pindar and Xenophon) that at Corinth slaves could belong to Aphrodite and serve her as prostitutes. Greek temples, here and there, owned a variety of enterprises, and a brothel was a particularly appropriate to Corinth, where prostitution was a major industry and Aphrodite the city-protecting god. We hear of a similar establishment at Eryx, in Elymnian (which is to say, Hellenized) territory, and Strabo (12.3.36) (with specific comparison to Corinth) gives an account of prostitutes in his own time owned by a temple in Comana in Armenia. None of this adds up to prostitutes in a temple, or to sex as part of a ritual obligation. The prostitutes belonging to temples are, like Greek prostitutes everywhere, slaves or at least unfree women, and they are enjoyed for recreation.

Justin's story is about something quite different: the prostitution of free women (thus violating the most fundamental categorical difference relevant to Greek women) in fulfillment of a vow. For this we have no Greek parallel in the Greek material. Herodotus (1.93–94) tells that the free girls of Lydia prostituted themselves before marriage in order to earn their dowries (the *nomoi* of the Lydians are "much like those of the Greeks except that they prostitute their daughters") and that at Babylon every woman had a religious obligation to prostitute herself in the temple before marriage (Herodotus 1.199), also that the daughter of an Egyptian pharaoh prostituted herself and built a pyramid with the proceeds. Strabo (11.14.16) (with specific reference to Herodotus) says that in his own time the Armenians had a custom like that of the Lydians, and also (17.1.46) tells a story of the ritual prostitution of a high-status maiden in Egypt. All these stories are more or less incredible (although we do have neo-Babylonian material showing that there, as elsewhere, women who had once been entertainers—and probably prostitutes as well—did sometimes later get married).[1] The stories fit into Herodotus's general sense of Near Eastern cultures as soft, luxurious, and lacking firm boundaries and secure structures of legitimate authority.

Clearchus of Soli, a notably sensationalistic writer, has an etiological story to tell about the Lydians: It seems that the Lydians lived luxuriously and gathered other people's wives and maidens into their gardens and outraged them. The result was that they became weak and feminine, so that they fell under the tyranny of one of the women they had outraged, Omphale; she took her revenge by forcing the free girls to lie with the slaves. The paragraph concludes:

> Not only the women of the Lydians who are turned loose to the first comer, but also those of the Epizephyrian Locrians, besides those of Cyprus and all those who turn their daughters to prostitution as an act of piety, all these seem to be truly in memory and expiation of some ancient outrage (*hubris*). (Athenaeus 516b)

[1] Cf. Kuhrt (1989), pp. 223–237.

This passage is often cited as evidence that Clearchus confirmed Justin's story, although Justin tells of something that didn't happen, while Clearchus tells of some kind of established custom. Actually it is not clear that the reference to Locri is from Clearchus; it may have been added by Athenaeus: The Omphale story, after all, is about forcing maidens, not turning them loose. The reference to "an ancient outrage," further, suggests that the author is thinking of the Locrian maidens at Troy, and that he has confused that story with something he had heard about the Epizephyrians.

Some other items have been interpreted as confirming Justin: Aside from Torelli's ill-considered suggestion that the U-shaped stoa was actually the brothel, we have references in the third-century temple archives of Olympian Zeus to income from certain sacred sources, feminine in grammatical gender (*hieraon*); these have been interpreted as "women" but are more plausibly "lands." Otherwise we have the material discussed earlier which suggests a Locrian sense of sisterhood between free women and prostitutes; this is certainly important material and tells us something about the Locrians which may indeed have contributed to the creation of the story that is transmitted to us by Justin—even fictions have to be motivated[2]—but in no realistic sense confirms that story.

I have saved for last, however, the most important piece of evidence: Pindar's *2nd Pythian*. Here the poet says that "the Locrian maiden now looks out in safety" because of Hieron. This, for once, is from the right period, and seems a critically important confirmation of the vow: The Locrians, by this reading, had vowed to prostitute their daughters; Hieron, however, intervened and spared them the sacrifice, and Pindar congratulates him.

Once again, however, it is important to pay attention to the context. The *2nd Pythian* is one of Pindar's most enigmatic epinicians; it is unclear what victory it celebrates, or even if it celebrates a victory at all; possibly it is a personal letter to Hieron in the form of an epinician.[3] In the text the reference to the Locrian maiden is placed between two exempla, Kinyras and Ixion:

> Different men have completed for different kings
> An echoing song, the recompense of excellence.
> Oftentimes the voices of the Cypriots sing
> About Kinyras, whom gold-tressed Apollo made affectionately his own,

[2] See p. 307.

[3] Burton (1962), pp. 111–114; "the curious nature of this poem . . . suggests that it was not meant for public performance but was a private communication."

That sacred beast (*ktilos*) of Aphrodite; grace takes the lead in reverence, in
recompense for friendly acts.
You, son of Deinomenes, the Zephyrian Locrian maiden invokes
Before her house, after the insoluble toils of war
Through your power looking forth in safety.
By divine decree they say that Ixion
Tells these things to mortals as he spins every way on his winged wheel:
"Set about to repay your benefactor with kind response."
He learned that correctly. By the favor of Zeus
He had acquired a sweet life, but his prosperity did not last long
Because in the madness of his wits he fell in love with Hera,
Who belonged in the delightful bed of Zeus. His insolence however sent
him
Into exceptional wrongdoing. Soon enough the man suffered
Fittingly an exceptional torment. His two crimes
Finished in pain: because he first of the heroes
Not without craft infected mortals with kindred murder
And because once in the great secret chambers
He attempted the wife of Zeus. One must learn from him
To look to the limit of each thing. His wrongful bedding
Cast him into disaster as he settled to sleep; he coupled then with a cloud
Pursuing a sweet falsehood, fool that he was:
In shape it resembled the proudest of the Ouranians,
Daughter of Cronos, but the guile of Zeus placed it there as a bait
A beautiful bane. He brought the four-spoked bond upon himself,
His own destruction, and falling into unbreakable fetters he shows
A lesson proper to all.
The cloud bore without the Graces a savage child,
Just one child, and hers alone, unrespected among gods or men,
And as she reared him she named him Centaur, and he mated
With Magnesian mares on the slopes of Pelion, and an amazing band
Came from him, like the mother below and the father above.

Pindar 2nd Pyth. 13–48

The poet is explicit about the crime of Ixion; he is less explicit about
Kinyras, and he leaves entirely to us the application of these two exempla to the case of the Locrian maiden.

Kinyras was famous for his riches (Tyrtaeus fr. 12.6), his beauty (Luc.
Rhet. Praec. 11.2 and Hyginus *Fab.* 270) and his guile (Apollodorus *Epitome* 3.9). He was also the heroic founder of the cult of Aphrodite on
Cyprus. This cult seems to have involved prostitution in some way, either because prostitutes brought obscene offerings to the goddess (Ar-
nobius *Adversus Nationes* 5.19) or because initiation into Aphrodite's

secrets required prostitution (Firmicus Maternus *de Errore Profanorum Religionem* 10.1); one source even speaks explicitly of a *pornē politis*, which is to say, a free citizeness prostitute (Clement of Alexandria *Protrepticus* 2.13.4). These are all hostile Christian sources, but we find some confirmation in the story of the foundation of Carthage as told in Justin: Here we learn (without reference to Kinyras) that "it was the custom in Cyprus that virgins before their marriage on certain stated days would, seeking money for their dowries, [like the Lydian girls in Herodotus; see above], be sent down to the seashore; here they were to sacrifice to Aphrodite the first-fruits of their modesty" (Justin 18.8.4). So it may seem that Kinyras instituted the ritual prostitution of free women on Cyprus, and that Pindar says that different men sing different songs because the Cypriots sing in praise of Kinyras for doing what Pindar praises Hieron for preventing. On the other hand, the women mentioned by Justin are Phoenician, not Greek.

This, moreover, leaves uninterpreted Ixion, who gets far the most space. Ixion, says Pindar, was the first to murder a kinsman (cf. Aeschylus *Eumenides* 441, 718); it seems that he murdered his father-in-law in order to avoid paying him the bride-price (schol. Lucian *Deor. Dial.* 6, pp. 216–219; Pherecydes apud schol. Appolonius Rhodius 3.62). Pindar only alludes to this story but tells the other one, in which Ixion was favored by Zeus—purified of his blood-guilt and admitted to Olympus, as Pherecydes told it—where (like Paris and many another legendary guest) he gave his host an ill return by attempting to seduce or rape his wife. The gods punished him by deceiving him into producing a monster, and then bound him forever to a wheel.

Pindar connects Ixion to Kinyras through the theme of grace, gratitude, *charis*; Ixion is an extreme case of ingratitude and he then experienced sex without *charis*, while in the case of Kinyras *charis* takes the lead in grateful recompense. It seems that while Ixion had the wrong sexual relation with Hera, Kinyras had the right relation with Aphrodite. It is not clear, however, what story about Kinyras Pindar has in mind; he refers, for example, to Apollo's protection of Kinyras, and therefore is obviously not thinking about the story that Kinyras competed in song with Apollo and thereby perished (Eustatius ad *Il.* 11.20). Similarly most of the stories about Aphrodite and Kinyras tell us of his bad relations with Aphrodite: that he had, for instance, three daughters who were driven by the wrath of Aphrodite to mate with improper men and therefore lived in Egyptian exile (Apollodorus *Library* 3.14.3). Sometimes Kinyras is the father of that Myrrha who, subject to the wrath of Aphrodite, seduced her father and bore Adonis, Aphrodite's nursling, lover, and victim (schol. ad Theocritus 1.107).

Here Kinyras is called "*ktilos* of Aphrodite." The *ktilos* in Homer is the fertile male animal kept with the herd, the ram, for instance, who leads the flock (*Iliad* 3.196–198). Kinyras led the worshippers of Aphrodite, and that may be sufficient to explain this odd word. Leonard Woodbury, however, noting that the verb *ktiloō* in Herodotus (4.113.3) means "to subdue sexually," suggests that Kinyras was Aphrodite's lover (a notion supported by an allusion in Clement of Alexandria: *Protrepticus* 2.56) and observes that his fortune would well match the *makron . . . olbon* given to Ixion, especially as "to marry Aphrodite" was proverbially a more-than-human blessing.[4] It seems that Kinyras was successful in a love above his station and founded a cult in gratitude therefore, whereas Ixion lost all his prosperity and honor by reaching for one beyond his grasp.

What is the relevance to these two exempla to Hieron? One answer springs to mind: Perhaps Hieron, like Dionysius after him, had hoped to marry a Locrian bride (before settling for a daughter of Anaxilas of Rhegion), and the message of the ode is that they are not for him; they belong to the Aphrodite of Locri and are not for export. Kinyras, indeed, was successful (at least up to a point; we do not know what further consequences may have been in Pindar's mind) but he belongs to an epichoric cult and in this sense was at home with the goddess. Hieron is a stranger to Locri; his proper role is to protect the maidens, not to appropriate one. As so often in Pindar, the praise of a Sicilian tyrant is shadowed by a warning. It is even possible that Pindar (who wrote at least one epinician for an Epizephyrian) had been commissioned by the Epizephyrians to write this ode of respectful but deeply serious caution. All this is of course conjectural, but at least it makes sense of more of the ode than the reading that connects it with Justin's story of the vow.

If we had solid evidence that the Locrians had ever made a vow to prostitute their daughters we would have to incorporate that fact into our understanding of their culture. I for one would find such a fact unintelligible in terms of what else I know about Locri—but historical facts are not infrequently unintelligible. However in this case no such solid evidence exists, and we need not torment ourselves. We have many strange stories about Locri, and each must be motivated; I have suggested a motivation for this one (see p. 307). More interesting, perhaps, is the readiness of modern scholars to accept Justin's story and even to go well beyond it, speaking of the religious prostitution of free women as an established institution at Locri. In fact we have slightly better evidence for ritual cannibalism at Locri, but that notion has attracted little interest—which tells us something not about the Locrians, but about us.

[4] Woodbury (1978).

Bibliography

(1973). *Economia e società nella Magna Grecia: atti del 12° convegno di studi sulla Magna Grecia, Taranto.* Naples: Arte Tipografico.

(1977). *Locri Epizefiri: atti del 16° convegno di studi sulla Magna Grecia, Taranto.* Naples: Tipografico.

(1982). *Megale Hellas: nome e immagine: atti del 21° convegno di studi sulla Magna Grecia, Taranto.* Taranto: Istituto per la storia e l'archeologia della Magna Grecia.

(1990). *La Magna Grecia ed il lontano Occidente 581–593: atti del 29° convegno di studi sulla Magna Grecia, Taranto.* Taranto: Istituto per la storia e l'archeologia della Magna Grecia.

Adamesteanu, D. (1974). *La Basilicata Antica.* [Cava dei Tirreni]: Di Mauro.

Angiolillo, S. (1983). "Pisistrato e Artemide Brauronia." *Parola del Passato* 32: 351–354.

Arias, P. A. (1941). "Euthymos." *Siculorum Gymnasium* 1 (2): 77–84.

Arias, P. E. (1947). "Locri (Piano Caruso) Scavi di case antiche." *Notizie degli Scavi di Antichità* series 8, 1: 165–171.

——— (1977). "L'arte locrese nelle sue principali manifestazioni artigianli." *Locri Epizefirii* (1977), 479–580. Naples.

Arthur (Katz), M. (1980–1981). "The Tortoise and the Mirror." *Classical World* 74: 53–65.

——— (1982). "Cultural Strategies in Hesiod's Theogony: Law, Family, Society." *Arethusa* 15: 63–82.

Asheri, D. (1966). *Distribuzioni di terre nell'antica Grecia.* Turin: Accademia delle scienze.

Ashmole, B. (1922). "Locri Epizephyrii and the Ludovisi Throne." *Journal of Hellenic Studies* 42: 248–253.

Barnes, J.W.B., and H. Lloyd-Jones (1964). "A Fragment of New Comedy: P. Antihoop. 15." *Journal of Hellenic Studies* 84: 21–34.

Barra Bagnasco, M. (1977a). "Lo scavo." In Barra Bagnasco, ed. (1977–1992), 1: 3–49.

——— (1977b). "Problemi di urbanistica locrese." In *Locri Epizefiri:* (1977), 375–408.

——— (1994). "Il culto di Adone a Locri, Epizefiri." *Ostraka* 3: 231–243.

———, ed. (1977–1992). *Locri I–IV.* Florence: Le Lettere.

Barron, J. P. (1972). "New Light on Old Walls." *Journal of Hellenic Studies* 92: 20–45.

Baur, P. (1912). *Centaurs in Ancient Art.* Berlin: Curtius.

Bell, M. (1981). *The Terracottas.* Princeton, NJ: Princeton University Press.

Blomquist, J. (1975). "The Dialect of Epizephyrian Locri." *Opuscula Atheniensia = Skrifter Utgivna av Svenska Instututet i Athen = Acta Instituti Atheniensis Regni Sueciae* OAth 11 = Skrifter 22: 17–35.

———— (1978). "Additional Remarks on the Locrian Bronze Tablets." *Opuscula Atheniensia* = *Skrifter Utgivna av Svenska Instututet i Athen* = *Acta Instituti Atheniensis Regni Sueciae* OAth 12 = *Skrifter* 25, 117–132.

Blümel, C. (1963). *Die archaisch griechischen Skulpturen der Staatlichen Museen zu Berlin.* Berlin: Akademie Verlag.

Boedeker, D. (1983). "Hecate: A Transfunctional Goddess in the Theogony?" *Transactions of the American Philological Association* 113: 79–83.

———— (1984). *Descent from Heaven: Aspects of Dew in Greek Poetry and Religion.* Chico, CA: Scholars Press.

Bömer, F. (1961). "Untersuchungen über die Religion der Sklaven. . . ." In *Ab. Geistes- und Sozial-Wiss. Kl,* vol. 4. Mainz: Akademie der Wissenschaft und der Literatur.

Bonacasa, N. (1990). *Lo Stile severo in Sicilia.* Palermo: Novecento.

Borgeaud, P. (1979). *Recherches sur le dieu Pan.* [Rome]: Institut Suisse de Rome.

Bouras, C. (1967). *I anastilosis tis stoa tis Brauronos.* Athens: Genikē Dieuthynis Archaiotōtēn kai Anastēlōseōs.

Bravo, B. (1980). "Sulan: Représailles contres des étrangers dans les cités greques." *Annali della Scuola Normale Superiore di Pisa* ser. 3 vol. X.3 (3): 675–987.

Brelich, A. (1959). "I Figli di Medea." *SMSR* 30: 213–254.

———— (1969a). *Paides e Parthenoi.* Rome: Ateneo.

———— (1969b). "The Symbol of a Symbol." In *Myth and Symbol: Studies in Honor of Mircea Eliade,* 195–207. Chicago: University of Chicago Press.

———— (1970). "La Corona di Prometheus." In *Homages à Marie Delcourt,* 234–292. Brussels, Latomus.

Bremmer, J. (1983). "Scapegoat Rituals in Ancient Greece." *Harvard Studies in Classical Philology* 87: 299–320.

Brendel, O. (1936). "Symbolik der Kugel." *Mitteilungen des Deutschen Archäologischen Instituts, Römische Abteilung* 51: 1–95.

Brommer, F. (1967). *Die Metopen des Parthenon.* Mainz: von Zabern.

Brown, P.G.M. (1993). "Love and Marriage in Greek New Comedy." *Classical Quarterly* n.s. 43: 189–205.

Burford-Cooper, A. (1974). "The Family Farm in Ancient Greece." *Classical Journal* 73: 162–175.

Burkert, W. (1966). "Kekropidensage und Arrhephoria Vom Initiationsritus zum Panathenaeenfest." *Hermes* 94: 1–25.

———— (1970 [1962]). *Lore and Science in Ancient Pythagoreanism.* Cambridge, MA: Harvard University Press.

———— (1982). "The Problem of Orphics and Pythagoreans." In *Jewish and Christian Self-Definition,* vol. 3, ed. E. P. Sanders, 1–22. Philadelphia: Fortress.

———— (1985). *Greek Religion.* Oxford: Blackwell.

———— (1993). "Concordia Discors: The Literary and the Archaeological Evidence on the Sanctuary of Samothrace." In Marinatos and Hägg (1993) 178–191.

Burton, R.W.B. (1962). *Pindar's Pythian Odes.* London: Oxford University Press.

Buschor, E. (1957). "Aphrodite und Hermes." *Mitteilungen des Deutschen Archäologischen Instituts, Athenische Abteilung* 72: 77–86.

Buxton, R.G.A. (1982). *Persuasion in Greek Tragedy.* Cambridge: Cambridge University Press.

Calame, C. (1977). *Les choeurs des jeunes filles.* Rome: Ateneo & Bizzari.

——— (1996). *L'Éros dans la Grèce antique.* Paris: Belin.

Cameron, H. D. (1968). "'Epigoni' and the Law of Inheritance in Aeschylus' *Septem.*" *Greek, Roman and Byzantine Studies* 9: 247–257.

Cantarella, E. (1991). "*Moicheia*: Reconsidering a Problem." In Gagarin (1991) 289–296.

Cardosa, M. (1999). "Introduzione: la classificazione." In Lissi Caronna et al. (1999) 210–214.

Carter, J. C., ed. (1998). *The Chora of Metaponto: The Necropoleis.* Austin: University of Texas Press.

Cartledge, P. (1979). *Sparta and Laconia.* London: Routledge and Kegan Paul.

——— (1981). "Spartan Wives: Liberation or License?" *Classical Quarterly* n.s. 31 (75): 84–105.

Casanova, A. (1979). *La famiglia di Pandora.* Florence: CLUSF.

Càssola, F. (1965). "Sull'alienabilità del suolo nel mondo greco." *Labeo* 11: 205–219.

Cavanaugh, W. G., and S.E.C. Walker, eds. (1995). *Sparta in Laconia.* 19th British Museum Classical Colloquium. London: British Museum, British School at Athens.

Caven, B. (1990). *Dionysius I, Warlord of Sicily.* New Haven: Yale University Press.

Cerchiai, L. (1988). "Sesso e classi di età nelle necropoli greche di Locri Epizefiri." In Gnoli and Vernant (1988), 289–298.

Chirassi (Colombo), I. (1968). *Elementi di culture precereali nei miti e riti Greci.* Rome: Ateneo.

Clement, P. (1934). "The Origin of the Iphigeneia Legend." *L'Antiquité Classique* 3: 393–409.

Cohen, D. (1990). "The Social Context of Adultery at Athens." In *Nomos,* ed. P. Cartledge, P. Millet, and S. Todd, 147–165. New York: University Press.

——— (1991). *Law, Sexuality, and Society: The Enforcement of Morals in Classical Athens.* Cambrige: Cambridge University Press.

Cohn-Haft, L. (1995). "Divorce in Classical Athens." *Journal of Hellenic Studies* 115: 1–14.

Coldstream, J. N. (1994). "Prospectors and Pioneers: Pithekoussai, Kyme and Central Italy." In Tsetkhladze and De Angelis (1994) 47–60.

Cole, S. G. (1984a). "Greek Sanctions against Sexual Assault." *Classical Philology* 79: 97–113.

——— (1984b). "The Social Function of Rituals of Maturation: The Koureion and the Arkteia." *Zeitschrift für Papirologie und Epigrafik* 55: 233–244.

Compernolle, R. van (1969). "Ajax et les Dioscures au secours des Locriens sur les rives de la Sagra." In *Homages à M. Renard,* ed. J. Bibauw, 2: 733–736. Brussels: Coll. Latomus.

Congdon, L.O.K. (1981). *Caryatid Mirrors of Ancient Greece.* Mainz am Rhein: P. von Zabern.

Conze, A. (1900). *Die attischen Grabreliefs,* vol. 2, Berlin: W. Spemann.

Cordiano, G. (1988). "I rapporti politici tra Locri Epizefirii e Reggio nel VI secolo A. C. alla luce di Arist. Rh. 1394b–1395a (= Stesichorus, Fr. 281b Page)." *Rendiconti Istituto Lombardo Accademia di Scienze e lettere* 122: 39–47.

Costabile, F. ed. (1991). *I ninfei di Locri Epizefiri*. Soveria Mannelli (Catanzaro): Rubbettino.

—— (1991a). "Culti e miti delle divinità fluviali: *Euthymos*, il *Kaikinos*, ed *Acheloos*." In Costabile (1991) 195–226.

—— (1991b). "Lo spazio religioso di Locri Epizefiri." In Costabile (1991) 227–233.

—— (1992a). "Redditi, terre e fonti finanzarie dell'*Olympeion*: tributi, imposte e rapporti contratuali." In *Polis ed Olympeion a Locri Epizefiri*, ed. F. Costabile, 160–174. Catanzaro, Rubbettino.

Costamagna, L., and C. Sabbione (1990). *Una città in Magna Grecia: Locri Epizefiri*. Reggio Calabria: Laruffa.

Cumont, F. (1924). "L'Aphrodite et la tortue." *Monuments et Mémoires publiés par l'Academie des Inscriptions et Belles-lettres* 27: 31–43.

D'Agostino, B. (1973). "Appunti sul funzione dell'artigianato nell'occidente greco dall'VIII al IV sec. a.C." In *Economia e società nella Magna Grecia* (1973), 221–229, 234–235.

D'Andria, F. (1979). "Salento Arcaico. La nuova documentazione archaeologica." In *Salento Arcaico*, ed. G. Congedo. Galatina: Congedo.

—— (1984). "Il Salento nell'VIII e VII sec. a.C.: nuovi dati archeologici." *Annuario delle Scuola Archeologica di Atene* 60 [1982]: 101–116.

Danforth, L. M. (1982). *The Death Rituals of Rural Greece*. Princeton, NJ: Princeton University Press.

Davidson, J. (1998). *Courtesans and Fishcakes*. New York: St. Martin's.

Davreux, J. (1942). *La légende de la profétesse Cassandre d'après les textes et les monuments*. Paris: Droz.

de Franciscis, A. (1972). *Stato e Società in Locri Epizefiri*. Naples: Libreria Scientifica.

—— (1979). *Il santuario di Marasà in Locri Epizefiri I. Il tempio arcaico*. Naples: G. Macchiaroli.

de la Genière, J. (1964). "Note sur la chronologie des nécropoles de Torre galli et Canale-Janchina." *Melanges de l'École Française de Rome: Antiquité* 76: 7–32.

—— (1985). "De la Phrygia à Locres Epizéphyrienne: Les chemins de Cybèle." *Melanges de l'École Française de Rome: Antiquité* 97: 693–717.

—— (1986). "Un ex-voto Locrese a Delfi?" *Annali della Scuola Normale Superiore di Pisa* ser. 3, 16: 345–409.

Denster, J.-M. (1982). *Le motif de banquet couché*. Rome: École française de Rome.

de Polignac, F. O. (1984). *La naissance de la cité greque*. Paris: Decouverte.

d'Errico, F., and A. M. Moigne (1985). "La faune classique-hellenistique de Locres: écologie, élevage, depeçage." *MEFRA* 97: 719–750.

Deubner, L. (1943). "Götterzwang." *Jahrbuch des deutschen archäologisches Museums:* 89–93.

de Ste. Croix, G.E.M. (1954). "The Character of the Athenian Empire." *Historia* 3: 1–41.

——— (1970). "Some Observations on the Property Rights of Athenian Women." *Classical Review* n.s. 20: 273–278.

Detienne, M. (1977 [1972]). *The Gardens of Adonis*, trans. Janet Lloyd. Garden City, NJ: Humanities Press. Originally published as *Les Jardins d'Adonis*. Paris: Gallimard.

Detienne, M., and J.-P. Vernant (1991 [1974]). *Cunning Intelligence in Greek Culture and Society*. Chicago: University of Chicago Press.

Diehl, E. (1964). "Fragmente aus Samos." *Archäologische Anzeiger*. 494–572.

Dowden, K. (1989). *Death and the Maiden*. London: Routledge.

Dressel, H., and A. Milchhofer (1878). *Die antike Kuntswerke aus Sparta und Umgebung*, vol. 2. Athens: Mittheilung des Archæol. Instituts.

DuBois, P. (1982a). *Centaurs and Amazons*. Ann Arbor: University of Michigan Press.

——— (1982b). "On the Invention of Hierarchy." *Arethusa* 15: 203–220.

Dunbabin, T. J. (1948). *The Western Greeks*. Oxford: Clarendon Press.

Durkheim, E. (1965). *The Elementary Forms of the Religious Life*. New York: Free Press.

École française d'Athènes (1991). *Guide de Delphes: Le musée*. Paris: Boccard.

Edgar, H. (1952). *Select Papyri*. Cambridge, MA: Harvard University Press.

Elderkin, G. W. (1930). "Jointed Dolls in Antiquity." *American Journal of Archaeology* 14: 455–479.

Fantham, E. (1975). "Sex, Status, and Survival in Hellenistic Athens: A Study of Women in New Comedy." *Phoenix* 29: 44–74.

Faraone, C. (1990). "Aphrodite's *Kestos* and Apples for Atalanta." *Phoenix* 44: 219–243.

——— (1999). *Ancient Greek Love Magic*. Cambridge, MA: Harvard University Press.

Ferrari (Pinney), G. (2002). *Figures of Speech: Men and Maidens in Ancient Greece*. Chicago: University of Chicago Press.

Figueira, T. J. (1981). *Aegina: Society and Politics*. Monographs in Classical Studies. New York: Arno.

——— (1985a). "The Theognidea and Megarian Society." In Figueira and Nagy (1985) 112–158.

Figueira, T. J., and G. Nagy, eds. (1981). *Theognis of Megara: Poetry and the Polis*. Baltimore: Johns Hopkins University Press.

Finley, M. I. (1954). *The World of Odysseus*. New York: Viking Press.

——— (1981 [1968]). "Sparta and Spartan Society." In *Economy and Society in Ancient Greece*, ed. B. D. Shaw and R. P. Saller, 24–40. Harmondsworth: Penguin.

Fitton, J. W. (1970). "That Was No Lady, That Was. . . ." *Classical Quarterly* n.s. 20 (64): 54–66.

Foley, H. (1982). "Marriage and Sacrifice in Euripides' *Iphigeneia in Aulis*." *Arethusa* 15: 159–180.

Fontenrose, J. (1968). "The Hero as Athlete." *Classical Antiquity* 1: 73–104.

——— (1978). "The Locrian Maidens." In *The Delphic Oracle*, 131–137. Berkeley: University of California Press.

Fossey, J. M. (1990). *The Ancient Topography of Opountian Lokris*. Amsterdam: Bieben.

Foti, G. (1977). "La topografia di Locri Epizefirii. In *Locri Epizefirii* (1977), 343–362.

Fourcart, P. (1889). "Inscriptions de l'Acropole." *Bulletin de Correspondence Hellenique* 13: 156–178.

Foxhall, L. (1989). "Household, Gender, and Property in Classical Athens." *Classical Quarterly* n.s. 39: 22–44.

——— (1991). "Response to Eva Cantarella." In Gagarin (1991) 287–303.

Francesco, A. M. d., and W. Frisatto (1986). "Utilisation de basalte provenant d'Etna dans les constructions de Locri Epizefiri—Centocamare." *Révue d'Achéometrie* 10: 25–32.

Frazer, J. G. (1898). *Pausanias' Description of Greece*. London: Macmillan.

Fried, M. H. (1967). *The Evolution of Political Society: An Essay in Political Anthropology*. New York: Random House.

Friis Johansen, K. (1951). *The Attic Grave-Reliefs in the Classical Period: An Essay in Interpretation*. Copenhagen: E. Munksgaaard.

Fuks, A. (1984). *Social Conflict in Ancient Greece*. Jerusalem: Magnes Press, the Hebrew University; and Leiden: E. J. Brill.

Gaca, K. L. (2000). "The Reproductive Technology of the Pythagoreans." *Classical Philology* 95: 113–132.

Gagarin, M., ed. (1991). *Symposion 1990. Vorträge zue griechischen und hellenistischen Rechtsgeschichte*. Cologne: Bohlau.

Gernet, L. (1968 [1954]). "The Marriages of Tyrants." In *The Anthopology of Ancient Greece*, ed. J.-P. Vernant, 289–302. Baltimore: Johns Hopkins University Press.

Gernet, L., and A. Boulanger (1932). *Le génie grec dans la religion*. Paris: A. Michel.

Ghali-Kahil, L. (1955). *Les enlèvements et le retour d'Hélène dans les documents figurés*. Paris: Boccard.

——— (1965). "Autour de l'Artemis Attique." *Antike Kunst* 8: 20–33.

——— (1977). "L'Artemis de Brauron: Rites et Mystere." *Antike Kunst* 20: 86–98.

Gianelli, G. (1963). *Culti e miti della Magna Grecia*. Florence: Sansoni.

Giangiulio, M. (1983). "Le tradizione legendarie intorno alla battaglia della Sagra." *Melanges de l'École Française de Rome: Antiquité* 95: 473–521.

Gigante, M. (1982). "Civiltà letteraria in Magna Grecia." In *Megale Hellas* (1982), 587–640.

Giudice, F. (1989). *Vasi e fragmenti "Beazley" da Locri Epizefiri*. Catania: Università di Catania, Istituto di archeologia.

Gnoli, G., and J.-P. Vernant, eds. (1988). *La mort, les morts dans les sociétés anciennes*. Cambridge and Paris: Cambridge University Press and Éditions de la Maison des Sciences de l'Homme.

Gould, J. (1980). "Law, Custom, and Myth: Aspects of the Social Position of Women in Classical Athens." *Journal of Hellenic Studies* 100: 38–59.

Graf, F. (1978). "Die lokrischen Madchen." *Studi Storico Religiosi* 2 (1): 61–79.

——— (1979). "Das Götterbild aus dem Taurerland." *Antike Welt* 4: 33–41.

Graham, A. J. (1964). *Colony and Mother City in Ancient Greece.* Manchester: Manchester University Press.

Gronigen, B. A. von (1977). *Euphorion.* Amsterdam: Hakkert.

Gruppe, O. (1921). "Lokris." *Bursian's Jahresbericht* 186: 344–349.

Guarducci, M. (1970). "Cibele in un' epigrafe di Locri Epizefiri." *Klio* 52: 133–138.

——— (1985). "Nuove riflessioni sulla laminetta 'Orfica' di Hipponion." *Rivista di Filologia e d'Istruzione* 113: 385–397.

Gullini, G. (1980). *La cultura architettonica di Locri Epizefirii.* Taranto: Istituto per la storia e archeologia della Magna Grecia.

——— (1982). "Il trono Ludovisi: Un' ipotesi." In *Aparchai: Nuovi ricerche e studi Sulla Magna Grecia e la Sicilia antica in onore di Paulo Enrico Arias,* ed. M. L. Gualandi, L. Massei, and S. Settis, 1: 305–318. Pisa: Giardini.

——— (1988). "L'architettura Greca." In Settis (1988), pp. 349–402.

Halperin, D. M., J. J. Winkler, and F. Zeitlin, eds. (1990). *Before Sexuality.* Princeton, NJ: Princeton University Press.

Hampe, R. (1951). *Die Stele aus Pharsalos im Louvre.* Berlin: W. de Gruyter.

——— (1955). "Eukleia und Eunomia." *Mitteilungen des deutsches archaiologisches Institut—Roma* 72: 107–123.

Hanson, V. D. (1995). *The Other Greeks: The Family Farm and the Agrarian Roots of Western Civilization.* New York: Free Press.

Harrison, A.R.W. (1968). *The Law of Athens.* Oxford: Clarendon Press.

Hatzfeld, J. (1940). *Alcibiade.* Paris: Presses universitaires de France.

Helbig, W. (1913). *Führer durch die öffentlichichen sammlungen klassicher Altertümer in Rom.* Leipzig: B. G. Teubner.

Herington, C. J. (1963). "Athena in Athenian Literature and Cult." *Greece and Rome* 10 supplement: 61–73.

Hermann, A. (1979). "The Biter: A Late Hellenistic Astragal Player." In *Studies in Classical Art and Archeology: A Tribute to Peter Heinrich von Blanckenhagen,* ed. Günter Kopke and Mary B. Moore, 163–173. Locust Valley, NJ: J. J. Angustin.

Higgins, R. A. (1954). *Catalogue of the Terracottas in the Department of Greek and Roman Antiquities, British Museum, I.* London: British Museum.

Hiller von Gärtringen, F. (1906). *Inschriften von Priene.* Berlin: Reiner.

——— (1930). *Gnomon* 6: 426–428.

Hodkinson, S. (1989). "Inheritance, Marriage, and Demography: Perspectives upon the Success and Decline of Classical Sparta." In *Classical Sparta: Techniques behind Her Success,* ed. A. Powell, 79–121. London: Routledge.

Hofkes-Brukker, C., and A. Mallwitz (1975). *Der Bassai-Fries.* Munich: Prestel.

Hogarth, G., et al. (1908). *Excavations at Ephesus: The Archaic Artemesia.* London: British Museum.

Hughes, D. D. (1991). *Human Sacrifice in Ancient Greece.* London: Routledge.

Humphreys, S. C. (1974). "The Nothoi of Kynosarges." *Journal of Hellenic Studies* 94: 88–98.

Hunter, V. L. (1993). "Agnatic Kinship in Athenian Law and Athenian Family Practice." In *Law, Politics, and Society in the Ancient Mediterranean World,* ed. B. Halpern and D. W. Hobson, 100–121. Sheffield: Sheffield Academic Press.

——— (1994). *Policing Athens.* Princeton, NJ: Princeton University Press.

Huxley, G. (1962). *Early Sparta.* London: Faber & Faber.

——— (1966). "Troy VIII and the Locrian Maidens." In *Ancient Society and Institutions: Studies Presented to Victor Ehrenberg on His Seventy-fifth Birthday,* 147–164. Oxford: Blackwell.

Ianelli, M. T., and V. Ammendolia, eds. (2000). *I volti di Hipponion.* Catanzaro: Rubbettino.

Isler, H. P. (1984). "Der Tempel der Aphrodite." In *Studia Ietina,* ed. H. P. Isler, 2: 11–116. Zürich: Eugen Rentsch.

Jahn, O. (1846). *Peitho, die Gottin der Uberredung.* Greifswald: C. A. Kock.

Jameson, M. (1990). "Private Space and the Greek City." In *The Greek City from Homer to Alexander,* ed. O. Murray and S. Price, 171–195. Oxford: Clarendon Press.

Jarcho, V. (1979). "Pflicht und Genuss in den ehelichen Beziehungen der alten Athener." In *Actes du VIIe Congrès de la Fédération Internationale des Associations d'Études classiques,* ed. J. Harnatte, II: 357–373. Budapest: Budapest Akadémia Kládo.

Johnston, S. (1999). *Restless Dead: Encounters between the Living and the Dead in Ancient Greece.* Berkeley and Los Angeles: University of California Press.

Just, R. (1985). "Freedom, Slavery, and the Female Psyche." In *Crux: Essays in Greek History Presented to G.E.M. de Ste. Croix on His Seventy-fifth Birthday,* ed. P. A. Cartledge and F. D. Harvey, 169–188. Sidmouth, Devon: Imprint Academic.

Kaibel, G. (1878). *Epigrammata Graeca.* Berlin: Reiner.

Kastriotis, P. (1909). "Anaglypha entumbia meta plangonos." *Ephemeris Archaiologike.* 122–131.

Kekulé, R. (1905). *Echelos und Basile, attisches Relief aus Rhodos.* Berlin: G. Reimer.

Keller, O. (1913). *Die antike Tierwelt.* Leipzig: Wilhelm Engelmann.

Klaffenbach, G. (1935). "Bericht uber eine epigraphische Reise durch Mittelgriechenland und die Ionischen Inseln." *Sitzungsbericht der Preussichen Akademie der Wissenschaften* 13: 1–726.

Koch-Harnack, G. (1989). *Erotische Symbole.* Berlin: Gebr. Mann.

Kondas, I. D. (1967). "Artemis Brauronia." *Archaiologikon Deltion* 22: 156–199.

Konstan, D. (1987). "Between Courtesan and Wife: Menander's Perikeiromene." *Phoenix* 41: 122–139.

Kuhrt, A. (1989). "Women in the Late Babylonian Period." In *Women's Earliest Records,* ed. B. S. Lesko, 215–239. Atlanta: Scholars Press.

Kunze, E. (1950). *Archaische Schildbänder: Ein Beitrag zur frügriechiscen Bildesgeschichte und Sagenüberlieferung.* Berlin: de Gruyter.

Kurke, L. (1999). *Coins, Bodies, Games, and Gold.* Princeton, NJ: Princeton University Press.

Kyrieleis, H. (1993). "The Heraion at Samos." In Marinatos and Hägg (1993) 125–153.

Landi, A. (1967). "Sul termine *kôtios* a Locri Epizefiri." *Parola del Passato* 22: 110–112.

Larsen, J.A.O. (1968). *Greek Federal States.* Oxford: Clarendon Press.

Lattanzi, E. (1990). "L'attività archeologica in Calabria, 1989." In *La Magna Grecia ed il lontano Occidente 581–593* (1990).

Leaf, W. (1912). *Troy: A Study in Homeric Geography*. London: Macmillan.

——— (1914–1916). "The Lokrian Maidens." *Annual of the British School at Athens* 21: 148–154.

Leeds, A. (1977). "Mythos and Pathos: Some Unpleasantries on Peasantries." In *The Integration of Peasant Economies*, ed. R. Halperin and J. Dow, 227–256. New York: St. Martin's.

Lefkowitz, M. (1983). "Wives and Husbands." *Greece and Rome* n.s. 30: 31–47.

Leone, R. (1991). "*Anathemata* fittili di figura femminile nuda seduta." In *I ninfei di Locri Epizefiri*, ed. F. Costabile, 114–126. Soveria Manelli (Catanzaro): Rubbinetto.

Lerat, L. (1952a). *Les Locriens de l'ouest I: Topographie et ruines*. Paris: C. de Boccard.

——— (1952b). *Les Locriens de l'ouest II: Histoires, Institutions, Prosopographie*. Paris: C. de Boccard.

Letta, C. (1971). *Piccola coroplastica metapontina nel Museo Archeologico di Firenze*. Naples: Libraria Scientifica.

Lincoln, B. (1981). *Emerging from the Chrysalis: Studies in Rituals of Women's Initiations*. Cambridge, MA: Harvard University Press.

Linders, T. (1972). *Studies in the Treasure Records of Artemis Brauronia Found in Athens*. Lund: P. Aström.

Lissi (Caronna), E. (1961). "Gli scavi della Scuola nazionale di Archeologia a Locri Epizefiri." In *Atti VII Congresso Internazionale di Archeologia Classica*, II: 109–115. Rome: "L'Erma" di Bretschneider.

Lissi Caronna, E., C. Sabbione, and L. V. Borelli, eds. (1999). *I Pinakes di Locri Epizefiri*. Rome: Società Magna Grecia.

Littman, R. J. (1979). "Kinship in Athens." *Ancient Society* 10: 5–31.

Loraux, N. (1981). *Les enfants d'Athena: Idées Atheniennes sur la citoyennete et la division des sexes*. Paris: Maspero.

——— (1987 [1985]). *Tragic Ways of Killing a Woman*, trans. A. Foster. Cambridge, Mass.: Harvard University Press. Originally published as *Façons tragiques de tuer une femme*. Paris: Hachette.

Lorimer, H. L. (1903). "The Country Cart of Ancient Greece." *Journal of Hellenic Studies* 23: 132–155.

MacDowell, D. M. (1963). *Athenian Homicide Law in the Age of the Orators*. Manchester: Manchester University Press.

Mackil, E. (n.d.). "From Metropolitan Lokris to Apoikic Lokroi."

Maddoli, G., ed. (1982). *Temesa e il suo territorio*. Taranto: Istituto per la storia e l'archeologia della Magna Grecia.

Malkin, I. (1994). *Myth and Territory in the Spartan Mediterranean*. Cambridge: Cambridge University Press.

Mangien, V. (1936). "Le mariage chez les Grecs anciens. L'initiation nuptiale." *L'Antiquité Classique* 5: 115–138.

Marinatos, N. (2003). "Hermes and Aphrodite as Gods of Initiation." In *Initiation in Ancient Greek Rituals and Narratives*, ed. D. Dodd and C. Faraone. London: Routledge.

Marinatos, N., and R. Hägg, eds. (1993). *Greek Sanctuaries: New Approaches*. London & New York: Routledge.

Martin, A., and O. Primavesi (1999). *L'Empédocle de Strasbourg*. Berlin: Walter de Gruyter.

Martin, R. (1993). "The Seven Sages as Performers of Wisdom." In *Cultural Poetics in Ancient Greece*, ed. C. Dougherty and L. Kurke, 108–128. Cambridge: Cambridge University Press.

Meiggs, R. (1963). "The Political Implications of the Parthenon." *Greece and Rome* 10 supplement: 36–45.

Mele, A. (1979). *Il Commercio Greco Arcaico: Prexis ed Emporie*. Naples: Institut Français de Naples.

—— (1982). "La megále Hellás pitagorica: aspetti politici, economici, e sociali." In *Megale Hellas* (1982), 33–80.

—— (1983). "L'eroe di Temesa fra Ausoni e Greci." In *Forme di contatto e processi di trasformazione nella società antiche*, 848–887. Pisa/Rome: Scuola Normale/École Française de Rome.

Meloni, P. (1951). "Il soggiorno di Dionisio II a Locri." *Studi Italiani di Filologia Classica* 25: 149–168.

Merck, M. (1978). "The City's Achievements: The Patriotic Amazonomachy and Ancient Athens." In *Tearing the Veil: Essays on Femininity*, ed. S. Lipshitz. London & Boston: Henley & Routledge and Kegan Paul.

Merkelbach, R. (1972). "Aglauros (Die Religion der Epheben)." *Zeitschrift für Papyrologie und Epigrafik* 9: 277–283.

Molli Boffa, G. (1977). "Figura feminile nuda seduta." In Barra Bagnasco, ed. (1977–1992), 1: 231–238.

Momigliano, A. (1945). "The Locrian Maidens and the Date of Lycophron's *Alexandra*." *Classical Quarterly* 39: 49–53.

Montepaone, C. (1979). "L'arkteia a Brauron." *Studi Storico-religiosi* 3: 343–364.

Moreau, A. (1989). "Les ambivalences de Cassandre." In *Entre Hommes et Dieux: Le convive, le héros, le prophète*, ed. A.-F. Laurens, 145–167. Paris: Les Belles Lettres.

Morgan, C., and J. Hall (1996). "Achaian Poleis and Achaian Colonisation." In *Introduction to an Inventory of Poleis: Symposium August 23–26, 1995*, ed. M. Hansen, 164–232. Copenhagen: Royal Danish Academy of Sciences and Letters.

Morris, I. (1987). *Burial and Ancient Society: The Rise of the Greek City-State*. Cambridge: Cambridge University Press.

—— (1991). "The Early Polis as City and State." In *City and Country in the Ancient World*, ed. John Rich and Andrew Wallace-Hadrill, 25–57. London: Routledge.

Munson, R. (2001). *Telling Wonders: Ethnographic and Political Discourse in the Work of Herodotus*. Ann Arbor: University of Michigan Press.

Murray, O. (1990a). "Cities of Reason." In Murray and Price (1990) 1–25.

Murray, O., and S. Price, eds. (1990). *The Greek City from Homer to Alexander*. Oxford: Clarendon Press.

Musti, D. (1977). "Problemi della storia di Locri Epizefiri." In *Locri Epizefirii* (1977), 23–147.

—— ed. (1979a). *Le tavole di Locri*. Rome: Ateneo & Bizzarri.

—— (1979b). Remarks reported in "Cronaca." In Musti (1979a), 7–11.

——— (1984). "Le lamine orfiche e la religiosità d'area locrese." *Quaderni Urbinati di Cultura Classica* n.s. 16 (old series: 45): 61–83.

Nagy, G. (1979). *The Best of the Achaeans*. Baltimore: Johns Hopkins University Press.

——— (1985). "Theognis and Megara: A Poet's Vision of His City." In Figueira and Nagy (1985) 22–81.

——— (1990). *Pindar's Homer*. Baltimore: Johns Hopkins University Press.

Nash, E. (1959). "Über die Auffindung und der Erwerb des 'Bostoner Thrones.'" *Mitteilungen des deutschen archaiologischen Instituts—Römische Abteilung* 66: 104–130.

Neutsch, B. (1961a). "Tonball mit Totenkultszenen aus der italischen Necropole von Sala Consiliana." *Apollo. Bolletino dei Musei Provinciali del Salernitano* 1: 53–66.

——— (1961b). "Der Heros auf der Kline." *Mitteilungen des Deutschen Archäologischen Instituts, Römische Abteilung* 68: 150–163.

Nilsson, M. P. (1906). *Griechische Feste von religiöser Bedeutung*. Darmstadt: Teubner.

——— (1954–1955). "Das frühe Griechenland, von innen gesehen." *Historia* 3: 257–282.

——— (1960). "Wedding Rites in Ancient Greece." In *Opuscula Selecta*, 243–250. Lund: C.W.K. Gleerap.

Niutta, F. (1977). "Le fonti letterarie ed epigrafiche." In Barra Bagnasco, ed. (1977–1992), 1: 253–355.

Oakley, J. H. (1982). "The Anakalypteria." *Archäologischer Anzeiger*: 113–118.

Ogden, D. (1996). *Greek Bastardy in the Classical and Hellenistic Periods*. Oxford: Clarendon Press.

Oldfather, M. (1908). "Lokrika." *Philologus* 67: 411–472.

Orsi, D. P. (1994). *La lotta politica a Siracusa alla metà del IV secolo a.C.* Bari: Unipuglia.

Orsi, P. (1890). "Gerace Marina. Scoperta di un tempio ionico nell'area dell'antica Locri." *Notizie degli Scavi di Antichità* 9: 248–267.

——— (1909). "Locri Epizefiri. Resoconto sulla terza campagna di scavi Locresi." *Bolletino d'Arte* 3: 406–428, 463–482.

——— (1911a). "Locri Epizephyrii. Il tempio dorico a casa Marafioti." *Notizie degli Scavi di Antichità* 8 supp.: 27–62.

——— (1911b). "Locri Epizephyrii. La necropoli Lucifero." *Notizie degli Scavi di Antichità* 8 supp.: 3–26.

——— (1912). "Locri Epizephyrii." *Notizie degli Scavi di Antichità* supp.: 3–56.

——— (1913). "Scavi di Calabria nel 1913 (relazione preliminare), Locri Epizephyrii." *Notizie degli Scavi di Antichità* supp.: 3–54.

——— (1917). "Locri Epiz. Campagne di scavo nella necropoli Lucifero negli anni 1914 e 1915." *Notizie degli Scavi di Antichità* 14: 101–167.

Ortner, S. B. (1974). "Is Female to Male as Nature to Culture?" In *Women, Culture and Society*, ed. M. Zimbalist Rosaldo and L. Lamphere, 67–87. Stanford, CA: Stanford University Press.

Osanna, M. (1992). *Chorai coloniale da Taranto a Locri*. Rome: Istituto Poligrafico e Zecca dello Stato.

Osborne, R. (1985). *Demos: The Discovery of Classical Athens.* Cambridge: Cambridge University Press.

Padel, R. (1983). "Women: Model for Possession by Greek Daemons." In *Images of Women in Antiquity,* ed. A. Cameron and A. Kuhrt, 3–19. London: Croom Helm.

Pagenstecher, R. (1911). *Eros und Psyche.* Heidelberg: C. Winter.

Palaiokrassa, L. (1991). *To iero tis artemidos mounichias.* Athens: Athēnais Archaiologikē Hetaireia.

Paris, P., and Holleaux, M. (1885). "Inscriptions de Carie." *Bulletin de Correspondence Hellenique* 9: 324–348.

Parker, R. (1983). *Miasma: Pollution and Purification in Early Greek Religion.* Oxford: Clarendon Press.

Patterson, C. (1981). *Pericles' Citizenship Law of 451–50 B.C.* New York: Arno.

——— (1986). "Hai Attikai: The Other Athenians." *Helios* 13: 49–67.

——— (1990). "Those Athenian Bastards." *Classical Antiquity* 9: 40–73.

Pearlman, P. (1983). "Plato *Laws* 833c–834d and the Bears of Brauron." *Greek, Roman, and Byzantine Studies* 24: 115–130.

——— (1989). "Acting the She-Bear for Artemis." *Arethusa* 22: 111–133.

Pedley, J. G. (1990). *Paestum: Greeks and Romans in Southern Italy.* London: Thames and Hudson.

Peradotto, J. (1977). "Oedipus and Erichthonius: Some Observations on Paradeigmatic and Syntagmatic Order." *Arethusa* 10: 85–101.

Pericika, J. (1970). "The Polis of Chersonese in the Crimea." In *Ricerche storiche ed economiche in memoria di Corrado Barbagallo,* ed. Luigi De Rosa, 459–477. Naples: Edizioni scientifiche italiane.

Picard, C. (1943). "Sanctuaires, représentations, et symboles de Zeus Meilichios." *Revue de l'Histoire de Religions* 126: 97–127.

Piccaluga, G. (1981). "L'olocausto di Patrai." In Rudhardt and Reverdin (1980) 243–287.

Piccirilli, L. (1978). "Due ricerche Spartane." *Annali della Scuola Normale Superiore di Pisa* ser. 3, 8: 917–947.

Pipili, M. (1987). *Laconian Iconography of the Sixth Century B.C.* Oxford: Oxford University Committee for Archaeology 82–96.

——— (1995). "Archaic Laconian Vase-Painting: Some Iconographic Considerations." In Cavanaugh and Walker (1995).

Polanyi, K. (1944). *The Great Transformation.* Boston: Beacon.

——— (1957). "Aristotle Discovers the Economy." In *Trade and Market in the Early Empires,* ed. K. Polanyi, C. W. Arensberg, and H. W. Pearson, 64–96. Glencoe, IL: Free Press and Falcon's Wing Press.

Popham, M. R. (1994). "Precolonization: Early Greek Contact with the East." In Tsetkhladze and De Angelis (1994) 11–34.

Post, L. A. (1940). "Woman's Place in Menander's Athens." *Transactions of the American Philological Association* 71: 450–459.

Pouilloux, J. (1954). *Recherches sur l'histoire et les cultes de Thasos.* Paris: E. Boccard.

Powell, A., ed. (1990). *Euripides, Women, and Sexuality.* London & New York: Routledge.

Powell, B. (1906). *Erichthonius and the Three Daughters of Cecrops.* Ithaca, NY: Published for Cornell University by the Macmillan Company.

Pratt, L. (2000). "The Old Women of Ancient Greece and the Homeric Hymn to Demeter." *Transactions of the American Philological Association* 130: 41–65.

Prückner, H. (1968). *Die lokrischen Tonreliefs.* Mainz am Rhein: P. von Zabern.

Pucci, P. (1977). *Hesiod and the Language of Poetry.* Baltimore: Johns Hopkins University Press.

Pugliese Caratelli, G. (1987). "Epigrafi di Cos relative al culto di Artemis in Cnido e in Bargylia." *Parola del Passato* 42: 110–123.

——— (1989a). "Artemis Hyakinthotrophos a Taranto." *Parola del Passato* 44: 463–468.

——— (1989b). "Dedica metapontina ad Afrodite." *Parola del Passato* 49: 471–472.

——— (1990). *Tra Cadmo e Orfeo.* Bologna: il Mulino.

Putorti, N. (1929 and 1930). *L'Italia antichissima.* Messina: Pilva.

Quagliati, Q. (1908). "Rilievi votivi arcaici in terracotta di Lokroi Epizephyrioi." *Ausonia* 3: 136–234.

Rackham, O. (1990). "Ancient Landscapes." In Murray and Price (1990) 85–111.

Redfield, J. M. (1977–1978). "The Women of Sparta." *Classical Journal* 73: 146–161.

——— (1982). "Notes on the Greek Wedding." *Arethusa* 15: 181–201.

——— (1983). "Odysseus: The Economic Man." In *Approaches to Homer*, ed. C. A. Rubino and C. W. Shelmerdine, 218–247. Austin: University of Texas Press.

——— (1985). "Herodotus the Tourist." *Classical Philology* 80: 97–118.

——— (1986). "The Development of the Market in Archaic Greece." In *The Market in History*, ed. B. L. Anderson and A.J.H. Latham, 29–58. London: Croom Helm.

——— (1990). "From Sex to Politics: The Rites of Artemis Triklaria and Dionysus Aisymnetes at Patras." In Halperin (1990) 115–134.

——— (1993). "The Sexes in Hesiod." *Annals of Scholarship* 10 (1): 31–61.

——— (1995). "Homo Domesticus." In *The Greeks*, ed. J.-P. Vernant, 153–183. Chicago: University of Chicago Press.

Rehm, R. (1996). *Marriage to Death: The Conflation of Wedding and Funeral Rituals in Greek Tragedy.* Princeton, NJ: Princeton University Press.

Richter, G. (1945). "An Ivory Relief in the Metropolitan Museum of Art." *American Journal of Archaeology* 49: 261–269.

——— (1968). *Korai: Archaic Greek Maidens.* London: Phaidon.

Ridgway, D. (1992). *The First Western Greeks.* Cambridge: Cambridge University Press.

——— (1994). "Phoenicians and Greeks in the West: A View from Pithekoussai." In Tsetkhladze and De Angelis (1994) 35–46.

Rizza, G. (1960). "Stipe votiva di un santuario di Demetra a Catania." *Cronaca d'Arte* 45: 247–262.

Robert, C. (1914). "Pandora." *Hermes* 49: 17–38.

Robertson, M. (1963). "The Sculptures of the Parthenon." *Greece and Rome* 10 supplement: 46–60.

—— (1982). "Le arti in magna Grecia." In *Megale Hellas* (1982), 187–203.

Robertson, N. (1983). "The Riddle of the Arrephoria at Athens." *Harvard Studies in Classical Philology* 87: 241–288.

—— (1991). "The Betrothal Symposium in Early Greece." In *Dining in a Classical Context,* ed. W. J. Slater, 25–57. Ann Arbor: University of Michigan Press.

Robinson, D. M. (1933). "A New Greek Inscription from Macedonia." *American Journal of Archaeology* 37: 602–604.

Rolley, C. (1977). "Intervento." In *Locri Epizefirii.* (1977), 212–214.

—— (1982). *Les vases de bronze de l'archaïsme récent en grande-grèce.* Naples: Centre Jean Berard.

Romeo, I. (1989). "Sacelli archaichi senza peristasi nella Sicilia greca." *Xenia* 17: 5–54.

Rosellini, M. l., and S. Said (1978). "Usage de femmes et autres nomoi chez les 'sauvages' d'Herodote: essai de lecture structurale." *Annali della Scuola Normale Superiore di Pisa* ser. 3, 8 (3): 949–1005.

Rosivach, V. J. (1984). "APHAIRESIS and APOLEIPSIS." *RIPA* 31: 193–230.

Rubinich, M. (1999). "Storia e metodologia dell'attuale edizione." In Lissi Carona et al. (1999), I.1: 3–21.

Rudd, N. (1981). "Romantic Love in Classical Times." *Ramus* 10: 140–158.

Rudhardt, J. (1970). "Les mythes grecs relatifs à l'instauration du sacrifice: les rôles corrélatifs de Prométhée et de son fils Deucalion." *Museum Helveticum* 27: 1–15.

Sabatucci, D. (1979). *Saggio sul misticismo greco.* Rome: Ateneo and Bizzari.

Sabatucci, D., and O. Reverdin, eds. (1981). *Le Sacrifice dans l'Antiquité.* Geneva: Foundation Hardt.

Sabbione, C. (1976a). "L'attività achaeologica nelle province di Reggio Calabria e di Catanzaro." *Magna Grecia nell' età romani: Atti del 15° convegno degli studi sulla Magna Grecia, Taranto, 1975,* 569–598. Naples: Arte Tipografica.

—— (1977). "Nota sul territorio di Locri." In *Locri Epizefirii* (1977), 363–373.

—— (1982). "Le aree di urbanizzazione di Crotone e Locri Epizefiri nell VIII e VII sec. a. C." *Annuario della Scuola archeologica di Atene e delle Missioni italiane in oriente* 60: 251–259.

Sale, W. (1975). "The Temple Legends of the Arkteia." *Rheinsche Museum* 118: 265–284.

Samter, E. (1901). *Familienfeste der Griechen und Romer.* Berlin: Georg Reimer.

Scanlon, T. F. (1990). "Race or Chase at the Arkteia of Attica." *Nikephoros* 3: 73–120.

Schaps, D. (1977). "The Woman Least Mentioned: Etiquette and Women's Names." *Classical Quarterly* n.s. 27 (71): 323–330.

—— (1979). *Economic Rights of Women in Ancient Greece.* Edinburgh: University of Edinburgh Press.

Schenal Pileggi, R. (1999). "Gruppo 2—Introduzione." In Lissi Caronna et al. (1999), 2: 209–228.

Schmitt, J. (1921). "Freiwilliger Opfertod bei Euripides." *Religionsgeschichtliche Versuche und Vorarbeiten* XVII.2. Giessen: Verlag von Alfred Töpelmann.

Schmitt-Pantel, P. (1992). *La cité au banquet*. Rome: École Française de Rome.

Schumacher, R.W.M. (1993). "Three Related Sanctuaries of Poseidon: Geraistos, Kalauria and Tanairon." In Marinatos and Hägg (1993) 62–87.

Seaford, R. (1987). "The Tragic Wedding." *Journal of Hellenic Studies* 107: 106–130.

——— (1990). "The Structural Problems of Marriage in Euripides." In Powell (1990) 151–176.

Settis, S. (1966). *Chelone: Saggio sull'Aphrodite Urania di Fidia*. Pisa: Nistri-Lischi.

———, ed. (1988). *Storia di Calabria: La Calabria antica 1*. Rome: Gangemi.

Shapiro, H. A. (1995). "The Cult of Heroines: Kekrops' Daughters." In *Pandora: Women in Classical Greece*, ed. E. D. Reeder, 39–48. Baltimore and Princeton: Walters Art Gallery and Princeton University Press.

Simon, E. (1959). *Die Geburt der Aphrodite*. Berlin: de Gruyter.

——— (1977). "Criteri per l'esegesi dei pinakes locresi." *Prospettiva* 10: 15–21.

Sissa, G. (1990). "Maidenhood without Maidenhead." In Halperin (1990) 330–364.

Smith, J. Z. (1987). "The Domestication of Sacrifice." In *Violent Origins: Walter Burkert, René Girard and Jonathan Z. Smith on Ritual Killing and Cultural Formation*, ed. R. G. Hamerton-Kelly, 191–205. Stanford, CA: Stanford University Press.

Snell, B. (1960). *The Discovery of the Mind*. New York: Harper Torchbooks.

Snodgrass, A. M. (1994). "The Nature and Standing of the Early Western Colonies." In Tsetkhladze and De Angelis (1994) 1–10.

Sommerstein, A. (1980). "The Naming of Women in Greek and Roman Comedy." *Quaderni di Storia* 11: 395–418.

Sordi, M. (1972). "Le leggende dei dioscuri nella battaglia della Sagra e di Lago Regillo." *Contributi dell'Istituto di Storia Antica* 1: 47–70.

Sourvinou-Inwood, C. (1971). "Aristophanes, *Lysistrata* 641–647." *Classical Quarterly* 65 (new series 21): 339–342.

——— (1973). "The Young Abductor of the Locrian Pinakes." *Bulletin of the Institute of Classical Studies, University of London* 20: 12–19.

——— (1974a). "The Boston Relief and the Religion of Locri Epizephyrii." *Journal of Hellenic Studies* 94: 126–137.

——— (1974b). "The Votum of 477/6 and the Foundation Legend of Locri Epizephyrii." *Classical Quarterly* n.s. 24: 186–198.

——— (1978). "Persephone and Aphrodite at Locri: A Model for Personality Definitions in Greek Religion." *Journal of Hellenic Studies* 98: 101–121.

——— (1988). *Studies in Girls Transitions: Aspects of the Arkteia and Age Representation in Attic Iconography*. Athens: Kardamitsa.

Spigo, U. (1982). "Nuovi contributi allo studio di forme e tipi della coroplastica delle città greche della Sicilia ionica e della Calabria Meridionale." In *Lo stretto crocevia di culture; atti della 26° convegno di studi sulla Magna Grecia*, 275–335. Taranto: Istituto der la storia e l'archeologia della Magna Grecia.

Spyropoulos, T. G. (1995). "Pellana, the Administrative Centre of Prehistoric Laconia." In Cavanaugh and Walker (1995) 28–38.

Stazio, A. (1982). "Temesa—La documentazione numismatica." In *Temesa e il suo territorio*, ed. G. Maddoli, 93–101. Taranto: Istituto per la storia e l'archeologia della Magna Grecia.

Stinton, T.C.W. (1976). "Iphigeneia and the Bears of Brauron." *Classical Quarterly* 70 (new series 26): 11–13.

Sutton, R. F. (1981). "The interaction between Men and Women as Portrayed on Attic Red-Figure Pottery." Ph. D. diss., University of North Carolina at Chapel Hill.

Szegedy-Maszak, A. (1978). "Legends of the Greek Lawgivers." *Greek, Roman, and Byzantine Studies* 19: 199–209.

Szeliga, G. N. (1982). "The Dioscuri on the Roof." Ph.D. diss., Bryn Mawr College.

Tandy, D. W. (1997). *Warriors into Traders: The Power of the Market in Early Greece.* Berkeley and Los Angeles: University of California Press.

Taylor, A. E. (1928). *A Commentary on Plato's Timaeus.* Oxford: Clarendon Press.

Thériault, G. T. (1996). *Le culte de* homonoia *dan les cités greques.* Lyon: Maison de l'Orient Méditerranéen and Éditions du Sphinx.

Thompson, D. B. (1963). *Troy: The Terracotta Figurines of the Hellenistic Period.* Princeton, NJ: Princeton University Press.

Thompson, W. E. (1972). "Athenian Marriage Patterns: Remarriage." *California Studies in Classical Antiquity* 5: 211–225.

Tod, M. N., and A.J.B. Wace (1906). *A Catalogue of the Sparta Museum.* Oxford: Clarendon Press.

Torelli, M. (1977). "I culti di Locri." In *Locri Epizefirii* (1977), 147–184.

——— (1979). "Considerazioni sugli aspetti religiosi e cultuali." In Musti (1979a), 91–112.

Tsetkhladze, G. R., and F. De Angelis, eds. (1994). *The Archaeology of Greek Colonization.* Oxford: Oxford University Committee for Archaeology.

Turano, C. (1961). "Bruciaprofumi in bronzo da Locri." *Klearchos* 3: 108–117.

Turner, E. G. (1977). "The Lost Beginning of Menander, *Misoumenos.*" *Proceedings of the British Academy* 63: 315–331.

——— (1979). "Menander and the New Society of His Time." *Chronique d'Egypte* 54: 106–126.

Tyrell, W. B. (1984). *Amazons: A Study in Athenian Mythmaking.* Baltimore: Johns Hopkins University Press.

Uhlenbrock, J. P. (1989). "Concerning Some Archaic Terracotta Protomai from Naxos." *Xenia* 18: 9–26.

Ure, A. P. (1929). "Boeotian Geometrising Vases." *Journal of Hellenic Studies* 49: 160–171.

Vatin, C. (1970). *Recherches sur le marriage et la condition de la femme mariée à l'époque hellénistique.* Paris: E. de Boccard.

Vernant, J.-P. (1968). "Avant-propos." In *Problèmes de la guerre en Grèce ancienne,* ed. J.-P. Vernant. Paris/The Hague: Mouton.

——— (1973). "Le mariage en Grèce archaique." *Parola del Passato* 28: 63–80.

——— (1979 [1974]). "The Myth of Prometheus in Hesiod." In *Myth and Society in Ancient Greece,* trans. Janet Lloyd. Sussex: English Harvester Press; Atlantic Highlands, NJ: Humanities Press. Originally published as *Mythe et société en Grece ancienne "têxtes à l'appui,"* ed. Vidal-Naquet.

——— (1982–1983). "Étude comparée des religions antiques." *Annuaire du College de France* 83: 443–458.

——— (1985). *La mort dans les yeux.* Paris: Hachette.

——— (1988). "La belle mort et la cadavre outragé." In Gnoli and Vernant (1988), 45–76.

Versnel, H. S. (1981). "Self-Sacrifice, Compensation, and the Anonymous Gods." In Rudhardt and Reverdin (1981) 135–185.

——— (1987). "Greek Myth and Ritual: The Case of Kronos." In *Interpretations of Greek Mythology,* ed. J. Bremmer, 121–152. London: Routledge.

Vidal-Naquet, P. (1975). "Les esclaves immortelles d'Athena Ilias." In *Le Monde Grec: Pensée, littérature, histoire, documents,* ed. Jean Bingen, Guy Lambier, and Georges Nachtergael, 496–507. Brussels: Editions de l'Université de Bruxelles.

——— (1986 [1981]). *The Black Hunter.* Baltimore: Johns Hopkins University Press.

Vinogradoff, J. G. (1991). "Zur sachlichen und geschictlichen Deutung der Orphiker-Plättchen von Olbia." *Recherches et rencontres* 3: 77–102.

Walbank, M. B. (1981). "Artemis Bear-Leader." *Classical Quarterly* 75 (n.s. 31): 276–281.

Walcot, P. (1987). "Married Love and True Love." *Ancient Society* 18: 5–33.

Wallerstein, I. (1979). *The Capitalist World Economy.* Cambridge: Cambridge University Press.

West, M. L. (1983). *The Orphic Poems.* Oxford: Clarendon Press.

——— (1985). *The Hesiodic Catalogue of Women.* Oxford: Clarendon Press.

Wilamowitz von Möllendorf, U. (1883). "Die Beiden Elektren: Excurs. Iphigeneia." *Hermes* 18: 249–263.

Wilhelm, A. (1911). "Die lokrische Mädcheninscrift." *Jahreshefte des Österreichisches Archäologisches Institut in Wein* 14: 163–256.

Will, E. (1973). "La grande Grèce, mileau d'échanges. Reflexions méthodologiques." In *Economia e Società nella Magna Grecia* (1973), 21–67.

Willetts, R. F. (1969). *Everyday Life in Ancient Crete.* London: Batsford & Putnams.

Williams, D., and J. Ogden (1994). *Greek Gold.* New York: Abrams.

Williams, T. (1961). "Menanders Epitrepontes im Spiegel der griechischen Eheverträge aus Ägypten." *Wiener Studien* 74: 43–58.

Williamson, M. (1990). "A Woman's Place in Euripides' *Medea.*" In Powell (1990) 16–31.

Wolff, H. J. (1944). "Marriage Law and Family Organization in Ancient Athens." *Traditio* 2: 43–95.

Woodbury, L. (1978). "The Gratitude of the Locrian Maidens." *Transactions of the American Philological Association* 108: 285–299.

Wuilleumier, P. (1935). *Tarante des origines à la conquète romaine.* Paris: E. de Boccard.

Wycherly, R. E. (1978). *The Stones of Athens.* Princeton, NJ: Princeton University Press.

Zancani Montuoro, P. (1935). "Il giudizio di Persephone in un pinakion locrese." In *Paulo Orsi,* Rome.

——— (1940). "Tabella fittile Locrese con scena di culto." *Rivista del R. Instituto d'Arcaeologia e Storia dell' Arte* 7: 205–224.

——— (1954a). "Il rapitore di Kore nel mito locrese." *Rendiconti, Accademia di archeologia, Napoli* 29: 79–86.

—— (1954b). "La teogamia di Locri Epizefiri." *Primo Congresso Storico Cal-abrese. Naples.*

—— (1954c). "Note sui soggeti e sulla technica delle tabelle di Locri." *ASMG* n.s. 1: 71–106.

—— (1960). "Il corredo della sposa." *Archaeologia Classica* 12: 37–50.

—— (1964). "Persephone e Aprodite sol mare." In Essays in Memory in Karl Lehmann. *Marsvas* supp. 1, ed. L. F. Sandler, pp. 386 ff.

—— (1968). "La pariglia di Afrodite." In *Opuscula Karl Karenyi*, 15–23. Stockholm.

Zeitlin, F. (1982). "Cultic Models of the Female: Rites of Dionysus and Demeter." *Arethusa* 15: 129–157.

—— (1985). "The Power of Aphrodite: Eros and the Boundaries of the Self in the Hippolytus." In *Directions in Euripidean Criticism*, ed. P. Burian, 52–111. Durham, NC: Duke University Press.

Zuntz, G. N. (1971). *Persephone: Three Essays on Religion and Thought in Magna Grecia.* Oxford: Clarendon Press.

Index